Historical Dictionary
of the
U.S. Army

EDITED BY
Jerold E. Brown

GREENWOOD PRESS
Westport, Connecticut • London

Library of Congress Cataloging-in-Publication Data

Historical dictionary of the U.S. Army / edited by Jerold E. Brown.
    p.   cm.
    Includes bibliographical references and index.
    ISBN 0–313–29322–8 (alk. paper)
    1. United States. Army—History—Dictionaries. I. Brown, Jerold E.
UA25.H67   2001
355'.00973'03—dc21   00–022373

British Library Cataloguing in Publication Data is available.

Library of Congress Catalog Card Number: 00–022373
ISBN: 0–313–29322–8

First published in 2001

Greenwood Press, 88 Post Road West, Westport, CT 06881
An imprint of Greenwood Publishing Group, Inc.
www.greenwood.com

Printed in the United States of America

The paper used in this book complies with the
Permanent Paper Standard issued by the National
Information Standards Organization (Z39.48–1984).

10 9 8 7 6 5 4 3 2 1

In memory of
Spec. 4 Ronald W. Brunson
23 December 1946–1 September 1969

CONTENTS

PREFACE

The U.S. Army has evolved, changed, and matured over the past two and a quarter centuries to become the premier military force in the world. During that time, the American soldier has served loyally and faithfully in war and peace, contributing to the development of the nation and fighting for freedom and American ideals on battlefields around the world. The Army's heritage is rich in history, tradition, and lore.

Compiling and editing this one-volume historical dictionary of the U.S. Army has been a challenge and an opportunity. The opportunity has been to bring to the interested reader, student, and researcher a broad cross section of military terms, concepts, arms and equipment, units and organizations, campaigns and battles, and individuals who have contributed significantly to the U.S. Army. The challenge has been to select those entries that will be of greatest value to users of this volume.

I began the selection of entries with a list of terms and names that I had accumulated from student questions and concerns during my more than twenty years of teaching both graduate and undergraduate courses in American and military history. I further selected entries suggested or recommended by my colleagues at the Combat Studies Institute, U.S. Army Command and General Staff College; by scholars and historians I invited to contribute to the volume; and by officers, teachers, and archivists with extensive knowledge of U.S. Army history and historiography. Unfortunately, space made it impossible to include all of the proposals I received; I had to omit a number of excellent submissions. I am fully responsible for the final selection of entries.

The terms, names, and concepts common to the U.S. Army are to be found in a wide variety of sources. These sources include books—both nonfiction and fiction; biographies; autobiographies; memoirs; monographs; general and military histories; articles and essays in professional and popular periodicals; journals; magazines; official, semiofficial, and private unit, organizational, and installation histories; U.S. Army and joint doctrinal publications and regulations; movies; television and stage productions; and the everyday language of soldiers on the parade ground and in the field. Even a brief perusal of the sources at the back of this volume will demonstrate the breadth of sources where one can find Army terms and usages.

With a few exceptions, each entry in this volume is followed by a reference or references. For users of this volume who choose to learn more about specific terms, names, and concepts, the references place the terms in context and serve as initial sources for further research. The references contain only the short title and date of publication for each work cited. A full citation of each book or article in the references can be found in the sources at the back of the volume.

While all terms in this dictionary can be found in published sources, some terms are predominantly part of the spoken language of soldiers. While U.S. Army veterans, serving soldiers, and most other uniformed service members will instantly recognize and understand these terms, I did not supply references I considered unnecessary or too obscure.

The use of acronyms and abbreviations in the U.S. Army is ubiquitous. Finding one's way through the maze of abbreviations and acronyms can be a serious challenge for anyone unfamiliar with military literature, especially the non-military reader or researcher. A number of official and commercially published guides are available to assist readers with this type of military terminology. See, for example, U.S. Army Regulation 310-50, *Authorized Abbreviations, Brevity Codes, and Acronyms* (Washington, D.C.: Department of the Army, 1985), and Fernando B. Morinigo, *The Acronym Book: Acronyms in Aerospace and Defense* (Washington, D.C.: American Institute of Aeronautics and Astronautics, 1990). Keep in mind, however, that acronyms frequently have more than one meaning and that they change meanings from time to time. Users of this volume will find a convenient list of the acronyms and abbreviations in Appendix A.

Many of the weapons, arms, equipment, units, organizations, historical events, and concepts included in this volume are commonly known by more than one term or name. To facilitate the use of this volume, I have included numerous cross-references. In each case, however, I endeavored to associate the definition with the most commonly used variation of the term. An asterisk (*) in the definition or explanation of a term indicates that the preceding term has its own entry in the dictionary.

In the course of compiling and editing this volume, I have incurred many debts. Many friends and colleagues assisted me with this project; some made valuable recommendations and suggestions for entries or sources, while others provided encouragement and moral support. I regret that I cannot thank everyone individually. I would, however, be remiss if I did not mention a few names that were particularly instrumental in supporting me over the past six years. Above all, I thank Mildred "Mim" Vasan, former Senior Editor, Social and Behavioral Sciences, at Greenwood Press for offering me the opportunity to undertake this project. When Mim retired, Cynthia Harris took over supervision of my project, and she has shown infinite patience with my progress. I owe both of these fine editors my deepest thanks.

I greatly appreciate the support of the directors of the Combat Studies Institute at the U.S. Army Command and Staff College. Colonels Richard Swain, Jerry D. Morelock, and Clay Edwards not only allowed me the freedom to work on this project when it did not interfere with my other duties but contributed entries to the volume. I owe much to my colleagues at the Combat Studies Institute: Chris Gabel, Bob Baumann, Tom Huber, Gary Bjorge, Jack Gifford, Larry Yates, and many former Army and Air Force officers of CSI contributed entries; others provided ideas, suggestions for entries, and assistance with sources and references. Special thanks goes to Mr. Donald Gilmore, editor at the Combat Studies Institute, who helped in innumerable ways. I greatly appreciate the assistance of Professor Pete Maslowski, University of Nebraska, and Professor John J. Contreni, Purdue University, for recruiting some of their best graduate students to write entries for the dictionary.

The staff at the Combined Arms Research Library at Fort Leavenworth, Kansas, performed above and beyond the call of duty in their efforts to assist me. Without the help of Dan Dorris, Joanne Knight, Pat Wells, Dorothy Rogers, Mary Jo Nelson, Dianne Karis, Bernie Brose, John Rogers, and a host of others too numerous for me to list here, I would still be searching for necessary references in distant corners of the library.

I wish to thank all of the contributors to this dictionary. Their hard work, attention to detail, and knowledge of the U.S. Army is clearly evident in the pages of this volume. All errors are mine alone.

Finally, I thank my wife, Shirley, for putting up with me over the years I have devoted to this project. Without her support, it would never have been finished.

A BRIEF HISTORY OF THE U.S. ARMY

The U.S. Army traces its heritage back to the 1600s and the period of colonization. From the first, England's colonies in North America differed from those established by the other European powers. The colonies founded by France and Spain were primarily intended to extract wealth and send it back to the mother country; hence, those colonies were populated by fortune seekers, priests, administrators, and soldiers. In contrast, the English colonies in North America consisted of farmers, craftsmen, merchants, and their families. These colonists were intent on starting new lives, not on extracting wealth.

England sent very few soldiers to her colonies in North America. When the colonists needed military protection, they generally had to provide it themselves. Most colonies enacted militia laws, which required every able-bodied man to provide himself with a weapon and report to periodic training sessions. In wartime, individuals would volunteer, or be selected, for active duty. Two concepts that still shape the American military can be traced to this period. The first is the idea of the citizen soldier, who picks up his gun in wartime and returns to civilian pursuits in peace. The second is the concept of universal obligation, under which every citizen is eligible for military service.

During the period of colonization, the militia conducted defensive and offensive operations against the Indians. When Britain got involved in European wars, colonial militias frequently mounted operations against French Canada, Spanish Florida, and the Indian tribes allied with those two powers. Not until the Seven Years' War (which in North America began in 1754) did the British king send a sizeable contingent of regular troops to North America. These troops stayed on after the war. The presence of Regular British troops in the American colonies contributed to popular unrest, and eventually to the American Revolution,* which began in 1775. Ever since colonial days, many Americans have disliked the idea of maintaining a standing army in peacetime.

Colonial military forces in the American Revolution took two forms. The first was the Continental Army,* which its commander, George Washington,* strove to transform into a professional, European-style force. The U.S. Army traces its lineage to the Continental Army. The second element of military force was the militia. Militia forces reinforced the Continental Army in battle, but they also waged guerrilla warfare on their own. British commanders found it difficult to cope with the dual American threat. If they massed forces to face the Continental Army, the militia could control the countryside. If the British scattered garrisons through the countryside in order to control the militia, the Continental Army could attack and defeat those garrisons piecemeal.

Our founding fathers incorporated into the Constitution of 1787 this complimentary relationship between the Regular Army, under central control, and the citizen-soldiers of the militia, under state control. Today, the U.S. Army consists of both full-time regulars and part-time citizen soldiers of the National Guard* and Army Reserve.* George Washington was personally responsible for introducing another enduring tradition—political noninvolvement. Individual soldiers, as citizens, participate in the political process, but the Army as an institution traditionally stays out of partisan politics and willingly subordinates itself to civilian authority. Article II, section 2 of the Constitution designates the president of the United States as the commander in chief of all military forces. On the other hand, Article I, section 8 provides that Congress shall raise and support armies, at the same time limiting military appropriations to no more than two years. State governors still retain a degree of control over the militia, while both the states and the federal government contribute to their maintenance.

From the end of the American Revolution until the beginning of the 20th century, the U.S. Army's primary mission did not involve waging war against foreign armies. Its main duty was to occupy and patrol the frontier between white settlements and American Indian territories. In other words, if the Army has had one formative experience that shaped its institutional character, it was frontier duty. Soldiers surveyed the vast territories of the American West, erected posts, patrolled trails, and from time to time fought against the Indians. Today, many Americans seem to believe that the U.S. Army waged a massive campaign of genocide against the American Indian. In reality, more Indians died fighting other Indians than perished in combat against the Army. One of the Army's more difficult tasks was to keep Indian tribes at peace with each other. Then as now, frontier duty was a thankless, unappreciated mission.

Three major wars interrupted the century-long frontier experience. The War of 1812* was largely a litany of military misfortunes and disasters, including the capture of Washington, D.C., by British troops. Have you ever wondered why the president of the United States lives in a mansion called the "White House"? Ever since British troops burned it in 1814, it has been painted white to hide the smoke stains. In fact, the United States was fortunate to emerge from this war intact. Still, the War of 1812 had relatively little impact on American military policy, except to reaffirm the need for a standing army.

Of much greater significance to the Army and the nation was the Mexican

War* of 1846–1848. The conflict had its origins in 1836, when American-born settlers in the Mexican province of Texas rebelled against Mexican rule and set up Texas as an independent republic. The epic stand of 186 Texans against 6,000 Mexican soldiers at the Alamo, while not involving U.S. Army troops, has nonetheless become a legend in American military history. The United States annexed Texas in 1845 and soon found itself at war with Mexico. The conflict started over a border dispute but quickly became a war of conquest.

The Army that marched into Mexico was the most professional force that the United States had ever sent to war. Graduates of the U.S. Military Academy* filled many of the company* and field-grade commands, as well as key staff positions. Many of the troops were long-service volunteers, hardened by service on the frontier. Discipline was good, and morale was high. Enthusiastic but poorly trained volunteer troops helped fill the ranks. One field army,* under Zachary Taylor,* defeated the Mexican army threatening Texas, thus securing the Rio Grande as the border between Texas and Mexico. When negotiations failed to end the conflict, Winfield Scott* led another field force in an amphibious landing at Veracruz and then on a campaign inland to Mexico City.* Meanwhile, other forces secured a vast area extending all the way from Texas to the Pacific Ocean. Ultimately, the Mexican government agreed to a peace treaty that yielded the New Mexico Territory and California to the United States in return for thirteen million dollars.

The Mexican War represents a milestone in American history, because the territories gained in that conflict touched off a debate over the expansion of slavery that ultimately led to civil war. It is a critical episode in the history of the U.S. Army, because many of the young, academy-trained officers who fought under Taylor and Scott would ultimately become general officers in the Civil War.* In a sense, the Mexican War was the training ground for Civil War generals. Some scholars feel that the Mexican conflict made war seem too easy and painless to these future generals and thus contributed to the bloodbath that began in 1861.

The Mexican War was truly the Regular Army's war. Although there were sizeable bodies of volunteer troops, most of the significant fighting was done by the regulars. In contrast, the Civil War was a people's war. When the war began in 1861, the U.S. Army numbered about 16,000 men. By the end of the war, the Federal army alone numbered well over a million men, the great majority of them volunteers. Although Regular Army officers filled most of the top command positions in both the Northern and Southern armies, the identity of the regular force was swamped by the influx of volunteers. In both armies, the vast majority of enlisted men, as well as company and field-grade officers, were citizen soldiers. More than a few general officers earned their appointments through political power rather than military experience. Old Regulars bemoaned the amateurism of the vast volunteer armies, which compared poorly to the professional army that had invaded Mexico just fifteen years earlier.

Ironically, many historians argue that the citizen volunteers who filled the ranks made better soldiers than their academy-trained generals deserved. During the war, field armies of 60,000 men were common—some grew to more than 100,000 troops—yet the generals who came to command those armies had little or no experience with formations larger than a thousand-man regiment.* The Army offered no formal education for command or staff work at such levels. The drill manuals that constituted the only written doctrine* were oriented to the company level. Thus the first two years of the Civil War paired masses of brave, enthusiastic volunteer troops with generals who were learning the art of command "on the job." These factors, coupled with increases in weapon lethality since the last war, resulted in huge casualty lists and indecisive campaigns. In a two-day battle at a place called Shiloh* in the spring of 1862, the number of Americans killed in action equalled the American battle deaths from the War of 1812 and Mexican War combined. At the battle of Antietam* later that year, 25,000 soldiers were killed or wounded in one day. Yet both sides replaced their losses, and the war continued. When volunteers stopped coming forward, both sides resorted to conscription—the first national conscription in American history. The U.S. Army also began enlisting escaped slaves and other blacks. By war's end, approximately 20 percent of the Union Army consisted of all-black regiments.

In the early stages of the war, generals focused their attention on the capture of decisive places. After all, Scott had won the Mexican War by taking the enemy capital. When the capture of strategic places proved impossible or indecisive, generals shifted their attention to the destruction of enemy armies, in the manner of Napoleon. But the huge field armies of the Civil War, sustained by national mobilization and supplied by a new invention called the railroad, were almost impossible to destroy. By 1864, generals had begun to focus on the ability and will of the enemy nation to continue the struggle. The foremost Southern general, Robert E. Lee,* hoped that if he avoided defeat long enough and inflicted enough casualties, the Northern population would tire of the war. Northern generals, especially Ulysses S. Grant* and William T. Sherman,* remembered a lesson learned in previous Indian conflicts—destruction of the opponent's economic resources eventually compels him to give up the struggle. In 1864 and 1865, Northern armies, in conjunction with the blockade mounted by the U.S. Navy, set about the systematic destruction of the Southern economy. When the war finally ended in the spring of 1865, the only remaining vestiges of the Confederate States of America were its ever-shrinking field armies, which remained defiant until the Southern economy, government, and public will had all been shattered. By the time it was all over, more than 600,000 Americans had lost their lives.

Historians sometimes view the Civil War as the first modern "total" war, but it is doubtful that the professional soldiers who conducted it viewed it in those terms. When the war ended, the huge citizen-soldier armies went home, and the professional soldiers went back to their prewar duties on the frontier and to occupation duties in the South. Institutionally, the U.S. Army behaved as if the war had never happened. By the 1890s, however, when the last Indian bands went to their reservations for good and the frontier essentially ceased to exist, a new attitude of professionalism began to take hold within the Army. A new peacetime mission replaced the duties of the frontier—preparation for war against the armies of foreign powers. Officers undertook the systematic study of foreign armies, began to study the works of European military theorists, and shared their knowledge in the pages of professional journals. The Army adopted modern, magazine-fed firearms, the Krag-Jorgenson* for example, and began to modernize its other branches, as well. Soldiers practiced marksmanship and participated in unit training exercises. The Army opened new schools to improve the proficiency of the officer corps. The School for the Application of Infantry and Cavalry* opened its doors at Fort Leavenworth in 1882; by 1902, it had evolved into a staff college.

A new era began for the Army in 1898, when Congress declared war on Spain. The Army's initial mission was to evict Spanish forces from Cuba, thus securing independence for that island. But the war quickly became a struggle for empire, as the U.S. Navy and the Army took over Spanish possessions in the Caribbean and the Pacific. Defeating the Spanish forces did not take long, but U.S. troops quickly found themselves involved in the long-term work of a colonial army. Prior to 1898, American soldiers had stayed within the borders of the United States, except for wartime expeditions against Canada and Mexico. Since 1898, the Army has maintained a global presence. In another sense, however, the job of policing the far-flung outposts in the Caribbean and the Philippines resembled the Army's old mission of guarding the western frontier.

Starting about 1900, Congress undertook a series of institutional reforms to correct deficiencies revealed in the Spanish-American War* and to meet the challenges of being a global military power. In order to coordinate better the activities of the administrative bureaus with those of the field forces, Congress created the position of chief of staff. A war college was established to train officers in the highest levels of strategy. Soon, an embryonic general staff began the job of drafting war plans for various contingencies. The position of the National Guard was formalized within the nation's defense establishment, and federal resources were provided to bring National Guard units up to Regular Army standards, at least in theory. The National Defense Act of 1916* gave the president the authority to call up the National Guard for federal duty. Troop training was made more realistic and came to include large-scale field maneuvers. The Leavenworth faculty published field manuals* to standardize procedures across the Army and to incorporate new changes brought about by technology.

When World War I* broke out in Europe in 1914, the Wilson administration declared a policy of neutrality, which it struggled to enforce for two and a half years. Military mobilization did not begin until Congress declared war in April 1917, and it had not yet reached its fullest impact when the war ended in November 1918. Were it not for the reforms of the preceding twenty years, it is doubtful that a sizeable American army would ever have reached the battlefront in Europe. Manpower mobilization was quite effective. While the federalized National Guard brought entire divisions into the military establishment, conscription provided the bulk of wartime manpower, which totaled about four million men by the time the war ended. Economic mobilization was less successful. Even though the United States was by far the world's leading industrial power in 1917, the U.S. Army had to rely on French and British industry for about half of its small arms, most of its artillery, and virtually all of its aircraft and tanks. Shipping for men and materiel was another shortcoming, a problem made worse by the presence of German U-boats in the North Atlantic.

Not until September 1918 did a complete American field army take its place in the trenches of France. John J. Pershing,* commander of the American Expeditionary Force* (AEF), had deliberately resisted the advice of French and British officers who knew firsthand how the machine gun and modern artillery had changed the battlefield. In their first test against a world-class foreign army since the War of 1812, the Americans did not fare very well. Out of a total of two million men in the theater, the AEF suffered over 120,000 casualties in just two months of offensive warfare. The war ended before American troops could attain levels of tactical proficiency comparable to those of the European powers. Even so, it is probably fair to say that the belated intervention of American forces was a significant factor in ending the stalemate on the western front and persuading Germany to sue for peace.

When World War I ended, the Army wanted to capitalize upon its hard-won lessons and undertake measures to maintain its readiness for war. But the American public had been told that World War I was the "war to end all wars." As had been the case after the Civil War, the mass army of citizen soldiers was quickly demobilized, and military funding was cut back to near-prewar levels. The U.S. Senate refused to ratify the Versailles Treaty and rejected membership in the League of Nations. For the next twenty years, the Army was starved for manpower and money. But even when they lack resources to buy new technology and fully man field units, soldiers can think and plan. Theorists such as William "Billy" Mitchell* explored the capabilities of airpower and pressed for the creation of an independent air force. Others, such as Adna R. Chaffee, Jr.,* conducted small-scale experiments in the employment of armored forces. The general staff, in conjunction with the Navy, maintained a series of war plans covering various contingencies, and they prepared mobilization plans that would preclude the confusion and delays of 1917. The Leavenworth Staff College shifted to a two-year curriculum for part of the interwar period. Individual officers, such as Dwight D. Eisenhower* and George S. Patton, Jr.,* compensated for their shortage of experience with troop units by engaging in individual study and professional reading. On the surface, the U.S. Army made little progress between the world wars, but for many of its officers this was a dynamic and creative period.

By 1939 the world was again at war. Japan had invaded China in 1937, and

Germany had gone to war against Poland, France, and Britain. This time the Army did not wait for a declaration of war to begin preparing for war. In 1938 and 1939, under the political leadership of President Franklin D. Roosevelt, the armed forces began a limited modernization and expansion program. When Germany defeated France in a stunning blitzkrieg campaign in 1940, Congress enacted legislation that allowed large-scale mobilization to begin in earnest. Roosevelt federalized the National Guard, and the first peacetime conscription in American history began. The Army Chief of Staff, George C. Marshall,* established the Armored Force in 1940 and initiated a program of large-scale training exercises. The Army's air service became autonomous in 1941, under the name Army Air Forces.* In September 1941 the Army conducted a series of maneuvers in Louisiana that pitted entire field armies against each other in unscripted exercises. By the time the United States entered World War II* that December, the Army (including the Army Air Forces) numbered 1.6 million men. Before the war was over, the total would be about eight million.

Economic mobilization for World War II was even more impressive than the manpower mobilization. This time, Americans armed not only themselves but provided massive quantities of supplies and equipment to their Allies through a program known as Lend Lease. Even by today's standards, the accomplishments of American industry in World War II are staggering—the Army alone procured 88,000 tanks, 230,000 aircraft, and 2.4 million trucks between 1941 and 1945.

Moreover, Army and Navy war planners entered the conflict with a clear idea of strategic priorities and a general concept of operations. Even before Pearl Harbor, the United States had reached agreement with its future British allies on a policy of "Germany First." The war in Europe would get top priority, and only after victory over Germany would the Allies turn their combined might against Japan. The Pacific war would fall principally under the control of the U.S. Navy, while the Army would focus upon the great land campaigns in Europe. Although actual events compelled the generals and admirals to modify these plans in practice, the Army focused the bulk of its attention and resources upon Germany.

Although General Marshall wanted to invade German-occupied Europe as early as 1942, circumstances compelled the diversion of troops to the Pacific, North Africa, and Mediterranean theaters in 1942 and 1943. But in 1944 the great invasion of Europe, which was the focal point of the Army's war effort, finally got under way.

Some historians assert that the U.S. Army in the European campaign of World War II exhibited many of the traits that had characterized it in previous wars. As in the Civil War, the Army's objective was to destroy the enemy's ability and will to fight, through direct offensive action and the destruction of the enemy's economic power. But this campaign also forecast the future. The Army of today is the direct descendent of the force that Dwight D. Eisenhower commanded in Europe. Characteristics common to 1944 and today include a heavy reliance on airpower and firepower, extensive motorization, and a preference for swift, decisive, offensive action. Today's division* structure is descended directly from the armored divisions that helped liberate Europe in World War II.

The U.S. Army never completely demobilized at the end of World War II. Occupation troops stayed in Germany and Japan long after the war. The onset of the Cold War,* with its strategies of deterrence and containment, called for the maintenance of sizeable forces, forward deployed in potential combat zones. Ever since colonial days the American military had operated under a policy of mobilization—wait for the war to start, then raise the forces necessary to fight it. In the four decades of the Cold War, the U.S. Army maintained a degree of combat readiness at all times.

Two factors made the Army's task a very difficult one. The development of atomic weapons during World War II and the creation of an independent Air Force in 1947 led many Americans to believe that ground forces had become obsolete. After the Soviet Union detonated its first atomic warhead in 1949, military power was calculated in terms of megatons rather than divisions or capital ships.

The fallacy of this view was driven home the hard way in 1950, when North Korea launched its invasion of the South. For tactical and diplomatic reasons, President Harry S Truman chose not to employ atomic weapons against the invaders. The Army maintained division-sized forces in theater, but they had been skeletonized and dispersed in occupation duties. With Douglas MacArthur* in command, Army forces fighting under the flag of the United Nations eventually stopped the North Korean invasion and liberated the South, only to be driven back again when the People's Republic of China intervened in the conflict. Veterans of World War II had difficulty recognizing that the goal in Korea was deterrence and containment, not unconditional surrender of the enemy. But although the Korean War* was fought under a new strategic concept, the conduct of operations resembled those that the Army had employed in World War II. When the war devolved into stalemate in 1951, it seemed that the trench warfare of World War I had been reinvented. Institutionally, the Korean War represented a new lease on life for the Army, with the weapon modernization and enhanced unit readiness that resulted from the defeats suffered in 1950. The Korean War also prompted a buildup of American ground forces in Europe under North Atlantic Treaty Organization* (NATO) command.

But the greatest military challenge of the Cold War came not in Europe but in Vietnam. At the instigation of President John F. Kennedy, the Army had developed capabilities for unconventional warfare, but when the U.S. Army deployed in force to South Vietnam in 1965, it went as a conventional, European-style army that bore a strong resemblance to the forces that had fought in World War II and Korea. Even now, a generation later, there is no clear consensus as to what went wrong in Vietnam. Some analysts claim that the Army was muzzled by political constraints and prevented from exercising its full, decisive, war-winning capabilities. Others claim that the war in Vietnam was essentially an insurgency, in which conventional military power was irrelevant. Whatever the truth of the matter, for the Army, as for the nation at large, Vietnam was a traumatic, humbling experience.

Following the U.S. withdrawal from Vietnam in 1973, the Army did not set about learning the lessons of the conflict just concluded. Instead, it shifted its attention to a different threat—the Warsaw Pact forces in Europe. Spurred on by information gained in the 1973 Middle East War, the Army embarked upon a massive modernization program designed to meet and defeat Soviet forces in Central Europe. A new doctrine called AirLand Battle* accompanied the buildup of Army strength under President Ronald Reagan. In many ways, AirLand Battle represented a refinement of World War II–style combat, though with increased emphasis on mobility, lethality, and deep battle. Just as significant was a new emphasis on realistic training, utilizing computer technology at training centers designed to make the preparation as realistic as possible.

The Army that trained under AirLand Battle won a resounding victory in the Gulf War, but today's leaders face a painful dilemma—should the Army of the future carry AirLand Battle to higher levels of mobility and lethality, or does the future call for enhanced capabilities in military operations other than war,* such as peacekeeping and humanitarian relief? In other words, should the Army build upon the legacy of World War II and Desert Storm,* or should it draw upon its history as a frontier constabulary force and a colonial army?

—Christopher R. Gabel

A

A TEAM

The Special Forces* A Team, currently referring to an operational detachment, represents the lowest organizational echelon of a Special Forces group. The basic A Team consists of a captain, a warrant officer,* and ten noncommissioned officers* (NCOs). Each team is self-contained, with individuals trained and experienced in operations, intelligence, engineering, medicine, weapons, and communications. The historical roots of the concept rest with the OSS Operational Groups* of World War II,* whose primary mission was to organize and direct partisan guerrillas in area interdiction. The teams were originally configured to operate deep behind enemy lines for extended periods with little or no need for outside support. Current A Team missions include guerrilla warfare, direct action, special reconnaissance, and coalition building.

Reference. Ian D. W. Sutherland, *Special Forces of the United States Army, 1952–1982*, 1990.

Joseph R. Fischer

ABERDEEN PROVING GROUND

Established by presidential proclamation in 1917, Aberdeen Proving Ground, Maryland, is a major U.S. Army research, development, testing, and evaluation center for arms, tracked and wheeled vehicles, and general equipment. The center was formally confirmed on 9 January 1919 when War Department General Order No. 6 authorized the installation as a permanent military post, to be named Aberdeen Proving Ground. Expansion during World War II* resulted in the 1943 development of the Ordnance Research and Development Center (ORDC). Two years later, ORDC split into three major units: Development and Proof Services, the Ballistic Research Laboratory, and the Aberdeen Ordnance Depot. In July 1971, the Proving Ground and Edgewood Arsenal* were consolidated, thus creating a diversified military installation with one of the foremost testing and research facilities in the world.

References. William R. Evinger, ed., *Directory of U.S. Military Bases Worldwide*, 3d ed., 1998. Warren D. Hodges, "New Role for Aberdeen," *Ordnance*, September–October 1971, 132–135.

Luke Knowley

ABRAMS, CREIGHTON W. (1914–1974)

One of the U.S. Army's premier tankers during World War II,* Creighton W. Abrams began his career as a middling cadet at the U.S. Military Academy* in 1936. In 1940, however, he was assigned to the 1st Armored Division, organized in response to German panzer success in the invasion of France. As a tanker, Abrams's talents shone, first as a trainer of tankers and then as commander of the 37th Tank Battalion. The 37th spearheaded the 4th Armored Division in the breakout from Utah beachhead in July 1944 and became Lieutenant General George S. Patton, Jr.'s lead battalion in Third Army's* advance across France. In December 1944, during the German Ardennes offensive,* Abrams broke through to relieve the besieged 101st Airborne Division* at Bastogne. This prompted Patton to remark: "I'm supposed to be the best tank commander in the Army, but I have a peer—Abe Abrams."

A tough, cigar-smoking, loud-swearing warrior, Abrams became supremely adept at sensitive operations as well, demonstrating great finesse when he commanded federal troops during racial unrest in the South during the 1960s, and as commander of U.S. forces in Southeast Asia during the pullout and Vietnamization in the Vietnam War.* During his tenure as Chief of Staff* of the Army (1972–1974), Abrams led the service in its efforts to improve its professional, ethical, and racial climate in the new All-Volunteer Force.*

References. Lewis Sorley, *Thunderbolt*, 1992, and "Creighton Abrams and Active-Reserve Integration in Wartime," *Parameters*, Summer 1991, 35–50.

Donald L. Gilmore

ABRAMS TANK. *See* M1 Abrams Tank.

ABSENT WITHOUT LEAVE

Under the provisions of Article 86 of the Uniform Code of Military Justice* (UCMJ), it is a criminal offense for a service member to fail to go to, or to go from, his appointed place of duty without authority or to absent himself from his unit, organization, or place of duty at which he is required to be at the time prescribed. A service member in violation of Article 86 is said to be absent without leave, or AWOL.

References. Alfred Avins, *The Law of AWOL*, 1957. Alan Levy, Bernard Krisher, and James Cox, *Draftee's Confidential Guide*, 1957.

ACQUISITION CORPS

Based on the findings of the Packard Commission and the mandate of the Goldwater-Nichols Act* of 1986, the U.S. Army established the Acquisition Corps in 1989 and implemented it a year later under the Defense Acquisition Workforce Improvement Act. The Corps currently operates under Title IX, U.S. Code, Chapter 87. Previously, officers from various branches had spent one or possibly two assignments working in the acquisition community. This proved problematic, for example, in that a tour in procurement or acquisitions for an infantry* officer often was a career-ending assignment. Recognizing the need to establish a group of officers who were not part-time members of the acquisition community, the Army identified an alternative career path, enabling its members to compete effectively for promotion. The officers had to have basic qualification as captains, but they would move along a defined career path—competing as program managers rather than battalion* commanders. This allowed officers to focus on jobs and schooling that improved their ability to work in acquisitions.

References. "Acquisition Corps Established," *Army Logistician*, May–June 1990, 2–3. Charles R. Henry, "New Acquisition Corps Enhances DOD Procurement Functions," *Defense* 92, July–August 1992, 53–55.

Jim Martin

ACTIVE DEFENSE

The term Active Defense describes the doctrine* adopted by the U.S. Army in the mid-1970s for possible battle in a European environment. Based on a systems analysis approach, this doctrine was developed under the leadership of General William E. DePuy and then Major General Donn Starry. It differed from previous defensive doctrine in that it was neither purely positional nor a mobile defense; rather, it was a combination of both. The most salient difference in the new doctrine was that it called for units to fight outnumbered and win. Active Defense assumed that a force fighting outnumbered—in this case the U.S. Army—would have advantages in superior technology, logistics, command and control, communications, intelligence, and training. Implying a great deal of mobility inherent in the defending force, this doctrine also assumed that an armored counterattack was the key to any successful defense.

Drawing from the experience of the 1973 Arab-Israeli War and West German army tactical doctrine of the time, Active Defense was also firmly planted in a mathematical system of analysis that embodied four key principles: threat, terrain, ambush, and attack. It divided the battlefield into three areas: the covering force, the main battle area, and the rear area. The U.S. Army officially adopted Active Defense as its tactical doctrine in July 1976, with the publication of Field Manual 100–5, *Operations*. Emerging doctrines replaced the Active Defense in the 1980s.

References. Paul H. Herbert, *Deciding What Has to Be Done*, 1988. Robert E. Wagner, "Active Defense and All That," *Military Review*, August 1980, 4–13.

Chris Clark

ADJUTANT GENERAL. *See* Adjutant General's Corps.

ADJUTANT GENERAL'S CORPS

With the creation of the Continental Army,* the Continental Congress provided a staff generally corresponding to the British army staff of the period. On 16 June 1775, the Continental Congress commissioned Horatio Gates as a brigadier general and appointed him Adjutant General (AG)—thus the Adjutant General's Corps claims to be the second oldest branch in the U.S. Army. Each of the separate armies under George Washington's* command had a comparable position, whose primary responsibilities included serving as key advisor and assistant to the commanding general. Congress abolished the position of Adjutant General when it reduced the size and role of the Army following the American Revolution.*

Responding to weaknesses in the Army demonstrated by a series of reverses in the War of 1812,* Congress passed several reforms in the War Department,* approved an expansion of the Army's staff, and re-created the AG's office. Over the next century, the AG became one of the most important bureaus of the War Department; its rises and declines were closely tied to the influence and prestige of the successive individuals appointed to the office. The AG conducted most of the nonsupply functions of the War Department staff, maintained records, defined policy, coordinated the other bureaus, and, at one time, spoke on behalf of the commander. However, the Root Reforms brought about the first major change in the AG's role, reducing the position's importance and transferring many of its functions to other agencies. In 1950, Congress designated the Adjutant General's Corps as one of fourteen services in the Department of the Army,* and in 1958 the AG lost statutory status and became a special staff officer.

Today, Adjutant General's Corps officers serve in a wide variety of administrative positions primarily dealing with personnel, training, records maintenance, recruitment, and other personnel services. The branch insignia* is a shield with thirteen embossed stars over six vertical stripes that symbolize the Army's trust in the Adjutant General's Corps and its members' authority to speak "for the commander."

References. Lawrence P. Crocker, *Army Officer's Guide*, 46th ed., 1993. Maurice Matloff, ed., *American Military History*, 1969.

ADVANCED COURSE

The advanced course is the second step in the U.S. Army's progressive officer education program. All commissioned officers are required to attend a branch-specific advanced course between their selection for promotion to captain and taking company-level command, normally prior to completing nine years of commissioned service. Graduation from the advanced course prepares the officer for the next level of responsibilities, including company-level command and assignment to a battalion* or brigade* staff, and it is a prerequisite for selection to attend the Combined Arms and Services Staff School* (CAS³) and later the Command and General Staff College.*

References. Arthur S. Collins, Jr., *Common Sense Training*, 1978. John W. Masland and Laurence I. Radway, *Soldiers and Scholars*, 1957.

ADVANCED INDIVIDUAL TRAINING

Advanced individual training (AIT) is the phase of training every new soldier undergoes after completing basic combat training* (BCT). Drill sergeants staff the combat-arms AIT units and apply the same rigorous discipline and training standards as in BCT. Depending on the branch and skill level, AIT courses range from five to twenty-two weeks. AIT trainees receive classroom instruction as well as practical training on the weapons and systems necessary for their Military Occupational Specialty* (MOS). Soldiers who change or reclassify their MOS may also attend additional AIT courses. Generally, however, prior service personnel do not attend the same classes as Initial Entry Training (IET) trainees. Regardless of the status, AIT is a school assignment, and the soldier's job is to learn. Those who do not master the required skills may be held back ("recycled"), sent to another AIT course, or processed out of the service. Upon graduation from AIT, soldiers are awarded their MOS and assigned to units throughout the Army and around the world. The top graduates from each class, designated as distinguished graduates or honor graduates, may be rewarded by accelerated promotion or further schooling opportunities.

References. Raymond K. Bluhm, Jr., and James B. Motley, *The Soldier's Guidebook*, 1995. Frank Cox, *Enlisted Soldier's Guide*, 4th ed., 1996. George C. Wilson, *Mud Soldiers*, 1989.

Michael G. Knapp

AID STATION

An aid station is the farthest-forward medical facility in the U.S. Army's hospital and evacuation system. Typically it is the first point at which wounded and injured soldiers receive medical care. At the aid station, a doctor, medical officer, or medic* provides first aid and establishes priority for subsequent evacuation to the rear. Although Jonathan Letterman made substantial reforms in the regimental hospital system during the Civil War,* not until the mobilization for the Spanish-American War* in 1898 did the predecessor of the modern aid station appear. Colonel Charles R. Greenleaf, chief surgeon of the Army in the field, drew heavily on Letterman's ideas and designed a system that included litter bearers to pick up casualties on the battlefield, move them two or three miles behind the front to collecting stations where they would receive first aid, then evacuate them to field hospitals in ambulances. Later, medical officers and trained enlisted personnel assumed responsibility for the collecting stations. In World War II,* aid stations, also called clearing stations, moved closer to the battle area.

References. Graham A. Cosmas and Albert E. Cowdrey, *Medical Service in the Eu-*

ropean Theater of Operations, 1992. Mary C. Gillett, *The Army Medical Department, 1865–1917*, 1995.

AIR ASSAULT

With the proliferation of nuclear weapons on the battlefield in the 1950s, the need for increased mobility intensified. Decisive results on the nuclear battlefield called for an ability to mass forces rapidly yet quickly disperse them to deny lucrative targets for weapons of mass destruction. These maneuver requirements, coupled with the tactical applications of other new technologies, primarily the helicopter, defined the U.S. Army's new battlefield architecture.

Present-day air assault includes the movement of forces on the battlefield by helicopters, to be airlanded or discharged while still airborne by rapelling. Attack aviation assets normally provide fire support for such operations. In most cases, forces with an airmobility capability can transport about one-third of the total force in one lift. Air assault training may be provided to a variety of combat and combat support troops, to include infantry,* Rangers,* and special operations forces.* However, the preponderance of the capability is normally located in a designated infantry division.* Traditionally, this has been the 101st Airborne Division (Air Assault).*

References. John E. Miller, "Going Deep," *Military Review*, April 1993, 2–12. Dennis Steele, "The 1994 Air Assault Challenge," *Army*, January 1995, 14–20.

Gary Bounds

AIR CAVALRY

Air cavalry is a term applied to U.S. Army units whose generic mission is to use aerial means to augment ground unit reconnaissance and security missions and to perform offensive, defensive, and delaying actions in lightly defended areas or terrain. After intense experimentation in the 1950s, air cavalry units were formally created each, as a troop* within the armored cavalry squadron* of a division,* under the Reorganized Objective Army Division* (ROAD) reorganization of 1962. A captain, later a major, commanded an air cavalry troop that contained twelve commissioned officers, nineteen warrant officers,* and 112 enlisted men. Troop aircraft consisted of nine OH-13s and sixteen Huey UH-1* helicopters. Troop organization included a headquarters, flight operations, aeroscout platoon,* aerorifle platoon, aeroweapons section,* and service platoon.

Air cavalry units are currently found within a divisional cavalry squadron and the regimental aviation squadron of the armored cavalry regiment.* The air cavalry troop of the divisional cavalry squadron may perform route reconnaissance, screen security, movement to contact, or facilitate movement of other units. The air cavalry troops of the regimental aviation squadron performs route, zone, and area reconnaissance, screen security, movement to contact, and hasty attack missions.

References. Simon Dunstan, *Vietnam Choppers*, 1988. Lawrence H. Johnson III, *Winged Sabers*, 1990.

Walter Kretchik

AIR CORPS

The U.S. Army Air Corps represented a stage in the evolution of military air power in the United States. Two camps carried on the public debate over the role of air power in the United States during the early years of military aviation. One side, most closely identified with Brigadier General William "Billy" Mitchell,* advocated an independent air force and argued that airpower alone could attack and destroy an enemy amphibious invasion fleet. Those opposed to an independent air force, principally in the General Staff,* believed that the role of military aviation was to support attacking ground forces. The debate surfaced publicly when Mitchell was court-martialed for accusing Navy and War Department* leaders of "incompetency, criminal negligence, and the almost treasonable administration of the National Defense."

The issues raised by Mitchell's court-martial compelled President Calvin Coolidge to appoint a board, chaired by the highly respected New York banker Dwight W. Morrow, to investigate the role of airpower in the armed forces. The Morrow Board recommended the expansion and elevation of the Air Service* into a combatant corps equal to the existing combat arms—infantry,* cavalry,* field artillery,* and coast artillery*—with special representation on the General Staff. On 2 July 1926, Congress passed the Air Corps Act, codifying the Morrow Board's recommendations.

While retaining military aviation within the War Department, the Air Corps Act changed the name of the Air Service to the Air Corps, provided for aviation representation on the General Staff, and authorized a substantial increase in operational strength, to 17,000 officers and men and 1,800 aircraft. The creation of the Air Corps represented progress toward an independent air force, but the act contained several flaws, principally in funding the authorized strengths. These flaws were clearly demonstrated in 1933, when in a contract dispute with the nation's air lines President Franklin Roosevelt ordered the Air Corps to carry the air mail. The resulting fiasco led to some improvements, but not to an independent air force.

In March 1935, a General Staff reorganization brought into existence the General Headquarters (GHQ) Air Force, responsible for tactical and logistical operations, while the chief of the Air Corps retained responsibility for training. Although this organization resolved some problems, it created others. As both the Air Corps and GHQ were on the same echelon of command, conflict and misunderstanding arose between them. Not until 20 June 1941 were these problems resolved: at that time the Air Corps was renamed the Army Air Forces* (AAF), the AAF command structure was separated from the ground forces, an Air Staff was formed, and a chief of the Army Air Forces became directly responsible to the Chief of Staff.*

References. Maurer Maurer, *Aviation in the U.S. Army, 1919–1939*, 1987. Michael S. Sherry, *The Rise of American Air Power*, 1987. Jeffrey S. Underwood, *The Wings of Democracy*, 1991.

Edward L. Maier III

AIR DEFENSE ARTILLERY

The origins of the U.S. Army's Air Defense Artillery can be traced to 1917 when the Army assigned the new mission of air defense to the coast artillery,* because it had the only experience shooting at moving targets. By the end of World War I,* the Army had formed two gun battalions* and two machine-gun battalions trained by the French. In a four-month period, U.S. antiaircraft gunners—nicknamed "Archies"—shot down fifty-eight German aircraft. Nevertheless, postwar constraints reduced the Army's antiaircraft capability to near extinction, despite warnings of airpower advocates. The growth of the German Luftwaffe and the performance of Germany's Condor Legion in the Spanish Civil War, however, prompted defensive developments and establishment of the Army's Antiaircraft Artillery Command in 1940. During World War II,* U.S. Army antiaircraft artillerymen participated in every major campaign, worldwide. They defended London and Antwerp against Hitler's pilotless V-1 buzz bombs, employing new proximity-fuse munitions to destroy more than 80 percent of the vengeance weapons. The defense of the Remagen Bridge* in March 1945 signaled the climax of antiaircraft activity in World War II.

Strategic concerns dominated the Cold War* years following World War II. In 1953, the Army fielded the Nike Ajax missile system, followed in 1957 by the improved Nike Hercules. These systems were part of the North American Air Defense Command, designed to protect the continental United States from manned Soviet bombers. As missile technology grew, a new Safeguard system, designed to counter Soviet ballistic missiles, replaced the old Nike missile defenses. In 1975, the Sprint missile system was deployed, but it was disestablished shortly thereafter as a result of obsolescence and fiscal constraints.

The most advanced antiaircraft weapon system in the Army's inventory, the Patriot air defense system,* made history in January 1991, shooting down Iraqi Scud missiles aimed at coalition forces in Saudi Arabia. Later, Patriot units provided air defense for Israel and contributed to the diplomatic effort to keep that country out of the Gulf War.

References. Thomas E. Christianson, "Triple A," *Air Defense Artillery*, May–June 1994, 8–16. Charles Edward Kirkpatrick, *Archie in the A.E.F.*, 1984. Kenneth P. Werrell, *Archie, Flak, AAA, and SAM*, 1988.

Thomas Christianson

AIR SERVICE

On 1 August 1907, the U.S. Army established the Aeronautical Division of the Signal Corps* to operate both lighter-than-air and heavier-than-air aircraft. The Aeronautical Division accepted the Army's first airplane, a Wright Flyer, on 2 August 1909. On 18 July 1914, just days before war broke out in Europe, the Aeronautical Division was reorganized as the Aviation Section of the Signal Corps, the arrangement with which the U.S. Army entered World War I* in 1917. On 24 May 1918, just as U.S. air combat operations were commencing, the Aviation Section was renamed the U.S. Army Air Service. Although it had to obtain all of its aircraft from the French and British, and experienced innumerable problems with organization, training, and maintenance, the Air Service performed well during the final months of the war, conducting pursuit, bombing, and observation missions.

Following the war, the Air Service had a turbulent history. Demobilization left it short-handed, appropriations provided little money for modern aircraft, and the debate over the role of airpower in national defense left the air community divided. Based on recommendations by the Morrow Board, appointed by President Calvin Coolidge to investigate military aviation in the United States, on 2 July 1926 Congress passed the Air Corps Act, abolishing the Air Service and creating in its place the Air Corps.*

References. Alfred Goldberg, ed., *A History of the United States Air Force, 1907–1957*, 1957. Maurer Maurer, *Aviation in the U.S. Army, 1919–1939*, 1987.

Randall N. Briggs

AIRLAND BATTLE

The term AirLand Battle first appeared as the title of chapter 8 in the 1976 edition of Field Manual 100–5, *Operations*, the U.S. Army's "capstone" manual, outlining fundamental warfighting doctrine.* The 1976 edition resulted from the new lethality of the battlefield demonstrated in the 1973 Arab-Israeli War and changes wrought by the post–Vietnam War* reduction in Army strength. These events forced the Army's senior leadership to reevaluate the relevance of current Army doctrine based on superior numbers and technology. Army leaders realized that the service needed a more flexible doctrine, with stronger interservice integration. AirLand Battle came to describe this changing vision of the battlefield, from a solely ground-based perspective to one employing airpower in concert with ground forces. The U.S. Air Force fully endorsed this evolving doctrine.

Publication of the 1982 and 1986 editions of FM 100-5 solidified AirLand Battle as a concept centered on strong interservice coordination and a fluid battlefield framework—consisting of "deep" (forward of friendly troops), "close" (the main battle area), and "rear" (behind the combat force) areas. The focus was to attack enemy forces early (deep) with combined air assets and long-range artillery, wearing down enemy forces before they could reach the close fight. Thus, U.S. forces would be able to fight outnumbered and win. The edition of FM 100-5 continued to emphasize the importance of AirLand Battle in light of the fall of the Soviet Union and changing Army missions, although the term disappeared. The most current doctrine emphasizes full spectrum operations which allow a wide variety of operations, ranging from domestic support operations* to total war. The doctrine continues to evolve toward more dependence on operations involving more than one service, and toward more emphasis on combined operations involving U.S. forces and those of one or more allied nations. The current edition of FM 100-5 recognizes that the Army is the only force that can dominate the land battle for extended periods of time.

References. Paul H. Herbert, *Deciding What Has to Be Done*, 1988. John L. Romjue, *From Active Defense to AirLand Battle*, 1984.

                                                                            Robert J. Dalessandro

ALAMO SCOUTS

U.S. Army commanders in the Southwest Pacific Area* (SWPA) theater in 1943 realized at the conclusion of the hard-won New Guinea* campaign that the long march back to the Philippines would be excessively bloody unless improvements were made in the Army's intelligence-gathering apparatus. Aerial reconnaissance failed to provide a clear picture of what lay beneath the triple canopy jungles of the area. To meet the need for more accurate and timely intelligence, Lieutenant General Walter Krueger,* Sixth Army* commanding general, created his own organization of highly skilled soldiers who could infiltrate Japanese-held islands, locate enemy defensive positions, and report the locations to U.S. ground, sea, and air forces. Dubbed the Alamo Scouts, the first volunteers began training in November 1943.

Working directly for Krueger, each scout team consisted of a lieutenant and six or seven enlisted men. U.S. Navy patrol boats usually moved the teams to the vicinity of operations, with the final move to shore in inflatable rubber boats. Teams normally remained ashore only as long as it took to acquire the required information. The first Alamo Scout mission supported the 1st Cavalry Division's landing on Los Negros on 27 February 1944. By the end of World War II,* the Alamo Scouts had conducted eighty missions, killed eighty-four enemy soldiers, and captured twenty-four more, without losing a single scout. Although few in number, the scouts received forty-four Silver Stars,* thirty-three Bronze Stars,* and four Soldier's Medals.* Their most famous operation was the Cabanatuan raid* on a Japanese prisoner of war* camp in the Philippines on 30 January 1945.

References. Lance Q. Zedric, *Silent Warriors of World War II*, 1995, and "Prelude to Victory—The Alamo Scouts," *Army*, July 1994, 49–52.

                                                                            Joseph R. Fischer

ALASKAN HIGHWAY

Dreams of a trans-Alaskan highway that would span Canada and provide a land route to the "lower forty-eight" states started long before World War II.* After the purchase of Alaska from Russia in 1867, various U.S. Army units conducted scientific, meteorological, and mining studies there. The discovery of gold in 1880 expanded the Army's role in Alaska to maintain law and order. Many military and government agencies studied the building of a highway; however, the distance, harsh climate, and mountainous terrain made the cost prohibitive, and cheap sea transportation made the benefits uncertain. After the attack on Pearl Harbor, fear of a Japanese invasion of the West Coast, especially Alaska, increased the value of a highway to the northwest. With the approval of the Canadian government, plans moved ahead to build a road connecting Edmonton, Alberta, with Fairbanks, Alaska. Between 1942 and 1946, forty thousand U.S. military and civilian personnel descended on the Canadian northwest to construct the Alaskan Highway and a railroad through the harsh wilderness.

References. K. S. Coates and W. R. Morrison, *The Alaskan Highway in World War II*, 1992. Stan Cohen, *The Trail of 42*, 1979.

Don Denmark

ALEUTIANS CAMPAIGN

In June 1942, Japanese naval forces converged on the Aleutian Islands as part of an effort to destroy the U.S. Pacific fleet near Midway. Although they failed in the latter effort, the Japanese established a foothold on Attu and Kiska to deter U.S. air and sea attacks on the Kuril Islands and discourage Soviet-U.S. collaboration against Japan. Japan's success in the north did not go unchallenged. The Allies implemented a campaign to sever lines of communications that bound Japan to her island holdings. Attacks consisted of submarine strikes in the western Aleutians and naval and air bombardment of Kiska in the fall of 1942. By April 1943, the Allies had succeeded in tightening the air-sea noose around Japanese forces in the North Pacific. After several postponements due to poor weather, on 11 May 1943 the U.S. 7th Division conducted an amphibious landing on Attu. Although the defenders, fighting from prepared positions, inflicted heavy casualties on the landing force, by the end of May U.S. forces had overcome resistance, and the Japanese decided to cut their loses and abandon the Aleutians. When U.S. troops landed on Kiska in mid-August 1943, the Japanese had already evacuated the island.

References. Stetson Conn, Rose C. Engelman, and Byron Fairchild, *Guarding the United States and Its Outposts*, 1964. Brian Garfield, *The Thousand-Mile War*, 1969.

Steven D. Coats

ALL AMERICAN. *See* 82nd Airborne Division.

ALL-VOLUNTEER FORCE

The move to an all-volunteer U.S. military started in 1970 with the goal to reduce the draft call to zero by the end of 1973. Reflecting a presidential campaign promise to end the draft, the program was implemented a full six months prior to the end of the fiscal year. The U.S. Army received its last draftee on 29 December 1972. With the advent of the new year, the Army entered a new era, one in which it would be charged with maintaining a quality force composed entirely of volunteers.

The Modern Volunteer Army Project, dubbed VOLAR, ushered in a program encompassing both professionalism and enhanced quality of life. The program stressed a "back to basics" approach, educational opportunities, improved housing for soldiers and families, enhanced post services, and better pay. Early incentives and programs were integral parts of the all-volunteer force that has provided quality soldiers to the U.S. Army since the mid-1970s.

References. William Bowman, Roger Little, and G. Thomas Sicilia, eds., *The All-*

Volunteer Force after a Decade, 1986. Roger K. Griffith, Jr., *The U.S. Army's Transition to the All-Volunteer Force, 1968–1974*, 1997.

Gary Bounds

ALLEN, ETHAN (1737–1789)

Born on 10 January 1737 in Litchfield, Connecticut, Ethan Allen formed a ragtag band of irregulars, called the Green Mountain Boys, to fight the British during the American Revolution. Known for his colorful leadership style and profane vocabulary, Allen led his band in a succession of victories over British regulars, Tories, and pro-British settlers in New England. Allen conducted his military operations primarily in what would later become Vermont. His greatest victory was the siege and ultimate capture of the British garrison at Fort Ticonderoga.* George Washington* greatly admired Allen and supported his actions. Later however, Allen opposed Vermont's ratification of the U.S. Constitution, and he lobbied long and hard to maintain his state's sovereignty. Allen died on 12 February 1789 after a long night of drinking with his Green Mountain comrades.

References. Stewart H. Holbrook, *Ethan Allen*, 1958. Charles A. Jellison, *Ethan Allen*, 1969.

Don Denmark

ALLIN CONVERSION

Following the Civil War,* the War Department* decided not to adopt one of the breech-loading, metallic-cartridge, magazine-fed weapons then available, such as the Sharps carbine,* Spencer rifle,* or Henry rifle,* but to convert a number of rifled muskets (1861 Springfield)* then in its armories to breech loaders. E. S. Allin, a master armorer at the Springfield Arsenal,* proposed the design in which a rising breechblock hinged at the front was fitted to an opening milled into the breech of the weapon. The conversion retained the Springfield's furniture, lock plate, barrel, and stock. The new breech loader fired a .58-caliber copper cartridge, rim fire, with a ratchet extractor. Officially designated the U.S. Rifle Model 1865, it was commonly referred to the First Allin Conversion. Five thousand Allins were produced in 1865.

During field trials, several weaknesses became apparent with the Model 1865. The Springfield Arsenal subsequently made a number of design changes and, in 1866, began producing the 'Second Allin Conversion,' the U.S. Rifle Model 1866. In this version the caliber was reduced to .50 by brazing a liner in the barrel, the bolt and firing pin assembly was improved, and the weak extractor was replaced with one operated by a U-shaped spring. Twenty-five thousand Second Allin Conversions were produced between 1866 and 1868.

References. Arcadi Gluckman, *Identifying Old U.S. Muskets, Rifles & Carbines*, 1959, 1965. James E. Hicks, *U.S. Military Firearms, 1776–1956*, 1962.

AMERICAN CANNAE. *See* Cowpens.

AMERICAN EXPEDITIONARY FORCE

The American Expeditionary Force (AEF), commanded by General John J. Pershing,* constituted the U.S. military effort in France during World War I.* From the hastily organized 1st Division* in June 1917, by the November 1918 armistice the AEF had grown to almost two million "doughboys,"* organized into forty-two combat divisions,* seven corps,* and two armies.* The AEF buildup—an enormously complex and time-consuming task—required the creation, training, and equipping of a general headquarters, logistical base, and combat units. Only half a million U.S. troops were in France by mid-May 1918, and the first U.S. offensive action, a 1st Division attack at Cantigny, did not occur until 28 May.

The allies provided the AEF additional shipping in May 1918 to accelerate the manpower buildup, and over a million U.S. troops reached France during the last six months of the war. In June, AEF forces fought at Chateau-Thierry* and Belleau Wood. In July, AEF units battled along the Marne River and at Soissons; by the end of summer, two U.S. corps had joined the French in a general offensive against the Germans. Created in August, the U.S. First Army,* commanded by Pershing, reduced the St. Mihiel* salient in two days, and it participated in the Meuse-Argonne* campaign from 26 September until the armistice. Pershing created the U.S. Second Army* in mid-October and assumed command of both armies. Total AEF battle casualties numbered 52,947 killed and 202,628 wounded. After the armistice, the U.S. Third Army* was created to occupy a bridgehead across the Rhine River at Coblenz.

References. Edward Coffman, *The War to End All Wars*, 1986. Timothy K. Nenninger, "American Military Effectiveness in the First World War," *Military Effectiveness*, vol. 1, ed. Allan R. Millett and Williamson Murray, 116–156, 1988. Donald Smythe, *Pershing*, 1986.

Robert Ramsey

AMERICAN LEGION

The American Legion, an organization of U.S. war veterans, was founded in Paris, France, in March 1919. A committee, chaired by Lieutenant Colonel Theodore Roosevelt, Jr., led a delegation of combat and service units from the American Expedtionary Force* (AEF) that adopted the original charter. Membership requirements today are that one has served in a U.S. military service and received an honorable discharge.* The organization, headquartered in Indianapolis, Indiana, is nonpolitical and nonsectarian. The American Legion provides a forum for airing the organization's special interests, which include education, health, and industry.

The Legion was instrumental in establishing hospitals to provide vitally needed medical care for World War I* veterans. The Legion has also helped set up programs of compensation and pensions for the disabled and military widows and orphans. The Legion's lobbying resulted in the creation of the Veterans Administration* and passage of the G.I. Bill * for World War II* veterans—

later amended to include Korean War* and Vietnam-era veterans as well. These measures afforded university and vocational training for millions of veterans and also allowed them to purchase homes, under special loan provisions. These groundbreaking efforts served as a foundation for an effort that has continued to expand and improve over the past eighty years.

Today, the American Legion is a thriving organization with a membership of 3.1 million. The annual convention is one of the largest volunteer-group meetings in the United States, quite a legacy for an organization originally chartered by twenty-five World War I veterans.

References. Miles Z. Epstein, "Seventy-Five Years for God and Country," *The American Legion*, September 1994, 42–44. William Pencak, *For God and Country*, 1989.

Ralph Nichols

AMERICAN REVOLUTION

The American Revolution was the cradle of American democracy and the formative period in the history of the U.S. Army. Following the outbreak of fighting on 19 April 1775 at Lexington, the Continental Congress moved to assume authority over the armed host that had been confronting elements of the British army around Boston. After some delay, on 14 June 1775, Congress voted to adopt the New England army as the Continental Army* and, the next day it appointed George Washington* of Virginia as its commander in chief.* After lengthy debate, the defiant American colonists defined two political goals of the war: independence and expansion. The vision was of a nation independent of Europe and dominant in North America, and these aims were the foundation of Washington's military strategy, even as circumstances changed over time. Those differing circumstances and Washington's strategic concepts arising from them divided the war into four distinct periods.

The first phase of the American Revolution, from April 1775 to July 1776, was the revolutionary phase. It began with royal officials in charge of every province in North America; it ended with the rebels running thirteen unified colonies stretching from Canada to Florida, with not a redcoat remaining on U.S. soil. Instinctively at first, and then by plan, the colonists assailed British forces wherever they could get at them. They attacked Fort Ticonderoga,* Canada, Boston, Florida, the West Indies, and many other places. Revolutionaries are by definition aggressive; they must assault the constituted authority in order to displace it. Although the colonists were woefully weak, the British in North America were even weaker. To take advantage of those favorable conditions, Washington reasoned, the Continentals had to take great risks. His strategy was to go on the offensive, in every way and in every place that he could. The possible rewards made virtually any risk acceptable, for a repulse would have been no more than a minor setback. That offensive-mindedness wrested the thirteen colonies from Britain and came close to achieving more, for England retained Canada only by the narrowest of margins.

Having declared independence, the Americans at once had to defend their newly won country. England sent only two major expeditionary forces across the Atlantic, and both were during this second period of the war, from June 1776 to December 1777. The first, arriving in the summer of 1776, was the largest London had ever sent anywhere—nearly 50,000 British and German troops, backed by the Royal Navy. The Americans could muster less than half as many men, most of whom were militia or untrained recruits. Moreover, the colonists had no navy, other than a few raiders, to prey on enemy shipping. Given the suddenly altered situation, Washington changed his strategy.

The Continental Army had to fight—for the British could not be allowed to roam at will over the land—but more importantly, it had to survive. In the face of the new odds, a defeat could spell disaster, while a victory might only throw the enemy temporarily off balance. Keeping the army intact was a higher goal than gaining battlefield success. During this period, Washington earned his reputation as a Fabian general, one who constantly nips at the heels of a superior opponent but avoids decisive engagements.

The British struck along the Hudson River from both north and south. Rather easily they pushed the Continentals out of Canada and deftly wedged them out of New York City. Thinking that their sizeable army might simply awe the rebels into putting down their arms, the British failed to drive ahead ruthlessly and decisively. Unexpected resistance slowed them, and with the onset of winter the British northern army withdrew into Canada. Major General William Howe, commanding along the lower Hudson, followed the retreating Continentals across New Jersey to the Delaware River before halting. Washington had avoided disaster, but the Revolution was at a low ebb.

Then, in a ten-day campaign at Christmas, Washington turned on his lethargic foe, won victories at Trenton* and Princeton, and drove deep to occupy positions in the mountains of New Jersey, where he was unassailable. Now he stood on the flank of the British supply lines running across New Jersey. Howe had no choice but to withdraw to New York City, with little to show for all his efforts of 1776.

Reinforced in 1777 by another large contingent of fighting units, the British resumed their offensive. Major General John Burgoyne marched one wing south from Canada, while Howe took the other by sea to Philadelphia. That strategically questionable move put the two forces too far apart for mutual support. Washington led elements to defend Philadelphia, while Horatio Gates and Benedict Arnold* opposed the invaders in northern New York. Losing a series of battles around Philadelphia, Washington failed to hold Howe in that city, but he kept the Continental Army together and in the field. In the north, overextended and unsupported, Burgoyne surrendered after failing to break through American defenses above Albany.

The campaign of 1776 and 1777 turned the tide of the war. The rebels had withstood the best the British could throw at them. At that point, having been secretly providing support to the rebels, France decided to join them openly and declared war on England. Spain and Holland soon entered on the side of France, and England found itself in a worldwide war. This would lead to the third phase of the war, January 1778 to October 1781.

At winter camp at Valley Forge,* Pennsylvania, Washington realized that the war's circumstances had shifted fundamentally once more. Having France as a formal ally offered chances for joint operations with a fleet and perhaps a combined French and American army superior to any the British could field. In addition, the professionalization of the Continental Army, its growing experience, longer enlistments, and stronger focus on training, along with money and arms from France, had combined to forge a revitalized army able to match European troops in open battle. That was demonstrated in June 1778, when Continentals mauled British units evacuating Philadelphia. It became possible to think again of gaining decisive victory.

But coordinating coalition operations proved difficult. For three years, efforts to coordinate with the French fleet were uniformly frustrating; all attempts to deliver a joint blow were thwarted by an inability to synchronize the allied forces. Still, the arrival in 1780 of a French army under the Comte de Rochambeau provided a great morale boost to Americans who were tiring of the prolonged struggle, then in its sixth year. Washington and Rochambeau contemplated offensive operations for 1781.

Meanwhile, numerous military expeditions expanded the territory controlled by the rebels, particularly in the wilderness regions west of the Appalachian Mountains. Washington kept the bulk of the Continental Army coiled at or near West Point, on the Hudson. From this strategic central location—the single most important position in North America, in the minds of senior leaders on both sides—he threatened New York City and blocked any attempt to operate in the area from Pennsylvania to Massachusetts. The British, therefore, decided to send powerful detachments to recapture the southern states. Americans suffered more reverses than successes in the subsequent fighting, but the British were never able to consolidate their gains. Nathanael Greene* won laurels for brilliant Fabian operations similar to those Washington had conducted in 1776 and 1777. The result was that in 1781 a large army under General Lord Cornwallis found itself bottled up in coastal Virginia near Yorktown.* Just at that time, French Admiral François de Grasse announced his intention to cooperate with the allied land forces in the area.

Washington and Rochambeau rapidly marched their armies southward. When they and the French fleet arrived simultaneously at Yorktown, Cornwallis was trapped. Besieged by land and cut off at sea, he surrendered. That was the decisive victory Washington had long sought. The king and his ministers decided to accept the independence of the former colonies.

Although conflict continued in other theaters, little fighting occurred in North America during the last phase of the war, from November 1781 to December 1783. Yet it was a time fraught with danger for the young nation. In some ways, it was the most dangerous part of the long war. Complacency and war weariness could well have caused everything won on the battlefield to be lost at the negotiating table. Washington struggled to prevent the Continental Army from disintegrating, and he personally defused a movement to turn the army against the civilian government. As a result, American negotiators obtained a favorable settlement. The Treaty of Paris recognized the independence of the United States and gave the new nation sovereignty over all the land between Canada (which remained British) and Florida (which went to Spain). The western boundary was the Mississippi River. Essentially, the goals of the American Revolution had been attained.

References. John R. Alden, *A History of the American Revolution*, 1972. Don Higginbotham, *The War of American Independence*, 1971. Dave R. Palmer, *The Way of the Fox*, 1975. Howard H. Peckham, *The War for Independence*, 1958.

Dave R. Palmer

ANACONDA PLAN

At a cabinet meeting on 29 June 1861, Lieutenant General Winfield Scott,* general-in-chief of the U.S. Army, proposed a military strategy for defeating the Confederacy. Rather than invade the South, Scott proposed encircling the Confederate states by blockading the coasts and splitting the Confederacy by controlling the Mississippi River. Scott's plan would isolate the South from all sources of supply, debilitate it economically, and allow for the growth of anti-secessionist sentiments. This plan, however, would require a large increase in the U.S. Navy and the creation and training of an army to control the land along the Mississippi. He estimated four and a half months would be required to prepare and implement such a strategy. Scott further proposed that should his strategy not succeed, the Union create a 300,000-man army that could invade the South and win the conflict in two or three years.

The Northern press dubbed Scott's strategy the "Anaconda Plan," after the serpent that slowly squeezes its victims to death. Public opinion held that the war would be short, and it demanded an invasion to destroy the rebellion. At the same cabinet meeting, Brigadier General Irvin McDowell, commander of the Army of Northeastern Virginia, proposed to attack and destroy the Confederate army assembling in the vicinity of Manassas Junction. Northern newspapers trumpeted "On to Richmond" (the Confederate capital) and expected a victorious Union Army soon to march into that city. Scott's plan was disregarded, and McDowell's was accepted. The result would be Union defeat at First Bull Run.*

A Union naval blockade of the South was imposed in April 1861, but it was ineffectual; as late as 1864 one in three blockade runners got through. In March 1862, the U.S. Army launched a campaign to open the Mississippi from the north, while a joint Army-Navy force captured New Orleans in April. By 9 July 1863, with the fall of Vicksburg* and Port Hudson* in Louisiana, the entire Mississippi was opened to Union traffic. These aspects of Scott's "Anaconda Plan" were vital to the ultimate defeat of the Confederacy, but it was still necessary to destroy the Confederate armies to force the South to surrender.

References. Herman Hattaway and Archer Jones, *How the North Won*, 1983. James M. McPherson, *Battle Cry of Freedom*, 1988.

Richard L. Kiper

ANDERSONVILLE

In February 1864, when prison facilities in Richmond became overcrowded, Confederate authorities opened Camp Sumter, widely known as Andersonville Prison, northeast of Americus, Georgia. The original prison was a sixteen-and-a-half-acre plot—later expanded to twenty-six acres—straddling a small stream and surrounded by a log stockade. Inside, parallel to the stockade, was a small fence that marked the "deadline," beyond which prisoners would be shot. The prison housed only enlisted soldiers, who received the same rations as Confederate soldiers. However, unlike their 2,300 guards, who were mostly raw militia, prisoners could not forage for additional supplies, and the commandant, Captain Henry Wirz, refused gifts of provisions for the prisoners from the local population. Shelters erected by the prisoners were nothing more than dugouts covered with rags. A prisoner gang called the "Raiders" terrorized the inmates. No precise figures for the total number of men who entered Andersonville exist, but the mean strength in August 1864 was 32,899. The hospital mortality rate was 83 percent. The Andersonville National Cemetery holds 12,912 graves, but actual deaths far exceeded this number. In October 1864, Sherman's advance prompted the movement of healthy prisoners to Millen, Georgia. After the war, Henry Wirz was tried by Federal military authorities, convicted of war crimes, and executed.

References: Ovid L. Futch, *History of Andersonville Prison*, 1968. William Marvel, *Andersonville*, 1994.

Charles Heller

ANTIETAM

On 4 September 1862, General Robert E. Lee,* commanding the Confederate Army of North Virginia, entered Maryland with 51,800 men. His objectives were to bring relief to Virginia farmers whose lands were being ravaged; draw Maryland into the Confederacy; weaken Northern will; cut the North's east-west rail line; and capture the Harpers Ferry* arsenal. After Union soldiers found a copy of Lee's Order 191 dividing his army into four columns, Major General George B. McClellan,* with 87,100 troops, moved to the South Mountain passes to destroy Lee's columns in detail. Surprised at his opponent's aggressiveness, Lee attempted to delay Union forces while consolidating his army near Sharpsburg. There Lee placed his small force in a semicircle, flanks anchored on the Potomac. On 16 September, McClellan's army occupied the heights overlooking Antietam Creek. Instead of attacking, McClellan hesitated until the following morning, when at 0600 he began a series of uncoordinated attacks. Lee, with interior lines, maneuvered his outnumbered forces to block the fragmented assaults. The initial engagements took place in the East Woods, through a corn field, around Dunker Church, and into the West Woods. In the early afternoon, intending to reinforce the morning assaults, Union forces drove the Confederates from what became known as the the Bloody Lane at Lee's center, then halted. After delaying for most of the day, Union troops on Lee's right crossed the Lower Bridge—known since as Burnside's Bridge. With a Union victory in sight, Confederate forces arriving from Harpers Ferry repelled this final assault. Nevertheless, Lee retired across the Potomac. Casualties included 12,469 Union and 10,292 Confederate killed, wounded, and missing, making this the bloodiest day of the Civil War.* The battle of Antietam (called Sharpsburg by the Confederates) marked the war's turning point, in that after this Union victory Lincoln issued the Emancipation Proclamation on 1 January 1863, ending any chance of foreign recognition for the Confederacy and making a vast pool of black manpower available to the Union armies.

References. John Cannan, *The Antietam Campaign*, rev. ed., 1994. John W. Schildt, *Drums along the Antietam*, 1972. Stephen W. Sears, *Landscape Turned Red*, 1983.

Charles Heller

ANVIL

Anvil was the code name for the Allied invasion of southern France in the summer of 1944. The proposal for such an invasion surfaced at the Trident Conference in May 1943, but a long debate among Allied leaders over the appropriate strategy for the defeat of Germany, availability of forces, and priorities for landing craft delayed a firm decision until the end of June 1944. The Anvil plan called for landings between Toulon and Cannes, seizure and development of a major port, and exploitation northward up the Rhone valley. The initial landings took place on 15 August, with the landing force consisting of the U.S. VI Corps and elements of the First French Army. Eventually, the U.S. Seventh Army* joined the First French Army under 6th Army Group, commanded by General Jacob L. Devers, in a campaign to liberate southern France and link up with 12th Army Group for the final assault into Germany.

Shortly before the landings in southern France in August 1944, the code name for the operations was changed to Dragoon.* In the historical literature, however, Anvil is more commonly used.

References. Jeffrey J. Clarke and Robert Ross Smith, *Riviera to the Rhine*, 1993. Maurice Matloff, *Strategic Planning for Coalition Warfare, 1943–1944*, 1959.

ANZIO

In the early morning of 22 January 1944, the U.S. VI Corps began landing at Anzio, thirty-three miles south of Rome, Italy. Codenamed Operation Shingle, the Anzio assault was a politically inspired operation designed to outflank the German Gustav Line.* This operation had become attractive when the Allied 15th Army Group, under Field Marshal Sir Harold Alexander, stalled in front of the formidable defensive line in bitter fighting at Cassino. This long-debated turning movement began with every expectation of success. The amphibious assault at Anzio would be joined by an attack against the Gustav Line in the Liri Valley. In theory, this would link both forces for a drive on Rome. The landings at Anzio, behind German lines, initially achieved complete surprise; there was only one weak German regiment within twenty-five miles. Field Marshal Albert Kesselring had just weakened the area by committing two German panzer divisions to the Cassino fight. He had, however, made contingency plans for just such an Allied move and rapidly began executing those plans. He recalled units from the front and from as far away as France and placed them under the command of General Eberhard von Mackensen, who eventually controlled nine divisions.

Major General John P. Lucas, unaware how few German forces opposed him, continued to consolidate his beachhead in an area fifteen miles wide by seven miles deep. His failure to seize the Alban Hills behind the beachhead and the main road to Rome is often cited as a reason for his later lack of success. Whether he had the forces necessary to seize the Alban Hills is debatable, but by nightfall on the 22d the Allies had come under increasing pressure. From 2 to 10 February, the Germans conducted a series of counterattacks against the British salient at Campoleone; they could not break through. The Germans again tried to pierce the defenses on the Albano Road in attacks from 16 to 20 February. Bitter fighting and counterattacks finally halted the Germans. Allied superiority in artillery and morale were factors in holding the beachhead until the two Allied forces in Italy linked up.

References. Martin Blumenson, *Anzio*, 1963. Carlo D'Este, *Fatal Decision*, 1992. Fred Sheehan, *Anzio*, 1964.

George Mordica II

ANZUS PACT

On 1 September 1951, Australia, New Zealand, and the United States signed the Pacific Security treaty. The treaty, which has become known as the ANZUS Pact, was similar to the NATO* agreement and obliged each member of the pact to aid the others in case of attack by an outside party. The treaty also established the Pacific Council, with the members to meet once a year, or more if necessary. A military representative from each member was to advise the Council on current military affairs. For the Australians and New Zealanders, ANZUS was a major diplomatic step: for the first time, both countries had joined an alliance not associated with Great Britain. This reflected the changing alignment of powers in the Pacific following World War II.* The ANZUS Pact continued in force until the mid-1980s. The electoral victory of the Labor party in New Zealand caused difficulties for the pact when the new government declared New Zealand a nuclear-free zone. For security reasons, the U.S. government refused to declare which of its naval vessels entering New Zealand ports carried nuclear weapons, thus creating an impasse. When the two countries could not come to an agreement, the treaty was left in abeyance.

References. Richard W. Baker, ed., *The ANZUS States and Their Region*, 1994. Jacob

Bercovitch, ed., *ANZUS in Crisis*, 1988. Joseph A. Camilleri, *The Australia New Zealand US Alliance*, 1987. Frank P. Donnini, *ANZUS in Revision*, 1991.

Trevor Brown

APACHE AH-64

A symbol of U.S. air power, this two-person helicopter has over the years provided the United States with a first-class reconnaissance and attack vehicle. McDonnell Douglas began test flights in 1975 and delivered the first Apache in 1984. Specifications for the Apache are: overall length 48 feet 2 inches (14.68 meters); height 16 feet 1 inch (4.9 meters); empty weight 11,387 pounds; (5,165 kg); cruising speed 182 mph (293 kmh/158 knots), with a maximum speed of 227 mph (365 kmh/197 knots); service ceiling 21,000 feet (6,400 meters); operating range 300 miles (482 km); and a fuel reserve of 30 minutes. Armament includes: an M239 chain-gun 30 mm autocannon that fires high-explosive (HE) or high-explosive dual-purpose (HEDP) rounds at a rate of 625 per minute; sixteen Hellfire antitank missiles, or seventy-six 2.75 mm folding-fin aerial rockets (FFAR); or a combination of the above, depending on the mission.

The Apache has been upgraded three times. The B version appeared in 1991 and included improved navigation equipment, new rotor blades, new targeting equipment, and Sincgras radios; the Cs were equipped with new engines. The D, named the Longbow, mounted a millimeter-wave radar and had new Hellfire missiles with better targeting equipment. The Apache saw action in Desert Storm* and today serves on the front line in the Army's air cavalry* units.

References. Douglas W. Nelms, "The Awesome Apache," *Army*, January 1987, 38–47. George Sullivan, *Military Aircraft*, 1993.

Trevor Brown

APOTHECARY GENERAL

The position of Apothecary General was written into the March 1813 reorganization of the War Department* staff "for the better superintendence and management of the hospital and medical establishment of the army of the United States." The Apothecary General was to assist the Physician and Surgeon General; receive and manage all stores, medicines, instruments, and dressings; account for supply distribution; compound, prepare, and issue medicines; and pay enlisted wages. Doctor Francis LeBaron was appointed Apothecary General on 11 June 1813, recognizing his acomplishment of the same duties in an unofficial capacity since February 1812. His tenure was marked by all the problems expected from a purchasing system that was centralized but beyond his control. At one point, the secretary of war* warned that additional complaints would see "the government discontinue your services." Congress eliminated the position in 1821, leaving the Surgeon General* to organize the Medical Department as necessary for the procurement of medical supplies.

References. Mary C. Gillett, *The Army Medical Department, 1775–1818*, 1981; and *The Army Medical Department, 1818–1865*, 1987.

David A. Rubenstein

APPOINTMENT IN A COMBAT ZONE. *See* Battlefield Commission.

ARDENNES OFFENSIVE

After breaking out of the the Normandy lodgment area at the end of July 1944, the Allied armies raced across France. Due to the distances and limited Allied logistics capability, however, the offensive finally ground to a halt. By December 1944, the Allies faced the Germans along a front from the North Sea to the Swiss border. The Allied commander, General Dwight D. Eisenhower,* chose an area in Belgium, the Ardennes, to rest his bloodied divisions* and to prepare green ones for combat by keeping them in a relatively quiet sector until needed. Thus, the U.S. VII Corps was stretched out along an eighty-mile front. Eisenhower's decision was clearly a calculated risk, based on Allied intelligence estimates about German capabilities and the terrain.

As early as July 1944, Adolf Hitler secretly began planning a counteroffensive in the West. The continued pressure on the Eastern Front and successful Allied landings at Normandy had convinced Hitler that he must take measures to stabilize the West, and then turn east. Hitler deceived Allied intelligence about his planned offensive by calling it "Watch on the Rhine" and reappointing the defensive-minded Field Marshal Gerd von Rundstedt as Supreme Commander West. The plan called for a surprise attack through the heavily wooded Ardennes in Belgium. The attack would defeat and isolate the 21st Army Group by seizing the crossings at the Meuse River, take Brussels, and eventually seize Antwerp. Hitler hoped that this success would split the Allies and lead to a negotiated peace.

Army Group B, under the command of Field Marshal Walter Model, looked impressive on paper. It included the Sixth Panzer Army in the north, the Fifth Panzer Army in the center, and the Seventh Panzer Army in the south. Hitler exercised personal control of the offensive. Model launched the attack on 16 December 1944 in severe weather conditions to limit interference by superior Allied air forces. The avenues of approach and the central towns of the Ardennes collectively became the focus of the battle. Small, well-led, and desperate Allied detachments defended these centers and disrupted the exact timetable calculated by the Germans as necessary for success. The Allied response in redistributing forces, rushing reserves to the crisis, and exploiting their artillery superiority defeated the German attack. By 3 January 1945, after tremendous sacrifices on both sides, the offensive was over, and the Allied front was reestablished by 16 January. The Ardennes offensive represented a desperate gamble by Hitler that only delayed, for a short time, the Allied advance on Germany. The loss of men and weapons exhausted Germany's last chance for a coordinated defense of its borders.

References. Hugh M. Cole, *The Ardennes*, 1965. Jerry D. Morelock, *Generals of the Ardennes*, 1994. Russell Weigley, *Eisenhower's Lieutenants*, 1981.

George Mordica II

ARLINGTON NATIONAL CEMETERY

Arlington National Cemetery, located on a wooded hillside across the Potomac River from Washington, D.C., is one of the nation's most revered shrines. The cemetery holds the remains of veterans from every U.S. war from the American Revolution* to the present. It was established during the closing months of the Civil War* on the estate of Robert E. Lee; Quartermaster General Montgomery Meigs selected the site as retribution for Lee's "treasonous act" of resigning his commission and fighting for the Confederacy. Thousands of Americans and foreign tourists visit the cemetery each year to view the Tomb of the Unknown Soldier* and John F. Kennedy's burial site.

References. Owen Andrews, *A Moment of Silence*, 1994. Philip Bigler, *In Honored Glory*, 1987. John Vincent Hinkel, *Arlington*, 1965. James Edward Peters, *Arlington National Cemetery*, 1986.

Don Denmark

ARMED FORCES JOURNAL. See Army and Navy Journal.

ARMED FORCES JOURNAL INTERNATIONAL. See Army and Navy Journal.

ARMED FORCES STAFF COLLEGE

The requirement to prepare officers specifically for the planning, conduct, and command of joint (multiservice) and combined (multinational) operations, identified during World War II,* led to the establishment of the Army-Navy Staff College in 1943. On 13 August 1946, the Joint Chiefs of Staff* (JCS) established the Armed Forces Staff College (AFSC) to continue the preparation of officers for joint and combined assignments. Currently located in Norfolk, Virginia, AFSC is one of four institutions, designated to conduct advanced joint and combined education, that constitute the National Defense University.* The mission of the AFSC's two schools is to provide instruction to officers of all the armed forces for service on joint and combined staffs. The Joint and Combined Staff Officer School (JCSOS) provides Joint Professional Education (JPE) Phase II instruction to field-grade officers. The Joint Command, Control, and Electronic Warfare School (JCEWS) conducts courses on the more technical aspects of joint operations. Passage of the Goldwater-Nichols Act* increased the importance of joint military education and training. Completion of Phase II at the AFSC and a successful joint tour of duty may lead to an officer to selection as a joint service officer.

References. John W. Masland and Laurence I. Radway, *Soldiers and Scholars*, 1957. Ike Skelton, "JPME," *Military Review*, May 1992, 2–9.

J. G. D. Babb

ARMOR

The U.S. Army Tank Corps was created on 26 January 1918, with Colonel Samuel D. Rockenbach as chief. Colonel George S. Patton, Jr.,* soon commanded the first U.S. tanks in battle and later the 304th U.S. Tank Brigade. He also was responsible for developing the first U.S. Army tank training center in France. The Tank Corps proved effective in battle at St. Mihiel* and the Meuse-Argonne.*

Following World War I,* the National Defense Act of 1920* abolished the Tank Corps and delegated responsibility for the development of tanks to the chief of infantry. The Infantry Tank Board continued testing tank modifications and new equipment. In 1927, while observing maneuvers by a British experimental force, Secretary of War* Dwight Davis was so impressed that he directed the General Staff* to organize a similar U.S. unit. Major Adna R. Chaffee, Jr.,* was assigned to help organize the mechanized force. Colonel Daniel Van Voorhis, commander of the new force at Fort Eustis, Virginia, established the basic principles of the Armored Force in 1931—earning him the title "Grandfather of the Armored Force." Although the War Department* disbanded the Mechanized Force in 1931, other branches carried on the work of mechanization specifically for their needs.

Chaffee continued to campaign for mechanization, and in 1938 he assumed command of the newly created 7th Cavalry Brigade (Mechanized) at Fort Knox,* Kentucky. At its inception on 10 July 1940, Chaffee became the first chief of the Armored Force. The 7th Cavalry Brigade (Mechanized) was the backbone of the new force. Early armor doctrine* was heavily cavalry oriented; little attention was given to field artillery or even to tank gunnery. The arrival of Major General Jacob Devers, a field artillery* officer, who became the second chief of the Armored Force in August 1941, changed the focus of the force. The Armored Force was redesignated the Armored Command on 2 July 1943, under the command of Major General Alvan C. Gillem, Jr., and armored training activities became more closely coordinated with Army Ground Forces. During World War II* the Armored Force comprised sixteen armored divisions and sixty-three separate tank battalions.* Cavalry was officially included as part of the Armor Branch in 1950. The home of armor/cavalry today is Fort Knox.

References. George F. Hofmann and Donn A. Starry, eds., *Camp Colt to Desert Storm*, 1999. Mary Lee Stubbs and Stanley Russell Connor, *Armor-Cavalry, Part I*, 1984.

George Mordica II

ARMOR DIVISION

An armor division is a military organization of all arms built around the tank. Such an organization first emerged in 1936 as a proposal to create a mechanized cavalry division* but was rejected at that time. In the spring of 1940, after the Germans defeated Poland using the new *blitzkrieg* tactics, the U.S. Army experimented with a provisional armored division formed by combining the cavalry's mechanized brigade* and the infantry's* tank regiments* during the Louisiana Maneuvers.* Following a conference in the Alexandria, Louisiana, schoolhouse, General George C. Marshall* recommended the creation of an armored force and armored divisions.

The 1st and 2d Armored Divisions were organized in July 1940, with the first being formed from infantry tank regiments. Before World War II* was over, the U.S. Army had formed and fielded sixteen armored divisions, in two different configurations. The first, known as a heavy division, consisted of two armored (tank) regiments of six battalions,* one armored infantry regiment of one battalion, three armored artillery battalions, and other supporting formations. The second, the light division, with greater communications capability, accounted for fourteen of the sixteen divisions; it consisted of three tank battalions, three armored infantry battalions, three armored artillery battalions, and supporting formations.

Following World War II, the armored division was renamed the armor division, retaining the basic organization of the light division. Later, under the Reorganized Objective Army Division (ROAD)* concept, the armor division grew to a total of nine maneuver battalions, generally five armor (tank) and four mechanized, the model it retains today. The primary purpose of the armor division is to close with and destroy the enemy by fire, protected by maneuver, and shock effect in offensive combat.

References. Mary Lee Stubbs and Stanley Russell Conner, *Armor-Cavalry, Part I*, 1984. John B. Wilson, *Maneuver and Firepower*, 1998.

John Broom

ARMORED CAR M-8

Developed during World War II,* the M-8 armored car was designed to provide high speed, mobility, defensive firepower, and crew protection for reconnaissance missions. Ford Motor Company completed the first production M-8 in 1943; it remained in production until 1945. Used extensively by U.S. and Allied forces, the M-8's hull was constructed of welded steel with a centrally mounted, open-top turret. The vehicle's primary protection consisted of 7/8-inch frontal and 3/8-inch side armor. Normal armament was one M6 37 mm gun, one coaxially mounted M1919A4 .30-caliber machine gun, and one M2 heavy-barrel .50-caliber machine gun on a pedestal mount for antiaircraft protection. The M-8 carried a crew of four, with interior space for ammunition storage and two radios.

References. Emory A. Dunham, *Tank Destroyer History*, 1946. B. T. White, *Tanks and Other Armored Fighting Vehicles of World War II*, 1983.

David Zoellers

ARMORED CAVALRY ASSAULT VEHICLE

The armored cavalry assault vehicle (ACAV) was an adaptation of the M113 armored personnel carrier* (APC) employed during the Vietnam War.* The M113, equipped with a gun shield around the commander's station, mounted a .50-caliber machine gun, pedestals and shields for two to four side-mounted M60 7.62 mm machine guns, and a front-facing, flat gun shield. Some ACAVs also carried a "hurricane fence" as a defense against rocket-propelled grenades*

(RPG). Significantly lighter than a medium or main battle tank, the ACAV was more maneuverable in the difficult Vietnamese countryside. The firepower of the multiple machine guns and the vehicle's good mobility combined to create a surrogate light tank. ACAVs could accompany reconnaissance and infantry* units, while their armor protection made them useful in a close-support role.

While Army of the Republic of Vietnam (ARVN) units had modified the M113 as early as 1963, the 11th Armored Cavalry was the first U.S. Army unit to implement this modification before arriving in Vietnam in 1966; the idea was quickly adopted by many other units, and many M113s were modified in South Vietnam. The armored cavalry assault vehicle remained in service into the early 1980s, when it was replaced by the M2/3 Bradley series of fighting vehicles.

References. John H. Hay, Jr., *Tactical and Material Innovations*, 1974. Donn A. Starry, *Mounted Combat in Vietnam*, 1978.

John Broom

ARMORED CAVALRY REGIMENT

The armored cavalry regiment (ACR) is the descendent of the horse cavalry* and dates to the period between the world wars. The ACR's mission is to perform reconnaissance, provide security for the main force, and engage in offensive, defensive, and delaying operations. Currently, an ACR consists of squadrons that are a mix of the M3 Bradley armor fighting vehicle and and the M1 Abrams tank,* plus artillery and aviation assets and other supporting units. They may operate as independent units or as attachments to other units. The importance of the ACR's role was especially evident in the deployment of two ACRs along the old inter-German border, where they were an integral part of the strategy for the defense of Western Europe during the Cold War.* In the event of Warsaw Pact aggression, these units were to detect and engage attacking forces in delaying actions until North Atlantic Treaty Organization* forces could be deployed. Armored cavalry saw service in World War II* and the Korean War.* In Vietnam, armored cavalry troopers often rode into combat. Since the end of the Cold War, the German-border mission has been rendered moot; however, armored cavalry units still play a significant role. Most recently, armored cavalry saw action in Desert Storm.* Despite the deactivation of some units due to overall force reduction, armored cavalry regiments remain a part of the Army's force structure.

References. Tom Clancy, *Armored Cav*, 1994. Michael D. Mahler, *Ringed in Steel*, 1986. Mary Lee Stubbs and Stanley Russell Conner, *Armor-Cavalry, Part I*, 1984.

James E. Franklin

ARMORED DIVISION. *See* Armor Division.

ARMORED PERSONNEL CARRIER

As armies became more mobile and the use of tanks became more common, the ability to move infantry* quickly over the battlefield with some protection became necessary. Armored personnel carriers (APCs), a loose family of vehicles that includes both wheeled and tracked vehicles, was the solution to this problem. The M113 is the most widely used APC in the Western world. Manufactured by FMC Corporation, the M113 is used as an infantry carrier, command-post vehicle, air defense weapons platform, armored ambulance, and in many other varients. As employed extensively in the Vietnam War,* the drawback to the M113 was the inability of troops to fight from it. Although armed with a .50-caliber machine gun, it provided no protection to the gunner or passengers while they fired. An interim solution to this problem was the armored cavalry assault vehicle * (ACAV), a modification of the M113, and the longer-range development of the infantry fighting vehicle (IFV) and the cavalry fighting vehicle (CFV), which have similar mobility but offer a flexible fighting platform to passengers and crew. APCs, especially the M113 family, are still in use in many armies of the world.

References. Scott R. Gourley, "M113A3," *Armada International*, August/September 1992, 22. John H. Hay, Jr., *Tactical and Materiel Innovations*, 1974. Mike Sparks, "M113s Maximize Mechanized Infantry Mobility and Firepower in Contingency Ops," *Armor*, January–February 1995, 6–14.

Jim Martin

ARMORED RECOVERY VEHICLE

The introduction of heavier tanks and other armored vehicles during World War II* led to the requirement for heavier recovery and repair vehicles that could also survive on the more lethal battlefield. The first generation of armored recovery vehicles (ARVs) in the U.S. Army, put into service in 1942, was a modified Grant M3 medium tank.* Except for the bow machine gun, all armaments were removed, and a crane arm replaced the main gun on the turret. Removal of the M3's turret permitted an A-frame jib to be mounted on the hull for more strength and flexibility in retrievals; additional armament was added, including an 81 mm mortar* to provide smoke screens; a redesigned suspension provided more stability for winching and lifting. A winch inside the ARV could be employed for direct hauling or hoisting over the crane arm. Various compartments for tools and spare parts were added to the exterior of the hull. When production of the M3 ceased in 1943, the Army developed an improved ARV, the M32, on Sherman M4 medium tank* chassis.

The appearance of even heavier tanks in the U.S. inventory after World War II demanded even more powerful and versatile ARVs. In 1953, the Army fielded the M74. The M74 still had the A-frame jib, but it was now hydraulically powered; a second winch was added inside the hull; a bulldozer-type blade was added on the vehicle's bow as a stabilizer; and special towing bars and mounts were added aft. Armed with one 7.62 mm and one .50-caliber machine gun, the M74 was able to defend itself on the battlefield. In the 1960s, a family of heavier and more powerful armored recovery vehicles, the M88 series, replaced the M74.

Reference. George Taylor, "Army Gets Improved Tank Recovery Vehicle," *Army Logistician*, January–February 1993, 34–35.

ARMY

The origins of the numbered armies in the U.S. Army can be found in the World War I* field armies* General John J. Pershing organized in the American Expeditionary Force* (AEF). Commanded by full generals, armies were composed of two or more corps* and associated support units to enable them to sustain combat operations indefinitely. Numbered armies were again employed in World War II.* After World War II, numbered armies were maintained in occupation roles, although several numbered armies returned to the continental United States. After the Vietnam War,* the designation army was dropped as a command echelon, although two still exist in Europe and Korea as administrative headquarters. Numbered armies remain as administrative and training headquarters in the continental United States, but their principal mission is the readiness of the Army Reserve.

References. George W. McCaffrey, "Progress toward Decentralized Command," *Military Review*, November 1951, 45–52. John D. Stuckey, "Echelons above Corps," *Parameters*, December 1983, 39–41.

Andrew N. Morris

ARMY AIR FORCES

On 1 March 1935, General Headquarters Air Force (GHQAF) was formed and assumed command and control over most Air Corps* tactical units, previously under the command of widely scattered Army corps.* Henceforth, the Office of the Chief of the Air Corps (OCAC) and GHQAF operated as parallel headquarters, with both reporting, albeit separately, to the Army Chief of Staff.* The GHQAF commander was responsible for tactical training and combat operations, while the OCAC kept control of air acquisition, logistics, training schools, and doctrine.* As a separate entity within the Army, the GHQAF was relatively short-lived, lasting only until 1 March 1939, when the OCAC absorbed it, again centralizing command of the entire Army air arm. Events in Europe prompted an unprecedented Air Corps expansion beginning the same year. Plans called for the procurement of 10,000 aircraft, of which 7,500 would be combat types, a threefold increase over the pre-1939 force levels. The new aircraft would equip eighty-four combat groups manned by 400,000 airmen by 30 June 1942.

With such expansion, Air Corps leaders lobbied for establishment of an independent air arm. Thus, on 19 November 1940 the General Headquarters was removed from the authority of the OCAC and given separate and equal status under the command of the Army Field Forces. Seven months later, General George C. Marshall,* Army Chief of Staff, formally established the U.S. Army Air Forces on 20 June 1941, to control both the Air Corps and the Air Force Combat Command (formerly GHQAF). The final step prior to separate-service status came under a War Department* reorganization on 9 March 1942 that created three autonomous Army commands: Army Ground Forces,* Services of Supply,* and Army Air Forces. The reorganization dissolved the Office of the

Chief of the Air Corps and the Air Force Combat Command, thus merging all elements of the air arm into the Army Air Forces.

References. Wesley Frank Craven and James Lea Cate, eds., *The Army Air Forces in World War II*, vol. 1, 1948. Alfred Goldberg, ed., *A History of the United States Air Force, 1907–1957*, 1957.

Keith B. Bartsch

ARMY AND AIR FORCE EXCHANGE

Commonly known as AAFES, the Exchange, or PX (for post exchange), the Army and Air Force Exchange is a general merchandise retailer that provides goods to Army and Air Force personnel in the United States and overseas. It is one of the largest retailers in the world. In 1775, the Articles of War granted civilian traders exclusive commissions to sell tobacco, blankets, knives, and other small items to soldiers at posts or in the field. For the next 100 years, these sutlers, as they were known, were the most common source for whatever the individual soldier might want. Inevitable abuses arose in such a system, and various reforms were tried, but in 1895 the War Department* abandoned it and adopted a system of military control. Commanders were ordered to establish post exchanges modeled after the British system, offering billiards, cards, and other games as well as small items for purchase. In 1948, the Army Exchange Service merged with the Air Force Exchange Service to form the current organization. AAFES operates over 10,000 retail facilities in twenty-five countries, including theaters, food operations, automobile service stations, clothing sales, and class-six (spirit and beer) stores, and it has a long tradition of support to the front lines. Headquartered in Dallas, Texas, a major general oversees AAFES operations.

Reference. Donna Miles, "AAFES Turns 100," *Soldiers*, July 1995, 50–52.

Kelvin Crow

ARMY AND DEPARTMENT OF THE GULF

The Army and Department of the Gulf was constituted on 23 February 1862 from Federal troops occupying the Gulf states. It experienced several reorganizations, with the creation of the Nineteenth Army Corps in January 1863 and the addition of the Thirteenth Army Corps from the Army of the Tennessee* in August 1863. Army of the Gulf forces conducted the Red River campaign* in March 1864. Although its constituent units changed frequently, the Army and Department of the Gulf maintained a separate existence until it was merged into the Military District of Western Mississippi after the surrender of the Confederacy.

Reference. Frank J. Welcher, *The Union Army, 1861–1865*, vol. 2, 1993.

Tamas Dreilinger

ARMY AND NAVY JOURNAL

The *Army and Navy Journal*, a weekly paper first published in New York on 29 August 1863, provided a vehicle for reviewing and voicing military concerns of the day. The original subscription price was five dollars per year, or ten cents per issue. On 13 May 1950 the publication changed its name to *Army-Navy-Air Force Journal*. Its name changed again on 17 March 1962 to *The Army-Navy-Air Force Journal and Register*. On 4 July 1964, the name again changed to *The Journal of the Armed Forces*. Four years later, on 6 July 1968, the name changed to *Armed Forces Journal*, and the subtitle changed from "Spokesman of the Service since 1863" to "Defense Weekly." In August 1971, the *Armed Forces Journal* became a monthly rather than a weekly publication, and in February 1973 the publication added the word "International," to become *Armed Forces Journal International*.

References. Donald Nevius Bigelow, *William Conant Church & The Army and Navy Journal*, 1952. Michael E. Unsworth, ed., *Military Periodicals*, 1990.

L. Lynn Williams

ARMY COMMENDATION MEDAL

War Department Circular 377 established the Army Commendation Ribbon on 18 December 1945; General Order No. 10 changed the award to the Army Commendation Medal (ARCOM) in 1960 and added a medal pendant. The ARCOM can be awarded to any member of the Armed Forces who is distinguished through heroism, meritorious achievement, or meritorious service. The ARCOM is the Army's lowest award for valor; it is awarded for heroic actions not deserving a Bronze Star.* As an achievement or service medal, it ranks above the Joint and Army Achievement Medal but below the Joint Service Commendation and Meritorious Service Medals.

References. Evans E. Kerrigan, *American War Medals and Decorations*, 1964. John E. Strandberg and Roger James Bender, *The Call of Duty*, 1994.

Robert J. Dalessandro

ARMY FIELD FORCES. *See* Army Ground Forces

ARMY GROUND FORCES

As World War II* progressed, it became increasingly evident that the peacetime organization of the War Department* was inadequate for directing a major war effort. Consequently, in March 1942, the Chief of Staff,* General George C. Marshall* initiated a sweeping reorganization of the War Department. In addition to significant reorganization of the Army staff, including an expanded War Plans Division,* two new commands were created, Army Ground Forces (AGF) and Services of Supply,* later renamed the Army Service Forces (ASF). AGF assumed the training mission for all combat forces within the United States, a mission formerly under the General Headquarters; it was also charged with developing equipment characteristics, preparation of training publications, and military characteristics and organization for the combat forces. Lieutenant General Lesley J. McNair* was the first AGF commanding general. In 1946,

AGF was reorganized as the Army Field Forces (AFF), and in 1955 the Continental Army Command* (CONARC) replaced the AFF. Training and Doctrine Command (TRADOC)* subsequently absorbed many CONARC functions.

References. Joseph I. Greene, *What You Should Know about Army Ground Forces*, 1943. Kent Roberts Greenfield, Robert R. Palmer, and Bell I. Wiley, *The Organization of Ground Combat Troops*, 1947.

Gary Bounds

ARMY GROUP

The term "army group" refers to a command echelon that controls two or more field armies.* Primarily associated with the World War II* army groups in the European Theater of Operations (ETO), the origins of the army group can be found in General John J. Pershing's command of the First and Second Armies in France in World War I.* In World War II, a full general commanded an army group. Since 1974 the closest organization to an army group is found only in NATO,* where three multinational commands have controlled separate geographical areas.

References. Robert W. Coakley and Richard M. Leighton, *Global Logistics and Strategy, 1943–1945*, 1968. John D. Stuckey, "Echelons above Corps," *Parameters*, December 1983, 39–41.

Andrew N. Morris

ARMY INDUSTRIAL COLLEGE. *See* Industrial College of the Armed Forces.

ARMY-McCARTHY HEARINGS

The 1954 Army-McCarthy hearings in the U.S. Senate represented the first time that any organization seriously challenged the unsubstantiated charges of "communist" or "soft on communism" issued by Senator Joseph McCarthy. The hearings concerned charges that G. David Schine, a close friend of McCarthy's chief aide, Roy Cohn, had been denied a commission and harassed by the Army solely because of his anticommunist crusade. The charge that the U.S. Army was "soft on communism" was palpably absurd. The Army had bent every regulation to give Private Schine privileges extraordinary for a draftee.

When Secretary of the Army* Robert Stevens hired Robert Welch to represent the Army in the hearings in the spring of 1954, the fully televised hearings proved riveting theater for the nation. The climax came when McCarthy talked about the supposedly leftist leanings of a member of Welch's law firm; Welch objected, saying "Let us not assassinate this lad further. You have done enough. Have you no sense of decency, sir, at long last?" McCarthy did not long survive this public debacle; he was censured by the Senate later that year and died of alcoholism in 1957.

References. William Bragg Ewald, Jr., *Who Killed Joe McCarthy?* 1984. Michael Straight, *Trial by Television and Other Encounters*, 1979.

Stanley Sandler

ARMY-NAVY-AIR FORCE JOURNAL. See *Army and Navy Journal.*

ARMY-NAVY-AIR FORCE JOURNAL AND REGISTER. See *Army and Navy Journal.*

ARMY-NAVY STAFF COLLEGE. See Armed Forces Staff College.

ARMY NURSE CORPS

Although it was not until 1910 that the Army Nurse Corps (ANC) became a permanent, integral element of the U.S. Army, women and men nursed incapacitated soldiers from the earliest days of the American Revolution.* During the Civil War* legislation authorized the hiring of untrained women nurses by the superintendent of female nurses, Dorothea L. Dix. These women and countless other volunteers provided necessary nursing services in a harsh climate. During the brief but fateful Spanish-American War,* trained nurses served in the Army for the first time. Anita Newcomb McGee, a physician representing the Daughters of the American Revolution, selected nurses to serve in the training camps within the United States, in Cuba, Puerto Rico, Hawaii, and the Philippines. Their contributions highlighted the wisdom of maintaining a permanent cohort of trained nurses.

The Army Reorganization Act of 1901 (31 *Stat.* 753) established the ANC on 2 February 1901 and directed that it include a body of nurses, a superintendent, and a nurse reserve. Members of the ANC had their first opportunity to serve in combat in hospitals during the Punitive Expedition* on the Mexican border. During World War I,* nurses served in almost every care setting, from the front lines in France to cantonments within the United States. ANC strength peaked at 21,480 on 11 November 1918. Congress granted the Army nurses relative rank in 1920 and authorized nurses retirement for service and disability in 1926 and 1930, respectively.

The ANC again mobilized during World War II.* More than 57,000 Army nurses served around in the world in every theater, and 201 of them died. Over sixty Army nurses became prisoners of war.* In 1947, Congress enacted the Army-Navy Nurse Act, which provided Army nurses with permanent commissioned-officer status. During the Korean War,* over 500 members of the ANC served in combat, advancing and retreating with the troops in the most difficult circumstances. In 1962, Army nurses first reported to Vietnam, and thousands subsequently provided nursing care there until the fall of Saigon. Army nurses have participated in almost every action since Vietnam. They contributed to successful missions in Grenada, Panama, and the Gulf War, and have served in Bosnia, Somalia, and Haiti. The heritage of the Army Nurse Corps is a proud story of extraordinary dedication and heroism.

References. Robert V. Piemonte and Cindy Gurney, eds., *Highlights in the History of the Army Nurse Corps*, 1987. Mary M. Roberts, *The Army Nurse Corps, Yesterday and*

Today, 1957. Mary T. Sarnecky, "A History of Volunteerism and Patriotism in the Army Nurse Corps," *Military Medicine*, July 1989, 358–364.

Mary T. Sarnecky

ARMY OF THE CUMBERLAND

The Army of the Cumberland experienced several changes of name from its inception in the summer of 1861 through October 1862. Organized within the Department of Kentucky, later the Department of the Ohio, under the command of Major General Don Carlos Buell, it embraced the states of Ohio, Michigan, Indiana, all of Kentucky east of the Cumberland River, and the state of Tennessee. On 27 October 1862, when Major General William S. Rosecrans assumed command, it was redesignated the Army of the Cumberland. Rosecrans oversaw the reorganization of the army's original three wings into three corps* (XIV, XX, and XXI). Prior to the Tullahoma campaign,* Rosecrans added a reserve corps. After the battle of Chickamauga* in September 1863, two corps from the Army of the Potomac* joined the Army of the Cumberland and, along with Ulysses S. Grant's* Army of the Tennessee,* broke the siege of Chattanooga.* In October 1863, Major General George H. Thomas* replaced Rosecrans. The Army of the Cumberland, consisting of IV, XIV, and XX Corps, made up the bulk of William T. Sherman's* army during the Atlanta campaign.* Following the fall of Atlanta, IV Corps moved to Nashville under Thomas, while the remaining corps accompanied Sherman's march* to the sea.

References. Thomas B. Van Horne, *History of the Army of the Cumberland*, 1875, 1988. Frank J. Welcher, *The Union Army, 1861–1865*, vol. 2, 1993.

Edward Shanahan

ARMY OF THE JAMES

Unlike the other named armies that constituted the Union Army from 1861 to 1865, the "Army of the James" was an unofficial, but commonly used, designation of the Army of the Department of Virginia and North Carolina, created when the Department of Virginia, constituted in May 1861 from troops in or near Fort Monroe,* Virginia, merged with the Department of North Carolina. Headquartered at Fort Monroe, which remained in Union hands throughout the Civil War,* Army of the James's troops participated in several campaigns along the Atlantic coast and in the final assault against Richmond. Following the Confederate surrender at Appomattox, the Army of the James continued to serve on occupation duty long after other Union armies had demobilized. Not until February 1866 were all white troops in the Army of the James discharged; the last black regiments* did not leave the area around Richmond until the summer of 1866, when they departed for service on the Rio Grande.

Both contemporaries and historians have characterized the performance of the Army of the James, comprising both white and black troops, as mediocre and its leadership as lackluster. To some extent, this evaluation is a result of the army's performance in the 1864 campaign against Richmond and the highly political nature of its senior leadership—it had more political generals than in any other Union army. To some extent, its performance may be attributed to the fact that the Army of the James existed for only the last sixteen months of the war and operated in the shadow of the Army of the Potomac.*

References. Edward G. Longacre, *Army of Amateurs*, 1997. Frank J. Welcher, *The Union Army, 1861–1865*, vol. 1, 1989.

Tamas Dreilinger

ARMY OF THE MISSISSIPPI

The Army of the Mississippi, constituted on 23 February 1862 under the command of Major General John Pope, consisted of five infantry* divisions,* several cavalry* brigades,* and a flotilla brigade. It operated on the Mississippi River from New Madrid, Missouri, to Corinth, Mississippi, during the spring and summer of 1862. When Pope left to assume command of the newly created Army of Virginia* on 26 June 1862, Major General William S. Rosecrans took command of the Army of the Mississippi. On 26 October the army was deactivated when most of its troops were transferred to the Army of the Tennessee.* The designation "Army of the Mississippi" was briefly revived in December 1862, when Major General John A. McClernand arrived from the north and took command of several existing formations in preparation for an attack on Arkansas Post on the Red River. McClernand's two corps, however, were soon redesignated as XIII and XV Corps, Army of the Tennessee.

Reference. Frank J. Welcher, *The Union Army, 1861–1865*, vol. 2, 1993.

Tamas Dreilinger

ARMY OF THE MOUNTAIN DEPARTMENT

The Mountain Department, created on 11 March 1862, included parts of six states—Virginia, Maryland, Tennessee, Kentucky, Ohio, and Michigan—taken from the Department of Western Virginia and part of the Department of the Ohio. John C. Frémont* assumed command on 29 March 1862 at Wheeling, West Virginia, but soon learned that he controlled only some of the troops in his district. Major Generals Don Carlos Buell, James A. Garfield, and Henry W. Halleck* did not report to Frémont, although they operated within his department. Therefore, "Army of the Mountain Department" was not an official designation but merely referred to Frémont's command. Soon after its formation, Frémont led his army into the Shenandoah Valley in the campaign against Thomas J. "Stonewall" Jackson.* His failure to engage and destroy Jackson's forces led to the extension of the Mountain Department eastward on 8 June to include more territory in Maryland and Virginia. The Mountain Department was abolished on 26 June 1862, and the department's troops were redesignated I Corps of the new Army of Virginia.*

Reference. Frank J. Welcher, *The Union Army, 1861–1865*, vol. 1, 1989.

Tamas Dreilinger

ARMY OF THE OHIO

The designation "Army of the Ohio" referred to three separate field armies* during the Civil War.* First organized from Department of the Cumberland troops then in Kentucky, Major General Don Carlos Buell commanded the Army of the Ohio from 15 November 1861 until 24 October 1862, fighting at Shiloh,* Corinth, and Perryville.* On 24 October 1862, the troops of the Army of the Ohio were transferred to the recently re-created Department of the Cumberland under Major General William S. Rosecrans and were officially designated XIV Corps, Department of the Cumberland.

On 11 April 1863, Major General Ambrose E. Burnside* designated the two divisions of IX Corps and other miscellaneous units serving under him in the Department of the Ohio as the Army of the Ohio. Over the next year, the Army of the Ohio participated in a series of actions, including the pursuit of John H. Morgan's raiders in the Ohio valley and the East Tennessee and Knoxville campaigns.* In April 1864, IX Corps left for the east, and on 9 April Major General John M. Schofield* assumed command of XXIII Corps, Department of the Ohio. Throughout the remainder of the war, Schofield's XXIII Corps was known as the Army of the Ohio. XXIII Corps participated in the Atlanta Campaign* in 1864 and was preparing for further operations when the Confederacy collapsed in April 1865.

References. Gerald John Prokopowicz, "All for the Regiment," 1994. Frank J. Welcher, *The Union Army, 1861–1865*, vol. 2, 1993.

Edward Shanahan

ARMY OF THE POTOMAC

The Army of the Potomac was constituted on 25 July 1861 as the Military District of the Potomac. Redesignated the Army of the Potomac on 15 August 1861, it contained fourteen brigades* (later expanded into divisions*), a provisional brigade, a provost guard, and a cavalry* command that had previously fought at First Bull Run.* It was reorganized in March 1862 into several corps*—the number of which varied from time to time. A cavalry division was added in July 1862; it was later expanded into a corps. Involved in nearly every battle fought in the critical Washington-Richmond corridor, the Army of the Potomac stood down on 28 June 1865.

References. Warren W. Hassler, Jr., *Commanders of the Army of the Potomac*, 1962. Robert Garth Scott, *Into the Wilderness with the Army of the Potomac*, rev. and enl. ed., 1992.

Tamas Dreilinger

ARMY OF THE SHENANDOAH

At least three Union armies were called the "Army of the Shenandoah" during the Civil War.* Two of these armies bore the name as a descriptive rather than official title: the army Major General Robert Patterson led into Virginia in July 1861 during the First Bull Run* campaign, and the army Major General David

Hunter led up the Shenandoah Valley in June 1864. The only official designated "Army of the Shenandoah" was created in August 1864 for the express purpose of driving Confederate General Jubal Early from the Shenandoah Valley. Commanded by Major General Philip H. Sheridan,* it consisted of troops from the Middle Military District, VI Corps (Army of the Potomac*), two divisions* of XIX Corps (Army of the Gulf), a cavalry corps (Army of the Potomac), troops from the Department of West Virginia, and the Army of West Virginia.* This army fought a number of engagements in September and October, but it was not officially recognized as the Army of the Shenandoah until 17 November 1864. After Sheridan left in February 1865 to participate in the final campaign against the Confederacy, the Army of the Shenandoah underwent several reorganizations, but it continued to exist until most of its troops mustered out of service in August 1865.

Reference. Frank J. Welcher, *The Union Army, 1861–1865*, vol. 1, 1989.

Tamas Dreilinger

ARMY OF THE TENNESSEE

On 14 February 1862, Major General Ulysses S. Grant* assumed command of the newly created District of West Tennessee, Department of the Missouri, with his headquarters at Fort Donelson, Kentucky. The following week, troops within the district were reorganized into four divisions* in the Army of the District of West Tennessee. After several changes of command, Grant again resumed command of the Army of the District of West Tennessee and began referring to his army as the Army of the Tennessee, a designation that became official on 21 April 1862. In 1862, the Army of the Tennessee fought at Shiloh* and saw sporadic action in western Tennessee during the summer and early fall. The creation of the Department of the Tennessee from the District of West Tennessee in October 1862 led to reorganization of the troops under Grant's command. XIII Corps, created on 24 October 1862, was for a time synonomous with the Army of the Tennessee, but two months later XIII Corps was reorganized into four separate corps. In 1863 and 1864, the Army of the Tennessee fought in the Vicksburg,* Chattanooga,* and Atlanta *campaigns. The Army of the Tennessee marched in the final grand review in the nation's capital, and its last regiments* were mustered out of service on 28 July 1865 at Louisville, Kentucky.

References. Thomas Lawrence Connelly, *Army of the Heartland*, 1967. Frank J. Welcher, *The Union Army, 1861–1865*, vol. 2, 1993.

Tamas Dreilinger

ARMY OF THE UNITED STATES. *See* United States Army.

ARMY OF THE WEST

When President Abraham Lincoln called for 75,000 volunteers on 15 April 1861 to put down the southern rebellion, Missouri governor Claiborne Jackson, staunch Democrat and secessionist, refused to send Missouri regiments* and instead called out the Missouri state militia. On 10 May, Captain Nathaniel Lyon, temporary commander of the Federal forces at St. Louis and an adamant antislavery advocate, surrounded the militiamen's camp and arrested them. When riots ensued in St. Louis, Lyon's men killed a number of local Southern sympathizers. This action made Lyon a Union hero and prompted the War Department* to promote him to brigadier general and place him in command of all Union forces in Missouri. By mid-July Lyon had brought together forces from throughout the state and Fort Leavenworth,* Kansas, gathering them at Springfield. He officially designated his force the "Army of the West," although it comprised only four brigades.* Following the Union defeat and Lyon's death at Wilson's Creek* on 10 August, the Army of the West fell back to Rolla, then to St. Louis. From St. Louis the troops were dispatched to other commands, and on 19 August 1861 the Army of the West was discontinued.

References. Hans Christian Adamson, *Rebellion in Missouri, 1861*, 1961. Frank J. Welcher, *The Union Army, 1861–1865*, vol. 2, 1993.

ARMY OF VIRGINIA

On 26 June 1862, troops from the Mountain Department, the Department of the Rappahannock, the Department of the Shenandoah, and the Military District of Washington were consolidated in the Federal Army of Virginia under the command of Major General John Pope. Organized into three corps* and subsequently augmented by additional forces from the Army of the Potomac,* the Army of Virginia fought only one major battle, Second Bull Run,* where it was badly mauled by Confederate forces under Thomas J. "Stonewall" Jackson* and James Longstreet.* The Army of Virginia disappeared on 12 September 1862, when it merged with the Army of the Potomac.

Reference. Frank J. Welcher, *The Union Army, 1861–1865*, vol. 1, 1989.

Tamas Dreilinger

ARMY OF WEST VIRGINIA

An order dated 8 August 1864 created the Army of West Virginia (also known as the Army of Western Virginia) with two divisions* under the command of Brigadier General George Crook.* The army participated in the Shenandoah Valley campaign against Jubal Early's Confederate forces until October 1864. Some sources refer to the Army of West Virginia as VIII Corps, because some of the units had previously served in VIII Corps, but that designation is incorrect. The Army of West Virginia stood down on 19 December 1864, and its troops were distributed throughout the department.

Reference. Frank J. Welcher, *The Union Army, 1861–1865*, vol. 1, 1989.

Tamas Dreilinger

ARMY OF WESTERN VIRGINIA. *See* Army of West Virginia.

ARMY ORGANIZATION ACT OF 1950

On 28 June 1950, Congress passed the Army Organization Act of 1950, consolidating almost one hundred years of miscellaneous thought and action reflecting various requirements of Army organization. In essence, the Act provided a statutory authority for organizational reforms embodied in earlier legislation—the National Defense Act of 1916,* the First War Powers Act of 1941, the National Security Act of 1947,* and the Officer Personnel Act of 1947. The Act consisted of three sections: Title I—providing for a secretary, undersecretary, and two assistant secretaries of the Army; Title II—organization of the Army staff and delineation of duties, in general terms; and Title III—organization of the Army, to include the components, commands, and territorial organizations, basic and special branches, general staff officers, and the Women's Army Corps.* In some sources, the Army Organization Act of 1950 is incorrectly referred to as the "Army Reorganization Act of 1950."

References. G. Emery Baya, "Army Organization Act of 1950," *Army Information Digest*, August 1950, 28–37. Russell F. Weigley, *History of the United States Army*, 1967.

Lee Kruger

ARMY PHYSICAL FITNESS TEST

Physical conditioning and fitness have always been important in the training and readiness of the U.S. Army. The current Army physical training program includes unit and individual exercise, weight control, and stress management. To check the progress and status of individual physical fitness, the Army Physical Fitness Test (APFT) is administered every six months to all officers and enlisted personnel on active duty and annually to National Guardsmen and reservists. The contents of the APTF have changed from time to time. The current APTF includes three events—pushups, situps, and a two-mile run—designed to test an individual's endurance, strength, and cardio-respiratory efficiency. Scoring is based on a sliding scale determined by age and sex, with a maximum of a hundred points for each event; a minimum score of sixty is required to pass each event. A soldier with a physical limitation or "profile" may have one or more events waived or may be required to successfully complete alternate events, such as swimming, bicycling, or walking.

References. Raymond K. Bluhm, Jr., and James B. Motley, *The Soldier's Guidebook*, 1995. Frank Cox, *NCO Guide*, 4th ed., 1992.

ARMY REGISTER

The term *"Army Register"* refers collectively to a series of official rosters of U.S. Army officers issued under different titles from 1784 to 1985, including the *Official Army Register, Army Register of the United States, Register of the Army of the United States*, and *Official Army and Air Force Register* (used only in 1948 while the two services were in the process of separating). The Adjutant General's Office published the *Register* annually (except for 1917 and 1919, when no issues appeared) until 1950, when the Secretary of the Army* began publishing it. The *Register*'s contents are arranged variously by branch and seniority, unit and rank, lineal rank, assignment, and date of commission. Individual entries vary in content but normally include date and place of birth, residence at time of appointment or commissioning, service number, promotions, civilian and military education and schools, assignments and postings, and separate sections on casualties and retirements. Although the *Army Register* ceased publication in 1985 because of privacy issues, it remains one of the most important biographical sources on U.S. Army officers throughout the nation's history.

ARMY REGISTER OF THE UNITED STATES. *See Army Register.*

ARMY REORGANIZATION ACT OF 1950. *See* Army Organization Act of 1950.

ARMY REORGANIZATION ACT OF 1866
By July 1866, less than 12,000 of the 1,034,064 volunteers serving in the U.S. Army at the end of the Civil War* were still in uniform. The Regular Army consisted of less than 40,000 soldiers in nineteen infantry,* six cavalry,* and five artillery regiments.* On 28 July 1866, Congress passed the Army Reorganization Act of 1866, providing for an army whose missions now were frontier constabulary and Reconstruction. The act set the Regular Army's authorized strength at 54,302 men in forty-five ten-company infantry regiments, ten twelve-company cavalry regiments, and five artillery regiments. It directed that four of the infantry and two of the cavalry regiments were to be composed of blacks, and it authorized recruitment of 1,000 Indian scouts.* It set terms of enlistment at five years for cavalry and three years for artillery and infantry soldiers.

The act further mandated precommissioning examinations for new officers and specified that newly created regiments draw their officers from both Civil War volunteer and Regular Army ranks. New cavalry regiments were required to recruit two-thirds of their captains and field-grade officers from wartime volunteer units and one-third from the Regular Army. Infantry regiments were to draw one-half of their officers above lieutenant from volunteer units. All new officers were to have served honorably for at least two years during the war; ex-Confederates were barred from serving in the U.S. Army in any capacity.

Congress, however, failed to provide resources to fund the Army at the levels authorized in the Army Reorganization Act of 1866, and in 1869 it further reduced the number of infantry regiments to twenty-five and authorized strength to 45,000. From a peak strength of 56,815 officers and men in September 1867, the Army was reduced to 27,442 men in 1876, at which level it remained virtually until the Spanish-American War* in 1898.

References. Maurice Matloff, ed., *American Military History*, 1969. Allen R. Millett and Peter Maslowski, *For the Common Defense*, 1984. Russell F. Weigley, *History of the United States Army*, 1967.

William E. Bassett

ARMY RESERVE

The Army Reserve's origins lay in the years before World War I.* In 1908 Congress established a Medical Reserve Corps and four years later authorized the Regular Army Reserve. By 1916, the Medical Reserve numbered 1,900, but only twenty-seven enlisted men had joined the Regular Reserve. The National Defense Act of 1916* created an enduring reserve that General Staff* reformers sought as an alternative to the National Guard—a force that Guardsmen opposed. Hence, from 1916 to the 1960s the Reserve faced competition for funds and recognition from the Guard.

The 1916 law established an Officers' Reserve Corps (ORC), an Enlisted Reserve Corps, and the Reserve Officer's Training Corps (ROTC).* U.S. entry into World War I* occurred before the new act took effect. In early 1917 there were only 8,000 ORC officers, although 80,000 others earned reserve commissions at Officer Training Camps or through the ROTC during the war. Between the declaration of war and the end of 1917, some 80,000 joined the Enlisted Reserve Corps.

The 1920 amendment to the National Defense Act of 1916 abolished the prewar reserve forces and established the Organized Reserve, which included the ORC and the Enlisted Reserve, created nine corps areas in the continental United States, and provided that each area maintain one Regular Army, two National Guard, and three Organized Reserve divisions.* However, Congress failed to vote appropriations to develop these reserve divisions during the interwar period. The lack of enlisted men—only 5,100 in 1925, fewer than 4,500 a decade later—created an officer-only reserve. Reserve officers who sought training served with the Army or took correspondence courses. World War I veterans initially manned the ORC, but as they departed, ROTC graduates filled the gap, adding 5,000 to 6,500 men each year. The ORC grew steadily, rising from just over 95,000 in 1925 to 116,700 by 1939. These men and some 3,000 enlisted reservists were called to duty in 1940–1941 and played a crucial role in the war, providing thousands of company* and battalion* officers for wartime organizations.

In the decade following World War II,* reserve policy floundered. Congress passed four major acts between 1948 and 1957 but failed to sort out the muddle, although it did rename the Organized Reserve the Army Reserve in 1952. The Army viewed the Army National Guard and Army Reserve as a skeletonized mobilization base. A shortage of funds shaped this policy, but it left reserve units woefully undermanned and poorly equipped. Furthermore, while many wartime officers joined the reserves, few enlisted men took that option. The advent of peacetime selective service in the late 1940s created a vast pool of obligated Army reservists, peaking at over two million in 1959 and 1960, that the nation neither needed nor could afford.

Flaws in the system appeared first when the Korean War* required a substantial mobilization but not a full call-up. More Army reservists, largely World War II veterans mobilized as individuals, were called than were Guardsmen in organized units. The ensuing political uproar led to legislative reform in 1952 to set priorities for mobilization. This law created a Ready, Standby and Retired Reserve, but the categories pertained to individual obligations for a call-up, not to unit combat readiness. Moreover, the Army Reserve continued to have difficulty compelling prior service enlisted men to enroll in drill units.

An effort to reduce the size of the Army Reserve and National Guard while raising unit strength and improving readiness began in the late 1950s, but most of the reorganization came during the tenure of Secretary of Defense* Robert McNamara. While McNamara stumbled badly in his effort to merge the Army Reserve with the National Guard in 1965–1966—an effort thwarted by Reserve Officers Association* lobbying—his other reforms were effected. McNamara reduced the units and total strength of both reserve components but increased the Individual Ready Reserve (IRR) and manning levels of the remaining organizations. He assigned most reserve combat units to the National Guard and allotted combat support and combat service support organizations to the Army Reserve.

In an unintended way, MacNamara's decision to man reserve components to a 93–100 percent level worked well. President Lyndon Johnson's decision not to mobilize reserves for the Vietnam War,* despite the advice of the Joint Chiefs of Staff,* made reserve components draft-havens. Some Guardsmen and reservists—over 12,000 of the former and nearly 8,000 of the latter—were called up in 1968, but Johnson's policy overall gave the reserves a bad name. President Richard Nixon ended selective service in 1972, and Army Reserve strength dropped sharply in the ensuing six years, with the National Guard suffering similar losses.

The Army Reserve's fortunes changed dramatically following its nadir of the late-1970s. In light of the many problems the Army faced in the post-Vietnam years, Army and Department of Defense* leaders devised the Total Force* policy. The policy permitted larger active Army and Reserve components—fully manned, equipped, and trained to augment the regulars in war. Reserve forces were to provide combat support and service support units the Army did not maintain in peacetime, although the National Guard retained some combat forces. By 1990, the Army Reserve provided 300,000 of the active Army's 700,000 Selected Reserve and all of its 250,000 Individual Ready Reserves.

Desert Shield and Desert Storm saw 39,000 Army reservists deployed to the Persian Gulf, 6,000 more than the Guard sent. While the reserve call-up experienced some difficulties, the Gulf War witnessed the most effective mobilization and deployment of reserves in the nation's history. Despite the success of the Gulf War, the precise future of the Army Reserve remains unclear. Cutbacks in defense spending following the end of the Cold War* once again raise the competition for funds among the Army, National Guard, and Army Reserve. Reductions in force for all three components are inevitable. If the past is a indication, the Army Reserve might suffer disproportionately.

References. Martin Binkin and William W. Kaufmann, *U.S. Army Guard and Reserve*, 1989. Richard B. Crossland and James T. Currie, *Twice the Citizen*, 1984. Jeffrey A. Jacobs, *The Future of the Citizen-Soldier Force*, 1994.

Jerry Cooper

ARMY SERVICE FORCES. *See* Services of Supply.

ARMY TIMES

Army Times is an independent newspaper published every Monday by the Army Times Publishing Company. It is not an official publication of the U.S. Army. The fledgling newspaper went through several format and name changes before the first edition under the masthead *Army Times* appeared on 17 August 1940. The first issue was twelve pages long and sold for five cents. It carried two small advertisements and a lead story on the call-up of National Guard* and Army Reserve* units. Today, many active duty and retired servicemen rely on *Army Times* as a vital source of information on the Army. Some of the important topics *Army Times* covers are officer and enlisted promotion forecasts; issues that effect the benefits and quality of life of soldiers and retirees; current deployments; modernization projects; and policies and changes within the Department of Defense.*

Reference. Michael E. Unsworth, ed., *Military Periodicals*, 1990.

Bill Knight

ARMY TRAINING AND EVALUATION PROGRAM

The Army developed the Army training and evaluation program (ARTEP) to improve peacetime training for war in the aftermath of the Vietnam War.* The ARTEP provides table of organization and equipment* (TOE) units with training plans consisting of wartime tasks, conditions, and standards. The program emphasizes that because units fight as they train, they must train as they will fight. Individual manuals have been developed for different unit types and command levels detailing the tasks that units need to perform to standard to be prepared for war. For example, ARTEP 6-100, *The Field Artillery Cannon Battery*, details tasks for all field artillery* cannon batteries,* while ARTEP 6-400, *The Field Artillery Cannon Battalion*, does the same for all field artillery cannon battalions* and their headquarters elements. The Army is currently replacing the ARTEP manuals with mission training plans (MTPs), which are more unit specific. For example, ARTEP 06-037-30 *MTP Cannon Battery, 155-mm (3×6)*, applies to each howitzer battery in an eighteen-howitzer battalion. ARTEP also referred to the diagnostic collective training evaluations based on ARTEP manuals.

References. William R. Lynch III, "The Eight-Day ARTEP FTX," *Military Review*, December 1984, 12–22. James R. Whitley, "Unit Training Management," *Military Review*, August 1980, 53–58.

Jeffrey S. Shadburn

ARMY WAR COLLEGE

One of the institutions that emerged as part of the Root reforms at the beginning of the twentieth century was the Army War College. Elihu Root initially appointed an ad hoc War College Board, which acted as a nascent General Staff,* but the need for further reforms and education in the senior ranks of the Army led Root to propose, and Congress to accept, the establishment of an Army War College. In the years immediately after its founding in November 1903, the War College served not only for the study and education of military theory and practice but as a center for military planning as well, in effect serving as an extension of the General Staff. Military history, taught both in the classroom and on Civil War* battlefields, provided a central focus for the early War College curriculum. The staff of the historical section attached to the War College collected, prepared, and published extensive World War I* records, including the *Order of Battle of the United States Land Forces in the World War*.

The Army War College closed during World War II,* although the historical section continued to edit World War I documents and maintained a World War II chronology. After the war, the War College reopened at Fort Leavenworth,* Kansas, then moved to Carlisle Barracks* in 1951, where it is located today. The curriculum has continued to evolve as the role and importance of professional education for senior military officers in the U.S. Army have evolved. Military history is still an important element in studies at the War College but is no longer the central focus of the curriculum. The curriculum today is interdisciplinary and eclectic. Students take a common core of courses and select an individual area of concentration that includes an independent research project. Successful completion of the War College is considered essential for selection to higher level command and promotion to general officer.

References. Harry P. Ball, *Of Responsible Command*, 1984. George S. Pappas, *Prudens Futuri*, 1967.

ARNHEM. *See* Market-Garden.

ARNOLD, BENEDICT (1741–1801)

Benedict Arnold, born 14 January 1741 in Norwich, Connecticut, holds the dubious distinction of being the first American convicted of treason. Before the American Revolution,* Arnold was a successful druggist and merchant. He was known as a hot-blooded businessman who chafed at the trading restrictions mandated by British rule. With the closing of Boston Harbor after the Boston Tea Party, Arnold adopted a fiery political outlook that matched his approach to free trade. He was instrumental in forming and seeking recognition from the

General Assembly for a local militia composed of sixty-five merchants and traders, the "Governors Second Company of Guards." His efforts and generous financial support earned him the position of First Captain. As the revolution widened, Arnold quickly exhibited a penchant for battlefield doctrine,* winning converts to the cause, and political savvy in coordinating actions of the various militia units. Arnold participated in several early campaigns and demonstrated skill and bravery on the battlefield. The trust Arnold earned may have proved his undoing, as he quickly fell into disfavor with many revolutionary leaders. Historians are divided on Arnold's motivation, but ultimately he sold out to the British and even led British troops against colonial forces. He emigrated to England after the war rather than face American justice (he was sentenced to death in absentia). Arnold died of dropsy in Galleywood, England, on 12 June 1801. Popular sentiment has held that he requested burial in his old colonial uniform; however, there is no record to support this myth.

References. Clare Brandt, *The Man in the Mirror*, 1994. James Thomas Flexner, *The Traitor and the Spy*, 1953, 1975. Willard Sterne Randall, *Benedict Arnold*, 1990. Willard M. Wallace, *Traitorous Hero*, 1954, 1970.

Don Denmark

ARNOLD, HENRY H. (1886–1950)

Henry H. ("Hap") Arnold was one of the U.S. Army's first aviators. After graduation from the U.S. Military Academy* in 1907, Arnold was commissioned in the infantry* and assigned to the Philippines. Later, he applied for transfer to the Signal Corps* and returned to the United States for pilot training with the Wright brothers. In World War I,* because of his flying experience and knowledge of aviation, Arnold served on the Air Service* staff in Washington rather than deploying to France. From 1919 to 1935, Arnold commanded a number of units and bases, won the Mackey Trophy in 1934 (he had won it once before in 1912), and rose to assistant chief of the Air Corps. When Oscar Westover was killed in a plane crash in 1938, Arnold became chief of the Air Corps with the rank of major general; in 1941 he was named chief of the newly created Army Air Forces.* As a member of the Joint Chiefs of Staff,* he was responsible for advising on and implementing airpower strategy throughout World War II.* In 1944, Arnold was promoted to general of the army, one of only five men to attain that rank, and later general of the air force, the only officer to hold that rank. Arnold suffered several heart attacks during the war and retired from active service in 1946. He succumbed to yet another heart attack in 1950, a year after publishing his memoirs, *Global Mission*.

References. H. H. Arnold, *Global Mission*, 1949. Thomas M. Coffey, *HAP*, 1982. Flint O. Dupre, *Hap Arnold*, 1972.

ARTICLE 15

Article 15 is the section of the Uniform Code of Military Justice* (UCMJ) that provides commanders authority to impose punishment on members of their command for minor disciplinary infractions. Although the *Manual for Courts-Martial* is used to determine both the charge and occasionally the maximum punishment allowed, an Article 15 is a nonjudicial measure. No formal court-martial is convened to hear the soldier's case; the unit commander weighs evidence and determines guilt or innocence. An Article 15 benefits the soldier, because it is an administrative action, not a criminal conviction. Additionally, allowable punishments adjudged through Article 15 are lower than courts-martial punishments.

References. Edward M. Byrne, *Military Law*, 3d ed., 1981. Lee S. Tillotson, *Index-Digest and Annotation to the Uniform Code of Military Justice*, 4th ed., 1956.

Robert J. Dalessandro

ARTICLE 32

Article 32 of the Uniform Code of Military Justice* (UCMJ) requires that a formal investigation be conducted prior to the trial of any case by general court-martial. This investigation is commonly referred to as "the Article 32." According to the notes in the *Manual for Courts-Martial* (1984), the "primary purpose of the investigation . . . is to inquire into the truth of the matters set forth in the charges, the form of the charges, and to secure information on which to determine what disposition should be made of the case." Although a government representative (such as the prosecutor) may be present at the Article 32 hearing, the investigating officer's duty is to weigh impartially the evidence and make a recommendation as to disposition, not to perfect the government's case against the accused. The accused may affirmatively waive his right to this investigation and has the right to be present with counsel and present evidence on his behalf, if he chooses. The convening authority is not bound by the recommendations of the Article 32 investigating officer.

References. Edward M. Byrne, *Military Law*, 3d ed., 1981. James Finn, ed., *Conscience and Command*, 1971.

ARTICLES OF WAR

These were a body of regulations that governed the conduct of armies and the discipline of individual soldiers in both the United States and England. The Articles were not a criminal code to ensure justice but rules to help maintain discipline and dispense punishment. James II issued the first set of Articles of War in 1686, although their origins can be traced to ordinances issued to armies in times of war by kings as far back as Richard I. The issuing and enforcement of the Articles remained a royal prerogative. Together with the Mutiny Act of 1689, the Articles formed the basis of English military law until 1879, when they were combined into one bill called the Army Discipline Act, subsequently known as the Army Act.

In the United States, the Articles immediately came under legislative authority. The Continental Congress adopted the Articles of War, with some changes, for the Continental Army* in 1775. In 1789, acting under its constitutional

authority to raise and support armies, Congress confirmed the Articles and revised them in 1806 and 1874. The Uniform Code of Military Justice* (UCMJ)
superseded the Articles after World War II.*

References. James B. Jacobs, *Socio-Legal Foundations of Civil-Military Relations*,
1986. Lee S. Tillotson, *The Articles of War Annotated*, 1942.

                                                                        Timothy C. Dunwoody

ARTILLERY JOURNAL. See Field Artillery.

ASSOCIATION OF THE UNITED STATES ARMY

The Association of the United States Army (AUSA), founded on 5 July 1950,
include active duty, retired, National Guard,* and Reserve* soldiers, West Point
and ROTC *cadets, and civilians interested in national defense. The purpose of
the AUSA is to advance the security of the United States and consolidate the
efforts of those who support the position that the U.S. Army is an indispensable
means of national defense. Each year the AUSA conducts an industrial sym-
posium for manufacturers of military equipment and weapons and for individuals within the Department of the Army* who plan, develop, test, and use
weapons and equipment. The AUSA annually recognizes individuals for "self-
less service to the United States of America."

References. A. J. Drexel Biddle, "This Is AUSA," *Army Information Digest*, October
1959, 32–36. "The First Annual Meeting of the Association of the U.S. Army," *Armed
Forces Chemical Journal*, November–December 1955, 38–39.

                                                                          John Edgecomb

ATLANTA CAMPAIGN

In the spring of 1864, Major General William T. Sherman* began an advance
from Chattanooga, Tennessee, toward Atlanta, Georgia with the objective of
capturing that city and preventing Confederate forces in the western theater from
reinforcing the eastern front. Confederate General Joseph E. Johnston* conducted a skillful withdrawal, trading time for space and laying traps and ambushes along Sherman's path. The Confederates took up strong positions at
Kennesaw Mountain, northwest of Atlanta, in an attempt to turn the Federals
back. In spite of severe losses, however, Sherman continued a series of maneuvers that forced Johnston to fall back into the defense of Atlanta itself. At this
point, the Confederate high command replaced Johnston with the more aggressive John B. Hood. General Hood immediately took the offensive and attacked
Sherman's extended flanks, without success. Sherman invested the city, and after
a short siege Hood evacuated Atlanta, taking up positions in north-central Alabama threatening Sherman's supply lines. Sherman occupied Atlanta on 2 September and spent the next two months deciding what to do next. Finally, in
mid-November, he turned away from Hood and marched to the sea at Savannah.
Atlanta's capture, along with the Union success at Mobile Bay, bolstered the

war-weary North and helped ensure Abraham Lincoln's reelection in November 1864.

References. Samuel Carter III, *The Siege of Atlanta, 1864*, 1973. Albert Castel, *Decision in the West*, 1992.

George Knapp

ATTU

Japanese forces invaded Attu and Kiska, the westernmost islands of the Aleutian chain, in early June 1942. The Japanese intent was to draw the weakened U.S. Pacific Fleet away from Pearl Harbor prior to the Midway invasion, and to provide a Japanese defensive perimeter in the North and Central Pacific. A three-week naval and aerial bombardment preceded the U.S. effort to recapture Attu, codenamed Operation Sandcrab. On 11 May 1943, elements of the 7th Infantry Division landed unopposed at widely separated points on the eastern portion of Attu. Japanese forces held well-entrenched defensive positions on the high ground of the fog-shrouded island. Heavy fighting and frustration ensued for the American troops as they converged on enemy strongholds. An encircling U.S. force eventually pushed the Japanese to Chichagof Harbor. A frantic charge on the night of 29 May by 700 to 1,000 Japanese ended organized resistance and placed Attu once again in U.S. hands. Attu revealed the pattern of future battles against the Japanese.

References. Stetson Conn, Rose C. Engelman, and Byron Fairchild, *Guarding the United States and Its Outposts*, 1964. Brian Garfield, *The Thousand-Mile War*, 1969. [Dashiell Hammett et al.], *The Capture of Attu*, 1984.

Danny E. Rodehaver

AVIATION

The U.S. Army's aviation branch traces its origins to 6 June 1942, when the War Department* approved organic aviation as an adjunct of the field artillery.* Aviation spotter and liaison aircraft were used in all theaters of operations during World War II.* In 1946, the Army acquired its first helicopter, the Bell Model 47, designated the H-13. When the National Security Act of 1947* created the U.S. Air Force as a separate service, the field artillery assumed responsibility for the Army's remaining aviation functions. The Korean War* stimulated many aviation developments in the Army, among them the use of helicopter units for medical evacuation and transportation of high-priority materials behind the battlefield. In 1954, the Army Aviation School moved from Fort Sill* to Camp (later Fort) Rucker,* Alabama.

From 1954 to 1962 the Army continued to expand its aircraft inventory and aviation mission. In 1962, Lieutenant General Hamilton Howze headed a board formed to study airmobility capabilities within the Army. Based on Howze Board* recommendations, the Army formed the 11th Air Assault Division to test the new ideas. Following the successful testing period, the 11th was redesignated the 1st Cavalry Division (Airmobile) and equipped with over four hundred helicopters. Army aviation came of age during the Vietnam War.* The 1st Cavalry Division was perhaps the most effective U.S. unit involved in the conflict, repeatedly demonstrating the value of aerial mobility on the modern battlefield. Aviation units throughout South Vietnam proved their worth in the air cavalry,* troop transport, medical evacuation, and medium and heavy-lift roles.

Since the end of the Vietnam War, the Army has continued to develop and expand its aerial missions, and on 12 April 1983 it designated aviation as a separate combat arms branch. Aviation units have played key roles in operations such as Urgent Fury,* Just Cause,* and Desert Storm,* as well as numerous humanitarian and domestic support operations.*

References. James B. McKenzie, Jr., "Challenges for the Aviation Branch," *U.S. Army Aviation Digest*, December 1984, 10–13. Bobby J. Maddox, "Aviation Branch Implementation," *U.S. Army Aviation Digest*. August 1983, 2–9. Richard P. Weinert, Jr., *A History of Army Aviation—1950–1962*, 1991.

Randall N. Briggs

B

BAD AXE

Following the battle of Wisconsin Heights on 26 July 1832, a band of Sac and Fox Indians loyal to Black Hawk fled westward, seeking safety west of the Mississippi. On 1 August the band reached the Mississippi near the mouth of Bad Axe Creek but were prevented from crossing by a lack of canoes and the approach of an Army contract steamer, the sidewheeler *Warrior*. The Indians indicated a desire to surrender, but the steamer's captain believed that the Indians were setting an ambush and opened fire with his six-pounder gun. Although a low fuel supply forced the *Warrior* to return to Prairie de Chien that evening, the Indians made no further attempt to cross the river that night.

The next morning a pursuing force under the command of Brigadier General Henry Atkinson arrived in the area. At first the Indians attempted to decoy the soldiers into an attack on their empty encampment, while most of their number escaped across the river. This worked until a group of scouts discovered the main body of Indians. An attack on this body led to a near massacre of the Indians after several hours of hard fighting. Colonel Zachary Taylor's* arrival with additional troops completed the defeat of the Indian force; he attacked those braves who had managed to reach several small islands in the river. The battle of Bad Axe broke the Indians' resolve and was the last major action of the Black Hawk War.* Black Hawk himself was captured three weeks later.

References. K. Jack Bauer, *Zachary Taylor*, 1985. Fairfax Downey, *Indian Wars of the U.S. Army, 1776–1865*, 1963.

BAD CONDUCT DISCHARGE

A bad conduct discharge, or BCD, is a punitive discharge given to enlisted persons as punishment for misdemeanor crimes or a pattern of minor offenses. The sentence can only be given by a general or special court-martial convened for that purpose, with a military judge, representation for the accused, and a trial record. This discharge disqualifies the bearer for most veteran benefits and handicaps his future employment by branding him a poor employee. The BCD was incorporated into the 1949 revision of the Articles of War* to correct flaws apparent after World War II.* The concept was borrowed from the U.S. Navy and was designed to spare soldiers guilty of lesser crimes the stigma of a dishonorable discharge.*

References. William T. Generous, Jr., *Swords and Scales*, 1973. Lee S. Tillotson, *Index-Digest and Annotation to the Uniform Code of Military Justice*, 4th ed., 1956.

Kelvin Crow

BADGE OF MILITARY MERIT. *See* Purple Heart.

BAILEY BRIDGE

Developed in 1940 by the chief designer of the British Experimental Bridging Establishment, Sir Donald Coleman Bailey, this bridge was used extensively by the Allies in World War II.* Consisting of interchangeable ten-foot by five-foot panels, the bridge could be constructed to handle a maximum load of seventy-eight tons over a 120-foot span. The Corps of Engineers* adopted the Bailey Bridge in February 1943 and began using it extensively in 1944. The Bailey offered several advantages over U.S. bridging equipment. The flat shape of the Bailey's panels allowed for easy transport and assembly; its 600 pound panels weighed about half as much as the U.S. H-10 bridge. It could also support heavier loads than U.S. bridges. Also, it was wide enough to handle the new Sherman M-4 medium tank.*

References. Alfred M. Beck et al., *The Corps of Engineers*, 1985. Blanche Coll, Jean E. Keith, and Herbert H. Rosenthal, *The Corps of Engineers*, 1988.

Edward L. Maier III

BALLOON CORPS

The U.S. Balloon Corps came into existence in June 1861, the creation of Thaddeus Lowe, who had experimented with gas-inflated balloons and convinced President Abraham Lincoln of their utility and value to the Army as observation platforms. From a balloon at 300 feet an observer could survey an area nearly fifteen miles in all directions, observing troop movements or counting predawn campfires to determine enemy strength and intentions. With the addition of a telegraph key to the balloon's equipment, immediate information could be sent to Union headquarters. Despite the expected resistance from many Army officers, Lowe's balloons were used by Union forces at numerous battles in the East following their initial tactical use during the Peninsula Campaign.* The corps was even responsible for the first aircraft carriers in U.S. service: the barge USS *George Washington Parke Custis* was remodeled to serve as a waterborne launching platform for balloons on the James River. The Balloon Corps was disbanded in 1863.

References. Carroll V. Glines, ed., *Lighter-than-Air Flight*, 1965. Juliette A. Hennessy, *The United States Army Air Arm, April 1861 to April 1917*, 1985.

Jim Martin

BASIC COMBAT TRAINING

Basic combat training (BCT) is the initial instruction that all recruits receive upon entering the U.S. Army. From the founding of the Army in 1776, individual training had been the responsibility of the unit receiving a new soldier. During the early twentieth century, the General and Special Service Schools provided limited specialized training for technical jobs. Change came in World War II.* To mass produce soldiers from civilians, the War Department* adopted a program of basic training at replacement training centers. Beginning in March 1941, basic training, conducted in 250-man companies, followed a standard program of instruction based on the branch of service. This curriculum separated replacement training from unit training. After BCT, soldiers received additional specialty training in formal courses or in their units. Between 1941 and 1944, basic training varied from twelve to seventeen weeks in length. Based on combat experience in North Africa and the Pacific, special battle courses—such as infiltration, close combat, and field training exercises—were added to prepare the soldier better for battle. In late summer 1944, branch-immaterial training began. After World War II, the Army generally conducted basic training at training centers. However, at times it conducted BCT in units. Basic training courses varied in length but generally ran eight to nine weeks.

Current training is three-phased: basic soldier skills, drill, discipline, and physical training; basic rifle marksmanship; and field combat skills. Immediately upon completion of BCT, recruits receive advanced individual training* (AIT) in their military occupational specialty* (MOS). Combat arms soldiers receive a combined BCT/AIT, called one-station unit training (OSUT), at the post where the branch school is located. For example, infantry soldiers train at Fort Benning,* Georgia, while tankers receive instruction at Fort Knox,* Kentucky. The overall mission of basic combat training remains unchanged—to turn civilians into soldiers.

References. Leonard L. Lerwill, *The Personnel Replacement System in the United States Army*, 1954. Alan Levy, Bernard Krisher, and James Cox, *Draftee's Confidential Guide*, 1957.

Robert Ramsey

BASIC COURSE

The Basic Course is normally the first branch-specific course an officer attends. It emphasizes leadership and is designed to familiarize officers with the equipment, tactics, and techniques required for success at their first assignments. More recently, the term has been used to designate the first course an enlisted or noncommissioned officer attends in his specialty (e.g., Basic Noncommissioned Officers Course [BNOC]). Until the end of the Civil War,* most junior officers acquired their basic military knowledge and skills during their precommissioning studies, in informal small-group instruction after commissioning (the "Lyceum system"), or by self-study. The first formal course to prepare new officers after commissioning and before reporting to their first assignment was the Artillery School of Practice at Fort Monroe,* Virginia, established in 1824. In 1866, the Engineer School at Willets Point, New York, was founded for the same purpose. The School for the Application of Infantry and Cavalry* was established at Fort Leavenworth,* Kansas, in 1881 to provide standard, high-quality instruction for selected junior officers of the line, who then carried this knowledge back to their regiments.*

After the Spanish-American War,* the Root reforms included the establishment of a uniform curriculum at post schools, where all junior officers received training, and branch schools for more advance study. During World War I,* temporary "schools of the line" were set up in the United States and France to train the large numbers of newly commissioned junior officers. Under the National Defense Act of 1920,* thirty-one service schools were established to provide basic training for all commissioned officers, but the courses were suspended in 1922 for lack of funds. During World War II,* basic courses were reestablished, but graduates of Officer Candidate School* (OCS) did not attend, as the curricula were so similar. By 1944, the majority of officers were graduates of OCS, so basic courses were again eliminated. Basic courses were reestablished again after the Gerow Report of 1946, and they have remained essentially unchanged since that time.

References. John W. Masland and Laurence I. Radway, *Soldiers and Scholars*, 1957. Timothy K. Nenninger, *The Leavenworth Schools and the Old Army*, 1978. Robert R. Palmer, Bell I. Wiley, and William R. Keast, *The Procurement and Training of Ground Combat Troops*, 1948.

Kelvin Crow

BATAAN

When the Imperial Japanese Army landed at Lingayen Gulf on 22 December 1941 in a bid to take over the whole Philippine archipelago, U.S. and Philippine forces under General Douglas MacArthur* conducted an orderly withdrawal to the Bataan Peninsula, in accordance with the recently discarded War Plan Orange.* The withdrawal allowed U.S. forces to establish a concentrated defense across the base of the peninsula and deny the Japanese use of Manila Bay. U.S. forces entered Bataan in early January 1942 and established the first defensive line in the north, from Mabatang to Mauban, intesected by Mount Natib. The Japanese, however, breached this line, forcing U.S. troops to pull back to the Pilar-Bagac line, seven miles to the south.

General Masaharu Homma, commander of the Imperial Japanese 14th Army, pressed attacks against the new line without success. He then ordered an operational pause on 8 February to await reinforcements. Behind schedule and pressured by his superiors to reduce Bataan, Homma launched determined attacks again on 3 April, and this time the Pilar-Bagac line gave way. The apparent reason for the collapse was a shortage of food, which left the defenders debilitated and vulnerable to diseases, especially malaria.

Faced with annihilation, Major General Edward P. King, operational commander of U.S. forces on Bataan, surrendered to the Japanese on 9 April. U.S. elements on Corregidor, under Lieutenant General Jonathan Wainwright,* continued to resist until 6 May. Many of the troops taken prisoner on Bataan perished on the infamous Bataan Death March* on their way to internment at Camp O'Donnell,* north of Bataan.

References. Richard C. Mallonée II, *The Naked Flagpole*, 1980. John W. Whitman, *Bataan*, 1990. Donald J. Young, *The Battle of Bataan*, 1992.

Thomas M. Huber

BATAAN DEATH MARCH

On 9 April 1942, 10,000 U.S. servicemen surrendered to Japanese forces on the Bataan* Peninsula in the Philippines. This surrender represented the largest loss of troops ever suffered by U.S. military forces. Herded together with thousands of captured Filipino soldiers, the captives endured a six-day, sixty-mile trek on which over 11,000 prisoners were clubbed, bayonetted, or shot by Japanese guards or died of disease or exposure. The "death march" was conducted without food or water, and the penalty for impeding the pace was death. Survivors of the march were later shipped to forced-labor camps in Japan. The voyage was a nightmare of deprivation; nearly half of the remaining prisoners died of starvation, dehydration, or by drowning when their ships en route to Japan were sunk by U.S. torpedoes. At the conclusion of World War II,* less than 4,000 U.S. Bataan death march survivors returned home.

References. Stanley L. Falk, *Bataan*, 1962. Donald Knox, *Death March*, 1981. Manny Lawton, *Some Survived*, 1984. Lester I. Tenney, *My Hitch in Hell*, 1995.

Don Denmark

BATTALION

A battalion is the basic building block for all higher-level organizations in the U.S. Army. The smallest unit in the army authorized to have a dedicated staff, it usually consists of from 400 to 1,200 soldiers. It is organized in three to five line companies* or troops,* a headquarters company, and attachments, depending on specific missions. It is usually commanded by a lieutenant colonel. The commander's principal assistants are an executive officer,* normally a major—who serves as second in command and supervises the staff—and a command sergeant major*—who supervises the senior noncommissioned officers* (NCOs) of the companies and staff sections and acts as principal advisor to the commander. The staff consists of four or five officers and their staff sections. The S-1, or adjutant, is responsible for all personnel matters and administration. The S-2, or intelligence officer, collects and analyzes combat intelligence and monitors the physical security of sensitive and classified items in the battalion.

The S-3, or operations and training officer, is responsible for the near and long-term planning and conduct of all the training and combat operations of the battalion. The S-4, or logistics officer, is responsible for all supply, fuel, ammunition, transportation, and maintenance operations. At various times, especially when overseas or deployed, there may be an S-5, who is responsible for civil-military relations. In addition to these primary staff officers, battalions may have special staff officers, including a maintenance officer, chaplain, signal officer, transportation officer, or a physician's assistant (PA). These officers frequently lead specialty platoons* in the headquarters company. Battalion staff officers are normally majors, captains, or occasionally lieutenants. The PA is a warrant officer.*

Maneuver battalions typically include a combat support company with a scout platoon, a mortar platoon, and, in an infantry battalion, an antitank platoon, which has twelve to fifteen mobile antitank systems. Combat support and combat service support battalions may lack some or all of these specialty platoons, having purely branch specific companies that may operate under the commander's direct supervision or be attached to the various brigades* and combat batallions.

For combat operations, the battalion may have attached a forward air controller* (FAC), a combat engineer platoon, antiaircraft resources such as Redeye* or Stinger* missile teams or Vulcan* guns, ground surveillance radar, sniper teams, K-9 (dog) teams, smoke-generator teams, or other attchments. More important, infantry and armor battalions in the same brigade will cross-attach companies among themselves to achieve a mix of capabilities that best meets the needs of the assigned mission. Such mixed battalions are termed "task forces."

References. Kenneth J. Ayers, "Structuring a Combat Maneuver Battalion," *Armor*, May–June 1976, 50–51. John C. Binkley, "A History of US Army Force Structuring," *Military Review*, February 1977, 67–82.

Andrew N. Morris

BATTERY

A battery is a company-sized organization peculiar to the field artillery* and air defense artillery.*

References. Boyd L. Dastrup, *King of Battle*, 1992. Kenneth R. Knight, "DRS: A Battery Commander's Perspective," *Field Artillery Journal*, January–February 1979, 44–47. *See also* Company.

Andrew N. Morris

BATTLE ABOVE THE CLOUDS. *See* Lookout Mountain.

BATTLE COMMAND TRAINING PROGRAM

The U.S. Army established the Battle Command Training Program (BCTP) in 1986 to integrate the doctrinal lessons of the 1973 Arab-Israeli War and the rapidly expanding technology of the post-Vietnam era into its current operational-level training system. BCTP applies to levels of command from brigade* to corps* and employs a number of the Army's training assets, including the battle command battle labs (BCBL) now functioning at a number of military posts in the United States, and open-air classrooms, such as the National Training Center* (NTC) and the Joint Readiness Training Center* (JRTC). BTCP training focuses on organizing information, solving problems, and disseminating solutions as an expression of the commander's will in the conduct of military operations.

References. Neal H. Bralley, "Improving Battle Command Skills," *Military Review*, November–December 1994, 49–52. Gregory Stanley and David Snodgrass, "BCTP," *Engineer*, August 1996, 32–35.

BATTLE FATIGUE

"Battle fatigue" is a euphemism for neuropsychiatric (NP) disorders caused by prolonged exposure to ground combat in World War II.* The term was probably coined by soldiers to avoid stigmatizing their exhausted comrades by diagnosing them as victims of "shell shock."* Battle fatigue, as used in World War II, is virtually synonymous with other terms: "NP casualties" and "the Old sergeant's syndrome," of medical origin; "combat fatigue" and "the two-thousand-mile stare," of soldierly origin. Variations of this terminology could be found in the Army Air Forces* Fifteenth Air Force, where the condition was simply known as "the clanks." The wide variety of such euphemisms was indicative of the widespread nosological confusion in the Allied services concerning the psychodynamics of combat. In the Eighth Air Force, flight surgeons employed more than fifty different medical terms to describe various states of combat fatigue among air crews. Medical definitions notwithstanding, these terms were applied to combatants who, by a combination of subjective and objective circumstances, could no longer function in combat. The severity of these conditions ranged from complete physical and mental collapse, requiring intensive and long-term prophylactic therapy, to temporary phychological crises that could be alleviated by simple rest and momentary relief from the front lines.

References. Gregory Belenky, ed., *Contemporary Studies in Combat Psychiatry*, 1987. Brian H. Chermol, "Battle Fatigue," *Infantry*, January–February 1984, 13–15.

Roger J. Spiller

BATTLEFIELD COMMISSION

The practice of commissioning officers directly from the ranks of enlisted soldiers and noncommissioned officers* (NCOs) in the field has been employed throughout the history of the U.S. Army. Officially an "appointment in a combat zone," the most commonly used term for the practice is "battlefield commission," but the term "field commission" also refers to this type of commission. The process, however, was not codified until after World War II.* Soldiers and warrant officers* in a combat zone who exhibit "a high potential in leadership" are recognized by promotion to the temporary commissioned ranks. Such appointments are normally only for soldiers in combat and combat support arms. Earlier, these temporary appointments were for the duration of the emergency plus six months. Today, the recipient of a battlefield commission must retroactively meet all requirements for commissioned status, then apply to remain on active duty in his commissioned tank. The most famous example of a soldier commissioned on the battlefield was Audie Murphy,* the most decorated soldier in Army history.

Reference. Lawrence P. Crocker, *Army Officer's Guide*, 46th ed., 1993.

Lawyn C. Edwards

BAYONET

Historians believe that the bayonet (from the French *bayonette*) was introduced around 1640 in Bayonne, France, although some sources suggest it was used in the 1500s. The first bayonet was the plug bayonet, inserted directly into the muzzle of a musket. Effective in hand-to-hand combat and in defense against cavalry, the plug bayonet had two significant disadvantages: first, with the bayonet inserted, the musket could not be fired; second, if a soldier rammed it in too forcibly, the bayonet became stuck. It became standard equipment for certain regiments in the French army in 1671.

In 1688 French field marshal the Marquis de Vauban invented the socket bayonet. This bayonet had a slotted sleeve that was placed over the muzzle and secured by a notch on the barrel. The flintlock musket with socket bayonet spread throughout Europe and supplanted the pike. The socket bayonet also simplified infantry tactics. After the adoption of the bayonet and flintlock, a basic infantryman replaced the four varieties of infantrymen that existed previously: pikeman, musketeer, fusilier, and grenadier.

In North America, British regulars carried the bayonet, but colonial militia did not issue or require its members to supply a bayonet. Not until the American Revolution* did colonial militia begin to appreciate the value of the bayonet. At Valley Forge,* Baron Friedrich von Steuben* instructed Continental Army* troops in the use of the bayonet. This training, along with other military instruction, brought the Continentals to parity with the British regulars. On 15 July 1779, the Continental Army captured the fort at Stony Point with a bayonet charge.

By the Civil War,* the rifled musket's greater range and accuracy had extended the battlefield; thus frontal assaults became too costly, and opposing lines rarely closed to bayonet range. Bayonet wounds, surgeons noted, became infrequent. The advent of repeating firearms caused a further reduction in the usefulness of the bayonet. Although the U.S. Army still issued bayonets to troops during both world wars, the size of the bayonet had been greatly reduced, and its use had been relegated largely to opening cans and digging holes. Today, bayonets are issued only to soldiers who carry the M16 rifle* as their individual weapons.

References. Anthony Carter and John Walter, *The Bayonet*, 1974. Brent Nosworthy, *The Anatomy of Victory*, 1990. Donald B. Webster, Jr., *American Socket Bayonets, 1717–1873*, 1964.

James L. Isemann

BAZOOKA

Originally developed by Robert H. Goddard in 1918, the American rocket pioneer, the rocket launcher received little attention from the U.S. Army until World War II.* With the onset of war and the massive use of tanks by the Axis powers, the Army needed a light antitank weapon for individual soldiers. This need resulted in a reevaluation of Goddard's rocket launcher. With the perfection of the "hollow charge," the M1 Rocket Launcher, 2.36-inch, became the infantry's antitank weapon. Early in World War II, a popular American comedian, Bob Burns, used a complex wind instrument of his own design that he called a "bazooka"; at the Ordnance Department demonstration of the prototype, a spectator remarked on the striking similarity between Burns's instrument and 2.36-inch rocket launcher. Soldiers quickly dubbed the new weapon a "bazooka." The 2.36-inch rocket launcher weighed 13.25 pounds, fired a 3.4-pound rocket of 2.36-inch caliber, had a range of 400 meters, and was capable of penetrating 80 mm of armor plating. U.S. troops first used the bazooka in North Africa in 1942.

References. Terry J. Gander, *Bazooka*, 1998. Richard M. Ogorkiewicz, "Recoilless Guns and Tanks," *Armor*, September–October 1953, 26–31.

John Edgecomb

BEECHER ISLAND

During the Indian war of 1868–1869, Major General Philip H. Sheridan* detailed his aide, Major George A. Forsyth, to recruit and organize fifty "first class hardy frontiersmen" from the ranks of Civil War* veterans and plainsmen to protect the Kansas Pacific Railroad. The men were lightly equipped for rapid movement, well armed, and better-than-average marksmen. On the morning of 17 September 1868, 600 to 700 Sioux and Cheyenne warriors surprised these scouts on a small, brushy island in a dry streambed. Using Spencer carbines,* Forsyth's men repulsed three uncharacteristic frontal charges by the Indians. Over the course of the next seven days, almost half of the defenders and the majority of their horses were killed or wounded. Two pairs of scouts eventually reached Fort Wallace, eighty-five miles distant, and a relief column of 10th Cavalry "buffalo soldiers,"* under Captain Louis H. Carpenter, lifted the siege on 25 September. Forsyth reported thirty-five enemy killed and an additional one hundred wounded; Indian sources admitted to only six fatalities. Forsyth's command suffered six killed and fifteen wounded. The small island was named for Lieutenant Frederick Beecher, who was killed in the fighting.

References. Dee Brown, *Action at Beecher Island*, 1967. Paul Andrew Hutton, *Phil Sheridan and His Army*, 1985. Robert M. Utley, *Frontier Regulars*, 1973.

Jeffrey Prater

BEETLE BAILEY

The cartoon strip *Beetle Bailey* has entertained readers for fifty years. Begun in the 1950s as a college strip, Mort Walker, who as a lieutenant guarded German prisoners of war* (POWs) in Italy, depicted problems of Army life in World War II* with which he was familiar. Although the strip features a lazy private who is always looking for a place to sleep instead of doing the work assigned him by his sergeant, the strip contains many subtle messages. Walker's strip has changed along with the Army. Walker has introduced characters who represent women and minorities, reminding readers of the diversity in the modern Army. Through this diversity, *Beetle Bailey* will remain alive and relevant and continue to make people laugh.

References. Bill Blackbeard and Martin Williams, eds., *The Smithsonian Collection of Newspaper Comics*, 1977. Jerry Robinson, *The Comics*, 1974.

Trevor Brown

BELL, JAMES FRANKLIN (1856–1919)

Born near Shelbyville, Kentucky, on 6 January 1856, J. Franklin Bell attended public schools and graduated thirty-eighth in his class of forty-three cadets at the U.S. Military Academy.* Initially assigned to the 9th Cavalry, he soon transferred to the more famous 7th Cavalry. Like many officers of his day, Bell found promotions slow and left the Army to teach at Southern Illinois University. He returned to his regiment* in 1889, however, and progressed through the ranks via a variety of assignments. In 1898, Bell was posted to the Philippines, eventually commanding the 36th Regiment and earning the Medal of Honor* for his actions on Luzon on 9 September 1899. Bell's contributions to the U.S. Army may have been greatest during his tenure as the head of the Army Service Schools at Fort Leavenworth,* Kansas, from 1903 to 1906. As commandant, Bell increased rigor and substance in the curriculum, laying the foundation for the institution that would train officers to fight the two worlds wars that were to follow.

In 1906, Bell became the Army Chief of Staff, a position he held for four years. During his tour as Chief of Staff, Bell was extremely successful in devising and promoting a legislative program that improved the Regular Army by increasing pay, technical services, and reserve forces. He subsequently commanded the Army of Cuban Pacification and the Department of the Philippines. At the time of his death in 1919 in New York, he commanded the Eastern Department of the U.S. Army.

References. William Gardner Bell, *Commanding Generals and Chiefs of Staff 1775–1987*, 1987. Edgar F. Raines, Jr., "Major General J. Franklin Bell, U.S.A.," *Register of the Kentucky Historical Society*, Autumn 1985, 315–346.

Jim Martin

BENET-MERCIE MACHINE RIFLE

In 1909, the U.S. Army adopted the automatic machine rifle, caliber .30, M1909, commonly known as the Benet-Mercie after its designer, to serve as its standard light machine gun. The gas-operated, air-cooled, metallic strip-fed Benet-Mercie machine rifle was similar to the French Fusil Mitrailleur Hotchkiss Modèle 1909 (Mle 09) light machine gun used by several European armies, but it fired a .30-caliber round instead of the .303 round commonly used in Europe. Intended as a light machine gun to be carried forward by assaulting troops, the Benet-Mercie weighed about thirty pounds, including the bipod—somewhat heavy for a light machine gun. The Benet-Mercie saw action during the Punitive Expedition* of 1916, and a few deployed to France with the American Expeditionary Force* (AEF). However, due to unsatisfactory performance in the field, most notably a defective ammunition-feed system, in 1918 the Army replaced it with the Browning automatic rifle* (BAR), which weighed half as much and was more reliable.

References. Ian V. Hogg and John Weeks, *Military Small Arms of the 20th Century*, 1977. Melvin M. Johnson, Jr., and Charles T. Haven, *Automatic Arms*, 1941.

BICYCLE

The introduction of the Rover Safety Bicycle in England in 1885 marked the culmination of nearly eighty years of bicycle evolution. All of the elements of the modern bicycle had finally come together: a tubular steel diamond-shaped frame mounted on two wire-spoked wheels of equal diameter with pneumatic tires, handle bars that controlled the front wheel for steering, a saddle or seat for the rider, and a rear-wheel, roller bearing, chain-and-sprocket drive. The new bicycle offered an efficient and reliable means of moving its rider and cargo considerable distances much faster than any existing mode of land transportation. A number of the world's armies had already perceived the military value of the bicycle and had conducted experiments with the machine over the previous decade.

In 1891, Nelson A. Miles, commander of the Department of the Missouri, ordered the 15th Infantry to conduct a series of bicycle experiments. Although these trials were short-lived, Miles maintained his interest in bicycles, and in 1896, now Commanding General* of the Army, he officially formed the 25th Infantry Bicycle Corps from officers and men of the 25th Infantry (one of two black infantry* regiments*). Under the command of Second Lieutenant James A. Moss, the unit trained and conducted a number of cross-country rides, the longest and most ambitious from Fort Missoula, Montana, to St. Louis.

Although the 25th Infantry Bicycle Corps had proven the utility of the bicycle, other events, particularly the Spanish-American War* and the Philippine Insurrection* directed the attention of the nation and the Army elsewhere, and the U.S. Army never adopted the bicycle as a general means of transportation.

References. Jim Fitzpatrick, *The Bicycle in Wartime*, 1998. Don Miller, "The Handlebar Infantry," *Army*, September 1980, 38–40.

"BIG GREEN MACHINE"

"Big green machine" was a pejorative term used by soldiers during the Vietnam War* to refer to the U.S. Army. The term reflected the fact that virtually everything in the Army—uniforms, vehicles, field gear, and personal equipment—was a shade of green, and also the perception that the Army, like most bureaucracies, was impersonal and mechanical. In its extreme usage, the term implied that the Army was an inexorable and uncaring juggernaut that exploited whatever value people had, ground them down, and left nothing but carnage in its wake. A number of post–Vietnam War sources use the term "the green machine"—undoubtedly an extension of the Vietnam-era "big green machine"—with a less negative connotation and note that the term also refers to the Veterans Administration.*

References. Gregory R. Clark, *Words of the Vietnam War*, 1990. Paul Dickson, *War Slang*, 1994. Linda Reinberg, *In the Field*, 1991.

BIRD DOG, O-1

First flown in 1949, the Cessna Model 305A won a U.S. Army design competition and served as a light observation and liaison aircraft during the Korean War* and later in the Vietnam War.* Initially designated L-19A, the O-1 was widely known as the Bird Dog. Powered by a 213-horsepower Continental O-470 flat-six engine, the L-19A was redesignated O-1A in 1962. Army versions included the improved O-1E. Other variants were the O-1B and O-1C, used by the U.S. Marine Corps, and O-1D, O-1F, and O-1G used by the U.S. Air Force. Over 3,500 Bird Dogs were built.

References. W. B. Bunker, "Why the Army Needs Wings," *Army*, March 1956, 19–23. George L. Morelock, Jr., "Army Aviation," *Military Review*, January 1956, 53–64.

Randall N. Briggs

BLACK HAWK UH-60

The Sikorski UH-60 Black Hawk was chosen in 1976 as the replacement for the Bell UH-1 Huey.* Its composite-material, four-blade main rotor and two GE T700-700 turbine engines make the UH-60 faster and more maneuverable than its predecessors, as well as giving it a greater range. The Black Hawk has a crew of three and can carry eleven combat soldiers and an externally slung load of 8,000 pounds. With its eight troop seats removed, it can carry four litters. Normally armed with two 7.62 mm machine guns, the UH-60 can be fitted with external "winglets" that carry long-range fuel tanks, mines,* or up to sixteen Hellfire antitank missiles. The UH-60 entered service in 1979. Other versions of the Black Hawk include the U.S. Navy's antisubmarine SH-60 Seahawk, the EH-60 electronic warfare variant, and the MH-60 search and rescue/special forces–insertion helicopter.

References. Gene Costello, "Black Hawk," *United States Army Aviation Digest*, February 1978, 34–39. Richard R. Walker, "Fielding the Black Hawk," *Army Logistician*, November–December 1977, 24–25.

Benjamin H. Kristy

BLACK HAWK WAR

The Black Hawk War was fought in 1832 between a mixed band of Sauk, Potawatomie, Winnebago, Kickapoo, and Mesquakie and U.S. Army Regulars and Illinois militia. The conflict began when the sixty-five-year-old Sauk chief, Black Hawk, led his band, including old men, women, and children, across the Mississippi into Illinois on 6 April 1832. Illinois Governor John Reynolds had threatened Black Hawk the previous year, forcing the Sauk, under Keokuk and a peace faction, to leave Illinois permanently. In Iowa, however, the Sioux threatened the Sauk, who, on the verge of starvation, returned to Illinois. Upon Black Hawk's return, Governor Reynolds called for volunteers to defend the state. On 8 May 1832, Brigadier General Henry Atkinson, in command of the federal troops in the region, mustered 1,700 Illinois militia into service to add to his 340 Regular Army troops.

The first battle of the war was fought at Stillman's Run, located northeast of Saukenuk along the the Rock River. Only Illinois militia fought in this first encounter with Black Hawk, and they lost eleven killed and numerous wounded, while Black Hawk lost only three braves. Although this was an Indian victory, the federal troops in the area forced Black Hawk to continue his retreat northward.

The Indian Creek massacre occurred on 21 May, when forty Pottawatomi killed fifteen whites, including women and children, near Ottawa. On 21 July the Indians fought a rear-guard action against another militia-only force at Wisconsin Heights to allow time for the rest of their band to cross the Wisconsin River. The final battle of the war occurred at Bad Axe* on 2 August, where Atkinson, with 400 regulars and 900 militia, killed over 300 Indians and took 122 prisoners. U.S. casualties were eight killed and twelve wounded. Total casualties for the war were seventy-two whites and from 450 to 600 Indians killed. The Black Hawk War permanently cleared the area of hostile Indian tribes.

References. Fairfax Downey, *Indian Wars of the U.S. Army, 1776–1865*, 1963. Cecil Eby, *"That Disgraceful Affair," the Black Hawk War*, 1973. Roger L. Nichols, *Black Hawk and the Warrior's Path*, 1992.

James L. Isemann

BLACKS IN THE U.S. ARMY

Although black Americans have fought in every major U.S. conflict except the Mexican War,* they served in segregated units within the U.S. Army until the Korean War.* At the time of the American Revolution,* separate black volunteer military units formed but were disbanded with the end of hostilities. Black volunteer regiments* were formed once more during the Civil War* but again were disbanded when the Confederacy surrendered. In the post–Civil War South, state militias,* mostly black, attempted to enforce the mandates of Radical Reconstruction, provoking the violent and undying enmity of "unreconstructed" southerners. Congress did mandate the activation of four Regular Army "colored" regiments, two cavalry* and two infantry.* These regiments established enviable records on the Western frontier—away from population centers. They registered fewer desertion, drunkenness, and AWOL cases than their white counterparts, perhaps because so few opportunities were open to blacks in civilian life. With just four exceptions (excluding chaplains), all officers in the black regiments were white. The exceptions included three black graduates from the U.S. Military Academy*: Henry O. Flipper,* John Alexander, and Charles Young. Only Young had a distinguished career, rising to the rank of colonel, always in command of black troops.

During the Spanish-American War,* all four regular black regiments fought in Cuba, along with numerous volunteer black units. The 24th Infantry distinguished itself in the famous charge up San Juan Hill, although Theodore Roosevelt's Rough Riders* received most of the public credit. Black troops also distinguished themselves in the Philippine Insurrection*

World War I* marked the activation of the first all-black Army divisions,* the 92d and 93d. Only the 92d fought as a unit, and its record is still controversial. The division was deliberately assigned white officers "who knew how to handle Negroes," often with disastrous results. Blacks were given temporary commissions after segregated training at Fort Des Moines, Iowa. The worst military racial clash in U.S. history took place at this time, in Houston, Texas, when troops of the 24th Infantry shot up sections of the city after enduring hostility from the white population. Sixteen civilians died in the gunfire. Following hasty courts-martial, nineteen black soldiers were hanged, and others were sentenced to long prison terms.

After World War I, the Army decided, in the name of equality of sacrifice, to maintain segregated units under white officers. The only exceptions were the commissioning of Benjamin O. Davis, Jr., the first black to graduate from West Point in the twentieth century, and the promotion to brigadier general of his father, Benjamin O. Davis, Sr., in 1940. During World War II,* the Army insisted on racial segregation, modifying this policy only in the last weeks of the war in Europe, when decimated infantry platoons* were efficiently reconstituted with black volunteers. But black troops, in many instances strongly influenced by the militancy of the "New Negro" movement of the time, violently resisted segregation. Generally speaking, small all-black units, such as of tank destroyers, fared better in every way than larger black units.

In 1945, the report of the Gillem Committee on Army manpower advocated equal treatment for blacks. Three years later, President Harry Truman issued Executive Order 9981* mandating the Gillem Board's recommendations. The following year, Truman's Fahy Board made the first recommendation for full racial integration in the military. Still, a segregated army entered the Korean War in 1950, and the poorly trained, poorly led black 24th Infantry performed disappointingly in the early weeks of the war. But the Army was becoming increasingly aware that racial segregation had proven inefficient, aside from its moral failings. Under Far East commander Matthew Ridgway,* the Army began breaking up all-black units and assigning black troops to units irrespective of race. A year after the end of the Korean War, the Army announced that it was racially integrated, a full decade ahead of American society.

Since 1955, blacks in the U.S. Army have achieved further acceptance and recognition in the absence of official segregation. The military turmoil of the 1970s did spill over into serious racial confrontations and violence, but the coming of the all-volunteer force* provided a far more professional service whose members were concerned with their work rather than with racial matters. The accession of the first black chairman of the Joint Chiefs of Staff,* General Colin Powell, in 1989 was not remarked upon unduly in the ranks, although it was undoubtedly a cause of black pride.

References. Richard M. Dalfiume, *Desegregation of the U.S. Armed Forces*, 1969. Jack D. Foner, *Blacks and the Military in American History*, 1974. Ulysses Lee, *The Employment of Negro Troops*, 1966. Bernard C. Nalty, *Strength for the Fight*, 1986.

Stanley Sandler

BLISS, TASKER HOWARD (1853–1930)

A Pennsylvania native, Tasker H. Bliss graduated from the U.S. Military Academy* in 1875. Massive in size and scholarship, Bliss served as an instructor at West Point (1876–1879), the artillery school at Fort Monroe* (1885), and the Naval War College (1885–1888). During the Spanish-American War* he participated in the Puerto Rican campaign and was subsequently appointed collector of customs in Havana. His service in Cuba led to his promotion to brigadier general in 1902 and assignment to the Army War College Board. In 1903 he became president of the Army War College,* which served as a planning body for the General Staff.*

In 1905 Bliss was named governor of Moro Province in the Philippines. He returned to the United States in 1909 and commanded several departments. When the United States entered World War I,* he was an Assistant Chief of Staff but was soon named Chief of Staff,* although he still considered himself subordinate to the commander in chief, American Expeditionary Force* (AEF), General John J. Pershing.* Aided by his knowledge of French and Italian, he served ably on the Supreme War Council* in 1918. President Woodrow Wilson appointed him one of five commissioners heading the U.S. delegation to the Versailles Peace Conference, where he opposed European schemes for a greater intervention effort in Soviet Russia.

Steeped in the history of warfare, Bliss contributed significantly to the Army's developing educational system, the organization of the General Staff, and allied success in World War I. In retirement, he spoke out in favor of U.S. leadership in the League of Nations and international disarmament.

References. Richard D. Challener, *Admirals, Generals and American Foreign Policy, 1899–1914*, 1973. Frederick Palmer, *Bliss, Peacemaker*, 1934.

Claude Sasso

BOARD OF ORDNANCE AND FORTIFICATIONS

In 1888, Congress voted an appropriation to establish a Board of Ordnance and Fortifications to assess and implement the Endicott Board's 1885–1886 recommendations to improve U.S. coastal defenses. The Endicott Board, headed by Secretary of War* William Endicott, recommended refortifying twenty-seven principal harbors, at an estimated cost of $127 million. Major General John M. Schofield* served as the board's first chairman. Although the Board of Ordnance and Fortifications existed until 1920, it never completed the Endicott Board's recommendations. After the initial funding, the goals changed from refortifying the old sites in favor of earthworks, armor-plated concrete pits, and ten- and twelve-inch disappearing guns. But internal problems plagued the project. The board lost supervision of engineering expenditures in 1890 and 1891 and of ordnance expenditures in 1892. Without control of expenditures, the board could not achieve its goals.

References. James A. Huston, *The Sinews of War*, 1966. Russell F. Weigley, *History of the United States Army*, 1967.

L. Lynn Williams

BOLERO

As early as March 1942, General George C. Marshall* initiated a series of planning sessions directed toward a cross-Channel invasion of the continent. Although many issues could not yet be resolved—availability of shipping and landing craft, for example—the Combined Chiefs of Staff (CCS) carried on discussions, and the Joint Chiefs of Staff* (JCS) proceeded with preliminary planning. "Bolero" was the code name for the preparation phase of the proposed cross-Channel operation. Bolero included two subordinate plans, both of which the British had already initiated and given separate code terms. Study, coordination, allocation of resources, movement of troops, and establishment of an active front in 1943 was code-named "Roundup."* "Sledgehammer"* was the development of plans and preparations for an "emergency" cross-Channel operation as early as 1942 if it appeared that collapse of the Soviet Union was imminent. Insufficient forces to guarantee success of a cross-Channel assault in 1943, competing demands for resources in the Pacific and Mediterranean, and division among U.S. and British leaders ultimately caused a postponement of Roundup in 1943. Thus, Bolero gave way to a new phase of planning for the cross-Channel invasion—Overlord.*

References. Maurice Matloff and Edwin M. Snell, *Strategic Planning for Coalition Warfare 1941–1942*, 1953. Roland G. Ruppenthal, *Logistical Support of the Armies*, vol. 1, 1953.

BOWMAN, SARAH (d. 1866)

Perhaps the most famous Army laundress* was Sarah Bowman, also known as "the Great Western." In the Mexican War,* Sarah nursed the wounded and fed the men as she dodged cannon and musket fire during the siege of Fort

Brown. Allegedly, she defended one of the guns with a saber and continued to fire it when its crew was killed. These deeds earned her another nickname, "the Heroine of Fort Brown." By order of Lieutenant General Winfield Scott,* Sarah was breveted a colonel for her services during the war and was made a pensioner of the government. Upon her death in 1866, she was buried with full military honors in Fort Yuma's post cemetery, the first woman so honored.

References. J. F. Elliott, "The Great Western," *Journal of Arizona History*, Spring 1987, 1–26. Brian Sandwich, *The Great Western*, 1991.

Dana Prater

BOXER REBELLION

The Boxers were members of a Chinese secret society who wished to drive all foreigners from China and eradicate foreign influence. The movement gained momentum in the final years of the 19th century; by early June 1900, the foreigners in China, especially those in Peking, found themselves in grave danger. The United States, Great Britain, Russia, Germany, France, and Japan sent troops to protect them. On 10 June, a relief force of 2,100 troops tried to reach Peking, but it met with stiff resistance after leaving Tientsin and failed to get through. The movement against Westerners in Peking culminated on 20 June with the murder of the German minister; about 3,500 foreigners and Chinese Christians, fearing for their lives, took refuge in the foreign legation compound. About 600 military personnel and civilians proceeded to defend the compound, invested by thousands of Boxers. The great powers organized a force to relieve the legation and crush what had come to be known as the Boxer Rebellion.

The United States dispatched the 9th Infantry and a Marine battalion* to Taku on 7 July. Two battalions of the 9th joined contingents of the other powers in an attack on Tientsin, which fell on 13 July. On 4 August an allied force of about 19,000 left Tientsin for Peking. The U.S. contingent, some 2,500 troops under Major General Adna R. Chafee, Sr.,* consisted of the 9th and 14th Infantry regiments,* elements of the 6th Cavalry, the 5th Artillery, and a Marine battalion. In the siezure of the Outer City of Peking on 14 August, elements of the 14th Infantry scaled the outer Tartar Wall, planted the first foreign flag ever to fly there, and opened the way for British units to relieve the legation compound. On the following day, Reilly's Battery (Henry J. Reilly's Light Battery F, 5th Artillery) blasted open the gates in the U.S. front in an assault on the Inner City. Peking was again safely in foreign hands. After extensive discussions, the Boxer Protocol was signed on 7 September 1901, ending hostilities and providing for reparations to all foreign powers.

References. Peter Fleming, *The Siege at Peking*, 1959. Victor Purcell, *The Boxer Uprising*, 1963. Chester C. Tan, *The Boxer Catastrophe*, 1966.

Michael Davis

BOZEMAN TRAIL

Established in 1864 by prospectors John M. Bozeman and John M. Jacobs as a more direct route than had existed to the newly opened gold fields in western Montana, this wagon road left the Oregon Trail west of Fort Laramie,* Dakota Territory (in present-day Wyoming), to run north along the eastern slope of the Bighorn Mountains, then west along the Yellowstone River to Virginia City, Dakota Territory (near present-day Bozeman, Montana). Running directly through the favored hunting grounds of the Oglala Sioux, this trail became the focus of a conflict between the U.S. government and the Sioux leader Red Cloud. In 1866 the government sent Colonel Henry B. Carrington and his 18th Infantry to establish a series of three forts for the protection of travelers along the trail. Carrington detached one company at Fort Reno, established the previous year, before proceeding farther north to build Forts Phil Kearny* and C. F. Smith. From the outset, the Sioux and their Arapaho allies waged a relentless campaign of raids and ambushes, soon giving Fort Phil Kearney the reputation as the most dangerous post in the Army.

The Bozeman Trail was the site of numerous clashes between the U.S. Army and the Sioux, most notably the Fetterman Massacre,* the Hayfield Fight,* and the Wagon Box Fight.* In April 1868 a peace commission appointed by President Andrew Johnson assembled at Fort Laramie to resume negotiations with the Sioux and Arapaho. On 19 May 1868, Major General C. C. Augur, commander of the Department of the Platte, issued an order for the evacuation and abandonment of all forts along the Bozeman Trail. Some sources later stated that before the departing troops were out of sight, the Sioux had rushed in and set fire to the hated forts.

References. Ralph K. Andrist, *The Long Death*, 1964. Dee Brown, *The Fetterman Massacre*, 1971. Dorothy M. Johnson, *The Bloody Bozeman*, 1971. S. L. A. Marshall, *Crimsoned Prairie*, 1972.

Fred J. Chiaventone

BRADLEY, OMAR NELSON (1893–1981)

One of five U.S. officers to achieve five-star rank in World War II,* Omar Nelson Bradley commanded the 1.3 million men of the 12th Army Group in the U.S. Army's offensive against the German armies in France, Belgium, the Netherlands, and inside Germany in World War II. Born in Clark, Missouri, Bradley graduated from the U.S. Military Academy* in 1915 and served the next twenty-eight years in planning and training assignments before assuming combat commands in World War II. Called the "G.I.'s general" for his approachability and rapport with his men, he was also a soldier's general in his ability to achieve dramatic combat results without incurring excessive casualties. Bradley was also famous for his skill in getting along with Allied commanders and his own peers, and in providing a stabilizing presence.

In 1941, General George C. Marshall* chose Bradley to command the Infantry School at Fort Benning.* Bradley went on to a succession of commands before becoming the deputy of Major General George S. Patton, Jr.,* in the invasion of North Africa in 1943. After Patton's departure, Bradley assumed command of II Corps and defeated the Germans at Bizerte, Tunisia, in May 1943 and in

Sicily in August. In June 1944, General Dwight D. Eisenhower* named Bradley commander of First Army* in the Allied invasion of Normandy. Within two months, he was given command of the 12th Army Group—the largest force ever wielded by a U.S. commander.

After the war, President Harry S Truman appointed Bradley head of the Veterans Administration* (1945–1947) and chairman of the Joint Chiefs of Staff* (1949–1953). In the latter position, Bradley had an important role in the relief of General of the Army Douglas MacArthur* as supreme allied commander during the Korean War.* After retiring in 1953, Bradley became an executive with the Bulova Watch Company, and in 1958 its chairman. Omar Bradley passed away in 1981 at the age of eighty-eight.

References. Omar Bradley and Clay Blair, *A General's Life*, 1983. Russell F. Weigley, *Eisenhower's Lieutenants*, 1981.

Donald L. Gilmore

BRADLEY INFANTRY FIGHTING VEHICLE

The Bradley infantry fighting vehicle was the result of joint planning by two U.S. Army branches (armor* and infantry*) to produce a common vehicle to serve both as a cavalry scout and infantry fighting vehicle. FMC of Santa Clara, California, began producing both versions in 1979. The infantry version, the M2, is almost identical to its cavalry cousin, the M3. In service solely with the U.S. Army, the Bradley is equipped with a Cummins VTA-903T turbocharged eight-cylinder diesel engine, is 3.2 meters wide and 2.9 meters high, weighs more than 45,000 pounds combat loaded, has a maximum range of 483 kilometers, and has a top land speed of 66 miles per hour. Both versions of the Bradley carry a crew of three; the M2 can carry seven infantrymen and the M3 two passengers. Fully amphibious, the Bradley in many ways resembles a light tank, armed with one 25 mm gun, one 7.62 mm machine gun, and two TOWs (the M2 also has gun firing ports for 5.56 mm rifles). Both the M2/M3 were combat proven during Desert Storm.*

References. D. H. C. Jenkins, "Operating the Bradley Infantry Fighting Vehicle," *International Defense Review*, vol. 15, 1982, 1203–1206. Christopher E. Lockhart, "Modern Dragoons," *Infantry*, November–December 1992, 33–35. Robert P. Sedar, "Employing the IFV," *Infantry*, September–October 1981, 33–37.

Chris Clark

BRANDYWINE

Brandywine Creek is a slow-flowing stream in southeastern Pennsylvania where, on 11 September 1777, George Washington's Continental Army* unsuccessfully attempted to block General William Howe's advance to Philadelphia. Rather than attack southwest across New Jersey, where Continental soldiers could harass his right flank and rear, Howe elected to move by sea to Chesapeake Bay and take Philadelphia from the south. His men departed New York City on 23 July, but bad weather delayed their arrival. The move to the

Chesapeake only temporarily deceived Washington, and he was able to shift his army southward in time to contest Howe's advance.

Using the river as an obstacle, Washington placed his army in a good defensive position, taking particular care to cover the fords. The Continental Army's left flank rested on Brandywine Creek, but the right flank was anchored more precariously. Howe quickly realized that a frontal assault could succeed only with inordinate casualties. He settled on a plan that called for one of his subordinates, General Lord Cornwallis, to envelop the Continental right, while Lieutenant General Wilhelm von Knyphausen staged a holding action against the Colonial center. Howe's army executed the plan with notable proficiency, causing Washington's right to crumble. To bolster his threatened flank, Washington ordered Anthony Wayne's and Nathaniel Greene's units into action temporarily to stem the British advance, providing time for the Continental Army to stage an orderly withdrawal to Chester.

References. Samuel S. Smith, *The Battle of Brandywine*, 1976. Joseph Townsend, *The Battle of Brandywine*, 1969.

Joseph R. Fischer

BRIGADE

Originally a combat unit composed of two or more regiments and commanded by a brigadier general, the brigade nearly disappeared from the U.S. Army during World War II* and the Korean War.* It reappeared with the Reorganized Objective Army Division* (ROAD) of the 1960s as the major subordinate echelon of the division.* As currently organized, brigades owe more to the combat command of the early armor division* than to the brigades of the square division.* Commanded by a colonel, a divisional brigade is technically only a headquarters, to which may be attached any number or combination of the maneuver battalions* of the division. In practice, battalions are habitually assigned to specific brigades, but the principle remains. The brigade has a standard S staff; the executive officer* is a lieutenant colonel, and the principal staff members are majors. In combat, the brigade is augmented by attachments from the engineer, signal, medical, air defense, intelligence, and logistical support battalions.

A separate brigade is of similar size and composition, but it is commanded by a brigadier general. It is not routinely assigned to a division and can be given missions independent of those given the divisions in the corps.*

References. John C. Binkley, "A History of US Army Force Structuring," *Military Review*, February 1977, 67–82. Stephen N. Magyera Jr., "Troubleshooting the New Division Organization," *Military Review*, July 1977, 53–60.

Andrew N. Morris

BRONZE STAR

The Bronze Star was authorized by Executive Order 9419 on 4 February 1944. It is awarded to individuals in any branch of military service who, while serving in any capacity with the armed forces of the United States on or after 7 December 1941, distinguish themselves by heroic or meritorious achievement or service in connection with military operations, excluding aerial flight, against an armed enemy. On 24 August 1962, Executive Order 11046 modified the eligibility criteria for awarding the Bronze Star. This executive order added the following conditions: the action had to be performed while engaged in an action against an enemy of the United States; or while engaged in military operations involving conflict with an opposing foreign force; or while serving with a friendly foreign force engaged in armed conflict against an opposing armed force in which the United States is not a belligerent party. The latter criterion permits recognition of heroic deeds or meritorious achievement performed by U.S. service personnel serving in advisory positions or duties with a foreign country.

References. David Borthick and Jack Britton, *Medals, Military and Civilian of the United States*, 1984. Evans E. Kerrigan, *American War Medals and Decorations*, 1964. Philip K. Robles, *United States Military Medals and Ribbons*, 1971.

John Edgecomb

BROWN BESS

The term "Brown Bess" refers to all types of British flintlock muskets* made from 1720 to 1840. The .75-caliber Brown Bess derived its name from the bright reddish-brown color of its barrel and metal fittings; the color of the gun's metal was achieved by applying a special browning solution. Several types of Brown Besses were used in the American colonies, including the age-old Long Land Model and the newer Shorter Land Model. Light infantry, artillerymen, and officers carried lighter, short-barreled versions called fusils. The Brown Bess was the principal weapon of the provincial and Continental armies until 1778, but most were older models left over from the French and Indian War. Provincial gunsmiths produced excellent copies of the Brown Bess, called the Committee of Safety muskets. The Brown Bess continued to be the standard musket of British regiments through the Napoleonic Wars and was still in service in the Crimean War, by which time it had been fitted with a percussion lock.

References. Howard L. Blackmore, *British Military Firearms, 1650–1850*, 1961. M. L. Brown, *Firearms in Colonial America*, 1980.

Michael Davis

BROWN-SHOE ARMY

"Brown-shoe Army" was a pejorative term used during the Vietnam War* era by younger soldiers to describe many of the older noncommissioned officers* (NCOs) and officers who had been brought up in what was now considered to have been the traditional, old-fashioned Army in which everything had been performed "by the numbers" and discipline had been much stricter. Actually, the term is relative, since brown shoes were only worn by the U.S. Army for a short period of its history. The Army went from the use of black leather to russet—hence "brown"—in 1899 for shoes and then for all leather items by 1911. Russet was the standard color of all leather uniform items, including cap bills and shoes items, until the Army moved back to black in 1958.

References. John J. Betz, Jr., "Brown Shoe Army Payday," *Army*, February 1989, 54–57. Albert N. Garland, "Reflections of a Veteran Foot Soldier," *Army*, June 1992, 39–41.

Edwin Kennedy, Jr.

BROWNING AUTOMATIC RIFLE

Prior to World War I,* the U.S. Army did not have a satisfactory automatic rifle. The Benet-Mercie machine rifle* had proven inadequate during the Punitive Expedition* in 1916. To fill this need, John M. Browning designed an automatic rifle that could be fired from the hip during assaults and was relatively easy to manufacture. The Browning automatic rifle (BAR)'s heavy recoil action, however, made it difficult to handle and inaccurate when fired from this position. To compensate, a bipod allowed the BAR to be fired from the more stable prone position. It fired a .30-caliber bullet, employed a twenty-round magazine, had a firing rate of five hundred rounds per minute, and weighed twenty-two pounds, making it a very heavy weapon. Although full production of the Browning automatic rifle did not begin until 1918, just as the war ended, it was destined to be the Army's primary squad,* light automatic weapon until the 1950s.

References. Christopher Foss and T. J. Gander, *Infantry Weapons of the World*, 1977. Gale C. Livengood, "The Story of the BAR," *Infantry School Quarterly*, April 1953, 67–69.

John Edgecomb

BUENA VISTA

The Battle of Buena Vista was fought on 22–23 February 1847 between U.S. forces commanded by Major General Zachary Taylor* and Mexican troops commanded President Antonio Lopez de Santa Anna. Santa Anna, learning from a captured document that Major General Winfield Scott* was preparing to invade Mexico, decided to defeat Taylor before this could happen. Therefore, he marched his 20,000 men from San Luis Potosí north across the desert to engage Taylor, who was occupying Saltillo, some 250 miles away. Santa Anna lost nearly 5,000 troops on this arduous, poorly planned, three-week trek.

Surprised by Santa Anna's approach, Taylor decided to defend and positioned his 4,750 mostly green volunteers in a narrow gap south of Saltillo near the village of Buena Vista. On 22 February, Santa Anna sent a cavalry brigade around Taylor's left to cut his communications. The main battle commenced on the 23d and was a confused affair whose outcome long remained in doubt. After the volunteers pulled back, U.S. artillery fire halted the heroic Mexican infantry. A determined U.S. counterattack, in which Jefferson Davis's Mississippi Rifles distinguished themselves, turned the tide. Taylor's rear guard subsequently repulsed the enveloping Mexican cavalry, leaving Santa Anna little choice but to withdraw. Mexican casualties were 1,500 killed and wounded. U.S. losses were 743 men and officers.

References. John S. D. Eisenhower, *So Far from God*, 1989. David Lavender, *Climax at Buena Vista*, 1966.

Robert E. Connor

BUFFALO SOLDIERS

During the Civil War,* more than 180,000 blacks served in the Union Army. Afterwards, Congress approved an expansion of the Army, including recruitment of two regiments* of colored cavalry* and four (later two) of infantry.* These regiments formed and began operations between 1866 and 1869 against Indians on the western frontier, where they became known as "buffalo soldiers." The most popular story of how the buffalo soldiers received their name comes from the Indians themselves: the dark skin and curly hair of the black troops reminded the Indians of the buffalo.

Buffalo soldiers fought in all the campaigns against the plains and south-western Indian tribes and performed all the other tasks associated with peace-making and peacekeeping. From 1866 to the Spanish-American War,* more than 12,000 blacks served in the U.S. Army. Nearly one in every five soldiers on the western frontier was black. Eighteen buffalo soldiers and Seminole Indian negro scouts earned the Medal of Honor.* In the Spanish-American War, buffalo soldiers were instrumental in the victory at San Juan Hill and later served in the Philippines and on the Mexican border. Integration of the armed forces marked the end of the buffalo soldier era, but certainly not the end of contributions made by black Americans in the military. The Buffalo Soldier Monument at Fort Leavenworth,* dedicated in 1992, is a reminder of the service rendered by these men to their country.

References. William H. Leckie, *The Buffalo Soldiers*, 1967. Frank N. Schubert, *Buffalo Soldiers, Braves, and the Brass*, 1993. *See also* Blacks in the U.S. Army.

George Knapp

BUG OUT

The term "bug out" means to leave in a hurry, to retreat, to play the coward, or to fly an aircraft quickly away from an endangered area. It can also mean an act of desertion, an exit, or a way out. Although the term came into use briefly during World War II,* it did not gain widespread usage until the Korean War.* "Bugout Boogie" and "Bugout Blues" were epithets for Hank Snow's popular country song "Moving On," referred to by some soldiers as the anthem of the 2d Infantry Division,* especially the 24th Infantry Regiment, following the division's rout at Kunu-ri in November 1950.

References. Paul Dickson, *War Slang*, 1994. Alan Levy, Bernard Krisher, and James Cox, *Draftee's Confidential Guide*, 1957.

Randall N. Briggs

BUGLE CALLS

Military formations have used bugle calls since ancient times to communicate and signal to units on the battlefield. The Romans were the first to use the ancestor of the modern bugle. The bugle came into general use in the U.S. Army about the time of the Civil War.* After the war, the use of buglers was firmly established, and bugle calls signaled the beginning and ending of many activities in camps, posts, and forts. Bugle calls roused soldiers in the morning, called the officers together, alerted everyone in case of fire, and ordered lights out in the barracks at night. The use of buglers on the battlefield largely ended during World War I,* when tactics and other means of communications forced a change. However, many posts retained buglers until World War II* to play ceremonial calls. Today, recorded bugle calls amplified over speakers have replaced buglers and bandsmen at most military installations.

References. Gerald Keating, "Buglers and Bugle Calls in the U.S. Army," *Army Historian*, Summer 1993, 16–17. Kenneth E. Olson, *Music and Musket*, 1981.

Edwin Kennedy, Jr.

BULL RUN. *See* First Bull Run; Second Bull Run.

BULLARD, ROBERT LEE (1861–1947)

Born in Lee County, Alabama, on 15 January 1861, Robert Lee (christened William Robert) Bullard entered the U.S. Military Academy* in 1881 and graduated four years later. Assigned to the infantry,* he was undistinguished during the first thirteen years of his career, although he did participate in the campaign against Geronimo. During the Spanish-American War,* Bullard commanded the 3d Alabama Volunteers and earned a reputation as an effective leader and a fair but stern disciplinarian. Over the next seventeen years, he served in the Philippines as a battalion* commander and district governor; in Cuba; and along the Mexican border.

In June 1917, Bullard arrived in France, where he commanded a brigade* before becoming commanding general* of the 1st Division.* Under Bullard's command, the 1st Division conducted the attack at Cantigny, the first successful U.S. attack in the war. Based on this success, General John J. Pershing* gave command of III Corps to Bullard. Bullard commanded III Corps in September and October 1918 in the Meuse-Argonne* offensive, the largest U.S. operation in World War I.* Promoted to lieutenant general, Bullard took command of the newly organized Second Army* just prior to the armistice on 11 November 1918. Bullard continued on active duty until 1925, when he reached the compulsory retirement age of sixty-four. After retirement, he worked with veterans organizations and wrote his memoirs and other books on military topics. He died at New York City in 1947 and is buried at West Point.

References. Joseph Cummings Chase, *Soldiers All*, 1920. Allan R. Millett, *The General*, 1975.

BUNA

Following their successful Philippine campaign in May and June 1942, the Japanese expanded their perimeter in the central and southern Pacific. They planned to seize Port Moresby, the principal city of southern Papua, New Guinea. In early July, elements of the Japanese Eighteenth Army, under the command of Major General Tomitaro Horii, landed at Gona and Buna and attacked inland, driving Allied defenders back over the key pass through the Owen Stanley Mountains to within thirty miles of Port Moresby. Partly under pressure from the Australian 7th and U.S. 32d divisions and partly in compliance with instructions from the Japanese high command, Horii's forces fell back stubbornly over the mountains and established strong defensive positions in the swampy regions around Buna and Gona. The Japanese put up a stiff defense, and the Allied offensive bogged down. The U.S. and Australian troops were racked by disease, short of artillery ammunition and rations, and untrained in jungle warfare. Lieutenant General Robert L. Eichelberger,* placed in command by General Douglas MacArthur,* rallied the sagging Allied morale and took steps to rectify the logistical problems. The Australians, on the Allied left, successfully stormed Gona on 9 December, but Buna was much more heavily fortified, and the Japanese resisted the U.S. attacks. The yard-by-yard fighting resulted in high casualties for both sides, but the U.S. forces eventually advanced to within sight of the shore. A converging attack by U.S. and Australian forces finally overran the Japanese positions. Some of the Japanese escaped in boats, but most died in the fighting. Total Japanese casualties in the Buna-Gona operations were more than 7,000 dead, an unknown number of wounded evacuatees, and 350 wounded prisoners. The Allies lost 5,700 Australian and 2,783 U.S. killed and wounded. Both sides lost heavily from disease, the U.S. alone having about 60 percent of its 13,646 men incapacitated.

This campaign had significant impact on the remainder of the war in the Pacific. It demonstrated that Allied troops could defeat the hitherto invincible Japanese forces in jungle fighting. It also changed the direction of Allied strategy in the Southwest Pacific Area* (SWPA). MacArthur declared "No more Bunas!" Rather than attack Japanese strongholds directly, MacArthur decided to "leapfrog" around them to cut off their supply lines. Once that was accomplished, MacArthur moved to retake the Philippines.

References. Jay Luvaas, "Buna, 18 November 1942–2 January 1943: A 'Leavenworth Nightmare," in *America's First Battles, 1776–1965*, 1986. Lida Mayo, *Bloody Buna*, 1974. Samuel Milner, *Victory in Papua*, 1975.

James H. Willbanks

BUNKER HILL

The Battle of Bunker Hill was fought on 17 June 1775, during the American Revolution,* between forces of the British garrison at Boston, under Major General William Howe, and local militia forces commanded by Colonel William Prescott. After the fights at Lexington and Concord, about 16,000 New England militiamen besieged the British garrison of Boston, which by May numbered about 7,000. Learning that the British were going to occupy the Dorchester Heights south of Boston, the Colonials decided to counter by seizing the heights north of the city. On 15 June, Major General Artemus Ward, commander of the militia forces around Boston, ordered Prescott to occupy and fortify Bunker Hill, on the Charlestown Peninsula. Convinced at the scene of the need to position his men instead on lower Breed's Hill, Prescott threw up earthworks there on the night of the 16th. He had with him about 1,400 men. After bombarding the Colonial earthworks from three British warships, Howe decided on a frontal assault. Moving his force of 2,300 picked men ashore, he immediately formed his troops for the attack. The Colonial militia repelled the first attack with close and deadly fire. Undaunted, Howe reformed and made a second attempt at the heights. Again the militia met his brave and disciplined soldiers with a withering fire. Reinforced by an additional 400 men, Howe ordered a third assault. By this time, the militia, critically short of ammunition, were unable to face the British bayonets* and fell back toward Cambridge. After a short pursuit, Howe ended the action. British losses were 1,050 killed and wounded; the Colonial militia suffered approximately 440 casualties.

References. John R. Elting, *The Battle of Bunker's Hill*, 1975. Thomas J. Fleming, *Now We Are Enemies*, 1960. Richard M. Ketchum, *Decisive Day*, 1974.

Robert E. Connor

BURMA ROAD

The Burma Road was a 717-mile track linking Lashio, in eastern Burma (today Myanmar), with K'un-ming in Yunnan Province, China. Construction of the road began in late 1937 after the Japanese occupied several major Chinese seaports as part of their strategy to defeat China by isolating it. The road was completed in 1939 and, after the Japanese moved into northern Indochina in September 1940 and closed the Indochina-Yunnan Railroad, became China's sole land link to the outside world.

In 1941 the United States began sending lend-lease material to China through the port of Rangoon and up the Burma Road. In early 1942, the Japanese invaded Burma and closed this route. To encourage China to stay in the war, the United States began flying supplies from northeastern India to China over the Himalayas, a route known as "the Hump." During 1943, U.S. military strategy in the China-Burma-India theater* (CBI) focused on retaking northern Burma and building a road from Ledo in northeastern India to join the Burma Road near the Chinese border. This objective was achieved in 1944, and on 28 January 1945 the first convoy from Ledo reached the Burma Road and moved along it to K'un-ming.

By this time, however, the success of the U.S. advance across the central Pacific had greatly reduced the strategic importance of a land link to China. No longer was the U.S. thinking of landing ground forces in southeast China and pushing north to establish bases for invading Japan. Also, large numbers of transport aircraft were now available, and it actually cost less to fly supplies from India to China than to truck them overland. As a result, the Ledo-Burma Road became primarily a one-way delivery route for vehicles being sent to China. Nevertheless, its contribution to the war effort was significant. During 1945, 25,783 vehicles and 6,539 trailers passed over the Burma Road on their way to China, carrying 160,000 tons of cargo to points in Burma and nearly 40,000 tons into China.

References. Raymond Callahan, *Burma 1942–1945*, 1979. Ian Fellowes-Gordon, *The Magic War*, 1971. Tan Pei-Ying, *The Building of the Burma Road*, 1945.

Gary Bjorge

BURNSIDE, AMBROSE EVERETT (1824–1881)

Born on 23 May 1824 at Liberty, Union County, Indiana, Ambrose Everett Burnside graduated from the U.S. Military Academy* in 1847 and was commissioned in the artillery.* He served during the Mexican War* and on the frontier before resigning in 1853. Between 1853 and 1861 he worked on a breech-loading carbine that bore his name, served in his state militia, was nominated for Congress, and worked for George B. McClellan* on the Illinois Central Railroad. During the Civil War,* Burnside organized the 1st Rhode Island Infantry and commanded a brigade* at First Manassas. He led a series of successful amphibious expeditions along the eastern seaboard during the first year of the war and was promoted to major general in March 1862. He commanded IX Corps in the Antietam* campaign and was given command of the Army of the Potomac* in November 1862. He led his army at Fredericksburg* and on the abortive "Mud March." Replaced by Major General Joseph Hooker,* Burnside took command of the Department of the Ohio in March 1863 and captured Knoxville, Tennessee, in September. Burnside returned to the East and once again commanded IX Corps as an independent command during the Overland Campaign under Ulysses S. Grant.* After the siege of Petersburg,* Burnside was replaced as IX Corps commander. He resigned his commission in April 1865.

Burnside's popularity grew after the war, and he served three terms as governor of Rhode Island. He was also elected to the U.S. Senate, where he served until his death in September 1881.

References. William Marvel, *Burnside*, 1991. Julia Jenkins Morton, *Trusting to Luck*, 1992.

George Knapp

BURNSIDE CARBINE

Designed by Ambrose E. Burnside,* the Burnside carbine was a .54-caliber percussion, breech-loading weapon produced between 1857 and 1865. The carbine* utilized a tapered, copper or foil, unprimed cartridge that somewhat resembled an ice cream cone. The first models utilized a tape priming system, while the later models relied on the standard percussion-cap ignition. It was one of the best carbines available during the Civil War.* The War Department* purchased and issued 50,000 Burnsides and over 21 million cartridges to volunteer cavalry. However, because of the uniqueness of the ammunition, supply problems, and the appearance of other multishot carbines, the U.S. Army never officially adopted the Burnside carbine.

References. Joseph G. Bilby, *Civil War Firearms*, 1996. David F. Butler, *United States Firearms*, 1971. William B. Edwards, *Civil War Guns*, 1962.

Steven J. Allie

BUTTER BAR

This term was Vietnam-era slang for a second lieutenant, the lowest-ranking commissioned officer; it referred to the yellow color and rectangular shape of the dress rank insignia,* which loosely resembled a bar of butter. A second lieutenant was also known as a "second louie," "newby," "2lt," "boot," and "brown bar." The phrase is derisive and reminiscent of other insulting terms like "butterball" and "butter-and-egg man"; it may also be used as a form of friendly teasing. The earliest uses of "butter bar" in print are from the late 1960s to early 1970s. Once a junior officer was accepted, he was commonly referred to as "the lieutenant" or simply "the L. T."

References. Paul Dickson, *War Slang*, 1994. Linda Reinberg, *In the Field*, 1991.

Kelvin Crow

C

C-47

The most widely used aircraft of World War II,* the C-47 was known as the Skytrain by U.S. pilots and as the Dakota by the pilots of other nations. Developed as a military transport from the Douglas DC-3 airliner, the C-47 was used in every theater of the war as a cargo and troop transport and to carry paratroops into combat. C-47s played a major role in the Allied operations in North Africa, Sicily, the Normandy invasion, and the Pacific, and they were a major part of the airborne supply operations over "the Hump" from India to China. The C-47 had a stronger cabin floor, larger hatch, and more powerful engines than its civilian counterpart; one major variant, the C-53 Skytrooper, was designed to carry personnel. By the end of the war the Army Air Forces* had received 10,123 C-47s and C-53s—almost one-half of the total number of transport aircraft bought by the Army between 1940 and 1945—and employed roughly 200 civilian DC-3s (designated C-48 through C-52 and C-68 through C-84). With a crew of three (five on parachute operations), the Skytrain and Skytrooper could carry twenty-seven troops or eighteen to twenty-four litters at a top speed of 230 mph, with a 1,600-mile range. The C-47 remained in service through the 1970s but was replaced largely within the decade after the war.

References. Jeffrey L. Ethell et al., *The Great Book of World War II Airplanes*, 1984. René J. Francillon, *McDonnell Douglas Aircraft since 1920*, 1979. Bill Yenne, *McDonnell Douglas*, 1985.

Luke Knowley

CABANATUAN RAID

Guided by Alamo Scouts,* with Filipino guerrillas providing security along the march, elements of the 6th Ranger Battalion infiltrated through Japanese lines on 28 January 1945 and made their way across twenty-five miles of jungle and grasslands to the outer defenses of a Japanese prisoner of war* camp located at Cabanatuan in the Philippines. Inside the camp, 511 U.S. and Allied prisoners, many of them survivors of Bataan* and Corregidor,* clung to life. In the early evening of 30 January, the Rangers raided the compound. At the cost of two Rangers killed, the combined efforts of Alamo Scouts, guerrillas, and Rangers freed the prisoners and inflicted an estimated 523 killed and wounded on the Japanese defending the camp.

References. William B. Breuer, *The Great Raid on Cabanatuan*, 1994. Forrest Bryant Johnson, *Raid on Cabanatuan*, 1988.

Joseph R. Fischer

CADET COMMAND

Established in 1985, Cadet Command is responsible for recruitment and training of 70 percent of U.S. Army officers, through the Reserve Officer Training Command and Junior Reserve Officer Training Command. Headquartered at Fort Monroe,* Virginia, and commanded by a major general, Cadet Command's staff of 3,800 supervises 44,000 cadets on over 1,000 college and university campuses across the United States. Cadet Command's other mission is the supervision of instruction for 125,000 Junior Reserve Officer Training Corps* (JROTC) high school students in basic military skills and citizenship through teamwork and self discipline.

References. Arthur T. Coumbe and Lee S. Harford, *U.S. Army Cadet Command*, 1996. Hans J. Massaquoi, "Maj. Gen. Wallace C. Arnold," *Ebony*, September 1992, 90.

Kelvin Crow

CALHOUN, JOHN CALDWELL (1782–1850)

One of the most distinguished Americans of his era, John Caldwell Calhoun served his country for most of his adult life. First elected to the U.S. House of Representatives in 1810. Calhoun twice ran for president, served as vice president under both John Quincy Adams and Andrew Jackson,* as secretary of war* in James Monroe's cabinet, as secretary of state from 1844–1845, and as U.S. senator for sixteen years.

As secretary of war, Calhoun provided leadership at a critical period in the Army's history. He reformed the War Department's financial system, dealt with lingering Indian land claims east of the Mississippi, and sent expeditions to the northern border to deal with British fur traders operating in U.S. territory. He argued for better pay and resisted reducing the size of the Army, a tendency in all postwar periods in American history. He curtailed flogging and other abuses of soldiers and launched a program to modernize the nation's system of coastal fortifications. Perhaps most importantly, Calhoun championed professionalism in the U.S. Army. Although a strong republican, he was dismayed at the poor showing of many militia units during the War of 1812* and came to believe that national security depended upon a standing professional army. He became an ardent supporter of the U.S. Military Academy* and established the Artillery School of Practice at Fortress Monroe. In December 1820, Calhoun wrote, "War is an art, to attain perfection in which, much time and experience, particularly for officers, are necessary."

References. Irving H. Bartlett, *John C. Calhoun*, 1993. Margaret L. Coit, *John C. Calhoun*, 1950. Roger Spiller, *John C. Calhoun as Secretary of War*, 1977.

CAMP O'DONNELL

Located near the village of Capas, north of Manila, on the island of Luzon, Camp O'Donnell had been originally constructed as a training camp for a Philippine army division.* Following the surrender of U.S. and Filipino troops on Bataan* on 9 April 1942, the camp became the northern terminus for the infamous Bataan Death March.* The camp was not complete when the first prisoners of war* from Bataan arrived. The enclosure covered 617 acres, approximately half the area housing about 9,000 Americans and the other half holding nearly 50,000 Filipinos. Inside the perimeter, there were few trees and little shade, and outside were endless stretches of cogan grass. U.S. prisoners remained at Camp O'Donnell for seventy-one days, during which 1,253 of them died from mental and physical exhaustion, malnutrition, lack of medical facilities, and brutal and savage treatment at the hands of the Japanese. Thus, Camp O'Donnell has become synonymous with the most inhumane and dehumanizing conditions to which men can be subjected; it has been compared to Andersonville.* O'Donnell figured heavily in the case against General Masaharu Homma, commander of the Japanese 14th Army, who was charged with responsibility for the deaths of 1,522 Americans and 29,000 Filipinos at the camp. Homma was tried before the Tokyo War Crimes Tribunal, found guilty, and executed.

References. Gavan Daws, *Prisoners of the Japanese*, 1994. John E. Olson, *O'Donnell*, 1985.

John A. Hixson

CAMP ZAMA

In September 1945, Camp Zama, formerly the *Sobudai*—the Japanese equivalent of West Point—was occupied by U.S. Army forces. Since 1950 the site has served as the headquarters for U.S. Army Japan (USARJ), a component of U.S. Army Pacific (USARPAC), with headquarters at Fort Shafter,* Hawaii. Commander, USARJ, normally a lieutenant general, oversees and provides logistics support for the nearly 2,000 Army personnel in Japan. He also administers the war reserves and contingency stocks in Japan. Approximately 1,200 personnel are assigned to Camp Zama, located less than fifty miles from Tokyo. IX Corps, headquartered in Hawaii, historically has provided additional personnel to reinforce and exercise with USARJ. In addition to USARJ, United Nations Headquarters (Rear) is based at Camp Zama. This headquarters links the logistic and basing facilities to the United Nations mandate for the defense of the Republic of Korea.

References. Dan Cragg, *Guide to Military Installations*, 4th ed., 1994. Dennis D. Dexter and Russell B. Shor, "From Zama to Hohkaido," *Army Digest*, August 1970, 14–19.

J. G. D. Babb

CAR-15

Following the adoption of the M-16 rifle* by the U.S. Army for use in Vietnam, the army perceived the need for a shorter version of the rifle, as a substantial weapon for officers and others who normally carried the standard M1911A1 .45 pistol,* and also to provide a weapon suitable for thick jungle and close combat. A desire for commonality of ammunition with the M-16 led to the fielding of the Colt automatic rifle, commonly called the CAR-15 but also known as the Commando or (more technically) the XM177E2. The M-16 barrel was halved to ten inches, and a telescoping metal stock replaced its plastic stock. This reduced the overall length of the CAR-15 to twenty-eight inches, extendable to thirty-one inches. A round foregrip, anticipating that of the M16A2, replaced the asymmetrical forestock of the standard rifle. Although the weapons were mechanically identical, the shorter CAR-15 barely allowed the full charge of powder in the standard cartridge to burn before it cleared the oversized flash suppressor. Therefore, because its ballistics are inferior to the M-16, the CAR-15 is classified as a submachine gun.

References. Ian V. Hogg and John Weeks, *Military Small Arms of the 20th Century*, 1977. Charles Latour, "Small Arms," *NATO's Fifteen Nations*, June–July 1974, 62–68.

Andrew N. Morris

CARBINE

A carbine is a shortened shoulder arm typically used by mounted soldiers. Examples have been both smoothbore (also known as muskatoons) and rifled, single shot and repeating. Frequently, carbines are cut-down versions of a standard service rifles, firing the same cartridge. About the time of the adoption of the Springfield rifle* at the turn of the 20th century, U.S. carbines disappeared, subsumed into standard rifles that were considerably shorter than their predecessors. With the exception of the M1 series of World War II,* an experiment that was ultimately judged a failure, carbines have been entirely replaced by submachine guns and assault-type weapons.

References. Arcadi Gluckman, *Identifying Old U.S. Muskets, Rifles & Carbines*, 1959, 1965. Andrew F. Lustyik, *Civil War Carbines*, 1962.

Andrew N. Morris

CARLISLE BARRACKS

Military use of the area at Carlisle, Pennsylvania, dates to the period of the French and Indian War. The first officially used building was constructed in 1777 by Hessian prisoners of war* to store ordnance. Shortly thereafter the structure became a guardhouse and detention center. Carlisle has been the site of several military schools since its establishment, including the Cavalry Practice School, the Medical Field Service School, and the Army War College.* Carlisle Barracks was also the home of the Carlisle Indian Industrial School, a coeducational Methodist-Episcopal institute for higher learning established by Captain R. H. Pratt and funded by the U.S. government, for Indian children whose parents lived on reservations. Students were housed in the barracks, took both practical and domestic courses, and spent a year on a local farm. The school declined after Pratt's retirement in 1904. Today, Carlisle Barracks is known as the site of the Army War College, the Military History Institute,* and the General Omar Bradley Historical Holding.

References. Dan Cragg, *Guide to Military Installations*, 4th ed., 1994. Thomas G. Tousey, *Military History of Carlisle and Carlisle Barracks*, 1939.

Lee W. Eysturlid

CARTWHEEL

"Cartwheel" was the code name for the 1943 Allied operation to seize the Solomon Islands–New Guinea–New Britain–New Ireland area, with the reduction of Rabaul as the ultimate objective. Cartwheel called for an advance north through the Solomons to Bougainville by Admiral William F. Halsey's South Pacific forces, with an accompanying offensive up the northern coast of New Guinea and landings on western New Britain by Southwest Pacific Area* (SWPA) forces under General Douglas MacArthur.* Cartwheel was a carefully phased series of operations the ultimate intent of which was to advance to within bomber range of Rabaul. That goal would be accomplished by improving forward bases already in Allied hands, occupying and constructing air bases that could be secured without the commitment of large forces, and siezing bases on sites currently occupied by Japanese forces. All of these objectives were met, except that the Joint Chiefs of Staff* (JCS) decided not to capture Rabaul but to neutralize and bypass it.

Because Cartwheel involved the employment of forces from both SWPA and South Pacific Area, command arrangements caused initial problems. The JCS resolved this issue on 28 March 1943 by assigning MacArthur overall command, with Halsey following his strategic direction. Featuring almost every type of military and naval operation that characterized World War II,* Cartwheel successfully concluded on 20 March 1944 with the seizure of Emirau, on Saint Matthias Island.

References. Maurice Matloff, *Strategic Planning for Coalition Warfare, 1943–1944*, 1959. John Miller, Jr., *Cartwheel*, 1959.

John A. Hixson

CAVALRY

The mounted combat arm of the U.S. Army had its origins in a regiment* of Connecticut "light horse" that reported to George Washington* in August 1776. Although the unit did not see action, the following year Congress authorized the formation of four regiments of dragoons. These formed the basis for one of the Army's most glamorous and well-known branches, the cavalry. Following the American Revolution,* cavalry fell into disuse until Congress again authorized a company of dragoons on 5 March 1792. This unit saw service at the Fallen Timbers* in 1794. Disbanded in 1821, it was again authorized during the

Black Hawk War* in 1832 and later expanded to a battalion* of mounted rangers for service on the frontier. By the time of the Civil War,* this unit had grown to two regiments of dragoons, two regiments of cavalry, and one regiment of mounted riflemen.

After the Civil War, the cavalry, which had been greatly enlarged for the war, was again reduced in size until difficulties with the western Indian tribes forced Congress to expand the force, in the Army Reorganization Act of 1866.* The cavalry saw extensive combat and escort service throughout the Indian Wars* and was also employed by the government for constabulary duties in the South during Reconstruction and the violent labor strikes of the period.

Despite romantic accounts of the charge at San Juan Hill, most cavalry operations during the Spanish-American War* and subsequent Philippine insurrection* were dismounted. This was due to the logistical problems encountered in shipping and sustaining the large, grain-fed U.S. mounts. In 1916 seven regiments of cavalry crossed the Mexican border in the Punitive Expedition* against Pancho Villa, and Congress authorized the expansion of the cavalry to twenty-five regiments in anticipation of U.S. involvement in World War I.* Only the 2nd Cavalry was deployed to France, however, and then only to run supply depots handling remounts for horse transport units.

The appearance of the tank in World War I portended the end of the horse on the battlefield. Between the world wars, the tank was slowly integrated into the U.S. Army as it began to mechanize in the early 1930s. By 1940, armored vehicles had all but replaced the horse, and in March 1942 the War Department* officially abolished the cavalry as a branch of service. This was not, however, the end of cavalry, as it reemerged coincident with the arrival of the armed helicopter. During the Vietnam War,* units were designated as air or armored cavalry, with their personnel continuing the traditions of the branch (even to the wearing of spurs, gauntlets, and Stetson campaign hats). According to current Army doctrine,* the cavalry employs its combined attributes of firepower, mobility, and shock effect for the specific purposes of security, reconnaissance, and surveillance.

References. John K. Herr and Edward S. Wallace, *The Story of the U.S. Cavalry 1775–1942*, 1953. Hamilton H. Howze, "The Mobile Branch," *Armor*, January–February 1968, 4–9. Richard Wormser, *The Yellowlegs*, 1966.

Fred J. Chiaventone

CAYUSE OH-6

Officially designated the OH-6, the Cayuse was built in large numbers during the early 1960s as the U.S. Army's light observation helicopter (thus the aircraft's nickname, "Loach"). Built around a single Allison turbine engine and an egg-shaped fuselage that usually held only four people, Cayuses were small, nimble, and quick. Armed with a mixture of light weapons, they performed a wide variety of tasks and missions during the Vietnam War.* Although the Kiowa OH-58 replaced the OH-6, a redesigned version, the MH-6 called the

Little Bird MH-6,* entered Army service and saw action with the 160th Special Operations Aviation Regiment during Just Cause* and Desert Storm.* The M500-D, a larger, updated variant of the OH-6, is currently used by many large city police forces and the armed forces of several nations, including Israel and the Republic of Korea.

References. Simon Dunstan, *Vietnam Choppers*, 1988. Stephen Harding, *U.S. Army Aircraft since 1947*, 1997.

Benjamin H. Kristy

CEDAR CREEK

On 6 October 1864, Major General Philip Sheridan* withdrew his 30,829-man Army of the Shennandoah* toward Winchester, Virginia, having routed Confederate General Jubal Early. However, the Confederates shadowed Sheridan's Army and occupied Fisher's Hill. On 16 October, Sheridan left his command near Cedar Creek. Two nights later, Early sent three divisions north across the creek and two divisions up Valley Pike on the Federal left flank. With a force of 18,410 men, the Confederates struck in the early morning fog, driving first the Federal VIII and then XIX Corps back. VI Corps rallied briefly, then retreated, while the other corps reformed in VI Corps's rear. Early's divisions then drove VI Corps back a mile to Meadow Brook, and the Confederate victory seemed complete. Early had inflicted 1,300 casualties and captured eighteen artillery pieces. After being repulsed twice, another Confederate attack drove VI Corps farther back to a ridge north along Valley Pike, but distracted by reports that his men were looting the abandoned Federal camps, Early ignored pleas for a final attack. By the time Early ordered a last assault, Sheridan had arrived and had rallied units to reinforce VI Corps and repulse the Confederates. At 4 P.M. Sheridan unleashed a counterattack, fragmenting the Confederates and driving them back to Fisher's Hill. Early suffered 2,910 casualties, including 1,050 missing; Sheridan's casualties were 5,665, with 1,591 missing.

References. Thomas A. Lewis, *The Guns of Cedar Creek*, 1988. Jeffrey D. Wert, *From Winchester to Cedar Creek*, 1987.

Charles Heller

CEDAR FALLS

Operation Cedar Falls took place thirty miles northwest of Saigon in an area known as the "Iron Triangle." Thought by intelligence analysts to contain the Viet Cong (VC) headquarters for Military Region IV, the Triangle was heavily fortified and dominated Highways 13 and 14 as they approached Saigon from that direction. On 8 January 1967, soldiers from the U.S. II Field Force, accompanied by one Army of the Republic of Vietnam (ARVN) division, moved into the Triangle to seek out and destroy the headquarters. Another major objective was the destruction of the village of Ben Suc, believed to be the hub of VC activity in the region, after the inhabitants were evacuated.

The U.S. 25th Infantry Division established a blocking position about fifteen miles long on the southwest side of the Triangle, while elements of the U.S. 1st Infantry Division and 173d Airborne Brigade air-assaulted directly into it. They were joined on the ground by two squadrons of the 11th Armored Cavalry Regiment. One battalion* from the 1st Division landed directly inside Ben Suc. After the village had been secured, searches located a large cache of medical supplies and twenty-eight individuals identified as VC. A total of 5,987 people were evacuated to a resettlement camp at Phu Loi. Ben Suc was then destroyed.

When Cedar Falls ended on 26 January 1967, 720 VC had been killed and 280 captured, and twelve miles of tunnels had been destroyed. U.S. casualties were seventy-two killed and 337 wounded.

References. Clark Dougan and Stephen Weiss, *The American Experience in Vietnam*, 1988. Barnard William Rogers, *Cedar Falls–Junction City*, 1974.

Richard L. Kiper

CENTENNIAL CAMPAIGN

Named for the observance of the nation's one-hundredth anniversary of independence, the Centennial Campaign remains the most famous of the Indian Wars.* Also known as the Yellowstone Expedition and the Little Bighorn Campaign, it was the result of violations, real or preceived, of the Fort Laramie Treaty of 1868, the discovery of gold in the Black Hills, and the increasing pressure of white migration into the Great Plains. Frustrated and beset with other problems, the Grant administration sought to resolve the Indian problem through the use of military force, driving the hunting bands out of the unceded territory and onto their reservations. When several Indian bands failed to comply, the government ordered the U.S. Army to move the recalcitrant Indians forcibly back to the reservations.

Lieutenant General Philip Sheridan,* commanding the Department of the Missouri, devised a winter campaign plan featuring three converging columns. This would harass and tire the Indians, bringing them to battle or forcing them back onto the reservation. Locating a village on the Powder River in March Brigadier General George Crook's cavalry* attacked, but abominable weather conditions, heavy snow, and subzero temperatures proved to be the most formidable enemy, and the cavalry failed to win a decisive victory. The other two columns were still struggling to get into the field. Thus, the winter campaign became a summer campaign.

By the summer of 1876, all three columns were in the field. In addition to Crook's force, operating out of Fort Fetterman, Colonel John Gibbon had moved south to the Yellowstone River from Fort Ellis, Montana territory, and Major General Alfred Terry had moved up the Yellowstone from Fort Abraham Lincoln. Crook's command was the first to clash with the Indians. On 17 June, about one thousand braves fought Crook to a standsill on the Rosebud.* Eight days later, the 7th Cavalry, under the command of Lieutenant Colonel George A. Custer,* attacked a large village on the the Little Bighorn.* In the ensuing action, an overwhelming Indian force killed Custer and 250 men of the 7th

Cavalry. On 9 September, Crook's troops located and attacked a village near a rock formation called Slim Buttes but failed to win a decisive victory. The weather then turned bad, and with rations running out and horses dying daily, the march from Slim Buttes to Deadwood, often called the Mud March or the Horsemeat March, became a struggle for survival.

The Centennial Campaign was not a glorious episode in the history of the U.S. Army; however it did succeed in forcing most of the Indians back to their reservations and was instrumental in breaking the last vestige of Sioux power on the Plains.

References. John S. Gray, *Centennial Campaign*, 1988. Charles M. Robinson III, *A Good Year to Die*, 1995.

John A. Hixson

CENTER OF MILITARY HISTORY

As part of a general staff reorganization in 1973, the Office, Chief of Military History* (OCMH), a special staff agency created in 1950 from the World War II* Historical Division of the Military Intelligence Division (G-2) of the General Staff,* became a field operating agency, the Center of Military History (CMH). CMH assumed the functions of OCMH, coordinating and supervising the Army's historical efforts: preparing and writing annual histories, special studies, lineages and honors, and monograph series, including the unwritten volumes of *The U.S. Army in World War II* (the "Green Books"*) and on Vietnam; maintaining the Army research and archive collection located at the U.S. Army Military History Institute,* Carlisle Barracks;* and managing other historical properties, including the museum system. Further reorganizations in 1974 and 1975 brought additional functions to CMH; for example, formerly independent historical offices, such as the Medical Department Historical Unit, were transferred to CMH. CMH has retained control of its own budget and is headed by the Chief of Military History, a brigadier general, who reports to the Deputy Chief of Staff for Operations (DCSOPS). A Department of the Army* Historical Advisory Committee, composed of civilian scholars and military representatives, meets annually to advise the Chief of Military History, the Chief of Staff,* and the secretary of the army* on historical matters.

References. John E. Jessup, Jr. and Robert W. Coakley, *A Guide to the Study and Use of Military History*, 1979, 1988. Harold W. Nelson, "CMH," *Army*, October 1990, 208–210.

CENTRAL INTELLIGENCE AGENCY

The Central Intelligence Agency (CIA) is an arm of the U.S. government whose mission is to collect, analyze, and disseminate economic, military, and political information on foreign countries. The CIA also influences actions abroad in support of U.S. interests. Established in 1947 and modeled after the wartime organization known as the Office of Strategic Services* (OSS), the CIA utilizes various means to facilitate intelligence collection, including electronic eavesdropping, aerial photography, orbiting satellites, and the use of field agents. A more common form of intelligence gathering is simply to listen to radio and television broadcasts and to read general publications that would be available to the public (such as economic forecasts, weather reports, and population trends). The agency also often works closely with the military in covert-action operations. The CIA employs a permanent force of field operatives and support personnel and utilizes foreign nationals in intelligence-collection activities. These personnel are subverted through various means, which may include ideological persuasion, greed, and fear of exposure. The CIA is headed by a director, who is appointed by the president and reports to the National Security Council.

References. Rhodri Jeffreys-Jones, *The CIA and American Democracy*, 1989. John Ranelagh, *The Agency*, 1986. Thomas F. Troy, *Donovan and the CIA*, 1981. Stansfield Turner, *Secrecy and Democracy*, 1985.

Don Denmark

CEREMONY

A ceremony is a formal act or observance established by tradition and custom and prescribed by protocol, convention, or regulation. The U.S. Army conducts daily scheduled ceremonies such as reveille* and retreat* and annually observes Memorial Day, Independence Day, and Flag Day at all active posts around the world. Ceremonies are also conducted during special occasions, for example, promotions, retirements, weddings, receptions, funerals, dining-ins,* and the presentation of awards and honors. Military ceremonies frequently include the presentation and retirement of the national colors, playing of the national anthem, parades, invocations, toasts, the reading of proclamations and orders, and addresses and speeches by honored guests.

References. Frank Cox, *NCO Guide*, 5th ed., 1995. Lawrence P. Crocker, *Army Officer's Guide*, 46th ed., 1993.

CHAFFEE, ADNA ROMANZO, JR. (1884–1941)

The son of Adna R. Chaffee, Sr.,* the second Chief of Staff* of the Army, Adna Romanzo Chafee, Jr., graduated from the U.S. Military Academy* in 1906. Commissioned in the cavalry,* he served in typical assignments as a company-grade officer, although he was extremely active in the horse-show circuit and was considered one of the Army's best horsemen. During World War I* Chaffee was a student at the Command and General Staff College course at Langres, France, and later served as an instructor before being assigned as a staff officer with the 81st Division and III Corps. After the war, Chaffee attended the U.S. Army War College* before serving as deputy G-3 in the 1st Cavalry Division.

His involvement with the development of mechanization in the U.S. Army began in 1927 and ended only with his death in August 1941. Assigned to the War Department* staff, Chaffee participated in the study that resulted in the formation of the Experimental Mechanized Force in 1928. Later, he became the principal War Department spokesman on mechanization and the executive officer of the Detachment for Mechanized Cavalry Regiment. When he was assigned as the congressional budget and liaison officer in the War Department staff, he managed to channel funding to the mechanization efforts of both the cavalry and infantry. In 1938, Chaffee assumed command of the 7th Cavalry Brigade (Mechanized) and led it in a series of maneuvers beginning at Plattsburg, New York, in 1939 and culminating in the Louisiana Maneuvers* of 1940. The success of the maneuvers and the example of the German *blitzkrieg* in France in 1940 convinced General George C. Marshall* to create a service test organization, the Armored Force, from elements of the 7th Cavalry Brigade and the infantry's* tank regiments.* Chaffee became the Armored Force's first commander and guided its growth to four divisions* and several separate tank battalions.* Chaffee died of a brain tumor in August 1941 while still in command of the Armored Force. Today, Chafee is known as the "Father of American Armor."

References. H. H. D. Heiberg, "Organizing a Mechanized Force," *Armor*, September–October 1976, 8–11. Timothy K. Nenninger, "The Experimental Mechanized Forces," *Armor*, May–June 1969, 33–39.

John Broom

CHAFFEE, ADNA ROMANZA, SR. (1842–1914)

Adna Romanzo Chaffee, Sr. enlisted in the 6th U.S. Cavalry on 22 July 1861 and won a battlefield commission* in 1863. He was wounded at Gettysburg* and at Brandy Station, the biggest cavalry battle of the Civil War.* Later, he served on the Southern Plains, fighting many skirmishes with the Indians; he is remembered for his injunction to his troops during the Red River War (1874–1875): "If any man is killed I will make him a corporal." After twenty-seven years with the 6th Cavalry, he was promoted to major and assigned to the 9th Cavalry.

Chaffee was an instructor at Fort Leavenworth* when the Spanish-American War* began. Appointed a brigadier general of volunteers, he was sent to Cuba with V Corps and commanded a brigade at El Caney. After the war, as a major general, he became chief of staff for the military governor of Cuba. During the Boxer Rebellion,* Chaffee commanded the 2,500-man China relief expedition, winning respect for his protection of Chinese property rights after the capture of Peking in 1900. He was sent from there to the Philippines in July 1902 to assume command of U.S. forces. Although President Theodore Roosevelt had declared the insurrection ended, fighting continued in some areas. Charged with cleaning up these difficult regions, Chaffee sent Brigadier Generals John Franklin Bell* and Jacob W. Smith into Batangas Province and Samar. Both areas were soon pacified, but both generals were criticized for their brutal tactics, and Smith was court-martialed.

Promoted to lieutenant general in January 1904, Chaffee served as Chief of

Staff* of the Army until his retirement in 1906. He was highly respected for his honesty, determination, and selflessness.

References. William H. Carter, *The Life of Lieutenant General Chaffee*, 1917. Stanley Karnow, *In Our Image*, 1989.

Claude Sasso

CH-54. *See* Flying Crane.

CHAMBERLAIN, JOSHUA LAWRENCE (1828–1914)

Considered by many American historians to be the quintessential citizen soldier in our history, Joshua Lawrence Chamberlain was born in Brewer, Maine, on 8 September 1828, the scion of a line of patriot-soldiers going back to the American Revolution.* He received some training at the military academy in Ellsworth, Maine, before graduating from Bowdoin College and Bangor Theological Seminary. In 1855 Chamberlain returned to Bowdoin as an instructor in natural and revealed religion, and over the next seven years he held a number of faculty positions there. A fierce believer in the Union cause and freedom for all men, in 1862 Chamberlain enlisted in the 20th Maine and was commissioned a lieutenant colonel. In May 1863, he was promoted to colonel of the 20th Maine.

Chamberlain participated in two dozen battles and was wounded six times between 1863 and 1865. His most famous action was the defense of Little Round Top in the battle of Gettysburg,* for which he received the Medal of Honor.* A year later, during the Petersburg* campaign, Lieutenant General Ulysses S. Grant* promoted him to brigadier general for his heroism and leadership on the field. For his assault on Lee's right on 29 March 1865 he was breveted major general of volunteers, and two weeks later was designated to receive the surrender of the Confederate Army of Northern Virginia.

At the end of the Civil War,* Chamberlain declined an offer of a colonelcy in the Regular Army and returned to his home in Maine. He subsequently served four terms as governor of Maine and twelve years as president of Bowdoin College. He also became a major-general of the state militia, American commissioner to the Universal Exposition in Paris (1878), and surveyor of the port of Portland. Among his writings is *The Passing of the Armies* (1915), a volume of personal reminiscences on the Army of the Potomac.*

References. Alice Rains Trulock, *In the Hands of Providence*, 1992. Willard M. Wallace, *Soul of the Lion*, 1991.

CHAMPION (CHAMPION'S) HILL

The Battle of Champion (or Champion's) Hill occurred during the Vicksburg* campaign, in May 1863. After the Battle of Jackson, Major General Ulysses S. Grant's Army of Tennessee* turned westward to face a Confederate force of 23,000 that emerged from the defenses of Vicksburg. On 16 May, Grant's intelligence sources reported Confederates under John C. Pemberton at Edwards Station, east of the Big Black River. Pemberton had countermarched to link up with General Joseph E. Johnston's army and, on the morning of the 16th he was deployed along a ridge above Jackson Creek. The Confederate column stretched for three miles, from just below the Raymond Road to Champion Hill. Grant ordered his seven divisions* (32,000 men) forward in three parallel columns to converge on Edwards Station.

About 7 A.M., Grant's southernmost column made contact with enemy cavalry pickets east of the Davis Plantation, focusing Pemberton in that direction. Grant, accompanying Major General James B. McPherson's corps,* approached the Confederate left flank, prompting Pemberton to reinforce his small element on Champion Hill. In the meantime, on the upper road, both sides continued to deploy and build their battle lines. Grant established his headquarters near the Champion House. The Federal movement forced the Confederates back and threatened to roll up Pemberton's flank, but a timely counterattack drove the Federals back, reestablishing the Confederate line. The Confederates then pursued the retreating Federals, but the pursuit quickly culminated and, not being reinforced, was driven back by a second Federal assault.

After nearly being run off the field, Grant sensed victory and tried to close the noose around Pemberton. However, he could not get his forces on the middle and lower roads in motion in time to trap the Confederates, who retreated back to their Big Black River defensive line. The victorious Federal troops marched into Edwards Station that night. Grant's casualties stood at 2,442, while Pemberton lost 4,602 men and twenty-seven guns.

References. Edwin C. Bearss, *The Campaign for Vickburg*, vol. 2, 1986. Earl S. Miers, *The Web of Victory*, 1955.

Edward Shanahan

CHANCELLORSVILLE

Following the Union repulse at Fredericksburg* in December 1862, the Army of the Potomac,* under its new commander, Major General Joseph Hooker,* slipped west to outflank the Army of Northern Virginia under Robert E. Lee.* Hooker's plan was for approximately one-third of his army to launch a diversionary attack against the Confederates, while another third conducted the envelopment. The remainder of the army was to be in reserve to reinforce whichever attack was successful.

Outnumbered more than two to one, Lee faced the prospect of being defeated and driven from his defensive position, thus leaving the road open to Richmond. His bold plan was to split his army, leave only 10,000 men to face Hooker's army of 40,000 at Fredericksburg, then to march with the remaining 43,000 against Hooker's 75,000 at Chancellorsville. Hooker crossed the Rappahannock on 1 May 1863 but, surprised by Lee's move, lost his nerve and established a defensive position. Lee decided to split his army once again. Leaving 17,000 men to face Hooker's front, he sent Thomas J. "Stonewall" Jackson's* 26,000

Confederates on a daring envelopment of Hooker's right flank. Jackson's attack at dusk on 2 May demolished the Federal right and forced Hooker to contract his defensive position. That night Jackson was mortally wounded by fellow Confederates while conducting a reconnaissance of the Federal lines. Hooker subsequently attacked and drove the Confederates west toward Fredericksburg, but he made only feeble attempts to break out of his position facing Lee. By the evening of 6 May, the entire Federal force had withdrawn north of the Rappahannock. Lee then began preparing for the invasion of the north that would culminate at Gettysburg* two months later.

References. Ernest B. Furgurson, *Chancellorsville, 1863*, 1992. Stephen W. Sears, *Chancellorsville*, 1996. Edward J. Stackpole, *Chancellorsville*, 1958.

Richard L. Kiper

CHAPARRAL

First fielded in 1969, Chaparral was the Army's short-range air defense (SHORAD) surface-to-air missile system for more than twenty years. It was the counterpart to the Soviet SA-9 and SA-13 systems introduced in the late 1960s and 1970s. Chaparral relied on a modified Sidewinder missile with an infrared-homing guidance system and was mounted on a tracked carrier that produced excellent cross-country mobility. This capability was imperative for low-level air defense to forward-deployed divisions* and corps.*

The Chaparral weapon system depended on visual target detection and tracking; the gunner used an Identification Friend or Foe (IFF) system to assist him in identifying targets. Each system had four ready missiles on launch rails and eight missiles in storage. A forward-looking infrared night sight (FLIR) fielded in the 1980s gave the system improved adverse weather and night capability. The Avenger system replaced the Chaparral in the active force in the early 1990s, although some National Guard* units still have Chaparral.

References. William O. Staudenmaier, "Division Air Defense," *Infantry*, September–October 1974, 10–12. Christopher Witt and David L. Priddy, "Target: Chaparral!!" *Air Defense Magazine*, January–March 1977, 6–11.

Thomas Christianson

CHAPLAINS CORPS

Chaplains have been serving in the U.S. Army since the American Revolution,* when just over a hundred chaplains volunteered to counsel and care for soldiers on the battlefield. In 1775, the chaplains were transferred from state sponsorship to the Continental Army,* which then paid their twenty-dollar monthly wages. Throughout the 19th century, chaplains (Baptist, Episcopalian, and Presbyterian) were considered part of the medical branch. Although the first Chief of Chaplains was appointed in July 1920, the Chaplains Corps was not formally established until November 1941. During World War II* just under nine thousand men of the cloth served with the Army on all fronts. These men were not only responsible for their own faith but knowledge of all other faiths as well. Today, chaplains not only provide spiritual guidance but have become professional counselors for soldiers and their families, an important function in every Army community.

References. Roy J. Honeywell, *Chaplains of the United States Army*, 1958. *The United States Army Chaplaincy*, 5 vols. 1997.

Trevor Brown

CHARLESTON

(American Revolution) In January 1776, the Continental Congress realized that a British attack on the city of Charleston, South Carolina, was possible and ordered its defenses increased. By the time the British struck in June, approximately 6,500 troops and militia, along with an assortment of artillery, were inside and around the city. The attacking British force consisted of several frigates and a number of transports commanded by General Sir Henry Clinton. After several days of reconnaissance, Clinton decided to concentrate his attack on Fort Sullivan. Located on Sullivan's Island at the entrance to the harbor, Fort Sullivan was only half completed, and its commander, Colonel William Moultrie, had resorted to palmetto log walls filled with sand, because better materials were unavailable.

On 16 June Clinton landed about 2,000 troops on undefended Long Island (present-day Isle of Palms), immediately north of Sullivan's Island, only to find the channel separating them uncrossable. Unable to assault the fort with infantry, the effort switched to Admiral Sir Peter Parker's gunships. Parker's attack occurred on 28 June, with four ships and one bomb ketch concentrating on the fort. Following the preliminary bombardment, three other vessels attempted to slip around the island to assault the fort's unprotected rear. However, all three ships ran aground. Furthermore, the fort's walls, especially the palmetto logs, absorbed the cannonade. By the end of the day, a combination of determined resistance and well-directed fire by the garrison had gained the upper hand; the British withdrew, burning one of the grounded vessels.

The Colonial victory was due primarily to good fortune and Clinton's poor judgment, especially considering the half-prepared state of Fort Sullivan. The success did ensure, however, freedom of Colonial operations in the South until Clinton's return in 1780.

References. Walter J. Fraser, Jr., *Patriots, Pistols and Peticoats*, 2d ed., 1993. Franklin B. Hough, ed., *The Siege of Charleston*, 1975.

Lee W. Eysturlid

(Civil War) Possessing a protected harbor and served by three rail lines radiating northwest, west, and southwest, Charleston, South Carolina, was a major center of commercial activity in 1861. Charleston Harbor was defended by a U.S. Army garrison at Fort Moultrie, a structure dating back to the American Revolution.* When South Carolina seceded in 1860, Major Robert Anderson abandoned Moultrie and moved to unfinished Fort Sumter,* in the middle of the harbor. On 12 April 1861, South Carolina militia gunners under the command of General Pierre G. T. Beauregard opened fire on Sumter. The following day, a Federal relief convoy appeared, but it did not attempt to pass through the bombardment. Short of food and unable to silence the shore batteries, the garrison abandoned Sumter. There had been no casualties on either side, but the Civil War* had begun.

On 16 April, President Abraham Lincoln declared a blockade of southern ports, and Federal warships served notice of the blockade of Charleston on 28 May 1861. Despite the blockade, blockade runners plied their trade for nearly four years. In 1863, the Union Army tried to close Charleston by capturing Battery Wagner at the mouth of the harbor. To accomplish this, the 54th Massachusetts Volunteer Infantry, a black regiment,* made a gallant but unsuccessful assault on Wagner over open ground. After two months of stalemate, however, the Confederates withdrew to new defenses, and Union troops captured Morris Island. Their success slowed, but did not stop, the blockade runners. Finally, in January 1865, William T. Sherman's forces cut Charleston's rail connections. On 12 February, Confederate authorities began evacuating the city, and on the night of 17 February 1865, the last ship left Charleston. The next morning, Union troops swarmed into the city.

References. E. Milby Burton, *The Siege of Charleston, 1861–1865*, 1970. Robert N. Rosen, *Confederate Charleston*, 1994.

William H. Carnes

CHATEAU-THIERRY

By the end of May 1918, a German offensive had pushed the French Sixth Army westward, nearly routing it and threatening to break through on the road to Paris, only fifty miles to the southwest. In response to pleas from Marshal Ferdinand Foch, General John J. Pershing* agreed on 30 May to release five U.S. divisions* to help shore up the French lines. The next day, the doughboys* from the 3d Division went into action near the small town of Chateau-Thierry, followed by troops of the 2d Division, with its twin brigades* of Regulars and Marines under the French VII Army Corps. This was the baptism of fire for most of the Americans. Over the next two months they proved themselves in hard fighting, with little rest, against a tenacious enemy. Chateau-Thierry was finally retaken on 21 July, and the German offensive, which had come so close to breaking the allies,* petered out. Although many faults were exposed in the American Expeditionary Force (AEF), Chateau-Thierry stands as the first major U.S. contribution to the allied victory in World War I.*

References. Edward M. Coffman, *The War to End All Wars*, 1986. Laurence Stallings, *The Doughboys*, 1963.

CHATTANOOGA

Following the Confederate success at Chickamauga* in September 1863, Major General William S. Rosecrans's Army of the Cumberland* retreated into

Chattanooga, where Braxton Bragg's Army of Tennessee* besieged it. The newly appointed commanding general of the Army of the West,* Major General Ulysses S. Grant,* relieved Rosecrans and replaced him with Major General George H. Thomas,* a position Thomas would hold for the remainder of the war. Both sides jockeyed for an advantage and conducted numerous mounted and amphibious raids and operations. Bragg eventually ordered James Longstreet's* corps* to attack the Union forces at Knoxville, just as Major General Joseph Hooker* with two corps arrived from Virginia, followed by Major General William T. Sherman* with 17,000 troops from Mississippi. Reinforced, the Union forces broke out of the city in a three-day battle, 23–25 November 1863. Bragg's army suffered its only rout and panic of the war and was forced into northern Georgia. The defeat led to Bragg's relief from command. Grant was called to Washington, promoted to lieutenant general, and placed in command of the total Union military effort for 1864.

References. John Bowers, *Chickamauga and Chattanooga*, 1994. Fairfax Downey, *Storming of the Gateway*, 1960. James Lee McDonough, *Chattanooga*, 1984.

Andrew N. Morris

CHEMICAL CORPS

The Chemical Corps traces its origins to the trenches of World War I,* when General John J. Pershing* directed the creation of a Gas Service on 5 July 1917. The First Gas Regiment was formed and deployed to support U.S. Army operations in 1918. On 28 June 1918, the War Department* established the Chemical Warfare Service* (CWS), and Congress made it a permanent branch of the Army in 1920. Between World War I and World War II,* the CWS oversaw all chemical weapons and activities, including research and development on chemical offensive and defensive capabilities. During World War II, the CWS developed and deployed flame and incendiary weapons, fielded smoke generators for air and force protection, and adapted the 4.2-inch chemical mortar to deliver smoke and high explosives for close-support fire missions for the infantry* and armor* forces. In 1942, the CWS assumed responsibility for managing biological warfare. In 1946, the CWS was redesignated the Chemical Corps. The Chemical Corps's role in Korea remained the same as that in World War II. As Cold War* tensions heightened during the 1950s, the Chemical Corps's defensive mission became more important. During the Vietnam War,* the Chemical Corps's flame devices again played an important role, clearing large areas of mines,* preparing helicopter landing areas, and conducting defoliation operations to deny the enemy cover and concealment. The Chemical Corps continues to play an important role, especially in nuclear, biological, and chemical* (NBC) defense.

References. Frederic J. Brown, *Chemical Warfare*, 1968. Victor A. Utgoff, *The Challenge of Chemical Weapons*, 1991.

John Edgecomb

CHEMICAL WARFARE SERVICE

The introduction of gas warfare during World War I* necessitated the creation of an agency to control gas weapons and develop countermeasures. On 28 June 1918, War Department* established the Chemical Warfare Service (CWS) to centralize authority for chemical warfare, which had previously been under the Bureau of Mines. The CWS was to provide chemical materials, toxic and non-toxic gasses, smoke and incendiary materials, and gas defense equipment. It was charged with the storage, maintenance, and issue of chemical materials and gas defense equipment. It also inspected troops when they were using chemical materials, to ensure proper procedures. It investigated all injuries resulting from interaction with chemical agents. The CWS also provided chemical components for chemical weapons used by other military services. The Chemical Warfare Service was not recognized as a separate branch until World War II.* It was redesignated the U.S. Army Chemical Corps* on 2 August 1946.

References. Leo P. Brophy and George J. B. Fisher, *The Chemical Warfare Service: Organizing for War*, 1959. Leo P. Brophy, Wyndham D. Miles, and Rexmond C. Cochrane, *The Chemical Warfare Service: From Laboratory to Field*, 1959. Brooks E. Kleber and Dale Birdsell, *The Chemical Warfare Service: Chemicals in Combat*, 1966.

Rebecca S. Witte

CHENNAULT, CLAIRE LEE (1890–1958)

Born in Commerce, Texas, in 1890, Claire Lee Chennault grew up in rural Louisiana and joined the U.S. Army soon after the United States entered World War I.* Selected for officer training, then flying training, he received his wings in April 1919. Discharged in April 1920, he soon accepted a regular commission in the newly established Air Service.* Known as a daring fighter pilot, Chennault loved acrobatic flying and believed that pursuit aircraft could shoot down any bomber. This opinion ran counter to the prevailing view within the Air Service (after 1926 the Air Corps*) that the bomber was unstoppable, and the fervor with which he promoted his position hurt his Army career. In 1937, his hearing severely damaged by years of flying in open cockpits, Chennault retired at the rank of captain.

After his retirement, the Chinese government hired Chennault as a technical consultant to their fledgling air force. Promoted to the rank of colonel, Chennault was instrumental in creating and leading the American Volunteer Group (AVG)—the Flying Tigers—which began flying for China in late 1940. In April 1942, the Air Corps ordered Chennault to active duty and soon promoted him to brigadier general. In July, when the AVG was dissolved and the China Air Task Force (CATF) of the Army Air Corps was created, Chennault became its commander. In March 1943, the CATF became the Fourteenth Air Force, with Chennault in command with the rank of major general. An advocate of air-power's ability to defeat Japan, Chennault disagreed with General Joseph W. Stilwell,* who focused on building the Chinese army. Chiang Kai-shek, however, supported Chennault, and for a time his ideas formed the basis for U.S.

strategy in China. A controversial figure to the end, Chennault retired in July 1945 rather than accept a position of lesser responsibility.

References. Martha Byrd, *Chennault*, 1987. Daniel Ford, *Flying Tigers*, 1991. Duane Schultz, *The Maverick War*, 1987.

Gary Bjorge

CHICKAMAUGA

By the end of June 1863, Braxton Bragg's Confederate Army of Tennessee had been driven from Tennessee into northern Georgia by Major General William S. Rosecrans's Army of the Cumberland.* Rosecrans followed Bragg, crossed the Tennessee River, and by 4 September he had spread his three corps* over a forty-mile front in an attempt to cut off the Confederate retreat. Bungling by Bragg and his subordinates prevented an isolated Union corps from being defeated. By 19 September, Rosecrans had concentrated two corps on the west side of Chickamauga Creek. Bragg crossed the creek and attempted to envelop the Union right. Neither Bragg nor Rosecrans, however, had an accurate picture of the other's dispositions, and the envelopment turned into a series of confused frontal attacks.

On 20 September, Bragg, joined by James Longstreet's corps from the Army of Northern Virginia, which had just arrived by rail, launched uncoordinated attacks all along his line. Union reinforcements were able to blunt the Confederate drive until about 1130, when Longstreet's corps fell on the Union center. It struck a portion of the line vacated by a division* Rosecrans had mistakenly ordered to reinforce Major General George H. Thomas* on the Union left. Two Union divisions moving toward the vacated position were struck in the flank by the attack, and the entire Union center and right were soon routed. Believing the battle lost, Rosecrans fled to Chattanooga* with much of his army. Only Thomas's corps remained a cohesive force. Thomas established a defensive position on Snodgrass Hill and held off repeated Confederate assaults throughout the afternoon. Without a reserve, Bragg was unable to drive Thomas from the hill. By the evening of 21 September, the Army of the Cumberland had withdrawn into Chattanooga, and Bragg had occupied Lookout Mountain and Missionary Ridge. The two armies would face each other there until late November.

References. John Bowers, *Chickamauga and Chattanooga*, 1994. Peter Cozzens, *This Terrible Sound*, 1992. Glenn Tucker, *Chickamauga*, 1961.

Richard L. Kiper

CHICKASAW BAYOU

The Chickasaw Bayou campaign was the first major effort by Union forces under Major General Ulysses S. Grant* to seize the city of Vicksburg.* In December 1862, while he moved overland, Grant sent Major General William T. Sherman* with a force of 32,000 troops from Memphis down the Mississippi to the Yazoo River just north of Vicksburg. Sherman landed at Johnson's Plantation on 26 December and soon made first contact with Confederate forces near

Chickasaw Bayou, a swampy, wooded area cut by numerous small lakes and streams. On the 29th, Sherman ordered a full assault on the Confederate defenses, but despite hard fighting and heavy casualties his troops were unable to break the Confederate lines. Poor Union morale and leadership problems combined with excellent Confederate generalship and tenacious defense in dense fog and rugged terrain to defeat the Union effort. Confederate cavalry raids on Grant's line of communications forced Grant to retreat and enabled the Confederates to concentrate against Sherman's force at Chickasaw Bayou. Sherman then called off further attacks and reembarked on 1–2 January 1863. Sherman lost 1,776 men at Chickasaw Bayou. After reviewing the campaign, Grant determined that in the future fixed lines of communications would be unnecessary to supply his army, thus lulling the Confederates into a false sense of security and ultimately contributing to their defeat at Vicksburg.

References. Edward C. Bearss, *The Campaign for Vicksburg*, vol. 1, 1985. Gray M. Gildner, *The Chickasaw Bayou Campaign*, 1991.

Edward Shanahan

CHIEF, ARMY RESERVE

In the reorganization of the U.S. Army Reserve during the early 1950s, the executive for reserve and ROTC affairs became the Chief, Army Reserve (CAR). Appointed by the president with the advice and consent of the Senate, for a four-year term, the CAR holds the rank of major general, Army of the United States, and serves as the Commander, U.S. Army Reserve Command (USARC), and deputy commanding general for Reserve Affairs, Forces Command* (FORSCOM). Working through the Office of the Chief, Army Reserve (OCAR), the CAR develops and executes Army Reserve plans, policies, and programs; administers U.S. Army Reserve (USAR) personnel; and is the director for three USAR appropriations—pay and allowances, operations and maintenance, and construction funds. In this capacity, he directs USAR planning to provide trained units and soldiers in support of Army mobilization plans. The Chief, Army Reserve, also advises the Army Chief of Staff* on USAR matters, represents the USAR in relations with governmental agencies and the public, and advises Army staff agencies in formulating and developing Department of the Army* (DA) policies affecting the USAR. He is also a member of DA and Office of Strategic Development (OSD) committees as required, and is directly responsible to the chief of staff for matters pertaining to the development, readiness, and maintenance of USAR forces.

Reference. Richard B. Crossland and James T. Currie, *Twice the Citizen*, 1984.

Bill Knight

CHIEF OF STAFF

This term refers normally to the senior officers of the U.S. Army and U.S. Air Force, responsible to their respective service secretaries. Other definitions refer to the principal staff officer in a brigade* or higher echelon of the Army or Marine Corps or a unit of the Navy, commanded by a rear admiral or his superior. Modern usage of the term "chief of staff" originated with the reorganization of the War Department* by Secretary of War* Elihu Root, commonly known as the Root Reforms. Prior to this reorganization, the commanding general* headed the Army. Considerable disagreement, however, existed about the responsibilities of the secretary, the commanding general,* and the various departments. Normally, operations, control, and disciplinary matters were under the commanding general, while the secretary handled fiscal matters directly with the various departments. The lack of unity of command was, in large part, instrumental in bringing about the Root reorganization. On 14 February 1903, Congress passed an act to increase the efficiency of the Army and establish the General Staff.* General Staff members were placed under the supervision of the chief of staff, who, under the direction of the president and secretary of war, supervised the troops of the line and the main departments of the Army. Additional duties included preparing war plans, ensuring Army efficiency, and advising the secretary of war.

Today, the Chief of Staff of the Army holds four-star rank and is the principal officer of the Army. Appointed by the president with the advice and consent of the Senate, he serves at the pleasure of the president for a period of four years and performs his duties under the direction of the secretary of the Army.* He presides over the Army Staff and is a member of the Joint Chiefs of Staff.* Additionally, he is charged with organizing, training, and sustaining Army forces to be provided to combatant commanders for military operations.

References. William Gardner Bell, *Commanding Generals and Chiefs of Staff, 1775–1987*, 1987. James E. Hewes, Jr., *From Root to McNamara*, 1975.

Gary Bounds

CHINA-BURMA-INDIA THEATER

In the summer of 1941, the U.S. government sent the American Military Mission to China (AMMISCA) to facilitate Chinese acquisition and use of U.S. lend-lease aid. After the Japanese attacked Pearl Harbor, the United States moved to strengthen relations with China and improve U.S.-Chinese military cooperation. In March 1942, General Joseph W. Stilwell* arrived in China to serve as chief of staff to the supreme commander of the Chinese theater, Chiang Kai-shek, and as commanding general* United States Army Forces in the Chinese Theater of Operations, Burma, and India. Stilwell took over the personnel of AMMISCA and established the Headquarters of American Army Forces, China, Burma, and India. In June 1942, with U.S. logistical support and Army Air Corps* personnel in India increasing rapidly, the War Department* authorized Stilwell to establish a U.S. theater of operations, with himself as theater commander. This theater, the China, Burma, and India theater, was commonly known as the CBI.

Stilwell's mission was to keep China in the war and improve the fighting ability of the Chinese army. Chiang and Stilwell, however, disagreed on strategy, objectives, and the use of U.S. resources flowing into China. Progress in the war against Japan did not eliminate tensions within the coalition, and in October 1944, at the insistence of Chiang Kai-shek, President Franklin Roosevelt decided to relieve Stilwell as commander of CBI and recall him to the United States. At the same time, Roosevelt directed that the CBI be dissolved; he created the China theater and the India-Burma theater. China had always been a secondary theater of operations, and the speed of the U.S. advance across the central Pacific had reduced its importance in U.S. strategic plans.

References. Edward Fischer, *The Chancy War*, 1991. Don Moser, *China-Burma-India*, 1978. Barbara W. Tuchman, *Stilwell and the American Experience in China, 1911–45*, 1971.

Gary Bjorge

CHINOOK CH-47

The CH-47, a tandem-rotor, medium-lift helicopter built by Boeing Helicopters, was first accepted by the U.S. Army in 1962, as the Chinook. Powered by two T-55 engines mounted in pods aft outside the fuselage, the Chinook has an unobstructed, full-length cabin for cargo and personnel. The Army received 762 A, B, and C models during the Vietnam War* period, each with progressively more powerful engines and better flight characteristics. Since 1982, Boeing has built 472 CH-47D Chinooks for the Army. These feature upgraded engines, avionics, flight controls, refueling equipment, and cargo-handling capacity. The D model can carry over 22,000 pounds of cargo on three external cargo hooks. The latest Chinook model, the MH-47E, is equipped with aerial refueling capability and navigational equipment for long-range penetration missions for Special Operations Forces.*

References. Truxtun R. Baldwin, "The Improved Chinook," *U.S. Army Aviation Digest*, December 1967, 22–27. Leonard R. Wilson, "The Chinook," *U.S. Army Aviation Digest*, April 1964, 18–20.

Randall N. Briggs

CHIPPAWA

Soon after crossing the Niagara River into Canada in July 1814, General Winfield Scott* captured Fort Erie, encamped along the river, and on the 5th staged a belated 4th of July dinner and parade. A British force under General Phineas Riall then mounted an attack on the Americans, confident that it would once again scatter the "provincials," but as the U.S. troops moved steadily into battle formation in the face of his cannonade, Riall exclaimed, "Those are regulars, by God!" Scott's lighter guns soon smashed the British batteries, and Scott calmly swung his two flanks toward the advancing British, catching them in a crossfire. The British attack collapsed, and the battle was over in thirty minutes. Scott's 1,300 well-drilled regulars had bested 1,500 British regulars in a stand-up fight in the open, inflicting 148 killed and 221 wounded at a cost of 44 U.S. lives and 224 wounded. The victory in the Battle of Chippawa gave the British further evidence that U.S. regulars could stand up to the best troops that they could put into the field,

References. Jeffrey Kimball, "The Battle of Chippawa," *Military Affairs*, Winter 1967–1968, 169–186. John K. Mahon, *The War of 1812*, 1972.

Stanley Sandler

CHOCTAW H-34

"H-34" was the official designation for a series of transport helicopters used by the U.S. Army beginning in 1955. Known as the Choctaw, the H-34 was a twelve-to-sixteen-passenger, cargo, and light tactical transport helicopter manufactured by the Sikorski Aircraft Division, Stratford, Connecticutt. Powered by one Curtiss-Wright R-1820–84 radial engine capable of producing 1,425 horsepower, the Choctaw's maximum speed at sea level was 107 knots, with a normal cruising speed of 95 knots. Maximum range was 318 nautical miles, and the rate of climb was 1,100 feet per minute. The Army produced a total of 437 A through C–model Choctaws from 1955 to 1965. The VH-34 was used as a VIP transport notable as the first helicopter used by the Presidential Flight Detachment. The Choctaw carried a crew of three.

References. *Army Aviation*, 1992. Stephen Harding, *U.S. Army Aircraft since 1947*, 1997.

David Zoellers

CHOSIN RESERVOIR

The Changjin Reservoir, an artificial lake in the high mountainous region of northeastern North Korea, had been named Chosin by the Japanese during their long occupation of that country. In late November 1950, Chinese forces intervening in the Korean War* surrounded and badly mauled elements of U.S. X Corps advancing northward to the Yalu. Task Force Faith, built around the 1st Battalion, 32d Infantry, 7th Infantry Division, attempting to engage what were supposedly "remnants of Chinese divisions fleeing north" on the east side of Chosin, was almost annihilated in an attack that began on the night of 27 November. The 1st Marine Division, advancing more cautiously on the west side of Chosin, was able to survive the Chinese assault. Joined by surviving Army elements, the marines conducted a fighting withdrawal to Hagaru, where 5,400 wounded were airlifted to safety by 6 December. From there they fought their way in bitterly cold weather to Kot'o-ri, where an additional 600 wounded were flown out. The soldiers and Marines dubbed the withdrawal the "retreat from the frozen Chosin." A relief column met the force just north of Chinhung-ni on 9 December, and together they reached the seaport of Hungnam on 11 December. There the survivors were evacuated by sea.

References. Roy E. Appleman, *East of Chosin*, 1987, and *Escaping the Trap*, 1990. Eric M. Hammel, *Chosin*, 1990.

Randall N. Briggs

CHROMITE. *See* Inchon.

THE CITADEL

The Citadel was founded in Charleston, South Carolina in 1842 in reaction to the Denmark Vesey slave revolt. South Carolinians wanted an arsenal for use against servile insurrections, but they did not want to pay a full-time garrison or call on federal troops. Originally called the Military College of South Carolina, the Citadel served as an institution where young men of middle or lower-class families could receive a degree in engineering. The state remitted tuition for the South Carolina Corps of Cadets in exchange for the cadets' training and service. The school's initial building, located on Broad Street and constructed in the Spanish-Moorish style, was intended to give the impression of a fortress. Two Citadel cadets were to fire the first salvo at the *Star of the West*, the opening shots of the Civil War.* The Corps of Cadets subsequently participated in several engagements around South Carolina, earning an excellent reputation. During Reconstruction, the federal government closed the Citadel; it did not reopen until the 1880s. The present campus on the periphery of Charleston opened in 1923. The Citadel operates today as a full-time, degree-granting institution with approximately 2,500 men and women in its Corps of Cadets.

References. O. J. Bond, *The Story of the Citadel*, 1936, 1989. Tommy Thompson, *The Citadel*, 1993.

Lee W. Eysturlid

CIVIL ADMINISTRATION

The term "civil administration" refers to one of the two principal areas of civil affairs—the other being civil military operations. Civil administration, also called civil affairs administration, deals with military support to foreign civilian governments. Among other activities, civil administration consists of assistance to foreign governments in rehabilitating or building government or socioeconomic infrastructure; the coordination and supervision of the distribution of U.S. resources to meet essential civil requirements; oversight of contacts between military forces and civil authority and the population, to the extent required by the mission; coordination of essential funding programs with appropriate U.S. government agencies; and coordination and assistance in the return of government and administration to the host nation civil authority as soon as practicable. Civil administration in friendly territory supports, reinforces, and restores a friendly government. Recent examples are Panama and Haiti. Civil administration in occupied territory, also known as military government, is required under international law, which states that the occupying power, within its capabilities, must maintain an orderly government in the occupied territory. Examples are the occupations of Germany and Japan following World War II.*

References. John T. Fishel, *Civil Military Operations in the New World*, 1997. United States Department of Defense, Joint Published 3–57, *Doctrine for Joint Civil Affairs*, 1995.

John T. Fishel

CIVIL AFFAIRS

The U.S. Army has been involved in a surprising number of civil affairs, civic action, and military government activities throughout its history. During the 19th century, the United States was in many respects underdeveloped, and the main source of technically educated persons with management experience of large numbers of workers, other than immigrants, were the graduates of the U.S. Military Academy.* Army engineers laid out roads and telegraph lines, protected westward immigrants, built bridges, and enlarged the U.S. Capitol and its dome. In the 1930s the Army operated the camps of the Civilian Conservation Corps* (CCC) for unemployed youths, who were mobilized to plant shelter belts and improve the national parks. Even at the end of the 20th century, the United States was the only industrialized nation whose coasts, rivers, and harbors were regulated and often improved by its army. The Corps of Engineers* continues to control and development of the nation's waterways, including the massive Tennessee Valley Authority.

The Army has administered friendly, neutral, and enemy civilian governments, from the most isolated towns to national capitals, in each of its conflicts, beginning with the American Revolution.* The most difficult governance was of fellow Americans during the post–Civil War Reconstruction period. During World War II,* the Civil Affairs Division (CAD) in the European Theater of Operations* (ETO) assumed responsibility for no less than eighty million civilians, orphans, displaced persons, refugees, and the homeless. After the war, the Army established military governments for the occupations of Germany and Japan and laid the foundations for the democracies that emerged in the second half of the 20th century.

During the Korean, Vietnam, and Gulf Wars, civil affairs officers worked with allied governments to defend and strengthen their sovereignty. The Army also administers newly liberated territories and rebuilds national infrastructures, utilizing a wide range of military and civilian expertise mobilized from both the active-duty and the far larger reserve components.

References. Jeffrey J. Clarke, *Advice and Support*, 1988. Harry L. Coles and Albert K. Weinberg, *Civil Affairs*, 1964. Alfred H. Hausrath, "Civil Affairs and Military Government," in *A Survey of Military Institutions*, vol. 2, ed. Roger W. Little, 1969.

Stanley Sandler

CIVIL WAR

Nearly all American historians consider the Civil War the pivotal event in American history. Fought between 12 April 1861 and 9 April 1865—but arguably spanning the years 1855 to 1875—the war was fought between sections divided by differing ideologies. As the war progressed, however, social, political, and economic ideologies diminished in importance, and by late 1862 slavery had become the paramount issue.

The Civil War epitomized the term "brother's war." Although the opposing armies generally represented the division of the nation between North and South and free versus slave states, the division of the population in many areas, especially the border states, was not so clear. Many accounts exist of brother pitted against brother, father against son, brother against sister. An example of this tragic situation was Mary Todd Lincoln, President Abraham Lincoln's wife, who had four brothers and three brothers-in-law fighting for the Confederacy. Although an undetermined number of persons served in both armies, estimates are that more than 620,000 combatants perished during the Civil War—360,000 in the North, 260,000 in the South—more than died in all U.S. wars from the American Revolution* through the Korean War.*

Some historians see the origins of the Civil War in "bleeding Kansas," where abolitionists and proslavery elements clashed as early as 1855, when John Brown led an assault at Pottawatomie Creek, killing five proslavery settlers. The next year, Congressman Preston Brooks confronted Senator Charles Sumner of Massachusetts in the Senate chamber over the Kansas issue and caned him senseless. Sumner was absent from the Senate for nearly four years recovering from the beating. Over the next several years, a series of crises and events— the Dred Scott decision, the Lincoln-Douglas debates, and John Brown's raid at Harpers Ferry—fueled the nation's divisions and created a passion for war. The final crisis was the election of a Republican to the presidency in November 1860. In December, South Carolina seceded from the Union, followed by ten more states. Lincoln's call for 75,000 volunteers to put down the rebellion sealed the nation's fate and assured civil war.

At the onset of war, the North boasted a population of twenty-two million, while the South's population was only 9.5 million—of which nearly four million were of African descent. The North, moreover, possessed more than 90 percent of the nation's manufacturing capacity, controlled the preponderance of financial houses, and contained two-thirds of the nation's 30,000 miles of rails. Although a significant percentage of the Regular Army officers resigned their commissions to fight with the Confederacy, nearly all professional naval officers continued to serve aboard Union vessels. The North, therefore, had a decided advantage in resources and manpower, although the military talent was divided between North and South.

The Civil War armies fought more than 4,000 separate engagement; however, only a small number can be considered major battles or campaigns. Major campaigns were fought in three theaters—the eastern, western, and trans-Mississippi. The first battle of significance occurred near the small Virginia town of Manassas. On 18 July 1861, at the Battle of First Bull Run*—also known as First Manassas (the Confederates tended to name battles after the nearest town or city, while the Federals tended to name them after the nearest body of water)—22,000 Confederates under General Pierre T. G. Beauregard defeated more than 35,000 Union troops under Major General Irvin McDowell. The Federal troops had been under the mistaken impression that the Rebel forces would disintegrate at their approach. As Washington picnickers watched the battle, initial Union success turned into chaos as Confederate forces counterattacked

McDowell's fatigued troops, sending them pell-mell back toward Washington. At First Bull Run, General Thomas J. Jackson received the sobriquet "Stonewall," and Union troops first heard the famous "Rebel yell."

Perhaps the most important battle of 1862 was fought near Sharpsburg, Maryland, along Antietam* Creek. On 17 September 1862, more than 84,000 Federals under Major General George B. McClellan* narrowly defeated 40,000 troops under General Robert E. Lee.* By objective standards, Antietam was not well fought tactically by either side. Lee should not have backed his forces against Antietam Creek, allowing himself no escape: conversely, with twice as many men, McClellan should have been able to annihilate Lee's army. Nevertheless, strategically victory belonged to the Union, and it served as a vehicle for Lincoln to issue the Preliminary Emancipation Proclamation on 22 September 1862. Publication of the Emancipation Proclamation on 1 January 1863 freed all slaves in Confederate-occupied territory and focused the war on a single cause, the abolition of slavery. Many historians consider this the critical event of the Civil War.

One of the most operationally and tactically sound battles of the war took place at Chancellorsville,* Virginia, from 1 to 6 May 1863. Lee's army of 43,000 men defeated 73,000 Union soldiers under Major General Joseph Hooker* in a costly battle that saved Richmond. Although outnumbered nearly two to one, Lee and Jackson devised a plan to split their forces; Jackson conducted a flank march with 26,000 troops to envelope Hooker's forces anchored on the Rapidan and Rappahannock Rivers. Jackson's audacious maneuver worked, but Jackson died five days later from wounds received during a lull in the battle. He had been one of the South's most capable generals, and his death was a severe blow to the Confederacy as well as a personal loss to Lee.

Two Confederate defeats in the first week of July 1863 clearly marked the turning point in the war. From 1 to 3 July, more than 90,000 Union soldiers under the command of Major General George G. Meade* faced Lee's Army of Northern Virginia, nearly 43,000 strong, near the small Pennsylvania town of Gettysburg.* The battle culminated in Pickett's charge, an assault by 15,000 Confederate soldiers across a mile of open fields in a desperate attempt to save the battle, perhaps already lost. After three days of bloody fighting, more than 58,000 Americans from both sides—more soldiers than the United States lost in the Vietnam War*—lay dead or wounded on the battlefield. Gettysburg represented the northernmost advance of the Confederate armies and their last significant action on Union soil. A Confederate victory might have changed the course of the war and breathed new life into the Southern cause, but Lee was never again able to take the war to the North.

On the heels of the loss at Gettysburg, more bad news awaited the Confederacy. On 4 July Vicksburg, Mississippi, capitulated after a seven-month siege. Vicksburg was significant for several reasons; it has been referred to as the nail that held the Confederacy together. Once it fell, the Confederacy was doomed. After the fall of such strategic locations as Forts Henry and Donelson in the north and New Orleans to the south, Vicksburg had been the only remaining Confederate stronghold on the Mississippi. Once the entire river was in Union hands, the South lost its primary communications line with the trans-Mississippi west. Additionally, the victory at Vicksburg brought Ulysses S. Grant* to Lincoln's attention and led to his rise to command all the Union armies. Perhaps most importantly, the loss of Vicksburg and the defeat at Gettysburg sealed a British decision not to extend aid to the Confederacy.

The year 1864 brought a new face to the war between North and South. Not only was Grant, far more aggressive and tenacious than any of his predecessors, now in command, but the Union Army was now enlisting tens of thousands of former slaves and free blacks (180,000 by the end of the war), replacing its losses of the previous year and swelling its ranks for the bloody and climactic battles to come. In addition to the assault on Lee's Army of Northern Virgina, Grant sent Major General William T. Sherman* into the South to attack the Confederate armies there. The result was Sherman's Atlanta campaign,* a march from Tennessee through Georgia and then north into South Carolina, a campaign that epitomized the war in its last year. Sherman's initial mission was to attack General John Bell Hood's army and destroy it. Unable to pin down Hood's army, however, Sherman let it move to the west and focused his attention on Atlanta. Taking the war directly to the people, Sherman, in his own words, made "Georgia howl." Sherman's March* proved to the South and the world that the Confederacy was unable to stop a Union army moving deep in its countryside with impunity. It was also a harbinger of war in the future.

Within four months after Sherman reached the sea, the Civil War effectively ended when Lee surrendered his army in a small private parlor at Appomattox Court House, Virginia. For more than a half-century after the guns fell silent, families would listen to firsthand accounts of the horrible battles and the great sacrifices of this war.

Depending on one's perspective, the American Civil War has many meanings: it was the first "modern" war; it was a war between industrialism and agrarianism; it was a war of states rights versus federalism; it was the war for Southern independence. The many perceptions notwithstanding, the Civil War had two notable and enduring effects on American society: the United States would remain a unified and indivisible state, and an entire race of people were freed from bondage forever.

References. Herman Hattaway and Archer Jones, *How the North Won.* 1983. Robert Leckie, *None Died in Vain*, 1990. Gerald F. Linderman, *Embattled Courage*, 1987. James M. McPherson, *Battle Cry of Freedom*, 1988. Charles P. Roland, *An American Iliad*, 1991.

Krewasky A. Salter

CIVILIAN CONSERVATION CORPS

After Franklin D. Roosevelt's first inauguration in March of 1932, he proposed a series of measures, known as the New Deal, to battle the Great Depression. The goal of the New Deal was to provide people with productive jobs and put money into circulation. On 31 March 1933, Congress passed a bill creating the Civilian Conservation Corps (CCC); it authorized the employment of young, unmarried men for conservation and beautification projects, to plant trees, fight forest fires, and build and maintain roads in the nation's forests. CCC volunteers received thirty dollars a month, room and board, and medical benefits. The CCC reached a peak strength of 500,000. The U.S. Army was given responsibility for organizing and supervising the CCC. The experience many officers gained working with the CCC became invaluable when the United States began to mobilize for World War II.* A total of three million men worked in the CCC before it was abolished in 1942.

References. Perry H. Merrill, *Roosevelt's Forest Army*, 1981. M. Chester Nolte, ed., *Civilian Conservation Corps*, 1990. John A. Salmond, *The Civilian Conservation Corps*, 1933–1942, 1967.

Trevor Brown

CIVILIAN IRREGULAR DEFENSE GROUPS

The Civilian Irregular Defense Groups (CIDG) program began in Vietnam, in the Central Highlands village of Buon Enao. U.S. advisors had long-feared Viet Cong (VC) attempts to dominate the Central Highlands and split South Vietnam in two. To forstall this, U.S. embassy and Special Forces* personnel developed a plan to send Special Forces A Teams* and South Vietnamese government special forces teams into the region. The Central Highlands region was populated by such mountain tribes as the Rhade, Jarai, Bru, Sedang, Mnong, Stieng, Chau Ma, Bahnar, Katu, and other ethnic groups known collectively by their French name of *Montagnards* (literally, mountain dwellers). The Vietnamese often referred to them disdainfully as "*moi*," or savages.

Special Forces teams trained villagers in local defensive measures, organized teams of strike forces, and kept thousands of villages at least nominally on the side of the government. At the height of the effort in 1966, the Special Forces had a total of 72,400 paramilitary indigenous forces (including village forces, strike forces, and regional and popular forces) at command. Often the best CIDG soldiers joined the Mobile Strike Forces, which served as "fire brigades" for isolated camps under attack. The CIDG program was a cost-effective program that used indigenous forces and a handful of U.S. advisors to great effect.

References. Francis J. Kelly, *U.S. Army Special Force, 1961–1971*, 1985. Shelby L. Stanton, *Green Berets at War*, 1985.

Richard Stewart

CLARK, GEORGE ROGERS (1752–1818)

George Rogers Clark, American frontiersman, military leader, and older brother of William Clark,* was born near Charlottesville, Virginia. Trained in surveying by his grandfather, Clark plied the trade with settlers in the Ohio Valley from 1772 to 1774. In the latter year he became a scout for Lord Dunmore in his campaign against the Indians in Kentucky. In 1775, when he was twenty-three, Clark led colonists in Transylvania (Kentucky and parts of Tennessee) in a revolt against their North Carolinian proprietors. He later successfully petitioned Virginia to accept Kentucky as a colony and to allot funds for its defense.

During the American Revolution,* Clark, now a lieutenant colonel in the militia, organized a campaign against the British and their Indian allies in the Northwest. In 1778, with a force of less than 200 men, he captured Kaskaskia and Vincennes.* Two years later, he defeated the British at Cahokia. In 1782, Clark, now a general, triumphed over the Shawnee at Piqua and Chillicothe. After the war, Clark became a commissioner of Illinois land grants. Soon thereafter, James Wilkinson, Continental Army* general who coveted Clark's position, began a campaign to discredit him; Congress removed Clark from his commissionership in 1787. In subsequent years, Clark attempted to found a colony west of the Mississippi and later participated in a failed plan to recapture Louisiana for France. In 1799 Clark returned to Kentucky and died at Louisville in 1818.

References. John Bakeless, *Background to Glory*, 1957. Lowell H. Harrison, *George Rogers Clark and the War in the West*, 1976. Walter Havinghurst, *George Rogers Clark*, 1952.

Joseph R. Fischer

CLARK, MARK WAYNE (1896–1984)

Mark Wayne Clark, the controversial commander of the Fifth Army* in its campaign against the Germans in Italy during World War II,* began his life at Madison Barracks, New York, the son of a U.S. Army colonel. After graduating fron the U.S. Military Academy* in 1917, Clark fought in France with the 11th Infantry and was wounded. Only a major in 1939 at the outbreak of World War II,* by July 1942 Clark had become chief of staff* of Army Ground Forces* and commanded American Ground Forces in Europe with the rank of major general. Later, as General Dwight Eisenhower's deputy, he was chief planner of the November 1942 invasion of North Africa. He traveled by submarine to a secret rendezvous with pro-Allied French officers in Morocco, obtaining intelligence from them for the upcoming landings. In 1943 Eisenhower appointed Clark as Fifth Army commander for the invasion of Italy. Landing at Salerno against heavy German resistance, Clark commanded his troops at the beachhead, personally leading an infantry counterattack against eighteen German tanks to relieve pressure on his position. For his heroism he received the Distinguished Service Cross.* In the drive up the Italian peninsula—600 miles of rugged, mountainous terrain—Clark led a multinational, often-outnumbered force against twenty crack German divisions under the command of Field Marshal Albert Kesselring. Clark's conduct of the campaign—especially in the battles at Anzio,* Rapido River,* and Rome—have received much criticism; however, his military peers, who understood the difficulties that faced him in his theater, have abstained from censure. On 2 May 1945, as commander of 15th Army Group, Clark received the German surrender of Italy.

After serving as United Nations commander in Korea (1952–1953), Clark retired, completing his career as president of the Citadel* from 1954 to 1966.

References. Martin Blumenson, *Mark Clark*, 1984. Mark W. Clark, *Calculated Risk*, 1950.

Donald L. Gilmore

CLARK, WILLIAM (1770–1838)

The son of a prosperous Virginia planter and younger brother of Jonathan and George Rogers Clark,* William Clark was born in Caroline County, Virginia, on 1 August 1770. The family moved when William was fifteen to Kentucky, when that "dark and bloody ground" was still the frontier. Before he was twenty, William had accompanied several militia expeditions against hostile Indians in the Ohio valley. In 1792, Clark was commissioned lieutenant of infantry and served the next four years under Major General Anthony Wayne, fighting a number of Indians battles, including Fallen Timbers,* and carrying out several diplomatic missions to the Spanish on the southern Mississippi. During this period he met and made friends with another young officer, Meriwether Lewis.*

In 1803, Clark received a letter from Lewis proposing that Clark join him in an expedition; President Thomas Jefferson was sending him to explore the vast territory recently purchased from France and to seek a route to the Pacific Ocean. The expedition left St. Louis on 14 May 1804. In one of the great epic journeys of history, Lewis and Clark led twenty-seven men up the Missouri River and over the Rockies to the headwaters of the Columbia River. Lewis was in command of the expedition, but Clark's skill as a frontiersman, knowledge of Indians, and ability to inspire subordinates were instrumental in the success of the mission. On 23 September 1806, two and a half years after their departure, Lewis and Clark returned to St. Louis (against the odds and to the delight of their countrymen). The value of the Lewis and Clark expedition to the future development of the nation is immeasurable.

After completing his reports, Clark resigned a second time from the Army on 27 February 1807 and returned to private life. Over the next several decades, however, Clark continued to serve the nation. He was appointed brigadier general of militia for the Louisiana Territory, superintendant of Indian affairs at St. Louis, and governor of Missouri Territory in 1813. In the War of 1812,* Clark led a force of regulars and militia up the Mississippi against the British and established Fort Shelby in what is now the state of Wisconsin. After the war, he devoted much of his time to establishing peaceful relations with the Indians of the upper Mississippi valley. He died at his son's home on 1 September 1838.

References. Stephen E. Ambrose, *Undaunted Courage*, 1996. Jerome O. Steffen, *William Clark*, 1977.

Donald L. Gilmore

CLASS A

The "class A" is an Army green service uniform authorized for year-round wear by all officer and enlisted male and female personnel. It is considered the normal duty uniform, unless the nature of duties require a soldier to wear one of the utility uniforms. The class A (or B version) may be worn when on duty, off duty, or during travel and is acceptable for wear during informal social functions after retreat,* unless other uniforms are prescribed by the host. The class A uniform for males consists of the Army green coat and trousers, a long or short sleeve Army green-shade (415) shirt, a black four-in-hand necktie, and authorized accessories. For females, it is the Army green classics coat and skirt or slacks, long or short sleeve shirt, a black neck tab, and authorized accessories. Soldiers should consult AR 670–1, *Wear and Appearance of Army Uniforms and Insignia*, for guidance and authorized changes in the appropriate wear and display of uniforms and insignia.

References. Frank Cox, *NCO Guide*, 4th ed., 1992. Lawrence P. Crocker, *Army Officer's Guide*, 46th ed., 1993.

Bill Knight

CLAYMORE MINE

The M18 (T48) antipersonnel weapon, or claymore mine, was designed in the late 1950s to provide a simple method to destroy a large attacking force. Weighing less than three pounds, the lightweight, rugged weapon produces a barrage of shrapnel in a fan-shaped zone two meters high, thirty meters wide, and thirty meters deep. The twenty-three-by-nine-centimeter, rectangular-shaped weapon rests on a tripod and can be detonated by either a nonelectric booby-trap device or by a hand-held electric detonator operated by an individual soldier.

References. Larry Grupp, *Claymore Mines*, 1993. James L. Murphy, "More on Claymore," *Marine Corps Gazette*, September 1966, 42–44. George L. Robson, Jr., "Claymore," *Infantry*, January 1960, 14–16.

Edward L. Maier III

CLEARING STATION. *See* Aid Station.

CLOSE AIR SUPPORT

Close air support, or CAS, is the direct support of ground troops with ordnance from fixed-wing aircraft. CAS is delivered in the immediate vicinity of ground troops—that is, close enough to be seen by them. To identify targets positively and reduce the danger of losses from friendly fire, CAS missions are normally directed by a tactical air controller party (TACP), an air liaison team deployed with the supported ground force. Fires delivered by rotary-wing aircraft are generally not considered close air support, even when provided in direct support of ground troops.

The U.S. Air Force applies the term "close air support" much more broadly than does the Army. To the Air Force, any ground-attack mission flown short of the fire support coordination line (FSCL) is considered CAS. The FSCL may be established anywhere from thirty to one hundred kilometers in front of friendly troops. Much of what the Air Force considers CAS would be described by the Army as battlefield air interdiction (BAI), missions flown beyond the vicinity of frontline ground troops but short of the FSCL. Air Force doctrine* no longer recognizes this distinction.

CAS dates back to World War I,* but CAS did not have a decisive impact on ground operations until World War II.* Between the world wars, the Air Corps* displayed little interest in the CAS mission. Air doctrine emphasized strategic bombing and considered ground support a secondary task. During World War II, the Air Corps gradually modified its position and devoted substantial assets to CAS, which proved enormously effective in all theaters and was one of the keys to the U.S. Army's success. Procedures developed for employing CAS in World War II remain the basis for modern close air support doctrine.

References. Benjamin Franklin Cooling, ed., *Case Studies in the Development of Close Air Support*, 1990. Richard G. Davis, *The 31 Initiatives*, 1987. Daniel R. Mortensen, *A Pattern for Joint Operations*, 1987.

Scott McMeen

COAST ARTILLERY

Until 1901 the Artillery Corps was a single arm consisting of both coast and field artillery. The renewed interest in coastal defense generated by the Spanish-American War* led Congress to reorganize the Artillery Corps into two sub-branches—Coast Artillery and Field artillery* (FA). Artillerists, however, both officers and enlisted men, could be assigned to either branch. Coast Artillery had 126 companies, while Field Artillery consisted of only thirty batteries, including field, mountain, and horse. With World War I* raging in Europe, Congress enacted the National Defense Act of 1916,* providing for an expansion of the Coast Artillery Corps (CAC) to 263 companies over the next five years. There was, however, little danger of a direct threat to the United States from the sea, and the Coast Artillery was seen primarily as an adjunct to the Navy. Therefore, Major General Erasmus Weaver, chief of Coast Artillery, proposed that the CAC assume responsibility for large-caliber or heavy mobile artillery, for which it was better suited than Field Artillery. In October 1917, the new antiaircraft artillery mission was assigned to Coast Artillery.

By the outbreak of World War II,* the Coast Artillery represented over 10 percent of the Army's total strength. Again, there was little need for coastal defense guns, so the branch focused on the antiaircraft mission. As Allied forces achieved air superiority, however, antiaircraft artillery (AAA) units were employed as light artillery in direct support of ground units. Based on the recommendation of the Patch Board, Congress reconsolidated Coast Artillery and Field Artillery in the Army Organization Act of 1950,* although AAA and FA unit designations were retained until 1954. During the Vietnam War,* the Army separated the artillery branch into Air Defense Artillery* and Field Artillery.

References. Larry H. Addington, "The U.S. Coast Artillery and the Problem of Artillery Organization, 1907–1954," *Military Affairs*, February 1976, 1–6. Boyd L. Dastrup, *King of Battle*, 1992.

Edward Shanahan

COBRA

Operation Cobra was Lieutenant General Omar Bradley's* plan to break through the German defenses that were bottling up First Army* in the Cotentin Peninsula following the Allied landings on D-day. Using J. Lawton Collins'* VII Corps for the initial assault, Bradley planned to strike southward toward Coutances, unhinge the German defenses, and exploit as far as Avranches, at the base of the Cotentin, thus opening the way into Brittany. The plan called for tactical air strikes by B-17 and B-24 heavy bombers against forward enemy positions just prior to the infantry* assault.

Weather delayed the attack several days, including a delay on 24 July after the bombers were already in the air. These bombers hit U.S. troops, killing twenty-five 30th Infantry Division soldiers; Bradley nonetheless decided to proceed with Cobra the next day. Shaken by the air strike and without reinforcements (the German operational reserves were tied up farther east by a British attack on Caen), the Germans nevertheless held for another day against the three assaulting divisions.* When Collins committed two more divisions the next day and a third the day after, the German defenses began to disintegrate. A breach opened through which Bradley sent a torrent of U.S. forces. By the end of July, both VII and VIII Corps had advanced thirty miles, had reached Avranches, and were poised to break into the open country beyond. Cobra had become the breakout the Allies had only dared to believe possible just a few weeks earlier.

References. Martin Blumenson, *Breakout and Pursuit*, 1984. Ulick Hallinan, *From Operation Cobra to the Liberation of Paris*, 1988.

COBRA AH-1

The Cobra AH-1 helicopter, developed in 1965 by Bell Helicopter to meet the Army's requirement for a fast, heavily armed helicopter to escort troop-carrying helicopters during the Vietnam War,* is still in service with the U.S. Army, Marine Corps, and several foreign countries. Originally designed to provide fire support for air assault* and air mobile operations, the Cobra at first possessed no antiarmor capability. To remedy this deficiency, in 1972 the Cobra was upgraded with the tube-launched optically tracked wire-guided missile (TOW) to allow it to attack tanks. The Army has continued to modify the Cobra with enhanced firepower, increased horsepower, and advanced avionics to improve its lethality and survivability. The latest version is the "modernized" AH-

1S, still in production for the United States and seven foreign countries. The Cobra has a single engine and carries a crew of two.

References. Doug Richardson, *AH-1*, 1987. George Sullivan, *Modern Combat Helicopters*, 1993.

Kenneth Turner

COLD HARBOR

Following Lieutenant General Ulysses S. Grant's* bloody encounter with Robert E. Lee's* Army of Northern Virginia at the Wilderness* in early May 1864, to the astonishment of many of his commanders Grant ordered the Army of the Potomac* to continue moving south toward Richmond. Throughout May, Grant pushed on, sidling to the southeast in search of Lee's right flank and a route to the Confederate capitol. A series of almost continuous engagements— Yellow Tavern, Spotsylvania,* North Anna, and Totopotomy Creek—slowed but did not check the Federal advance. As the end of May approached, one more sidestep brought Grant's and Lee's armies to a small, inconsequential tavern on the road from White House to Richmond just north of the Chickahominy. The name of this dry, dusty crossroads was Cold Harbor.

Union cavalry* under Major General Phillip H. Sheridan* made first contact with Confederate forces near Cold Harbor on 31 May. Grant immediately ordered Major General Horatio Wright's VI Corps to march to his left flank and detached Major General William "Baldy" Smith's XVIII Corps from the Army of the James,* floating it down the James to reinforce the troops gathering at Cold Harbor; all this brought Union strength to nearly 40,000. Grant intended to attack at dawn the following day, 2 June, catching the Confederates unprepared and in the open. The friction of war, however, delayed the attack. Inefficient staff work, misunderstood orders, a lack of a sense of urgency, the poor road network, and difficult terrain caused a twenty-four-hour delay—a delay that proved disastrous.

Lee understood the value of Cold Harbor as well as Grant and, using his interior lines, quickly moved forces to meet the threat, using the extra day to build formidable and effective defensive positions. When the Federals finally attacked, early on the morning of 3 June, they met a storm of fire and iron like no other they had experienced. Confederate fire ripped and tore the Union lines to pieces, leaving 7,000 blue-clad soldiers dead and wounded on the field within thirty minutes. Of all the assaults he ordered during the Civil War,* Grant regretted this one the most. In spite of the losses, however, Grant did not withdraw but continued to press Lee back toward the critical communications center of Petersburg and, ultimately, Richmond.

References. R. Wayne Maney, *Marching to Cold Harbor*, 1995. Noah Andre Trudeau, *Bloody Roads South*, 1989.

COLD WAR

Dating from the end of World War II,* the forty-four-year period of tension and antagonism between the two global powers—the United States and the

Soviet Union—came to be known as the Cold War. The Cold War originated in Europe divided into a western zone dominated by the United States and its NATO (North Atlantic Treaty Oreganization) allies and an eastern zone dominated by the Soviet Union and its Warsaw Pact allies. The boundary between the two zones became known as the "Iron Curtain," a term first used by Winston Churchill to describe the closure of the Soviet zone. With the Truman Doctrine of 1947, which stated that the United States would "support free peoples who are resisting attempted subjugation by armed minorities or by outside pressure," the West formally declared the Cold War. Emerging nuclear weapons in both camps prevented open combat that could easily have proved disastrous for the entire world. Americans and Soviets alike lived under the constant fear of nuclear war, as both nations built and maintained huge arsenals of atomic weapons capable of mass devastation. Thus, each side utilized surrogates when conflicts erupted into fighting. The Korean and Vietnam Wars exemplify the workings of the Truman Doctrine and conflicts in which the United States and Soviet Union opposed one another.

Historians disagree as to who was responsible for the onset of the Cold War, alternately blaming the Soviets and the Americans. The period marked a time of unprecedented peacetime military growth in the United States and instant readiness to meet the enemy whenever and wherever necessary. Marked by such diplomatic and theoretical terms as "containment" and "massive retaliation," the Cold War constantly threatened to become hot.

The Cold War came to a close in 1989, when peaceful democratic revolutions inside the Soviet Union and other Warsaw Pact nations caused the fall of the "Iron Curtain," and the tension that had existed between the two sides ceased. Symbolic of this cessation of tensions was the fall of the Berlin Wall, which had divided that German city into Allied and Soviet zones since the end of World War II.

References. Michael J. Hogan, *The End of the Cold War*, 1992. Walter Lafeber, *America, Russia, and the Cold War 1945–1980*, 4th ed., 1980. Bernard W. Weisberger, *Cold War, Cold Peace*, 1984.

Jim Martin

COLLINS, JOSEPH LAWTON (1896–1987)

Joseph Lawton Collins, an aggressive, hard-driving corps* commander in World War II,* was born in New Orleans, Louisiana, and graduated from the U.S. Military Academy* in 1917. He served in increasingly responsible positions until he assumed command of the 25th Infantry Division (Tropic Lightning)* in May 1942. By late 1942 Collins's division* was engaged in the campaign against the Japanese on Guadalcanal* and the Solomon Islands, during which Collins won the Silver Star.* From his division's lightning-bolt shoulder patch and his vigorous style of warfare, Collins earned the nickname "Lightning Joe."

Collins's distinguished achievements in the Pacific led General Dwight D.

Eisenhower* to select him to command VII Corps, one of the two corps that landed in Normandy (Operation Neptune*) on 6 June 1944. A brave and dynamic fighter, Collins spearheaded the breakout at St. Lô, referred to by General George C. Marshall* as "one of the greatest feats of American arms." Collins's valor earned him an Oak Leaf Cluster for his Silver Star. Collins's forces subsequently attacked through Belgium and across Germany, advancing all the way to the Elbe River, where they linked up with the Soviet army.

In 1949 President Harry S Truman selected Collins to be Chief of Staff* of the Army. During the Korean War,* Collins was one of the service chiefs who encouraged George C. Marshall* and Truman to relieve General of the Army Douglas MacArthur* as supreme allied commander. Later, Collins served as the U.S. representative on the Military Committee and Standing Group of NATO,* retiring in 1956.

References. J. Lawton Collins, *Lightning Joe*, 1979. Russell F. Weigley, *Eisenhower's Lieutenants*, 1981.

Donald L. Gilmore

COLT AUTOMATIC RIFLE. *See* CAR-15.

COLT NAVY. *See* Pistol, Colt Navy.

COLT SINGLE-ACTION ARMY

The Colt single-action army and frontier revolver, commonly called the "Colt Single-Action Army," was the most successful handgun produced in the United States in the 19th century. It was also known as the "Peacemaker," the "Frontier Six-Shooter," and "the gun that won the West." The U.S. Army purchased approximately 37,000 .45-caliber center-fire Single-Action Armys between 1873 and 1891. The military model was normally fitted with a seven-and-one-half-inch barrel, but some were later cut down to five and one-half inches. Civilian models of this famous revolver were of various calibers from .32 to .45, and barrel lengths from five and one-half inches to sixteen inches (the "Buntline Special"); a detachable, extended stock allowed some models to be fired as carbines. In addition to its general durability and reliability, the Single-Action Army's had an ejector assembly, a spring-loaded rod under the right side of the barrel, that allowed for rapid removal of spent rounds and reloading. This was a particularly desirable feature for both soldiers and peace officers on the frontier. Colt discontinued the manufacture of the Single-Action Army in 1941 but, due to popular demand, resumed production in 1955.

References. Bern Keating, *The Flamboyant Mr. Colt and His Deadly Six-Shooter*, 1978. James E. Serven, *Colt Firearms from 1836*, 1979. R. L. Wilson, *Colt*, 1990.

COLT WALKER DRAGOON PISTOL

Although several sidearms used by the U.S. Army were known as "dragoon pistols"—because they were issued to dragoons, or mounted soldiers—the revolver commonly associated with the term is the Colt dragoon pistol adopted in 1847. Based on a Colt design, the Whitneyville-Walker—generally referred to as the "Walker," for Captain Samuel H. Walker of the Mounted Rifles, who initiated the contract—was produced by Eli Whitney. One thousand pistols were purchased and issued to the Regiment of Mounted Rifles. The Colt Walker was a six-round, single-action revolver that fired a .44-caliber ball. Following the initial contract, Colt went on to produce dragoon revolvers well into the 1850s. The third and last variation had a detachable shoulder stock. The entire dragoon series of pistols was heavy, and thus they were carried on the saddle. Improved designs of revolvers by both Colt and others produced lighter revolvers that could be kept in belt holsters, making the large dragoons obsolete.

References. James E. Hicks, *U.S. Military Firearms, 1776–1956*, 1962. James E. Serven, *Colt Firearms from 1836*, 1954, 1979. R. L. Wilson, *Colt*, 1990.

Steven J. Allie

COLUMBUS, NEW MEXICO

Columbus, New Mexico, located about eighty miles west of El Paso, Texas, is best known as the site of a raid by the Mexican revolutionary Pancho Villa. Villa's hostility to the United States had resulted from President Woodrow Wilson's recognition of Villa's rival, Venustiano Carranza, in October 1915. Villa's revolutionary movement depended on his ability to control northern Mexico. His designs on Columbus were driven by a cache of food, arms, ammunition, and horses there, guarded by elements of the U.S. 13th Cavalry. Early on the morning of 9 March 1916, Villa and 485 followers attacked Columbus and its garrison. The attack was uncoordinated, and after an initial surprise the garrison put up a fierce resistance, killing sixty-seven Mexicans, with eight Americans killed and two wounded. U.S. cavalrymen pursued Villa, killing another seventy-five Villistas before they reached the border.

Along with the military defeat, Villa now suffered an enormous political disaster. President Wilson ordered forces under General John J. Pershing* across the Mexican border to search for and destroy Villa. The Punitive Expedition* would eventually total over 100,000 men, and although Villa escaped, he never again raided north of the border.

References. Clarence C. Clendenen, *The United States and Pancho Villa*, 1961. Haldeen Braddy, *Pancho Villa at Columbus*, 1965.

Thomas Christianson

COMANCHE

Foaled in 1862, "Comanche" was a bay cavalry mount with a white star and black tail and mane. The horse belonged to Captain Myles W. Keogh, 7th U.S. Cavalry, and gained notoriety as the only survivor of Lieutenant Colonel George Armstrong Custer's* immediate command at the Little Bighorn* in June 1876. The badly wounded animal was found on the battlefield two days after the fight and was returned to Fort Abraham Lincoln, Dakota Territory, with wounded soldiers aboard the steamer *Far West*. The care and attention of farrier Gustave Korn and Captain Henry J. Nowland allowed the horse to recover fully by the spring of 1877. On 10 April 1878, General Order No. 7 granted Comanche special care as the symbol of the regiment's heroic action at the Little Bighorn. The horse was never ridden again but traveled with the regiment to duty stations in the Black Hills and Kansas. At 1:30 A.M. on 7 November 1891, Comanche died at Fort Riley,* Kansas. At the request of the officers of the 7th U.S. Cavalry, L. L. Duche of Kansas University mounted the remains into a life-like figure that can still be seen at the university's Museum of Natural History, at Lawrence.

References. Anthony A. Amaral, *Comanche*, 1961. David Dary, *Comanche*, 1976.

Jeffrey Prater

COMANCHE RAH-66

First conceived in 1982, the RAH-66 Comanche helicopter was designed to replace three older helicopters in the U.S. Army inventory, the Cobra AH-1,* the Kiowa OH-58,* and the Cayuse OH-6,* and also to provide an armed reconnaissance capability for attack helicopter and air cavalry* units. The Comanche's improved capabilities were developed specifically to provide a significant advantage in all battlefield environments, including adverse weather and night combat. The Comanche is capable of self-deployment up to 1,260 nautical miles, a dramatic improvement. Standard mission equipment includes a turret-mounted cannon, a night-vision pilotage system, an electro-optical target-acquisition system, helmet-mounted displays, and aided target recognition. The Commanche's maiden flight was on 4 January 1996.

References. Stephen Harding, *U.S. Army Aircraft since 1947*, 1997. Eric S. Johnson, "RAH-66 Commanche: Eyes and Ears for the 21st Century," *Field Artillery*, May–June 1996, 22–25.

David Zoellers

COMBAT

This critically acclaimed weekly television drama aired on ABC from 1962 through 1967. Television's longest-running World War II* series, *Combat* followed the exploits of Second Platoon, Company K, from the beaches of Normandy across France and Germany. Noted for its gritty realism, *Combat* offered an American infantryman's perspective of ground combat in Europe during 1944 and 1945. It featured actors Vic Morrow, as Sergeant Chip Saunders, and Rick Jason, as Lieutenant Gil Hanley. Other regular cast members were Pierre Jalbert as Caje, Jack Hogan as Kirby, and Dick Peabody as Littlejohn. Although production ended in the spring of 1967, the series has been subsequently aired in syndication. *Combat* is currently owned by ABC Television and distributed by Worldvision.

References. Alex McNeil, *Total Television*, 4th ed., 1996. Jeff Rovin, *The Great Television Series*, 1977.

William E. Bassett

COMBAT CAR M1

When Chief of Staff Douglas MacArthur* ordered all branches of the U.S. Army to pursue mechanization, the cavalry* had to find a way to carry out MacArthur's order and yet comply with the National Defense Act of 1920,* which authorized tanks only for the infantry.* The result was an armored, tank-like vehicle standardized in 1935 for use with mechanized cavalry. Initially developed by Colonel Danial Van Vooris and Lieutenant Colonel Adna R. Chaffee, Jr,* they adopted the term "combat car" as a subterfuge to evade the legal restriction. It was developed concurrently with the M2A1 light tank. The only significant difference between the two designs was in armament: the M1 was armed with two machine guns in a single turret, while the M2 series had twin turrets. The M2 later carried a 37 mm cannon. Both were powered by a 250-horsepower, air-cooled Continental radial engine and possessed volute suspension systems.

J. Walter Christie's combat car T4 was the major competitor to the Ordnance Department–designed combat car M1—or T5, as it was known in development. Early in the competition between the two vehicles, the cavalry, whose primary advocate was Chaffee, supported the Christie design. Although Christie's personality had a great deal to do with the decision to procure the T-5, the exact rationale has never been sufficiently explained. By 1941, the M2 and the combat car would evolve into the M3 and M5 series of light tanks used by the U.S. Army and its Allies during World War II.*

References. Peter Chamberlain and Chris Ellis, *Pictorial History of Tanks of the World 1915–45*, 1972. Kenneth Macksey and John H. Batchelor, *Tank*, 1971.

John Broom

COMBAT ENGINEERS

The delineation between combat engineer units—those conducting tasks directly related to engaging enemy forces, such as minelaying, obstacle clearing, and preparing vehicle fighting positions—and other Army engineer organizations is not sharply defined. Combat engineers are generally a permanent part of maneuver division,* brigade,* or regimental structures, or are corps* units assigned in support of these organizations. Combat engineer missions are categorized as mobility (e.g., countermine/counterobstacle, gap crossing, and light road construction and maintenance), countermobility (minelaying and obstacle installation), or survivability (construction of fighting positions and protective emplacements). Other engineering organizations are categorized as general engineering or topographical engineer units. The former are characterized by their heavier and more construction-oriented equipment; their work includes major road construction and maintenance, production of such building materials as asphalt and gravel, and development of support facilities. Although their missions are typically more construction oriented, these units are at times referred to as "combat heavy" engineers. Topographical engineers focus on terrain analysis, survey work, and map production.

U.S. combat engineers trace their origins to the American Revolution.* On 27 May 1778, Congress authorized three companies of sappers and miners. These units supported operations against the British, including construction of field fortifications and participation in George Washington's* successful October 1771 siege of Yorktown.*

References. Alfred Beck, et al, *The Corps of Engineers: The War against Germany*, 1985. United States Army, Corps of Engineers, *The History of the US Army Corps of Engineers*, [1986].

Russell W. Glenn

COMBAT INFANTRYMAN'S BADGE

The Combat Infantryman's Badge (CIB) was instituted on 15 November 1943. The original criteria for awarding the badge were prescribed by War Department* Circular No. 186, 11 May 1944, made retroactive to 7 December 1941. The badge consists of a silver musket mounted on a blue-enameled rectangle one-half inch wide and three inches long, superimposed on a silver wreath of oak leaves open at the top. Subsequent awards of the CIB are indicated by the addition of stars between the open points of the wreath. The CIB is awarded to infantry* or special forces* soldiers of colonel of below who have "satisfactorily performed duty while assigned as a member of an infantry, ranger, or special forces unit of brigade, regimental, or smaller size during any period such unit was engaged in active ground combat." The criteria for the CIB have been modified somewhat since its inception to recognize soldiers who, though not infantrymen or of the special forces, performed the duties of an infantryman, as did some advisors in Vietnam.

In 1944 Congress authorized an additional ten dollars per month for recipients of the badge. Amendments to this bill authorized the CIB for members of all ground forces who qualified. Award of the badge, however, was left to the War Department, which kept the badge for infantrymen only. The CIB remains the most prestigious badge in the U.S. Army.

References. Albert N. Garland, "The Combat Infantryman Badge," *Infantry*, July–August 1996, 17–21. Evans E. Kerrigan, *American Badges and Insignia*, 1964.

Robert E. Connor

COMBAT MEDICAL BADGE

Authorized by the General Staff* on 1 March 1945, the Combat Medical Badge was awarded to Medical Department personnel who shared the same dangers as combat infantrymen. Because of concerns over the medics' noncombat status under the Geneva Convention, medics were not eligible for the Combat Infantryman's Badge* (CIB). The General Staff tried to rectify this limitation with the creation of the Combat Medical Badge. The one-inch by one-and-one-half-inch badge, struck in oxidized silver, displayed a horizontal stretcher placed behind a caduceus with a cross of the Geneva Convention placed at the junction of a pair of wings. The Combat Medical Badge mirrored the Combat Infantryman's Badge in its importance and special pay benefits. Recipients of the Combat Medical Badge originally received an extra five dollars a month for the first award and ten dollars a month for the second.

References. Frank Cox, *NCO Guide*, 4th ed., 1992. Evans E. Kerrigan, *American Badges and Insignia*, 1964.

Edward L. Maier III

COMBAT STUDIES INSTITUTE

The U.S. Army established the Combat Studies Institute (CSI) in June 1979 as a directorate of the U.S. Army Command and General Staff College* (CGSC) at Fort Leavenworth,* Kansas. CSI missions include teaching general and special history courses for the Command and General Staff Officers Course at CGSC; conducting research on topics of interest to the U.S. Army and CSI faculty members; publishing monographs, anthologies, bibliographies, compendia, and special studies written or edited by CSI faculty and other military historians; and designing, developing, supporting, and leading staff rides* for CGSC and other units throughout the U.S. Army, National Guard,* and Army Reserve.* CSI's Leavenworth Papers are recognized throughout the military and academic communities for their outstanding scholarship and balanced treatment of their subjects. The CSI faculty includes professional historians and serving officers who have advanced degrees and specialized knowledge in history.

Reference. Roger J. Spiller, "War History and the History of Wars," The *Public Historian*, Fall 1988, 65–81.

COMBINED ARMS AND SERVICE STAFF SCHOOL

Originating in a review of education and training for officers study, the Combined Arms and Service Staff School (CAS³) has the mission of educating all U.S. Army captains in staff procedures and decision making. Colonel Harold Fraley became director of CAS³ in August 1980, presided over the creation of the curriculum, and taught the first class. CAS³ is located at Fort Leavenworth,* Kansas, as part of the U.S. Army Comand and General Staff College.* The first students arrived for the CAS³ pilot course in 1981.

Originally designed as a course for officers not selected for the resident Command and General Staff Officers Course (CGSOC), CAS³ has evolved into a mandatory course for all Army officers. The course consists of Phase I, 140 hours of nonresident study, and Phase II, 307 hours of resident study over nine weeks (later reduced to six weeks). The program utilizes small-group instructional techniques, with a maximum of twelve students in each group. This allows for an interactive educational experience, requiring each student to participate fully in order to successfully complete the course.

References. Charles W. Cox III, "CAS³," *Military Police Journal*, Spring 1986, 41–42. J. Steve Patterson, "CAS³," *Military Review*, May 1994, 24–28.

Jim Martin

COMMAND AND GENERAL STAFF COLLEGE

The U.S. Army Command and General Staff College (CGSC) is the U.S. Army's senior tactical institution and the keystone of the Army's school system. It is responsible for developing officers, from captain to general, able to lead fighting units at the tactical and operational levels of war. CGSC has achieved worldwide recognition as a professional graduate-level military school, and it is accredited by the North Central Association of Colleges and Schools as a master's degree–granting institution. It was established as the School for the Application of Infantry and Cavalry* in 1881; the first class of officers graduated in July 1883. Located at Fort Leavenworth,* Kansas, the school underwent several name changes until the Army selected the present designation in 1947. By 1987, CGSC had expanded to five separate schools: the Command and General Staff School (CGSS); the Combined Arms and Services Staff School (CAS³)*; the School of Advanced Military Studies (SAMS); the School of Command Preparation (SCP); and Nonresident Studies. The staff and faculty of these five schools include selected officers of all the armed services and reserve components, civilian academics, and exchange instructors and liaison officers from about a dozen allied armies.

References. Boyd L. Dastrup, *The US Army Command and General Staff College*, 1982. John E. Miller, "Training and Educating Leaders for the Future," *Military Review*, January 1991, 10–17.

Bill Knight

COMMAND POST

A command post, commonly referred to as the CP, is the hub of all military activities undertaken by an operational unit. Commanders and their staffs conduct most routine, field-related military duties there. Each level of command—from platoon* to army group*—has a command post. A small command post may be manned by a single individual—a platoon leader, for example—and his vehicle. He or she may be joined on occasion by his or her platoon sergeant, driver, or radio operator. A large command post may be located in a hardened bunker with elaborate equipment; it may consist of more than a hundred personnel to assist the Commander.

References. Frederick J. Kroesen, "What Should a Command Post Do?" *Army*, January 1993, 32–35. Kenneth A. McDevitt, "Why Standardize Command Posts?" *Military Review*, July 1990, 54–59.

Krewasky A. Salter

COMMAND SERGEANT MAJOR. *See* Sergeant Major.

COMMANDER IN CHIEF

The Constitution of the United States (Article II, section 2) designates the president "Commander in Chief" of the armed forces. As such, he is not a field commander; rather, he makes military policy and strategy, together (in the modern organization) with his National Security Advisor, the service secretaries, and the service chiefs. The precise limits of the president's powers as Commander in Chief have caused considerable debate, since the Constitution gives Congress the power to "declare war." Many presidents, including Jefferson, Lincoln, Truman, and Johnson, sent U.S. forces into hostilities without congressional declarations of war. A Supreme Court decision during the Civil War* concluded that the president may, without consulting Congress, send U.S. forces into combat when reacting to an attack.

All post-1945 U.S. military actions have taken place without a declaration of war, although in 1991 Congress formally endorsed President George Bush's actions in the Gulf War. The Korean and Vietnam Wars, especially, raised questions about the limits of the president's war powers. In 1973 Congress passed the War Powers Resolution, requiring congressional consent whenever the president sends U.S. forces into hostilities for more than sixty days. All presidents since then have denied the resolution's constitutionality.

George Washington* held the title "Commander-in-Chief" from 1775 to 1783, as a military rank, in a different usage of the term than that defined above.

References. Edwin S. Corwin, *The President*, 1957, and *Presidential Power and the Constitution*, 1976. Ann Van Wynen Thomas and A. J. Thomas, Jr., *The War-Making Powers of the President*, 1982.

Mark H. Danley

COMMANDING GENERAL

This term applied to the senior officers who succeeded George Washington* after 1783. Secretary of War* John C. Calhoun* formalized the position of Major General Commanding the Army of the United States, or Commanding General, following the Act of 2 March 1821, which reorganized the War Department.* Although assigned to command the Army, with a headquarters subordinate to, but distinct from, the War Department, the Commanding General's duties remained ambiguous, and relations with the secretary of war and the War Department bureaus were often strained. By the end of the 19th century, the office had been reduced to an empty title, with the adjutant general replacing the Commanding General as the president's primary military advisor. The Commanding General's authority was based on regulations and precedent; it was never precisely defined or confirmed by statute. The position was abolished in the Root Reforms of 1903.

References. William B. Skelton, "The Commanding General and the Problem of Command in the United States Army, 1821–1841," *Military Affairs*, December 1970, 117–122. Robert F. Stohlman, Jr., *The Powerless Position*, 1975.

Lee W. Eysturlid

COMMANDING OFFICER

The term "commanding officer" (CO) is synonymous with "commander" and "leader" when used in a military context. He or she is the highest-ranking com-

missioned officer in an organized military unit. For example, at the platoon*
level, the commanding officer is a lieutenant, the platoon leader. At the company,* battery,* or troop* level, the commanding officer is the captain in charge
of the unit. At the divisional level, the commanding officer is the general serving
as the divisional commander. The commanding officer establishes the intent,
direction, and tone for his or her unit. He or she is responsible for carrying out
the mission, caring for unit personnel and property, and for overseeing all actions that occur within the unit. The commanding officer can delegate authority
to subordinates but always retains responsibility for the unit.

References. Aubrey S. Newman, *Follow Me*, 1981, 1990. Ches Schneider, *From
Classrooms to Claymores*, 1999.

Krewasky A. Salter

COMMISSARY

The commissary is the element of an installation responsible for acquiring,
storing, issuing, selling, and accounting for supplies required for consumption
by personnel authorized to subsist at government expense, and by organizations,
activities, and personnel authorized to purchase therefrom. The term "commissary" dates back to the American Revolution,* when a commissary was an
official responsible for some facet of administration within the military organization—for example, the Commissary General of Stores and Provisions. This
official, frequently a civilian, was responsible for the supply of food. Other
"commissaries" were responsible for financial records, care and feeding of the
fleet (horses), and prisoners of war.* By 1812, these commissary missions were
performed by the Subsistence Department, headed by the Commissary General
of Subsistence,* who was responsible for supplying rations to the Army. Rations
were issued from warehouses under the control of the commissary general. This
is the basis for the current term "commissary," which describes the military-
supported supermarkets on military bases around the world.

References. James A. Huston, *The Sinews of War*, 1966. Walter E. McNamara, "You
and Your Commissary," *Airman*, June 1962, 15–18.

Lee Kruger

COMMISSARY GENERAL OF SUBSISTENCE

One of three staff positions established by Congress when it organized the
Continental Army,* the Commissary General of Subsistence, also referred to as
the Commissary General of Purchase, was to secure and deliver to the troops
rations of food, drink, soap, and candles prescribed by Congress. The breakdown
of the commissary system, along with the collapse of Continental currency, was
largely responsible for dissatisfaction among the troops and several mutinies
during the American Revolution.* Following the Revolution, a system of private
contractors replaced the Commissary General, but problems experienced during
the War of 1812* and the First Seminole War led Congress in 1818 to reestab-

lish the Commissary General of Subsistence at the head of the Subsistance Department.

Over the next ninety-four years, the Subsistence Department was responsible for feeding the Army while fiercely maintaining its independence from other staff departments, especially the Quartermaster General. But a major scandal—the embalmed-beef scandal—following the Spanish-American War* and reorganization under the Root Reforms led to the merger of the Subsistence Department and the Quartermaster Corps* in 1912. Although the Subsistence Department disappeared, and along with it the Commissary General of Subsistence, its tradition of independence in the procurement and research of subsistence persisted for many years in the Subsistence Branch and the Subsistence Research Laboratory.

References. Erna Risch, *The Quartermaster Corps*, vol. 1, 1953. Russell F. Weigley, *History of the United States Army*, 1967.

COMMON TABLE OF ALLOWANCES

The origins of the common table of allowances (CTA) can be found in the mobilization planning for World War II,* when the Office of the Quartermaster General set about the task of estimating materiel requirements for a mass army. On 1 October 1941, the War Department* issued T/BA (Table of Basic Allowances) 21 covering clothing and individual equipment. In 1943, the War Department had published tables of equipment (T/Es) designating the initial equipment issue for each type of organization, such as infantry,* armor,* or signal. T/Es were later combined with the tables of organization (T/Os) to create tables of organization and equipment* (T/O & Es), greatly simplifying the task of ordering and distributing equipment to newly mobilized units.

Today, the common table of allowances (CTA) is a document authorizing issue of items of materiel for common or specific usage to individuals and units with a table of organization and equipment (TOE), table of distribution and allowances (TDA), and joint table of allowances. The purpose of the CTA is to provide a flexible basis for acquiring items included on the CTA—CTA 50-900 for uniforms, equipment, and field gear, and CTA 50-909 for field and garrison furnishings, for example—but not authorized as part of a TOE or TDA. It is the only authority for such items. Requisition of common table of allowances items, however, is discretionary, not mandatory. They should be ordered only in minimum quantities for efficient operation of the unit or accomplishment of the mission.

Reference. Erna Risch, *The Quartermaster Corps*, vol. 1, 1953.

COMMUNICATIONS ZONE

The communications zone, commonly referred to as the "CommZ" or "ComZ," is the area within a theater of operations, from the rear areas to the front lines, in which the Army's support elements control logistical efforts and the flow of supplies and replacements to the combat forces at the front. It includes transportation services, such as aircraft, railroads, and trucks, under the CommZ commander. Within the CommZ, responsibilities are divided into districts or bases. During World War II,* the European Theater of Operations* (ETO) CommZ was divided into sections. One section, the Normandy Supply Base, for example, moved the supplies off the beaches, and another section shipped the supplies to the front lines. In other theaters of operations, including the Mediterranean and the Pacific, CommZs operated according to local command requirements and needs.

References. Gayton E. Germane, Joseph O. Carter, and William E. Rogers, *A New Concept of Transportation Movement*, 1959. Steve R. Waddell, *United States Army Logistics*, 1994.

Trevor Brown

COMPANY

The company is the smallest organizational element of the U.S. Army authorized to have a commander. It consists of between 40 and 250 soldiers, usually organized in platoons.* A captain usually commands a company, although in larger companies, such as aviation* and Pershing missile companies, a major commands. The senior noncommissioned officer* is the first sergeant,* who acts as the commander's principal assistant. Normally a senior lieutenant serves as company executive officer* (XO). He or she is second in command of the company and usually has responsibility for the maintenance of the company's vehicles and other equipment. Three or more companies are typically organized as a battalion.*

References. Harold P. Leinbaugh and John D. Campbell, *The Men of Company K*, 1985. C. M. Virtue, *Company Administration*, 22d ed., 1953.

Andrew N. Morris

COMPANY CLERK

Until the mid-1970s, when automation and computerization rendered the position obsolete, the company clerk was an indispensable member of every company, battery, troop, or detachment. An enlisted person or noncommissioned officer,* the company clerk served as the administrative assistant to the commanding officer* and first sergeant.* He managed the routine paperwork and suspenses for the unit; prepared the morning report and other special reports; typed orders and correspondence; maintained and updated files, documents and bulletins; posted the unit bulletin board; kept office supplies and blank forms; acted as mail clerk when necessary; and served as receptionist and general font of knowledge about the unit. The company clerk's domain was the orderly room. With the advent of SIDPERS (Standard Installation/Division Personnel System) in 1975, all personnel administrative functions were consolidated in the Personnel Administration Center (PAC) at the battalion level. With the exception of a few special units, the company clerk disappeared, and the military occupational specialty* (MOS) 75B, unit clerk, was redesignated "personnel administration specialist." Nevertheless, a number of clerical and administrative tasks remain at the company level that the first sergeant alone could not handle. Many company-sized units, therefore, assign a "shadow clerk"—typically a soldier from a line platoon* who possesses typing and computer skills—to the orderly room to complete many of the tasks previously performed by the company clerk.

References. John C. Bahnsen, "The Shadow War in the Army's Orderly Rooms," *Army*, January 1987, 14–17. C. M. Virtue, *Company Administration*, 22d ed., 1953.

CONGRESSIONAL MEDAL OF HONOR. *See* Medal of Honor.

CONSCIENTIOUS OBJECTOR

Those who for religious, philosophical, or political reasons object to military service are classified as conscientious objectors. The liberal attitudes of the United States in this respect began in colonial Pennsylvania, whose government was controlled until 1756 by Quaker pacifists. Since the Civil War* and the enactment of the first U.S. conscription law, some form of alternative service has been granted to those unwilling to bear arms. The Selective Service and Training Act of 1940 granted conscientious objectors some form of service unrelated to and not controlled by the military, but the status was based solely on being a member of a recognized pacifistic religious sect. Philosophical, political, or personal moral objections were not valid reasons for refusing military service. During the Korean War,* exemption was no longer granted, and an alternative service program was set up for objectors. A slightly larger proportion of objectors appeared under this law than during World War II.* The United States dropped the religious requirement in 1970, recognizing objection based on strong ethical principles but refusing to allow objection to a particular war, such as the Vietnam War.*

References. Cynthia Eller, *Conscientious Objectors and the Second World War*, 1991. Gerald R. Gioglio, *Days of Decision*, 1989. Charles C. Moskos and John Whiteclay Chambers II, eds., *The New Conscientious Objection*, 1993.

Michael Davis

CONSTITUTIONAL BASIS OF THE ARMY

The legal basis of the U.S. Army, in all its components, is found in the several articles and amendments, as well as the preamble, of the Constitution of the United States of America, ratified 17 September 1787. In fact, one of the principal reasons for adopting a constitution was to "provide for the common defense," an essential requirement for any independent nation and something that the Articles of Confederation had proved ineffective in achieving. To avoid the potential tyrannies that might be wrought by the unauthorized use of a large standing army should a power elite co-opt its leadership, the Constitution's framers reserved to the Congress, as the elected representatives of the people, the power to provide for the common defense and general welfare. This congressional power included the sole right "to declare War, grant Letters of Marque and Reprisal, and make Rules concerning Captures on Land and Water," the framers also specified that "no Appropriation of Money to that Use shall be for a longer Term than two Years." To strengthen congressional oversight and control over the military (including local militia forces when called into Federal service), Congress reserved to itself the right "to make Rules for the Government and Regulgation of the land and naval Forces; To provide for calling forth the Militia to execute the Laws of the Union, suppress Insurrection and repel Invasions."

Lest the individual states be tempted to create military organizations that might potentially challenge the central government, the framers established congressional control over the organization and use of the militia, giving Congress the power "to provide for organizing, arming, and disciplining, the Militia, and for governing such Part of them as may be employed in the Service of the United States." The states, however, would be able to provide for "the Appointment of the Officers and the Authority of training the Militia," but only "according to the discipline prescribed by Congress." The Constitution also gives Congress the ability to extend Federal control over the real property of the military, regardless of its physical location by awarding it "Authority over all Places purchased by the Consent of the Legislature of the State in which the same shall be, for the Erection of Forts, Magazines, Arsenals, dock-Yards, and other needful Buildings." To ensure that the intent of the Constitution's framers was clearly understood with regard to Congress's military powers, states were specifically prohibited from "granting Letters of Marque and Reprisal" and were denied the right to "keep Troops or Ships of War in time of Peace . . . or engage in War, unless actually invaded."

To accomplish the daily management and oversee the normal operations of the Army, the Constitution placed the armed forces within the executive branch of the government and established the principle of civilian control of the military, declaring, "The President shall be Commander in Chief of the Army and Navy of the United States, and of the Militia of the several States, when called into the actual Service of the United States." The Constitution further provided the president with the authority to exert control over the military by giving him the "Power, by and with the Advice and Consent of the Senate . . . to appoint . . . Officers of the United States." However, when all military officers are commissioned, they swear an oath "to protect and defend the Constitution of the United States against all enemies, foreign and domestic," clearly establishing that the officer's first and overriding loyalty is to the Constitution, not to any individual person, including the president who appointed them.

References. Constitution of the United States of America. Edwin S. Corwin, *Total War and the Constitution*, 1947, 1970. John Lehman, *Making War*, 1992. Gary M. Stern and Morton H. Halperin, eds., *The U.S. Constitution and the Power to Go to War*, 1994. Francis D. Wormuth and Edwin B. Firmage with Francis P. Butler, *To Chain the Dog of War*, 1986.

Jerry D. Morelock

CONTINENTAL ARMY

The Second Continental Congress estabished the Continental Army, which became the nucleus of colonial defense, on 14 June 1775. Congress authorized the raising of ten companies* (around seventy men each) of riflemen from Pennsylvania, Virginia, and Maryland. Congress then assumed command of the New England militia, which was already deployed around Boston. On 15 June Congress unanimously approved George Washington* as the commander in chief of the newly formed army, and on the following day Washington accepted the commission.

Between 16 and 19 June 1775, Congress adopted a plan of organization for the army that created and filled a number of positions: four major generals, eight brigadier generals, one adjutant general, one commissary general, one paymaster general, and others. Washington assumed command of the Continental Army at Cambridge, Massachusetts, on 3 July and immediately attempted to organize and discipline the unruly army of 14,500 men. Throughout the war Congress was responsible for appointing the Army's generals managing its administration, deciding upon its organization, and setting its size. The number of soldiers actually in the Continental Army never reached the numbers Congress allotted; its size fluctuated between one-third and one-half of the prescribed strength. Washington never commanded more than 26,000 men at one time; most of the time he had less than 10,000. Infantry battalions* and artillery brigades* composed the bulk of Washington's force. As the war progressed, a few cavalry regiments* were incorporated into the army.

The Continental Army consisted of three major divisions: the main army, under Washington, operating primarily in the middle colonies; the Northern Army, responsible for northern New York and Canada; and the Southern Army, operating in the colonies south of Virginia. Although Washington was commander-in-chief of the entire Continental Army, the generals in charge of the Northern and Southern departments received their orders directly from Congress. A number of difficulties plagued the Continental Army—for example, the perennial problem of recruiting to replace losses due to desertions and expired enlistments, and the lack of trained and experienced officers of every grade. The army was also constantly short of supplies and discipline. During the American Revolution,* approximately 231,000 soldiers served in the Continental Army.

References. Don Higginbotham, *The War of American Independence*, 1971. Jonathan G. Rossie, *The Politics of Command in the American Revolution*, 1975. Russell F. Weigley, *History of the United States Army*, 1967. Robert K. Wright, Jr., *The Continental Army*, 1983.

James L. Isemann

CONTINENTAL ARMY COMMAND

Following World War II,* field army* headquarters were brought back to the continental United States and assigned geographical areas of responsibility. Under the Army Field Forces (formerly Army Ground Forces),* the continental armies were principally responsible for training and readiness of the forces

within their respective areas. In 1955, the continental armies came under the
newly created Continental Army Command (CONARC). CONARC had five
primary missions: command control over the six continental armies and the
Military District of Washington; military education for the Army in the field;
training and organization of the Army Reserve* and National Guard;* development of tactics,* doctrine,* organization, and some equipment and weapons
to serve the Army's future needs; and mobilization in the event of national
emergency. In the post-Vietnam reorganization of 1973, two new commands
replaced CONARC, Training and Doctrine Command* (TRADOC)* and Army
Forces Command* (FORSCOM). TRADOC assumed CONARC's educational
and training missions, while FORSCOM became the Army's component of
Readiness Command under the Joint Chiefs of Staff* (JCS). It commands all
CONUS active and Reserve forces, including the remaining four—later reduced
to three—continental armies.

References. John G. Blair, "CONAC: Organization with a Mission," *Army Information Digest*, October 1955, 14–17. Ralph E. Haines, Jr., "Vast CONARC," *Army*, October 1972, 26–33. Willard G. Wyman, "New and Old Tasks of CONARC," *Army*, December 1957, 40–44.

Andrew N. Morris

CORONET

Operation Coronet was the code name for the anticipated invasion of the
Japanese island of Honshu in World War II.* It was to follow Operation Olympic, the invasion of Kyushu. Together, the two invasions constituted Operation
Downfall, the invasion of Japan and the culmination of the war in the Pacific.
In June 1944, U.S. war planners first studied the possibilities of occupying
Honshu and seizing the Tokyo plain. Counting on the rapid collapse of Germany
to free up resources for use in the Pacific, the planners orignally envisioned a
target date of December 1945. With continued German resistance, however, this
was later revised to March 1946. The rationale behind the invasion reflected the
political demand for the unconditional surrender of Japan and the military belief
that aerial bombardment and sea blockade would not be sufficient to defeat
Japan. The plans for the invasion of Honshu called for the U.S. First and Eighth
Armies to land with twelve divisions* in the first wave, with eleven divisions
in reserve. The Twentieth Air Force and the Pacific Fleet would lend the necessary support. Projections of U.S. casualties ranged from half a million to a
million. The rapid surrender of Japan following the dropping of the atomic
bombs in August 1945, however, rendered Coronet unnecessary.

References. John H. Bradley and Jack W. Dice, *The Second World War*, 1984. Robert W. Coakley and Richard M. Leighton, *Global Logistics and Strategy, 1943–1945*, 1968.

Timothy C. Dunwoody

CORPS

A corps is a combat and administrative organization larger than a division.*
It can operate independently or as part of a larger force, usually labeled a field

army,* although this term disappeared in the post-Vietnam reorganization. Commanded by a lieutenant general, a corps typically consists of two or more divisions* or armored cavalry regiments,* one or more separate brigades,* a corps artillery, and a corps support command (COSCOM). The size of its staff varies, depending on the mission and theater. Currently, the corps is the largest purely U.S. element in the U.S. Army. All larger units are international, in that they include Allied as well as U.S. forces.

References: Lewis I. Jeffries, "A Blueprint for Force Design," *Military Review*, August 1991, 20–31. Jacob L. Riley, Jr., "What Is a Corps?" *Military Review*, October 1956, 12–19. John D. Stuckey, "Echelons above Corps," *Parameters*, December 1983, 39–41.

Andrew N. Morris

CORPS OF ENGINEERS

The Corps of Engineers is a branch of the U.S. Army that has significant civil responsibilities, in addition to its mission of supporting forces during combat and noncombat military operations. The corps traces its foundation to 16 June 1775, when Congress authorized the Continental Army* and provided for a chief engineer and two assistants with the Army and a similar allocation of engineers should an additional department be created. Congress formally established the Corps of Engineers as a separate branch on 16 May 1802 in the same legislation that created the U.S. Military Academy,* and it assigned the engineers responsibility for that institution. The corps retained that obligation until 1866, when Congress allowed for occupation of the superintendency by other than engineer officers.

Corps of Engineers missions in support of combat operations include the building of field fortifications, obstacle breaching, bridging, construction and maintenance of support facilities and roads, and topographical operations. Historical examples of other defense-related corps activities include the building of coastal defense fortifications between 1794 and the 1860s and supervision of construction in support of the Manhattan Project* and the space program. Engineer officers provided terrain analysis and mapping support for the Army as early as the American Revolution,* but topographic engineers were not formally made part of the peacetime Army engineer establishment until 1818, when they were subordinated to the Engineer Department. These topographers worked as surveyors, cartographers, and explorers during the 19th century, notably in support of the nation's westward expansion.

Civil works efforts in which the Corps of Engineers played a major role include the building of the Cumberland Road, between Cumberland, Maryland, and Wheeling, [West] Virginia, completed in 1818; lighthouse construction, beginning in 1831; maintenance of navigable waterways; flood control and hydropower development; and the establishment of national parks. Corps officers also assisted in the completion of the Panama Canal and have participated in numerous additional engineering projects in nations throughout the world.

References. Blanche D. Coll, Jean E. Keith, and Herbert H. Rosenthal, *The Corps of*

Engineers, 1988. U.S. Army, Corps of Engineers, *The History of the US Army Corps of Engineers* [1986].

Russell W. Glenn

CORPS OF TOPOGRAPHICAL ENGINEERS

On 2 March 1813, Congress authorized eight topographical engineers ("Topos," as they became known) and eight assistants to be attached to the War Department* staff. All but two Topos were discharged at the end of the War of 1812.* Congress soon recognized the importance of the topographical expertise, especially in an expanding nation, where the Army would have a considerable role in exploration and development, and it restored three Topo positions in April 1816. In 1818, the Topos were placed under the Engineer Department, where they worked for almost a decade until Secretary of War* Peter B. Porter established an independent Topographical Bureau within the War Department.

Congress created the Corps of Topographical Engineers in 1838, with a staff of thirty-six officers. Their tasks involved surveying and mapping; construction of civil works, roads, harbors, bridges, canals, tunnels, water projects, and lighthouses; and the development of Washington, D.C. In the 1850s, the Topos declined in prestige and power as the Corps of Engineers* assumed a considerable role in civil works. Although its strength peaked in 1861 at forty-five officers, the Corps of Topographical Engineers declined in importance during the Civil War,* and Congress abolished it and merged its functions with the Corps of Engineers in 1863.

References. Frank N. Schubert, ed., *The Nation Builders*, 1988. Adrian George Traas, *From the Golden Gate to Mexico City*, 1993.

CORREGIDOR

Corregidor is a rocky, heavily fortified, two-square-mile island astride the entrance to Manila Bay in the Philippines. Having no resources, Corregidor has been used almost exclusively by military forces to control and protect this valuable harbor. Corregidor was under U.S. military control from 1898 until 1942, when Lieutenant General Jonathan Wainwright* surrendered all U.S. forces in the Philippines to the Japanese after four months of bitter fighting. The U.S. Army recaptured Corregidor in 1945 with a daring airborne operation that caught the Japanese totally by surprise. Today, Corregidor stands as a World War II* memorial in honor of U.S. and Filipino forces who fought in defense of the Philippines.

References. Gerard M. Devlin, *Back to Corregidor*, 1992. Edward M. Flanagan, *Corregidor*, 1988. Eric Morris, *Corregidor*, 1981.

Don Denmark

COUNTERBATTERY FIRE

Counterbattery fire is the technique of attacking the enemy's artillery with one's own artillery to limit damage to friendly forces during an engagement.

Development of effective counterbattery fire was a product of the Napoleonic Wars, when armies massed artillery fires against portions of an enemy line. In addition to breaking up enemy infantry before an assault, attacking artillery fired on enemy artillery positions. The advent of effective indirect fire in the early 20th century accelerated the development of counterbattery-fire techniques. Enemy artillery firing from "over the hill," however, had to be located before it could be attacked. Thus, forward observation, aerial observation, and sound and flash ranging became important target-acquisition tools in World War I.* Communication and unobserved fire procedures also enhanced the ability of artillery units to perform counterbattery fire.

Counterfire, the current version of counterbattery fire, expands the traditional counterbattery role from enemy artillery to the total enemy fire support system, and it involves all friendly fire support systems. It includes enemy mortars,* helicopter forward operating bases, fire support command and control, artillery, rocket and missile systems, and sustainment installations. The counterfire attack can also be undertaken by all fire support assets, both lethal and nonlethal. Radars,* intelligence systems, photo imagery, and space-based systems have been added to the acquisition arsenal.

References. Vollney B. Corn, Jr., "The Counterfire Battle," *Army*, July 1989, 39–41. Bruce I. Gudmundsson, *On Artillery*, 1993. David K. Hugus, "Counterbattery," *Armed Forces Journal International*, October 1989, 105–110.

Jeffrey S. Shadburn

COUNTERFIRE. *See* Counterbattery Fire.

COURT OF MILITARY APPEALS

The Articles of War* governed the administration of military justice from the American Revolution* to the introduction of the Uniform Code of Military Justice* (UCMJ) in May 1950. Those Articles provided commanders with the responsibility, authority, and power to administer justice and maintain discipline. Commanders held the power to initiate and direct court-martial* proceedings, adjust sentences, and retry cases, with limited oversight by higher authority.

Congress revised the Articles of War in 1920 following public debate led by the Acting Judge Advocate General* (JAG) Samuel T. Ansell, concerning the lack of review of cases by qualified legal personnel, and insufficient due process. After World War II,* criticism arose over the extent of command influence and the striking differences between the civilian and military justice systems. In response, Secretary of Defense* James Forrestal formed the "Morgan Committee" to draft the UMCJ, which Congress enacted in May 1950.

The creation of the Court of Military Appeals, under Article 67, remains a major feature of the UMCJ. Three civilian judges constitute the court. In the years since its formation, the court has slowly, but increasingly, addressed service members' constitutional rights, as well as statutory rights, under the UCMJ.

Since 1984, an appeal of courts-martial judgments to the Supreme Court has been allowed in certain cases.

References. Jonathan Lurie, *Arming Military Justice*, vol. 1, *The Origins of the United States Court of Military Appeals, 1775–1950*, 1992. John T. Willis, "The United States Court of Military Appeals," *Military Law Review*, Winter 1972, 39–93.

Danny E. Rodehaver

COURT-MARTIAL

Military courts for the trial of persons subject to military law are known as courts-martial. The background for U.S. military justice can be traced to Richard I, Gustavus Adolphus, and the 1765 British Articles of War. The Continental Congress enacted the Articles of War* in 1776 to provide commanders the means to enforce discipline and administer justice. The Articles detailed the offenses, commander's authority, responsibility, and procedures for courts-martial.

Article 1, Section 8, of the Constitution of the United States empowered Congress to establish laws to govern and regulate the military. Congress codified military law in 1806 with the revised Articles of War that clearly set courts-martial apart from the civilian court system. These Articles stood, with minor and periodic modification, until 1916, when they were completely revised. The experience of World War I* prompted public debate, especially between the Judge Advocate General* (JAG), Enoch Crowder, and Acting JAG Samuel T. Ansell over the philosophy and administration of military law. As a result, in 1920 Congress revamped the Articles of War to address Ansell's proposals for a statutory power of the JAG Office to review and revise courts-martial proceedings.

Major criticism of the administration of military justice during World War II* focused largely on command influences over courts-martial and disparity in sentencing. After the war, Secretary of Defense* James Forrestal decided to press for the creation of the Uniform Code of Military Justice* (UCMJ), which would modernize the system. Two primary goals were to protect individual rights without hampering the military function and to boost public confidence in the military justice system. Congress enacted the UCMJ in 1950. The Military Justice Acts of 1968 and 1983 introduced additional reforms.

References. William T. Generous, Jr., *Swords and Scales*, 1973. Alexander Holtzoff, "Administration of Justice in the United States Army," *New York University Law Quarterly Review*, January 1947, 1–18. Luther C. West, *They Call It Justice*, 1977.

Danny E. Rodehaver

COWPENS

The battle of Cowpens, sometimes called the "American Cannae" (recalling Hannibal's decisive defeat of the Romans in 216 B.C.), was fought between colonial troops under Brigadier General Daniel Morgan and a British force commanded by Colonel Banastre Tarleton. On 20 December 1780, the newly appointed commander of colonial forces in the South, Major General Nathanael Greene,* decided to disrupt the expected British invasion of North Carolina by splitting his own force and sending slightly more than 1,000 men under Morgan on a wide westward sweep through the interior of South Carolina. Lord Cornwallis, British commander in the south, acceded to Tarleton's persuasive arguments and sent him with 1,100 men after Morgan.

The two forces met at a place called Hannah's Cowpens, in extreme north-central South Carolina near the Broad River, on 17 January 1781. Ingeniously exploiting the strengths and weaknesses of his mixed militia and Continental infantry,* Morgan deployed his men to receive Tarleton's mixed force of British regulars, including two light field guns, and Tarleton's own dreaded British Legion. On a low rise 150 yards from where his regular infantry was formed, Morgan placed his militia, with riflemen to the front. When Tarleton's force attacked, it met rifle fire from the skirmishers and a volley from the militia, which then retired behind the Continentals. Believing they were now pursuing a fleeing enemy, the British ran into the Continentals and were double-enveloped by Morgan's cavalry and militia. Ninety percent of Tarleton's men became casualties or prisoners, while Morgan lost twelve killed and sixty wounded.

References. Lawrence E. Babits, *A Devil of a Whipping*, 1998. Burke Davis, *The Cowpens–Guilford Courthouse Campaign*, 1962. Kenneth Roberts, *The Battle of Cowpens*, 1958.

Robert E. Connor

CRAIG, MALIN (1875–1945)

Born in St. Joseph, Missouri, on 5 August 1875, Malin Craig graduated from the U.S. Military Academy* in 1898. Commissioned in the infantry,* he served with the 6th Cavalry in the Santiago campaign* during the Spanish-American War* and subsequently with the 4th, 10th, and 1st Cavalries. After attending the General Staff School at Fort Leavenworth* from 1904 to 1905, Craig served in a series of assignments, attended the Army War College* from 1909 to 1910, stayed as an instructor the next year, and served as chief of staff of the 41st Infantry Division, I Corps, and the Army of Occupation in Germany during and after World War I.*

After the war, Craig reverted to his permanent grade of major, but he rose once again to brigadier general after several successful assignments. Among other positions, over the next fourteen years, he served as commandant of the Cavalry School, Assistant Chief of Staff (G-3) of the Army, and commandant of the Army War College. In October 1935, President Franklin D. Roosevelt selected Craig to be Chief of Staff* of the Army, where he was instrumental in warning Congress of the Army's lack of preparedness. He focused Army mobilization planning and, within the constraints imposed by the Congress and the times, was instrumental in preparing the Army for World War II.*

Malin Craig retired from active service in August 1939 but was recalled to active duty in 1941 to head the War Department's* Personnel Board, a group responsible for selecting individuals to receive direct commissions* in the Army. He died on 25 July 1945 in Washington, D.C.

Reference. William Gardner Bell, *Commanding Generals and Chiefs of Staff 1775–1987*, 1987.

John A. Hixson

CREEK WAR

During the War of 1812* a number of Indian tribes had an opportunity to strike at encroaching white settlements. In the southern Mississippi Territory, the Creek Indians, who had allied themselves with the British, attacked a number of settlements in the summer of 1813. The most successful attack, on 30 August, killed more than half of the 500 man garrison at Fort Mims, on the Alabama River thirty-five miles northeast of Mobile. Major General Andrew Jackson,* having just dissolved his 2,000-man force of Tennessee volunteers at Natchez, quickly reconstituted it and moved to strike the Creek at Tallahatchee (3 November) and Talladega (9 November). Difficulties with supply and terrain, however, and defeat by the Creek greatly demoralized the militia, and Jackson was forced to go into a defensive position at Fort Strother, in northern Mississippi. There he attempted to reorganize the volunteers while awaiting the arrival of reinforcements from the Regular Army. In March 1814, with the arrival of a regiment* of Regulars, Jackson moved against the Creek, gathered at Horseshoe Bend on the Tallapoosa River. Taking the field on 27 March 1814 with a force of 2,000 militia, 600 Regulars, and several hundred Indian allies, Jackson launched a devastating attack on 900 warriors, killing all but about 200, who fled south into Spanish territory. The combined force of Regulars and militia suffered 201 casualties. On 9 August 1814, the Treaty of Fort Jackson ended the Creek War, and Andrew Jackson was commissioned a major general in the Regular Army.

References. H. S. Halbert and T. H. Ball, *The Creek War of 1813 and 1814*, 1895. Joel W. Martin, *Sacred Revolt*, 1991.

Fred J. Chiaventone

C-RATIONS

Between 1937 and 1939, U.S. Army researchers under the direction of Lieutenant Colonel Rohland Isker, at the Subsistence Research Laboratory at the Chicago Quartermaster Depot, launched a program to develop a more nutritious and palatable combat ration. The "Reserve Ration," consisting of canned meat and canned hardbread and known to 1918-era doughboys* as hardtack and "corned willie," had been in use since World War I* and was nutritionally insufficient. No effort had been made to provide a better combat ration since the early 1920s. The result of Iskar's research program, dubbed C-rations for "Combat type," was first fielded in 1940. C-rations were issued in sets of six cans, three containing the M component (meat) and three containing the B component, or biscuit—actually biscuits or crackers, instant coffee, sugar, and hard candy. Until 1943, the meat components came in only three varieties: meat and vegetable hash, meat and vegatable stew, and meat and beans. The result of such a limited fare was rapid troop dissatisfaction when C-rations were used for any length of time. By 1944, menu items of the M component had been expanded to twelve varieties, including ham and lima beans, spaghetti and meatballs, chicken and vegetables, and others. Foil pouch accessory packs, including cigarettes, matches, toilet paper, and halazone water-purification tablets, were also added. The complete C-ration (three meals), if consumed in its entirety, provided 3,800 calories. C-rations remained the Army's primary combat meal until replaced by Meals Ready to Eat* (MRE) in the early 1980s.

References. Franz A. Koehler, *Special Rations for the Armed Forces, 1946–53,* 1958. Erna Risch, *The Quartermaster Corps,* vol. 1, 1953. Harold W. Thatcher, *The Development of Special Rations for the Army,* 1944.

Stephen C. McGeorge

CREST

Crests are metal and enamel devices authorized for units or organizations permitted to have distinctive shoulder insignia. Many, but not all, armies,* corps,* divisions,* brigades,* and regiments* have adopted crests. The design of the crest may be similar to, or have the same colors as, the shoulder insignia: however, they may be completely different in design and often have a unit motto and are more decorative than the shoulder insignia. Crests are worn on the right breast pocket of Class A,* Class B, and dress uniforms of both officers and enlisted men, and on overseas caps.

References. Barry Jason Stein, *U.S. Army Heraldic Crests,* 1993. John B. Wilson, Corp., *Armies, Corps, Divisions and Separate Brigades,* 1987.

CRIMINAL INVESTIGATION COMMAND

The U.S. Army Criminal Investigation Command (USACIDC or CID) is the Army's sole agent for worldwide investigations of crimes committed by members of the Army or against the Army. CID was officially established by General Order No. 217, Headquarters, American Expeditionary Force,* in France on 27 November 1918, under the Provost Marshal General. Disbanded after World War I,* it was reactivated for a limited role in 1942. In December 1943, the Provost Marshal General was charged with providing staff supervision over all criminal investigations. CID agents accompanied combat troops in all theaters and participated in all major campaigns. Following World War II,* CID was centralized at theater army and area-command level. The 1964 Project Security Shield study recommended the centralization of Army criminal investigation. USACIDC was formed on 17 September 1971. Today it is a major Army command, with headquarters in Fort Belvoir, Virginia, with agents supporting units throughout the world. The CID special agent, a soldier-detective, uses the latest investigative equipment, systems, and techniques to pursue suspects.

References. Paul Boyce, "The Army's Investigators," *Soldiers,* September 1996, 40–

43. Barry W. Collins, "Covering Force," *Soldiers*, December 1987, 34–36. Eugene R. Cromartie, "Boosting Combat Readiness by Fighting Crime in the Army," *Army*, October 1989, 152–155.

Daniel G. Karis

CROOK, GEORGE (1818–1890)

George Crook graduated from the U.S. Military Academy* in 1852 and spent his pre–Civil War career as an Indian fighter in California and Oregon. During the Civil War,* he distinguished himself in action at Antietam* and Chickamauga.* Appointed brigadier general of volunteers in 1862, he went on to command the Department of West Virginia and later VII Corps of the Army of the Shenandoah.* Captured in 1865, he was returned in a prisoner exchange and finished the war as major general of volunteers and commander of the Cavalry Corps of the Army of the Potomac.*

Following the Civil War, Crook was appointed a lieutenant colonel in the Regular Army and returned to the frontier, where he participated in a number of successful Indian campaigns in Idaho, Oregon, and California. His most notable successes were as commanding general of the Department of Arizona (1871–75), where he conducted a brilliant and unconventional campaign against the Apache. In this campaign, Crook developed a unique approach to frontier warfare. It included the use of trains of pack mules for logistics, the employment of Indian Scouts* against their own tribesmen, and the conduct of winter campaigns, when hostile movements were restricted by weather and lack of forage.

In 1875, Crook was appointed commander of the Department of the Platte and participated in the Centennial Campaign.* As part of a three-pronged thrust against the Sioux and their allies, Crook's column met stiff resistance at the Battle of the Rosebud* on 17 June 1876, and although he remained in control of the field, he withdrew temporarily from the operation. His victory at Slim Buttes on 9 September was the first success in a heretofore spotty campaign that included the defeat of the 7th Cavalry at the Little Bighorn. After the campaign, Crook remained in the department until 1882, when he was reassigned to the Department of Arizona, where he conducted another successful campaign against Geronimo, Chato, and Nana in the Sierra Madre. Geronimo's flight from the reservation in 1885 again put Crook into the field; in 1886 he was able to bring most of the renegades back under government control. Worsening relations between Crook and Lieutenant General Phillip H. Sheridan,* who disapproved of Crook's unconventional methods, led Crook to request relief and reassignment. He moved again to the Department of the Platte, then assumed command of the Division of the Missouri.

Crook excelled in the use of Indian scouts and developed a reputation for honesty and openess in dealing with Indians. This frequently put him at odds with his superiors and westerners. In his later career, he became an outspoken champion of the Indian and insisted that dishonesty and corrupt government practices were at the root of the most of the Indian wars. His innovative approach to pack-mule logistics continued to be used by the U.S. Army through World War I.*

References. John G. Bourke, *On the Border with Crook*, 1891, 1971. Paul A. Hutton, *Soldiers West*, 1987. Charles King, *Campaigning with Crook*, 1964.

Fred J. Chiaventone

CUSTER, GEORGE ARMSTRONG (1839–1876)

A controversial figure in American history, George Armstrong Custer graduated at the bottom of his U.S. Military Academy* class in 1861 and was commissioned a lieutenant in the 2d Cavalry. He quickly established a reputation as an aggressive and reckless cavalry* officer, earning early promotion to captain and then brevet brigadier general in the Regular Army. He was repeatedly cited for "gallant and meritorious service" at the battles of Gettysburg,* Yellow Tavern, Winchester, and Five Forks. By the end of the war he had been promoted to brevet major general of volunteers and commanded the Third Cavalry Division of the Army of the Potomac.* A flamboyant and successful cavalry commander, he was the darling of the Northern press, which dubbed him the "boy general."

At the conclusion of the Civil War,* Custer was appointed a lieutenant colonel in the Regular Army and served in a series of Reconstruction-era posts in Texas and Kentucky before taking command of the 7th Cavalry at Fort Riley,* Kansas, in October 1866. His tenure with the 7th Cavalry was marked by controversy; there was a series of disputes with senior and subordinate officers who objected to his unorthodox leadership style. Despite its many detractors, the 7th Cavalry maintained a reputation as the elite cavalry unit in the Army, and the oft-cited incidences of internal rivalry were in fact commonplace for all Army units of the period. Custer's foibles were probably overstated.

Much of the criticism of Custer as a commander seems to stem from his conduct of operations on the Washita* (November 1867) in which he destroyed Black Kettle's village of Cheyenne. Custer's success at the Washita was marred by the loss of Major Joel Elliot and his detachment, who were cut off from the main command and massacred. The onset of darkness and snow slowed the search for the missing men, and when Custer discovered a large body of Cheyenne, Arapaho, Kiowa, and Comanche warriors closing in on the command, he decided to withdraw from the area rather than risk additional casualties. In command of the Yellowstone expedition of 1873 and the Black Hills expedition of 1874, he was one of few officers to become intimately familiar with the Indians, studying their culture and becoming adept at sign language. He also wrote a series of articles on his experiences for Eastern magazines under the pseudonym of "Nomad," later published in a book titled *My Life on the Plains*. Relieved of command by order of President Ulysses S. Grant* (who was incensed by Custer's testimony before Congress on the corrupt practices of the "Indian Ring"), he was recalled to duty for the Sioux campaign of 1876.

Commanding the 7th Cavalry again under Major General Alfred Terry, Custer was moving against an expected 800 hostile Sioux warriors when, on 25 June 1876, he found a large village of Sioux, Cheyenne, and Arapaho on the Little Bighorn. Confronted by a force of 1,500 to 2,000 Indians, Custer divided his command into three battalions* to assault the village. Custer's wing, consisting of five companies* of cavalry,* was overwhelmed by superior numbers and destroyed. The two other battalions, under Major Marcus Reno and Captain Frederick Benteen, assumed a defensive position and managed to hold out for two days until relieved by the arrival of the remainder of Terry's force.

George Armstrong Custer's life, death, and the Battle of the Little Bighorn have become integral parts of the legend of the American West.

References. Robert M. Utley, *Cavalier in Buckskin*, 1988. Jeffrey D. Wert, *Custer*, 1996.

Fred J. Chiaventone

D

DAKOTA. *See* C-47.

DAVIS, BENJAMIN O., SR. (1880–1970)

Benjamin O. Davis, Sr. was the first black general officer in the U.S. Army. Born in Washington, D.C., on 28 May 1880, Davis recruited soldiers for the 8th U.S. Volunteer Infantry for the Spanish-American War* and was appointed a first lieutenant as a reward for his efforts. Later, he applied to the U.S. Military Academy* but was rejected. He then enlisted in the 9th Cavalry, where he quickly rose to the rank of sergeant major.* Commissioned a second lieutenant in 1901, he was assigned to the 10th Cavalry.

Davis served in the Philippines and on the Mexican border, was a tactics instructor at Tuskegee Institute and Wilberforce University, advised the Ohio and New York National Guards, and was military attaché to Liberia. In 1940, President Franklin D. Roosevelt appointed Davis brigadier general and commander of the 2d Cavalry Division at Fort Riley,* Kansas. He retired in June 1941 but was soon recalled. Assigned to the Inspector General's* office during World War II,* Davis traveled throughout the Army, focusing on racial problems and the morale of black soldiers. After the war, he participated in planning for the postwar place of blacks in the Army.

Davis retired again in 1948, spending his last twenty years serving on government boards, the Battle Monuments Commission, and as a representative in Liberia. Davis's career of nearly fifty years is one of the longest in U.S. military history. He balanced his opposition to racism with professionalism and used his personal skills to advance the cause of equality in the U.S. Army. His son, Benjamin O. Davis, Jr., became the Army's first black lieutenant general.

References. Marvin E. Fletcher, *America's First Black General*, 1989. Ulysses Lee, *The Employment of Negro Troops*, 1966.

George Knapp

DAVIS, JEFFERSON (1808–1889)

Born in Kentucky in 1808, Jefferson Davis graduated twenty-third of thirty-three in the U.S. Military Academy* class of 1828. He served on the Northwest frontier until he resigned from the Army in 1835 to settle in Mississippi as a planter. His first wife, the daughter of Zachary Taylor,* died three months after their marriage. In 1845 he married Varina Howell and was elected to Congress. He resigned from Congress the next year to serve in the Mexican War,* where he distinguished himself in command of volunteers and was wounded at the battle of Buena Vista.* After the war he returned to politics and was elected to the U.S. Senate. He later served as secretary of war* in Franklin Pierce's administration. His tenure was marked by significant advances in weapons and equipment for the Army and by frequent disagreements with the Commanding General,* Winfield Scott.*

Davis returned to the Senate and served there until Mississippi seceded from the Union in January 1861. He was elected the first president of the Confederacy, a position he held for the entire Civil War.* He tended to be inflexible in his administration, especially with his state governors and in military matters, about which he thought himself well qualified. He fled Richmond in April 1865 with his cabinet and was finally captured by Federal cavalry in northern Georgia in early May. Incarcerated at Fort Monroe,* he was held for two years without trial. After his release, he lived in Biloxi, Mississippi, and published his great work, *The Rise and Fall of the Confederate Government*, in 1881.

In the years after the war, many southerners blamed Davis for the Confederacy's failure. However, while he would have preferred a general's commission, he had served honorably and energetically in the duty given him by the South. His imperious style was not widely successful in the states rights–conscious Confederacy. Eventually, he emerged as one of the heroes in the Confederate pantheon. Latter day historians have moderated their criticisms of Jefferson Davis by viewing his whole career and measuring his considerable achievements.

References. William C. Davis, *Jefferson Davis*, 1991. Clement Eaton, *Jefferson Davis*, 1977. Paul D. Escott, *After Secession*, 1978.

George Knapp

DAVY CROCKETT

The Davy Crockett was an early 1950s recoilless rifle* design that attempted to provide frontline infantry* with a mobile nuclear warhead–delivery system. The M28 120 mm version weighed 116 pounds, had a range of one and a half miles, and was served by a three-man crew. The M29 version, with a 0.25-kiloton atomic warhead, weighed 379 pounds and had a range of three miles. The weapon could be airlifted, mounted on a Jeep,* mechanical mule, or armored personnel carrier* (APC), or hand carried for use with a tripod. It could also fire a conventional warhead. Unfortunately, above-ground atomic tests in Nevada demonstrated that the range of the Davy Crockett was too short to prevent atomic blast and radiation injuries to the crew and the frontline infantry they were supporting. Consequently, although in theory highly useful to the new atomic battlefield tactics of the time, the Davy Crockett never entered service.

References. Thomas B. Cochran, William M. Arkin, and Milton M. Hoenig, *Nuclear Weapons Databook*, vol. 1, *U.S. Nuclear Forces and Capabilities*, 1984. James F. Dunnigan and Albert A. Nofi, *Shooting Blanks*, 1991.

John R. Finch

DEFENSE INTELLIGENCE AGENCY

A product of Secretary of Defense* Robert S. McNamara's desire to reorganize and consolidate duplicated functions within the Department of Defense* (DOD), the Defense Intelligence Agency (DIA) was established on 1 August 1961. Originally charged with meeting and coordinating all of the intelligence requirements of the joint services, the DIA saw its responsibilities expanded in 1964 to include coordination and consolidation of both raw and finished intelligence from DOD and non-DOD sources, data processing and systems design, and limited espionage operations. To accomplish these tasks, the DIA was divided into five large directorates: Resources and Systems, Joint Chiefs of Staff* (JCS) Support, Management and Operations, Intelligence and External Affairs, and Foreign Intelligence. The DIA reports directly to the secretary of defense through the JCS.

The agency has been criticized since its inception. Several congressional investigations have suggested its abolition, the most notable and recent being the Pike Committee (1975). Both military and civilian critics have charged that the DIA has too many broad-ranging agendas to allow it to meet demands for mission-specific, timely information required at the tactical level by the various branches it supports. Headquartered in the Pentagon,* DIA employs approximately 4,500 civilian and military personnel and 1,000 defense attachés who report to DIA.

References. Jeffrey Richelson, *The U.S. Intelligence Community*, 1985. Ernest Volkman, *Warriors of the Night*, 1985.

Robert Rook

DEMILITARIZED ZONE

The Demilitarized Zone (DMZ) is the physical boundary separating the Republic of Korea (South Korea) and the Democratic People's Republic of Korea (North Korea). This geographic area is a strip of land approximately four kilometers wide running the width of the Korean Peninsula. The centerline of the DMZ divides the two countries along the frontline truce positions of the United Nations forces and those of the Communist Chinese and North Koreans when the armistice ending the fighting in the Korean War* took effect in August 1953. Each side of the DMZ, a two-kilometer zone, is patrolled by the forces of the respective Koreas. Both sides are limited by the provisions of the armistice agreement as to the size and composition of forces that can be introduced into the DMZ. The North Koreans have frequently violated the provisions regarding the DMZ over the years, and United Nations forces have erected an extensive set of barriers to prevent infiltration to the south.

References. Daniel P. Bolger, *Scenes from an Unfinished War*, 1991. Michael Keon, *Korean Phoenix*, 1977.

Edwin Kennedy, Jr.

DENTAL CORPS

Dental care for soldiers was considered an individual responsibility from the founding of the U.S. Army until 4 April 1872, when the Army appointed an enlisted hospital steward, William Saunders, as dentist to the U.S. Military Academy.* Emergency dental care was commonly provided by physicians and enlisted hospital stewarts until 1901, when the Surgeon General* employed thirty contract dentists. These dentists held no rank but wore uniforms of the Medical Corps, with a silver "D.S." insignia,* and enjoyed many of the privileges of officers.

On 3 March 1911, legislation established the Army Dental Corps, with officers initially given the rank of first lieutenant. John S. Marshall became the first commissioned dentist in April 1911. During World War I,* active-duty dental officers from the regular and reserve component expanded from eighty-six in April 1917 to 4,620 by November 1918. Major William H. G. Logan was appointed first chief of the Army Dental Corps, in August 1917. The size of the Dental Corps reached an all-time high of 15,292 officers on active duty during World War II* The Korean War* saw active Dental Corps strength reach 2,641 officers; during the Vietnam War,* it peaked at 2,810.

References. John M. Hyson, Jr., *The United States Military Academy Dental Service*, 1989. George F. Jeffcott, *United States Army Dental Service in World War II*, 1955.

John King

DEPARTMENT OF DEFENSE

A 1949 amendment to the National Security Act of 1947* specified the establishment of the Department of Defense (DOD). Separate cabinet-level departments of War and Navy had been established in the nation's earliest days, but a history of clashes and compromises between the president and Congress, the War and Navy Departments, and Army and Navy leaders had demonstrated the need for a more unified defense establishment. Following the Spanish-American War,* significant efforts were made to combine the Navy and War Departments, and a Joint Board was established. Over the next several decades, both military and civilian individuals and groups exerted pressure to streamline the military bureaucracy and enhance cooperation between the services.

World War II,* however, provided the real impetus for a single, civilian, executive agency for national defense. The National Security Act of 1947 created the National Military Establishment, headed by a civilian, cabinet-level secretary, over the Departments of the Army* and Navy and the newly instituted

Department of the Air Force. This basic legislation has evolved through amendments and executive orders to invest more control and direction over the armed forces in the secretary of defense.* Current DOD functions are to maintain and employ the armed forces to support and defend the Constitution of the United States against all enemies, foreign and domestic; to ensure, by timely and effective military action, the security of the United States, its possessions, and areas vital to its interest; and to uphold and advance the national policies and interests of the United States. To perform its national security role, DOD has its own staff; nine combatant commands (unified command*); fourteen agencies responsible for a variety of intelligence, research, and development, logistics and support functions; and seven field activities for service members, service families, and civilian employees.

References. C. W. Borklund, *The Department of Defense*, 1968. Alice C. Cole et al., eds., *The Department of Defense*, 1978. James E. Hewes, Jr., *From Root to McNamara*, 1975.

J. G. D. Babb

DEPARTMENT OF THE ARMY

With the end of World War II,* government and military leaders recognized a need to reorganize the national security system to meet the needs of a changing world. During the war, ad hoc measures helped ensure centralized control, but the need for a centralized authority directly under the president to manage the myriad activities and operations of air, land, and sea forces led to the passage of the National Security Act of 1947.* Although DOD's authority was wide-ranging in some respects, in reality the military services retained much of their autonomy, since they were each separate departments.

The National Security Act renamed the War Department* the Department of the Army* (DA) and created the National Military Establishment, with the president at its head. The DA is headed by a secretary, with an under secretary and a number of assistant secretaries that deal with specific functional areas. The Chief of Staff* of the Army is the highest-ranking officer assigned to duty within the Army. He is supported by a special staff of four deputy chiefs, one each for personnel, intelligence, operations and plans, and logistics. Department of Defense* Directive 5100.1, "Functions of the Department of Defense and Its Major Components," articulates DA functions. Foremost among these is to organize, train, equip, and provide forces for the conduct of prompt and sustained combat operations on land—specifcally, forces to defeat enemy land forces and to seize, occupy, and defend land areas.

References. Alice C. Cole et al., *The Department of Defense*, 1978. James E. Hewes, *From Root to McNamara*, 1975.

Gary Bounds

DEPARTMENT OF VETERANS AFFAIRS. *See* Veterans Administration.

DEPUY, WILLIAM E. (1919–1993)

William E. DePuy began his remarkable military career in the South Dakota National Guard. Commissioned into the infantry* from the Reserve Officer Training Corps* (ROTC) at South Dakota State University, he landed on Utah Beach on D+1 as the S-3 (Operations Officer) of the 1st Battalion, 37th Infantry. After six months of combat, at the age of twenty-five, DePuy was given command of that unit; he distinguished himself in combat, earning three Silver Stars,* two Purple Hearts,* and the Distinguished Service Cross.* Twenty years later, DePuy commanded the 1st Infantry Division* in Vietnam. His stellar career crested in 1973, when he assumed command of the U.S. Army's Training and Doctrain Command* (TRADOC), an organization that he had envisioned and created. DePuy's legacy is evident today in his continued influence upon TRADOC. As a result of his efforts, the U.S. Army has a dynamic and progressive warfighting doctrine,* as reflected in Field Manual* (FM) 100–5. This doctrine served as the foundation for a training revolution developed in the 1980s. DePuy was a leading proponent and enthusiastic advocate for the development and fielding of five major weapon systems—the Apache* and Black Hawk* helicopters, the M1 Abrams Tank,* the Bradley infantry fighting vehicle,* and the Patriot* air defense system. These proved crucially effective in Operation Desert Storm.* He continued to serve his country in retirement, publishing probing articles that reflected his wide-ranging interests until his death in 1993.

References. Romie L. Brownlee and William J. Mullen III, *Changing an Army*, [1986]. Paul H. Herbert, *Deciding What Has to Be Done*, 1988.

Ralph Nichols

DESERT STORM

Desert Storm was the designation of the multinational military operation conducted from 17 January to 3 March 1991 under joint U.S.-Saudi Arabian command to free the emirate of Kuwait from Iraqi occupation. The immediate origin of the crisis was Iraq's attempt on 2 August 1990 to resolve both immediate financial shortfalls and long-term geographic ambitions by seizing its small, oil-rich neighbor. This aggressive action threatened the Kingdom of Saudi Arabia and the West's Persian Gulf oil supply. Moreover, it occurred at a time when the forty-five-year Western preoccupation with the Soviet menace to Western Europe was ending. As a consequence of German reunification in December 1990, the United States had an unusually large and otherwise idle military capacity, which it turned immediately to redress the Iraqi action. Ultimately, thirty-five states contributed resources to the coalition, with the principal military forces provided by the United States, Saudi Arabia, Egypt, Great Britain, France, and Syria.

Iraq's aggression and continued miscalculations by its leader, Saddam Hussein, served to isolate Iraq from the beginning. As early as 2 August, the United Nations* (UN) condemned the Iraqi attack. Through the diplomatic efforts of

U.S. President George Bush and Secretary of State James Baker, Egyptian President Hosni Mubarak, and King Fahd of Saudi Arabia, the UN Security Council first imposed an economic quarantine of Iraq on 6 August (Resolution 661), then moved to a vote on 29 November (Resolution 678) that set a deadline (15 January 1991) for Iraq to withdraw from Kuwait. The resolution permitted the use of "all necessary means" by the growing coalition if Iraq failed to respond. In January, after a month of debate, the U.S. Congress authorized the president to use force.

The coalition's war plan called for a four-phased offensive. Three phases were entirely oriented to the destruction of the Iraqi military by the massive and precise use of air power; the fourth phase was a ground envelopment. The air offensive began on 17 January, with the destruction of Iraq's military command-and-control system in and around Baghdad; it continued for thirty-eight days, concluding with a massive air-ground preparation to disrupt the Iraqi forces in Kuwait. As much as one-third of the allied air effort was ultimately diverted to Scud hunting; the crude Scud missile was the one Iraqi strategic capability that the coalition was unable to master.

On the day the air offensive began, General Norman Schwarzkopf, commander in chief of Central Command, ordered the U.S. Third Army* to shift its two corps,* assembled over a period of six months from bases in the United States and Europe, west to the Iraq-Kuwait border. The Iraqis were thought to have elements of forty-three divisions* positioned, primarily in Kuwait proper. The allied ground plan called for the concealed movement to the west of the U.S. VII and XVII Corps (including British and French divisions), a sweep around the Iraqi defenses, and an attack deep into the Iraqi rear beyond the Kuwait border to destroy the Iraq theater reserve. Simultaneously, two U.S. Marine Corps divisions, reinforced by an Army tank brigade,* and the Arab coalition forces would attack the Iraqi defenses along the Saudi-Kuwait border to liberate Kuwait City.

The ground offensive began in the early morning hours of 24 February. It was halted by President Bush at 8. A.M. on 28 February after it had destroyed a large portion of the Iraqi force or forced it into a small pocket around the Iraqi city of Basrah. Cease-fire talks held on 3 March at Safwan in southeastern Iraq ended the active phase of Operation Desert Storm. UN forces then moved in to protect Kuwait from any returning Iraqi forces and, later, occupied a major part of northern Iraq to protect rebellious Kurds from Iraqi reprisals. Although the Iraqi nuclear, chemical, and biological* program was thrown open to international inspection and a new impetus was given to settlement of long-standing Arab-Israeli conflicts, Saddam Hussein remained in power with a formidable, if greatly reduced, capability in an oil-rich part of the world. Economic sanctions continue. Desert Storm proved to be a testing ground for a range of new precision and high-tech weapons that led many to proclaim the existence of a revolution in military affairs.

References. Rick Atkinson, *Crusade*, 1993. Dilip Hiro, *Desert Shield to Desert Storm*, 1992. Robert H. Scales, Jr., *Certain Victory*, 1993. Richard M. Swain, *"Lucky War,"* 1994.

Richard Swain

DESERTION

Under the provisions of Article 85 of the Uniform Code of Military Justice* (UCMJ), it is a criminal offense for a service member to go or remain absent from his unit, organization, or place of duty with the intent to remain absent permanently, or to quit his unit, organization, or place of duty to avoid hazardous duty or to shirk important service. This offense is commonly referred to as "desertion." A soldier who is absent without leave* (AWOL) for thirty days is normally charged with desertion. During a time of war, desertion and attempted desertion may be punishable by death.

References. Edward M. Byrne, *Military Law*, 3d ed., 1981. Robert F. Elliott, "Commitment or Cop Out?" *Soldiers*, November 1971, 4–6.

DETACHMENT 101

With a two-fold mission of conducting espionage and guerrilla war against the Japanese forces in Burma, Detachment 101 became the first Office of Strategic Services* unit to take the field in Asia, deploying to the China-Burma-India* theater in 1942. Under the command of Major General Carl Eifler, the small detachment worked directly for General Joseph Stilwell.* Stillwell's guidance to Eifler was simple and direct: "All I want to hear from you are booms coming from the Burma jungle."

After some initial failures, Eifler and his men succeeded in developing a sophisticated intelligence network behind Japanese lines. Of particular importance was Detachment 101's ability to organize and direct the Kachins, one of Burma's indigenous highland peoples, against the Japanese. The combination of Detachment 101's expertise and Kachin enthusiasm proved an effective weapon in Stilwell's arsenal. Their accomplishments were impressive; they became the eyes and ears of the Tenth Air Force, finding nearly 80 percent of the targets selected for bombardment. Following air strikes, the Kachins frequently conducted the bomb-damage assessments critical to subsequent mission planning. The pilot-recovery network Detachment 101 established provided a valuable lifeline for downed pilots. In terms of ground combat, Detachment 101 eventually directed 10,800, mostly guerrilla, soldiers in an active and successful war against the Japanese.

References. Richard Dunlop, *Behind Japanese Lines*, 1979. David W. Hogan, Jr., *U.S. Army Special Operations in World War II*, 1992.

Joseph R. Fischer

DEUCE AND A HALF

The 2½-ton, medium, 6 × 6 truck, commonly known as the "deuce and a half," was the workhorse for the U.S. Army from the early 1940s until the mid-

1980s. Many of these vehicles still move equipment and soldiers today. The deuce and a half was one of five chassis the Army selected when it standardized its truck fleet in response to expected logistics needs on the eve of World War II.* The General Motors Corporation won the original contract and, after a design freeze in 1942, was able to assemble great numbers of deuce and a halfs, with component parts from other manufacturers such as Bendix, Hercules, Borg-Warner, and Timken-Detroit. The deuce and a half combined good road performance with better than adequate cross-country mobility, a combination that the Army had been lacking since the inception of motorization. Of the nearly 2.5 million trucks delivered to the U.S. Army during World War II, almost 25 percent (800,000) were deuce and a halfs. This vehicle provided the majority of the transportation lift needed to win the war in Europe and, along with the Willys-Jeep,* was the most important military wheeled vehicle produced in the United States this century.

References. Daniel R. Beaver, "Deuce and a Half," in *Feeding Mars*, ed. John A. Lynn, 1993. Fred W. Crismon, *U.S. Military Wheeled Vehicles*, 1983.

Jim Martin

DEVIL'S BRIGADE. *See* First Special Service Force.

DICK ACT

The Dick Act of 1903, sponsored by Congressman Charles William Dick of Ohio (later elected to the U.S. Senate and chair of the Committee on Militia), revised the Militia Act of 1792,* reformed the state militia as the National Guard* and Reserve Militia, and provided for extensive federal involvement in the new organizations. While the act retained many militia customs, such as pay, legal liability, and court-martial authority, it called for each state or territory to have an Adjutant General* who would report annually to the Secretary of War.* It made available federal funds and authorized the secretary of war to provide the same arms and equipment to the Guard as it issued to the Regular Army. The act required the Guard to meet periodically throughout the year for the purpose of drill and marksmanship training, authorized Guardsmen to attend Regular Army encampments for training, and made funds available for officers to attend military schools. It set guidelines for examinations for commissions in the volunteers and established rules governing age and eligibility requirements. It further extended pension benefits to members of the militia—or their survivors—wounded or killed in the line of duty. The Dick Act, however, fell short of resolving all of the issues that plagued the use of militia, especially the restrictions on the call-up of the militia and control of Guard personnel. Further legislation in 1908 and 1914 was necessary to meet the full intent of Dick's original House bill.

References. Louis Cantor, *The Creation of the Modern National Guard*, 1963. Maurice Matloff, ed., *American Military History*, 1969.

Michael G. Knapp

DINING-IN

A dining-in is a formal social event held by a military unit or organization. Although the tradition of formal dinners in regimental messes dates back to the 18th century in the British army, the U.S. Army did not conduct such formal occasions until World War I.* A dining-in may serve a number of purposes. It may be held to welcome newcomers, bid farewell to departing members of the mess, celebrate historic events, honor special guests or dignitaries, or recognize individual achievements of significance to the unit; or it may simply bring the officers of the command together to build esprit de corps and unit cohesion. Detailed planning and formal invitations normally precede the dining-in. Formal attire is usually prescribed, and rules of conduct are strictly observed. The evening typically begins with the president or senior officer receiving members and guests, followed by a cocktail hour, during which members and guests socialize in a relaxed and congenial atmosphere. Established protocol dictates the evening's formal activities: seating of members and guest by rank and precedence; presentation of the national colors and standards; the invocation by the chaplain; toasts; dinner; and after-dinner remarks, speeches, or presentations of awards. Informal activities after dinner normally include planned or impromptu entertainment and games.

References. Lawrence P. Crocker, *Army Officer's Guide*, 46th ed., 1993. Oretha D. Swartz, *Service Etiquette*, 4th ed., 1988.

DIRECT COMMISSION

Appointment from civilian life is one way the U.S. Army fills its continuing need for commissioned officers who have special professional and technical competence. Physicians and surgeons, for examples, as well as chaplains, lawyers, and other professionals, are offered commissions at grades appropriate to their professional achievements, age, and background. Appointment may or may not be members of the active or reserve components prior to appointment. The U.S. Code authorizes the president to appoint qualified persons to any commissioned grade, except warrant officers* and grades above major general or rear admiral, during war or national emergency declared by Congress or the president. Such appointments are known as "original appointments." During World War II,* battlefield commissions* were authorized for warrant officers and enlisted soldiers who demonstrated high potential leadership in combat.

References. Sheldon R. Eisnitz, "Challenge with Choice," *Army Information Digest*, August 1965, 38–47. Monro MacCloskey, "Paths to a Commission," *Army*, December 1964, 35–39.

Andrew L. Giacomini, Jr.

DIRECTOR GENERAL OF THE HOSPITAL DEPARTMENT

When the Continental Congress established the Continental Army's* Medical Department on 27 July 1775, medical care and hospitals for the soldiers were in considerable disarray and completely inadequate. Medical personnel were insufficient in both numbers and training, supplies of drugs and bandages were chronically short, and food and clothing were limited and of poor quality. To head the Hospital Department, Congress appointed a Director General and Chief Physician, a title that was subsequently reduced to Director General of the Hospital Department. The position, however, was responsible directly to the Congress, not to Commander in Chief of the Army, George Washington.*

Contending factions within the Congress continued to meddle in the affairs of the Hospital Department and prevented the Director General from becoming an effective leader in developing adequate medical care for the Continental Army. The first incumbent, Benjamin Church, was suspected of collaborating with the British and was forced from office. John Morgan, Church's successor, served for fifteen stormy months before Congress dimissed him. The third Director General, William Shippen, Jr., entered office with the support of Washington and most of Congress, but his administration too was highly controversial. Because of the problems that plagued the Directors General and the limited success of a series of reforms and reorganizations of the Hospital Department, Congress eventually abolished the offices of Director General and Apothecary General* and replaced them with the Surgeon General* who had more authority and could bring a greater degree of professionalism to the task of providing medical care for the U.S. Army.

Reference. Mary C. Gillette, *The Army Medical Department, 1775–1818*, 1981.

DISHONORABLE DISCHARGE

The dishonorable discharge is the most severe punitive discharge. It may be applied only to enlisted members, noncommissioned officers* (NCOs), and warrant officers* by a general court-martial. Its purpose is to separate from the service those guilty of the most serious offenses, generally equivalent to a civilian felony conviction. Originally borrowed from the British Articles of War, it has been an element of U.S. military law since the 18th century.

References. Edward M. Byrne, *Military Law*, 3d ed., 1981. William T. Generous, Jr., *Swords and Scales*, 1973. Lee S. Tillotson, *Index-Digest and Annotations to the Uniform Code of Military Justice*, 1956.

Kelvin Crow

DISMOUNT ELEMENT. *See* Dismount Team.

DISMOUNT TEAM

With the adoption of the Bradley infantry fighting vehicle,* the strength of U.S. Army's mechanized infantry* squad* was reduced to eight soldiers: a driver, two men to operate the turret weapons, and five men to fight dismounted—the dismount team, or the dismount element. The squad, organized as a single fighting team, fires ball-mounted weapons derived from the M-16* while in the vehicle, and a grenade launcher (M203), a squad automatic weapon (SAW-M249), and M-16s once they dismount. According to current doctrine,* the dismount team is always prepared to exit the Bradley and operate under the cover of its heavy weapons, conduct an attack, clear obstacles, fight in urban or fortified areas, or occupy defensive positions. The dismount team is led by the second-ranking noncommissioned officer* (NCO) in the squad, normally a sergeant or corporal.

References. Harry C. Andress, "The Bradley Challenge," *Infantry*, January–February 1991, 18–21. Allen L. Tiffany, "Proposed Rapidly Deployable, Tactically Mobile, Motorized Infantry Brigade," *Military Review*, February 1994, 74–77.

Andrew N. Morris

DISTINGUISHED SERVICE CROSS

"The [Distinguished Service Cross] DSC is awarded to any person who, while serving in any capacity with the Army, distinguishes himself by extraordinary heroism not justifying the award of the Medal of Honor."* The DSC is for combat gallantry only. The act or acts of heroism must have occurred while engaged in an action against an armed enemy of the United States and "must have been so notable and have involved risk of life so extraordinary as to set the individual apart from his comrades." The DSC ranks only second to the Medal of Honor. Established by President Woodrow Wilson in 1918 and ratified by Congress the same year, the Distinguished Service Cross is also the second-oldest award in the armed forces' hierarchy of medals and decorations.*

References. Evans E. Kerrigan, *American War Medals and Decorations*, 1964. J. Strandberg and R. Bender, *The Call of Duty*, 1994.

Frederic L. Borch III

DIVISION

The division is the largest combat unit with a permanent organization. It is equipped and organized to conduct extended combat operations under various geographical and threat environments. When augmented by support elements from a corps* or larger headquarters, called a "division slice," it can operate independently for indefinite periods. There are various specialized types of divisions in the U.S. Army to address differing threats. An example is the heavy division such as the armored or mechanized infantry division equipped with modern tanks, artillery, and armored infantry vehicles. Every soldier in a heavy division can ride to war. Light divisions include the light, airborne, and air assault* divisions. In these units, infantry* provides the predominant combat power and, though infantrymen may ride Air Force or Army aircraft to the vicinity of the fight, they actually conduct combat operations on foot.

Historically the division has consisted of from 5,000 to over 20,000 soldiers. Under current tables of organization and equipment* (TOE), the division is commanded by a major general, with two assistant division commanders, one of whom usually supervises the manuever forces (ADC-M), the other the support force (ADC-S). The division staff reports to a chief of staff. Unlike the S staffs at battalion* and brigade,* the division staff has a G prefix, indicating the staff of a general officer. Officially designated the assistant chief of staff, the G-1 is responsible for personnel matters; the G-2 is responsible for collecting and analyzing intelligence on the enemy terrain; the G-3 plans operations and training; the G-4 is responsible for logistical planning; and the G-5 handles civil-military operations and relations.

A division's major subordinate elements include three maneuver brigade headquarters, an aviation brigade, and brigade-sized division artillery (DIVARTY) and support commands. (DISCOM). To the brigade headquarters are assigned the organic battalions of the division. Although most brigade-battalion relations are habitual, the design of the division allows the commander to tailor his brigades for specific operations by changing the mix of battalions in any specific brigade. An infantry, airborne, or air assault division typically has nine infantry battalions. A mechanized infantry division has five mechanized infantry and five tank battalions. An armor division* has an additional tank battalion, assigned to a brigade headquarters as deemed necessary. The aviation brigade has battalions of cargo and attack helicopters. The DIVARTY always has three direct support battalions of howitzers 105-mm (M102),* one for each brigade. Additionally, it has a general support unit of battery* or battalion size, with heavier and longer-ranged artillery or missiles. The DISCOM has the medical, transportation, and maintenance battalions that sustain the division.

References. Richard F. Kolasheski, "Division Restructuring," *Armor*, November–December 1978, 18–23. John B. Wilson, *Maneuver and Firepower*, 1998, and "Influences on U.S. Army Divisional Organization in the Twentieth Century," *Army History*, Fall 1996, 1–17.

Andrew N. Morris

DOCTRINE

Doctrine is an authoritative and fundamental statement of how an army approaches, and fights in, war. It establishes a professional culture; facilitates communications between staffs, commanders, and subordinates; describes how forces are to think about applying the principles of war;* sets direction and standards for the conduct of operations; and serves as a basis for officer education. Doctrine must be enduring, relevant, and sufficiently solid to provide guidance for forces on the battlefield, but it must also be flexible to address diverse and varied situations in a changing world. Doctrine requires individual judgment and initiative in application.

In the U.S. Army, doctrine is expressed in a number of official sources, including field manuals,* Department of State publications describing how the United States should respond to international situations, pamphlets issued periodically by the the service chiefs and the chairman of the Joint Chiefs of Staff,* and the curricula of the Army War College* and the Command and General Staff College.*

References. Aaron Blumenfeld, Air Land Battle Doctrine, 1989. Henry Jerry Osterhoudt, "The Evolution of U.S. Army Assault Tactics, 1778–1919," 1986.

DOG ROBBER

"Dog robber" is an Old Army* term applied to men from the ranks hired as officers' household servants. The practice arose in response to the relative shortage and instability of civilian domestic servants at frontier posts. Although "dog robber" was more derisive, it was used interchangably with the term "striker," and it implied connotatively a willingness to scavenge from animals if necessary to procure needed materials. Hiring servants form the ranks was made illegal in 1870, but the practice continued possibly as late as the early 1890s. Dog robbers were relieved of some routine tasks, and their extra pay ranged from five to ten dollars a month, depending upon the duties required. Although scorned by other soldiers, some strikers found life in the officers' households more serene and comfortable than that in a noisy, bare barracks. Some served officers for years and became valued parts of their families.

References. Edward M. Coffman, *The Old Army*, 1986. Don Rickey, Jr., *Forty Miles a Day on Beans and Hay*, 1963. Robert Wooster, *Soldiers, Sutlers, and Settlers*, 1987.

Jeffrey Prater

DOG TAGS

The unofficial use of identification tags in the U.S. Army can be documented as early as the Civil War.* Sources, however, differ as to the official origins of the metallic identification tag. One source suggests that they became official when General Order 204 designated the tag as part of the uniform and specified what information it should include. General Order 204 was amended in 1917 to require twin tags. Another source states that tags were advocated as early as 1899, but Army regulations did not make them mandatory until 1913. In either case, by the end of World War I,* combat soldiers wore identification discs on chains around their necks. In 1940, the current oblong-shaped tags—commonly called dog tags—replaced the metal discs.

The two dog tags that soldiers wear today differ little from the 1940 model. Embossed on each is the bearer's name, blood type, social security number, and religious preference. In case of injury or death, one tag stays on the casualty, while the other is used for administrative purposes to mark a casualty's temporary location. Dog tags are no longer the sole method of identification. Medical and dental records are the primary means of casualty identification; DNA methods are being developed. Soldiers are, however, still required to wear dog tags.

References. Robert W. Fisch, *Field Equipment of the Infantry, 1914–1945*, 1989. Gerard C. Wilson, "Simple Little Things," *Soldiers*, April 1990, 50–52. Richard W. Wooley, "A Short History of Identification Tags," *Quartermaster Professional Bulletin*, 1988, 16–17.

Lee Kruger

DOMESTIC SUPPORT OPERATIONS

The U.S. Army has been engaged in what today are known as "domestic support operations" since its inception. The secretary of defense* has designated the secretary of the army* as executive agent for most domestic support operations. These operations have been divided into four broad types: disaster assistance, community assistance, law enforcement support, and environmental assistance. Disaster assistance refers to actions taken by the Army to support civil authority with respect to both natural and man-made disasters, such as hurricanes and terrorist acts. Community assistance refers to applying military resources to community projects, such as construction of various types of public works and the establishment of mutual support agreements concerning police, medical, and emergency services. Law enforcement support refers to the ways in which the Army supports the Civilian police in a variety of activities, such as counterdrug operations or riot control; such activities are governed by the Posse Comitatus Act of 1878, which severely restricts the use of federal forces to enforce public law. Environmental assistance refers to activities involving the protection, conservation, and restoration of the environment. These activities may be initiated under disaster assistance or undertaken under separate authority. Generally, the force of choice in the first instance for domestic support operations is the National Guard* in a nonfederal status. Active-component forces are usually called only when the National Guard cannot handle a situation.

Reference. U.S. Department of Defense, Joint Pub 3–57, *Doctrine for Joint Civil Affairs*, 1995.

John T. Fishel

DONIPHAN, ALEXANDER WILLIAM (1808–1887)

Born in Maysfield, Kentucky, in 1808, Alexander William Doniphan graduated from Augusta College and established a law practice in Missouri, where he soon acquired a reputation as one of the best trial lawyers in the state. Doniphan's reputation as a man of conviction and integrity increased when, leading a Missouri militia unit in response to a threat by members of the Church of Jesus Christ of Latter-day Saints, he refused the governor's order to execute a number of Mormon leaders, including Joseph Smith.

When the United States declared war against Mexico, Doniphan was appointed colonel to command the 1st Missouri Volunteers. After organizing and training at Fort Leavenworth,* the regiment* accompanied Stephen Kearny's expedition to Mexico. Doniphan's march down the Santa Fe Trail was a remarkable feat, covering over 2,000 miles in nearly six months. The irregular volunteers were accustomed to voting on their courses of actions; in the words of a British observer, it was a unit in which "the most total want of discipline was apparent in everything."

Shortly after leaving Santa Fe, Doniphan's command confronted a force of Mexican lancers near El Brazito. The Missourians routed the lancers, killing over a hundred while losing only one militiaman. Doniphan then proceeded to El Paso, where he learned that a Mexican force was assembling at Chihuahua. Passing through the barren deserts of southern New Mexico, including a three-day trek across the infamous *Jornado del Muerto*, Doniphan's 1,500 men marched on Chihuahua against a Mexican force of nearly 3,000 men with nineteen guns under General Garcia Conde. On 28 February 1847, Doniphan skirted the left of the Mexican position and smashed into its flank. Doniphan's stunning defeat of the superior enemy force cost over 300 Mexican lives and all the Mexican artillery but only two Missouri militiamen. Doniphan occupied Chihuahua on 1 March.

By the time the Missourians made their way back to Fort Leavenworth, they had marched over 6,000 miles and won, outnumbered, two major battles—all under the leadership of a ragged, red-haired giant of a trial lawyer who pitched his own tent and cooked his own meals. Upon his return to Missouri, Doniphan was lauded by many as "the Missouri Xenophon." He died at his home in Liberty, Missouri, in 1887.

References. John S. D. Eisenhower, *So Far from God*, 1989. John T. Hughes, *Doniphan's Expedition*, 1962. Roger D. Launius, *Alexander William Doniphan*, 1997.

Fred J. Chiaventone

DONOVAN, WILLIAM J. (1883–1959)

Colonel William J. Donovan, a World War I* Medal of Honor* winner, was sent by President Franklin D. Roosevelt in 1940 on several low-key fact-finding tours. The most important of these tours was to Berlin, to assess the ability of the British to resist the expected German invasion. Donovan accurately predicted British resolution in the coming battle. He also pointed out the need for a centralized office for the collection and processing of foreign intelligence and that potential U.S. involvement in the war required an agency to plan or conduct special operations, such as unconventional warfare, counterintelligence, psychological operations, propaganda, sabotage, subversion, and espionage. In July 1941 Roosevelt authorized the establishment of the Office of the Coordinator of Information (COI) and appointed Donovan to the post. Although holding the rank of colonel (later brigadier general), he did not answer to the military chain of command. He quickly built up his office to include branches on research and analysis, economic intelligence, special information, domestic morale, and a supplementary activities branch for refugee interrogations, communications, and "projects." Not content with adhering to a strict intelligence-collection role, Donovan began adding sections on special operations, sabotage, subversion, propaganda, and even commando operations. He dispatched subordinates to Britain to learn about such operations from the British Special Operations Executive (SOE). Before the U.S. entered World War II,* Donovan had laid the basis for an active strategy of taking unconventional war to the enemy. During the war, he supervised the multifarious activities of the Office of Strategic Services* (OSS) in virtually every theater of war. He served as the only director of the OSS until its abolition in October 1945.

References. Anthony Cave Brown, *The Last Hero*, 1982. Richard Dunlop, *Donovan*, 1982.

Richard Stewart

DOOLITTLE BOARD

In 1946, the secretary of war* asked retired General James Doolittle, former World War II* Air Corps* leader and commander of the Tokyo Raid, to head a commission on officer-enlisted relationships. Doolittle later attributed the necessity for the board to the long and costly world war, claiming that the public was fed up with the military and the strict discipline associated with it. Popularly known as the "GI Gripes Board," the Doolittle Board looked into complaints and alleged incidents of abuse and ill treatment of enlisted men at the hands of officers. The Board's recommendations provided for a transition to a peacetime Army the public could live with, and they were generally adopted, even though many old-line officers predicted they would lead to an ill-disciplined and second-rate Army.

References. James H. Doolittle, with Carroll V. Glines, *I Could Never Be So Lucky Again*, 1991. Quentin Reynolds, *The Amazing Mr. Doolittle*, 1953.

Thomas Christianson

DOUGHBOY

U.S. infantrymen during World War I* were called "doughboys." The origins of the term remain clouded in obscurity, but one of the more plausible explanations is that the term evolved during the Civil War,* when it referred to the large, globular brass buttons on infantry* uniforms,* and to the boys who wore them. A second explanation traces the origin of the term as far back as 1854, when infantrymen wore white belts and cleaned them with "dough" made of clay. A third possible theory claims that U.S. soldiers operating around the Mexican border during the Punitive Expedition* would become covered in "adobe" dust. The soldiers began to be called "adobes," which was shortened to "doughies," then to "doughboys."

References. Connell Albertine, *The Yankee Doughboy*, 1968. Laurence Stallings, *The Doughboys*, 1963.

Edward L. Maier III

D-RATION

Field Ration D, commonly known as the D-Ration, replaced the emergency or iron rations that the U.S. Army had used since before World War I.* Like the emergency ration, the D-ration was a stop-gap ration bar based on the high energy of fortified chocolate. Developed from 1934 to 1936 under the direction of Captain Paul D. Logan, the D-ration, initially called the Logan Bar, was like its predecessor designed to provide nutrition during limited periods of combat. When the Army tested the first production run in 1937, it found the bars— intentionally designed to be unpalatable to preclude troops from using them as snacks—to be so bad that no one could eat them. Modifications to the recipe the next year rendered the bars edible. Large-scale production began in 1940, and D-rations were issued throughout World War II.* The complete D-ration, three 4-ounce fortified chocolate bars in a cardboard and cellophane package, contained 1,800 calories.

Reference. Erna Risch, *The Quartermaster Corps: Organization, Supply, and Services*, vol. 1, 1953.

Stephen C. McGeorge

DRAGOON

Throughout late 1943 and the first half of 1944, the Allies debated the necessity of landing troops in southern France; the United States advocated such landings, the British opposed them. Nevertheless, planning for an amphibious operation in southern France proceeded, with the landings to occur just before or just after Overlord.* Originally code named Anvil,* the highly controversial landings had security problems that caused Allied planners to change the code name to Dragoon shortly before the actual landings, which took place on 15 August 1944. By this time, however, the Allies had broken out of the Normandy lodgement area and were pursuing the defeated German forces across northern France. General Jacob L. Devers's 6th Army Group quickly routed German resistance in the south and linked up with 12th Army Group for the final assault on Germany.

In an attempt to avoid confusion, historians have often used terms Anvil and Dragoon interchangably. To some degree, however, this attempt has created confusion for the casual student of World War II.*

References. William B. Breuer, *Operation Dragoon*, 1987. Jeffrey J. Clarke and Robert Ross Smith, *Riviera to the Rhine*, 1993.

Don Denmark

DROP ZONE

A drop zone (DZ) is an area designated for landing airborne troops or delivering supplies by parachute from aircraft. In combat operations, Army pathfinder* teams or Air Force combat control teams precede the main units into the DZ to reconnoiter and mark it with visual and electronic signal devices. A drop zone is normally rectangular in shape, with the long axis oriented to the flight path of approaching aircraft. It varies in size depending on the size of the unit or type of air drop.

Reference. Nancy Harrington and Edward Doucette, "Army after Next and Precision Airdrop," *Army Logistician*, January–February 1999, 46–49.

DUCK. *See* DUKW.

DUKW

Universally known as the DUCK, the DUKW was a 6×6, wheeled, 2½-ton amphibious truck used in World War II,* produced by General Motors Corporation. "DUKW" was a acronym of the GMC model-code letters. The vehicle used components of the GMC 2½-ton truck (deuce and a half*) and was initially intended to be a light, wheeled cargo vehicle that could ferry supplies from ships anchored off shore to the beach and then continue across the beach to delivery locations. A GMC 269.5-cubic-inch, in-line, overhead valve, six-cylinder engine powered the DUKW, and a five-speed manual transmission gave it a maximum land speed of fifty miles per hour. A twenty-five-inch-diameter propeller, driven by the three lower gears, provided amphibious mobility, giving the DUKW a maximum water speed of 6.4 miles per hour. A permanent rudder provided steering in the water. The first DUKW operations occurred in the Pacific in March 1943; use in the European Theater of Operations* (ETO) followed.

References. Thomas Berndt, *Standard Catalog of U.S. Military Vehicles, 1940–1965*, 1993. Joseph Bykofsky and Harold Larson, *The Transportation Corps*, 1957. Fred W. Crismon, *U.S. Military Wheeled Vehicles*, 1983.

John Edgecomb

DUSTER M-42

The M-42 Duster antiaircraft system was the standard U.S. Army motorized antiaircraft platform from the mid-1950s through the 1960s. Based on the M-41 tank chassis, the Duster was armed with two 40 mm Bofors guns mounted in an open turret at the center of the vehicle. The guns had a maximum range of six kilometers, were aimed using conventional optical sights, and had a rate of fire of 240 rounds per minute (480 rounds of ammunition carried in the vehicle). While never actually used in combat for aircraft defense, Dusters served in the Vietnam War* in a variety of roles. Their mobility and firepower were great assets in base perimeter defense and convoy-escort missions. Withdrawn from active service during the 1970s, Dusters continued to serve in Reserve and National Guard* units into the early 1980s.

References. Edward B. Atkeson, "New Life for Duster," *Army*, August 1963, 45–46. Tom Gervasi, *America's War Machine*, 1984.

Benjamin H. Kristy

E

EASTERTIDE OFFENSIVE

One of the bloodiest military operations of the Vietnam War,* the Eastertide Offensive began on 30 March 1972, when North Vietnam invaded South Vietnam with twelve divisions. North Vietnamese Army (NVA) objectives were the provincial capitals of Quang Tri in the north, Kontum in the Central Highlands, and An Loc in the south. After reorganizing its army along conventional lines in late 1971, North Vietnam had decided that the combination of the U.S. withdrawal and presidential election in 1972 and unpreparedness of the Army of the Republic of Vietnam (ARVN) to defend the nation itself indicated that a major NVA conventional invasion could topple the South Vietnamese government in 1972. Following initial NVA success in the north, however, ARVN defenses, heavily supported by massive U.S. firepower and logistics, defeated the NVA forces in detail, from the initial attack through Quang Tri's recapture on 17 September. The NVA lost about half of its committed tanks and artillery, along with nearly 100,000 troops. ARVN losses totaled approximately 50,000. Less than three years later, after first ensuring that U.S. firepower and logistical support would be minimal, the NVA was victorious with another conventional invasion, this time concentrating on dividing South Vietnam by capturing the Central Highlands.

References. Ngo Quang Truong, *The Easter Offensive of 1972*, 1980. Gerald H. Turley, *The Easter Offensive*, 1985.

John R. Finch

EDGEWOOD ARSENAL

Located on the Maryland shore of Chesapeake Bay, with the Susquehanna River to the north and the Gunpowder River to the south, Edgewood Arsenal was established by presidential proclamation in 1917 as a research and testing facility for ammunition, arms, general equipment, and vehicles for the U.S.

Army. General Order No. 6 made the post permanent in 1919. It was subsequently divided into two areas: Aberdeen Proving Ground* to the north of the Bush River, and Edgewood Arsenal to the south. The Arsenal was reorganized and expanded during World War II.* The expansion included the creation of the Ordnance Research and Development Center (ORDC) and the construction of ENIAC, the world's first electronic computer. In an effort to remain on top of research and testing, Aberdeen and Edgewood merged in 1971 into a single installation. During the recent base closings, Edgewood Arsenal fell to the budget ax, thus ending eighty years service as a U.S. Army facility.

References. "Fifty-Year-Old Edgewood Arsenal Develops New Equipment." *Ordnance*, July–August 1968, 30. "Forty-nine Years for Edgewood Arsenal," *Ordnance*, July–August 1967, 90.

Trevor Brown

EICHELBERGER, ROBERT LAWRENCE (1886–1961)

Robert Lawrence Eichelberger, born in Urbana, Ohio, on 9 March 1886, graduated from the U.S. Military Academy* in 1909 and was assigned to the 10th Infantry Regiment at Fort Benjamin Harrison,* Indiana. He served with the 10th during the Punitive Expedition* in Mexico and later in Panama. During World War I,* Eichelberger served on the staff of the 8th Division, which was sent to Siberia, not Europe. Feeling that his career was at a standstill, Eichelberger transferred from the infantry* to the Adjutant General's Corps* in 1924. Over the next sixteen years, he attended the Command and General Staff* School at Fort Leavenworth* and the Army War College.* He held a number of staff positions, including adjutant general and secretary of the Academic Board at the Military Academy, and secretary, General Staff, under the Chief of Staff* of the Army. In October 1940 Eichelberger became the Academy's superintendent. In January 1942, as a major general, he took command of the 77th Infantry Division. Seven months later, Eichelberger and his staff sailed for Australia. From 1942 to 1944, he commanded I Corps, participating in the New Guinea* and New Britain campaigns and the reconquest of the Philippines. From 1944 to 1948 he commanded the Eighth Army* and the Allied and U.S. Ground Forces, Japan. He retired as a lieutenant general on 31 December 1948 but returned to government service in 1950 as an advisor to the under secretary of the army, providing advice and counsel during the early stages of the Korean War.* Retiring again in 1951, Eichelberger lived in Ashville, North Carolina, until his death on 27 September 1961.

References. Paul Chwialkowski, *In Caesar's Shadow*, 1993. John F. Shortal, *Forged by Fire*, 1987.

John Edgecomb

EIGHTH ARMY

The Eighth Army was the principal U.S. ground force in Asia at the opening of the Korean War* in June 1950. Commanded by Lieutenant General Walton

Walker, it consisted of the 2d, 24th and 35th Infantry Divisions and the 1st Cavalry Division. Before June 1950 the Eighth was, in many ways, an army in name only: understrength, equipped with aging World War II* material, its men soft from easy occupation duty. The disaster that befell Task Force Smith,* the initial U.S. ground unit to clash with the North Korean invaders, pointed out the deficiencies of the Eighth Army, as did the dispiriting retreat to the Pusan Perimeter* in the summer of 1950 despite complete U.S. air control and even, eventually, UN numerical superiority. After some success following the Inchon* landings in September, the Eighth once again found itself in full retreat to below the 38th parallel, although this retreat never degenerated into a rout. A new Eighth Army commander, Lieutenant General Matthew B. Ridgway,* brought new and aggressive leadership to the force and in early 1951 Eighth Army began a careful offensive that took it back to the 38th parallel and recaptured Seoul a second time. Soon thereafter, Ridgway took steps to integrate racially the Eighth Army, a move followed by the rest of the U.S. Army. By the summer of 1951, the battle lines had hardened into a "fighting while negotiating" stalemate. Under Ridgway's successors, Lieutenant Generals James Van Fleet* and Maxwell Taylor,* the Eighth Army held up well, repelling enemy offensives and mounting its own thrusts, until an armistice was signed on 27 July 1953.

References. S.L.A. Marshall, *The River and the Gauntlet*, 1953. G. S. Meloy, Jr., "The Eighth Army Story," *Army Information Digest*, June 1963, 3–13.

Stanley Sandler

82D AIRBORNE DIVISION

The 82d Airborne Division today is the U.S. Army's premier response force for contingency operations. Stationed at Fort Bragg,* North Carolina, the division* consists of three airborne infantry* brigades,* three artillery* battalions,* and various supporting battalions of engineers, air defense artillery,* aviation,* air cavalry,* and logistical support. Formed on 25 August 1917 as part of the American Expeditionary Force* (AEF), the 82d remains prepared to deploy with air force support to any crisis area in the world. The 82d's nickname, the "All American" division, derived from the fact that its original members hailed from all forty-eight states. In 1918, the division distinguished itself in two major campaigns and boasted the nation's most famous soldier, Medal of Honor* winner Alvin York.* The 82d was deactivated in 1919.

On 25 March 1942, the 82d was reactivated for World War II* and became the U.S. Army's first airborne division. It participated in the Sicily, Salerno, Anzio,* Normandy,* Holland, Ardennes,* and Germany campaigns. After the war, the 82d moved to Fort Bragg, where it became part of the U.S. strategic reserve and participated in the Vietnam War,* Power Pack,* Urgent Fury,* Just Cause,* and Desert Storm.*

References. Forrest W. Dawson, comp. and ed., *Saga of the All Americans*, 1946. John K. Mahon and Romana Danysh, *Infantry*, 1972. Leroy Thompson, *The All Americans*, 1988.

Douglas P. Scalard

EISENHOWER, DWIGHT DAVID (1890–1969)

Dwight David Eisenhower was born in Denison, Texas, in October 1890. His family moved to Abilene, Kansas, when he was a few months old. A quiet young man who exuded a sense of dignity and warmth, Eisenhower entered the U.S. Military Academy* in 1911 and was commissioned in the infantry* upon graduation in 1915. Eisenhower, or "Ike," as he was called, had an unremarkable career prior to World War II.* Forced to sit out World War I* in secondary staff roles, he seemed to rotate from one "soft" staff assignment to the next. While Eisenhower did not impress his superiors with battlefield acumen, superiors and peers took note of his quite efficiency and his exceptional ability to forge teams oriented toward a common goal.

When World War II erupted in Europe, the U.S. Army responded to the looming challenge. First assigned as the chief of staff* of the Third Division, Eisenhower quickly assumed a rapid succession of increasingly more responsible positions, which culminated in his selection as Supreme Allied Commander. This selection was not based on any demonstrated excellence in the act of war; it was a reflection of his ability to mediate the nonstop disputes fueled by the egos of wartime Allied commanders on both sides of the Atlantic. Historians give Ike ample credit for his strategic vision, as well as his ability to visualize prolonged campaigns.

Eisenhower retired from the U.S. Army in July 1952 to launch his campaign for the presidency. Swept into office by residual wartime adulation, he began a series of diplomatic efforts that reflected his belief that wars should be fought on the "political and economic" fields of battle. Reelected in 1956, Eisenhower became a strong supporter of civil rights and emerging democracies. Following a series of heart attacks, Eisenhower died at Walter Reed Army Medical Center* on 28 March 1969.

References. Stephen E. Ambrose, *Eisenhower*, 2 vols., 1983–84. Robert F. Burk, *Dwight D. Eisenhower*, 1986. Blanche Wiesen Cook, *The Declassified Eisenhower*, 1981. Dwight D. Eisenhower, *At Ease*, 1967. Martin J. Medhurst, *Dwight D. Eisenhower*, 1993.

Don Denmark

ELECTRIC STRAWBERRY. *See* Tropic Lightning.

ENGINEER SCHOOL OF APPLICATION

In the summer of 1865, the U.S. Army established an engineer post at Willets Point, later Fort Totten, New York. At the suggestion of the chief of engineers, Brigadier General Andrew A. Humphreys, the Engineer School of Application was created in 1866. The status of the school was informal until 1885, when the War Department* officially recognized it. Instruction at the school for both enlisted men and officers included practical training in mapping, astronomy, photography, submarine mines, and pontoon and permanent bridge construction. In 1879 an astronomical observatory was added to the other facilities. The school also served as a laboratory, where the staff conducted experiments and developed new equipment. In 1890 the name was changed to United States Engineer School, but it once again became the Engineer School of Application, United States Army in 1900, a year before the school moved to Washington Barracks (later renamed Fort McNair).* In 1903, a shortage of engineer officers forced classes to be suspended; they did not resume until early 1906. In 1919 the school moved to Fort Belvoir, where it remained until 1989. Today, the Engineer School is located at Fort Leonard Wood,* Missouri.

References. Henry L. Abbot, *Early Days of the Engineer School of Application*, 1904. David M. Dunne, "The Engineer School: Past and Present," *Military Engineer*, November–December 1949, 411–416. United States Army, Corps of Engineers, *The History of the US Army Corps of Engineers* [1986].

ENTRENCHING TOOL

Entrenching tools—commonly called "E-tools"—have been used in one form or another throughout the ages to dig field fortifications. Until the end of the Civil War,* U.S. soldiers relied on traditional civilian digging tools—shovels, axes, and picks—and their bayonets* to construct field fortifications. In 1875, the Army Board adopted a trowel bayonet, a combination bayonet and entrenching tool. Although ill received, the trowel bayonet confirmed the need for a dedicated, individual entrenching tool. Until the turn of the century, the U.S. Army sporadically issued the trowel bayonet and the Hagner entrenching tool (a small, garden-spade–variety tool) to each soldier. In 1910, the Army adopted the larger T-handle shovel for individual use. It was modified to a folding shovel during World War II* and to a trifold, aircraft-aluminum shovel following the Vietnam War.* Today, the E-tool is an issue item to every soldier, providing basic protection on the battlefield.

References. Stephen J. Allie, *All He Could Carry*, 1991. Robert W. Fisch, *Field Equipment of the Infantry, 1914–1915*, 1989. Douglas C. McChristian, *The U.S. Army in the West, 1870–1880*, 1995.

Robert J. Dalessandro

EUROPEAN THEATER OF OPERATIONS

In June 1942, General George C. Marshall* announced the establishment of the European theater of operations of the U.S. Army (ETOUSA). Based on the principle of unity of command within a specific geographical area, the ETOUSA was to be a joint command of all U.S. Army and Navy forces assigned to the theater. The boundaries of the European Theater of Operations (ETO) began at 15° west, 70° north, moved south along 15° west, angled west to include Iceland, then south to 43° 45' West, then due east just north of Spain to take in all of the United Kingdom, France, Germany, the low countries, the Baltic states, Czechoslovakia, and Poland; it then moved north along the Polish-Soviet border, to include Finland, Norway, and Sweden. After March 1945, the southern boundary was extended to include Spain and Portugal. The Commanding General, ETOUSA, was responsible for planning and operational control of all U.S. forces in the theater. He was directed to cooperate with British and other allied

162   EXECUTIVE OFFICER

leaders but was to proceed on the principle that U.S. forces "are to be maintained
as a separate and distinct component of the combined forces." Dwight D. Eisenhower* was named first commander of the ETO.
   References. Franklin M. Davis, Jr., *Come as a Conqueror*, 1967. W. Victor Madej,
ed., *U.S. Army Order of Battle*, vol. 1, 1983. Maurice Matloff and Edwin M. Snell,
Strategic Planning for Coalition Warfare 1941–1942, 1953.

                                                                          Trevor Brown

EXECUTIVE OFFICER

   An executive officer (XO) is normally the second in command in battalion,*
brigade,* and company*-level units throughout the Army. The XO carries out
duties analogous to those of the deputy commander and the chief of staff* in
higher-level units. He or she serves as the principal assistant to the commanding
officer,* directs and supervises the unit staff section, and speaks for the commander in his or her absence. The XO may also be assigned additional duties:
for example, the XO frequently serves as the unit material readiness officer and
conducts special courts-martial. At the company level, the XO is normally the
senior lieutenant; at the battalion level he is a major, at the brigade level a
lieutenant colonel. A tour as executive officer is generally considered essential
for selection to battalion and brigade command.
   References. Lawrence P. Crocker, *Army Officer's Guide*, 46th ed., 1993. George E.
Keenan and Paul R. Reed, "Do We Need an Exec?" *Infantry*, July–August 1962, 34–35.

EXECUTIVE ORDER 9981

   On 26 July 1948, President Harry S Truman signed Executive Order 9981.
It called for "equality of treatment and opportunity for persons in the armed
services without regard to race, color, religion, or national origin," and it set up
the President's Committee on Equality of Treatment and Opportunity in the
Armed Services to oversee the process of ending discrimination in the military.
Executive Order 9981 did not call for the end of segregation as such, but that
was the ultimate effect. The President's Committee struggled with the Army
leadership until 1950 to convince it that under segregation, minorities had limited chances to go to specialist schools, because their separate units had no
requirements for 198 of the 490 Army Military Occupational Specialties*
(MOS). Eventually the Army conceded and formally issued a new policy statement, Special Regulation 600–629–1, "Utilization of Negro Manpower in the
Army," on 6 January 1950. It ordered minorities with special skills to be "assigned to any . . . unit without regard for race or color."
   References. Richard M. Dalfiume, *Desegregation of the U.S. Armed Forces*, 1969.
Morris J. MacGregor, Jr., *Integration of the Armed Forces, 1940–1965*, 1981.

                                                                          Luke Knowley

EXPERT FIELD MEDICAL BADGE

   The Expert Field Medical Badge, previously called the Medical Badge, is
awarded to medical personnel who pass the required technical tests and physical

challenges. Once or twice each year, posts and larger units with medical personnel host Expert Field Medical Badge competitions, which include field first aid, litter carrying, and other field skills. As with the Expert Infantryman's Badge* (EIB), relatively few military personnel earn the Expert Field Medical Badge. It is the highest peacetime qualification badge that a medical professional can earn.

References. Evans E. Kerrigan, *American Badges and Insignia*, 1967. Ruth J. Spaller, "Earning the Badge," *Soldiers*, June 1994, 42–43.

Jim Martin

EXPERT INFANTRYMAN'S BADGE

The Expert Infantryman's Badge (EIB) is awarded to enlisted members with a military occupational specialty* (MOS) of infantryman and officers assigned to the infantry* branch who have demonstrated a high proficiency in weapons marksmanship, infantry skill and knowledge, and physical fitness. Lieutenant General Lesley J. McNair,* then commanding general of Army Ground Forces,* established the EIB in October 1943 to foster and acknowledge greater levels of achievement in combat preparation. The badge shows a pattern 1816 flintlock musket enclosed in a three-inch-wide blue-enamel rectangle edged in silver. It is worn on both fatigue and dress uniforms on the left breast above the ribbon bar.

References: Bruce N. Bant, "EIB," *Soldiers*, July 1978, 28–31. Harry Inker, "Improved EIB," *Infantry*, March–April 1985, 15–17.

Kelvin Crow

F

F TROOP

F Troop was a farcical television series involving a troop of incompetent cavalrymen and a tribe of peaceful but capitalistic Indians. In the opening episode, we learn that Captain Wilton Parmenter—played by Ken Berry—had been mistakenly promoted for leading a decisive and victorious charge during the Civil War.* In fact, Parmenter's horse had bolted toward enemy lines as a result of a bee sting. Decorated with a Silver Star* (which was in fact not created until World War II*), Parmenter was assigned to Fort Courage, where he met Sergeant Morgan Sylvester O'Rourk (Forrest Tucker—a veteran of the U.S. horse cavalry* in World War II) and Corporal Randolph Agarn (Larry Storch). This trio is interested solely in making money. O'Rourk Enterprises involves selling souvenirs made by the Heckawi (as in, "Where the heck are we?") Indians. Many episodes involved the plot device of trying to make the peaceful Heckawi look warlike in order to keep Fort Courage from being closed. Frank Dekova played Chief Wild Eagle until his death after the first season, and Edward Everett Horton played Medicine Man Roaring Chicken. The series has often been compared to another noted series based on an Army theme, the *Phil Silvers Show*, with its main character Sergeant Bilko.*

References. Erik Barnouw, *Tube of Plenty*, 1975. Alex McNeil, *Total Television*, 4th ed., 1996.

Rod Cooley

FAIR OAKS. *See* Seven Pines.

FALAISE GAP

After Third Army* broke out at the base of the Cherbourg Peninsula on 31 July 1944, Hitler decided to counterattack at Mortain* to isolate the U.S. Army in Brittany. Field Marshal Guenther von Kluge's Army Group B attacked on 6

August, but the Allies, with air superiority, quickly halted the German westward thrust. The offensive weakened the German position in the north along the British-Canadian front as the right wing of the westward-moving U.S. Army turned northward. The Allied encirclement created a large pocket, trapping most of the German army before it could retire. The Allies, however, failed to complete the encirclement, and the Twelfth SS Hitler Youth Division held a supply route open from 14 to 19 August. On 19 August, the Allies sealed the fifteen-mile-wide gap near Falaise, through which nearly 35,000 Germans had escaped. Although the Germans left behind most of their heavy equipment, 50,000 prisoners, and 10,000 killed, at the Falaise Gap, the Germans denied the Allies the decisive victory they sought.

References. Martin Blumenson, *The Battle of the Generals*, 1993. William B. Breuer, *Death of a Nazi Army*, 1985. Eddy Florentin, *The Battle of the Falaise Gap*, 1967.

James L. Isemann

FALL OF THE PHILIPPINES. *See* Philippines, Fall of.

FALLEN TIMBERS

In keeping with traditional fears of a standing army, following the American Revolution* Congress all but disbanded the Continental Army.* Congress soon realized, however, that a continuing threat from hostile Indian tribes on the frontiers required a response beyond the rudimentary capabilities of the militia. In October 1790, the Miami Indians launched a series of raids against white settlers in the Northwest Territory (present-day Ohio and Indiana). A punitive expedition of 320 Regulars and 813 militiamen under Josiah Harmar, general in chief of the Army, proved unsuccessful; the Indians routed the militia and decimated the Regulars. A second expedition under Arthur St. Clair, governor of the Northwest Territory, with fifteen hundred militia and six hundred Regulars, was even more disastrous. On 4 November 1791, the hostiles, led by Little Turtle, surprised St. Clair's force on the banks of the Wabash and destroyed it. The victorious Indians butchered over 637 soldiers, including nearly the entire infantry* strength of the Regular Army.

Responding to the emergency, in June 1792 Congress authorized the formation of the Legion of the United States, to consist of eight infantry battalions,* four rifle battalions, four companies of dragoons, and one battery* of artillery.* General Anthony Wayne, commander of the Pennsylvania Line during the American Revolution, was called out of retirement to command the new organization. Wayne spent most of 1793 training and equipping this force and bringing it to peak readiness: in August 1794, he moved against the hostiles. On 20 August, the Legion caught the main force outside of Fort Miami, an illegal British garrison near present-day Toledo, Ohio. The Miami had taken up defensive positions in a densely wooded area characterized by a tangle of blown-down trees (hence the name Fallen Timbers). With his cavalry* deployed along the flanks, Wayne's Regulars launched a fierce bayonet* charge at the enemy's center, driving the Indians into open grasslands, where the cavalry cut them down. The Legion went on to destroy the Miami stronghold and surrounding villages, breaking their resistance. The subsequent Treaty of Greenville, signed on 3 August 1795, ended the war and ceded all Miami lands in the Ohio Valley to the U.S. government.

References. Harrison Bird, *War for the West, 1790–1813*, 1971. Fairfax Downey, *Indian Wars of the U.S. Army, 1776–1865*, 1963. Richard Raymond III, "St. Clair's Defeat," *Army*, December 1983, 62–65.

Fred J. Chiaventone

FATIGUES

Throughout most of its history, soldiers in the U.S. Army were attired in the same uniform* for dress, fatigue duties, and combat. The first fatigue, or specifically working uniform, was the sack coat, issued to soldiers in all branches of the Union Army during the Civil War.* Loosely fitted and manufactured in only four sizes, the sack coat was made of stout wool, either lined or unlined; it replaced the dress frock coat for all but formal occasions. Following the Civil War, however, the Army reverted to an all-purpose uniform. Beginning in the early 1900s, Army regulations prescribed work or fatigue clothing of blue and brown denim, but it was reserved for soldiers in particularly dirty rear-echelon organizations, stevedores, construction engineers, and other noncombat service personnel.

Blue denim fatigues remained the standard fatigues until 1940, when the Army developed fatigue or utility clothing of virtually identical patterns, constructed of green herringbone twill cotton material. In 1941, the Army introduced the "field jacket," based on a civilian windbreaker design, to replace the dress blouse on field duty and in combat. In 1943, additional items were added to the fatigue uniform, including matching field trousers, a sweater, and the "Ike jacket" (seldom worn in combat). From the 1950s through the early 1980s, the Army wore fatigues in garrison and in the field, attempting to make the fatigue uniform serve double duty by requiring the fatigue or work uniform to be heavily starched and creased. The camouflaged "battle dress uniform" (BDU), following the model of the Vietnam-era jungle fatigues (themselves patterned after the 1942 parachutist uniform), replaced the standard green fatigue uniform, beginning in 1982.

References. Griffin N. Dodge, "When New Fatigues Come In, Can #10 Cans Be Far Behind?" *Army*, September 1983, 44–49. Lana Ott, "Spit & Polish," *Soldiers*, May 1980, 6–9.

Stephen C. McGeorge

FETTERMAN MASSACRE

In November 1866, Captain William J. Fetterman arrived at Fort Phil Kearny,* one of three forts established the previous summer to provide security along the Bozeman Trail.* Frustrated and angry at what he perceived as a lack of aggressiveness in dealing with hostile Indians on the part of Colonel Henry B. Carrington, the fort's commander, Fetterman boasted that given eighty men he could ride through the entire Sioux nation. On the morning of 21 December, when a party of Indians attacked the wood train a few miles from the fort, Fetterman requested command of the relief force. With forty-nine infantrymen armed with 1862 Springfield muskets (muzzle-loaders), twenty-seven cavalry-men armed with Sharps carbines,* two officers, and two volunteer civilian buffalo hunters—a total of eighty men—Fetterman left the fort. Despite Carrington's repeated warnings not to engage in offensive action and not to venture beyond Lodge Trail Ridge, Fetterman saw his chance to end the hostile raids once and for all. The attack on the wood train, however, had been a ruse to lure the relief force beyond the range of the fort's artillery—a ploy Red Cloud, the Indian leader, had unsuccessfully tried earlier in the month. When Fetterman pursued the decoys across Lodge Trail Ridge, a force of approximately a thousand warriors sprang an ambush on what is today known as Massacre Ridge.

Since there were no white survivors, the course of the battle is open to conjecture. Evidence suggests that there were two separate fights: one with the slow-firing infantrymen, who died several hundred yards behind the cavalry, and the second with the mounted troops, who held their ground until infiltration by small groups of warriors sealed their fates. Until the Battle of the Little Bighorn ten years later, this was the most significant Indian victory in the Indian Wars* on the Great Plains.

References. Cyrus Townsend Brady, *Indian Fights and Fighters*, 1971. Dee Brown, *The Fetterman Massacre*, 1971.

Tamas Dreilinger

FIELD ARMY

The U.S. Army employed named or numbered field armies from the Mexican War* through World War II.* Commanded by a full general, field armies were composed of two or more corps,* with associated support units to enable them to sustain combat operations indefinitely. Although field armies existed in the Army's organizational plans after World War II, in 1972, with the primary focus on Europe and NATO,* the U.S. Army dropped field armies as a command echelon.

References. Karl R. Bendetsen, "A Plan for Army Reorganization," *Military Review*, January 1954, 39–60. Lewis I. Jeffries, "A Blueprint for Force Design," *Military Review*, August 1991, 20–31.

Andrew N. Morris

FIELD ARTILLERY

A congressional act of 25 January 1907 established field artillery as an independent branch of the U.S. Army, separate from coast artillery,* and authorized the War Department* to form six regiments* of artillery, with two battalions* per regiment. Until 1907, batteries* were the largest artillery units, and artillerymen were rotated among field and coast artillery regardless of individual expertise. The 1907 act also allowed the War Department to improve training, specialization, and assignment of personnel. Subsequently, from one to three artillery regiments were assigned to each division until World War I,* when the organization stabilized at a Field Artillery brigade of three regiments per division.*

The School of Fire at Fort Sill had been closed after six years of mixed results in 1916, but the need for trained personnel prompted the War Department to reopen it in 1917 and to establish the office of Chief of Field Artillery in 1918. Major General William J. Snow, the first Chief of Field Artillery, centralized all training and equipping of field artillery at replacement depots, established brigade firing centers and schools of instruction for specialists and mechanics, and personally supervised the School of Fire. Training centers were also established in France to complete field artillery training.

After World War I,* the School of Fire and its successor, the Field Artillery School, contributed significantly to the development of new field artillery weapons, organization, motorization, mechanization, and the fire direction center* (FDC). The success of these developments proved invaluable in World War II,* when a forward observer* could mass the firepower of an entire corps.* Nevertheless, the Field Artillery School continued to improve artillery support techniques throughout World War II.

As part of the Army's restructuring after World War II, the Army Organization Act of 1950* merged the field artillery and coast artillery (which included antiaircraft artillery) into a single artillery branch. The new branch focused on the development of guided missiles, free-flight rockets, and atomic warheads for its weapons. Organizationally, it sought to economize, until the late 1950s, when it finally had to begin developing and fielding new equipment to replace its aging guns. The Vietnam War* highlighted the problems associated with consolidating field and coast artillery. Responding to the Artillery Branch Study of 1966, in 1968 the Army once again separated the artillery, this time into field artillery and air defense artillery.* Over the past three decades, the field artillery has pioneered developments in automation, precision guided munitions, improved warheads, and more effective weapons and organizations. Today, the field artillery branch encompasses U.S. Army tube-artillery systems, surface-to-surface missile systems, free-flight rocket systems, and, until recently, tube-delivered tactical nuclear weapons. The branch is managed by a major general with a headquarters and the Field Artillery School at Fort Sill,* Oklahoma.

References. Boyd L. Dastrup, *King of Battle*, 1992, and *The Field Artillery*, 1994. Bruce I. Gudmundsson, *On Artillery*, 1993.

Jeffrey S. Shadburn

FIELD ARTILLERY

Field Artillery: A Professional Bulletin for Redlegs, is currently a bimonthly professional bulletin published by Headquarters, Department of the Army* un-

der the auspices of the U.S. Army Field Artillery Center at Fort Sill,*
Oklahoma. First published as *Artillery Journal* in 1911, then as *Field Artillery
Journal* until 1987, *Field Artillery* is similar in purpose and intent to other
branch journals, such as *Infantry Journal*, published at the Infantry School at
Fort Benning,* Georgia, and *Armor*, published at the Armor Center at Fort
Knox,* Kentucky. Its stated purpose is to "publish a journal for disseminating
professional knowledge and furnishing information as to the field artillery's*
progress, development and best use in campaign; to cultivate, with the other
arms, a common understanding of the power and limitations of each; to foster
a feeling of interdependence among the different arms and of hearty cooperation by all; and to promote understanding between the Regular and militia
forces by a closer bond; all of which objects are worthy and contribute to the
good of our country." Although it is an official bulletin, the views of the articles
are the authors' and do not necessarily reflect the official positions of the U.S.
Army.

Reference. Michael E. Unsworth, ed., *Military Periodicals*, 1990.

Jerry D. Morelock

FIELD ARTILLERY JOURNAL. *See Field Artillery.*

FIELD COMMISSION. *See* Battlefield Commission.

FIELD MANUAL

A field manual (FM) is an official publication that contains fundamental principles, together with the tactics,* techniques, and procedures, needed to guide
military operations across the spectrum, during peace, conflict, and war. FMs
are organized in a hierarchical table consisting of keystone, capstone, combined-
arms, proponency, employment procedures and training, and reference
publications. The keystone manual describe the conduct of campaigns, major
operations, battles, engagements, and military operations other than war.* FM
100–5, *Operations*, is the Army's keystone manual. Capstone manuals describe
operational principles, while combined-arms publications describe tactics and
techniques for combined-arms operations. Proponency manuals describe principles, tactics, and collective training tasks in greater detail. Training
publications address specific aspects of the individual soldier's duties and the
systems operated in the performance of those duties. The doctrine* contained
in the Army's FMs drives the development of subordinate doctrine, training,
organizational initiatives, material acquisition and development, and leader development.

References. John R. Cameron, "Turf Philosophy Hard on Doctrine Cohesion," *Army*,
August 1982, 20–23. Ben Harrell, "Toward a Total Land Combat System," *Army*, October 1966, 57–61. Thomas E. Johnson, "Reconstitution," *Military Review*, September
1989, 36–47.

Gary Bounds

FIELD OFFICER OF THE DAY

The field officer of the day (FOD) is a commissioned officer of the rank of major or above who is responsible for representing the commander in the commander's absence. During his tour of duty, which is normally a twenty-four-hour period, the FOD is responsible for physical security of the unit or installation and other duties assigned by the commander, depending on local directives. These duties consist of tasks ranging from security checks, posting of guards, and responding to unforeseen circumstances that arise.

Reference. U.S. Army, FM 22–6, *Guard Duty*, 1971.

Kenneth Turner

FIELD SERVICE REGULATIONS

Prior to the 20th century, Army Regulations did not address military formations larger than a regiment.* Although the Army had experienced difficulty in the command and control, training, movement, and sustainment of larger units during the Civil War,* it tended to overlook these problems when it reverted to its normal, small, peacetime size after Appomattox. A recurrence of many of the same problems in the Spanish-American War* prompted Congress to pass a series of reforms, including the creation of the General Staff.* One of the first tasks confronting the new General Staff was the absence of written guidance for higher-level commanders. In 1905, the General Staff published *Field Service Regulations of the United States Army* to ensure the coordination and cooperation of the several combat and supporting arms in the conduct of operations and to develop the teamwork necessary for success on the battlefield. The title *Field Service Regulations* remained in use through the publication of the 1941 edition of FM 100-5. However, it was discarded during World War II.* Today, FM-100-5 is titled simply *Operations*.

References. Robert A. Doughty, *The Evolution of US Army Tactical Doctrine, 1946–76*, 1979. Maurice Matloff, ed., *American Military History*, 1969.

John A. Hixson

FIFTH ARMY

Fifth Army was activated at Oudjda, French Morocco, on 5 January 1943, under the command of Lieutenant General Mark Clark.* Clark commanded Fifth Army until December 1944, when he assumed command of 15th Army Group; he was succeeded at Fifth Army by Major General Lucian Truscott. The first Allied army to land on Hitler's *Festung Europa*, Fifth Army was the most cosmopolitan of Allied forces: in addition to eleven U.S. divisions* that served under it at one time or another, there were also British, New Zealand, Indian, Canadian, South African, French, Brazilian, and Italian divisions. On 9 September 1943, Fifth Army assault units landed at Salerno, commencing the longest continuous campaign of any U.S. field army* in World War II.* After the Allied landings at Normandy on 6 June 1944, the press quickly turned its attention away from the Italian campaign to northern Europe, and many Fifth Army soldiers came to believe that they were fighting in the Forgotten Army. In twenty months of combat, Fifth Army troops fought in some of the most difficult and demanding terrain and weather conditions encountered in World War II and suffered 189,000 casualties, including 31,000 killed in action (19,475 U.S.). In August 1945, Fifth Army began turning over responsibility for the military government of Italy to the Allied Commission. It was deactivated at Camp Myles Standish, Massachusetts, on 2 October 1945.

References. Edmund F. Ball, *Staff Officer with the Fifth Army*, 1958. George Forty, *Fifth Army at War*, 1980. Chester G. Starr, *From Salerno to the Alps*, 1979.

5307TH COMPOSITE UNIT (PROVISIONAL). *See* Merrill's Marauders.

FINANCE CORPS

The Finance Corps is the branch of the Army that specializes in pay and other financial matters. The Finance Corps traces its roots to the Pay Department,* organized on 16 June 1775. The Quartermaster Corps* (QMC) absorbed the Pay Department in the 1912 Army reorganization. World War I* experience, however, indicated a need for a separate pay organization, and the Finance Service was established in 1919. The following year it was renamed the Finance Department and designated a separate branch of the War Department.* In World War II,* the Finance Department, less than one-fifth of 1 percent of Army strength, accomplished the enormous task of paying millions of soldiers worldwide in dozens of regular and special currencies.

The end of the war ushered in an era of change unprecedented in Finance Corps history. In 1949 the Army implemented the Military Pay Record System, replaced it in 1959 with the Military Pay Voucher System, and in 1964 phased in the Centralized Automated Military Pay System. Finally, in 1971 the Joint Uniform Military Pay System came on line, thus completing the process of automating Army pay started in 1949. In 1950, the Finance Department became the Finance Corps, a basic branch within the Army. The Finance Corps continues to refine its pay and financial management systems. From Vietnam to Operation Desert Storm,* finance personnel have seen their systems tested and have modified them as needed. The Finance Corps expects change and strives to adapt for the future.

References. Walter Rundell, Jr., *Military Money*, 1980. U.S. Army Finance School, *History and Organization of the Finance Corps*, 1971.

William H. Carnes

FIRE AND MANEUVER

"Fire and maneuver" is commonly defined as a "method of attack in which one element of a command moves while being supported by the fire of another element or elements." However, the terms "fire" and "maneuver" are normally treated as separate but related entities in military doctrinal publications. Maneuver is an essential element of combat power. It contributes significantly to sustaining the initiative, exploiting success, preserving freedom of action, and reducing vulnerabilities. Its object is to concentrate forces in a manner designed to place the enemy at a disadvantage, thus achieving results that would otherwise be more costly in men and material. To be successful, maneuver normally requires the application of fires. There are five forms of maneuver: penetration, envelopment, turning movement, frontal attack, and infiltration. Maneuver seeks a decisive impact on the conduct of a campaign and typically requires protection from enemy airpower. Tactical maneuver sets the terms of combat in a battle or engagement. At both levels, maneuver is vital to achieving superior combat power.

Fire is uniformly described in authoritative Army doctrinal publications as "firepower." Unlike maneuver, which is one of the nine principles of war,* firepower is normally a supporting function that contributes to the success of other elements on the battlefield, such as maneuver, suppression of enemy defenses, destruction of enemy firepower capabilities, and attrition of enemy equipment and personnel. Its effectiveness is measured by its destructiveness, accuracy, and timeliness. Firepower may be used independently of maneuver to destroy, delay, or disrupt uncommitted enemy forces. Modern weapons and means of massing fires make firepower devastatingly effective against troops, material, and facilities.

References. William L. Hauser, "Fire and Maneuver in the Delta," *Infantry*, September–October 1970, 12–15. James T. Westwood, "Maneuver," *Military Review*, March 1983, 15–19.

Gary Bounds

FIRE DIRECTION CENTER

Today, the fire direction center (FDC) is the nerve center of field artillery* batteries* and battalions.* It provides tactical and technical fire control of field artillery fires. Tactical fire direction determines firing unit(s), shell/fuze combinations, volume of fire, method of engagement, and method of fire. A fire control element (FCE) performs tactical fire direction above battalion level. Technical fire direction employs computers to calculate gunnery solutions. Most technical fire direction is accomplished in platoon* operation centers (POC).

The need for fire direction centers arose during World War I,* with the emergence of predicted fire and attacks on unobserved targets with indirect fire. While existing gunnery methods accounted for atmospheric conditions, weapon and ammunition variations, the rotation of the earth under a shell in flight, gun range, direction to the target, and location of seen targets, multiple artillery units could not mass their fires on individual targets without adjusting individual units onto the target. In the 1930s, two successive directors of the Gunnery Department at the Field Artillery School, Majors Carlos Brewer and Orlando Ward, pioneered the creation of centralized indirect-fire methods. Ward overcame significant resistance from the field artillery community and adopted the innovative method of centralizing the computation and control of fires at battalion FDCs.

References. Boyd L. Dastrup, *King of Battle*, 1992. Bruce I. Gudmundsson, *On Artillery*, 1993. Blaise X. Schmidt and Lawrence E. Broughton, "We Mean Business," *Field Artillery Journal*, July–August 1985, 23–25.

Jeffrey S. Shadburn

FIRE TEAM

The smallest organizational element in the infantry* is the fire team. Adopted from the U.S. Marine Corps after World War II,* it has been included in every infantry table of organization and equipment* since. Common to all types of infantry, except the current mechanized infantry* squad,* it consists of either four or five soldiers armed with rifles, grenade launchers, and a squad automatic weapon (M240), led by a sergeant or corporal. Two fire teams make up a squad.

References. R. C. Morrow, "Does the Fire Team Need Reorganizing?" *Marine Corps Gazette*, February 1969, 28–30. W. H. Russell, "Before the Fire Team," *Marine Corps Gazette*, November 1984, 71–78.

Andrew N. Morris

FIRING TABLES

Firing tables have been used by artillerymen since the 17th century to provide to gunners the data, such as tube elevation and powder charges, wind and temperature variations, and projectile characteristics, necessary for accurate fire. Today, firing table data is computed in the fire direction center* (FDC) by the Field Artillery Digital Automatic Computer (FADAC) and sent to the gunners electronically or by voice radio. Artillerymen, however, still learn manual computation from firing tables, as a backup in case of computer failure and to understand more fully how their guns work.

References. Boyd L. Dastrup, *King of Battle*, 1992. Arthur R. Wilson, *Field Artillery Manual*, vol. 2, rev. ed., 1928.

FIRST ARMY

The U.S. First Army was organized in July 1918 and became operational on 10 August at La Ferte-sous-Lovarre, France, nominally under the command of General John J. Pershing.* From September to November 1918, First Army took part in three campaigns: Lorrain 1918, St. Mihiel,* and Meuse-Argonne.* Major General (later Lieutenant General) Hunter Liggett assumed command of First Army on 16 October, a post he held until First Army stood down on 30 April 1919. Reconstituted in the mobilization for World War II,* First Army participated in five campaigns, landing at Normandy and fighting across France, Belgium, and Germany. In the early 1970s, First Army's mission shifted from installation activities to assisting Army Reserve* and National Guard *units enhance their readiness status.

References. Glenn D. Walker, "First U.S. Army," *Army*, October 1973, 72–76. John B. Wilson, comp. *Armies, Corps, Divisions and Separate Brigades*, 1987.

Trevor Brown

FIRST BULL RUN

On 8 July 1861, the Army of Northeastern Virginia, 35,000 Union troops under the command of recently promoted Brigadier General Irvin McDowell, was ordered to move against Confederates located near Manassas Junction, while another Union force, 18,000 men under Brigadier General Robert Patterson, kept the Confederate army at Harpers Ferry* occupied. Impeded by the inexperience of officers and men, shortages of supplies, and maddening delays of all sorts, McDowell postponed his march until 16 July and lost the element of surprise. Confederate forces, split into three independent commands (P.G.T. Beauregard, with 21,000 men facing Washington; Joseph Johnston, with 11,000 men defending Harpers Ferry; and Theophilus H. Holmes, at Aquia Creek), began concentrating by road and rail at Manassas. McDowell's battle plan was well conceived, it called for turning the Confederate eastern flank. A skirmish and minor defeat of McDowell's forces at Blackburn's Ford, however, alerted the Confederates and caused further Union delay. McDowell then wasted two days at Centerville reorganizing and developing a new plan. He now planned to demonstrate with a major force at the stone bridge on the Warrenton Turnpike and outflank Confederates to the northwest, sending two divisions across Bull Run at Sudley Springs and Poplar Fords undetected. The plan proved difficult to execute.

After initial Union success on the morning of 21 July, Colonel Nathan G. Evans checked McDowell's attack at the stone bridge. The arrival at Henry House Hill of Thomas J. Jackson's brigade from Johnston's army stiffened Confederate resistance at a critical point in the battle, which was undecided until late in the day, when the arrival of the last brigade of Johnston's army by rail sealed the Federals' fate. This last brigade enveloped McDowell's flank, causing the Union Army to break and flee in panic back to Washington. Only a fierce rearguard action by a small force of Regulars under Major George Sykes and the confused and disorganized state of Confederate forces prevented a worse disaster. A major Confederate victory, the Battle of Bull Run convinced both sides and observers overseas that this would be long and bloody conflict. After the two armies fought again in the same area in 1862, the 1861 battle became known as First Bull Run in the North, First Manassas (a nearby town) in the South.

References. William C. Davis, *Battle at Bull Run*, 1977. Alan Hankinson, *First Bull Run 1861*, 1991. William G. Robertson, "First Bull Run, 19 July 1861," in *America's First Battles, 1776–1965*, eds. Charles E. Heller and William P. Stofft, 1986.

George Mordica II

1ST INFANTRY DIVISION

Known as the "Big Red One," the 1st Infantry Division traces its origins to 24 May 1917, when the War Department* organized the First Expeditionary Division. Elements of the First Expeditionary Division sailed for France in June and became the first U.S. division* in combat in World War I.* Redesignated the 1st Division, American Expeditionary Force* (AEF), in July 1917, the division took part in six campaigns from June to November 1918. Again, in World War II,* the "Fighting First" was the first U.S. division to deploy to the European Theater of Operations* (ETO). The Big Red One fought in both Africa and Europe, participating in eight campaigns from Torch* in November 1942 to the surrender of Germany in May 1945. After a decade of occupation duty in Germany, the 1st Division returned to the United States and its new home at Fort Riley,* Kansas. During the Vietnam War,* the 1st Division was among the first divisions to arrive in the Republic of Vietnam. From 1965 to 1970, units of the 1st Division took part in nearly every significant campaign of the war. After Vietnam, the Big Red One returned to Fort Riley. In 1996, the division headquarters and one brigade* redeployed to Europe.

The division's insignia is a red numeral 1 on an olive-drab shield with a pointed base, whence it derives it nickname.

References. George C. Dellinger, "1st Infantry Division," *Infantry*, March–April 1978, 18–23. H. R. Knickerbocker et al., *Danger Forward*, 1947, 1980. Joseph Dorst Patch, *A Soldier's War*, 1966.

Trevor Brown

FIRST MANASSAS. *See* First Bull Run.

FIRST SEMINOLE WAR. *See* Seminole Wars.

FIRST SERGEANT

First sergeant was one of five noncommissioned officer* (NCO) positions defined in 1779 in Baron Friedrich von Steuben's* *Regulation for the Order and Discipline of the Troops of the United States Army*. Although the duties of the first sergeant are now more complex, they remain very similar to those of the position Steuben described. The first sergeant is the senior NCO in companies,* batteries,* and troops.* He is responsible for motivation and discipline among the enlisted ranks and for routine company administration, such as mornings reports and duty rosters; he assists the company commander in conducting operations. Until the post–World War II* period, although they held positions of much greater responsibility, first sergeants were not paid significantly more than privates. Congress did not rectify this discrepancy until it added two NCO pay grades, E-8 (the current pay grade for first sergeants) and E-9, in 1958.

Selection of first sergeants has always been based on personal leadership qualities, past performance, dedication to duty, moral character, integrity, and military bearing. Today, education is an increasing consideration in selection of soldiers for first sergeant positions. Since the War of 1812,* the distinctive insignia of the first sergeant has been a diamond with three chevrons worn on the sleeve. Today, the first sergeant wears three chevrons with three "rockers" surrounding the diamond.

References. L. R. Arms, *A Short History of the NCO*, [1989]. Arnold G. Fisch, Jr., and Robert K. Wright, Jr., eds., *The Story of the Noncommissioned Officer Corps*, 1989. Bobby Owens, *The Diamond, 1993.*

FIRST SPECIAL SERVICE FORCE

Originally activated at Fort William Henry Harrison, the First Special Service Force was a combined U.S.-Canadian brigade-sized unit of 2,194 men and 173 officers intended for action against strategic targets in German-occupied Norway and Romania. Trained and commanded by Colonel Robert T. Frederick, the First Special Service Force consisted of highly trained, exceptionally conditioned parachute infantry,* closely akin to the Ranger* regiment* currently found in the U.S. Army. Unfortunately, by the time the unit was ready for combat, the mission it had prepared for had been cancelled. Rather than wait for something else to turn up, Frederick actively sought a mission for his impatient men. They participated in the landings at Kiska in the Aleutians, then redeployed to the Italian theater, where the unit established an unmatched reputation for excellence. At Anzio,* the First Special Service Force eventually anchored the beleaguered Allied right flank, earning the nickname "the Devil's Brigade." Later, in the Allied offensive up the Italian boot, elements of the brigade scaled the 3,120-foot-high prominence of Monte la Difensa to assault German defensive positions at the summit. The Devil's Brigade also fought in the Rome-Arno, southern France, and Rhineland campaigns. Because of extensive casualties, the First Special Service Force was disbanded on 5 December 1944.

References. Robert H. Adleman and George Walton, *The Devil's Brigade*, 1966. Robert D. Burhans, *The First Special Service Force*, 1947, 1981.

Joseph R. Fischer

FLEXIBLE RESPONSE

"Flexible response" is the term given to the U.S. national security policy originating in the early 1960s. The growth of the Soviet nuclear arsenal during the 1950s seemed to negate the U.S. threat of massive retaliation, which had been based on the assumption that strategic superiority deterred overt hostile acts. At the same time, Soviet sponsorship of wars of national liberation led policy makers to expect limited wars to be the pattern for the future, making nuclear weapons an unlikely solution for every aggressive act. The policy of flexible response permitted the United States the use of nuclear weapons as one of its core concepts; indeed, nuclear warheads and their delivery means must remain available at all times for strategic and tactical use should the need arise. The main function of these nuclear forces continues to be deterrence of the use of nuclear weapons by a potential enemy.

Flexible response also required the United States to maintain large conventional standing forces. This was good news to the U.S. Army, whose nuclear role was seen as incidental and had maintained only a limited number of divisions.* Until the advent of tactical—short-to-medium-range—nuclear weapons, the Army's primary role had been air defense. Now, the mission of conventional forces was deterrence against conventional attack or, if necessary, to fight limited wars. In the event of an overwhelming assault by opposing conventional forces, the United States hinted that it might escalate to the use of tactical nuclear weapons to prevent being overrun.

Technical advancements in transportation and communications that allowed more units and larger equipment to be transported by air or more quickly by sea provided the means by which a response could be truly flexible. This meant that major Army units could be retained in the United States, keeping costs down, but be quickly brought to bear should a crisis erupt. Flexible response allowed the United States to apply the amount of force necessary to control a crisis or attack without either losing or having to escalate because of a lack of alternatives.

References. Robert Dallek, *The American Style of Foreign Policy*, 1983. Richard Smoke, *National Security and the Nuclear Dilemma*, 1984.

Arthur T. Frame

FLIPPER, HENRY O. (1856–1940)

Henry Ossian Flipper holds the distinction of being the first black graduate of the U.S. Military Academy.* Born in a slave family on 21 March 1856 in Thomasville, Georgia, Flipper entered West Point in 1873. There he experienced social ostracism, but he claimed that treatment he received in military and academic matters was impartial and fair. He graduated in 1877 and received a commission in the cavalry.* While serving with Company A, 10th Cavalry, at Fort Sill,* Fort Elliott, and Fort Davis, Indian Territory (Texas), Flipper's performance was satisfactory, but his business practices created problems. In 1881, while acting commissary officer at Fort Davis, a shortage surfaced in his commissary account. An investigation of the case led to Flipper's court-martial for embezzlement and conduct unbecoming an officer. The court-martial cleared him on the charge of embezzlement but recommended dismissal because his attempts to conceal the shortage constituted misconduct. President Chester A. Arthur concurred with the findings.

After his dismissal from the Army, Flipper remained in the Southwest as an engineer and government agent dealing with land claims. His success in this capacity eventually led to his appointment as assistant secretary of the Interior in 1920. In 1923, he assumed an executive position with an American firm in Latin America. In 1931, Henry Flipper returned to his home in Atlanta, where he died on 3 May 1940.

References. Jane Eppinga, *Henry Ossian Flipper*, 1996. Henry Ossian Flipper, *The Colored Cadet at West Point*, 1878.

Danny E. Rodehaver

FLYING ARTILLERY. *See* Flying Battery.

FLYING BANANA. *See* Shawnee H-21.

FLYING BATTERY

In 1838, Major Samuel Ringgold was authorized to form a light or flying battery by mounting all gunners of a field artillery* battery* on horses, thus giving them the mobility of cavalry.* Previously, teams of six horses had pulled the guns while the gunners followed on foot or, in extreme cases, rode on the limber boxes. Individual mounts increased the gunners' speed and mobility. During the Mexican War,* two batteries were equipped as flying or horse artillery. Due to the expense of maintaining the extra horses, however, the flying batteries, also known as flying artillery, were discontinued after the war, only to be reestablished during the Civil War.*

References. Boyd L. Dastrup, *King of Battle*, 1992. Lester R. Dillon, Jr., *American Artillery in the Mexican War, 1846–1847*, 1975.

Steven J. Allie

FLYING CRANE

The Sikorski CH-54, officially designated the Tarhe, but commonly known as the Flying Crane, was one of the most unusual helicopters ever employed by the U.S. Army. Weighing less than 20,000 pounds, the CH-54 could lift more than twice its own weight in externally underslung cargo. Powered by twin Pratt & Whitney turbine engines and a massive six-blade rotor system, the Flying Crane could lift the 20,000-pound Universal Military Pod, which held up to forty-five troops, twenty-four litters, a complete field surgical unit, or a field communications and command post. Its height-adjustable tricycle landing gear allowed the CH-54 to accommodate oversized cargoes that other helicopters could not. In April 1965, a CH-54 set a world record when it carried a pod holding ninety passengers. During the Vietnam War,* CH-54s recovered 380 crashed aircraft. Today, although no longer used by the U.S. Army, CH-54 Flying Cranes continue to be used in the forestry and construction industries.

References. Stephen Harding, *U.S. Army Aircraft since 1947*, 1997. Richard K. Tierney, "The Flying Crane," *U.S. Army Aviation Digest*, November 1964, 12–15.

Benjamin H. Kristy

FORCES COMMAND

U.S. Army Forces Command (FORSCOM) was activated on 1 July 1973 as part of a reorganization of the Army's major commands. FORSCOM is responsible for the training and combat readiness of all active Army forces and Army Reserve* (USAR) units. It also oversees and advises the training of Army National Guard* units, but it commands them only when they are called to active duty. On 1 July 1987, FORSCOM acquired new duties, including the planning and conduct of joint exercises and the defense of CONUS. On 1 October 1993, FORSCOM's mission changed again, to include response to natural disasters within the United States and support of all U.S. involvement in United Nations peacekeeping operations.

References. Richard E. Cavazos, "FORSCOM Hones as It Modernizes," *Army*, Oc-

tober 1982, 34–39. Robert M. Shoemaker, "The Changeover to 'Go to War' Management," *Army*, October 1980, 28–32.

William H. Carnes

FORD, JOHN (1894–1973)

John Ford was a Hollywood filmmaker well known for his interpretations of
American history. His military service made him especially receptive to film
story lines dealing with martial themes; some of his more popular films chron-
icled army life during the 19th century, these included his "cavalry trilogy" (*Fort
Apache*, 1948; *She Wore a Yellow Ribbon*, 1949; and *Rio Grande*, 1950). *Fort
Apache* depicts a massacre reminiscent of the Little Bighorn,* against a back-
drop of duty to the regiment* and the making of legends. *She Wore a Yellow
Ribbon* portrays events shortly after the Little Bighorn, depicting an aging officer
who chooses to resolve a military situation without resort to force of arms. *Rio
Grande* represents Colonel Ranald S. Mackenzie's 1873 raid on Remolino, Mex-
ico, within the context of "officially unsanctioned" military operations on foreign
soil. Ford's last works on the mounted arm of the Army included *The Horse
Soldiers*, 1959; *Sergeant Rutledge*, 1960; and *Cheyenne Autumn*, 1964. *The
Horse Soldiers* depicts Colonel Benjamin Grierson's April 1863 raid through
Mississippi during the Vicksburg* Campaign. *Sergeant Rutledge* treats the buffalo soldiers* of the 9th Cavalry and the sensitive area of racial and sexual
relations during the period. *Cheyenne Autumn* relates the Dull Knife–Little Wolf
outbreak from the Cheyenne-Arapaho Reservation in 1878–89 by contrasting
the needs of reservation Indians and an insensitive and unresponsive government
bureacracy. Ford's depiction of 19th-century army life was relatively accurate,
but his use of uniforms, equipment, and accoutrements is uneven—much of
what is seen represents later periods. Ford largely ignored technical advice and
borrowed from Frederic Remington, among others, for his film composition.

References. Tag Gallagher, *John Ford*, 1986. J. A. Place, *The Western Films of John
Ford*, 1974. Andrew Sinclair, *John Ford*, 1979.

Jeffrey Prater

FORREST, NATHAN BEDFORD (1821–1877)

Considered by many the greatest American cavalryman, Nathan Bedford Forrest began his remarkable career early in the Civil War.* Forrest raised and
equipped a Confederate cavalry* regiment* from his own considerable resources
in 1861. Forrest and his regiment first saw action during the siege of Fort Donelson, slipping away before the garrison surrendered. The regiment was largely
responsible for the initial Confederate success at Shiloh,* and he protected the
Confederate Army as it returned to Corinth. In July 1862, Forrest began the
strategic raiding that typified his brilliance. Forrest regularly suffered poor treatment by his superiors and was forced to raise and equip new forces at the
expense of the enemy. He repeatedly fought outnumbered, yet he consistently
prevailed. Some of his more noteworthy accomplishments were his victory over

Colonel Abel Straight in April 1863, his work at Chickamauga* the same year, his ferocious yet controversial fighting at Fort Pillow, and his stunning accomplishments against Brigadier General Samuel D. Sturgis at Brice's Crossroads in 1864. Having no formal military training, Forrest formulated his own means of waging war. His targets were generally lines of communications, and he tenaciously seized and maintained the initiative in any engagement. He was a superb logistician who cared for his men and animals with the single intent of being more agile and maneuverable than his enemy—what he described as an attempt "to get there first with the most men." Despite his postwar inclination toward peaceful cooperation with federal authorities, events pushed Forrest into leadership of the Tennessee Ku Klux Klan—a role that has tended to overshadow his brilliant military exploits.

References. Jack Hurst, *Nathan Bedford Forrest*, 1993. Brian Steel Wills, *A Battle from the Start*, 1992.

Jeffrey Prater

FORT BENJAMIN HARRISON

In March 1903, Congress established a military post thirteen miles northeast of Indianapolis, Indiana, to serve as the home of an infantry* regiment.* The post had no official name until 1906, when President Theodore Roosevelt chose to honor former president and Indianapolis resident Benjamin Harrison. Fort Benjamin Harrison was in World War I* a training camp for officers; later it was the home of the 10th, 11th, 20th, 23rd, 40th, 45th, and 46th Infantry Regiments. In World War II,* the fort hosted a reception station, schoolhouse, military prison, and prisoner of war* camp. Inactivated in 1947, Fort Benjamin Harrison became Benjamin Harrison Air Force Base from 1948 to 1950, but it reverted to Army control in 1951 and became the home of the Army Finance Center, the Defense Information School, the Adjutant General's Corps, and the Soldier Support Institute. Fort Benjamin Harrison closed in 1996.

References. Dan Cragg, *Guide to Military Installations*, 4th ed., 1994. Warren J. Le Mon. "Fort Benjamin Harrison," *Army Information Digest*, November 1965, 17–24.

David A. Rubenstein

FORT BENNING

Established following World War I,* Fort Benning is approximately seven miles south of Columbus, Georgia, on former Indian land sold during the Georgia land lottery of 1827. The federal government purchased and consolidated several small holdings in 1919 for a military reservation and named it in honor of Brigadier General Henry L. Benning, Confederate States Army. Benning, known as "The Old Rock" for his coolness and daring under fire, had fought with great distinction through the Virginia campaigns and finally commanded his own brigade,* called "the Rock Brigade." Fort Benning presently occupies approximately 180,000 acres in Georgia and Alabama and includes some of the finest and most modern training facilities available in the U.S. Army today. Benning is currently home to the 3d Brigade of the 24th Infantry Division (Mechanized), the 36th Engineer Group, and the 3d Battalion, 75th Ranger Regiment. Fort Benning's Lawson Army Airfield supports the largest types of U.S. Air Force transport aircraft,* facilitating rapid deployment missions anywhere in the world. The National Infantry Museum, honoring the U.S. Army infantryman, is located at Fort Benning.

References. Thomas E. Conrad, "Fort Benning, Home of the Infantry," *Infantry*, May–June 1975, 24–30. Orwin C. Talbott, "The Home Where Nobody Ever Rests," *Army*, March 1970, 34–41. John M. Wright, Jr., "Fort Benning 1918–1968," *Infantry*, September–October 1968, 4–11.

David Zoellers

FORT BLISS

Founded at El Paso, Texas, in 1849, Fort Bliss was part of a chain of forts in New Mexico and Texas to protect settlers, miners, and emigrants traveling westward against the periodic raids of the Mescalero Apache. Fort Bliss was named for William Wallace Bliss, a veteran of the Seminole and Mexican Wars and later private secretary to President Zachary Taylor.* Notable among the fort's commanders and officers were future Confederate leaders James Longstreet* and George Pickett. In 1861, Bliss and other Texas posts were surrendered to the Confederacy. The post served as headquarters for the ill-fated Confederate campaign into New Mexico and was subsequently burned by Confederates in late 1862. The U.S. Army reoccupied Bliss in 1865 and has remained there to the present. Fort Bliss has been called the "training ground for generals." Following Pancho Villa's attack on Columbus, New Mexico,* General John J, Pershing* led the Punitive Expedition* from Fort Bliss, and four future Chiefs of Staff—Hugh L. Scott, Peyton C. March,* Pershing, and John Leonard Hines—served there. During World War I,* Bliss served as an important training base for officers and troops and became a major antiaircraft training center, forerunner of the U.S. Army Air Defense Center. Today, Fort Bliss is a major U.S. Army Training and Doctrine Command* (TRADOC) installation and hosts the 3d Armored Cavalry Regiment, with a tradition that spans the 19th and 20th centuries; the 11th Air Defense Brigade; the German Air Force Training Command; and the U.S. Army Sergeant Majors Academy (USASMA).*

References. Arthur Van Voorhis Crego, *City on the Mesa*, 1969. Leon C. Metz, *Fort Bliss*, 1981, and Desert Army, 1988.

Thomas Christianson

FORT BRAGG

Known as the "Home of the Airborne" and the heart of of the Army's special operations community, Fort Bragg is one of the nation's largest military installations, with over 50,000 active-duty personnel. Located near Fayetteville, North

Carolina, Fort Bragg lies next to Pope Air Force Base and close to Camp Mackall training area. XVIII Airborne Corps, with four divisions—82d Airborne* at Fort Bragg, 101st (Air Assault)* at Fort Campbell,* Kentucky, 10th Mountain at Fort Drum,* New York, 3d Mechanized at Fort Stewart—and a host of corps* support units, is the major headquarters at Fort Bragg. U.S. Army Special Operations Command, headquarters for all Special Forces* groups, psychological operations groups, civil affairs brigades,* the 160th Special Operations Aviation Regiment, and other support units, is also located on the post. Thus, Fort Bragg is referred to as "the center of the universe" for airborne and special operations soldiers. Established as an artillery training site during World War I* and named for Braxton Bragg, a noted Civil War commander, Camp Bragg became a permanent post in 1922. The post grew rapidly in World War II,* when thousands of paratroopers from all five airborne divisions trained at Bragg. Today, Fort Bragg is a growing installation, with projects under way and plans for an even more dynamic future.

References. William R. Evinger, ed., *Directory of U.S. Military Bases Worldwide*, 3d ed., 1998. Heike Hasenauer, "Bragg 2000" *Soldiers*, June 1994, 24–25, and "Building Up Bragg," *Soldiers*, June 1997, 28–31.

                                                                        S. A. Underwood

FORT CAMPBELL

Located astride the Kentucky-Tennessee border, approximately sixty-five miles northwest of Nashville, Fort Campbell was named in honor of Brigadier General William Bowen Campbell, remembered for his cry, "Boys, follow me!" as he led his regiment* in the storming of Monterrey* in 1846. Initially developed to accomodate one armor division* and support troops, today Campbell is home to the 101st Airborne Division* (Air Assault), the 5th Special Forces Group, and some of the U.S. Army's finest training facilities and ranges. Fort Campbell's training reservation—an area in excess of 105,000 acres, including drop zones,* tactical landing strips, and a fully modernized array of small arms, antiarmor, and artillery ranges—permits fully integrated, combined-arms training exercises. Fort Campbell's airfields support the largest types of U.S. Air Force transport aircraft,* ensuring that the installation's units can rapidly deploy anywhere in the world.

References. Dan Cragg, *Guide to Military Installations*, 4th ed., 1994. Phil Prater, "The Good Neighbor Post," *Soldiers*, March 1992, 34–36.

                                                                        David Zoellers

FORT CARSON

At nearly 7,000 feet above sea level, Fort Carson, the "Mountain Post," is located five miles south of Colorado Springs, Colorado, in the eastern lee of the Rocky Mountains. Many officers and soldiers who have served at Carson—known for its beautiful setting, moderate year-round climate, and favorable cost of living—consider it the best duty station in the Army. Named after the famous frontiersman Kit Carson, the post opened in May 1942 as an infantry* training center. In recent decades, Fort Carson has been most closely associated with the 4th Infantry Division* (Mechanized), which replaced the 5th Infantry Division at Carson after returning from Vietnam at the end of 1970. As the Army downsized after Desert Storm,* however, the 4th ID (M) left Fort Carson in 1996, to be replaced by the 10th Special Forces Group and the 7th Armored Cavalry Regiment.

References. Steve Abbott, "High in the Rockies," *Soldiers*, July 1978, 34–38. Dan Cragg, *Guide to Military Installations*, 4th ed., 1994. Tony Nauroth, "In the Shadow of Cheyenne Mountain," *Soldiers*, August 1991, 48–51.

Phil Bradley

FORT CHAFFEE

Fort Chaffee, located five miles east of Fort Smith, Arkansas, was established in 1941 and named in honor of Major General Adna Chaffee, Jr.,* the first chief of Armored Forces and commanding general of I Armored Corps. The post served as a training site for armored forces preparing for World War II* and, later, as a prisoner of war* camp. Inactivated in 1947, Chaffee reopened in 1948 as home of the 5th Armored Division. In 1957, the 5th Armored stood down, and Fort Chaffee became a dual training center for the field artillery* and the Army Reserve.* From 1958 to 1961, Headquarters XIX Corps was the only unit at Chaffee. Since 1961, the post has seen a wide variety of missions, including Vietnam and Cuban refugee reception and holding force-on-force training for light infantry units, and regional training for the Army Reserve.

References. Dan Cragg, *Guide to Military Installations*, 4th ed., 1994. William R. Evinger, ed., *Directory of U.S. Military Bases Worldwide*, 3d ed., 1998.

David A. Rubenstein

FORT DEVENS

Established in September 1917 as a reception station and training center, Fort Devens, Massachusetts, thirty-five miles northeast of Boston, was named in honor of Major General Charles Devens, a Massachusetts native, Civil War* division* commander, and state supreme court justice. The 76th Infantry Division trained at Devens in World War I* and the 1st, 32nd, and 45th Divisions trained there in World War II* before deploying overseas. Other World War II tenants included a Women's Army Corps* (WAC) training center, army nurse basic training, and a cadet nurse program. The post also hosted a prisoner of war* camp. After the war Devens closed, but the site housed the University of Massachusetts (Fort Devens) in response to the massive influx of veterans attending college on the G.I. Bill.* In 1951, the Army Security Agency School became the major tenant, and in 1968 the 10th Special Forces Group arrived at Devens. Once slated to become the home of the Army's Information Systems Command, Devens was selected for closure by the Base Realignment and Closure Committee, but Army Reserve units still use the training areas.

References. Dan Cragg, *Guide to Military Installations*, 4th ed., 1994. "Fort Devens," *Army Digest*, June 1966, 51–52.

David A. Rubenstein

FORT DIX

Fort Dix, New Jersey, fifty miles east of Philadelphia, was established in 1917 as a training site for troops deploying to France. It was the largest Army training center in the United States. Named in honor of Major General John Adams Dix, a veteran of the War of 1812* and the Civil War,* New York senator and governor, and oft-appointed presidential representative, Camp Dix was designated a permanent garrison in 1939. It became the Army's major basic combat training* (BCT) center in the Northeast. For more than three decades after World War II,* Fort Dix continued to train new army recruits for infantry* units around the world.

In the the downsizing of the 1990s, the Base Realignment and Closure Committee placed Dix on the list of bases to be closed. The Fort Dix reservation remains the largest military installation in the northeastern United States, and it shares common boundaries with McGwire Air Force Base and Lakehurst Naval Air Engineering Station. Today, Fort Dix's BCT area is a training center for the Army Reserve* and National Guard.* Navy and Coast Guard organizations have found new homes on the post, and the hospital has been turned over to the Air Force.

References. Dan Cragg, *Guide to Military Installations*, 4th ed., 1994. Gerri Taylor, "Fort Crossroads," *Soldiers*, May 1986, 34–36.

David A. Rubenstein

FORT DONELSON. *See* Forts Henry and Donelson Campaign.

FORT DRUM, N.Y.

Fort Drum was established in 1908 nine miles from Watertown, New York, and was later named in honor of Lieutenant General Hugh Drum, primary planner of the St. Mihiel* offensive and commanding general of First Army* during World War I.* Throughout its history, Fort Drum has served as a training center for Army Reserve* and New York National Guard* units, a cold-weather training and experimentation site for U.S. Army, Marine, and Canadian forces, and a tactical equipment storage site for Reserve and Guard organizations. In 1995, the post completed an extensive construction program resulting from its designation as home of the newly reactivated 10th Mountain Division (Light Infantry). It also received units relocating from the 1995 closure of Fort Devens,* Massachusetts, and it remains a major training site for Army Reserve* and National Guard* units in New York and the New England area.

References. Fletcher H. Griffis, "Revamping Fort Drum," *Military Engineer*, September–October 1986, 502–505. Keith Trohoske, "The Beat of a Different Drum," *Soldiers*, October 1987, 34–36.

David A. Rubenstein

FORT DRUM, P.I.

Called the Army's "Concrete Battleship," Fort Drum, Philippine Islands, was a dreadnought-shaped fortification protecting Manila Harbor. It was completed in 1913 and armed with four 12-inch guns mounted in armored turrets and four 6-inch guns in two double-deck casements; no less than twenty feet of reinforced concrete protected Drum's flanks. In spite of heavy enemy artillery and air bombardment, Drum's fire broke up heavy concentrations of Japanese troops on Bataan and denied the Japanese navy access to Manila Harbor from January to May 1942. Drum surrendered with the capitulation of all Corregidor* forts. By the time U.S. forces returned to the Philippines, Fort Drum had undergone at the hands of its former owners a far heavier air bombardment than anything the Japanese had inflicted. U.S. forces eventually cleared a small Japanese garrison from the fort by pumping in and igniting a flammable liquid mixture. There were no Japanese survivors. Today, Fort Drum lies derelict, picked apart by metal salvagers but basically as imperishable as the Pyramids.

References. Francis J. Allen, *The Concrete Battleship*, 1988. R. Ernest Dupuy, "The Concrete Battleship," *Army*, August 1973, 28–32.

Stanley Sandler

FORT GEORGE G. MEADE

Fort Meade, Maryland, located between Baltimore and Washington, D.C., was established in May 1917 and named in honor of Major General George G. Meade, commanding general of the Union Army at Gettysburg.* The post was renamed Fort Leonard Wood in 1928, but complaints forced War Department* officials to reinstate the original name. During World War I,* Meade served as a training site for doughboys* deploying with the American Expeditionary Force* (AEF). It served a similar mission in World War II.* The fort currently houses units from all services and the Federal government, including National Security Agency,* Defense Courier Service, the Air Force's 694th Intelligence Wing, and the Navy's Security Group Activity. The major Army tenant is Headquarters, First Army.* Fort Meade will grow during the current military downsizing with the arrival of the Defense Information School from Fort Benjamin Harrison* and the Operational Security Evaluation Group from Vint Hall Farm, Virginia.

References. Dan Cragg, *Guide to Military Installations*, 4th ed., 1994. William R. Evinger, ed., *Directory of U.S. Military Bases Worldwide*, 3d ed., 1998.

David A. Rubenstein

FORT GREELY

In June 1942, the U.S. government established an airfield, Station 17, 106 miles southeast of Fairbanks, Alaska, for the transfer of Lend-Lease aircraft to the Soviet Union. Deactivated after World War II,* the post was transferred to the Army. In 1948 it was reactivated, under the name Big Delta, as the Army's Arctic indoctrination school and equipment test and evaluation station. The

Army Chemical Corps Arctic Test Team began operation at the site in 1952. In 1955, the Army designated the post Fort Greely, in honor of Major General Adolphus Greely, a Civil War* veteran, arctic explorer, chief of the Army Signal Corps,* director of relief operations following the San Francisco earthquake, and recipient of the Medal of Honor.* Today, Fort Greely hosts the Northern Warfare Training Center and the Cold Regions Test Center.

References. James A. Bell, "Grizzly Flight—We Do It Right," *U.S. Army Aviation Digest*, July–August 1994, 18–20. Tom Williams, "Mountains, Glaciers and Rivers," *Soldiers*, August 1984, 42–45.

David A. Rubenstein

FORT HOOD

Fort Hood, Texas, is the largest armor training installation in the free world. On 15 January 1942, the War Department* announced the selection of the central Texas site for the Tank Destroyer Tactical and Firing Center. Camp Hood, as it was originally called (for Confederate Brigadier General John B. Hood), encompassed 108,000 acres and officially opened on 18 September 1942. By the end of 1942, 45,000 troops were living and training at Camp Hood. It reached its wartime peak strength of 95,000 troops in June 1943, by which time an additional 50,943 acres had been added to the training area. Activity at Hood's Infantry Replacement Training Center slowed as World War II* came to an end and the post turned to equipment reclamation and demobilization planning. In January 1946, the 2nd and 20th Armored Divisions arrived from overseas, but the 20th was rapidly inactivated, and the post population dropped to less than 5,000.

During the early 1950s, Hood continued to train recruits and provide individual replacements for Army units worldwide. In 1954, III Corps moved to Fort Hood, where it remained until deactivated in May 1959. Hood again became a two-division post with the arrival of the 1st Armored Division in 1962. During the Vietnam War,* Fort Hood trained many units and individuals for duty in Southeast Asia. In 1971, the 1st Cavalry Division, returning from Vietnam, replaced the 1st Armored Division, which deployed to Germany. During the Persian Gulf crisis of 1990, Fort Hood mobilized, trained, and deployed 25,000 active and reserve soldiers from the 1st Cavalry Division, the 2nd Armored Division, and supporting units to the Middle East for Desert Shield and Desert Storm.*

References. Dan Cragg, *Guide to Military Installations*, 4th ed., 1994. Odie B. Faulk and Laura E. Faulk, *Fort Hood*, 1990.

James H. Willbanks

FORT HUACHUCA

On 3 March 1877, Captain Samual M. Whitsides, with two companies* of the 6th Cavalry, located a temporary post in the Huachuca Mountains in southeast Arizona, fifteen miles north of the Mexican border. The post gained permanent status in January 1878 and was formally designated Fort Huachuca in 1882. Nelson A. Miles* used the post as a headquarters and supply base for his campaign against Geronimo, and after Geronimo's capture, Huachuca remained active to cope with border troubles. The 10th Cavalry (buffalo soldiers*) arrived in 1913 and joined General John J. Pershing's* 1916 Punitive Expedition* into Mexico. During World War I,* the post guarded the U.S.-Mexican border, and during World War II* troops destined for both the Pacific and European theaters trained there. On 15 September 1947, the government declared Huachuca surplus and transferred it to the state of Arizona. The post was reopened in 1951, closed again in 1953, and finally reopened in 1954. In 1967, Fort Huachuca became the headquarters for the Army Strategic Communications Command and, in 1971, the site of the Army Intelligence Center and School. The original post area was declared a National Historic Landmark in March 1977.

References. Robert W. Frazer, *Forts of the West*, 1965. Lana Ott, "Secrets of Fort Huachuca," *Soldiers*, May 1979, 17–20.

L. Lynn Williams

FORT HUNTER LIGGETT

In the mid-1920s, William Randolph Hearst purchased large ranch holdings south of Monterey, California, extending from the Pacific Ocean to over forty miles inland. The remote and underdeveloped land, with its variable terrain, made an ideal staging ground for realistic combat training. In 1940, the War Department* acquired the Hearst holdings for twelve dollars per acre, but range-safety concerns required an exchange of land with the U.S. Forestry Service, resulting in the loss of all coastline property. In 1941, the Army established Fort Hunter Liggett (named for Major General Hunter Liggett,* commander of First Army* in World War I*), on the site as a training support area for Fort Ord.* In the early 1950s, units trained at Hunter Liggett for deployment to Korea. In 1956, Hunter Liggett became the field laboratory for specialized experimental weapons training. Both missions continue at Hunter Liggett.

References. Dan Cragg, *Guide to Military Installations*, 4th ed., 1994. Steve Hara, "Tomorrow's Battles Fought Today," *Soldiers*, June 1985, 36–39.

David A. Rubenstein

FORT JACKSON

Fort Jackson, near Columbia, South Carolina, was established in 1917 and named for Andrew Jackson,* hero of the battle of New Orleans* and seventh president of the United States. The fort's motto, "Victory Starts Here," is associated with its first unit, Company E, 1st South Carolina Infantry Regiment, which used the site to train for deployment with the American Expeditionary Force* (AEF) in World War I.* The 1st Provisional Infantry Regiment (Colored) also organized and trained at Jackson, with the 81st Infantry Division. Controlled by the Cantonment Lands Commission after the war and used extensively by the South Carolina National Guard, Camp Jackson reverted to War Department* control as an infantry* training center during World War II.* Army downsizing during the 1990s resulted in significant growth at Fort Jackson, with the arrival of the Chaplain's School and Soldier Support Center from other posts and the continuing missions of the 1st Basic Training Brigade and 4th Training Brigade.

References. Dan Cragg, *Guide to Military Installations*, 4th ed., 1994. William R. Evinger, ed., *Directory of U.S. Military Bases Worldwide*, 3rd ed., 1998.

David A. Rubenstein

FORT KNOX

Although better known to the American public as the site of the United States Bullion Depository, Fort Knox, Kentucky, is one of the U.S. Army's most important training installations. The War Department* selected the site in 1918 for a National Army Cantonment, because of its central location, access to transportation facilities, and the availability of cheap adjacent land for expansion. Named for Henry Knox, George Washington's* close friend, advisor, and successor as Commanding General,* and secretary of war,* Camp Knox served as V Corps Area training camp for Reserve Officer Training Corps* (ROTC) and National Guard* units after World War I.* Camp Knox became a permanent post in 1932 and was redesignated Fort Knox. Situated on 110,000 acres twenty-five miles south of Louisville, today Fort Knox is home of the U.S. Army Armor Center, U.S. Army Recruiting Command,* the Patton Museum, and the 1st Armor Training Brigade.

References. Mildred Hanson Gillie, *Forging the Thunderbolt*, 1947. Tom Kaser, "More than Gold," *Travel*, September 1962, 49–52.

Lawyn C. Edwards

FORT LARAMIE

Located on the left bank of the Laramie River within a mile of its junction with the North Platte River, in present-day Wyoming, Fort Laramie was established as a fur trading post in 1834. Originally named Fort William (for William Sublette, William Anderson, and William Patton) and renamed Fort John (probably for John B. Sarpy), the post was purchased on 26 June 1849 and garrisoned with two companies of the Regiment of Mounted Rifles and one company* of the 6th U.S. Infantry. The post assumed the name of Fort Laramie from the nearby river (named for French trapper Jacques Laramie, killed by Arapaho warriors near its headwaters in 1821). The fort protected travelers along the Oregon Trail and controlled the Indians on the northern plains. The Army abandoned the post on 2 March 1890; the last part of the military reservation was transferred to the Interior Department on 9 June 1890. Fort Laramie has been partially restored and today is a national monument.

References. Paul L. Hedren, *Fort Laramie in 1876*, 1988. Robert A. Murray, *Fort Laramie*, 1974. Remi Nadeau, *Fort Laramie and the Sioux Indians*, 1967.

Jeffrey Prater

FORT LAWTON

Fort Lawton, Washington, five miles south of downtown Seattle, was established in 1897 as the first and principal of four forts protecting the entrance to

Puget Sound and the frontier centers of Olympia, Tacoma, and Seattle. It served, in turn, as a coast artillery,* infantry,* engineer, transportation corps,* and air defense post. It was named in honor of Major General Henry Lawton, whose long career included chasing Geronimo deep into Mexico, marching on Santiago, Cuba, commanding the 2nd Infantry Division, and tracking down the Philippine insurgent Emilio Aguinaldo. Lawton was killed in December 1899 during the Philippine Insurrection.* Fort Lawton originally comprised 640 acres; the 1972 transfer of a large tract to the city of Seattle for use as a nature preserve and park reduced it to seventy-five acres. Today Fort Lawton houses the 124th Army Reserve* Command and 104th Training Division.

Reference. William R. Evinger, ed., *Directory of U.S. Military Bases Worldwide*, 3d ed., 1998.

David A. Rubenstein

FORT LEAVENWORTH

Fort Leavenworth, Kansas, is one of the most historic U.S. Army posts still on active duty. It was the second post established west of the Missouri River, and the first permanent one. Colonel Henry Leavenworth, who is buried in the Fort Leavenworth* National Cemetery, established Cantonment Leavenworth on the Missouri River in May 1827 as a base of operations for a regiment* of dragoons protecting wagon trains moving along the Santa Fe Trail. When national development and technology reduced the western trail's importance in the late 1840s, the fort's mission changed; it became an arsenal, supplying guns, powder, cannon balls, and other items to more western posts. Leavenworth's third mission began in May 1881, when Commanding General* William T. Sherman,* who had lived at Leavenworth before the Civil War,* directed the establishment of the School for the Application of Infantry and Cavalry* at Leavenworth, forerunner of today's U.S. Army Command and General Staff College.* Today, Fort Leavenworth is home of the Army's Combined Arms Center and the U.S. Disciplinary Barracks.*

References. J. H. Johnston III, *Leavenworth*, 1976. John W. Partin, ed., *A Brief History of Fort Leavenworth 1827–1983*, 1983. George Walton, *Sentinel of the Plains*, 1973.

John Reichley

FORT LEE

Although Fort Lee has been the name of posts from Massachusetts to Oregon, Fort Lee, Virginia, located three miles from Petersburg, is the only one named in honor of the great Civil War* commander and Virginian, Robert E. Lee.* During World War I,* Fort Lee served as a center for mobilizing and training Europe-bound divisions. After the war, Lee was turned over to the state for use as a game preserve and part of the Petersburg National Military Park. By World War II,* the site once again became a military post, housing the Quartermaster and Medical Replacement Training Center. Before the war's end, the Quartermaster School and an Officer Candidate School* (OCS) were established at Lee.

In 1962, Fort Lee became the home of the Quartermaster Corps,* under the Second Continental Army Command. It now falls under the Army's Training and Doctrine Command* (TRADOC) and houses the Army's Combined Arms Support Command, which is responsible for training officers and soldiers in all facets of logistical support. Other major tenants include the Quartermaster Center and School, Army Logistics Management College, and Defense Commissary Agency.

References. Dan Cragg, *Guide to Military Installations*, 4th ed., 1994. William R. Evinger, ed., *Directory of U.S. Military Bases Worldwide*, 3d ed., 1998.

David A. Rubenstein

FORT LEONARD WOOD

Fort Leonard Wood, the home of the U.S. Army Engineer Center, is located in the Ozark hills region of south-central Missouri, 125 miles southwest of St. Louis. The post covers approximately 63,000 acres and is manned by 13,500 active-duty personnel, including the 132d and 136th Engineer Brigades, the 3d Basic Training Brigade, and the 1st Engineer Battalion. Construction on the VII Corps Area Training Center began in December 1940 in the Big Piney River area of the Clark National Forest. The post's 1,600 buildings were completed in a five-month period. On 3 January 1941, the new post was redesignated Fort Leonard Wood, in honor of Major General Leonard Wood, a Medal of Honor* winner famous for his service in the Indian Wars,* Cuba, the Philippines, and as Chief of Staff. During World War II,* the post trained nearly 300,000 engineer troops; the 6th, 8th, 70th, 75th, and 97th Infantry Divisions, and housed a prisoner of war* camp. Deactivated in 1946 and used for summer training by the National Guard,* Fort Leonard Wood was reactivated in 1950 to train troops for the Korean War.* In 1956 it was designated the U.S. Army Training Center, Engineer, and made a permanent installation. The Engineer Officers School transferred from Fort Belvoir to Fort Leonard Wood in 1988.

References. Dan Cragg, *Guide to Military Installations*, 4th ed., 1994. Steve Hara, "Show Me Fort Wood," *Soldiers*, August 1986, 6–8.

Kelvin Crow

FORT LEWIS

Located in the Puget Sound region of Washington state, ten miles south of Tacoma, Camp Lewis was established in July 1917 on 70,000 acres donated to the federal government by Pierce County. Named for Captain Meriwether Lewis,* it was the largest training camp constructed in World War I.* It was designated a permanent installation in 1927 and, during World War II,* was expanded by an additional 16,000 acres, called "North Fort," to train combat divisions* and Army Service Forces. In 1943, a prisoner of war* camp was erected on the post. Following the war, Fort Lewis served as a separation center for returning soldiers and training center for overseas occupation troops. During the Korean War,* both Canadian and U.S. troops trained at Fort Lewis. Today, Fort Lewis is the home of the I Corps and the 9th Infantry Division.

References. Michael Brown, "All-Terrain Post," *Soldiers*, March 1985, 13–17. Janet Hake, "Fort Lewis and Other Sites of the Sound," *Soldiers*, February 1979, 46–49.

Kelvin Crow

FORT McCLELLAN

Camp McClellan was established on 18 July 1918 adjacent to Anniston, Alabama, as a mobilization and training site for the 29th National Guard Division. Named for Major General George B. McClellan,* general in chief of the U.S. Army from 1861 to 1862 and twice commanding general, Army of the Potomac,* the post was redesignated Fort McClellan in 1929. In 1940, the 27th Infantry Division trained at Fort McClellan before shipping out to the Pacific; subsequently, 500,000 troops trained there during World War II.* In 1943, the Branch Immaterial Replacement Training Center became the Infantry Replacement Training Center, and an internment camp for prisoners of war* opened at McClellan. Deactivated in 1947, McClellan reopened in 1951 and has hosted a number of activities since that time: the U.S. Army Chemical Center and School; the Women's Army Corps* (WAC); the U.S. Army Combat Development Command Chemical-Biological-Radiological Agency; an advanced individual training* (AIT) brigade*, the U.S. Army Military Police School; and the U.S. Army Chemical School. Fort McClellan was redesignated the U.S. Army Chemical and Military Police Centers and Fort McClellan on 1 March 1983.

References. "Ft. McClellan—46 Years of Service," *Armed Forces Chemical Journal*, June 1963, 18–19. William H. McMichael, "The Best Kept Secret in the Army," *Soldiers*, December 1991, 46–49. Alan Moore, "Redeveloping Fort McClellan," *Soldiers*, June 1996, 15–16.

Edward Shanahan

FORT McCOY

Fort McCoy is the only currently active U.S. Army installation in Wisconsin. Located near Sparta, the post was founded in 1909 and named for Spanish-American War* veteran, lawyer, and promoter Robert McCoy. The camp became a favorite of the field artillery.* During World War I,* new facilties, including barracks, stables, mess halls, and warehouses, signaled its permanent status as a fort rather than a camp. During the 1920s, McCoy first became an Ordnance Depot, then reverted to the Department of Agriculture. The barracks were dismantled, and active Army strength dwindled to less than ten men. Troops continued to train during the summers, however, and, in the 1930s, the site served as a supply base for the Civilian Conservation Corps* (CCC). As war clouds loomed in Europe, the Army rebuilt the barracks, and Second Army* conducted maneuvers at McCoy in August 1940. In World War II,* thousands of troops trained at McCoy prior to deployment, including the 100th Infantry Regiment, Hawaiian National Guardsmen of Japanese descent. Following the war, more than 240,000 G.I.s* were demobilized at McCoy. Deactivated after the war, the Korean War* prompted reactivation of the post. In the 1980s, McCoy housed more than 15,000 Cubans, part of Fidel Castro's "Freedom Flotilla." Currently, Fort McCoy hosts National Guard* units from the Midwest for annual training.

References. Dan Cragg, *Guide to Military Installations*, 4th ed., 1994. Bill Roche, "The Real McCoy," *Soldiers*, January 1990, 42–44.

Thomas Christianson

FORT McHENRY

Following the burning of Washington in August, 1814, Vice Admiral Sir Alexander Cochrane directed his Royal Navy squadron and 4,500 troops toward Baltimore, situated on the Patapsco River. Baltimore was the third-largest city in the United States, and its defenses were anchored on Fort McHenry, which guarded the water approaches to the city. The burning of Washington had caused panic among the populace of Baltimore, who expected the same fate. Maryland's governor gave command of the city's defenses to sixty-two-year-old Senator Samuel Smith. A veteran of the American Revolution,* Smith inspired the citizens to fight for their city. On 12 September the Royal Navy disembarked Major General Robert Ross and 4,700 troops at North Point, about fourteen miles from Baltimore. Later that afternoon, Ross was killed by sharpshooters as he led his men toward 3,000 Maryland militia blocking the road to the city. Putting up a stout defense, the militiamen slowly gave way and retired to the main defensive lines east of Baltimore.

The British plan was for Cochrane's flotilla to sail past Fort McHenry and bombard the rear of the U.S. lines while the land forces assaulted the front. The fort's commander, Major George Armistead, and the garrison of one thousand were determined to stop the British. Cochrane opened fire at dawn on 13 September from beyond the range of the fort's guns. Armistead's men stoically withstood the heavy barrage. When dawn arrived the following day, Cochrane realized the futility of his efforts to batter the fort into submission and persuaded Colonel Arthur Brooke, Ross's replacement, to break off the assault. The defense of Fort McHenry saved the city of Baltimore and marked the end of British attacks along the shores of Chesapeake Bay. More important, the flag flying defiantly over the fort during the bombardment inspired Francis Scott Key to pen the lyrics of the "Star Spangled Banner."

References. Walter Lord, *The Dawn's Early Light*, 1972. John K. Mahon, *The War of 1812*, 1972.

Richard Barbuto

FORT McPHERSON

Named for Major General James Birdseye McPherson, commander of the Army of the Tennessee* killed on 22 July 1864 in the battle of Atlanta, McPherson Barracks opened in 1867 on the present-day site of Spellman College in Atlanta, Georgia. The 4th Artillery moved to the present site in 1889, and on 4 May that year the post was designated Fort McPherson. During the Spanish-American War,* McPherson became an important training center and the site of a general hospital; in World War I* an internment camp for German prisoners of war* operated at the fort. In 1941, a general depot and reception center were developed at McPherson to facilitate mobilization for World War II.* Following the war, McPherson served as a separation and reassignment center, and in December 1947 Headquarters, Third Army,* moved to McPherson. In 1991, Headquarters, U.S. Army Reserve Command* (USARC), was activated at Fort McPherson.

References. Dan Cragg, *Guide to Military Installations*, 4th ed., 1994. William R. Evinger, ed., *Directory of U.S. Military Bases Worldwide*, 3d ed., 1998.

Edward Shanahan

FORT MONROE

Fort Monroe, the Army's third-oldest operating fort, occupies a natural defensive position at the mouth of Chesapeake Bay. First occupied by settlers from Jamestown in 1609, the present fort was begun in 1819 and named in honor of James Monroe, then president of the United States. It was the largest stone fort in the United States and one of few Union forts in the South that did not fall to the Confederacy during the Civil War.* Following the war, Confederate President Jefferson Davis was imprisoned at Monroe for two years. During World War I,* the fort served as Headquarters, Harbor Defenses of Chesapeake Bay, and it later became the home of the Army's Coast Artillery School. Currently, Fort Monroe is home of the U.S. Army Training and Doctrine Command* (TRADOC).

References. Irvin Haas, *Citadels, Ramparts, & Stockades*, 1979. Phyllis Sprock, "Freedom's Fort," *Soldiers*, January 1988, 20–23. Richard P. Weinert, Jr., and Robert Arthur, *Defender of the Chesapeake*, 1989.

David A. Rubenstein

FORT MOULTRIE

Fort Moultrie was one of three defensive structures strategically located at the harbor mouth of Charleston, South Carolina, on Sullivan's Island at the northeast entrance to the harbor. Moultrie sat just one mile from the more imposing Fort Sumter* and was named after Colonel William Moultrie, whose command of then Fort Sullivan had been credited with turning back a British attack in 1776. Constructed in the post-Revolutionary period, the brick fort was not particularly strong. Designed to repel a seaward invasion, the fort was a series of barbettes giving protection forward; its rear was open. Because of its limited military importance, Moultrie was in poor repair when South Caroilina seceded in 1860, and it fell without a fight when its commander determined it indefensible.

The secessionists quickly rearmed and began improving the fort. Moultrie's guns, aided by several other batteries on Sullivan's Island, played a key role in the defense of Charleston from 1861 to 1865. The batteries engaged Union ships and monitors on several occasions and suffered numerous casualties. The Confederates finally abandoned Moultrie and Sullivan's Island on 18 February 1865; Federal forces occupied them almost immediately. After the Civil War,* Fort Moultrie was refitted and became part of the U.S. coastal defense system until after World War II.* Today, the site is a museum.

Reference. E. Milby Burton, *The Siege of Charleston 1861–1865*, 1970.

Lee W. Eysturlid

FORT MYER

Fort Myer, located in Arlington, Virginia, adjacent to Arlington National Cemetery, was established as Fort Whipple in 1863 for the defense of Washington, D.C. First named in honor of Brigadier General Amiel Whipple, brigade* and division* commander in the defense of Washington, in the late 1860s the Signal Bureau (later the Signal Corps*) took it over. On 4 February 1881, Fort Whipple was renamed Fort Myer, in honor of Brigadier General Albert Myer, an Army surgeon who was the Army's first chief signal officer.

At the turn of the century, Quarters One at Fort Myer became the residence of the Army's Chief of Staff,* and on 3 September 1908 the parade field became the site of the world's first military aviation test flight, when Orville Wright conducted a one-minute demonstration for the Army. Two weeks later First Lieutenant Thomas Selfridge was killed when the Wright plane crashed at Myer; Selfridge became the world's first aviation fatality. During World War II,* Myer was a processing station for troops and home of the Army Band School. Today, the 3rd Infantry (the Old Guard*), the U.S. Army Band, and Headquarters, Military District of Washington are stationed at Fort Myer.

References. Dan Cragg, *Guide to Military Installations*, 4th ed., 1994. William Gardner Bell, *Quarters One*, 1988.

David A. Rubenstein

FORT NIAGARA

As early as 1669, the French built the first fortification at the mouth of the Niagara River, a strategic choke point that controlled water traffic into the interior of North America. In 1759, during the French and Indian War, Fort Niagara fell to the British and their Iroquois allies. During the American Revolution,* Butler's Rangers, a loyalist unit, and their Iroquois allies raided colonial frontier settlements from Fort Niagara as far east as New Jersey. The Jay Treaty ceded Fort Niagara to the United States in 1796; the British then built Fort George, across the river in Upper Canada, within cannon shot of Niagara. Fort Niagara anchored the U.S. defensive line along the river until the night of 18–19 December 1813, when a force of 562 British troops entered the fort through a door carelessly left unlocked and inadequately guarded. Surprising the 433-man garrison, the British conducted a bayonet* assault, overwhelming the defenders. Over the next two weeks the British burned virtually every building on the U.S. side of the river, sending the occupants fleeing into the interior. Sir Gordon Drummond, the British commander in Upper Canada, noted that the Americans on the Niagara frontier had sheltered soldiers in their homes since the beginning of the war. Thus, he felt, these civilian homes were legitimate targets.

The Americans were disinclined to lay seige to the strong fort and chose instead to attack along the Canadian shore in July 1814. This offensive, under Major General Jacob Brown, ultimately failed, although it was the most serious threat to Upper Canada during the War of 1812.* The Treaty of Ghent called for a return to the status quo ante bellum, and the British relinguished Fort Niagara to the United States in May 1815. The usefulness of Fort Niagara decreased in 1825, when the Erie Canal bypassed the fort and connected the upper Great Lakes to the Atlantic Ocean. Today, Fort Niagara is a museum, maintained much as it was during its heyday as a strategic fort dominating the passageway between lakes Erie and Ontario.

References. Brian Leigh Dunnigan, *Forts within a Fort*, 1989, and *A History and Guide to Old Fort Niagara*, 1985.

Richard Barbuto

FORT ORD

For Ord, located a hundred miles south of San Francisco on Monterey Bay, was established in 1917 and named in honor of Major General Edward O. C. Ord. The rolling sand dunes and plains on the coast and sharp inland hills offered ideal terrain for maneuver training. Two generations of recruits received their basic combat training* and advanced individual training* at Ord. In 1974, Fort Ord became the home of the reactivated 7th Infantry Division (Light) and assumed responsibility for nearby Camp Roberts, Fort Hunter Liggett,* and the Presidio* of Monterey. Many soldiers who served there considered Fort Ord to be the most beautiful setting of any U.S. Army post. In 1991, the Base Realignment and Closure Commission designated Fort Ord for closure; it closed in 1994.

References. Dan Cragg, *Guide to Military Installations*, 4th ed., 1994. Matt Glasgow, "Bullets, Beaches, and Bayonets," *Soldiers*, June 1979, 45–48.

David A. Rubenstein

FORT PHIL KEARNY

On 13 July 1866, Colonel Henry B. Carrington selected a site 243 miles north of Fort Laramie* at the foot of the Bighorn Mountains, between Big and Little Piney Creeks, to build the second of three forts protecting the Bozeman Trail.* Originally called Fort Carrington, it was renamed Fort Phil Kearny in honor of Major General Philip Kearny, who had been killed on 1 September 1862 at the Battle of Chantilly, Virginia. The fort was well constructed, with an eight-foot log palisade wall, but the surrounding hills provided good observation for the enemy. Best known for the massacre of Captain William Fetterman's command by hostile Indians in December 1866, Fort Phil Kearny existed for only two years. The Fort Laramie* Treaty of 1868 with the Sioux required the Army to abandon all three Bozeman forts. The site of Fort Phil Kearny is now administered by the state of Wyoming.

References. Dee Brown, *The Fetterman Massacre*, 1971. Robert W. Frazer, *Forts of the West*, 1965.

Jeffrey Prater

FORT PICKENS

In January 1861, Fort Pickens was one of three forts that controlled the entrance to Pensacola Bay. Hearing of the surrender of Pensacola's Navy Yard, First Lieutenant Adam Slemmer spiked the guns at Forts McRea and Barrancas and moved his force of eighty men to Fort Pickens on Santa Rosa Island. Although unused since the Mexican War* and in disrepair, the stone fort was still an imposing defensive structure. Until after the firing on Fort Sumter* in April, the Confederates did not directly threaten the reinforced garrison at Pickens. Following the outbreak of the war, however, General Braxton Bragg and the newly formed 8,100-man Army of Pensacola resolved to capture Fort Pickens. Between 12 April 1861 and 9 May 1862, the Confederates assaulted Pickens five times. In October 1861, for example, Bragg sent 1,000 infantry in a night assault against Pickens. Called the Battle of Santa Rosa Island, the action failed to eject the Federals. Eventually accepting the stalemate, the Confederates destroyed their positions and abandoned Pensacola in May 1862. The Federals reoccupied the port for the duration of the war, using it as a base for the West Gulf Squadron, thereby denying the Confederacy the best naval facility south of Norfolk.

References. Edwin C. Bearss, "Civil War Operation in and around Pensacola," *Florida Historical Quarterly*, January 1961, 231–255. Irvin Haas, *Citadels, Ramparts, & Stockades*, 1979.

Lee W. Eysturlid

FORT POLK

Located in central Louisiana, Fort Polk was established in 1941 and named in honor of Lieutenant General Leonidas Polk, Episcopal Bishop of Louisiana (1841–1861), and Civil War* Confederate commander. The fort's initial mission was to support the Louisiana Maneuvers,* for which the area provided open plains for armored and mechanized forces and thickly vegetated areas for dismounted training. Following World War II,* Polk closed and reopened several times. The active Army trained at Polk during the Korean War* and the Berlin crisis, while the Army Reserve* used it during summer training periods. During the 1960s, basic combat training* and advanced individual training* brigades* at Polk prepared infantry* replacements for Southeast Asia. It was the home of the 5th Mechanized Infantry Division from 1974 to 1994. Since 1993, the Joint Readiness Training Center* (JRTC) has operated at Fort Polk.

References. Steve Hara, "The Polk Word: New," *Soldiers*, December 1985, 13–16. Thomas E. Kerscher, "The Rebirth of Fort Polk," *Military Engineer*, November–December 1975, 329–330. Ralph E. Ropp, "Ft. Polk," *Army*, April 1978, 46–50.

David A. Rubenstein

FORT RICHARDSON

Fort Richardson, adjacent to Anchorage, Alaska, was established in 1940 and named in honor of Brigadier General Wilds P. Richardson, early Alaskan explorer. Originally located on the current site of Elmendorf Air Force Base, Richardson's first mission was to support the delivery of Lend-Lease aircraft to the Soviet Union. In 1947, Headquarters, U.S. Army Alaska, was established at Richardson, and the present post was constructed in 1950. In the 1950s, Richardson assumed a new role, overseeing a number of Nike Hercules air defense missile sites across Alaska. In 1961, the U.S. Modern Biathlon Training Center opened at Richardson and trained U.S. athletes for the next three Olympics. The post remained the home of the 6th Infantry Division (Light) until 1990. Today, one battalion* of the 6th remains at Fort Richardson, along with Alaska Defense Command and the Arctic Support Brigade.

References. Bill Branley, "I'm Going Where?" *Soldiers*, November 1981, 31–33. Dan Cragg, *Guide to Military Installations*, 4th ed., 1994.

David A. Rubenstein

FORT RILEY

Captain Charles S. Lovell, 6th U.S. Infantry, established Fort Riley, Kansas, on the north bank of the Kansas River at the junction of the Smoky Hill and Republican Rivers, a site recommended by Colonel Thomas T. Fauntleroy, 1st U.S. Dragoons. Fauntleroy had suggested that the site was of such merit that a post would permit abandoning Forts Leavenworth, Scott, Atkinson, Kearny, and Laramie. Originally called Camp Center—it was very close to the geographical center of the United States—the post was designated Fort Riley on 27 June 1853, in honor of Colonel Bennett Riley, 1st U.S. Infantry, who had died on the 9th of that month. A permanent cavalry post was erected in 1855 under the direction of Captain Edmund A. Ogden, 8th U.S. Infantry. Fort Riley has served continuously since that time. Today, Fort Riley is home to the 1st Brigade, 1st Infantry Division, and the 3d Brigade, 1st Armor Division.

References. Robert W. Frazer, *Forts of the West*, 1965. Heike Hasenauer, "Fort Riley History," *Soldiers*, April 1991, 38–41. Francis Paul Prucha, *A Guide to the Military Posts of the United States*, 1964.

Jeffrey Prater

FORT RUCKER

Fort Rucker occupies 64,349 acres ninety miles south of Montgomery, Alabama, and houses the U.S. Army's Aviation Center and School. Its primary mission is to train the Army's helicopter and fixed-wing pilots, maintenance personnel, and air traffic controllers. Established in 1942 as the Ozark Triangle Division Camp on land purchased in 1935, the post was renamed Camp Rucker in 1943 in honor of Confederate General Edmund Winchester Rucker, a long-time businessman in Montgomery. The camp was inactive from 1946 to 1950 but was reactivated during the Korean War.* In 1954, the post again closed until 1955, when the Army Aviation School moved there from Fort Sill.* Camp Rucker was redesignated Fort Rucker the same year. Today, over 9,000 active-duty soldiers and civilian workers serve at Fort Rucker, the "Home of Army Aviation."

References. Steve Hara, "Fort Rucker," *Soldiers*, March 1988, 19–21. John Kitchens, "Camp Rucker Selected as Home of Army Aviation," *U.S. Army Aviation Digest*, January–February 1994, 30–38.

Kenneth Turner

FORT SAM HOUSTON

U.S. Army troops first occupied San Antonio, Texas, and established a depot around the Alamo in 1845. A fort was built within the city in 1876, and the depot moved to its new storage facilities in 1879. In 1886, the Apache leader Geronimo and his band were held in the fort's Quadrangle until they were relocated to Florida. Four years later, the post was renamed Fort Sam Houston, in honor of Sam Houston, first president of the Republic of Texas. Lieutenant Colonel Theodore Roosevelt trained his regiment of Rough Riders at Sam Houston in 1898, and First Lieutenant Benjamin D. Foulois flew the first Army aircraft on the main parade field in 1910. Second Lieutenant Dwight D. Eisenhower* came in 1915 to Sam Houston, where in October he met Mamie Doud; their first quarters were on the Infantry Post. Colonel William "Billy" Mitchell* was sent to Sam Houston in 1925 in an attempt to keep him from the media spotlight. Fort Sam Houston is currently the home of Headquarters, Fifth Army,* and the Army Medical Department and its tenent units: Health Services Command (1973–95), Army Medical Command, Army Medical Department Center and School, Brooke Army Medical Center, and the Institute of Surgical (Burn) Research.

References. Roger N. Conger et al., *Frontier Forts of Texas*, 1966. Mary Olivia Handy, *History of Fort Sam Houston*, 1951. Terri Wiram, "Fort Sam," *Soldiers*, March 1983, 46–48.

David A. Rubenstein

FORT SHAFTER

Fort Shafter, near Honolulu, was the first permnent, Army installation in Hawaii. Built in 1907, today Fort Shafter houses the headquarters for the United States Army, Pacific (USARPAC)—the Army component of U.S. Pacific Command (PACOM), commanding all Army units in the Pacific theater outside of Korea—the Pacific Ocean Division of the U.S. Army Corps of Engineers,* and

U.S. Army Support Command, Hawaii. The post is named for General William Rufus Shafter (1835–1906), who served in the Civil War,* fought several campaigns during the Indian Wars,* and commanded V Corps in the Spanish-American War.*

References. Stetson Conn, "Guardian of the Pacific," *Army Information Digest,* July 1960, 14–23. Dan Cragg, *Guide to Military Installations,* 4th ed., 1994.

J. G. D. Babb

FORT SHERMAN

In April 1878, the U.S. Army established Fort Coeur D'Alene in the city of Coeur D'Alene, Idaho. In April 1887, the post was renamed Fort Sherman for William Teeumseh Sherman,* then Commanding General of the U.S. Army. One of Sherman's initiatives was to consolidate Army units at strategic locations instead of spreading them thinly across the western frontier. One such site was on Lake Coeur D'Alene's north shore, at its junction with the Spokane River. As a consolidated site, the post had a threefold mission: to present a military presence near the U.S.-Canadian border; maintain order in northern Idaho and eastern Washington; and protect crews working on the Walla Walla railroad and Bozeman Trail telegraph. Fort Sherman served as a catalyst for the city of Coeur D'Alene until it closed as an active post in 1890.

Reference. Robert W. Frazer, *Forts of the West,* 1965.

David A. Rubenstein

FORT SILL

On 8 January 1869, Lieutenant General Philip H. Sheridan* staked out a site near Lawton, Oklahoma, for a military post. Originally named Camp Wichita, on 1 August 1869 the post officially adopted the name Fort Sill, in honor of Sheridan's U.S. Military Academy* classmate Brigadier General Joshua W. Sill, who had been killed in the Battle of Stones River* in the Civil War.* The post's original purpose was to pacify the Indian tribes located on the southern Great Plains. The 10th Cavalry and the 6th Infantry were the first units to garrison the fort. Fort Sill's role, however, began to change in January 1902, when the 29th Battery of field artillery reported to the post. The last cavalry* unit left in 1907, and the Army established the Field Artillery School at Fort Sill in 1911. Today, Fort Sill in known as the "Home of the field artillery."

References. Numa P. Avendano, "Fort Sill Fifty Years Ago," *Field Artillery Journal,* March–April 1978, 44–47. W. S. Nye, *Carbine and Lance,* 1937.

James L. Isemann

FORT SNELLING

Fort Snelling is located at the juncture of the Minnesota and Mississippi Rivers in present-day St. Paul, Minnesota. Built by soldiers of the 5th Infantry Regiment between 1819 and 1825 and named for its first commander, Colonel Josiah Snelling, the fort served as the northwestern link of a chain of forts between Lake Michigan and the Missouri River. Soldiers from Snelling policed the frontier, controlled the fur and liquor traffic in the upper Mississippi valley, pacified local Indian tribes, and protected travelers along northern roads. As the frontier moved west, the fort was reduced to a supply depot; it was sold to private developers in 1858. Plans to build a town on the site were abandoned at the outbreak of the Civil War,* and the government reacquired the area. Snelling served as a training center for Minnesota volunteers. After the Civil War, Fort Snelling served as a headquarters and supply base for the Department of Dakota. Snelling's soldiers fought in the Indian Wars* and the Spanish-American War,* and Snelling was a recruiting center in the two world wars. Decommissioned in 1946, Fort Snelling was designated Minnesota's first national historic landmark in 1960 and has since been restored with public and private funds.

References. Steve Hall, *Fort Snelling*, 1987. Evan Jones, *Citadel in the Wilderness*, 1966.

Douglas P. Scalard

FORT SUMTER

Fort Sumter was a pentagonal brick and masonry fort located in Charleston Harbor. It measured about 300 feet on each side and mounted forty-eight guns. After South Carolina seceded from the Union in December 1960, Major Robert Anderson occupied Sumter with about a hundred soldiers and refused South Carolina's demands that he evacuate the fort. By the first week of April 1861 the line had been drawn, and Sumter was the primary focus of the nation's attention. On 10 April, General P.G.T. Beauregarde demanded that Anderson immediately evacuate the fort and warned that the Confederate batteries surrounding the harbor would open fire at 4:20 A.M. on the 14th. At 4:30 that morning the bombardment began, an act generally cited as the beginning of the Civil War.* Without a relief force Fort Sumter could not be saved, and Anderson surrendered after 4,000 shells fell on the fort in thirty-four hours. President Abraham Lincoln used the attack on Fort Sumter to justify calling for 75,000 volunteers to put down the rebellion. Sumter became the key position in the Confederate defense of Charleston and withstood fierce attacks by Union forces during the latter part of the war. Reduced to rubble, the fort stood as a defiant symbol of the rebellion until the Confederates abandoned it in early 1865. Today, Fort Sumter is a national monument operated by the National Park Service.

References. Robert Hendrickson, *Sumter*, 1990. W. A. Swanberg, *First Blood*, 1957.

George Knapp

FORT TICONDEROGA

Originally constructed by the French in 1755 and called Fort Carillon, the stone fortress at the junction of Lakes Champlain and George guarded a major water route into Canada. After failing to take it in 1758, the British succeeded

in 1759 and renamed it Ticonderoga. In one of the American Revolution's*
opening blows, Ethan Allen's* and Benedict Arnold's* forces captured the undermanned fort on 10 May 1775. That winter the colonials transported over fifty
artillery pieces from Ticonderoga south to use against the British, besieged in
Boston.

Driven from Canada in the spring of 1776, the colonials bolstered Ticonderoga and fortified Mount Independence on the Vermont shore to stem a British
invasion, while Arnold drew the British into a lengthy shipbuilding race. By
autumn 1776 British forces had abandoned their offensive. The following summer, Tinconderoga slowed British General John Burgoyne's offensive, but lacking the supplies and manpower for prolonged resistance, the colonials withdrew
from the fort on the night of 6 July. Although the withdrawal was seen as a
defeat, Fort Ticonderoga's former defenders became the nucleus of the army
that eventually defeated Burgoyne at Saratoga.* Plundered by local settlers for
building supplies after the war, the restored fort is today a private museum.

References. Edward P. Hamilton, *Fort Ticonderoga*, 1964. Robert B. Roberts, *New
York's Forts in the Revolution*, 1980.

Stanley Adamiak

FORT UNION

Lieutenant Colonel Edwin Vose Sumner, 1st U.S. Dragoons, established Fort
Union on 26 July 1851 on the Santa Fe Trail, about twenty-four miles northeast
of Las Vegas, New Mexico. Along with other posts in the New Mexico territory,
Fort Union protected settlers, miners, and immigrants moving west from Jicarilla
Apache and Ufe Indians. In 1861, Colonel Edward R. S. Canby, 19th infantry,
erected a new post, better prepared to withstand an expected Confederate assault.
Fort Union soldiers met Confederate forces under H. H. Sibley at Glorieta Pass
in March 1862, destroyed the Confederate supply train, and forced Sibley to
withdrew from New Mexico. Following the Civil War,* Fort Union soldiers
fought in numerous skirmishes with Indians and local thieves, and Fort Union
served as an ordnance and supply depot before arrival of the railroad in the
1880s. The last U.S. Army soldier left Fort Union in 1891.

References. Chris Emmett, *Fort Union and the Winning of the Southwest*, 1965. Irvin
Haas, *Citadels, Ramparts, & Stockades*, 1979. Herbert M. Hart, *Tour Guide to Old
Western Forts*, 1980.

Thomas Christianson

FORT WAINWRIGHT

Fort Wainwright, adjacent to Fairbanks, Alaska, was established in 1941 as
Ladd Army Airfield, a stopover on the Lend-Lease route to the Soviet Union.
After World War II,* the U.S. Air Force assumed control of Ladd and its sub-
installation, Eielson Air Force Base, as supply depots supporting Distant Early
Warning (DEW) radar* sites and experimental stations above the Arctic Circle.
When the Air Force relinquished control of Ladd in January 1961, the Army

reoccupied the base and named it Fort Wainwright, in honor of General Jonathan M. Wainwright,* defender of Bataan* and Corregidor.* As an Army post, Wainwright has served as home to the 171st Infantry Brigade (Mechanized), the 172d Infantry Brigade, a Nike-Hercules battalion,* the Cold Regions Research and Engineering Laboratory, and Headquarters, 6th Infantry Division (Light), which moved from Fort Richardson* to Fort Wainwright in 1990. Following the 6th Infantry Division's inactivation in 1994, the division's* First Brigade remained at Fort Wainwright.

References. Bill Branley, "I'm Going Where?" *Soldiers*, November 1981, 31–33. Dan Cragg, *Guide to Military Installations* 4th ed., 1994. William R. Evinger, ed., *Directory of U.S. Military Bases Worldwide*, 3d ed., 1998.

David A. Rubenstein

FORT WILLIAM McKINLEY

In 1902, just as the Philippine Insurrection* was coming to a close, the U.S. Army began construction on Fort William McKinley. Situated on 8,151 acres bordering the Pasig River, the post was six miles from downtown Manila, near the town of Guadaloupe in the province of Rizal, Luzon. Fort McKinley featured housing for officers and troops, an excellent road system, hospital, post exchange, bakery, chapel, fire department, and gymnasium. Training facilities were also available, including Class A and B target ranges. The first commander, Lieutenant Colonel C.A. Booth, along with 293 officers and men of the 7th Infantry and supporting units, occupied the fort on 25 February 1904. The 31st Infantry formed at McKinley on 1 August 1916; the 45th and 57th Regiments of the Philippine Scouts* formed there in 1918. During World War I,* an officer candidate school* and the Philippine National Guard Division moved to the post. Prior to World War II,* McKinley served as headquarters for the Philippine Division, commanded by Major Jonathan M. Wainwright,* and it hosted a variety of specialized training programs for the Philippine army. During the war, it served as a key organizing point and command post for the defense of the Philippines and a supply depot for operations on Bataan.*

Immediately after World War II, the Philippine government expressed opposition to locating U.S. military bases in metropolitan areas, particularly Manila. Complying with Filipino wishes and in accordance with the 1947 Military Base Agreement, the U.S. Army vacated Fort William McKinley in August 1947.

References. William E. Berry, Jr., *U.S. Bases in the Philippines*, 1989. Charles J. Sullivan, *Army Posts & Towns*, 1935.

John Quinlivan

FORTS HENRY AND DONELSON CAMPAIGN

In February 1862, Albert Sidney Johnston commanded all Confederate forces west of the Appalachian Mountains, approximately 43,000 poorly equipped troops—mostly Tennesseans. Johnston's task was to defend a line from the

Cumberland Gap in the east, to Bowling Green, Kentucky, in the west, a task complicated by his "violation" of Kentucky's "neutrality." Johnston proceeded to establish a series of forts along this line, including Fort Henry on the Tennessee River, and Fort Donelson on the Cumberland River, just below the Kentucky-Tennessee state line. Forts Henry and Donelson presented the greatest weakness in Johnston's defenses. In large part because of lackadaisical efforts to finish the positions, they were still incomplete when U.S. forces under Brigadier General Ulysses S. Grant* attacked Fort Henry on 6 February 1862. Escorted by armored steamers, under the command of Flag Officer Andrew H. Foote, Grant attempted to outflank the defenders of Fort Henry, while the gunboats bombarded the Confederate position. Outnumbered, outgunned, and in an earthen fortification that was largely under water from the Tennessee River's winter floods, the remaining defenders surrendered to a Navy party that entered by rowing in through a sallyport. Most of the garrison had retreated to Fort Donelson, which had been reinforced by a significant number of Confederate troops. On the 13th, Grant surrounded Donelson and attempted to shell it into submission, but the Confederate gunners, firing from higher ground, damaged every ship in the attacking squadron, forcing Grant to retreat. In spite of his success, the Confederate commander, John B. Floyd, was convinced that his position was untenable and attempted a breakout two days later. Led by cavalry forces under Nathan Bedford Forrest,* Floyd nearly succeeded, but he lost his nerve and returned his men to their starting positions. Grant, who had been visiting the wounded Foote when his army was assailed, returned to his men and closed the breech. He prepared to finish the assault the next day.

Floyd decided to surrender, a decision backed by his second in command, Gideon J. Pillow; however, neither of them was willing to actually take the responsibility. That onus fell to the third in command, Simon B. Buckner. The two senior officers and two to three thousand men of their own brigades escaped from the doomed fort that night, leaving sixteen to seventeen thousand irreplaceable soldiers to lay down their arms at Grant's demand for "unconditional and immediate surrender." The success at Forts Henry and Donelson launched Grant's career, bringing him to President Abraham Lincoln's notice. It also led to the permanent loss to the Confederacy of Kentucky, western Tennessee, and, most critically, Nashville, the second most important city in the western Confederacy.

References. Benjamin Franklin Cooling, *Forts Henry and Donelson*, 1987. Roy P. Stonesifer, Jr., The Forts Henry-Heiman and Fort Donelson Campaigns, 1965.

Andrew N. Morris

FORTS MONTGOMERY AND CLINTON

Forts Montgomery and Clinton, located in the Hudson Highlands on the west side of the Hudson River several miles below West Point, were the primary defenses of the upper river. The two earthen works sat on either side of Popolopen Creek and overlooked a massive iron chain that spanned the river, blocking it to oceangoing vessels. Montgomery's heavy artillery threatened any vessel trying to pass the chain. However formidable the forts were to ships, their land approaches were vulnerable to attack from the west.

In 1777, the British planned simultaneous advances along the Lake Champlain–Hudson River approach and east along the Mohawk toward Albany. Although it was not specified in the plan, it was assumed that General William Howe's army in New York City would assist by staging an attack against the Hudson Highlands, with the possibility of uniting British forces at Albany. Howe believed, however, that the army in the north would not need his assistance; he sailed to the Chesapeake Bay to launch a campaign to seize Philadelphia. When the advance down the Mohawk stalled outside Fort Stanwix, Major General Horatio Gates forced John Burgoyne's army to give battle near Saratoga.* In an attempt to relieve pressure on Burgoyne, General Sir Henry Clinton, Howe's second in command at New York, used his garrison forces to attack Forts Montgomery and Clinton. A British force of 3,500 men carried the two forts in a brief but bloody engagement and advanced toward Kingston, but Burgoyne's eventual surrender rendered further advance superfluous.

References. Harrison Bird, *Attack on Quebec*, 1968. Bruce Grant, *American Forts Yesterday and Today*, 1965. Richard M. Ketchum, *Saratoga*, 1997.

Joseph R. Fischer

FORWARD AIR CONTROLLER

The forward air controller (FAC), a key member of the close air support team, coordinates air strikes against enemy targets in the close battle area. Basic techniques utilizing ground-based or airborne FACs emerged during World War II* and were extensively tested and refined during the Korean War.* In Korea, FACs served as members of tactical air control parties (TACP), made up of Army and Air Force personnel assigned to coordinate tactical airpower with ground troops directly engaging the enemy. Controversy, fueled by interservice disputes over techniques, equipment, and command, eventually diminished with experience and with the evolution of clear policies. By the end of the war, FACs had proven that close coordination between air and ground forces was essential and could be effective. Nevertheless, interservice friction between the Army and Air Force concerning the FACs' missions continued into the Vietnam War* years. In 1965, a joint agreement assigned a TACP, consisting of an air liaison officer, a forward air controller, and a radio operator, to Army units from the field army* to the battalion* level. Today, the forward air controller is an essential member of the joint combined-arms team.

References. Benjamin Franklin Cooling, ed., *Case Studies in the Development of Close Air Support*, 1990. William A. Jacobs, "Tactical Air Doctrine and AAF Close Air Support in the European Theater, 1944–1945," *Aerospace Historian*, Spring–March 1980, 35–49. Riley Sunderland, *Evolution of Command and Control Doctrine for Close Air Support*, 1973.

Danny E. Rodehaver

FORWARD EDGE OF THE BATTLE AREA

Current U.S. Army doctrine* organizes the tactical battlefield into three areas of operation: deep, close, and rear. Each of these areas is further subdivided to effect coordination of fire and maneuver.* The close area of operations includes the forward edge of the battle area, or FEBA, within the main battle area, where ground combat troops are closest to the enemy. While the FEBA has more significance in an area defense, it is also important in a mobile defense. The commander coordinates fire support, commits combat power, and launches counterattacks along the forward edge of the battle area.

References. Robert A. Doughty, *The Evolution of US Army Tactical Doctrine, 1946–76*, 1979. John M. Fawcett, Jr., "Which Way to the FEBA?" *Airpower Journal*, Fall 1992, 14–24.

Kenneth Turner

FORWARD OBSERVER

A forward observer (FO) coordinates fire support activities for his supported unit. He locates and identifies targets, requests fire support, performs fire support coordination, and controls artillery* and mortar* fires. FOs normally accompany infantry* platoons,* but they also operate as aerial observers in helicopters and in independent combat observation laser teams (COLTs). The increasing use of indirect fire after the Franco-Prussian War of 1870–71 created the need for forward observers. All belligerents refined their forward observation techniques during World War I,* as accurate indirect fire became a necessity on the battle field and increasingly sophisticated communications systems became available. By the late 1930s, the use of surveyed firing tables* and centralized fire-direction centers* at the battalion level, along with greatly improved radio communications, effectively enabled FOs to control the fires of several battalions simultaneously. Today, forward observers, equipped with radios and computer systems, operate as integral parts of fire support teams that coordinate fire support for companies and higher units.

References. Boyd L. Dastrup, *King of Battle*, 1992. Bruce I. Gudmundsson, *On Artillery*, 1993. Sean E. Harris, "Company Fire Support Matrix," *Field Artillery*, May–June 1997, 17–20.

Jeffrey S. Shadburn

4TH INFANTRY DIVISION

The 4th Infantry Division was constituted on 19 November 1917 and organized on 10 December at Camp Greene, North Carolina. Troops of the Ivy Division—after the Roman numeral IV—fought at the Aisne-Marne, St. Mihiel,* Meuse-Argonne,* and the battles of Champagne and Lorraine. Demobilized in September 1921, the 4th was reactivated in June 1940 as part of the pre–World War II* buildup. Designated the 4th Division [Motorized] in August 1940 and the 4th Motorized Division in July 1941, it was redesignated 4th Infantry Division in August 1943. The 4th landed on Utah Beach on D-Day and fought in every campaign in Europe, returning to the United States in July 1945. Deactivated in March 1946, the 4th was reactived sixteen months later at Fort Ord,* California. It deployed to Vietnam in 1966; there it participated in numerous operations and campaigns until it returned to the United States in 1972. Until 1995, the 4th was located at Fort Carson,* Colorado. In December 1995, it relocated to Fort Hood,* Texas.

The 4th Infantry Division's motto is "Steadfast and Loyal." Its insignia, four green ivy leaves—symbols of fidelity and tenacity—are connected by an open circle arranged in a cross on a khaki square.

References. Herb "Chick" Fowle, *The Men of the Terrible Green Cross*, 1991. Gardner N. Hatch, ed., *4th Infantry "Ivy" Division*, 1987. Edward Hymoff, *Fourth Infantry Division, Vietnam* [1968].

FRANKFORD ARSENAL

The Frankford Arsenal was established on 27 May 1816 in Frankford, Pennsylvania, just outside of Philadelphia. By 1830, the arsenal had become an major small-arms-ammunitions production plant and a munitions development and testing center for the U.S. Army. When identifying headstamps began to be placed on shell casings in 1877, Frankford Arsenal ammunition was identified by the letter F and the month and year of manufacture. In 1902, Frankford's designation was changed to F A and, in 1917 the month of manufacture was dropped from the headstamps. By 1897, Frankford's production capacity was 50,000 cartridges per day and up to 15,500,000 ball and blank cartridges per year. In the 20th century, Frankford Arsenal has produced armaments, chronometers, instrument guidance systems, pilot ejection catapults, and direct-fire weapons, and it has served as an ordnance research and engineering center. The arsenal originally consisted of two buildings on twenty acres of land, a series of expansions increased its size to 110 acres and 234 buildings. The growth of Philadelphia's suburbs around the arsenal, however, limited future expansion and development of the facility. On 24 November 1974, the Secretary of the Army* ordered Frankford Arsenal to be closed by 1977, and in 1983 about 170 buildings and 80 acres were sold to a Massachusetts developer.

References. James J. Farley, *Making Arms in the Machine Age*, 1994. James A. Huston, *The Sinews of War*, 1966.

L. Lynn Williams

FRANKLIN, TENNESSEE

The battle of Franklin was the first of two major battles in the Franklin and Nashville Campaign.* After the fall of Atlanta in September 1864, the Confederate Army of Tennessee under General John Bell Hood attacked the Federal lines of communication back to Nashville. William T. Sherman* sent two corps* under George H. Thomas* to deal with Hood. On 29 November, XXIII Corps, commanded by Major General John M. Schofield,* slipped past Hood's forces at Spring Hill, Tennessee, and marched through the night to Franklin. Outraged,

Hood ordered a pursuit, but by the time his forces reached Franklin the Federals had entrenched in an arc about a mile and a half long, with both flanks anchored on the river. Disregarding advice to the contrary, Hood ordered a two-division assault on the Federal lines. The Confederates struck two brigades astride the Columbia Pike, driving the Federals back and opening a gap in the line. After fierce fighting, however, the Federals repelled the Confederates and closed the breach. Fighting continued into the night, but Schofield withdrew unmolested into Nashville the next day. Federal casualties were 2,326, while the Confederates lost 6,252 men, including five generals.

References. Jacob D. Cox, *Sherman's March to the Sea*, 1994. Winston Groom, *Shrouds of Glory*, 1995. James Lee McDonough and Thomas L. Connelly, *Five Tragic Hours*, 1983.

Edward Shanahan

FRANKLIN AND NASHVILLE CAMPAIGN

After the Federal capture of Atlanta,* Georgia, in September 1864, Confederate General John B. Hood decided to withdraw the Army of Tennessee into north-central Alabama, from where he threatened Lieutenant General William T. Sherman's* lines of supply. Sherman did not want to chase Hood and was not willing to remain in Atlanta. Hood's army, on the other hand, was not strong enough to challenge Sherman in a pitched battle. The stalemate was broken in October, when Hood began to move toward Sherman's rail lines in northwest Georgia. Sherman followed Hood briefly, then broke off the pursuit. Hood believed that if he could threaten Nashville and the Ohio River, Sherman would have to abandon Atlanta. Sherman detailed sufficient forces, however, to contain Hood and, two weeks after Lincoln's reelection, began his march to the sea. Hood continued into central Tennessee, still believing that he could force Sherman to withdraw. Nevertheless, Sherman reached Savannah on 10 December. Hood subsequently attacked the Federal position at Franklin, Tennessee,* on 30 November, but suffered heavy casualties. He did not have the strength to attack the fortifications around Nashville. Over the next two weeks, reinforcements augmented Major General George H. Thomas's* command, and he finally attacked Hood's badly weakened army on 15 and 16 December. In defeating Hood, Thomas achieved one of the few decisive Union battlefield victories of the war. Hood's survivors regrouped in Alabama but were never again a serious threat in the West.

References. Stanley F. Horn, *The Decisive Battle of Nashville*, 1956. James L. McDonough and Thomas L. Connelly, *Five Tragic Hours*, 1983. Wiley Sword, *Embrace an Angry Wind*, 1991.

George Knapp

FREDERICKSBURG

After his defeat at Antietam,* Robert E. Lee* withdrew his army into Virginia. Major General George McClellan's* slow pursuit prompted President

Abraham Lincoln to replace him as commander of the Army of the Potomac*
with Major General Ambrose Burnside.* Burnside's plan was to move toward
Fredericksburg, Virginia, to threaten Richmond and force Lee to fight. At first
Burnside moved quickly, and on 17 November 1862 his leading units reached
Falmouth, across the Rappahannock River from Fredericksburg. Although only
a few Confederate troops occupied Fredericksburg, Burnside waited for pon-
toons to arrive. On 21 November, while Burnside hesitated, a Confederate corps
occupied the town; it was joined by a second corps on 30 November. Not until
10 December did Burnside attempt to cross the river, by which time Lee's army
was well entrenched on Marye's Heights overlooking the river and the town.
By 12 December, Burnside had almost 100,000 men across the river, they faced
about 70,000 Confederates. Burnside's main attack began on 13 December, one
division was able to penetrate the Confederate right, but it was driven back by
timely counterattacks. Fog and rain delayed Burnside's advance on the right,
but by late morning his forces were deployed in front of Marye's Heights.
Withering fire from Confederates along the Heights and from behind a stone
wall at the base of the ridge shattered the Union assault. Burnside withdrew
across the river the following night. Burnside sustained about 12,500 casualties;
Confederate losses approached 5,500. In January, Lincoln replaced Burnside
with Major General Joseph Hooker.*

References. Jay Luvass and Harold W. Nelson, eds., *The U.S. Army War College
Guide to the Battles of Chancellorsville and Fredericksburg*, 1988. Edward J. Stackpole,
The Fredericksburg Campaign, 2d ed., 1991.

Richard L. Kiper

FREE-FIRE ZONE

A free-fire zone (also known as a free-fire area) is an operational term used
to designate an area into which any weapon may be fired without coordination
with higher headquarters. They are established to expedite fires and allow aircraft to dispose of munitions that could not be used on their intended targets.
A free-fire zone is represented on a military map by a solid black line, with the
headquarters that established it and the time it became effective. When possible,
the free-fire zone is located on an easily identifiable terrain feature. If this is not
possible, it is identified by grid coordinates on maps and military overlays.

References. James S. Olson and Randy Roberts, *Where the Domino Fell*, 1991. Ches
Schneider, *From Classrooms to Claymores*, 1999. Neil Sheehan, *A Bright Shining Lie*,
1988.

Kenneth Turner

FRÉMONT, JOHN CHARLES (1813–1890)

Born in Savannah, Georgia, in 1813 and expelled from college for "incorri-
gible negligence," John Charles Frémont lived a life of alternating successes
and failures. After gaining experience in 1836 as a railroad surveyor, Frémont
was commissioned in the U.S. Topographical Corps. In 1841 he married Jesse

Benton, daughter of Thomas Hart Benton; both would assist in advancing his career. Frémont achieved early fame as an explorer in the Rockies. His published accounts of his adventures were extremely popular and earned him the sobriquet "the Pathfinder."

His 1846 expedition in California encouraged the Bear Flag Revolt; Frémont assumed command and captured Cahuenga. Promoted to lieutenant colonel and made governor of the state, he fell afoul of Brigadier General Stephen Watts Kearny and was court-martialed for disobedience in 1848. Although cleared by President James K. Polk, Frémont retired and led two further, although less successful, western expeditions in 1848 and 1853. In 1856, Frémont became the first Republican candidate for the presidency, but he lost to James Buchanan. In 1861, Frémont was commissioned a general and appointed commander of the Western Department, to retain control of Missouri for the Union. He failed to make effective use of his superior forces and was relieved of his command. As a political concession to the Radicals, Frémont was given command of the newly created Mountain Department, a secondary theater throughout the remainder of the war. Appointed governor of Arizona from 1878 to 1883, John C. Frémont died in New York City in 1890, known as a more successful explorer than military commander.

References. Allan Nevins, *Frémont*, 1939. Andrew Rolle, *John Charles Frémont*, 1991.

Lee W. Eysturlid

FRENCH 75 MM

Introduced in 1897, the French 75 mm gun combined recent technological advancements with a novel recoil system to produce the first modern quick-firing cannon. Like other contemporary guns, the French "75" featured a steel barrel, an improved breech-loading mechanism, and fixed ammunition, using white or smokeless powder. Its revolutionary feature was a dual hydraulic, or "long," recoil system that kept the carriage perfectly still when the gun fired. The barrel was placed in a cradle, or slide, separated from the carriage by a hydraulic brake, or buffer, causing the barrel to slide back three or four feet when fired, then return rapidly to its original position. Because it did not have to be resighted for the next shot, the French 75 could fire twenty to thirty rounds per minute. A shield attached to the stationary carriage also provided protection for the crew. The French 75 mm design, with its superior recoil system, longer range, and greater accuracy, influenced the U.S. Army in a series of experiments in 1901 to find a replacement for its obsolete M1897 3.2-inch fieldpiece.

References. Boyd L. Dastrup, *The Field Artillery*, 1994, and *King of Battle*, 1992. Ian V. Hogg, *A History of Artillery*, 1974.

Timothy C. Dunwoody

FULDA GAP

The Fulda Gap extends from the small plain just north of Frankfurt am Main in the state of Hesse east-northeastward into the Thüringen Wald. The small

German manufacturing city of Fulda lies on Fulda River, eighty kilometers northeast of Frankfurt, in about the middle in this gap. During the Cold War,* it was considered one of three primary corridors for a Warsaw Pact advance into West Germany. Its defense was the primary responsibility of the United States. Over more than four decades, U.S. Army troops patrolled and manned a series of defensive positions across the Fulda Gap. The Fulda Gap, however, became more than just a place where U.S. soldiers looked over barbed-wire and concrete obstacles at their Soviet counterparts; it became a symbol of the Cold War itself. To the hundreds of thousands of U.S. soldiers who served in the Federal Republic of Germany, the Fulda Gap meant the most rigorous and demanding field conditions of any duty post in the Army. To military planners and doctrine writers, the potential for a Soviet attack through the Fulda Gap— and how to meet that threat outnumbered in both men and tanks—was always a factor to be considered. The Fulda Gap scenario was integrated into training from the officer basic course to the Army War College,* in tactical exercises without troops (TEWTs), command-post exercises (CPXs), staff battle exercises (SBEs), and field exercises at all levels. Officers, from lieutenant to general, who never served in Germany knew the plans and practiced in the classroom and in the field to defend the Fulda Gap.

References. John M. Collins, *American and Soviet Military Trends since the Cuban Missile Crisis*, 1978. Stephen P. Gehring, *From the Fulda Gap to Kuwait*, 1998.

Lawyn C. Edwards

FUNSTON, FREDERICK (1865–1917)

Born in Ohio on 9 November 1865, Frederick Funston was raised in Kansas. He began his military career as a volunteer captain on the side of the Cubans in their revolt against Spain. Funston rose to the rank of lieutenant colonel before returning to the United States because of illness brought on by wounds he had received in over twenty-two engagements. In 1898, when the United States declared war against Spain, Funston raised the 20th Kansas Volunteers for service in the Philippines. Promoted to colonel, he received the Medal of Honor* for his actions at Calumpit, where he and forty-five men drove 2,500 of the enemy from an entrenched position. He was also credited with capturing the insurgent leader Emilio Aguinaldo. He was promoted to Brigadier general of volunteers.

Receiving a commission in the Regular Army, Funston rose to the rank of major general. As commander of the Department of California, he figured prominently in the relief work following the 1906 San Francisco earthquake. In February 1915, Funston assumed command of the Southern Department and, therefore, exercised general command along the Mexican border during the Punitive Expedition of 1916. Frederick Funston died unexpectedly of a heart attack while still on active duty at San Antonio, Texas, on 19 February 1917.

References. Thomas W. Crouch, *A Yankee Guerrillero*, 1975. Brian M. Linn, "Guerrilla Fighter," *Kansas History*, Spring 1987, 2–16.

Steven J. Allie

G

GALAHAD. *See* Merrill's Marauders.

GARAND. *See* M1 Garand.

GATLING GUN

The Gatling gun was the U.S. Army's first rapid firing "machine gun." It was invented by Dr. Richard Gatling (1818–1903) and patented in November 1862. Early models saw limited use by Federal forces in the Civil War.* It initially consisted of four rifled musket barrels, but later models had six or ten barrels mounted in a circle within a frame. Turning a crank on the right side of the breech housing rotated the barrels; each had its own lock, and cartridges were fed by gravity from a hopper on top of the frame. Originally .58 caliber, later models ranged from one inch to 6 mm. The 6 mm guns, manufactured at the end of the century, achieved a rate of fire of 800 rounds per minute.

References. Joseph Berk, *The Gatling Gun*, 1991. Paul Wahl and Donald R. Toppel, *The Gatling Gun*, 1965.

John Edgecomb

GENERAL HEADQUARTERS

A General Headquarters (GHQ) was first formed during World War I* to handle many of the problems surrounding the mobilization, administration, and general employment of U.S. troops. Between the world wars, GHQ was a shadow organization, minimally staffed within the War Department.* Theoretically, upon mobilization it would be filled out and assume command of all deployable and deploying U.S. Army units, then itself deploy overseas to assume command of the field forces, with the Chief of Staff* serving as Commander, GHQ. As it turned out, however, the worldwide commitments and deployments during World War II* made this impracticable. Under the direction of its chief of staff, Lieutenant General Leslie J. McNair,* GHQ assumed responsibility for organizing and training all U.S. Army units within the United States, preparing them for deployment, and deploying them to the various theaters, where they came under the direct command of the theater commanders. GHQ was subsequently reorganized and renamed Army Ground Forces,* responsible for all combat and combat support forces. As a concept, GHQ was outpaced by events, but as a functioning agency it was a success within its limited role; it was a model for today's Army Forces Command* (FORSCOM), charged with maintaining the readiness of units based in the continental United States for deployment to overseas theaters.

References. Kent Roberts Greenfield, Robert Palmer, and Bell I. Wiley, *The Organization of Ground Combat Troops*, 1947. Otto L. Nelson, Jr., *National Security and the General Staff*, 1946.

John Broom

GENERAL STAFF

Congress created the first War Department* General Staff in 1813, to provide a management staff for the secretary of war.* Under the General Staff were the Topographical Engineers, Adjutant General's Corps, Inspector General's* Corps, Ordinance, Hospital, Purchasing, and Pay Departments, the Judge Advocates, Chaplains, the U.S. Military Academy,* and the commanding generals of the military districts. In 1816, Congress added the Quartermaster General* to the Staff. This staff, however, did little more than assume the housekeeping and routine administrative duties of the War Department clerks, who had previously been responsible for them. The bureau chiefs remained autonomous and reported directly to the secretary of war.*

The modern General Staff of the U.S. Army can be traced to the General Staff Act of 1903, one of several post–Spanish-American War* reforms initiated by Secretary of War Elihu Root.* Heavily influenced by the Prussian/German Great General Staff that had proved so effective in the German wars of unification, the purpose of the new staff was to supervise and coordinate War Departments bureaus and departments and to provide a nexus for contingency planning.

Numerous reforms and reorganizations—some mandated by Congress, others initiated by farsighted Chiefs of Staff*—have updated and streamlined the General Staff throughout the 20th century. Perhaps the most important reorganization was the post–World War I* realignment of duties and responsibilities along functional lines, i.e., G-1, Personnel; G-2, Intelligence; G-3, Operations and Training; G-4, Supply; and the War Plans Division* (WPD). With the addition of G-5 (Civil Affairs), this remains the basic organization of the General Staff today. The General Staff Corps, composed of officers assigned to the staff for specific tours of duty, has increased significantly, from the forty-five members stipulated by the General Staff Act to several thousand officers today.

References. Otto L. Nelson, Jr., *National Security and the General Staff*, 1946. William R. Roberts, "Loyalty and Expertise," 1979.

GERMANTOWN

As part of Major General Sir William Howe's plan for the defense of Philadelphia in the fall of 1777, British forces established ten redoubts north of the city. In order to provide depth to the defenses, Howe positioned approximately 9,000 soldiers in the vicinity of Germantown, Pennsylvania. George Washington,* believing that this exposed segment of the British army was vulnerable to surprise attack, devised a daring plan, one that was arguably beyond the capabilities of the Continental Army.* He intended to attack his opponent with four converging columns. He instructed John Armstrong and his Pennsylvania militia to conduct a feint by the way of the Ridge Road against the British left. A second column, under William Smallwood and David Dorman, would take the Old York Road and strike the British right. John Sullivan's and Nathanael Greene's* columns would provide the coup de grace against the British center.

The plan came remarkably close to fruition. Armstrong's and Smallwood's militia made not very noteworthy contributions, but Sullivan's and Greene's columns smashed into the British encampment in the fog of the early morning of 4 October 1777, driving their surprised opponents before them. British troops managed to slow Sullivan by holding and fortifying a stone house astride the Colonial line of advance. The attack degenerated over the hours that followed. The confusion produced by poor visibility, and the vulnerability of their flanks due to the failure of the militia, combined to stymie the Colonial advance. When the British counterattacked, Sullivan's men gave ground first, followed by Green's. By midmorning, Washington accepted the obvious and ordered a general retreat, effectively bringing the engagement to a conclusion.

References. John W. Jackson, *With the British Army in Philadelphia, 1777–1778,* 1979. John S. Pancake, *1777,* 1977.

Joseph R. Fischer

GEROW, LEONARD TOWNSEND (1888–1972)

Leonard Townsend Gerow, was born in Petersburg, Virginia, and graduated with honors from Virginia Military Institute* (VMI) in 1911. During World War I,* Gerow was the Signal Corps* purchasing and disbursing officer in France; after the war, he filled a variety of increasingly responsible positions. In 1940, Gerow became chief of the War Plans Division* of the General Staff, where he developed strategic plans for the United States in the event of a general war. In 1942, he was promoted to major general and assigned to command the 29th Infantry Division, which soon shipped out to England.

Named commander of V Corps in July 1943, Gerow organized and trained his men for the upcoming invasion of Europe for nearly a year before it landed on Omaha Beach on 6 June 1944. Assailing the heavily fortified German positions in Normandy, Gerow's two divisions,* the 1st and the 29th, bravely battled their way inland. Two months later, Gerow presided over the German surrender of Paris. He then advanced his troops across the Meuse River, through Luxembourg, and onto the Cologne plain. On 1 January 1945, Gerow was promoted to lieutenant general and assumed command of the newly created Fifteenth Army. He commanded the Fifteenth Army through the early period of the German occupation. After commanding of the Second Army at Fort George G. Meade,* Maryland, in 1950, he retired. A general of serious demeanor and surpassing accomplishments, Gerow received his fourth star at Fort Lee,* Virginia, in 1954.

References. Cole C. Kingseed, "A 'Formidable Array of Warriors,' " *Army*, May 1996, 46–53. Russell F. Weigley, *Eisenhower's Lieutenants*, 1981.

Donald L. Gilmore

GETTYSBURG

After his great victory at Chancellorsville,* Confederate General Robert E. Lee* had three choices. He could remain in place along the line of the Rappahannock River and wait for the Federals to resume their offensive; he could detach part of his army and send it to the western theater, where it might reverse Union gains before Vicksburg and central Tennessee; or he could take his army into the North in an effort to relieve pressure on Virginia and, possibly, cause the Union to relax its hold in the West. Lee chose the third option. He planned to conduct a large-scale raid into Pennsylvania, threaten Washington, Baltimore, Philadelphia, and New York, and draw the Union Army into the open, where he could destroy it.

After the defeat at Chancellorsville, the Federal commander, Major General Joseph Hooker,* was willing to resume the offensive in northern Virginia, but his political capital was exhausted. President Abraham Lincoln turned first to Major General John Reynolds and then, when he refused command, offered command to Major General George G. Meade.* Meade assumed command late in June; Lee was already on the march. Thus, Meade had very little influence on the campaign before the battle.

The two armies collided to the west of Gettysburg on 1 July 1863. Lee did not want a general engagement, but he committed more and more troops as the day wore on. Reynolds, commanding the nearest Union troops, rushed toward Gettysburg to establish positions before the Confederates could concentrate. Although bested on 1 July, the Federals retained the commanding ground south of town and reinforced during the night and next day. Lee chose to resume his offensive on 2 July and unsuccessfully attacked both Union flanks. On 3 July, after an extensive artillery preparation, Lee again attacked the Federal center. The assault, conducted by George Picketts division, was a disaster. Lee withdrew back to Virginia. Meade pursued but was unwilling to risk another major fight. Federal loses were 23,000 of 88,000 engaged; Confederater loses were 28,000 of 75,000 engaged. The battle at Gettysburg is generally regarded as the turning point in the American Civil War.*

References. Edwin B. Coddington, *The Gettysburg Campaign*, 1968. Edward J. Stackpole, *They Met at Gettysburg*, 1956.

George Knapp

G.I.

The use of the term "G.I." originated in the 1930s to designate government-issue items provided to U.S. Army troops. It became more prevalent when the Army began to mobilize in 1940. In 1941 "G.I." began replacing "doughboy"* as a slang term for an enlisted soldier, usually a draftee. A caption for a 1941 cartoon, "G.I. Joe," popularized the term. As the war progressed, G.I. referred to anything associated with enlisted soldiers, such as "G.I. haircut."

References. Lee Kennett, *G.I.*, 1987. Ralph G. Martin, *The GI War, 1941–1945*, 1967. Frank F. Mathias, *G.I. Jive*, 1982.

Charles Heller

G.I. BILL

Congress passed the Servicemen's Readjustment Act of 1944, commonly known as the G.I. Bill, at the urging of President Franklin D. Roosevelt and the American Legion,* to provide benefits for returning soldiers in World War II.* Congress itself acted with mixed motives. Fearing wild behavior among G.I.s,* some members proposed creating demilitarization centers where warlike instincts could be tamed. Fortunately, however, most politicians acknowledged the nation's debt to its soldiers. The G.I. Bill provided veterans with temporary unemployment benefits of twenty dollars per week, hiring preferences in civil service jobs, health benefits, low-interest business and home loans, and tuition and living stipends for college and vocational education. This program paid out nearly four billion dollars in unemployment benefits during the postwar years. Over two million veterans matriculated in colleges and universities, half of the total male enrollment, and another six million attended technical and vocational schools on the G.I. Bill. School benefits included $110 per month, plus an allowance for dependents, and tuition payments. When the program ended in 1956, the Veterans Administration* had spent about fourteen billion dollars on schooling. The skills acquired by this generation of veterans boosted job mobility and incomes, and the government recouped much of its outlay through higher income-tax collections.

References. Theodore R. Mosch, *The G.I. Bill*, 1975. Keith W. Olson, *The G.I. Bill, the Veterans, and the Colleges*, 1974.

Luke Knowley

GLIDER

The U.S. Army first used gliders, or motorless aircraft, to deliver soldiers and supplies to the battlefield in World War II.* Gliders had been employed earlier by the Germans; the U.S. Army organized its first glider units at Fort Benning,* Georgia, in March 1942, after General Henry H. Arnold* directed the development of gliders to carry twelve to fifteen combat-equipped troops or loads of military supplies. In May 1942, Arnold initiated a glider pilot training program, and in August the Army established glider infantry* regiments* in the newly organized 82d and 101st Airborne Divisions. Trained at Fort Bragg,*

North Carolina, with the new Waco CG-4A, glider units participated in numerous campaigns and operations from 1943 to 1945, including the invasions of Sicily, Normandy,* southern France, Market-Garden,* the relief of Bastogne, support of the Chindits in southeast Asia, and the liberation of the Philippines. More than 13,900 Waco gliders were built during World War II. Despite advances in glider technology, the use of assault gliders ceased after World War II.

References. Gerard M. Devlin, *Silent Wings*, 1985. John L. Lowden, *Silent Wings at War*, 1992. Alan Wood, *History of the World's Glider Forces*, 1990.

Randall N. Briggs

GOLDEN KNIGHTS

The U.S. Army Parachute Team, universally known as the Golden Knights, was created in 1959 both for public relations and competition. The Golden Knights consist of two demonstration teams, Black and Gold, and two competition teams, Style & Accuracy and Relative Work. Aviation and headquarters sections round out the eighty-four-member unit. The Golden Knights include both men and women, all enlisted personnel; each member on entry has averaged about 2,000 jumps. The only officers are the commander and the pilots. The Golden Knights perform throughout the United States and around the world, at air shows, military open houses, and aerial competitions, for millions of spectators annually. Perfection in all of their work is the goal of the Golden Knights, the Army's "goodwill ambassadors."

References. R. C. Murray, *Golden Knights*, 1990. Dennis Steele, "The Golden Knights," *Army*, August 1989, 36–39.

GOLDWATER-NICHOLS DEPARTMENT OF DEFENSE REORGANIZATION ACT

In the Goldwater-Nichols Department of Defense Reorganization Act, commonly referred to as "Goldwater-Nichols," Congress moved to fix a number of systemic problems within the Department of Defense* (DOD). Goldwater-Nichols dramatically increased the powers of the position of chairman of the Joint Chiefs of Staff,* little more than a "first among equals" or a committee chairman prior to the act, and designated it the highest military link in the chain of command. In addition, Goldwater-Nichols created the office of vice chairman, increased powers of the regionally oriented commanders in chiefs (CinCs) of the European, Pacific, South American, Middle East, and Atlantic areas, and authorized "consideration . . . [of] creation of a unified combatant command for special operation missions." With passage of the Cohen-Nunn Amendment to Goldwater-Nichols, Congress mandated the creation of the U.S. Special Operations Command (USSOCOM) as a joint command of all Special Operations Forces,* and of an assistant secretary of Defense for Special Operations/Low Intensity Conflict.

References. John E. Grady, "No More Pickup Games," *Army*, July 1994, 28–30. James

R. Locher III, "Taking Stock of Goldwater-Nichols," *Joint Force Quarterly*, Autumn 1996, 10–16.

Richard Stewart

GOOD CONDUCT MEDAL

Executive Order 8809 established the Good Conduct Medal on 28 June 1941. It is awarded to enlisted soldiers who have completed three continuous years of active service subsequent to 26 August 1940 and who are recommended by their commanding officers* for exemplary behavior, efficiency, and fidelity. Award-ees must have a character and efficiency rating of excellent or higher throughout the qualifying period, including time spent attending service schools, and cannot have been convicted by court-martial. During limited periods of World War II* and the Korean War,* the award was authorized for less than three years' service. Personnel separating from the service after less than three years, if their separation is for physical disability incurred in the line of duty, and personnel departing the enlisted ranks with less than three years' service for a warrant officer* or officer-producing school or academy, may also be awarded the Good Conduct Medal. A second award is indicated by a bronze clasp with two loops or knots, a sixth award by a silver clasp with one loop, and an eleventh award by a gold clasp with one loop.

References. Evans E. Kerrigan, *American War Medals and Decorations*, 1964. Philip K. Robles, *United States Military Medals and Ribbons*, 1971.

John Edgecomb

GOTHIC LINE

The Gothic, or Green Line, was a German defensive zone twelve to fourteen miles deep, complete with pillboxes, minefields, and bunkers, in northern Italy. Generally following the line of the northern Apennine Mountains, the defenses were about two hundred miles long, starting in the valley of the Magra River on the Mediterranean and ending at Pesaro on the Adriatic. Adolph Hitler ordered construction of the line in September 1943, following the Allied invasion of Italy. The Allies opened an offensive against the Gothic Line on 25 August 1944. Despite some initial successes by the British 8th Army and the U.S. Fifth Army,* the Allied drive petered out by the end of October. A stalemate ensued throughout the winter, but in April 1945 a renewed offensive dislodged the Germans and broke the Gothic Line.

References. Carlo D'Este, *World War II in the Mediterranean, 1942–1945*, 1990. Trumbull Higgins, *Soft Underbelly*, 1968. Douglas Orgill, *The Gothic Line*, 1967.

Timothy C. Dunwoody

GRAFENWÖHR

This small town in eastern Bavaria, twenty-one miles southeast of Bayreuth, has become infamous in the G.I.* lexicon. After World War II,* a European tour was hardly considered complete without enduring a training cycle at "Graf," with its legendary test of marksmanship and stories of heat and cold, mud and dust. Consisting of ranges capable for firing everything from the 9 mm pistol to the multiple-launch rocket system to the weapons of the AH-1 Cobra,* this daunting piece of Germany has maintained the readiness of U.S. infantrymen, artillerymen, and tankers at the highest level as long as most of today's soldiers can remember.

References. Michael Brown, "Graf on Target," *Soldiers*, January 1985, 23–25. Dan Cragg, *Guide to Military Installations*, 4th ed., 1994.

Jim Martin

GRAND GULF

After failing to take Vicksburg* from the north during the winter of 1862–63, Major General Ulysses S. Grant* ordered two corps* to march down the west side of the Mississippi, from Milliken's Bend to Hard Times, Louisiana. From there Grant intended to conduct an amphibious assault against Grand Gulf to effect a lodgment on the eastern shore for operations against Vicksburg from the south. During the nights of 16 and 23 April, Admiral David D. Porter's fleet ran the gauntlet of the Vicksburg batteries to support Grant's landings. Grant ordered Colonel Benjamin H. Grierson's 1,700-man cavalry* force on a diversionary raid through Mississippi to Baton Rouge, with a faint against Snyder's and Hayne's bluffs, to fix the Confederates in the north.

The Confederate defenses at Grand Gulf consisted primarily of two strong points: Fort Cobun, the upper battery, at the northern end; and Fort Wade, the lower battery, on a terrace above the town's ruins. Each battery had four heavy guns, while three brigades* of infantry* and three field batteries covered the interval between. Porter's ironclads, organized into two squadrons, attacked on 29 April at 0825 and by 1100 had silenced Fort Wade's battery; the upper battery, however, proved too strong. After six hours of fighting, Grant called off the engagement and the assault landings. During the night, Porter's fleet steamed downstream to Disharoon Plantation, where Grant learned of an alternate landing site. On 30 April, Grant landed unopposed at Bruinsburg, secured his beachhead, and moved inland. Port Gibson* fell on 1 May, forcing the Confederates to abandon Grand Gulf two days later.

References. Edwin C. Bearss, *The Campaign for Vicksburg*, vol. 2, 1986. Phillip Thomas Tucker, *The Forgotten "Stonewall of the West,"* 1997.

Edward Shanahan

GRANT, ULYSSES SIMPSON (1822–1885)

There is little in the early life of Ulysses S. Grant to suggest that he might emerge as a great general. He was born Hiram Ulysses Grant; an administrative error during processing into the U.S. Military Academy* changed his name to Ulysses Simpson Grant. He graduated twenty-first of thirty-nine in the class of 1843 and served with distinction in the Mexican War,* but he resigned from the Army in 1854 and moved to Missouri to live with his wife and children. He tried farming and several business undertakings without success.

At the beginning of the Civil War,* Grant volunteered his services and rose quickly to command the Union force attempting to penetrate the South along the Tennessee and Cumberland Rivers. His victories in the Forts Henry and Donelson Campaign* and at Nashville* elevated him to national prominence. He temporarily lost command of the army following his surprise and narrow victory at Shiloh* in April 1862. He resumed command in July 1862 and led his army in the campaign that captured Vicksburg* a year later. He was next sent to the break the siege of Chattanooga,* which he accomplished in November 1863.

In March 1864, Grant was promoted to lieutenant general and given overall command of the Union armies. He devised a strategy to end the war by advancing simultaneously with several armies to prevent the Confederates from shifting forces from one theater to another. He personally accompanied the Army of the Potomac* in its advance toward the Confederate capital at Richmond, Virginia. In a series of the war's bloodiest battles, culminating with the siege of Petersburg,* Grant finally forced the surrender of Robert E. Lee's* Army of Northern Virginia at Appomattox Court House in April 1865. The war ended shortly thereafter.

After the war, Grant became General of the Army and, in 1868, he was elected president of the United States. His two terms as president were marked by a series of poor cabinet choices and by scandals. After leaving the White House, he started a brokerage business, but his venture ended in bankruptcy in 1884. He barely finished his *Personal Memoirs* before dying of throat cancer in July 1885.

References. A. L. Conger, *The Rise of U.S. Grant*, 1931, 1996. William S. McFeely, *Grant*, 1981. Geoffrey Perret, *Ulysses S. Grant*, 1997.

George Knapp

GRANT M3 MEDIUM TANK

The M3 medium tank was developed in response to the successes of the German panzers in the early years of World War II.* Commonly known as the Grant in the United States, its production began in 1941 and continued until December 1942. Over 6,000 Grants were built. Under the Lend-Lease program, the United States sent many M3s to the British, who called them General Lees. The major difference between the U.S. and British versions was the turret configuration. Both versions were similarly armed, with a 75 mm main gun located on the right side of the hull in a semitraversable rotor assembly, a 37 mm gun mounted in a fully traversable turret on top of the vehicle, and three or four .30-caliber machine guns. Grants remained in service through 1944 and saw action in North Africa and the Pacific.

References. Peter Chamberlain and Chris Ellis, *British and American Tanks of World War II*, 2d ed., 1981. R. P. Hunnicutt, *Sherman*, 1978.

Kenneth Turner

GREAT WESTERN. *See* Bowman, Sarah.

GREEN BERETS

On 20 June 1952, the 10th Special Forces Group, commanded by Colonel Aaron Bank, was activated at Fort Bragg,* North Carolina. Soon thereafter, one detachment of the group began wearing black berets in the field as distinctive headgear. On 11 November 1953 the group split, with one half deploying to Germany; the group in Germany then began wearing the green beret in the field. The unit remaining at Fort Bragg was redesignated the 77th Special Forces Group. In 1954, the 10th Special Forces Group commander approved the beret as unit headgear. The commander of the 77th Special Forces Group then applied to the Continental Army Command* (CONARC) for authorization to have the green beret designated as official headgear, but the request was disapproved. The group, however, continued to wear the green beret unofficially until 25 September 1961, when President John F. Kennedy authorized the green beret as distinctive headgear for all Special Forces* soldiers.

References. Aaron Bank, *From OSS to Green Berets*, 1986. Hans Halberstadt, *Green Berets*, 1988. Charles M. Simpson III, *Inside the Green Berets*, 1983.

Richard L. Kiper

GREEN BOOKS

The *United States Army in World War II*, commonly referred to as the Green Books because of the color of the covers, is the U.S. Army's history of its involvement in World War II.* The seventy-six volumes published to date are divided into twelve subseries covering every aspect of the war from strategy to logistics, mobilization, technical developments, and combat. The concept for the series and research on the initial volumes arose among a group of historians working in the Office of the Chief of Military History* at the end of World War II. A generation of historians, many too young to remember the war, have contributed many of the later volumes to the series. Sources for the Green Books have come from the Army's archives, unpublished histories, service journals, personal papers, oral history projects, and published monographs. Although not an "official" history, the series was originally published by the Office of the Chief of Military History and is now published by the Center of Military History.*

Reference: Harold W. Nelson, "CMH," *Army*, October 1990, 208–210.

Trevor Brown

GREENE, NATHANAEL (1742–1786)

Nathanael Greene was a key architect of the victory over the British during the American Revolution.* A charming and personable man, he was greatly admired by most revolutionary leaders and was George Washington's* designated successor, should he have fallen in battle. Born on 7 August 1742 (Julian calendar) in Rotowomut, Rhode Island, Greene sought to shake off his conservative Quaker upbringing. Restricted by his father to a "utilitarian" education, Greene secretly read everything he could find. In this way he gained broad knowledge in economics, law, international relations, and finance. These skills, coupled with his demonstrated leadership, brought Greene to the forefront of colonial politics. As a strategist, he correctly assessed the dependence of the British army on the Royal Navy—a dependence that prevented the British army from undertaking an extensive internal ground campaign. His visionary strategy is credited with the key victories at Cowpens* and Guilford Courthouse,* which set the stage for the ultimate defeat of Lord Cornwallis at Yorktown.* Greene amassed great political and economic influence after the war and was very influential in forming the new government. His untimely death on 19 June 1786 in Savannah, Georgia, was a loss to the young nation.

References. Joseph B. Mitchell, *Military Leaders in the American Revolution*, 1967. Theodore Thayer, *Nathanael Greene*, 1960. David A. Tretler, "The Making of a Revolutionary General, Nathanael Greene: 1742–1779," 1986.

Don Denmark

GRENADE. *See* Hand Grenade.

GRENADE LAUNCHER M79

The M79 grenade launcher is a shoulder-fired, breech-loading, single-shot weapon that fires a 40 mm antipersonnel fragmentation grenade. Weighing only 5.95 pounds unloaded, the M79 can be fired from the prone, kneeling, or standing position. It has a minimum range of fifty meters and a maximum range of 400 meters. A well trained soldier can hit a window of a building at 150 meters; however, at greater ranges the accuracy diminishes, due to the high-arching trajectory required. The Springfield Arsenal* began development of the M79 in 1952 to fill a void between the maximum range of the hand grenade* and the minimum range of the the 60 mm mortar.* M79 production began in 1959, and the first weapons reached U.S. Army units in 1961. Used extensively in the Vietnam War,* the M79 grenade launcher is no longer in service with U.S. forces, but it is still used in numerous foreign armies.

Reference. Charles R. Baker, "The Rifle Squad's Artillery," *Infantry*, September–October 1969, 39–41. R. B. Marlin, "M-79," *Infantry*, March–April 1963, 31–40.

Kenneth Turner

GRIFFEN RIFLE. *See* Ordnance Rifle.

GRIMSLEY SADDLE

Thorton Grimsley of St. Louis provided saddles of a Spanish design to the Regiment of Dragons, formed in 1833. The first pattern of Grimsley saddle featured a rawhide-covered tree with a horned pommel. It was padded and skirted, with an English-style girth. In 1841 and 1842, the Ordnance and Ringold patterns of European hussar design replaced the Grimsley. Grimsley then introduced a second saddle of the Spanish design, but with the outward appearance of the preferred European models. For this pattern Grimsley relied on a rawhide-covered tree for strength, but the pommel was no longer horned, and the entire saddle was covered and double skirted in black leather, with a padded leather seat and brass binding on both the pommel and cantle. The Army adopted this saddle in 1845. The dragoons and cavalry* used it until 1861, and the artillery* used it as both driver and valise saddles until 1885.

References. R. Stephen Dorsey and Kenneth L. McPheeters, *The American Military Saddle, 1776–1945*, 1999. Randy Steffen, *United States Military Saddles, 1812–1943*, 1973.

Steven J. Allie

GUADALCANAL

Guadalcanal, located in the Solomon Islands 300 miles southeast of Bougainville, was the site of the first U.S. offensive operation in the Pacific during World War II.* The concept called for the U.S. Marines to make an amphibious assault on the island and capture an airfield, known to U.S. forces as Henderson Field, then under construction by the Japanese. Seizure of the airfield would deny the Japanese a staging base for bombing Australia, and it would provide the Allies with a springboard for air operations throughout the Solomons. U.S. Army troops followed the Marines onto Gaudalcanal. During the six-month campaign, in which both sides committed all available resources, the U.S. Navy fought seven sea battles. The air forces of both sides lost nearly 1,200 aircraft, and over 37,000 combatants were reported killed or missing in action (7,100 Allied and 30,000 Japanese). Ultimately, Guadalcanal set the tone for future operations, with the Japanese relying on suicidal massed attacks against U.S. Army and Marine units supported by artillery and air assets.

References. Richard B. Frank, *Guadalcanal*, 1990. Eric M. Hammel, *Guadalcanal*, 1987. Edwin P. Hoyt, *Guadalcanal, 1982*.

Don Denmark

GUARD MOUNT

Guard mount is a formal or informal inspection by the commander of the relief, the sergeant of the guard, or the officer of the guard detail prior to the guard tour and the assignment of guards to their posts. Typically, during guard mount one member of the guard detail is selected as a supernumerary to serve as an alternate in case a member of the guard cannot continue his or her tour, or to perform special, honorary duties, such as colonel's orderly, as prescribed by unit directive.

References. Alan Levy, Bernard Krisher, and James Cox, *Draftee's Confidential Guide*, 1957. U.S. Army, FM 22–6, *Guard Duty*, 1971.

GUILFORD COURTHOUSE

In the two months preceding the battle at Guilford Courthouse on 15 March 1781, Major General Nathanael Greene* had drawn Lord Cornwallis far from his logistics bases in South Carolina. Determined to avenge his lieutenants' defeats at King's Mountain* and Cowpens,* Cornwallis burned his supply wagons and pursued Greene into Virginia. Cornwallis, however, failed to engage decisively and destroy Greene's army. With the arrival in early March of reinforcements, mostly militia and inexperienced recruits, Greene maneuvered back into North Carolina. Greene decided to fight on a piece of ground near Guilford Courthouse and planned to repeat Daniel Morgan's successful double envelopment at Cowpens. He arrayed his force in three lines. On 15 March, Cornwallis approached from the west and attacked the Colonial line head on. In spite of stiff fighting by the Colonials, the British and Hessian troops pressed forward. At a pivotal point in the fight, Cornwallis fired his artillery into the mass of struggling soldiers, inflicting heavy casualties on foe and friend alike. Greene, who might have gained a victory by counterattacking with his reserves, decided instead to preserve his force and began withdrawing from the field. Although the battle was tactically a British victory, Greene had inflicted more than 25 percent casualties on Cornwallis's army, prompting Charles James Fox to exclaim in Parliament, "Another such victory would destroy the British Army." The battle at Guilford Courthouse signaled the beginning of the end for British forces in the American Revolution.*

References. John Buchanan, *The Road to Guilford Courthouse*, 1997. Henry Lumpkin, *From Savannah to Yorktown*, 1981.

S. A. Underwood

GULF WAR. *See* Desert Storm.

GUSTAV LINE

The Gustav Line was among the most formidable defensive positions constructed during World War II.* Overlooking the Rapido and Garigliano Rivers, the Gustav Line ran from the vicinity of Gaeta on the west to Ortona on the east coast of Italy. The key and dominant terrain along the line was Monte Cassino. In addition to its natural strength, the Gustav Line boasted wooden mines,* steel-covered machine-gun positions, and an abundance of barbed wire. The Germans built the line to keep the Allies from breaking out of southern Italy and capturing Rome, thus opening the door to a southern invasion of Europe proper. Initially it served its purpose well. Beginning in January 1944, the Allies made four attempts to break the Gustav Line, but not until May 1944, after protracted artillery and aerial bombardment, was the breakthrough achieved.

References. Martin Blumenson, *Salerno to Cassino*, 1969. Ernest F. Fisher, Jr., *Cassino to the Alps*, 1989.

Krewasky A. Salter

H

HALF-TRACK

The half-track was a lightly armored vehicle with open (topside) troop and cargo areas; it had a wheeled front axle (for steering) and a track rear-end drive assembly. The U.S. Army half-track can be traced to 1925, when the Ordnance Department* purchased a French Citroën half-track. This vehicle, used in trials, was further developed and modified during the 1930s. Initial production began in 1940. The M2 and M3 models differed slightly. The M3, ten inches longer, carried thirteen rather than ten troops and driver, had a rear door, and employed the M25 pedestal machine-gun mount rather than the skate ring. Machine guns were the half-track's primary armament, either .30-caliber weapons placed around the top of the hull on pedestals or a single M2 .50-caliber machine gun* mounted above the driver's compartment. The M25 pedestal allowed the .30-caliber guns to be fired in any direction. The half-track also served as a platform for other weapons: an 81 mm mortar,* 37 mm and .50-caliber antiaircraft guns, and turret-mounted quad 50s (four .50-caliber machine guns) for infantry* support. The half-track's body armor was a quarter inch thick, and the windshield was armored to half inch thickness. The final series M3, half-track, the M3A2, accommodated a variety of crews and equipment depending upon the mission. During World War II,* Autocar, White Motor Company, Diamond T Motor Company, and International Harvester manufactured half-tracks.

References. Thomas Berndt, *Standard Catalog of U.S. Military Vehicles, 1940–1965*, 1993. Fred W. Crimson, *U.S. Military Tracked Vehicles*, 1992.

John Edgecomb

HALLECK, HENRY WAGER (1815–1872)

Henry Wager Halleck was born in Oneida County, New York, in 1815. Educated at Union College and the U.S. Military Academy,* Halleck had a scholarly mind and was known in the Army as "Old Brains." Halleck graduated third in the class of 1839 and served as an engineer officer until he left the service in 1854. When the Civil War* began, Halleck was offered a commission as a major general and given command of the Department of the Missouri, where he restored order after the confusion left by John C. Frémont.* The success of Ulysses S. Grant* and William T. Sherman* in the West propelled Halleck to the position of general in chief in Washington, where a preoccupation with the safety of Washington and poor advice to his field commanders hampered his job performance. Named chief of staff* upon Grant's arrival in Washington, Halleck proved to be a competent staff officer, effectively dealing with administrative matters while Grant accompanied the army in the field. After the war, Halleck commanded various divisions of the Army. He died in Louisville, Kentucky, in 1872.

References. Stephen E. Ambrose, *Halleck*, 1962. T. Harry Williams, *Lincoln and His Generals*, 1952.

Jim Martin

HAMBURGER HILL

Applied to a feature officially known as Hill 937 to the Americans and Dong Ap Bia to the Vietnamese, the name "Hamburger Hill" derived from the heavy losses sustained by the North Vietnamese Army's (NVA) Twenty-ninth Regiment and three U.S. and one Army of the Republic of Vietnam (ARVN) battalions that fought there for ten days in May 1969. The A Shau Valley was an important staging area for NVA attacks on the coast, and its proximity to the Ho Chi Minh Trail and sanctuaries in nearby Laos made it a high-priority target for allied forces. Unfortunately, the attempt to take Hill 937 turned into a battle of attrition. The U.S. public was outraged when, following its bloody conquest, U.S. forces abandoned Hamburger Hill and the NVA reoccupied it a month later. The outcry in Congress was further fueled by the photographs of 241 U.S. soldiers killed in less than a week during the Hamburger Hill fight and elsewhere in Vietnam. Following this battle there was a marked reduction in large-scale U.S. ground combat actions, as the Vietnamization policy was implemented. In 1987, Paramount Pictures released a major motion picture, *Hamburger Hill*, based on the controversial battle.

Reference. Samuel Zaffiri, *Hamburger Hill, May 11–20, 1969*, 1988.

John R. Finch

HAND GRENADE

A hand grenade is a small explosive device, normally weighing about one pound, typically used by the infantry* in close combat. Hand grenades were used in North America as early as the French and Indian War, but they did not receive significant attention until the Civil War,* when numerous designs were patented. The best-known Civil War hand grenade was the Ketcham, a cylinder with stabilizing fins to ensure it would land nose first, to activate the simple percussion-point fuse system. In World War I,* the now-familiar Mark 1 pineapple grenade,* with a serrated iron shell to ensure even fragmentation, was developed for the U.S. Army. The Mark 1 employed the French Bouchon fuse system, with an arming lever that permitted safe handling of the grenade even after the safety pin was removed. Upon release from the thrower's hand, the lever separated and a spring-loaded firing pin started the fuse train to the main charge, normally in five seconds. The Mark II, an improved version of the Mark I, saw widespread use in World War II,* along with a variety of new, special-purpose grenades: smoke, illumination or signal, incendiary, chemical agent, and concussion. The latter, known as offensive grenades, relied more on blast effect than fragmentation to produce casualties, minimizing the chance of being wounded by fragments from one's own grenade.

References. Bruce N. Canfield, *U.S. Infantry Weapons of World War II*, 1996. J. P. Driver, "Hand Grenades," *Marine Corps Gazette*, March 1963, 43–45. K.J.W. Goad and D.H.J. Halsey, *Ammunition (including Grenades and Mines)*, 1982.

Stephen C. McGeorge

HAND RECEIPT

A hand receipt is a document used to record receipt and responsibility for U.S. Army equipment or property under the provisions of Army Regulation 735–5, *Property Accountability*, and DA Pam 710–2-1, *Using Unit Supply System*. Every officer and noncommissioned officer is familiar with DA Form 2062, Hand Receipt, although several other forms may also serve as hand receipts or sub–hand receipts. Most officers learn very early in their careers the vital importance of maintaining accurate and up-to-date hand receipts. More than one officer's career has been damaged or ruined due to poor hand-receipt maintenance.

Reference. Harold D. Baker, Jr., "Hand-Receipt Procedures," *Infantry*, November–December 1996, 41–44.

HARDEE'S *TACTICS*

Major William J. Hardee (later Confederate lieutenant general) published a manual in 1855 under the title *Rifle and Light Infantry Tactics*. Secretary of War* Jefferson Davis* had directed Hardee to write the work following the general trend of military writing in Europe which now emphasized increased tactical mobility for the infantry in response to the threat of the rifled musket. Hardee emphasized speed more than mass in battle; he recommended doubling the rate of advance to 180 steps per minute. Furthermore, Hardee put forward the theory that small-unit cohesion was the most important factor in battle. During the Civil War,* Hardee's *Tactics* became the small-unit manual for both armies. The pocket-sized edition was especially popular with officers. Although the war proved Hardee wrong regarding speed—attackers simply could not cross fields of fire quickly enough to overcome properly prepared defenders armed with rifled muskets—his notions about small-unit cohesion did find fertile ground and formed the basis for later tactical manuals that took the U.S. Army away from mass-unit maneuver on the battlefield.

References. Paddy Griffith, *Battle Tactics of the Civil War*, 1989. Grady McWhiney and Perry D. Jamieson, *Attack and Die*, 1982.

George Knapp

HARLEM HEIGHTS

After being driven from New York City by British land and naval forces in September 1776, George Washington* entrenched his defeated army along Harlem Heights, a chain of hills bisecting Manhattan Island. On the morning of 16 September, after his rangers probed enemy lines, Washington sought to draw some forward British units into a trap. While a small force lured the redcoats into a hollow between the two armies, a force of rangers and riflemen enveloped the position. Unfortunately, the flanking troops misjudged their position and entered battle too soon. Both sides fed additional units into the fighting, but Washington, not wanting a major battle, broke off the engagement by mid-afternoon. Though little more than a skirmish, in which each side suffered some 150 casualties, Harlem Heights demonstrated that despite its poor performance on Long Island, the Continental Army* remained an effective fighting force.

References. Bruce Bliven, Jr., *Battle for Manhattan*, 1956. Henry P. Johnston, *The Battle of Harlem Heights*, 1897.

Stanley Adamiak

HARPERS FERRY ARSENAL

In 1796, Congress passed a bill appropriating funds to establish arsenals and magazines for the manufacture of arms for the U.S. Army. There was general agreement that one of these arsenals should be located at Springfield, Massachusetts, but the sites of the other arsenals were hotly disputed. President George Washington* wanted a single arsenal located at Harpers Ferry, Virginia (today West Virginia), at the confluence of the Potomac and Shenandoah Rivers. Secretary of War* Henry Knox and his supporters argued for several armories rather than just one at Harpers Ferry. Although Washington did not prevail for nearly three years, construction finally commenced in 1799, and most of the buildings' exteriors were complete by 1800. Production, however, was slow to start, because much of the machinery and many of the skilled artisans were not yet in place. Once in operation, the Harpers Ferry Arsenal produced arms and munitions for the U.S. government for nearly six decades, although not as efficiently as the Springfield Arsenal* and not without controversy.

The role of the Harpers Ferry Arsenal in American history, however, is more closely identified with events just before and during the Civil War* than with its contribution to American arms manufacturing. In October 1859, the abolitionist John Brown siezed the arsenal in an attempt to inspire a slave uprising in the South. After a brief battle, federal troops under the command of Colonel Robert E. Lee* captured Brown, who was later hanged for his crimes. The town of Harpers Ferry changed hands numerous times during the war; successive waves of Union and Confederate troops looted, burned, and razed the armory. The only building to survive the war intact, the small engine house where John Brown made his final stand, is today a national historic structure operated by the National Park Service.

References. Chester G. Hearn, *Six Years of Hell*, 1996. Merritt Roe Smith, *Harpers Ferry Armory and the New Technology*, 1977. Paul R. Teetor, *A Matter of Hours*, 1982.

HARRISON, WILLIAM HENRY (1773–1841)

Born in Virginia in 1773, William Henry Harrison joined the U.S. Army in 1791 and served in the Indian campaigns in the Northwest Territory, learning from the highly competent General Anthony Wayne,* for whom he acted as aide-de-camp. Harrison resigned from the Army in 1798, accepting appointments in turn as secretary of the Northwest Territory, delegate to Congress, and governor of Indiana. As governor, he was given authority to negotiate treaties with the Indians and was instructed by President Thomas Jefferson to acquire as much land as possible. In a series of treaties culminating with the Treaty of Fort Wayne (1809), he acquired most of Indiana. The Shawnee leader Tecumseh and his brother the Prophet formed a powerful Indian confederation to reverse these losses. Encouraged by the British, the Indians encamped near the junction of Tippecanoe Creek and the Wabash River. Harrison marched in with 1,000 men, mostly volunteers, and defeated the forces under the Prophet, who had launched a surprise attack. This victory brought Harrison fame. When the War of 1812* broke out, he embarked on a campaign to recover the Northwest Territory after the surrender of Detroit to Tecumseh and the British. On 5 October 1813, Harrison defeated the British and Tecumseh (who was killed) at the Battle of Thames River in Canada. Resigning his commission in May 1814, Harrison resumed his political career, serving as a state senator (1819–1821) and a U.S. senator (1825–1828). He was elected president of the United States in 1840 but died of pneumonia a few weeks after assuming office, in 1841.

References. Freeman Cleaves, *Old Tippecanoe*, 1939. Dorothy Burne Goebel, *William Henry Harrison*, 1926.

Claude Sasso

HASHMARK

Soldiers have traditionally worn service stripes on their uniforms to denote accomplishments. In the U.S. Army, such stripes have signified the number of enlistments, wounds, and wartime or overseas service. Prior to World War II,* enlistment stripes, one for each three years of service, were diagonal ribbons worn beneath the war-service chevrons on the left sleeve. After World War II, gold lace, gold bullion, or gold-color rayon stripes on an olive-green background replaced the ribbons. Still worn diagonally on the bottom of the left sleeve of the Class A* uniform coat, each service stripe denotes three years of honorable service. Service stripes are commonly referred to as "hashmarks," a term that doughboys* may have derived from the French *hacher* (to chop up) in World War I,* or that may refer to the amount of hash a soldier eats to earn one.

Reference. Frank Cox, *NCO Guide*, 4th ed., 1992.

Lawyn C. Edwards

HAYFIELD FIGHT

The Hayfield Fight took place on 1 August 1867 at Fort C. F. Smith on the Bighorn River, about two miles from where it exits the mountains. To sustain live stock at the post during the bitter winters, the garrison found it necessary to put up hay. The best hay was some distance from the post; there a corral, with heavy logs at the base, formed a campsite and base of operations. Indians under the Sioux chief Red Cloud, who had harassed the soldiers from the time the fort was built, attempted to overrun the hay detail. The soldiers, recently armed with the new Allin conversion* breechloaders, and civilian hayers with repeating rifles, beat off a series of attacks and killed between eight and forty attackers, for the loss of three soldiers killed.

References. Barry J. Hagan, *"Exactly in the Right Place,"* 1999. J. W. Vaughn, *Indian Fights*, 1966.

Jack Gifford

HEARTBREAK RIDGE

Heartbreak Ridge is a long, narrow ridge in Korea that runs from north to south between the Mundung-ni Valley on the west and the Sat'ar-ri Valley on the east. In 1951, the ridge was located in the eastern sector of U.S. Eighth Army's* defensive line in an area known as the Punchbowl. On 13 September, the 23d Infantry conducted an attack to seize this strategic line in order to prevent enemy assaults against X Corps positions to the west. It met heavy resistance, and a French battalion reinforced the 23d Infantry. The 9th Infantry was also committed to the initial attack. From 13 to 27 September these units conducted piecemeal frontal attacks, without success. On 5 October, the 2d Infantry Division's* 9th, 23d, and 38th Infantry Regiments conducted a coordinated attack. This attack was successful, and the ridge was seized on 13 October. During the battle, news correspondents named the ridge Heartbreak Ridge. One of the bloodiest battles of the Korean War,* Heartbreak Ridge marked the end of major United Nations offensive operations in the conflict. The North Korean People's Army's (NPKA) 14th Regiment attempted to retake the ridge on 3 November 1952, but UN units fought off the attackers and retained control of Heartbreak Ridge for the remainder of the war.

References. Arned L. Hinshaw, *Heartbreak Ridge*, 1989. Richard Whelan, *Drawings the Line*, 1990.

John Edgecomb

HEAVY EQUIPMENT TRANSPORTER

A heavy equipment transporter, or HET, is a tractor/trailer combination intended to haul armored and oversized vehicles over long distances that would destroy tracks and take precious miles off a tank's life. The U.S. Army's M1911 tractor and M747 semitrailer, designed in the 1970s to haul the M60-series tank, proved not strong enough to carry the M1 family of main battle tanks during Desert Storm.* In January 1990, the Department of Defense* awarded the first in a series of contracts for a new heavy equipment transport system, or HETS, composed of the M1070 tractor and M1000 trailer, capable of carrying the heaviest tanks, self-propelled artillery, and other armored vehicles. Initial deliveries were scheduled for July 1997. While many of the world's militaries procure a tank and a HETS as a single weapons system, the U.S. Army still acquires the two separately, and it has fallen short of its overall HETS requirements. The procurement of new HETS is an important step in maintaining tank readiness.

References. Joe A. Fortner, Jules T. Doux, and Mark A. Peterson, "Bring on the HETs!" *Military Review*, January 1992, 36–45. Karen E. Good, " 'Ghostbusters' in the Saudi Desert," *Army Logistician*, May–June 1993, 14–17.

Jim Martin

HELLCAT. *See* Tank Destroyer M18

HENRY RIFLE

The Henry rifle was the first magazine-fed firearm employed by the U.S. Army. The Henry had a round, tubular magazine which held sixteen .44-caliber rim-fire rounds and utilized a lever action to eject the spent shell casing and load a new round in the chamber. The War Department* purchased 1,731 Henrys and 4,610,400 cartridges during the Civil War.* State militias and volunteer units purchased approximately 10,000 additional Henrys during the same period. Confederates referred to the Henry as "that damned Yankee rifle that could be loaded on Sunday and fired all week." Because it was underpowered—only twenty-five grains of powder propelled the .44-caliber, 216-grain round—the U.S. Army never officially adopted the Henry. After the Civil War, Winchester bought B. Tyler Henry's New Haven Arms Company and reintroduced the Henry rifle in 1866, with a side-loading gate, as the Model 1866 Winchester.

References. Joseph G. Bilby, *Civil War Firearms*, 1996. Arcadi Gluckman, *Identifying Old U.S. Muskets, Rifles, and Carbines*, 1959, 1965.

Steven J. Allie

HERALDRY

Heraldry dates to the Middle Ages, when individual men-at-arms began painting distinctive insignia,* or coats of arms, on their shields so that they could be readily identified in combat. Coats of arms became highly stylized, consisting of ordinaries and subordinaries, with rules for design, color, and arrangement, and depicting real and mythical animals, religious symbols, and historical events. Eventually, nobles, families, clans, towns, and guilds adopted coats of arms. Although some heraldic devices came to colonial America from Europe, few survived the American Revolution* and the rise of the new nation.

The War Department* approved, and U.S. Army units adopted, distinctive shoulder insignia for the first time during World War I.* In 1924, the Quartermaster General* assumed responsibility for the Army's heraldry program, and by World War II* many units had adopted both shoulder insignia and crests. In 1960, the Institute of Heraldry was established to centralize the research, design, standardization, and control of heraldic devices for all branches of the armed forces and other agencies of the U.S. government. By 1964, the Institute had also assumed supervision over production and control of official dies for the manufacture of heraldic items.

References. Barry Jason Stein, *U.S. Army Heraldic Crests*, 1993. John B. Wilson, comp., *Armies, Corps, Divisions, and Separate Brigades*, 1987.

HEROINE OF FORT BROWN. *See* Bowman, Sarah.

HERSHEY, LEWIS B. (1893–1977)

Lewis B. Hershey, born in Steuben County, Indiana, and educated at Tri-State College, directed the Selective Service System* (SSS)—the military draft—under six presidents over a period spanning three wars. After beginning his service in several inconspicuous positions, in 1936 Hershey was appointed secretary to the Joint Army-Navy Selective Service Committee, to organize a readiness plan in case of war. In this capacity, Hershey traveled the globe examining the effectiveness of various draft systems. In 1940, he became deputy director of the newly formed Selective Service System, and in 1941 President Franklin D. Roosevelt appointed him its director.

Hershey's early tenure in the Selective Service System was marked by harmony in a country imbued with patriotism and dedicated to the overthrow of the Axis powers. During the Korean and Vietnam Wars, however, political dissidents increasingly assailed the Selective Service System for sheltering the privileged through educational, occupational, and religious deferments that discriminated against the poor, black, and uneducated. Responding to the criticism, Hershey initiated a draft lottery in 1969. Nonetheless, he was uncomfortable with the new program and, partly at President Richard Nixon's insistance, left his post the next year to become Nixon's adviser on manpower mobilization. In 1972 Hershey, much decorated, retired at four-star rank.

References. George Q. Flynn, *Lewis B. Hershey*, 1985. Harry A. Marmion, *Selective Service*, 1968.

Donald L. Gilmore

HERSHEY BAR

An overseas service bar, commonly—and sometimes pejoratively—referred to as a "hershey bar" is worn on the lower right sleeve of the Class A* or Army green uniform coat to denote six months of active service in certain locations outside the continental United States during specified periods of time. First awarded during World War II,* service bars are gold lace, bullion, or rayon. The term "hershey bar" may have originated from the resemblance of the overseas bar to the chocolate ration bar with its yellow wrapper and the fact that they were as easy to obtain as the chocolate bar.

Reference. Frank Cox, *NCO Guide*, 1992.

HIGGINS BOAT

Beginning in the late 1930s, Higgins Industries, Inc., a small boat-manufacturing firm in New Orleans, designed and built a family of small vessels, known as Higgins boats, for the U.S. Navy, including patrol-torpedo boats and landing craft.* In May 1941, Higgins demonstrated a shallow-draft tank lighter with a forward ramp capable of landing a vehicle onto and withdrawing from, a beach. Based on the demonstration, the U.S. Navy's Bureau of Ships and the U.S. Marine Corps requested further development of the ramped-boat design. This led Higgins to design and begin production of the landing craft, vehicle, personnel (LCVP). Commonly called the Higgins boat by both G.I.s* and Marines in World War II* and the Korean War,* the LCVP participated in amphibious landings from Sicily to Normandy and from the Philippines to Inchon.* It was 36 feet in length, 10 feet 5¼ inches in beam, weighed 9 tons, carried 36 troops or 6,000 pounds of cargo, and drew 3 feet aft and slightly more than 2 feet forward. The Higgins boat was the most widely used and successful landing craft in history.

References. A. D. Baker III, *Allied Landing Craft of World War Two*, 1944, 1985. John W. Mountcastle, "From Bayou to Beachhead," in *In Defense of the Republic*, ed. David Curtis Skaggs and Robert S. Browning III, 1991. Jerry E. Strahan, *Andrew Jackson Higgins and the Boats That Won World War II*, 1994.

HIGH-MOBILITY MULTIPURPOSE WHEELED VEHICLE

By the late 1970s, the U.S. Army clearly recognized the need to replace and modernize its fleet of aging tactical vehicles, including—after nearly four decades of service—the most successful vehicle in the Army's history, the Jeep.* Three manufacturers responded to the Army's specifications for a high-mobility multipurpose wheeled vehicle (HMMWV); AM General's Hummer—according to AM General, this name derived from high-utility maximum-mobility easy rider—won the initial contract. AM General employed the latest automotive technology in the Hummer's design and construction, including a double A-frame independent-coil suspension, a precombustion chamber on a General Motors V-8, water-cooled, diesel engine to reduce noise and increase efficiency, a three-speed automatic transmission, and space-age metals to reduce weight and add strength. The first HMMWVs entered the Army inventory in late 1983 and early 1984. The Hummer can be configured to meet a variety of tactical requirement, including crew, cargo, ambulance, and TOW (wire-guided missile) weapons carriers. By the mid-1990s, the Army had purchased over 91,000

HMMWVs, and the other services had purchased 3,000. Although "Hummer" is the most commonly used name for the vehicle today, it is also known by several other variants of the original acronym, including Humvee and Humm-V.

References. J. Philip Geddes, "High Mobility," *International Defense Review*, 5/1982, 581–584. Scott R. Gourley, "U.S. Army Transport in Transition," *Armed Forces Journal International*, May 1993, 38–40.

HODGES, COURTNEY HICKS (1887–1966)

Born in Perry, Georgia, on 5 January 1887, Courtney Hicks Hodges entered the U.S. Military Academy* in 1904 but was dismissed after failing geometry. He enlisted in the infantry* in 1906 and gained a commission three years later. In World War I,* Hodges commanded a battalion* in the 5th Infantry Division and earned the Distinguished Service Cross.* Hodges was a major from 1920 to 1934 and attended the usual General Staff and Army War College* courses. Early in 1941, he went to the War Department* to head its Infantry Bureau.

From mid-1942 to the end of 1943, Hodges successively commanded the X Corps and Third Army,* and he advanced to lieutenant general. For the invasion of Europe, he relinquished the Third Army to George S. Patton, Jr.* Highly esteemed, Hodges went to England early in 1944 as deputy head of First Army.* Groomed as the senior U.S. ground commander for the invasion, he took over First Army on 1 August 1944, directing it in a swift drive across France to the German border. Less celebrated than Patton's Third Army, First Army was nevertheless the first Allied army to cross the German border, breach the Siegfried Line,* capture an important German city, and meet the westward-moving Soviet army at the Elbe River.

Promoted to full general in April 1945, Hodges was reassigned with First Army headquarters to General of the Army Douglas MacArthur's command in the Pacific. Following the Japanese surrender, First Army assumed its peacetime role as an area defense and training army, headquartered at Governors Island in New York Harbor. Hodges retired to San Antonio, Texas, early in 1949. He died there on 16 January 1966.

References. G. Patrick Murray, "Courtney Hodges," *American History Illustrated*, January 1973, 12–25. Russell F. Weigley, *Eisenhower's Lieutenants*, 1981.

Luke Knowley

HOHENFELS

Hohenfels is the U.S. Army Europe's largest maneuver training area in Germany. In 1989, Hohenfels became part of the U.S. Army's Combat Training Center system, as the Combat Maneuver Training Center (CMTC). The CMTC is located in the state of Bavaria, in the district of Oberfalz, in the former *landkreis* of Parsberg, now Neumarkt; it is named after the town of Hohenfels. Originally established by the Wehrmacht in 1937, the site was selected because of its low population, lack of minerals, poor soil and water supply, and limited transportation system—that is, its undesirability for civilian purposes. A total of 544 properties and farms were acquired or taken over to establish the training area. Hohenfels served as a limited training area and prisoner of war* camp throughout World War II.* On 22 April 1945, the U.S. Army captured Hohenfels without a fight and freed over 7,000 internees. After the war Hohenfels was used for repatriation, immigration, and resettlement of refugees, until it was closed in 1949. In 1951, U.S. forces reclaimed the area for military training.

Currently the training area has fifty-two ranges, capable of handling most conventional weapons in the U.S. arsenal. Covering some 40,000 acres of low ridges, twisting valleys, meadows, woods, and limestone plains, Hohenfels is a unique area in Europe, where armor and infantry units can replicate maneuver on the modern battlefield.

References. Kevin McAndrews, "The Hohenfels Experience," *National Guard*, February 1996, 20–24. Donna Miles, "Hail the New Hohenfels," *Soldiers*, October 1990, 44–48.

George Mordica II

HONORABLE DISCHARGE

An honorable discharge is a separation from military service with honor, it is the most favorable type of discharge a service member can receive. A service member who receives an honorable discharge at the conclusion of service is entitled to all post–active duty benefits offered by his service department and the Veterans Administration.* Disciplinary actions, including Article 15* of the Uniform Code of Military Justice* and convictions by court-martial, do not necessarily disqualify a service member from receiving an honorable discharge. A soldier's entire service record determines the type of discharge to be awarded. More than 95 percent of all soldiers earn honorable discharges.

References. Frank Cox, *NCO Guide*, 4th ed., 1992. Chuck Noland, "What Money Can't Buy," *Soldiers*, November 1971, 24–25. Norman Oliver, "The Honorable Thing to Do," *Soldiers*, September 1983, 34–36.

HOOKER, JOSEPH (1814–1879)

Born in Hadley, Massachusetts, on 13 November 1814, Joseph Hooker graduated from the U.S. Military Academy* in the class of 1837. Following service in the Second Seminole War* and the Mexican War,* he resigned from the Army in 1853. When President Abraham Lincoln called for volunteers in April 1861, Hooker quickly wrote the War Department* offering his services. When no commission was forthcoming, he appealed directly to Lincoln, who appointed him a brigadier general of volunteers. In 1862, Hooker rose from brigade* to corps* comander, seeing action at Williamsburg in the Peninsular Campaign,* during the Seven Days* Battle in June, at South Mountain and Antietam* in September, and at Fredericksburg* in December. Wounded at Antietam, Hooker earned the sobriquet "Fighting Joe" for his aggressiveness during the Seven Days.

When Ambrose Burnside* was relieved in January 1863; Lincoln gave Hooker command of the Army of the Potomac.* Hooker then planned and led his army on a campaign against Robert E. Lee's army around Fredericksburg. The plan went well at first, but Lee's adroitness at meeting the threat and an uncharacteristic loss of nerve by Hooker led to the Army of the Potomac's defeat at Chancellorsville* and its withdrawal back to its original position. At his own request, Hooker was relieved of command in June 1863; he was replaced by George G. Meade.* Hooker continued to serve in the Union Army and commanded corps in several campaigns, including Chattanooga* and the Atlanta Campaign.* He headed several departments after the Civil War,* but he retired as a major general in 1868 due to the effects of war wounds.

References. Walter H. Hebert, *Fighting Joe Hooker*, 1944. T. Harry Williams, *Lincoln and His Generals*, 1952.

"HOUGH"

"Hough" (hoo-a), the familiar Army greeting or response, means roughly "can do" or "good-job." It has its origins with the Second Dragoons in Florida in 1841. In an attempt to end the Second Seminole War,* a meeting was arranged with Chief Coacoochee. After the meeting, a banquet ensued at which officers of the garrison made a number of toasts, such as "Here's to luck!" and "The old grudge," before drinking. Coacoochee's interpreter explained to the chief that the toast meant "How d'ye do!" Whereupon, with great dignity, the chief lifted his cup and, elevating it above his head, exclaimed in a deep gutteral and triumphant voice, "HOUGH." During the Mexican War,* when the officers and men of the U.S. Army gathered for the first time in decades, "HOUGH" spread through the ranks and became a universal Army toast.

References. Samuel E. Chamberlain, *My Confession*, 1956. Theodore F. Rodenbough, comp., *From Everglade to Cañon with the Second Dragoons*, 1875.

Steven J. Allie

HOWARD, OLIVER OTIS (1830–1909)

After graduating from the U.S. Military Academy* in 1854, Oliver Otis Howard served as an instructor of mathematics from 1855 until June 1861, at which time he resigned his commission to become colonel of the 3rd Maine Regiment. Howard saw action at First Bull Run,* the Peninsula campaign* (where he lost his right arm at Fair Oaks [Seven Pines*] in 1862), South Mountain, Antietam,* Fredericksburg,* Chancellorsville,* Gettysburg,* the Chattanooga* campaign, and Sherman's march* through Georgia. He was awarded the regular rank of brigadier general and held the brevet rank of major general when Andrew Johnson appointed him commissioner of the Freedmen's Bureau in 1865.

Howard served as commissioner until the Freedmen's Bureau was disbanded in 1872. In 1872 Howard University was named after him, and he served as its president from 1869 to 1873. In 1872 he acted as President Ulysses S. Grant's* emissary to treat with Cochise, the Chiricahua Apache chief. Two years later Howard returned to active duty as commander of the Department of the Columbia, in which capacity he prosecuted the campaign against the Nez Percé in 1877 and the Bannock the following year.

Howard served as the superintendent of West Point from 1881 to 1882; commander of the Department of the Platte from 1882 to 1886; and commander of the Division of the East until his retirement in 1894. In 1893 he was awarded the Medal of Honor* for his actions at Fair Oaks. During his lifetime he published *Nez Perce Joseph* (1881), *Fighting for Humanity* (1898), *My Life and Experiences among Our Hostile Indians* (1907), and his *Autobiography* (1907). He was a deeply religious man, widely known throughout the Army for his piety.

References. John A. Carpenter, *Sword and Olive Branch*, 1964. Gerald Weland, *O. O. Howard, Union General*, 1995.

Jeffrey Prater

HOWITZER, 8-INCH M110

Designed to meet the U.S. Army's air-transportability needs, the M110 203 mm (8-inch) howitzer, self-propelled, entered the U.S. Army inventory in 1962. The first M110 battalion was formed in 1963. With a range of 16,800 meters, the M110 provided U.S. and NATO* units with long-range divisional artillery capable of firing a mix of munitions, including nuclear ordnance. Known for its accuracy and punch, the M110 was a favorite weapon against bunkers and built-up positions. Some gunners bragged that they could consistently fire rounds into a fifty-gallon barrel. The last improvement to the M110 program, the M110A2, added an entirely new family of projectiles to the howitzer's capability and increased the maximum range to 21,300 meters.

References. Boyd L. Dastrup, *King of Battle*, 1992. "A Guide to Army Equipment in Field Use or Development," *Army*, November 1968, 134–136.

Jeffrey S. Shadburn

HOWITZER 105 MM M102

In 1955, the U.S. Army identified a need for a lightweight towed howitzer to support airmobile operations. The then-current M101 105 mm howitzer used to support infantry* brigades* was too heavy for transport by the same helicopters that carried infantry into combat. The new M102 105 mm howitzer weighed only 1,496 kilograms (3,290 pounds), 762 kilograms less than the M101. An aluminum carriage accounted for most of the decrease in weight. A circular base plate under the howitzer's recoil mechanism shifted the recoil's burden off the carriage directly into the ground. The corresponding elimination of trails and spades, and the addition of a spherical roller at the end of the carriage, gave the gun a 360-degree firing capability. It was officially adopted in 1965, and the 1st Cavalry Division developed new airmobility tactics* to use the M102 in Vietnam, but relatively short range—11,500 meters—limited its effectiveness in fast-moving airmobile operations over extended distances.

References. Boyd L. Dastrup, *King of Battle*, 1992. Robert G. McClintic, "Army Artillery Slims Down," *Army Digest*, May 1969, 28–29.

Jeffrey S. Shadburn

HOWITZER 155 MM M1

The towed M1 155 mm howitzer, known as the "Long Tom," was one of several new field artillery* pieces to appear in 1942. The 155 mm howitzer, considered a medium artillery piece because of its caliber and weight (about 12,000 pounds) was mounted on a T64E1 howitzer motor carriage. Air-filled tires (pneumatic or balloon) on a split-trail carriage permitted more mobility (25 mph compared to 8) than its World War I* predecessor, the M1918 155 mm howitzer, mounted on a solid-tired carriage. The M1 fired a ninety-five-pound shell a maximum of 16,355 yards, about 4,000 yards farther than the M1918; it fired many different types of shells, including chemical, steel-shrapnel, high-explosive (HE), and armor-piercing. It saw action in both Europe and the Pacific in World War II and during the Korean War.* The M1 155 mm howitzer continued in service until the early 1960s, when it was replaced by the M114 155 mm howitzer.

References. Boyd L. Dastrup, *King of Battle*, 1992. Konrad F. Schreier, Jr., "The 'Long Tom' Story," *Ordnance*, November–December 1967, 281–283.

James L. Isemann

HOWITZER, SELF-PROPELLED, 105 MM M7

The U.S. Army developed the M7 105 mm howitzer, self-propelled, in 1941 to provide mechanized units with artillery able to keep up with mechanized maneuver forces. To speed development, the Ordnance Department adopted a modified M3 tank chassis for the carriage and reduced the gross weight by reducing the chassis armor, removing the closed turret, and forgoing a 360-degree traverse capability. An M2 105 mm howitzer was mounted to the right of center, and a pulpit-like machine-gun turret—giving the M7 its nickname, the Priest—was added for air defense. Under Lend-Lease, M7s were sent to the British in North Africa and first saw action in 1942. In 1943, a newly designed chassis, the M4, replaced the M3. Employed by the U.S. Army throughout World War II* in all theaters, the M7 proved the value of self-propelled artillery. More mobile than towed artillery, the self-propelled gun protected its crew from small-arms fire and fragmentation, thus it could be employed more aggressively and closer to the enemy.

References. Boyd L. Dastrup, *King of Battle*, 1992. Konrad F. Schreier, Jr., *Standard Guide to US World War II Tanks & Artillery*, 1994.

Jeffrey S. Shadburn

HOWITZER, SELF-PROPELLED, 155 MM M109

In the early 1960s the U.S. Army fielded a number of new artillery pieces with greater range, maneuverability, rates of fire, and a wider variety of ordnance. Among these, the M109 155 mm self-propelled howitzer was to become the workhorse of the field artillery for the next generation. Unlike its predecessor from the pentomic era, the M109 could not fire nuclear rounds, but a more reliable chassis, more powerful engine, higher angle of fire, 360-degree traverse, and more spacious turret more than compensated for any limitations. When a 1979 study identified serious deficiencies in U.S. artillery due to advances in Soviet armor, the Army, rather than designing an entirely new self-propelled gun, upgraded and improved the M109, increasing its range and survivability in the field and adding several new types of munitions. Currently, the M109A3 is the standard self-propelled gun in armor and mechanized divisions* throughout the U.S. Army. European armies, the German and Swiss armies particularly, have adopted and developed variants of the M109, including the M109G and M109U. The M109 has, therefore, been one of the most successful artillery pieces in U.S. Army history.

References: "M109-Series 155-mm Self-Propelled Howitzers," *Army*, May 1992, 53–54. Rupert Pengelley, "M109 Modernization Moves," *International Defense Review*, 2/1990, 193–195.

HOWZE BOARD

On the basis of the airborne concepts and techniques of World War II* and the technological advances made by the helicopter during and after the Korean War,* a few farsighted U.S. Army officers conceived a novel set of principles combining light infantry, supporting artillery, and rotary-wing aviation to achieve maximum shock-power and maneuver on the modern battlefield. Upon taking office in 1961, Secretary of Defense* Robert S. McNamara also believed that more could and should be done to develop and adapt Army aviation to airmobile capabilities. In April 1962, he directed the formation of an ad hoc task force to examine the role of Army aircraft requirements. The task force, officially named the U.S. Army Technical Mobility Requirements Board, but commonly referred to as the Howze Board after its president, Lieutenant General Hamilton H. Howze, was pivotal in the development of this new idea and the airmobile concept. The Howze Board investigated, tested, and evaluated the organizational and operational concepts of airmobility; it concluded that transition to the airmobile concept was inevitable. The principal tactical and organizational innovation recommended by the board was the air assault* division, with a fourfold increase in aircraft over the standard division.* This use of helicopters for scout, command and control, troop transport, escort, gunships, aerial rocket artillery, supply, and medical evacuation would do for maneuver what the internal combustion engine had done for mobility.

References. Perry Poe, "How's Air Mobility?" *Army*, June 1963, 25–28. John J. Tolson, *Airmobility, 1961–1971*, 1973. Claude Witze, "The Howze Board Issue Is Joined," *Air Force and Space Digest*, May 1963, 14–16.

Arthur T. Frame

HUEY UH-1

Commonly known as the "Huey" to U.S. troops during the Vietnam War*
and since, the UH-1 is a single-main-rotor, general-purpose helicopter. In 1955,
the Bell Model 204 won an Army design competition for a frontline helicopter.
The prototype, designated XH-40, first flew on 26 October 1956. The Army
designated the production version HU-1—thus the popular name Huey. When
the Army subsequently changed the official designation to UH-1 Iroquois, however, the term "Huey" was too deeply inbedded in the soldiers' lexicon to
change. U.S. Army versions of the UH-1 include the A, B, C, D, and H models,
powered by various turboshaft engines. The Huey served as troop carrier, logistical support and medical evacuation vehicle and gunship, with 2.75-inch
rockets and .30-caliber machine guns to provide fire support for ground troops.
The UH-1H, introduced near the end of the Vietnam War, was equipped with
a 1,400–shaft horsepower T-53-L-13 engine. It continued as the Army's primary
utility helicopter until the introduction of the UH-60 in the early 1980s. The
term Huey was later associated with UH-1's cousin, the Bell AH-1 Cobra.* The
Huey UH-1 remains in service today as a general support and training helicopter.

References. Michael J. Krisman, "Huey Is the Bird Known as the 'Can Do' Helicopter," *Army Digest*, July 1966, 12–16. Bill Siuru, *The Huey and Huey Cobra*, 1987.

Randall N. Briggs

HUMMER. *See* High-Mobility Multipurpose Wheeled Vehicle.

HUNDRED-MILE-AN-HOUR TAPE

Hundred-mile-an-hour tape, or green tape, is soldier slang for a woven cloth,
high-strength, all-temperature, waterproof tape, normally issued in a two-inch
width, but available from one to six inches wide, and olive drab or dark green
in color. Hundred-mile-an-hour tape is used to secure almost anything in any
situation. The term refers to the tape's ability to adhere even in gale force winds.

Kelvin Crow

HUSKY

Operation Husky was the code name for the Allied landings in Sicily in July
1943. The task was assigned to the U.S. Seventh Army* under Lieutenant General George S. Patton, Jr.,* along with the British Eighth Army and the Canadian
I Corps. Opposing them were ten Italian and two German panzer divisions. On
10 July, British troops landed on the southeastern corner of the island, followed
by U.S. landings to the west the next day. Driving northward, the Allies defeated
savage German counterattacks and seized the southern quarter of the island by
15 July. Allied successes compelled the Axis commander, Field Marshal Albert
Kesselring, to inform Benito Mussolini that Sicily would soon fall.

Concentrating on slowing the British advance, the Germans conducted a retreat toward Messina with the intention of evacuating to Italy. U.S. forces fought
determined Axis resistance over rough terrain, captured Palermo on 30 July, and

drove eastward along the coast. By early August, the Allies were attempting to cut off the German retreat toward Messina with additional U.S. amphibious landings behind German lines. On 17 August, the U.S. 3d Infantry Division captured Messina, but the bulk of German forces managed to escape across the Straits to Italy. Operation Husky cost the Allies 25,000 casualties (including 7,500 U.S.) while the Germans lost 12,000 men.

References. Carlo D'Este, *Bitter Victory*, 1988. Samuel W. Mitcham, Jr., and Fredrich von Stauffenberg, *The Battle of Sicily*, 1991. S.W.C. Pack, *Operation 'Husky,'* 1977.

James E. Franklin

I

IA DRANG

In what was known as the Ia Drang Valley or Pleiku campaign, from 19 October through 18 November 1965 the newly arrived 1st Cavalry Division (1st CAV) confronted North Vietnamese Army (NVA) regulars on the Pleiku Plateau in South Vietnam's central highlands. This series of engagements was the first time an NVA regular division* met a U.S. Army division* on the battlefield. The NVA objective was to destroy a series of Special Forces* camps and the South Vietnamese district headquarters in the western plateau of the central highlands, seize the city of Pleiku, and cut South Vietnam in half. The 32nd and 33rd NVA regiments kicked off the action on 19 October when they laid siege to the camp at Plei Me and waited to ambush the relief column. U.S. artillery and close air support* thwarted the plan and mauled the NVA regiments, sending them reeling toward Cambodia. Elements of the 1st Brigade of the 1st CAV fanned westward in search of the enemy, ambushing elements of the 66th NVA Regiment.

Following sporadic fighting and a search for the enemy through largely empty territory, the 3rd Brigade of the 1st CAV replaced the 1st Brigade on 9 November. Five days, later the 1st Battalion, 7th Cavalry (1/7th Cav) assaulted into an area near the Ia Drang River around the Chu Pong Massif. The battalion landing zone* at the base of the massif, later designated LZ X-Ray, was in the middle of the NVA staging area for a second attack on Plei Me. A bloody engagement between the 1/7th Cav (plus Company B of the 2/7th Cav) and two NVA regiments followed. By dawn of 16 November, the NVA attack had petered out; the 2/7th Cav and the remainder of the 2/5th Cav relieved 1/7th Cavalry at LZ X-Ray. On 17 November, the two cavalry units pulled out of LZ X-Ray as B-52 strikes took over the task of destroying the retiring NVA units. That night, the 2/7th Cav, moving toward LZ Albany to be airlifted out of the area, was caught in an NVA ambush and suffered heavy casualties before reinforcements could be rushed to the scene the next morning.

Despite this setback, from a doctrinal perspective the Ia Drang campaign validated the concept and tactics* of airmobile warfare. U.S. leaders were convinced that superior firepower and technology would allow the U.S. military to destroy sufficient enemy forces to compel an end to the war.

References. Steven M. Leonard, "Steel Curtain," *Field Artillery*, July–August 1998, 17–20. John Pimlott, *Vietnam*, 1990. Shelby L. Stanton, *Anatomy of a Division*, 1987.

Arthur T. Frame

INCHON

Conceived by General of the Army Douglas MacArthur* during some of the bleakest days of the Korean War,* when U.S. forces were being pushed back into the Pusan Perimeter,* Operation Chromite—the amphibious landing at Inchon, twenty-five miles southwest of Seoul, Korea—was one of the most brilliant military operations of modern times. Chromite was a classic end-run, designed to relieve pressure on Lieutenant General Walton Walker's Eight Army* fighting around Pusan, to recapture the new capitol of the Republic of Korea, and to allow South Korean farmers to harvest their rice crop. Initially, MacArthur's proposal was received with scepticism, particularly from the U.S. Navy; he had to sell the idea to both the Joint Chiefs of Staff*(JCS) and his subordinates.

In the early morning hours of 15 September 1950, the first elements of the 1st Marine Division assaulted Wolmi-do, a small island fortress in the channel approach of Inchon, subduing it in forty-five minutes and opening the way for landing ashore. The next day, the Marines secured Kimpo Airfield (Seoul's airport) as Eighth Army began a series of attacks to break out along the Naktong River. The U.S. Army's 7th Infantry Division began landing on the 17th and joined the Marines in clearing Seoul of North Korean People's Army (NKPA) troops. Over the next week, progress was slow in heavy fighting both around Seoul and on the Naktong. By the 23rd, however, the NKPA began to disintegrate and withdraw north from the Naktong, with the Eighth Army in pursuit. Units of the 1st Cavalry Division and 7th Infantry Division linked up near Suwon on 27 September, and the next day, Major General Edward M. Almond, commanding X Corps, declared Seoul secured. What had seemed an almost certain defeat for the United States and United Nations forces in the Korean Peninsula had turned to victory. MacArthur's gamble had paid off.

References. Michael Langley, *Inchon Landing*, 1979. Walter J. Sheldon, *Hell or High Water*, 1968.

INDIAN SCOUTS

Use by the U.S. Army of Indians to find and fight hostile Indians was commonplace from the colonial period through the end of the Indian Wars.* Indian scouts were most effective and best known for their service during the Indian

Wars of the 1870s and 1880s. They served as guides in unfamiliar territory and gathered information about the hostile Indians' strength and movements. They fought either in conjunction with Army troops or as independent agents, and they helped maintain or restore order on reservations. The status of the scout was formalized by General Order 56 on 1 August 1866. Scouts who enlisted after 1866 received regular Army pay and equipment, even though they were often regarded as temporary and remained separated from the regular troops and their routines. Scout uniforms* were similar to the cavalry* uniform but had scarlet and white facings instead of cavalry yellow. The crossed arrow insignia identified U.S. Scouts until 1942.

Generally, Indians scouted against other tribes, especially tribal enemies, but there are notable exceptions, such as the Apache scouts who were vital in the capture of the Apache chief Geronimo. In 1891, General Order 28 required that L Troop in each cavalry regiment* and I Company in each infantry* regiment be composed of enlisted Indians. Indian scouts continued to serve in the Army after the end of the Indian Wars; they participated in the Spanish-American War* and General John J. Pershing's* Punitive Expedition* against Pancho Villa in 1916. By 1924, only eight scouts remained on active duty, at Fort Huachuca.* The last Indian scouts retired from the U.S. Army in September 1947.

References. Fairfax Downey and Jacques N. Jacobsen, Sr., *The Red/Bluecoats*, 1973. Thomas W. Dunlay, *Wolves for the Blue Soldiers*, 1982.

L. Lynn Williams

INDIAN WARS

The term "Indian Wars" describes a series of conflicts between various Indian tribes and the United States and its allies. The cause of these wars was usually white migrations and the government's policy of restricting or relocating Indians to reservations, where they would not impede white expansion. Replete with stories of massacres, broken promises, and brutal tactics by both sides, the generally accepted dates—1866–1891—are derived from a 1905 decision by the U.S. Army to award campaign medals to soldiers who fought on the frontier during those years. Among the separate wars and campaigns that encompassed the Indian Wars were: the Bozeman Trail War (1866–1868); the Snake War (1866–1868); the Modoc War (1872–1873); the Centennial Campaign* (1876–1877); the Nez Percé War (1877); the Bannock War (1878); the Sheepeater War (1879); and the Ute War* (1879).

The final action of the Indian Wars occurred in December 1890, when the 7th Cavalry confronted a large group of Miniconjou Sioux who had gathered for the Ghost Dance on the Pine Ridge Reservation in South Dakota. When the soldiers attempted to disarm a number of Indians, a melee ensued. More than 150 Indians, including women and children, were killed along, with twenty-five soldiers. Brigadier General Nelson Miles's* arrival, with a force of over 3,000 men who quickly surrounded the area, convinced the Indians that they had no chance of escape; they formally surrendered on 15 January 1891 at White Clay Creek, ending a quarter-century of armed conflict.

References. Alan Axelrod, *Chronicle of the Indian Wars*, 1993. Richard H. Dillon, *North American Indian Wars*, 1983. Robert M. Utley and Wilcomb E. Washburn, *The American Heritage History of the Indian Wars*, 1977.

Tamas Dreilinger

INDUSTRIAL COLLEGE OF THE ARMED FORCES

As established by General Order 7 on 25 February 1924, the purpose of the Army Industrial College was to train senior officers in logistics and mobilization planning. Over the next fifteen years, faculty and student research projects contributed directly to the Industrial Mobilization Plan, a critical step in planning for World War II.* Renamed the Industrial College of the Armed Forces (ICAF) in May 1946 and relocated to Fort McNair, the secretary of defense* designated the school a joint educational institution in 1948. In 1975, ICAF merged with the National War College to form the National Defense University.* Today, ICAF's primary function is the study of management of national security resources. Students represent all of the armed services, various agencies of the U.S. government, and occasionally civilians from the private sector. Selection for the coveted ten-month course is based on past performance and potential for future leadership in managing national assets. Students are typically senior lieutenant colonels or colonels (or equivalent), and they receive senior service college credit. Most members of the annual class of 170 students attend courses at the Fort McNair campus, but a small number—usually about eight—participate in faculty-directed independent research programs in the nation's industrial and national command structure.

References. Stanley L. Falk, "The Little-Big School off Buzzard's Point," *Army*, April 1985, 46–50. Gregory D. Foster, "Educating for the 21st Century," *National Defense*, March 1992, 14–17. Dennis Steele, "Higher Learning," *Soldiers*, March 1986, 21–24.

Lawyn C. Edwards

INFANTRY

Since the earliest human conflicts, foot soldiers—both light troops equipped for maneuver and offensive action, and heavy troops for shock and defense— have played significant roles on the world's battlefields. Although the infantry's role has not always been preeminent, the appearance of gunpowder weapons on the battlefield in the early modern period assured the foot soldier a continuing and major place in warfare. In the 16th century, the English adopted the term "infantry" (from the French *infanterie*—meaning small soldiery) to describe these troops.

The infantry has always been an important arm of the U.S. Army. On 14 June 1775, the Continental Congress authorized ten companies* of riflemen (or infantry) to be raised in Pennsylvania, Maryland, and Virginia, and it later authorized another forty-nine infantry battalions* or regiments.* When George

Washington* assumed command of the Continental Army,* he met with a congressional committee that proposed raising twenty-six regiments of infantry. Although that number was never achieved, the precedent that infantry would be the most numerous of the combat arms was clearly established.

Throughout the 19th and first half of the 20th centuries, the infantry retained a predominant place in the U.S. Army. A series of drill manuals defined the basic infantry organization—the regiment was initially composed of ten companies, later twelve companies in three battalions.* At various times, the manuals called for grenadier and light infantry companies, and in the West dragoons (mounted infantry), to provide security along the Santa Fe and Oregon Trails and to fight fast-moving Indian warriors. Primarily, however, the infantry marched to the battlefield and formed the Army's main battle line.

The National Defense Act of 1920* created a chief of infantry to oversee infantry affairs; also it assigned the Army's tank corps to the infantry. Along with a newly created Infantry Board, the chief of infantry directed the development of the infantry during the interwar period, including new tables of organization and equipment* (TOEs), doctrine,* training, and weapons. World War II* saw new and innovative uses of infantry, particularly in airborne, glider, mechanized, ranger, and amphibious operations. The Army Organization Act of 1950* extended statutory recognition to the three combat arms, infantry, armor,* and artillery.* Ironically, the ratio of infantry in the U.S. Army was declining while it was assuming even more important and more sophisticated missions for the future. Infantrymen constituted about 10 percent of all U.S. Army forces deployed to Southeast Asia during the Vietnam War.*

Today, the infantry is still a vital and necessary element of the U.S. Army. Its mission is primarily to gain and hold ground, but it has many specialized tasks as well. One of seven combat arms in the U.S. Army, the infantry is variously known as "the Queen of Battle" and "the ultimate weapon."

References. John K. Mahon and Romana Danysh, *Infantry*, 1972. Gregory J. W. Urwin, *The United States Infantry*, 1988.

INFANTRY

Infantry, published by the U.S. Army Infantry School at Fort Benning,* Georgia, is distributed free of charge to U.S infantry* and infantry-related units and sold by subscription to other units and individuals. The professional bulletin of the infantry, *Infantry* originated in 1921 as the Infantry School *Mailing List* with a pamphlet called "Tactical Problems." Beginning with the 1930–1931 academic year, school material was collected and published semiannually in bound volumes. The *Infantry School Quarterly* replaced the *Mailing List* in July 1947, and in April 1957 the title was shortened to *Infantry*. In October 1959, *Infantry* began its current bimonthly schedule. Its mission is to provide current information on infantry organization, weapons, equipment, tactics, and techniques; provide a forum for the expression of profession ideas; and publish relevant historical articles. *Infantry* features original articles, letters to the editor, career notes for both officers and enlisted personnel, book reviews, and news items of particular interest to the professional infantryman.

References. Michael E. Unsworth, ed., *Military Periodicals*, 1990. [Stephen H. White], "Editor's Page," *Infantry*, April 1957, 2.

Gary Bounds

INITIAL PROTECTIVE FORCE

On 16 December 1936, Chief of Staff* Malin Craig* directed the General Staff* to begin work on a protective mobilization plan (PMP).* In 1937, the staff completed the first installment of the PMP. Section I called for an emergency defensive initial protective force (IPF) of 400,000 men, composed of 165,000 Regular Army and 235,000 National Guard* troops in the continental United States. Although the staff revised the numbers annually, the essence of the plan did not change. In 1939, Army planners estimated the number of troops available upon mobilization at 283,335, with another 151,280 men available in the first thirty days. However, prior to mobilization in 1940, the IPF's four Regular infantry* divisions* were not even at their authorized reduced peacetime strength; troops would have to be drawn from the other five, already-skeletonized, Regular Army divisions. Even severely cutting low-priority units failed to yield sufficient manpower for the four Regular divisions in the IPF. Some artillery* units existed only on paper, and others were missing batteries.* Planners concluded that raw recruits would have to fill units after mobilization. The IPF was inadequately manned and funded, but its primary value was to establish a force structure for the eventual procurement of men and material for World War II.*

References Marvin A. Kreidberg and Merton G. Henry, *History of Military Mobilization in the United States Army, 1775–1945*, 1955. Mark S. Watson, *Chief of Staff*, 1950.

Charles Heller

INSIGNIA

Military insignia are worn by military service members to indicate unit, rank or grade, branch, capacity, and special duty assignments. Insignia of grade— gold and silver bars for company-grade officers and warrant officers,*oak leaves and eagles for field-grade officers, and stars for general officers—are metallic devices worn on the shoulder epaulets of the dress uniform,* and embroidered cloth worn on the collar of the combat uniform. Enlisted and noncommissioned officer* (NCO) insignia of rank consist of one to three chevrons (points up), and rockers with stars and wreaths. Cloth rank insignia are worn on the upper sleeve of the dress uniform, while subdued metallic devices are worn on both collars of the combat uniform. Service members also wear distinctive branch insignia—crossed rifles for infantry,* for example—officers on both dress and combat uniforms, enlisted personnel and NCOs on the dress uniform only. Other insignia indicate special duties; officers wear such insignia in lieu of branch insignia when in that special duty status. Special insignia include inspector general,* General Staff,* and aide-de-camp. Officers assigned special duties, such as the General Staff and the* Joint Staff, also wear badges on the pockets of dress and Class B uniforms. Shoulder insignia (patches) worn on the upper-left sleeve indicate a service member's current unit, while soldiers who have served in combat are authorized to wear the appropriate unit patch on the upper-right sleeve.

References. Jack Britton, *Uniform Insignia of the United States Military Forces*, 1980. Evans E. Kerrigan, *American Badges and Insignia*, 1967. J. McDowell Morgan, *Military Medals and Insignia of the United States*, 1941.

Steven E. Clay

INSPECTOR GENERAL

During the American Revolution,* George Washington* and the Continental Congress realized that the Continental Army* needed improvement. Washington believed that a way to effect these improvements was to establish an inspecting mechanism. He proposed an office modeled on the European system; on 13 December 1777 Congress authorized the appointment of two general officers to report on the condition of the Army. The duties, responsibilities, and even the existence of the Office of the Inspector General have changed as the Army has matured. Today, the mission of the Inspector General (IG) is to determine and report on the overall readiness of units within the U.S. Army and to serve as a confidential advisor to the secretary of the Army.* The IG conducts periodic inspections of units to assess efficiency, morale, and level of training. At the completion of inspections, the IG forwards report on deficiencies to the units for corrective action and conducts follow-up inspections, if necessary, to ensure unit compliance. To assist the IG, each subordinate command down to division* level has an office of the inspector general. The office performs the same function at each level in regard to unit readiness and as a confidential advisor to the commander on issues affecting the unit.

References. David A. Clary and Joseph W. A. Whitehorne, *The Inspector General of the United States Army, 1777–1903*, 1987. Joseph W. A. Whitehorne, *The Inspectors General of the United States Army, 1903–1939*, 1998.

Kenneth Turner

INTELLIGENCE PREPARATION OF THE BATTLEFIELD

Intelligence preparation of the battlefield (IPB) is a continuous process of gathering and assessing data before and during a battle, with a view toward preparing specific products, often graphical in nature, to support the commander's decision-making process. The IBP process begins with a complete terrain analysis of the operational area and assessment of its effect on friendly and enemy courses of action. The analyst then assesses probable enemy capabilities and relates them to friendly capabilities and options. Possible courses of action are developed, war gamed for contingencies, and presented to the commander as a predictive possibility (what the enemy will most likely do). The IPB process prepares the commander and his staff for a new battlefield, sorts and presents new data in a useful framework, and, using templates of enemy units and formations, helps predict future enemy operations and possible friendly responses.

References. Gregory P. Rowe, "Integrating IPB into Paragraph Three (and Other OPORD Briefing Techniques)," *Armor*, January–February 1992, 44–46. Robert M. Toguchi and James Hogue, "The Battle Convergence in Four Dimensions," *Military Review*, October 1992, 11–20.

Richard Stewart

INVALID CORPS. *See* Veteran Reserve Corps.

IROQUOIS. *See.* Huey UH-1.

J

JACKSON, ANDREW (1767–1845)

Andrew Jackson, seventh president of the United States, was a capable politician and a ruthless fighter. Dubbed "Old Hickory," Jackson retained immense popularity among the American people throughout his life. Born on the South Carolina frontier to Irish immigrant parents, Jackson fought against the British during the American Revolution.* Orphaned at the age of fourteen, he was self-educated and passed the North Carolina bar Examination in 1787. Moving west, he settled near Nashville, Tennessee, where he built a plantation he called the Hermitage.

Jackson's rise was mercurial serving as Tennessee's first U.S. representative in 1796 and then as a senator from 1797 to 1798. Leaving the Senate, Jackson took a seat on Tennessee's supreme court from 1798 to 1804. In 1802, Jackson, now a major general in the state militia, gained fame for the suppression of the Creek Indians in the Mississippi Territory. He retired immediately thereafter, due to several ongoing personal feuds, but he was reappointed a major general in the Regular Army to fight in the last year of the War of 1812.* Jackson's enduring fame was achieved as the victor at the Battle of New Orleans* in 1815, even though the action had no influence on the war's outcome. Jackson next commanded the U.S. effort to suppress the Seminoles in Florida. His success in this endeavor assured U.S. acquisition of Florida and led to Jackson's appointment as military governor of the territory in 1821.

Fame as both an Indian fighter and foe of the British gave Jackson strength to reclaim his Senate seat in 1823 and to run for the presidency in 1824. Defeated in a hotly disputed contest, he ran again in 1828 and won; he was decisively reelected in 1832. A staunch Democrat and enemy of government interference, Andrew Jackson earned an enduring reputation as a representative of the common man.

References. Donald B. Cole, *The Presidency of Andrew Jackson*, 1993. Robert V. Remini, *The Life of Andrew Jackson*, 1988. Anthony F. C. Wallace, *The Long, Bitter Trail*, 1993.

Lee W. Eysturlid

JACKSON, THOMAS J. "STONEWALL" (1824–1863)

After graduating seventeenth of fifty-nine in the U.S. Military Academy* class of 1846, Thomas J. Jackson distinguished himself in the Mexican War.* In 1851, he became professor of natural and experimental philosophy at Virginia Military Institute* (VMI). In 1859, Jackson commanded the VMI cadet corps and attended the execution of the abolitionist John Brown. After Virginia seceded in 1861, he volunteered his services to his state and rose quickly to the rank of brigadier general.

Jackson secured his place in American military history at First Bull Run,* when his brigade became a rallying point for the retiring Confederate forces. "There is Jackson standing like a stone wall!" shouted General Bernard Bee. The epithet stuck. Jackson added to his fame in the spring of 1862 in a series of maneuvers and battles known as the Valley Campaign. His small force kept many times its number of Federal troops from reinforcing the main Union army advancing toward the Confederate capital at Richmond. At the critical moment, Jackson led his army to reinforce the Confederates defending Richmond and participated in the battle that forced the Federals to withdraw.

In the reorganization that followed, Jackson became one of the two corps* commanders in Robert E. Lee's* Army of Northern Virginia. Jackson's corps led the series of brilliant maneuvers that resulted in victory at Second Bull Run* and the capture of Harpers Ferry* in the summer of 1862. He participated in the battles of Antietam* and Fredericksburg.* His greatest moment came in May 1863, when his corps attacked the flank of the Army of the Potomac* during the battle of Chancellorsville.* His attack reversed the military situation and allowed Lee to regain the initiative and force a Federal withdrawal. However, while conducting a personal reconnaissance with his staff well forward of his own lines late on 2 May 1863, Jackson was mortally wounded by his own men. He died a week later.

Jackson was always at his best in independent command and when given freedom of action as a subordinate. His death at the height of military success established his place in American military history.

References. Bevin Alexander, *Lost Victories*, 1992. John Bowers, *Stonewall Jackson*, 1989. John Selby, *Stonewall Jackson as Military Commander*, 1968. Robert G. Tanner, *Stonewall in the Valley*, 1976.

George Knapp

JEDBURGHS

The Office of Strategic Services* (OSS) created ninety-three three-man "Jedburgh" teams in late 1943 to provide special-operations support for the Allied invasion of France, and six additional teams to support subsequent operations in the Netherlands. By early 1944, some 230 French, British, American, Belgian, Dutch, Canadian, and South African volunteers had assembled in Cambridge-shire, north of London, for training in behind-the-lines operations. British offi-cers headed the project; their headquarters and main training facility were at Milton Hall, outside the city of Peterborough. A typical three-man team con-sisted of a French officer, an American or British officer, and an enlisted radio operator. They received training in close combat, infiltration and exfiltration techniques, small-unit tactics,* light weapons, demolitions, and a host of skills necessary for survival behind German lines.

Approximately half of the Jedburgh teams deployed from England to northern France at or shortly after the Normandy landings (Overlord*), while the rest staged out of Algiers for the invasion of southern France (Dragoon*). Typically, Jeds arrived by parachute, dropping through the open bomb bays of bombers specially equipped for night operations. Other teams infiltrated by glider,* cargo plane, or boat. Ideally, members of the French Resistance met the teams at the landing zones.* On occasion, however, German Gestapo agents supported by the French *milice* (French collaborators) provided the welcoming party, ending an operation almost before it began. Even after linkup with the Resistance, however, the Jeds occasionally ran afoul of the tangled political disputes be-tween Gaullist and communist partisans. Because the Jeds offered partisans the surest access to air-dropped supplies, rival groups occasionally fought each other to secure a team and its all-important radio. In addition to equipment, the Jeds provided means to organize and direct partisan operations in support of Allied armies driving east and north toward the Rhine.

Jedburgh-led partisan groups destroyed rail lines, ambushed enemy convoys, cut telephone wires, and blew up bridges. When German resistance began to crumble, the Jeds found themselves hard pressed to keep an ever-growing num-ber of partisans equipped with weapons. Despite the occasional betrayal of the teams and inevitable casualties, the Jeds and their bands of French partisans harassed the enemy unmercifully. As a result, the Germans found it necessary to dedicate thousands of troops to the task of rear-area security. The last Jed-burgh team completed its mission in January 1945.

References. Aaron Bank, *From OSS to Green Berets*, 1986. William B. Dreux, *No Bridges Blown*, 1971.

Joseph R. Fischer

JEEP

The Jeep is by far the most immediately recognizable and well-known military vehicle of all time; its cachet is still being used by automotive manufacturers today. Undoubtedly more has been written about the design, origin, and pro-duction of the military Jeep than any other military transport vehicle in history. The genesis of the Jeep was in infantry* branch requirements for a high-horsepower, low-silhouette, all-terrain reconnaissance car. The Howe-Wiley

"Belly Flopper," a hybrid vehicle based on the light Austin motor car, built in 1937 and tested by the Infantry Board over the next three years holds claim as grandfather of the Jeep. By June 1940, an Army technical committee had determined the characteristics for a new vehicle and had issued an invitation to 135 automotive manufacturers to produce prototypes. Only two companies, Ford and Willys, responded, although American Bantam Motor Company had already developed a prototype.

After service test trials of 1,500 prototypes from each company in 1941, the Willys Model MA emerged as the strongest competitor. The result was extensive litigation by Bantam, which claimed that Willys had utilized much of its early design work. Further modification of the Model MA resulted in the Willys MB, the vehicle that became the World War II* Jeep. When Willys-Overland could not produce sufficient quantities of the new quarter-ton 4×4s, Ford received a contract to build its version of the Model MB, the Ford Model GPW—thus the term "Jeep." During World War II, Willys built 361,349 Model MBs, and Ford built 277,896 GPWs. Models including the M38, M38A1, and M151 were produced for military use until 1978. Rightly hailed as a "divine instrument of wartime locomotion" by correspondent Ernie Pyle,* the Jeep won praise from everyone, from privates to generals.

References Michael Clayton, *Jeep*, 1982. J.-G. Jeudy M. Tararine, *The Jeep*, 1981. Kurt Willinger and Gene Gurney, *The American Jeep in War and Peace*, 1983.

Stephen C. McGeorge

JEFFERSON BARRACKS

Built in 1826 just south of St. Louis, Missouri, as a recruitment and training center, Jefferson Barracks was originally named Camp Adams, but War Department* General Order 66 changed the name on 23 October 1826 in honor of the recently deceased President Thomas Jefferson. Many noted officers of the 19th century served at Jefferson Barracks during their careers. For a period in 1843, Jefferson Barracks was the largest military establishment in the United States. During the Civil War,* it served primarily as a hospital and recuperation center for 15,000 soldiers. Jefferson Barracks was the sixth-largest induction center during World War I* and World War II,* but it was closed in June 1946. Today Jefferson Barracks is a National Historic Park, and the grounds contain the second-largest national cemetery* in the United States.

References. Herbert M. Hart, *Pioneer Forts of the West*, 1967. Henry W. Webb, "The Story of Jefferson Barracks," *New Mexico Historical Review*, July 1946, 185–208.

L. Lynn Williams

JEFFERSON BROGANS

Brogans, also called "bootees," were the standard-issue U.S. Army footwear from the early 19th century until 1872. Inspired by Thomas Jefferson (thus "Jefferson brogans") who advocated a simple lace-up shoe, the brogan was produced with right and left lasts, a broad square toe, and an ankle-high quarter.

The early version came well above the ankle; the shoes were at times cut down by soldiers to prevent chafing. By the Civil War,* although the brogans were cut lower, the contractors sometimes sewed the soles rather than pegging them, as in the earlier version, thus producing a shoddier product. Brogans were issued to both foot and mounted troops until the late 1850s, when boots were introduced that had improved lasts and soles attached by brass screws. At that time, the term brogan, or bootee, was abolished and replaced by "shoe," thus ending the confusion between the issue shoe and the issue boot.

References. Sidney Brinkerhoff, *Boots and Shoes of the Frontier Soldier*, 1976. Frederick P. Todd, *American Military Equipage, 1851–1872*, 1980.

Steven J. Allie

JODY

"Jody" has two common meanings. First, it is the generic name for cadential marching songs. The soldier in charge of a formation typically chants one line of the song, which is then echoed by the entire formation. Jodies are especially popular during double-time marching. The subject of many jodies is "Jody," the mythical nemisis of all soldiers serving far from home. When a soldier is called away, Jody emerges to steal his girl, his job, his property, and generally destroy all chances for the soldier to return to the life he left behind. Jody—the mythical character—is aptly described in the following verse from a popular jody:

> Ain't no use in goin' home
> Jody's got your girl and gone.
> Ain't no use in lookin' back
> Jody's got your Cadillac.

Reference. Sandee Shaffer Johnson, ed., *Cadences*, 2 vols., 1983–1986.

Scott McMeen

JOHNSON, HAROLD KEITH (1912–1983)

Harold Keith Johnson, a highly decorated veteran of World War II* and the Korean War,* became Chief of Staff* of the U.S. Army during the Vietnam War* and presided over the Army during one of its most difficult periods. Born in Bowesmont, North Dakota, Johnson graduated from the U.S. Military Academy* in 1933 and advanced through the ranks quickly to become a major and commander of the 57th Infantry (the Philippine Scouts*) at the time of the Japanese attack on Pearl Harbor. During a dangerous mission in 1942 against the Japanese, he was captured and barely survived the Bataan death march.* He weighed only ninety pounds when liberated.

During the Korean War, Johnson commanded the 1st Provisional Infantry Battalion of the 1st Cavalry Division in the heavy fighting along the Pusan Perimeter* and north on the peninsula. Rising to the rank of colonel, Johnson became assistant chief of staff of I Corps, winning the Distinguished Service Cross* for extraordinary heroism in action.

As Army Chief of Staff in 1964, Johnson presided over the buildup of U.S. forces in Vietnam and the acceleration of the war. He believed the Vietnam War was winnable but differed with President Lyndon Johnson on how victory could be accomplished and at what cost. General Johnson opposed the president's "gradualist" approach to the bombing war in Vietnam and favored hitting the enemy quickly, with the heaviest blows possible. Harold K. Johnson retired in 1968 and died in 1983.

References. Martin Blumenson, " 'A Most Remarkable Man,' " *Army*, August 1968, 18–26. Lewis Sorley, *Honorable Warrior*, 1998.

Donald Gilmore

JOHNSTON, JOSEPH E. (1807–1891)

Born in Farmington, Virginia, in 1807, Joseph E. Johnson graduated thirteenth of forty-six cadets in the U.S. Military Academy* class of 1829. Commissioned a lieutenant in the artillery, Johnson resigned after eight years of service. Recommissioned later, he served with distinction in the Second Seminole War* and the Mexican War.* In 1860, he was appointed Quartermaster General with the rank of brigadier general, but Johnston offered his services to Virginia soon after secession and was appointed a brigadier general in the Confederate Army on 14 May 1861.

In July 1861, Johnston reinforced P.G.T. Beauregard's forces at Manassas (First Bull Run*) by rail. His timing and direction of the arriving troops proved to be the turning point in the Confederate victory. Promoted to full general, he assumed command of the Army of Northern Virginia on 31 August 1861. In the spring of 1862, Johnston defended Richmond during the Peninsula Campaign* and attacked George B. McClellan's* army at Seven Pines* at the end of May. Severely wounded, he left the army to recuperate but returned to service in November, in command of the Department of the West, where unclear authority and contradictory orders contributed to the loss of Vicksburg on 4 July 1863.

After Braxton Bragg's abandonment of Chattanooga in November 1883, Johnston was given command of the Army of Tennessee. Jefferson Davis, however, relieved Johnston in July 1864, replacing him with John Bell Hood because of Johnston's failure to stop Sherman's advance on Atlanta. After Hood's loss of Atlanta and the disastrous battles of Franklin and Nashville,* Robert E. Lee* restored Johnston to command. He was still in command in April 1865, when Lee surrendered. After the war Johnston wrote his memoirs, was elected to the House of Representatives after Reconstruction, and served as commissioner of railroads in the Grover Cleveland administration. He died in Washington, D.C., on 21 March 1891.

References. Gilbert E. Govan and James W. Livingood, *A Different Valor*, 1956. Jeffrey N. Lash, *Destroyer of the Iron Horse*, 1991. Craig L. Symonds, *Joseph E. Johnston*, 1992.

George Mordica II

JOINT ARMY-NAVY BOARD

In July 1903, the secretaries of war and the Navy established a joint board for "conferring upon, discussing, and reaching common conclusions regarding all matters calling for cooperation of the two services." Four officers from each service named by the secretaries, constituted the board. Although the board manifested some prestige in its early years, its importance declined, and in 1914 President Woodrow Wilson suspended it. Following World War I,* the Joint Army-Navy Board, as it was now formally named, was reorganized and directed to secure complete cooperation and coordination in all matters and policies involving joint action of the Army and Navy. Membership now comprised three ex officio members from each service. Army members were the Chief of Staff,* the director of the Operations Division (G-3), and the director of the War Plans Division.* Within the Joint Board, as it was commonly called, the Joint Planning Committee (JPC) was charged to investigate, study, and report to the board.

The Joint Board met continuously from 1919 until 1942. With the increasing importance of airpower, the board's membership was expanded to include the Army's deputy chief of staff for air and the Navy's chief of the Bureau of Aeronautics. The two services provided the board's coordinating secretary on an alternating basis. In 1939, President Franklin D. Roosevelt directed the Joint Board to exercise its functions under his direction and supervision. In May 1941, a Joint Strategic Committee was created under the JPC to study and prepare joint basic war and joint operations plans. The JPC thus became the institution through which the Joint Board could utilize Army and Navy planning staffs for interservice coordination. Furthermore, this arrangement provided the pattern for the planning committees subsequently set up under the Joint Chiefs of Staff* in 1942.

References. Ray S. Cline, *Washington Command Post*, 1951. Mark S. Watson, *Chief of Staff*, 1950.

John A. Hixson

JOINT BOARD. *See* Joint Army-Navy Board.

JOINT CHIEFS OF STAFF

The National Security Act of 1947* officially established the Joint Chiefs of Staff (JCS). Originally formed as the Joint U.S. Chiefs of Staff shortly after the United States entered World War II,* this organization coordinated strategic direction and planning with the British Chiefs of Staff Committee. At the end of the war, the legislative and executive process to formalize a joint command and staff structure was instituted. The size, function, and importance of the JCS and the role of the Chairman of the Joint Chiefs of Staff (CJCS) in national defense had grown significantly since its inception. With the passage of the Defense Reorganization Act of 1986 (the Goldwater-Nichols Act*), however, the CJCS became the "principal military advisor to the President, the Secretary of Defense,* and the National Security Council." Nevertheless, the CJCS still does not have executive authority to command combatant forces: combatant command resides in the commanders in chief of the unified commands.*

Today, the JCS consists of the Chairman (CJCS), the Chief of Staff of the Army, the Chief of Naval Operations (CNO), the Chief of Staff of the Air Force (CSAF), and the Commandant of the Marine Corps (CMC). The JCS, with its own supporting staff, the Joint Staff, is the immediate military staff of the secretary of defense.* The CJCS is responsible for strategic direction and planning, contingency planning, programming, and budgeting for military equipment. In addition, the CJCS is responsible for the development of joint doctrine* and education and training for the employment of joint forces provided by the services. He also provides the communication links for transmission of orders between the president and the secretary of defense—the National Command Authorities* (NCA)—and the unified commands.

Goldwater-Nichols significantly enhanced the position of the CJCS. In addition, the act created a vice chairman, who by law is the second-ranking member of the armed forces and replaces the chairman under specific circumstances. The military service chiefs have two roles. They serve as members of the Joint Chiefs of Staff and provide military advice to the NCA and National Security Council, but they are also responsible to their civilian department secretaries for the management of their respective services.

References. Lawrence J. Korb, *The Joint Chiefs of Staff*, 1976. Allan R. Millett et al., *The Reorganization of the Joint Chiefs of Staff*, 1986.

J.G.D. Babb

JOINT OPERATIONS

Joint operations are defined simply as military operations conducted by forces of two or more military services or departments. While there is a long history of military operations conducted in concert by land and sea forces, dating back to ancient times, an account of U.S. joint operations usually begins with the battle of Vera Cruz* during the Mexican War* and the Vicksburg* campaign during the Civil War.* However, the use of airpower and seapower to support land and amphibious campaigns in complex and difficult operations conducted over great distances in World War II* are the most notable examples of past joint operations.

Since 1945 the U.S. military has moved to integrate its military command and control structure. The National Security Act of 1947* is considered the most important piece of legislation in this regard. The failure in 1980 of the rescue attempt of hostages held in Iran by a joint force, and problems in command, control, and communications that surfaced in Grenada in 1983, prompted Congress to enact the Goldwater-Nichols Act* (the Department of Defense Reorganization Act of 1986). Goldwater-Nichols elevated the chairman of the Joint Chiefs of Staff* to be the principal military adviser to the president, the secretary of defense,* and the National Security Council,* and it gave combatant command for the conduct of military operations to the unified and specified commanders in chief (CINCs). Although the services still have a major role to play in organizing, training, equipping, and maintaining forces, the employment of those forces to further U.S. national interests now falls primarily on the unified, regional warfighting CINCs. Virtually all military operations since 1986 have been joint and commanded by the CINCs or joint task force (JTF) commanders under their direct command. This included Operation Just Cause* in 1989, Operation Desert Shield/Desert Storm* in 1990–1991 and various military operations other than war* (OOTW) in Somalia, Rwanda, northern Iraq, and Haiti.

References. Daniel R. Mortensen, *A Pattern for Joint Operations*, 1987. Robert W. RisCassi, "Doctrine for Joint Operations in a Combined Environment," *Military Review*, January–February 1997, 103–114.

J.G.D. Babb

JOINT READINESS TRAINING CENTER

The Joint Readiness Training Center (JRTC), the U.S. Army's premier training ground for light forces, provides a joint training environment for units in low to mid-intensity conflict, although the emphasis is on operations other than war* (OOTW). A three-week training scenario is designed for each unit, based on its brigade* commander's specific training objectives. Scenarios can include counterguerrilla operations, defense and offense against a conventional opposing force (OPFOR), and special unit training, such as military intelligence and civil affairs. Originally located at Fort Chaffee,* Arkansas, the JRTC outgrew the facilities there and moved to Fort Polk,* Louisiana, in 1993.

References. Geoffrey N. Blake, John Calahan, and Steven Young, "OPFOR Observations from the JRTC," *Infantry*, January–February 1995, 30–35. Robert A. Ivey, "Tough Lessons Learned at the JRTC," *Military Intelligence*, April–June 1990, 15–18.

JOURNAL OF THE ARMED FORCE. See Army and Navy Journal.

JUDGE ADVOCATE GENERAL

The Judge Advocate General was one of nine staff officers assigned to George Washington* upon the creation of the Continental Army.* Each separate army also had a judge advocate general, but each remained subordinate to the Judge Advocate of the main army and, later, the War Department.* The Judge Advocate General is responsible for providing legal advice to military commanders and staffs regarding the administration of military justice and other legal matters. Today, the acronym JAG refers to commissioned officers who are members of the Judge Advocate General's Corps; they are lawyers admitted to practice before a federal court and the highest court in at least one state, the District of Columbia, or Puerto Rico.

References. T. James Binder, "Their Battlefield Is the Courtroom," *Army*, November 1984, 48–52. U.S. Army, Office of the Judge Advocate General, *The Army Lawyer* [1975].

JUNCTION CITY

One of the largest combat operations of the Vietnam War,* Junction City, 22 February to 14 May 1967, was directed against a major enemy stronghold, War Zone C, in Tay Ninh province. The primary purpose of the operation was to search out and destroy elements of a Viet Cong (VC) division and a North Vietnamese Army (NVA) regiment, as well as enemy base camps and the Communist Central Office of South Vietnam (COSVN) headquarters. Elements of the U.S. 1st and 25th Infantry Divisions, the 173d Airborne Brigade, and the 196th Light Infantry Brigade, along with integrated Army of the Republic of Vietnam (ARVN) battalions, formed blocking positions in an inverted horseshoe around the operation area. The 11th Armored Cavalry Regiment and the 2nd Brigade of the 25th Infantry Division pushed into the open southern end of the horseshoe to conduct search-and-destroy* operations. Initially, two full ARVN regiments were to have been included, to provide ARVN forces the opportunity to observe and evaluate the combat standards of U.S. units. This was reduced to only four battalions, however, to eliminate information leaks experienced in the preceding operation, Cedar Falls,* in the adjacent "Iron Triangle."

Junction City was considered a success and a vindication of large-scale, multiunit operations. Yet while killing nearly 2,800 enemy, it demonstrated superficial U.S.-ARVN cooperation and combined action at best. COSVN headquarters and the VC/NVA units were not destroyed; they simply withdrew into Cambodian sanctuaries. U.S. commanders did all the planning themselves and relegated their Vietnamese counterparts to the role of blindfolded executioners. Operational plans on the Vietnamese side were merely translations of U.S. orders, and the tactical role of ARVN units was largely secondary. As for coordination at the top, the South Vietnamese Joint General Staff knew nothing about Junction City until it was launched, although the operational plan had been published a month in advance.

References. John Pimlott, *Vietnam*, 1990. Bernard W. Rogers, *Cedar Falls—Junction City*, 1974. Shelby L. Stanton, *The Rise and Fall of an American Army*, 1985.

Arthur T. Frame

JUNIOR RESERVE OFFICER TRAINING CORPS

The Junior Reserve Officer Training Corps (JROTC) program is a course of instruction taught for academic credit in high schools by retired officers and noncommissioned officers* (NCOs). In public schools, students enroll in JROTC as an elective course and are referred to as cadets. Participation in this program incurs no military obligation on the student. Some of the topics taught in JROTC are American citizenship, leadership, drug abuse prevention, map reading, American military history, first aid and hygiene, and techniques of communication. Some of the program's desired learning outcomes are understanding the ethics and principles underlying good citizenship, positive mental techniques (such as goal setting), knowledge of educational and vocational opportunities, and practical experience in leadership.

The National Defense Act of 1916* authorized the secretary of war* to issue equipment to secondary schools desiring military training programs. Subsequent legislation revalidated the JROTC concept, made it an integral part of the schools' curriculum, and most recently in 1993, expanded the number of programs from 856 to approximately 1,370 units.

References. Catherine Lutz and Lesley Bartlett, *Making Soldiers in the Public Schools*, 1995. Mavis McLeod, "Best in the Business," *Corrections Today*, April 1996, 16.

Bill Knight

JUST CAUSE

A few minutes after midnight on 20 December 1989, the United States launched a massive attack on the Republic of Panama designed to remove a corrupt military regime and protect the lives of U.S. citizens living there. General Manuel Noriega had been the virtual dictator of Panama since the death of General Omar Torrijos in 1981. In 1988, the United States had indicted Noriega on drug trafficking charges and placed severe economic sanctions on Panama in an effort to force him to resign. Noriega had nullified an election in May 1989 when unofficial counts indicated a clear victory by the opposition slate headed by Guillermo Endara. Noriega survived an aborted coup attempt on 3 October 1989.

The situation for the Americans, both military and civilian, living and working in Panama had become increasingly tenuous as Noriega stepped up his anti-American campaign. General Maxwell R. Thurman, Commander in Chief of U.S. Southern Command placed the command at a heightened state of readiness and updated contingency plans for combat operations in Panama. On 15 December 1989, the Panamanian National Assembly declared Noriega "maximum leader of national libersation." Noriega then declared that Panama was in a state of war with the United States. On 16 December 1989, Lieutenant Robert Paz, U.S. Marine Corps, was killed at a Panama Defense Force roadblock. Shortly thereafter, a U.S. Navy officer and his wife were arrested, interrogated, and roughed up by the Panama Defense Forces.

These two incidents were the catalysts that caused President George Bush to order Noriega's apprehension and the neutralization of the Panama Defense Force. Under Thurman's direction, Lieutenant General Carl Steiner, Commanding General, XVIII Airborne Corps, formed and led a joint task force of 26,000 U.S. troops in a complex operation to eliminate the Panama Defense Force, capture Noriega, and install the previously elected government of President Endara. Thurman's objective was to strike with sufficient force and suddenness to disable the Panama Defense Forces before they could mount a credible defense. The complex operation involved airborne and air assault* troops, airlifted from the United States, linking up in the hours of darkness with mechanized, light infantry, and special operations* units. More than 3,000 soldiers, including Army Rangers,* parachuted in—the largest airborne operation since World War II.* The operation was a resounding success. Twenty-three targets were seized almost simultaneously, virtually decapitating the Panama Defense Forces, and Guillermo Endara was installed as the duly elected president of Panama. Noriega sought refuge in the Vatican Embassy but gave himself up on 3 January 1990 to U.S. authorities, who escorted him to the United States to stand trial on drug charges. U.S. casualties in Operation Just Cause included twenty-three killed and 324 injured.

References. Thomas Donnelly, Margaret Roth, and Caleb Baker, *Operation Just Cause*, 1991. Edward M. Flanagan, Jr., *Battle for Panama*, 1993. Bruce W. Watson and Peter G. Tsouras, eds., *Operation Just Cause*, 1991.

James H. Willbanks

K

KASSERINE PASS

In January 1943, Field Marshall Erwin Rommel's Panzerarmee Afrika crossed the Libyan-Tunisian border to establish defensive positions at Mareth. The army's ten divisions were at half strength and critically short of supplies—especially fuel—after withdrawing before Field Marshall Sir Barnard Montgomery's British Eighth Army. Montgomery also had difficulties sustaining his large field force, and he failed to pursue Rommel after chasing his army into Tunisia. Monty's reluctance to pursue Rommel created an operational pause that gave Rommel time to reconstitute his withered fighting force. Rommel resolved to use his central position in Tunisia to launch a deep strike at the Allies. Rommel's plan featured a combined assault with Generaloberst Jürgen von Arnim's Fifth Panzer Army, but Arnim and Rommel were unable to agree on details. Field Marshall Albert Kesselring in Rome ordered the two to resolve their differences, but the results of their February meeting were muddled. Each would launch strikes in their respective areas: there would be no centralized command short of Kesselring.

The battle opened when Arnim's forces penetrated key salients, forcing U.S. Army units to withdraw from Sidi Bou Zid, give up the supply base at Sbietla, and evacuate the airfield at Thelepte. At this juncture, Rommel wanted to strike deep in the Allied rear and push U.S. forces off the Western Dorsal, but Arnim refused to agree. While the Germans bickered, the Allies moved troops and equipment forward. Frustrated by the repeated failure of his troops to break through the U.S. positions at Kasserine Pass, Rommel finally called off the offensive at the end of February.

Although the Allies eventually claimed victory at Kasserine Pass, the battle had demonstrated many deficiencies: Allied airpower had been ineffective; U.S. commanders had been indecisive; U.S. armor forces had been employed piecemeal; and units had withdrawn in panic, becoming intermixed. One result of the battle was that General Dwight D. Eisenhower* relieved the II Corps and 1st Armored Division commanders. For many G.I.s,* Kasserine Pass was the baptism of fire.

References. Martin Blumenson, *Kasserine Pass*, 1983. Charles Whiting, *Kasserine*, 1984.

Ralph Nichols

KENNESAW MOUNTAIN

Throughout May 1864, William T. Sherman* had maneuvered Joseph E. Johnston's* Confederate army out of successive delaying positions as the Federals drove into the heart of Georgia. Following three days of fighting at the end of May at New Hope Church, near Dallas, Georgia, Johnston withdrew once again, keeping his army between Sherman and Atlanta. On 19 June, Johnston pulled back to the Kennesaw (or Kenesaw) Mountain line and prepared defensive positions stretching about eight miles. With cavalry on his flanks and an infantry corps on the line, the position seemed impregnable.

Sherman decided to forgo his usual flanking strategy and directed a frontal assault against Johnston's line on 27 June. Sherman's plan called for two simultaneous assaults, the main attack by Major General George H. Thomas's* Army of the Cumberland,* and a supporting attack from Major General James B. McPherson's* Army of the Tennessee* McPherson's troops struck first, attacking eastward along Burnt Hickory Road. After about two hours and about 850 casualties. McPherson called his men back. Thomas's picked divisions assaulted an hour later up the steep mountainside toward a plateau on its peak. The Confederates devastated Thomas's infantry from their well-entrenched firing positions. The Federals failed to penetrate any of the Confederate defenses along what is known today as Cheatham Hill and the "Dead Angle." The attack cost Thomas about 1,500 casualties; Confederate losses were minimal. The Confederate victory at Kennesaw Mountain notwithstanding, Johnston elected to continue his withdrawal, and Sherman once again shifted his forces southward, seeking an open flank.

References Richard A. Baumgartner and Larry M. Strayer, *Kennesaw Mountain, June 1864*, 1998. Richard M. McMurry, *The Road Past Kennesaw*, 1972.

Edward Shanahan

KENTUCKY RIFLE

The Kentucky, or more accurately Pennsylvania, Rifle emerged as a hunting arm along the North American frontier by the mid-1700s. Pennsylvania's German immigrants modified traditional European designs, resulting in small-caliber long rifles that used a greased cloth patch to mate the round lead bullet to the rifling, in order to seal gasses. Despite popular mythology, however, the smoothbore musket,* not the long rifle, became the Continental Army's* principal longarm. Although a trained rifleman could hit his mark at two hundred yeards, four times a musket's range, rifles took far longer to load, lacked a bayonet* for self-defense, and, having no adjustable sights, required extensive practice and experience for accurate long-range fire. Riflemen served effectively as scouts, flankers, and snipers, gaining their adversaries' fear and respect. After the American Revolution,* the U.S. Army continued contracting rifles from Pennsylvania's gunmakers through the early 1800s.

References. J. George Frederick, "The Kentucky Rifle Myth," *National Guardsman*, August 1951, 8–10. Joe D. Huddleston, *Colonial Riflemen in the American Revolution*, 1978. Henry J. Kaufnman, *The Pennsylvania-Kentucky Rifle*, 1960.

Stanley Adamiak

KEPI

In 1851, the U.S. Army adopted a new uniform, including a tall kepi with band and pompon. Based on the French military hat of the period, the kepi was made of dark-blue cloth over a cardboard form with an attached visor, a close-fitting band, and a flat, round top that slanted to the front. The crown was not waterproofed; soldiers carried a waterproof cap cover for rain protection. Uniform* changes in 1861 replaced the stiff kepi with a low-crowned, dark-blue kepi. During the Civil War,* Confederate troops wore a grey-blue kepi with a blue band. In 1872, the Army officially adopted the chasseur kepi, a cap that many soldiers had worn unofficially for years. The flat-topped forage cap officially replaced the kepi in 1903.

References. Gordon Chappell, *The Search for the Well-Dressed Soldier 1865–1890*, 1972. Frederick P. Todd, *American Military Equipage 1851–1872*, 1980.

L. Lynn Williams

KEY WEST AGREEMENT

In March 1948, the Joint Chiefs of Staff* met to resolve differences on the precise roles and missions of their respective services. The Navy wanted to assure itself an air capability; the Army and Air Force disagreed philosophically on the role of airpower, with the Army stressing support of maneuver forces and the Air Force the strategic atomic capability; and the Air Force argued the obsolescence of Army weapons. Nor could the services agree on who should command and control air defenses. At Key West, Florida, the Joint Chiefs hammered out an agreement that recognized the obvious: the Army controlled land forces, the Navy the sea, and the Air Force the air. They also agreed that each service's secondary missions could overlap, but no service could develop weapons only for its secondary mission.

A subsequent conference later that year at Newport, Rhode Island, solidified the Key West Agreement. While the Navy was assured an air capability, the Army and Air Force remained at odds, particularly over the issue of air defense.

References. Robert F. Futrell, *Ideas, Concepts, Doctrine*, 1989. Kenneth Schaffel, *The Emerging Shield*, 1991.

Thomas Christianson

KILROY

"Kilroy" was the ubiquitous legendary character familiar to every G.I.,* airman, and sailor in World War II.* In virtually every location where U.S. armed forces went—isolated garrisons, remote atolls, or enemy towns and cities— arriving American servicemen found penciled, painted, or carved on walls, doors, fenceposts, kiosks—any surface at hand—the phrase KILROY WAS HERE, KILROY SLEPT HERE, KILROY ATE HERE, or some variation. Later a simple line drawing began to accompany Kilroy graffiti: a bald-headed, wide-eyed figure peering from behind a wall, with only a droopy nose and gripping fingers visible.

Several attempts were made to identify Kilroy. After the war, the American Transit Association sponsored a radio contest to find the best explanation for the Kilroy legend. Among the many claims, some sources consider James J. Kilroy, a inspector in the Bethlehem Steel Company shipyard at Quincy, Massachusetts, to be the most likely. Kilroy claimed that in 1941, while inspecting ship tanks and inner bottoms, he started marking hatches in yellow crayon with "Kilroy was here" to prevent reinspecting the same area a second time. The ships carried Kilroy's slogan around the world; those who saw it copied it. As plausible as this story is, other sources claim that the first KILROY WAS HERE sighting was as early as 1939, putting James Kilroy's claim in doubt. Today, Kilroy lore includes several books and numerous articles that recount the mythical fellow's travels and speculate on his real identity. While we may never know who he really was, Kilroy is surely the author of the most prolific graffiti in history.

References. William F. French, "Who Is Kilroy?" *Saturday Evening Post*, 20 October 1945, 6. "Who Is 'Kilroy'?" *New York Times Magazine*, 12 January 1947, 30.

KING, CHARLES (1844–1933)

Charles King so enjoyed his service as a drummer boy in the Civil War that he applied for an "at large" appointment to the U.S. Military Academy.* He graduated with the class of 1866. Upon commissioning in the artillery,* he served as an instructor before joining his battery.* In 1871, he transferred to the cavalry,* serving in Nebraska and Arizona, where he distinguished himself and won a brevet captaincy. Seriously wounded in 1874, King spent more than a year recovering before rejoining the 5th Cavalry just as it was taking the field against the Sioux on the Centennial Campaign.* Over the next year, King began adapting entries from his personal journal for a series of short articles in the *Milwaukee Sentinel*. He subsequently collected and republished these articles under the title *Campaigning with Crook: The Fifth Cavalry in the Sioux War of 1876*.

King served in the Nez Percé campaign of 1877, but his old wound, never fully healed but became progressively worse. The Army medically retired King in 1879, and he returned to Milwaukee, where he devoted much of his time to writing. Over the next thirty-four years, King produced fifty-three novels, four historical works, and nine volumes of short stories. He could not stay away from the military, however, and served in the Wisconsin National Guard, rising to the rank of brigadier general. He volunteered for service during the Spanish-American War,* and commanded the First Brigade, First Division of VIII Corps during the Philippine Insurrection.* Returning to the National Guard,* King continued to serve until his death at the age of eighty-nine. His seventy-year career remains one of the longest in the U.S. Army's history.

References. Paul L. Hedren, "Charles King," in *Soldiers West*, ed. Paul A. Hutton, 1987, 243–261. Charles King, *Campaigning with Crook*, 1964.

Fred J. Chiaventone

KING'S MOUNTAIN

Following the fall of Charleston, South Carolina, to the British in May 1780, Major General Charles Lord Cornwallis opened a campaign to subdue the Carolinas and bring them under British control. Cornwallis's plan called for extensive use of Loyalists to take and hold the back country. The result of this policy was civil war between Tories and Patriots, as both sides raised and trained militia units. On 7 October 1780, a Patriot force caught a Loyalist formation near the North Carolina border at King's Mountain, a flat-topped ridge 600 yards long and 60 to 100 feet wide at the summit. In a battle that lasted little more than an hour, the Patriots surrounded and soundly defeated the Loyalists who were under the command of Major Patrick Ferguson, the only professional soldier on the field. Tory casulties were 157 killed, including Ferguson, and 153 wounded among the 805 prisoners taken by the Patriots. The Patriots lost 28 killed and 62 wounded. The defeat of the Loyalist militia at King's Mountain was a serious blow to Lord Cornwallis and forced him to retreat toward Viginia, abandoning his plan to secure the Carolinas for the Crown.

References. Wilma Dykeman, *With Fire and Sword*, 1991. Hank Messick, *King's Mountain*, 1976.

KIOWA OH-58

In 1962, the Bell Model 206 lost to Hughes' Cayuse OH-6* in the Army's Light Observation Helicopter competition. When the Army reopened the competition in 1968, a modified and redesigned Bell Model 206 was selected to replace the Cayuse. Powered by a single Allison turbine and manned by a two-man crew, the Kiowa proved a very successful and adaptable aircraft. Bell built more than 2,200 of the new helicopters, designated the OH-58A Kiowa. Starting in 1976, Bell rebuilt 585As as the much improved and upgraded C model. The later D model had a more powerful engine, a four-blade main rotor, and could be equipped with a mast-mounted ball sensor array that contained a laser designator, TV and forward-looking infrared (FLIR) sensors, and an internal navigation system. Additionally, the D model carried the Hellfire antitank missile and Stinger* antiaircraft missile. C and D-model Kiowas currently serve as scouts, locating and targeting enemy vehicles for the larger Bell Cobra AH-1* or Hughes Apache AH-64* gunships to engage.

References. Bill Gunston, *An Illustrated Guide to Military Helicopters*, 1981. Stephen Harding, *U.S. Army Aircraft since 1947*, 1997.

Benjamin H. Kristy

KITCHEN POLICE

Until recently kitchen police duty, or KP, was a duty-roster mission rotated among garrison units and among enlisted soldiers within units. Soldiers detailed to KP provided support in the mess halls* in the preparation, serving, and cleanup of meals. Unit reports mention KP duty prior to World War I,* but it was during the two world wars that KP became a familiar duty to large numbers of American soldiers. While vignettes often portray KP as hard work over long hours, rarely did the soldiers pulling KP complain of a shortage of food. By the early 1980s, significant changes in food service preparation and delivery, including an increasing role for civilian contractors, in mess operations throughout the Army have relieved most soldiers of kitchen police duty.

References. Alan Levy, Bernard Krisher, and James Cox, *Draftee's Confidential Guide*, 1957. Mike Quinn, "KP," *Soldiers*, June 1983, 18–19.

Lee Kruger

KNOXVILLE CAMPAIGN

At the same time Major General William S. Rosecran advanced against Chattanooga* in August 1863, Major General Ambrose E. Burnside* advanced on Knoxville. Responding to Rosecrans's threat, Braxton Bragg ordered Simon B. Buckner, who was defending Knoxville, back to Chattanooga. Thus, Burnside's two corps, 24,000 men, entered Knoxville on 2 September without resistance. Burnside then conducted operations against Confederate forces in eastern Tennessee along an eighty-mile line from the Cumberland Gap to Louden, Tennessee.

After the Confederate victory at Chickamauga,* the Federals withdrew into Chattanooga, surrounded by Bragg on the high ground. Unable to force the Federals out of Chattanooga, however, on 4 November Bragg detached James Longstreet* to move against Burnside at Knoxville, in an attempt to reopen the most direct rail route to Virginia and force Major General Ulysses S. Grant* to reinforce Burnside by diverting troops from Chattanooga. Longstreet and Burnside parried for the next month; the Union soldiers in Knoxville came close to starvation. On 29 November, Longstreet assaulted a salient in the Federal defenses, Fort Sanders, a star-shaped, twelve-gun redoubt built on a hill and protected by a wide ditch and wire "tanglefoot" strung between tree stumps. The Federals repulsed the attack in less then thirty minutes at a cost of 813 attackers, compared to a loss of only thirteen defenders.

Following Bragg's defeat at Chattanooga, Grant dispatched two corps to relieve Knoxville. Learning of their approach, on 3 December, Longstreet withdrew into Virginia. Although Burnside did not pursue Longstreet, east Tennessee was now securely in Union hands.

References. Digby Gordon Seymour, *Divided Loyalties*, 1963. Frank J. Welcher, *The Union Army, 1861–1865*, vol. 2, 1989.

Edward Shanahan

KOREAN AUGMENTATION OF THE UNITED STATES ARMY

The Korean Augmentation of the United States Army (KATUSA) was an emergency program of the U.S. Far Eastern Command to overcome the drastic manpower shortage in Korea, as Republic of Korea (ROK) and U.S. forces fell back in some disarray early in the Korean War.* KATUSA initially provided for the incorporation of between 30 and 40,000 ROK recruits into the 24th and 25th Infantry Divisions and the 1st Cavalry Division in Korea and the 7th Infantry Division in Japan. The ROK paid and administered KATUSA recruits, but they received U.S. rations and special service equipment. To make the program work in the field, Far East Command encouraged the so-called "buddy system," the pairing of each KATUSA with a U.S. soldier who would train him in weapons and equipment use, unit drill, personal hygiene, even some words of English. Early recruits, many swept from the streets of Pusan and Taegu by ROK Army military police, received five days of training.

Initially, the system broke down in action. Unit commanders in most cases soon dropped the buddy system and organized their KATUSAs into separate subunits under ROK or U.S. officers. But the program simply needed more time, eventually the KATUSAs performed useful tasks for the U.S. units, and by 1951 KATUSA military skills had improved. By the end of the war, 23,922 augmentees were serving with U.S. units. The program is still in effect for carefully selected recruits.

References. Charles L. Bachtel, "The KATUSA Program," *Signal*, December 1968, 42–44. David C. Skaggs, "The KATUSA Experiment," *Military Affairs*, April 1974, 53–58.

Stanley Sandler

KOREAN WAR

The Korean War began at 0400 on 25 June 1950 when about 10,000 North Korean People's Army (NKPA) troops, a hundred tanks, and a like number of aircraft followed a short artillery bombardment across the 38th parallel into the Republic of Korea (ROK). ROK troops, equal in numbers to the NKPA, lacked heavy artillery, tanks, antitank weapons, and aircraft. Furthermore, many NKPA troops were veterans of either World War II* or the Chinese Civil War, while few ROK soldiers had any combat experience. In areas where the North Koreans could use their tanks, ROK resistance quickly collapsed. Premature demolition of the Han River bridges stranded most of the ROK motorized transport north of the river, and Seoul, the ROK capital, fell on the third day of fighting.

Under a United Nations mandate, U.S. forces joined the battle, first air and naval forces, then ground forces. A task force from the 24th Infantry Division engaged a North Korean armored column on 5 July, but the poorly trained and equipped infantrymen were quickly overrun. The 24th Division then fought a costly delaying action over the next month, while additional U.S. forces rushed to Korea. Over the next two months, UN forces conducted a desperate but ultimately successful defense along the Naktong River, while they built up troops and supplies through the port of Pusan.

Meanwhile, in Japan, General of the Army Douglas MacArthur* prepared an amphibious attack at Inchon,* far to the rear of the main NKPA force. The 1st Marine Division overcame numerous physical obstacles at the port and captured Inchon within thirty-six hours. Within two weeks, the Marines took Seoul and linked up with U.S. Army troops driving north from the Pusan Perimeter.* North Korean resistance in the South collapsed.

In early October, Chinese Communist units entered Korea while UN forces, moving north, crossed the 38th parallel and captured the North Korean capital on 19 October. A Marine landing at Wonson went awry when mines in the harbor delayed the landings until after ROK troops advancing overland had taken the city. In late October, Chinese forces decimated a regiment* of the 1st Cavalry Division,* stopping Eighth Army's* advance on the west coast, as Marines encountered strong resistance north of Wonson. After resuming its offensive in late November, Eighth Army ran into a Chinese ambush and took heavy casualties; attached ROK units were overrun and dispersed. The 2nd Division* tried to force a Chinese roadblock south of Kuni-ri and lost a third of its force. Eighth Army now retreated precipitously south to the 38th parallel, taking up its new positions in late December.

A nearly simultaneous Chinese attack on X Corps destroyed an Army regimental combat team* east of Chosin, but over the next week the Marines fought their way out of the trap and reached Hannung, a good harbor north of Wonson. The remainder of X Corps withdrew, except for the 3rd Infantry Division, which covered the Marines' west flank and evacuated at Hamnung, with 90,000 refugees, at the end of December. General Matthew Ridgway came from Washington, D.C., to assume command of Eighth Army after Lieutenant General Walton Walker died in a traffic accident. The year 1950 ended with a Communist attack along the 38th parallel that drove United Nations forces seventy miles south and took Seoul for the second time in the war.

Ridgway took steps to improve Eighth Army's fighting quality and assumed direct command of X Corps, moving it north from Pusan to cover Eighth Army's eastern flank. When the Communists outran their supply system, Ridgway launched probing patrols, then began to push north toward the Han River, making full use of his superior firepower. Checking Chinese attacks at Wonju and Chipyong-ni, Eighth Army pushed north toward the 38th parallel, retaking Seoul on 18 March 1951. The Chinese attacked again in April and May but suffered heavy losses against devastating counterattacks by Eighth Army, now under the command of Lieutenant General James Van Fleet.*

Badly hurt by their losses in men and supplies and falling back to the 38th parallel, the Communists suggested peace talks, and the UN accepted. With the opening of the peace talks, first at Kaesong then at Panmunjom,* the U.S. drive slowed, and the war of motion that had characterized the conflict's first year came to an end. A two-year stalemate began. The Truman administration desired to get out of the fighting as quickly, and with as few casualties, as possible. When Ridgway and Van Fleet felt that the Communists were stalling, however, they launched several heavy attacks. Undertaken in the most rugged terrain along the front, assaults on such positions as Heartbreak Ridge* and Bloody Ridge made minor gains, while attacks on more favorable locations made significant penetrations. Nevertheless, most of the fighting over the next twenty months took place at outposts, such as Old Baldy, Pork Chop Hill, and White Horse Hill. Only in the closing days of the war did the Communists make major counterattacks, to secure a better cease-fire line, driving UN forces back several miles in some areas.

Fighting in the Korean War ended in July 1953 when the delegations at Panmunjom agreed upon a truce. Under the terms of the armistice, both armies withdrew two kilometers from the truce line to establish a demilitarized zone* (DMZ) that is still recognized today. UN casualties during the Korean War were almost 95,000 killed and 455,000 wounded, including 33,629 U.S. killed and 103,284 wounded. Enemy casualties are estimated as high as 1,500,000, perhaps 900,000 of whom were Chinese.

References. Clay Blair, *The Forgotten War*, 1987. T. R. Fehrenbach, *This Kind of War*, 1963. John Toland, *In Mortal Combat*, 1991.

Jack Gifford

KRAG-JORGENSON

After a series of tests in 1892, the U.S. Army adopted its first rifle utilizing smokeless powder. Developed by the Danish firm Krag-Jorgenson, the rifle fired a .30-caliber headless, center-fire cartridge loaded in a five-round box magazine. A cut-off switch allowed rounds to be loaded individually, leaving the magazine as a reserve. Between 1892 and 1903, the Krag-Jorgenson was the Army's primary shoulder weapon. It was used in both Cuba and the Philippines. The Krag was produced in two lengths, the standard rifle for the infantry and the carbine* for the cavalry. The infantry weapon was equipped with one of two bayonets.* For tropical service, a bolo-shaped bayonet was employed, but the standard knife bayonet was more common in the field. The Krag had three major weaknesses: the headless shells were difficult to remove when jammed; the magazine was difficult to load quickly; and the weak receiver, secured by only one lug, tended to fail with high-powered ammunition.

References. William S. Brophy, *The Krag Rifle*, 1986. James E. Hicks, *U.S. Military Firearms, 1776–1956*, 1962.

Steven J. Allie

K-RATIONS

The K-ration was developed in 1940–1941 to provide a lightweight yet nutritionally complete "blitz ration" for parachutists and other highly mobile forces. The Army tested the K-ration, initially called the "Parachute Ration," at Fort Benning,* Georgia, in early 1942 and adopted a standardized package by May of that year. K-rations were issued in breakfast, lunch, and supper meals consisting of canned components, cheese, pork or veal, energy components, fruit, malt-dextrose or a chocolate bar, a biscuit component, and accessories, bouillon, instant coffee or lemon beverage powder, cigarettes, gum, and sugar cubes. The waxed cardboard inner container burned quite hot with little smoke and thus could be used to heat water for coffee. A complete K-ration provided 3,300 calories. Millions of K-rations were produced in World War II*—21 million in October 1943 alone—and became familiar to combat troops around the world. Although they generally approved of K-rations, the troops' most common complaint was that the lemon beverage powder was good only for bleaching barracks-room floors. Despite its advanced packaging, the K-ration's shelf life was relatively short—about a year. Millions of K-rations were on hand at the war's end, and they became a major item in relief efforts to feed displaced peoples throughout Europe and Asia.

Some sources claim that the K-ration was named in honor of Dr. Ancel Keys, who was instrumental in development of the K-ration. But official Army reports maintain that the designation K was used simply because it was phonetically distinct from C and D-type rations then in use.

References. Erna Risch, *The Quartermaster Corps*, vol. 1, 1953. Harold W. Thatcher, *The Development of Special Rations for the Army*, 1944.

Stephen C. McGeorge

KRUEGER, WALTER (1881–1967)

Walter Krueger was born in Flatow, West Prussia, in 1881 and migrated to the United States at the age of eight. He first enlisted in the U.S. Army during the Spanish-American War.* When he reenlisted in the Regular Army while serving in the Philippines, he was promoted to sergeant. In June 1901, he was commissioned a second lieutenant in the 30th Infantry. On returning to the United States, he attended the Infantry and Cavalry Schools and the Fort Leavenworth Staff School. He served with Major General John J. Pershing* during the Punitive Expedition* in 1916 and later as chief of staff of the 26th and 84th Divisions and assistant chief of staff of VI and IX Corps in France.

Promoted to brigadier general in 1936, Krueger commanded Third Army* and the Southern Defense Command as a lieutenant general in 1941. In January 1943, he assumed command of the Sixth Army* and commanded that organization until it was deactivated in January 1946. He was known as a skilled tactician and was one of General Douglas MacArthur's* principal ground commanders. The Sixth Army developed into a superb fighting force, seeing action throughout the Southwest Pacific Area* (SWPA). Krueger's forces were instrumental in the recapture of the Philippines in 1944 and spent the remainder of the war clearing those islands of remaining Japanese forces. Krueger retired in July 1946 and died in 1967.

References Arthur S. Collins, Jr., "Walter Krueger," *Infantry*, January–February 1983, 14–19. Walter Krueger, *From Down under to Nippon*, 1953.

Gary Bounds

L

LAM SON 719

Following the militarily successful but politically disastrous incursion into Cambodia in May and June 1970, all U.S. and Army of the Republic of Vietnam (ARVN) forces withdrew into South Vietnam. However, Hanoi continued to view all of Indochina as its theater of operations and established new lines of communication to replace those lost in the spring 1970 incursion. Successful enemy reconstitution efforts in Cambodia spurred the United States to press South Vietnam to launch a second cross-border operation, this time in Laos. The United States provided air, artillery, and logistic support to the ARVN forces, but no U.S. Army advisors took part in the Laos incursion.

Political pressure to hasten the process of Vietnamization (i.e., transfer of the bulk of the fighting from U.S. to ARVN forces) played a role in the planning of this campaign. The main feature of the campaign plan, known as Lam Son 719, was to sever the Ho Chi Minh Trail—the major line of communication, which continually supplied Communist fighters throughout the Vietnam War.* ARVN units performed poorly in Laos, losing nearly 2,000 men and a large quantity of equipment in a hasty and disorderly withdrawal. The U.S. Army lost 107 helicopters in the operation, the highest loss incurred during any single operation in the war. Lam Son 719 was not a complete failure; it delayed a planned Communist spring offensive in the northern provinces. Nevertheless, it failed disastrously to meet the military goal of severing Hanoi's logistics line of communications, or the political goal of achieving a military victory through Vietnamization.

References. Jeffrey J. Clarke, *Advice and Support*, 1988. Keith William Nolan, *Into Laos*, 1986. Roy R. Stephenson, "Road to Downfall," 1991.

Ralph D. Nichols

LANDING CRAFT

Landing craft is a general term applied to smaller boats and craft designed for beaching, loading and unloading troops, vehicles, weapons, and supplies on a hostile beach, and retracting from it. The U.S. Navy generally applies the term to non-seagoing vessels less than 200 feet long, distinguishing them from landing ships. Throughout World War II,* landing craft steadily increased in size until the larger types were capable of completing a passage on their own. Prior to World War II, Japan led the United States and Great Britain in the development and employment of amphibious operations and equipment. The requirements of War Plan Orange* fostered U.S. interest in landing craft and other aspects of amphibious operations prior to the war, and the nature of Allied operations in Europe and the Pacific from mid-1942 onward spurred the development of landing craft. The British Combined Operations Command was tasked to develop various types of landing craft for the conduct of amphibious operations.

By 1944, the Allies had designed and fielded a large number of specialized types of landing craft. These included the Landing Craft Infantry (LCI), Landing Craft Personnel (LCP), Landing Craft Tank (LCT), Landing Craft Mechanized (LCM), Landing Craft Flak (LCF), Landing Craft Gun (LCG), and Landing Craft Rocket (LCR). In addition to transporting various combinations of troops and equipment ashore, these craft provided support services ranging from casualty evacuation and hot meals to indirect rocket and gunfire, emergency repairs, and close air support* direction. Larger amphibious assault vessels, landing ships, included the Landing Ship Infantry (LSI), Landing Ship Tank (LST), Landing Ship Headquarters (LSH), Landing Ship Fighter Direction (LSF), Landing Ship Rocket (LSR), Landing Ship Dock (LSD), and various other specialized types. Although the Allies constructed thousands of landing craft and ships during World War II, there were never sufficient numbers to meet all the competing requirements. Frequently the decision to proceed with an operation depended on the availability of landing craft.

References. A. D. Baker III, *Allied Landing Craft of World War Two,* 1944, 1985. Norman O. Larson, "Faster Landing Craft," U.S. Naval Institute *Proceedings,* February 1966, 128–133.

John A. Hixson

LANDING ZONE

The term "landing zone" (LZ) is most closely associated with the Vietnam War,* because of the extensive use of U.S. Army helicopters in that war. Generally, a landing zone, or LZ, was the field landing site for helicopters involved in airmobile operations transporting ground troops, their equipment, and support from relatively secure sites to possible hostile locations in order for those troops to conduct combat operations. Landing zones varied in size, depending on the terrain and conditions, from just large enough to land a single aircraft to those capable of landing the normal air assault* contingent of ten aircraft. While any field landing site could be termed an LZ, they were normally specified by the terms PZ, or "pick-up zone," for a secure troop pick-up location, or LZ for a generally less secure drop-off site.

References. J. D. Coleman, *Pleiku*, 1988. Simon Dunstan, *Vietnam Choppers*, 1988. John J. Tolson, *Airmobility, 1961–1971*, 1973.

Arthur T. Frame

LAUNDRESS

The first women officially recognized by the U.S. Army, laundresses not only washed clothes but occasionally served in battle. The practice of hiring laundresses was inherited from the British army and officially adopted by the U.S. Army in 1802. Laundresses received rations of food and bedding straw and the services of the regimental surgeon. Appointed by company* commanders, their numbers were limited to four per company. A General Order of 1803 specified that they be "married women of good conduct." Fees for laundry services were set by the Post Council of Administration. To ensure the laundresses received their compensation, regulations specified that when a company mustered for pay, the laundress bill was to be deducted before payment of debts to the sutler. The institution of hiring laundresses was officially discontinued in 1878, but the practice continued unofficially for some years.

References. Samuel E. Chamberlain, *My Confession*, 1956. Patricia Y. Stallard, *Glittering Misery*, 1992. Miller J. Stewart, "Army Laundresses," *Nebraska History*, Winter 1980, 421–436.

Dana Prater

LEAVE

Leave is official permission for a soldier to be absent from duty, or the absence resulting from such permission. There are several types of leave, including ordinary leave, emergency leave, convalescent leave, environmental and morale leave, and excess leave. Often "leave" is used synonymously with "vacation."

References. Arthur S. Collins, Jr., "Take It—Don't Leave It," *Army*, December 1974, 8–9. JoAnn Mann, "On Leave and Pass," *Soldiers*, May 16–17.

LEE, "LIGHT-HORSE" HARRY (1756–1818)

One of George Washington's* favorite battlefield commanders, "Light-Horse" Harry Lee enjoyed a career that included accomplishments on the battlefield and in government. A cavalry commander during the American Revolution,* Lee employed daring, yet calculating, tactics* that secured both victories and acclaim. His capture of a British fort at Paulus Hook, New Jersey, and successes in the Carolinas during service with Nathanael Greene* were among his wartime accomplishments. Lee's units were noted for their discipline and loyalty, products of Lee's attention to supply and the well-being of his troops.

An avowed Federalist, Lee served in the Continental Congress as a member of Virginia's constitutional ratifying convention, as Virginia's congressman to the new federal legislature, and as governor of Virginia. He resumed military command in 1794, when he led federal troops during the Whiskey Rebellion.

Business failures later left Lee bankrupt and imprisoned for debt, and his opposition to the War of 1812* resulted in a severe beating by a Baltimore mob. These misfortunes led him to self-imposed exile in the West Indies. His legacy includes his funeral oration for Washington, in which he proclaimed the now-famous epitaph, "First in war—first in peace—and first in the hearts of his countrymen." Harry Lee was the father of Robert E. Lee.*

References Thomas Boyd, *Light-Horse Harry Lee*, 1931. Charles Royster, *Light-Horse Harry Lee and the Legacy of the American Revolution*, 1981.

Robert Rook

LEE, ROBERT EDWARD (1807–1870)

Born in Westmoreland County, Virginia, Robert E. Lee graduated second in the U.S. Military Academy* class of 1829. Commissioned in the engineers, as a captain Lee distinguished himself on Winfield Scott's * staff during the Mexican War* and later served as superintendent of the Military Academy. He transferred to the cavalry,* and he commanded the contingent of Marines that captured John Brown at Harpers Ferry in 1859. Lee was on duty in Texas in April 1861 when the South Carolina militia fired on Fort Sumter.*

Winfield Scott offered Lee command the Union Army in April 1861, but Lee felt that his duty to Virginia was the higher calling. He resigned his commission in the U.S. Army and accepted command of the defense of Virginia. During the first year of the Civil War,* he served primarily as military advisor to Jefferson Davis* but took command of the Confederate army defending Richmond when Joseph E. Johnston* was wounded during the Peninsula Campaign.* From that time, Lee was the dominant figure in the Civil War, commanding the victorious Army of Northern Virginia at Second Bull Run,* Fredericksburg,* and Chancellorsville.* Historians generally agree that Lee's defeat at Gettysburg* was the turning point in the war.

Lee is unquestionably one of the great soldiers of American history. He was aggressive and believed that the offensive was decisive, yet he defended with the greatest economy of force possible. He was willing to risk everything in bold maneuvers but capable of the greatest compassion for his soldiers. He took full responsibility for his failures. When the Civil War ended, he set the highest example for his fellow southerners. Lee became president of Washington College in Lexington, Virginia. He revised the curriculum and created departments of commerce and journalism—among the first in the nation. He urged his former comrades to be good citizens, even though his own citizenship was not restored during his lifetime. He died in 1870 and is buried on the campus of Washington and Lee University, subsequently renamed in his honor.

References. Thomas L. Connelly, *The Marble Man*, 1977. Gary W. Gallagher, ed., *Lee*, 1996. Emery M. Thomas, *Robert E. Lee*, 1995.

George Knapp

LEGION OF MERIT

The Legion of Merit is the Army's second highest peacetime award for service; only the Distinguished Service Medal* is higher. Established by an act of Congress in 1943, the decoration was created for two reasons. First, the War Department* wanted a decoration to honor Allied and other foreign military personnel. Second, it wanted to be able to reward U.S. military personnel for outstanding service. The decoration has four classes or degrees—Chief Commander, Commander, Officer, and Legionnaire. The first three categories are awarded to foreign personnel; only the last category—Legionnaire—may be awarded to U.S. personnel. Today, about 75 percent of U.S. Army recipients of the Legion of Merit (Legionnaire) receive it as an award at retirement for career service. The remaining 25 percent receive it for clearly exceptional service or achievement.

References. Evans E. Kerigan, *American War Medals and Decorations*, 1964. John E. Strandberg and Roger J. Bender, *The Call of Duty*, 1994.

Frederic L. Borch III

LEWIS, MERIWETHER (1774–1809)

Best remembered for his part in the exploration of the Louisiana Purchase, Meriwether Lewis served his country as a soldier as well. Lewis was five years old when his father, a lieutenant in the Continental Army,* died in 1779. The next year, his mother remarried, this time to a captain in the Army. When President George Washington* ordered forces to put down the Whiskey Rebellion in 1794, Lewis volunteered for service. In 1801, he was a captain when President Thomas Jefferson asked him to lead, with Captain William Clark,* the now-famous expedition to open the Louisiana Purchase. The trek lasted three years and was largely responsible for opening up the vast heartland of North America to further exploration and development.

After returning Lewis was preparing to write his memoirs when Jefferson appointed him governor of Upper Louisiana, a post Congress approved for three years. For the next two years, Lewis struggled to govern the territory, fend off political enemies who coveted his post, and publish his memoirs, which had run him deeply into debt. While governor of Upper Louisiana, Lewis died in 1809 at the age of thirty-five; his death, officially listed as a suicide (based merely on hearsay), remains clouded in mystery. No official investigation was conducted. Some historians argue that the evidence points to murder. Lewis is buried near Collinwood, Tennessee.

References. Stephen E. Ambrose, *Undaunted Courage*, 1996. Richard H. Dillon, *Meriwether Lewis*, 1965. Vardis Fisher, *Suicide or Murder?* 1962.

Trevor Brown

LEYTE

The dramatic return of U.S. forces to the central Philippines was preceded by the destruction of 700 Japanese planes and forty ships in wide-ranging preinvasion operations by Admiral William Halsey's U.S. Third Fleet and B-29 Superfortresses based in China. The U.S. Seventh Fleet—"MacArthur's Navy"— put the X and XXIV Corps of Lieutenant General Walter Krueger's* U.S. Sixth

Army,* 194,000 men, ashore on Leyte's east coast. Surprise was achieved, and the 21,500-man Japanese 35th Army offered scant resistance as U.S. forces seized port and coastal air facilities. The Japanese chose to fight in the north, digging in on "Breakneck Ridge" near the port of Carigara, engaging the X Corps in a month-long battle while 45,000 Japanese reinforcements poured in, mainly at the west-coast port of Ormoc.

The massive effort to eject U.S. forces, called by the Japanese *Sho-1*, or victory plan, failed; Lieutenant General George C. Kenney's Far East Air Forces and carrier-based planes from Halsey's Third Fleet choked off the stream of reinforcements. After the 7th Infantry Division crossed the center of the island, Kreuger split Japanese defenses by landing the 77th Infantry Division three miles south of Ormoc on 7 December 1944. The city fell on the 10th. The 7th and 77th Infantry Divisions linked up on the 11th, and organized resistance ended on Christmas Day. Although unexpected Japanese reinforcements and heavy rains had delayed the U.S. operation, the outcome was a major setback for the Japanese, who lost 67,000 men compared to 5,000 U.S. dead.

References. M. Hamlin Cannon, *Leyte*, 1954. Stanley L. Falk, *Decision at Leyte*, 1966. Ronald H. Spector, *Eagle against the Sun*, 1985.

Claude Sasso

LIFER

This term refers to a soldier who makes the army a career. Pejoratively, a lifer is anyone who stays in the army beyond the traditional twenty-year retirement period. "Lifer" is commonly associated with the acronym of "Lazy, inefficient, fouled up, expecting retirement."

References. Dale P. Jerzykowski, "A 'Lifer' Has His Say," *Soldiers*, August 1971, 42–43. Ches Schneider, *From Classrooms to Claymores*, 1999.

Scott McMeen

LIGGETT, HUNTER (1857–1935)

A Pennsylvania native, Hunter Liggett served on the northern plains and on the Mexican border after graduating from the U.S. Military Academy* in 1879. During the Spanish-American War,* he served as an assistant adjutant general; he then spent two years in the Philippines among the Moros on Mindanao as an infantry* battalion* commander. Promoted to lieutenant colonel at the age of fifty-two, he graduated from the Army War College* in 1910 and became its director. Four years later he was promoted to brigadier general and was named president of the War College. He commanded a brigade during the Mexican border crisis of 1914 and in the Philippines in 1915. In 1916–1917 he served as chief of the Department of the Philippines but was reassigned to command the Western Department in San Francisco.

Despite his girth and age, he went to Europe with the American Expeditionary Force* (AEF) as a division commander. Taking command of I Corps in January 1918 he ably led it in the Second Battle of the Marne, the St. Mihiel* operation, and the Meuse-Argonne* offensive. Wen General of the Armies John J. Pershing* assumed command of the army group* in October 1918, he gave Liggett command of First Army.* Liggett skillfully reorganized the shell-shocked army, rounding up an estimated 100,000 stragglers before resuming the offensive. Admired and respected like no other AEF combat commander by both officers and enlisted men, Liggett led the First Army forward until the armistice. On 20 April 1919, Liggett took command of the army of occupation on the Rhine. He retired as a lieutenant general in 1921.

References. Edward M. Coffman, *The War to End All Wars*, 1986. Basil H. Liddell Hart, *Reputations*, 1928, 1968.

Claude Sasso

LIGHT ANTITANK WEAPON M72

The M72 light antitank weapon (LAW) was developed as a series of one-man, nonreloadable, disposable antitank rocket launchers. The U.S. Army developed three versions, the M72, M72A1, and M72A2, the principal differences being in the effectiveness of their armor-penetration capabilities. The M72 consists of two collapsible tubes, mounting the sighting and firing mechanisms. The M72 series fires a 66 mm high-explosive antitank (HEAT) rocket with a point-detonated M18 warhead. The M18 warhead contains a three-quarter-pound shaped charge capable of penetrating approximately twelve inches of steel plate. In flight, the rocket is fin stabilized. The M72 system is a zero-recoil, smooth-bored weapon capable of effectively engaging stationary targets out to 300 meters and moving targets out to 150 meters, with a maximum range of 1,000 meters. The launcher and rocket weigh approximately 4.5 pounds and the tube is twenty-six inches in length closed and thirty-five inches when entended for use.

References. Dennis Culkin, "David and Goliath," *Defense & Foreign Affairs*, February 1984, 24–26. Michael R. Harris, "Tactical Employment of the Shoulder-Fired Rocket," *Infantry*, November–December 1996, 29–32.

David Zoellers

LINCOLN, BENJAMIN (1733–1810)

Born in Hingham, Massachusetts, Benjamin Lincoln was the son of a well-to-do farmer. He became a farmer himself, held local political offices, and was a member of the Massachusetts militia from 1755 to 1776. In May 1776, Congress voted him the rank of major general in the Continental Army.* As one of George Washington's* most trusted generals, Lincoln took an active part in the American Revolution* until 1777, when he was severely wounded during the Saratoga* campaign. In August 1778, he assumed command of the Continental forces in the South. Unfortunately, he failed to eject the British from Savannah, Georgia. In May 1780 he was cornered by the enemy in Charleston,* where he surrendered and was taken prisoner. He was widely criticized for the Charleston defeat, although no formal action was taken against him.

Released in a prisoner exchange, he was able to participate in the Yorktown* campaign in 1781.

In October 1781, he was made secretary of war,* a post he held for two years. In January and February 1787, he led the troops that put down Shay's Rebellion* in Massachusetts. He was later elected lieutenant governor of Massachusetts and then collector for the port of Boston. He died in Hingham in May 1810.

References. David B. Mattern, *Benjamin Lincoln and the American Revolution,* 1995. Clifford K. Shipton, "Benjamin Lincoln: Old Reliable," in *George Washington's Generals,* ed. George A. Billias, 1964.

Michael Davis

LITTLE BIGHORN

In June 1876, forces under Major General Alfred Terry were searching for hostile Indians in the Unceded Territory south of the Yellowstone River. Based on fresh reports from his scouts, Terry ordered Lieutenant Colonel George A. Custer* to lead the 7th Cavalry—625 men—up the Rosebud (south) to its headwaters, cross into the Little Bighorn valley (west), and push the hostiles northward toward the remainder of Terry's force (723 men under Colonel John Gibbon, coming up the Bighorn). For three days, Custer followed a trail of abandoned village sites. On the morning of 25 June, from a promontory in the Wolf Mountains, Custer's Arikara and Crow scouts spotted a large Sioux and Cheyenne village along the Little Bighorn River, near present-day Crow Agency, Montana. Fearing that he had lost the element of surprise, Custer decided to attack immediately rather than rest his men and hit the village the next morning. The 7th crossed the divide between the Rosebud and Little Bighorn vallies at noon. Custer detached Captain Frederick Benteen with three companies—125 men—to search the upper Little Bighorn for hostiles, while he and Major Marcus Reno, with 396 men, proceeded down what is today Reno Creek toward the village. Arriving near the mouth of Reno Creek, Custer ordered Reno to cross the Little Bighorn and attack the village with three companies (112 men) while he, Custer, took the remaining five companies (210 men) north to strike the village in the center, or north, end. He then sent a messenger ordering Benteen to rejoin the main command as quickly as possible.

Reno's assault down the valley met heavy resistance from Indian warriors defending their village, forcing Reno to break off the attack and seek safety on high ground east of the river. Benteen later joined Reno's troops there, and they repelled a number of Indian attacks until relieved by Gibbon's troops on 27 June. As Custer continued to move north, unable to assist Reno, large numbers of warriors began crossing from the village on Custer's left flank. The details of Custer's fight remain controversial, but it is possible that he once again split off two companies, under Captain George Yates, toward the main crossing point of the river while the other three companies sought a defensible piece of ground on the ridgeline above the valley. Faced with an overwhelming number of warriors, Custer's force was quickly reduced to about forty survivors, who made a stand on what is now known as Custer, or Last Stand, Hill. Archeological evidence and statements from Indian participants belie Hollywood's version of Custer's end, a glorious fight on Last Stand Hill. The Indian warriors overwhelmed the soldiers desperately fighting for their lives in small groups. The battle of the Little Bighorn was the U.S. Army's worst defeat of the Indian Wars.*

References. John S. Gray, *Custer's Last Campaign*, 1991. Charles M. Robinson III, *A Good Year to Die*, 1995. Wayne Michael Sarf, *The Little Bighorn Campaign*, 1993.

Tamas Dreilinger

LITTLE BIRD MH-6

In the 1980s, the U.S. Army developed the first in a series of light helicopters for special operations forces* (SOF) missions. In a highly secret program, the Army redesigned the McDonnel Douglas (Hughes) MD500/MG530—a civilian versions of the Cayuse OH-6,* recently replaced by the Kiowa OH-58* as the Army's light observation helicopter—to meet the SOF requirements. This aircraft is commonly known as Little Bird, though official designations have included OH-6A, MD Defender, AH-6, and MH-6. One of Little Bird's first known uses in combat came during Operation Urgent Fury,* when a national news magazine published a photo of one. They were reported active during the U.S. escort missions in the Persian Gulf during 1987, and press reports indicated that "little bird" helicopters were used to counter Iranian naval minelaying specifically during combat operations against the vessel *Iran Ajr*. The next major reference to these aircraft was during Operation Just Cause,* where "little birds" were a key component in the rescue of Kurt Muse from the so-called Carcel Modelo, where he was held prisoner. Undoubtedly, Little Birds were also active during Desert Shield/Desert Storm,* where part of Task Force 160 (later the 160th Aviation Regient), equipped with the latest in high-technology weapons, sensors, and communications, conducted a number of classified missions.

References. Thomas Donnelly, Margaret Roth, and Caleb Baker, *Operation Just Cause*, 1991. Stephen Harding, *U.S. Army Aircraft since 1947*, 1997.

John R. Finch

LOGAN BAR. *See* D-ration.

LONG-RANGE RECONNAISSANCE PATROL

Although U.S. Army Ranger* units were deactivated after World War II,* the need for highly skilled, elite infantry units continued. In 1961, the U.S. Seventh Army* activated a Long-Range Reconnaissance Patrol (LRRP) Company (Airborne) in Wildflecken, Germany under V Corps. Known as the "Victory Lerps," a VII Corps LRRP, the "Jayhawk Lerps," soon joined them. The concept proved successful, and on 15 May 1965 the units were given official standing as D Company, 17th Infantry (for the V Corps LRRP) and C Company, 17th Infantry (for the VII Corps LRRP).

During the Vietnam War,* patrolling and reconnaissance were considered vital to the success of U.S. operations. From 1966 to 1967, all U.S. divisions* in Vietnam had either a LRRP or Recondo (Reconnaissance Doughboy) reconnaissance unit. These units performed ranger duties, intelligence gathering, deep penetration, patrolling, and direct combat raids. In 1969, the LRRP units were redesignated Ranger companies. The value of these LRRP units in Vietnam, where they were credited with many reconnaissance successes, prompted the Army to reactivate and place all of the separate LRRP/Recondo units in the 75th Infantry Regiment. On 1 February 1969, thirteen of fifteen LRRP detachments assigned to divisions or separate brigades* were designated as Ranger companies under the 75th Infantry Regiment (Ranger).

References. Michael Lee Lanning, *Inside the LRRPS*, 1988. Shelby L. Stanton, *Rangers at War*, 1992.

Richard Stewart

LONG TOM. *See* Howitzer 155 mm M1.

LONGSTREET, JAMES (1821–1904)

James "Old Pete" Longstreet, also known as "Lee's Old War Horse," was born in Edgefield District, South Carolina, on 8 January 1821. He received an appointment to the U.S. Military Academy* and graduated fifty-fourth in his class of sixty-two in 1842. Commissioned in the infantry,* he served in the Indian campaign in Florida, where he was wounded and twice breveted. On 1 June 1861, Major Longstreet resigned from the U.S. Army to accept an appointment as brigadier general in the Army of the Confederate States of America.

After the Civil War,* Longstreet moved to New Orleans and returned to the service of the United States. In 1880, President Ulysses S. Grant* named him minister to Turkey: from 1881 to 1884 he was a U.S. marshal; and from 1884 until his death in 1904 he was a U.S. railroad commissioner. In 1896, Longstreet published his memoirs, *From Manassas to Appomattox*.

References. R. L. DiNardo and Albert A. Nofi, eds., *James Longstreet*, 1998. William G. Piston, *Lee's Tarnished Lieutenant*, 1987. Jeffrey D. Wert, *General James Longstreet*, 1993.

Edward Shanahan

LOOKOUT MOUNTAIN

Rising 1,500 feet above the valley and extending south into Alabama and Georgia from Moccasin bend just west of Chattanooga,* the heights of Lookout Mountain dominate the Tennessee River and the western approaches to the city. In the fall of 1863, troops under Braxton Bragg sat atop Lookout Mountain, besieging William Rosecrans's* Army of the Cumberland,* which had withdrawn into the city after the battle of Chickamauga. Major General Ulyssses S. Grant's* arrival at the end of October signaled a renewal of Union offensive operations in the area.

Grant ordered Major General Joseph Hooker's* XX Corps to assault Lookout Mountain on the army's right, while Major General William T. Sherman's* Army of the Tennessee* attacked Missionary Ridge on the left. With premonitions of disaster, Hooker's men moved toward the forbidding mountain on the morning of 24 November 1963, but fortune favored the Union soldiers that day, clouds and heavy mist shrouded their movements. Before the Confederate troops manning the rifle pits and abatis realized the situation, the Federals were above and behind them. Many Rebels retired or surrendered without firing a shot. Some fierce fighting did take place on the higher slopes, giving the day's action its epithet, "the battle above the clouds." By evening, Hooker's men had taken Lookout Mountain, and with far fewer casualties than expected. After the loss of his position overlooking Chattanooga, Bragg moved south, and he did not threaten Chattanooga again.

References. Peter Cozzens, *The Shipwreck of Their Hopes*, 1994. Wiley Sword, *Mountains Touched with Fire*, 1995.

LOUISIANA MANEUVERS

From 1940 to 1943, the area between Shreveport and Lake Charles, Louisiana, was the scene of many U.S. Army training exercises. By far the largest and best known were the GHQ maneuvers conducted in September 1941. Under Lieutenant General Lesley J. McNair,* these maneuvers involved two field armies* of eighteen divisions* and 400,000 men (Regular Army, National Guard,* and conscripts), including two armor divisions, three experimental antitank groups, a parachute company, and ten combat aircraft groups. For two weeks, these forces conducted a simulated war with blank ammunition, flour-bag bombs, and sound trucks that blared prerecorded battle noise. Umpire teams adjudicated the tactical action.

Taken with comparable maneuvers in the Carolinas two months later, the Louisiana maneuvers were an important milestone in the Army's efforts to overcome two decades of stagnation and prepare itself for the war raging overseas. The maneuvers also provided experience in large-scale operations and the employment of armored, antitank, and tactical air forces to a generation of officers who had come of age in the interwar Army, including Dwight D. Eisenhower,* George S. Patton, Jr.,* Mark W. Clark,* Walter Krueger,* and J. Lawton Collins.* Covered extensively and favorably by the media, the Louisiana maneuvers helped prepare the nation psychologically for World War II.*

References. Christopher R. Gabel, *The U.S. Army GHQ Maneuvers of 1941*, 1991. Mark S. Watson, *Chief of Staff*, 1950.

Christopher R. Gabel

LOW-INTENSITY CONFLICT

Low-intensity conflict (LIC) is currently defined as a politico-military confrontation between contending states or groups at a level below that of conventional war but above routine, peaceful competition. Political considerations in

LIC are invariably paramount to all others (e.g., military, economic, etc.), LIC is commonly assumed to encompass four categories: insurgency and counter-insurgency operations, combatting terrorism, peace operations (peacekeeping, peace enforecement, etc.), and peacetime contingency operations (e.g., limited raids, blockades, search and rescue operations, humanitarian assistance). LIC objectives may be political, military, economic, or social in nature, they are often limited by geographical, budgetary, equipment, legal, or operational con-straints. While LIC operations are most frequently conducted by special oper-ations units, conventional units are often called upon to participate. The term LIC, which superseded the term "small wars," is presently being superseded itself by the term "operations other than war"* (OOTW).

References. Edwin G. Corr and Stephen Sloan, eds., *Low Intensity Conflict: Old Threats in a New World*, 1992. James J. Gallagher, *Low-Intensity Conflict*, 1992. Max G. Manwaring, *Uncomfortable Wars*, 1991. Loren B. Thompson, *Low-Intensity Conflict*, 1989.

Fred J. Chiaventone

LUNDY'S LANE

Lundy's Lane was one of the bloodiest battles of the War of 1812.* In 1814, after two years of war with little to show for it, the U.S. faced a renewed enemy. With Napoleon's defeat, the British were free to redeploy thousands of Penin-sular veterans to North America. Hoping to gain decisive results before British reinforcements arrived, Major General Jacob Brown crossed the Niagara River at Buffalo on 3 July with the intention of clearing the enemy from the Niagara Peninsula and then driving on to York (modern Toronto). His plan depended upon resupply by Commodore Isaac Chauncey's Lake Ontario fleet, at the head of that lake.

On 5 July, Brown's lead brigade,* commanded by Brigadier General Winfield Scott,* handily defeated a smaller British force at Chippawa.* Brown marched on Fort George, where he waited in vain for Chauncey and the siege guns necessary to reduce the British fort. As Brown waited, British reinforcements arrived. Despairing of capturing the fort, Brown drew back to the Chippawa battlefield to be resupplied. Late in the afternoon of 25 July, Brown ordered Scott to march north along the portage road to threaten Fort George, but as Scott approached Niagara Falls he discovered Major General Phineas Riall's brigade drawn up along Lundy's Lane, which ran east-west, perpendicular to the portage road. Never one to refuse a fight, Scott launched his brigade in an impetuous attack against the center of the British line which was on a small rise topped by a church.

The fighting continued until after midnight, with Brown and Sir Gordon Drummond, Riall's superior, bringing large number of reinforcements of regu-lars and militia. As fresh forces arrived, both sides made repeated attacks, with soldiers firing at the muzzle flashes of their enemies. Eventually the fight cen-tered on the British battery positions at the church. Overwhelming the British artillerymen in a bayonet* assault, the 21st Infantry, under Lieutenant Colonel James Miller, seized the hill and the guns. The British maintained a solid front only yards below the summit and made three determined but unsuccessful attempts to recapture the guns. In the fighting, Brown, Scott, and Drummond were wounded, and Riall was captured. As the firing slackened, Brown, thinking that he had won the fight, ordered his division* to retire to camp for rest and supply. The next day U.S. forces reappeared on the battlefield only to find the British once more in command of the high ground. With Brown and Scott recovering from their wounds, the U.S. commander, Eleazer Ripley, declined to continue the contest and withdrew his forces into Fort Erie across the river from Buffalo. Casualties at Lundy's Lane amounted to nearly one-fourth of the forces involved. Lundy's Lane was the high-water mark of the last American attempt to seize Canada.

References. Donald E. Graves, *The Battle of Lundy's Lane*, 1993. F. G. Stanley, *The War of 1812*, 1983.

Richard Barbuto

M
***

MI ABRAMS TANK

In the early 1970s, the United States became concerned with Soviet tank evolution and the continuing threat of armored combat on the European battlefield. The U.S. Army established a test bed to develop a new tank, dubbed the MBT (main battle tank), to meet this threat. The high cost of new technology and differing opinions on what was needed ended the project after completion of two prototypes. In the late '70s, a new tank system began to evolve based on the latest technology in armor, suspension, engine design, and armament. The XM-1 project was the Army's answer to the perceived Soviet threat and the solution to the high-speed lateral movement on the battlefield called for by the new but short-lived doctrine* of Active Defense.* The XM-1, however, fit nicely into the next generation of doctrine,* AirLand Battle.* The M1 Abrams tank emerged from the XM-1 project. The M1 development involved the best minds in armored warfare theory, considerable armor community cooperation, and technology derived from competitions within NATO* and extensive field tests. Both the M1 and M1A1 imcorporate a 1,500-horsepower diesel turbine engine, chobham armor, and a laser range finder with thermal imagery. Both are built by General Dynamics. The primary difference between the M1 and M1A1 is the 105 mm rifled gun on the M1 and the 120 mm smooth-bore gun on the M1A1. The newer M1A1 is completely computer integrated.

References. Timothy Garth, "The Future Is Now," *Armor*, March–April 1992, 26–28. R. P. Hunnicutt, *Abrams*, vol. 2, 1990. Kevin D. Poling, "M1A2 Update," *Armor*, May–June 1996, 16–20.

George Mordica II

M-1 CARBINE

The M-1 carbine was designed and manufactured on short notice in 1941 to provide greater firepower to soldiers whose duties precluded the use of full-sized rifles. The M-1 was designed by Winchester, but a number of different companies manufactured six million of them, both semiautomatic and automatic versions, between 1941 and 1945. The M-1 carbine fired a rimless caliber .30 cartridge from either a fifteen or thirty-round box magazine. The M1 carbine remained in active service in the U.S. Army until the early 1960s and continues in use today in many third world countries.

References. Bruce N. Canfield, *U.S. Infantry Weapons of World War II*, 1994. Paul Wahl, *Carbine Handbook*, 1964.

Edwin Kennedy, Jr.

M1 GARAND

The M1 Garand rifle was an important milestone in the development of military small arms in the twentieth century. It was the first military semiautomatic rifle to be adopted by and issued to an army in large quantities. M1 issue was slow and began in small numbers in 1939; when the United State entered World War II* in 1941, M1s were still in short supply. Production expanded enormously, however, and by 1945 U.S. arsenals had manufactured over four million. A further 500,000 were produced during the Korean War.* The M1 remained in U.S. Army service until replaced by the M14* in 1957. Many NATO* countries adopted the M1 after 1948. Beretta, the Italian gunmaker, established a facility and manufactured more than 100,000 M1s. Although obsolescent and out of production for decades, the M1 Gerand continues in service with the National Guard* and many other countries, including Chile, Costa Rica, Denmark, Greece, Guatemala, Haiti, Honduras, Italy, the Philippines, Taiwan, Tunisia, and Turkey.

References. Bruce N. Canfield, *U.S. Infantry Weapons of World War II*, 1996. Edgar R. Fenstemacher and Eugene R. Webb, "From Musket to M1," *Infantry School Quarterly*, July 1953, 22–31.

Luke Knowley

M1 ROCKET LAUNCHER, 2.36 INCH. *See* Bazooka.

M2 MACHINE GUN. *See* Machine Gun, Cal. .50.

M2 MEDIUM TANK

In 1938, Rock Island Arsenal* initiated work on a new medium tank generally based on the design of the M2 light tank and using many of its components. Originally designated the T5, the redesigned model became the M2 medium tank in June 1939. Powered by a Wright nine-cylinder radial engine, the M2 carried a 37 mm gun in a central turret and six (later eight) machine guns cal. .30.* The suspension system consisted of three two-wheel units on either side of the vehicle, with the drive sprockets connected to the drive train at the front and a set of idler wheels at the rear. A crew of six—commander, driver, and four gunners—served the M2. The 25 mm armor plate in the front hull and turret was increased to 32 mm in the M2A1 model. Weighing almost twenty-four tons, the M2A1 measured 17 feet in length, and was 8.5 feet wide and 9.25 feet in height.

Chrysler opened a new tank plant, the Detroit Tank Arsenal, to manufacture the M2, and the government contracted for 1,000 vehicles in August 1940. Events in Europe, however, made the M2A1 obsolete, and the government cancelled the contract before production began. About a hundred M2A1s were eventually built at Rock Island Arsenal. The Grant M3 medium tank* superseded the M2A1.

James E. Franklin

M3 MEDIUM TANK. *See* Grant M3 Medium Tank.

M4 MEDIUM TANK. *See* Sherman M4 Medium Tank.

M5 STUART TANK

The M5 Stuart light tank was the ultimate embodiment of U.S. pre–World War II* tank design: tall silhouette, raised rear deck to accomodate an air-cooled engine, and volute-spring suspension. Apart from the twin Cadillac V-8 engines and the automatic transmission, the M5 was identical to the earlier M3 series of light tanks. Armed with a single gyrostabilized 37 mm gun in a power traverse turret and two machine guns cal. 30,* the thin-skinned M5 was ill suited for direct combat with heavier tanks. However, the M5 proved to be nimble, robust, reliable, and an excellent scouting tank. The M5's small size and maneuverability made it ideal for jungle terrain and other tight areas that were difficult for larger tanks to traverse. Nearly 9,000 M5s were built, many of which went to the British, who nicknamed it the Stuart.

References. Peter Chamberlain and Chris Ellis, *British and American Tanks of World War II*, 2d U.S. ed., 1969. Duncan Crow, ed., *American AFVs of World War II*, 1972. R. P. Hunnicutt, *Stuart*, vol. 1, 1992.

Benjamin H. Kristy

M-14 RIFLE

As a result of NATO's* decision to adopt a common cartridge in the 1950s, the U.S. Army adopted the M-14 rifle to replace the M1 Garand.* Capable of firing its twenty-round magazine in semiautomatic and fully automatic mode (M-14A1), the M-14 also replaced the Browning automatic rifle* (BAR). Problems associated with the fully automatic capability, however, plagued the M-14 throughout its design and production. Its light weight caused a great dispersion of bullets when fired; excessive recoil and muzzle climb contributed to overall inaccuracy; and without an interchangeable barrel, it was incapable of sustained firing in the automatic mode, because the barrel overheated. After a difficult five years, in which approximately 1,380,000 weapons were manufactured, Secretary of Defense* Robert S. McNamara terminated production in 1963. In the mid-1960s, after extensive use in the early years of the Vietnam War,* the

M-16* replaced the M-14 as the standard shoulder weapon of the U.S. Army. Initially some soldiers longed for the heavier, more durable M-14, but most preferred the lighter, handier M-16.

References. Frank F. Rathbun, "The Rifle in Transition," *Army*, August 1963, 19–25. R. Blake Stevens, *U.S. Rifle M-14*, 2d. rev. ed., 1991.

Thomas Christianson

M-16 RIFLE

M-16 denotes a series of lightweight, high-velocity, 5.56 mm–caliber weapons developed for and currently issued to U.S. military forces. The M-16 series of rifles accepts either twenty or thirty-round detachable magazines and has a full-automatic rate of fire of approximately 800 rounds per minute. Unlike previous U.S. military rifles, private industry developed the M-16. Eugene M. Stoner, an engineer at the ArmaLite Division of Fairchild Engine and Airplane Corporation, originally submitted the design for a lightweight, high-velocity rifle. In 1958, the U.S. Army received the initial prototypes, designated the AR-15, for testing and evaluation. Colt's Patent Firearms Manufacturing Company subsequently purchased the manufacturing rights to the design. In 1963, the Army adopted the CAR-15* (Colt Automatic Rifle-15) and designated it the M-16. Initially plagued with reliability problems, stemming largely from the rush to get the design through the testing and evaluation process, and from inadequate troop training, the M-16 eventually proved itself a reliable and effective weapon. The Army began fielding the current version, the M-16A2, in 1982.

References. Edward Clinton Ezell, *The Great Rifle Controversy*, 1984. Charles Latour, "Small Arms," *NATO's Fifteen Nations*, June–July 1974, 62–68.

David Zoellers

M48 PATTON TANK

First produced in 1952, the M48 series main battle tank (MBT), officially named the Patton, came in six variants (M48 to M48A5) and was used in the U.S. Army until the late 1980s. The M48A5 had an AVDS-1720–2D diesel engine, a crew of four, and a 105 mm main gun, with three 7.62 mm machine guns. Total production of the M48 was 11,703, with many of the same components used for the M88 tank recovery vehicle and the M53 self-propelled gun. In use worldwide, the M48 series has been combat proven by the U.S., Iranian, Jordanian, Lebanese, and Pakastani armies. Beginning in 1960, the M60 main battle tank* replaced the M48 series in the U.S. Army inventory.

References. Daniel B. Adams, "The New M48 Tank," *Infantry School Quarterly*, October 1954, 98–112. R. P. Hunnicutt, *Patton*, vol. 1, 1984.

Chris Clark

M-60 MACHINE GUN

The M-60 is a general-purpose machine gun that incorporates many of the best characteristics of both the German MG-42 machine gun and FG-42 assault rifle of World War II.* The M-60 utilizes a number of stamped and fabricated components, which contributes to its economy of manufacture and light weight. It was the first U.S. machine gun to have a functioning quick-change barrel. Firing the 7.62 mm NATO round and weighing approximately 27.7 pounds when configured with a hundred-round belt of ammunition, the M-60 has an effective rate of fire of 600 rounds per minute at an effective range of 600 meters (when fired from the bipod) and 1,450 meters (when fired from a tripod).

References. Jeffrey J. Gudmens, "The M60 Machinegun," *Infantry*, March–April 1994, 39–41. "M60-Series 7.62-mm Machine Gun," *Army*, June 1992, 52–53.

David Zoellers

M60 MAIN BATTLE TANK

In early 1956, the U.S. Army decided to improve the M48 Patton tank.* Improvements included increased range, mobility, armament, ease of maintenance, and fuel efficiency. In 1957, the Army tested a new compression-ignition engine, the AVAS-1790-P, at the Yuma Proving Ground* as the first step in the development of a new series of tanks. Other components developed for the new tank included the 105 mm M68 gun, a torsion-bar suspension system, live-action tracks, a coincidence range finder, and a mechanical ballistic computer.

Designated the Tank, M60, Main Battle, the new tank entered service in 1960, and in October 1962 the M60A1 went into production. The M60A1 included a redesigned turret that increased main-gun ammunition storage from 57 to 63 rounds, a nuclear-biological-chemical* (NBC) system with air filtration, and a commander's cupola. The last M60A1 was completed in May 1980. The M60A2 version had a limited production, with a 152 mm gun-launcher and missile system; it was followed by the M60A3, with a laser range finder, solid-state computer, built-in stabilizer, a RISE engine, and top-loading air cleaners. M60A3 production ended in 1985.

The production schedule for all M60 variations was kept at an artificially low rate, the minimum necessary to sustain the production base. Only after the 1973 Arab-Israeli War was production increased, to replace high Israeli losses and to increase U.S. war reserves. The M1 Abrams tank* began to replace the M60 in the U.S. active force, and by 1997 the remaining M60s in the U.S. inventory were declared surplus and designated for foreign sales.

References. R. P. Hunnicutt, *Patton*, vol. 1, 1984. Robert M. Parker, Jr., "M60A1," *Armor*, July–August 1965, 33–40.

George Mordica II

M79. *See* Grenade Launcher M79.

M113. *See* Armored Personnel Carrier.

MacARTHUR, ARTHUR (1845–1912)

During the Civil War,* Arthur MacArthur, not yet twenty years old, earned the Medal of Honor* and commanded the 24th Wisconsin Infantry. In 1866, he joined the Regular Army and spent most of the next three decades performing routine duties on the western frontier. When the Spanish-American War* began, the War Department* appointed MacArthur a brigadier general of volunteers. After successfully leading his brigade* against the Spanish in the battle for Manila, MacArthur commanded the 2d Division* in the Department of Northern Luzon during the Philippine Insurrection.* He replaced Major General Elwell Otis as commanding general of the Division of the Philippines and became military governor, a position he held for fourteen months. After three years in the archipelago, MacArthur returned to the United States, where he held several departmental commands and toured the Far East at the direction of the War Department. Three years before his retirement in 1909, he was promoted to lieutenant general, the senior rank in the U.S. Army at the time. Arthur MacArthur, the father of Douglas MacArthur,* died on 12 September 1912.

References. Richard E. Welch, Jr., *Response to Imperialism*, 1979. Kenneth Ray Young, *The General's General*, 1994.

Stephen D. Coats

MacARTHUR, DOUGLAS (1880–1964)

Douglas MacArthur was one of the most brilliant and controversial military figures in American history. In a career that spanned forty-eight years, he rose to the highest position in the U.S. Army and led U.S. forces as a general officer in two world wars and Korea. Yet, he is most remembered for his conflict with President Harry Truman and his relief from command.

Born on 26 January 1880, the son of Arthur MacArthur* and a southern belle, he graduated first captain in his U.S. Military Academy* class and won recognition early in his career. In 1917 he helped form the famed Rainbow Division,* the 42d Infantry Division, and later commanded it in France, where he won nine decorations for heroism. His achievements earned him appointment as superintendent of West Point in 1919, where he implemented a number of reforms. In 1930 he became Chief of Staff* of the Army.

In 1937 MacArthur retired from the active list and went to the Philippines to help create the new Filipino army. The War Department* recalled him to active duty in 1941. Critics have faulted him for being unprepared for the Japanese attack on the Philippines and abandoning his doomed army in early 1942. He subsequently organized Allied resistance in the Southwest Pacific Area* (SWPA) and ultimately led his forces back to the Philippines in October 1944. When World War II* ended, MacArthur was named supreme commander for the Allied Powers and received Japan's surrender on the battleship USS *Missouri*. As supreme commander, MacArthur instituted sweeping reforms to democratize and demilitarize Japan. The North Korean invasion of South Korea, however, interrupted his work and brought about the crisis that led to his relief.

Convinced that the only way to win was to strike directly at China, MacArthur said so publicly, in direct opposition to Truman's policy. Douglas MacArthur returned to the United States a hero, but his long career was over. In his declining years, he cautioned Presidents John Kennedy and Lyndon Johnson to avoid committing U.S. forces in Vietnam.

References. D. Clayton James, *The Years of MacArthur*, 3 vols., 1970–1985. Geoffrey Perret, *Old Soldiers Never Die*, 1996. Michael Schaller, *Douglas MacArthur*, 1989.

Douglas P. Scalard

McCLELLAN, GEORGE BRINTON (1826–1885)

Born in Philadelphia, Pennsylvania, on 3 December 1826, George Brinton McClellan graduated from the U.S. Military Academy* second in the class of 1846. He distinguished himself in the Mexican War,* served as an instructor at the Academy, and performed various engineer duties. As an observer, he studied European armies during the Crimean War and, upon his return, recommended adoption of a cavalry saddle copied from a Hungarian model; the McClellan saddle* became the Army standard for more than fifty years. McClellan resigned his commission in 1857 to become chief engineer of the Illinois Central Railroad. When the Civil War* began, he was commissioned major general of volunteers and served with such efficiency and success in his early commands that Abraham Lincoln selected him to succeed Winfield Scott* as general in chief of the Army.

McClellan, an adept organizer and planner, turned the great mass of Union volunteers raised during the first six months of the war into the Army of the Potomac.* He supervised everything and looked after the welfare of his soldiers, but he was less able as a field commander. In the spring of 1862, he conducted a brilliant movement, taking his army by water to Fort Monroe* and then across the Virginia Peninsula to threaten the Confederate capitol at Richmond. However, he failed to take advantage of his initial success and was eventually forced to withdraw after the Seven Days* battle before Richmond.

At the battle of Antietam,* near Sharpsburg, Maryland, in September 1862, McClellan failed to capitalize on his numerical advantage in the tactical battle, then compounded his failure by allowing the Confederates, under Robert E. Lee,* to withdraw unhindered into Virginia. This failure led Lincoln to relieve McClellan, who did not command again during the war. In 1864, the Democrats selected McClellan to run against Lincoln for the presidency. In the campaign, he advocated making immediate peace with the South even if that meant allowing secession to stand. After losing the election, McClellan traveled extensively and served as governor of New Jersey from 1878 to 1881.

McClellan's legacy as a military commander lies wholly in the area of organization, élan, and motivation. His soldiers regarded him highly, and later in the war, the mere suggestion that he had returned to command would raise the army's morale. In the field, however, he most often failed to realize and capitalize on opportunities placed before him. After Antietam, Lee was so convinced of McClellan's timidity that he remained on the field outnumbered more than two to one, daring McClellan to attack. McClellan died in 1885 and is buried in Trenton, New Jersey.

References. Warren W. Hassler, Jr., *General George B. McClellan*, 1957. Stephen W. Sears, *George B. McClellan*, 1988.

George Knapp

McCLELLAN SADDLE

While still a captain in the 1st U.S. Cavalry, George B. McClellan* was appointed to the U.S. Military Commission to the Crimea in 1854 to observe combat operations of the French and British armies in their war against imperial Russia. At the conclusion of the Crimean War, McClellan continued his mission with an inspection tour of European armies. Upon returning to the United States, he wrote to Secretary of War* Jefferson Davis* recommending that U.S. mounted units adopt a new type of saddle to replace the Grimsley Saddle.* The U.S. Army was already testing other saddles for possible use, among them the Hope (or Texas) modification of the Grimsley, and a design by Danial Campbell. McClellan's design, he claimed, was based on a Hungarian tree minus the heavy iron "furniture" used on similar Prussian saddles. More likely, however, the design was based on the popular Spanish tree saddle and incorporated features taken from both Campbell (whose saddle had been patented in 1855) and Captain Lewis Edward Nolan, a renowned British cavalry officer and horse trainer killed at Balaklava. Basically, the McClellan saddle consisted of a beechwood tree, composed of a pommel, cantle, and side rails with an elongated slot running down the center of the seat. Iron staples riveted to the tree supported stirrup leathers, and a leather cover stitched over rawhide covered the tree. Slots cut through the pommel and cantle allowed leather straps to be threaded through the saddle for the suspension of additional equipment, such as bedrolls, valises, and overcoats. A simple system of rings and studs allowed for the attachment of saddle bags, canteen, picket line, feed bag, and carbine. The 1858–1859 Army Ordnance Board formally adopted the McClellan as the standard cavalry saddle. With various modifications, the McClellan continued in U.S. Army service until 1942. When the Army adopted olive green as the official uniform color in 1902, the standard black leather cover was changed to russet. Experienced riders continue to favor the McClellan, because of its light weight and comfortable fit for the horse.

References. R. Stephen Dorsey and Kenneth L. McPheeters, *The American Military Saddle, 1776–1945*, 1999. Randy Steffen, *United States Military Saddles, 1812–1943*, 1973.

Fred J. Chiaventone

MACHINE GUN, CAL. .50

The designation applies to a variety of machine guns first fielded in 1926 by the U.S. Army. The machine gun, caliber .50, was intially designed as an antitank weapon but was quickly adapted to antiaircraft roles as well. A number of different models have been fielded over the years, including water-cooled and air-cooled models. The most common model, the M2, Heavy Barrel, Flexible, is still in service with the U.S. Army as its primary heavy machine gun.

References. Peter Chamberlain and Terry Gander, *Machine Guns*, 1974. Don Manning, "Getting to Know an Old Standby," *Army*, March 1992, 36–38.

Edwin Kennedy, Jr.

MACHINE GUN, CAL. .30

A joint Army-Navy board agreed upon .30 caliber as the U.S. military standard cartridge in 1898. The first standard machine gun adopted for U.S. Army use was the caliber .30 Model 1904 Maxim gun.* Subsequently, the Army fielded a variety of machine guns designated caliber .30, including water-cooled, air-cooled, tripod-mounted, and bipod-mounted models. Originally chambered for the .30–40 Krag-Jorgenson cartridge, later cal. .30 models used the .30–06, the standard cartridge of the Model 1903 Springfield rifle.* The U.S. discarded the cal. .30 series of machine guns when it adopted the NATO 7.62 mm standard cartridge in 1958. Many foreign armies still use U.S. cal. .30 machine guns, while others have rechambered and rebarrelled them for 7.62 mm.

References. Peter Chamberlain and Terry Gander, *Machine Guns*, 1974. Edward Clinton Ezell, *Small Arms of the World*, 1977.

Edwin Kennedy, Jr.

McNAIR, LESLEY JAMES (1883–1944)

Lesley James McNair, one of the U.S. Army's great trainers and organizers, was born in Verndale, Minnesota, in 1883 and graduated from the U.S. Military Academy* in 1904, eleventh in his class of 124. In 1916, he served with General John J. Pershing's* Punitive Expedition* in Mexico; during World War I* he was an artillery commander, rising to the rank of brigadier general in 1918. In July 1940, General George C. Marshall* appointed McNair chief of staff of General Headquarters* (GHQ). In 1942, McNair (then a lieutenant general) assumed command of Army Ground Forces,* created to train the large citizen army then being mobilized to fight around the globe. McNair ensured that training integrated the latest doctrine* and most advanced weapons. He insisted on realistic maneuvers under battlefield conditions and imbued the young troops with the spirit to fight and win. In 1943, during an inspection trip to North Africa, McNair was severely wounded by enemy shrapnel. On 25 July 1944, while observing preparations for Operation Cobra* near St. Lô, France, U.S. Eighth Air Forces heavy bombers undershot their target and killed McNair and a number of other Americans. Leslie J. McNair was the highest-ranking U.S. officer killed in action in World War II.*

References. Julius Goldstein, " 'Invincible' Lt. Gen. Lesley J. McNair," *Army*, August 1999, 43–44. E. J. Kahn, Jr., *McNair*, 1945. Brooks E. Kleber, "The Educator of the Army," *Army*, July 1980, 50–54.

Donald L. Gilmore

McPHERSON, JAMES BIRDSEYE (1828–1864)

Born in Clyde, Ohio, on 14 November 1828, James Birdseye McPherson graduated first in his class at the U.S. Military Academy* in 1853. Commissioned in the engineers, McPherson taught engineering at the Academy before serving in assignments on both coasts and working on harbor, river, and seacoast fortification projects. Promoted to captain in August 1861, he served as aide-de-camp to Henry Halleck* in Missouri and as chief engineer to Ulysses S. Grant* during the Forts Henry and Donelson Campaign* and at Shiloh* and Corinth. Promoted to colonel in the Regular Army in May 1862, brigadier general of U.S. Volunteers in August, and major general of U.S. Volunteers in October, McPherson commanded an engineer brigade* at Iuka and, in January 1863, assumed command of XVII Corps, Army of the Tennessee,* which he led during the Vicksburg* campaign. Promoted to brigadier general in the Regular Army in August 1863, he commanded the Army of the Tennessee during the Atlanta campaign.* Because of indecision at Resaca, Georgia,* in May 1864, McPherson missed an excellent opportunity to deliver a devastating blow against Joseph E. Johnston's* Confederate Army of Tennessee. James McPherson was killed in action during the Atlanta campaign on 22 July 1864.

Reference. Tamara Moser Melia, "James B. McPherson and the Ideals of the Old Army," 1987.

Edward Shanahan

MAHAN, DENNIS HART (1802–1871)

Dennis Hart Mahan graduated first in his U.S. Military Academy* class in 1824 and was immediately appointed to the faculty there. In 1832, he became professor of military and civil engineering, and of the science of war, a position he held until his death in 1871. Mahan's teachings and writings helped shape U.S. military thought during the nineteenth century and influenced the generation of officers who fought in the Civil War.* Mahan published a number of books on military engineering and fortification, including *A Complete Treatise on Field Fortification* (1836) and *An Elementary Treatise on Advanced-Guard, Out-Post, and Detachment Service Troops* (1847). Although heavily influenced by Baron Antoine Henri de Jominic (an interpreter of Napoleon) and by French tactical doctrine, and an admirer of Napoleon's offensive style of war, Mahan recognized that because of political, geographical, and cultural factors, the U.S. military could not duplicate the French system. Therefore Mahan advocated active defense and field fortifications to preserve the lives of U.S. soldiers and to simplify the task of command. Only after the enemy force had exhausted itself attacking the U.S. entrenchments should a counterattack be launched. Mahan took his own life in 1871.

References. R. Ernest Dupuy, *Men of West Point*, 1951. Thomas E. Griess, "Dennis Hart Mahan," 1968. Edward Hagerman, *The American Civil War and the Origins of Modern Warfare*, 1988.

Timothy C. Dunwoody

MAIN SUPPLY ROUTE

The term "main supply route" (MSR) refers to routes designated by U.S. Army units for logistical and administrative purposes. Normally extending forward from rear areas, an MSR is the lifeline of the combat unit, providing safe passage for supplies, equipment, and personnel replacements. MSRa are designated by theater, corps,* and division* staffs during their planning processes and are managed by the appropriate movement-control organization. Some main supply routes—for example, the route of the Red Ball Express* in northern France in World War II* and routes Dodge and Sultan, the lifelines from major ports in Desert Storm*—have attracted considerable historical attention.

References. John E. Edwards, *Combat Service Support Guide*, 2d ed., 1993. William G. Pagonis and Jeffrey L. Cruikshank, *Moving Mountains*, 1992.

Jim Martin

MAKIN

Makin Atoll, in the Gilbert Islands, lies near the equator 2,000 miles southwest of Hawaii. On 10 December 1941, the Japanese occupied Makin to use it as a seaplane base. U.S. carrier units struck the atoll in February 1942, the 2d Marine Raider Battalion landed on the main island of Butaritari on 17 August 1942, destroyed many installations, and wiped out most of the small garrison. After the raid, the Japanese reassessed their defenses in the Gilberts, dispatched reinforcements, and began fortifying Betio Island, Tarawa Atoll, and Butaritari, Makin Atoll.

In July 1943, the Joint Chiefs of Staff* (JCS) directed Admiral Chester W. Nimitz to capture the Gilberts. As part of Operation Galvanic, on 20 November two battalions* of the U.S. Army's 165th Regimental Combat Team (Reinforced), 27th Infantry Division, landed on the west coast of Butaritari and moved east along the long axis of the island. A third battalion came through the lagoon from the north and landed in the vicinity of the seaplane base. The Japanese fought tenaciously; the last pockets of resistance were not eliminated until 22 November, when, at 1130, Major General Ralph C. Smith, the division commander, signaled: "Makin Taken." U.S. casualties were sixty-six killed in action or died of wounds and 150 wounded. Japanese losses were over 400 killed and 104 prisoners—three of these were Japanese, the remainder were Korean laborers.

References. Philip A. Crowl and Edmund G. Lowe, *Seizure of the Gilberts and Marshalls*, 1955. Edwin P. Hoyt, *Storm over the Gilberts*, 1978. United States War Department, Historical Division [John M. Baker and George F. Howe], *The Capture of Makin*, 1946, 1990.

Brian D. Moore

MANASSAS. *See* First Bull Run; Second Bull Run.

MANHATTAN PROJECT

The Manhattan Project was the U.S. program during World War II* that culminated in the first fission (atomic) bomb. Many historians consider the Manhattan Project to be the largest and most complicated technological effort in the history of man. In the late 1930s, most physicists believed that atomic fission was theoretically possible but considered the question an esoteric classroom pursuit. As the German army moved across Europe, the issue became more important, because many emigrant scientists believed that Germany had a near-term solution to the problem—a notion that was subsequently disproved. In this atmosphere of urgency, the United States brought together some of the world's great physicists to explore the theory and potential applications of atomic fission. Led by Robert Oppenheimer, the project included scientists such as James Conant, Neils Bohr, Enrico Fermi, and Edward Teller—known as the father of the fusion (hydrogen) bomb. The concept of splitting an atom held morbid fascination for many of these key scientists; some believed that the first atom to be split would ignite a chain reaction that would consume the entire universe. Ultimately successful, the Manhattan Project culminated in the two atomic bombs dropped on Japan in August 1945, ending World War II.

References. Stephane Groueff, *Manhattan Project*, 1967. Vincent C. Jones, *Manhattan*, 1985. Richard Rhodes, *The Making of the Atomic Bomb*, 1986.

Don Denmark

MARCH, PEYTON C. (1864–1955)

Born in Easton, Pennsylvania, on 27 December 1864, Peyton C. March became the primary architect of the office of Chief of Staff.* Upon graduation from the U.S. Military Academy* in 1888, March was commissioned in the artillery.* He served in the Philippines and commanded forces at the battle of the Clouds at Tilad Pass on 12 December 1899. Following his promotion to lieutenant colonel of volunteers, March served two years as aide-de-camp to Lieutenant General Arthur MacArthur* and, from 1903 to 1907, served on the newly created General Staff* in Washington. After resigning his commission in the volunteers, March rose to the rank of brigadier general and in June 1917 was given command of the artillery of the American Expeditionary Force* (AEF) in France. Recalled to Washington in March 1918, March became acting Chief of Staff, then Chief of Staff. Despite opposition from General John J. Pershing,* commander of the AEF, who had been promoted to four-star rank ahead of March and resisted March's authority, March initiated a series of reforms that greatly shaped the role of the General Staff. In doing so, March strengthened the authority of the Chief of Staff as the supreme officer within the U.S. Army. March retired from the Army in January 1921, but he retained a keen interest in military and national affairs for the remainder of his life. He died in 1955.

References. Edward M. Coffman, *The Hilt of the Sword*, 1966. Peyton C. March, *The Nation at War*, 1932, 1970.

Edward L. Maier III

MARION, FRANCIS (1732?–1795)

In the wake of Continental Army* defeats at Charleston* and Camden in 1780, Colonial fortunes in the South appeared dim. Only the activities of partisan leaders, such as Francis Marion known as the "Swamp Fox," kept the British from pacifying the Carolinas. Marion and his men granted British and Tory forces no respite, hitting them in the dead of night, then fading into the swamps and woods of the Carolina backcountry. When George Washington* dispatched Nathanael Greene* with additional Continental regiments* to the area, the stage was set for one of the most successful campaigns of the American Revolution.* Using partisan forces to threaten British garrisons supporting Lord Cornwallis, Greene's army executed a brilliant delaying operation that eventually wore down its more numerous foe. Frustrated and short of supplies, Cornwallis was forced to pull his forces back to Wilmington, North Carolina. When Cornwallis turned his army northward toward Yorktown, Marion began the process of reducing British garrisons left behind in the Carolina backcountry.

References. Robert D. Bass, *Swamp Fox*, 1972. Hugh F. Rankin, *Francis Marion*, 1973. Russell F. Weigley, *The Partisan War*, 1970.

Joseph R. Fischer

MARKET-GARDEN

Operation Market-Garden was a plan for Allied forces to cut through Holland and cross the Rhine into Germany; it was intended to achieve the early defeat of Germany in World War II.* The campaign, initiated on 17 September 1944, was the idea of the notoriously cautious British Field Marshall Sir Bernard Law Montgomery. One of the most daring campaigns of the war, Market-Garden was unusually complex and relied on the sequential accomplishment of numerous supporting attacks. "Market" was the airborne portion of the plan; it involved the use of nearly 5,000 aircraft and more than 2,500 gliders. "Garden," the ground phase of the operation, was a thrust north from the Belgium border by British XXX Corps and two U.S. airborne divisions.* Equally challenging in complexity was the required integration of numerous combined, joint, and coalition doctrines, equipment, and logistic systems. Ultimately, Market-Garden proved a disastrous failure for the Allies, due in large part to the failure of advancing Allied ground forces to link up with, and relieve, the airborne forces that were holding critical choke points, bridges, and lines of communications in and around Arnhem. By 25 September, it was obvious that the operation was a failure and that Allied forces would not establish a bridgehead on the far side of the Rhine. After nine days, Market-Garden was called off after the loss of over 17,000 Allied casualties.

References. Peter Harclerode, *Arnheim*, 1994. Martin Middlebrook, *Arnhem 1944*, 1994. Cornelius Ryan, *A Bridge Too Far*, 1974.

Don Denmark

MARSHALL, GEORGE CATLETT (1880–1959)

Born in Uniontown, Pennsylvania, on the last day of 1880, to an old and distinguished family, George Catlett Marshall rose to be one of America's premier soldiers and foremost statesmen. In 1901, Marshall graduated from the Virginia Military Institute* (VMI) as first captain. Commissioned in the infantry,*

Marshall's early career included two tours in the Philippines; a stint at Fort Reno, Oklahoma; four years at Fort Leavenworth,* Kansas, where he attended both the Infantry and Cavalry School and the staff course before serving on the faculty for two years; an assignment with the Massachusetts militia; and command of a company in the 4th Infantry. By the time Marshall was promoted to captain in 1916, he had established a firm relationship with senior commanders, including Major Generals Hunter Liggett* and James Franklin Bell,* that would influence much of his later career.

After the United States declared war on Germany in April 1917, Marshall sailed for France with the 1st Division* as training officer. Over the next eighteen months he served in a number of staff positions, primarily in operations, and received the nickname "Wizard" for his logistics plans. After the Armistice of November 1918, Marshall stayed in France, worked on plans for the occupation of Germany, traveled extensively throughout Europe, and in the spring of 1919 became an aide to General of the Armies John J. Pershing*—another relationship that would prove valuable to Marshall's future career. In 1924, he went to China, where he served as executive officer* of the 15th Infantry, completing his experience in virtually every area of the world where U.S. Army troops operated before World War II.*

In 1927, Marshall returned to United States and reported to the Army War College,* beginning an association with the school house that would have a significant influence on an entire generation of U.S. Army officers. At the Infantry School at Fort Benning,* Georgia, Marshall emphasized the importance of history, especially the lessons of World War I,* rewrote the curriculum that would prepare infantry officers for the next war; and mentored or influenced more than 160 officers who would attain general-officer rank and lead U.S. forces during World War II.

After leaving the Infantry School in 1933, Marshall once again served in a number of assignments, including a battalion* command in the 8th Infantry, a tour as an instructor with a National Guard* unit, as supervisor of a Civilian Conservation Corps* (CCC) camp, a brigade* command, and as head of the War Plans Division* in Washington. In 1939, Marshall was named Chief of Staff* over a lengthy list of more senior generals. It was as Chief of Staff during the next six years that Marshall left his greatest impression on the U.S. Army. He worked tirelessly to prepare the Army for the coming war, and he provided wise and sound leadership throughout the most trying period of the nation's history.

Marshall retired from the Army on 20 November 1945 but almost immediately was called upon to serve as diplomat and peacemaker. President Harry Truman named Marshall secretary of state in 1946, just as the Cold War* was beginning. During Marshall's tenure, the United States proclaimed the Truman Doctrine, recognized Israel, began negotiations that resulted in the North Atlantic Treaty Organization (NATO),* and confronted the Soviet Union during the

Berlin Airlift. Marshall's greatest achievement, however, was the European Recovery Act, commonly known as the Marshall Plan, for the economic recovery of the war-ravaged countries of Europe. He resigned from State in 1949 because of ill health, but Truman once again called on Marshall, appointing him secretary of defense in September 1950, during a critical crisis of the Korean War.* He left Defense a year later, ending a half-century of service to his country. In December, 1953, Marshall accepted the Nobel Prize for Peace in Oslo, Norway, the first professional soldier to received that prestigious prize. On 16 October 1959, after an extended illness, Marshall passed away at Walter Reed Hospital in Washington. He is buried at Arlington National Cemetery.*

References. Ed Cray, *General of the Army*, 1990. Leonard Mosley, *Marshall*, 1982. Forrest C. Pogue, *George C. Marshall*, 4 vols., 1963–1987. Mark A. Stoler, *George C. Marshall*, 1989.

MARSHALL, SAMUEL LYMAN ATWOOD (1900–1977)

Born in Catskill, New York, seventeen-year-old Samuel Lyman Atwood Marshall enlisted in the U.S. Army shortly after the United States declared war against Germany in April 1917, beginning an association that would last more than fifty years. He served as an infantryman with the 90th Division at Soisson, St. Mihiel,* the Meuse-Argonne,* and Ypres-Lys and was commissioned a lieutenant in the infantry* in 1919. Following the war, Marshall returned to his home in El Paso, Texas, and drifted into journalism. It was a field in which he had no formal training, but he learned quickly and took a position with the *Detroit News* in 1927. Marshall successfully combined his life-long interest in military affairs with his skill as a journalist.

In World War II,* Marshall served first in the Office of War Information, then in the new historical service of the General Staff.* He visited frontline units in the Pacific and Europe, where he began formulating his ideas on the relationship of men and battle, a theme that would run through much of the body of literature he produced during the next thirty years. He saw action again during the Korean War and was promoted to brigadier general in the U.S. Army Reserve.* Although he retired in 1960, in 1966 "SLAM"—as he was known to many readers and students of military history—went to Southeast Asia and saw action in his fourth war.

Marshall believed that the true lessons of battle were subtle, but perishable. He pioneered and refined the post-action interview as a way to learn as quickly as possible what really occurred in combat. His theories stirred controversy among military historians and analysts, and critics point out that he frequently played fast and loose with the facts. Nevertheless, his thirty books, including such classic studies as *Men against Fire* (1947, 1978) and *The Soldier's Load and the Mobility of a Nation* (1950), and hundreds of articles are an immeasurable contribution to our understanding of man facing his ultimate challenge.

References. John Douglas Marshall, *Reconciliation Road*, 1993. S.L.A. Marshall, *Bringing Up the Rear*, ed. Cate Marshall, 1979. F.D.G. Williams, *SLAM*, 1990.

M*A*S*H

On 17 September 1972, *MASH* premiered on CBS Television. Based on the novel by Dr. J. Richard Hornberger, a Korean War* veteran writing under the pseudonym "Richard Hooker," and on the movie *M*A*S*H*, directed by Robert Altman, it became one of the most successful series in television history. *MASH* was an antiwar black comedy set in a mobile army surgical hospital, but its story lines were humorous and portrayed the human side of conflicts. To the characters, practical jokes and laughs were the key to survival in war. Episodes focused on the doctors, nurses, and wounded soldiers; through their eyes, the audience saw people struggling together, sometimes futilely, to persevere and preserve lives. While *MASH* was on the air, the Vietnam War* was drawing to an end—not a coincidence—and the series played an important role in the public's understanding of the effects of war on the human soul. On 28 February 1983, *MASH* closed its long run with the largest television audience in history.

References. Rick Mitz, *The Great TV Sitcom Book*, 1980. Ed Weiner, and Editors of *TV Guide, The TV Guide TV Book*, 1992.

Trevor Brown

MAULDIN, WILLIAM HENRY (1921–   )

As a World War II* cartoonist for *Stars and Stripes*,* William Henry Mauldin won a Pulitzer Prize for his depiction of two combat-weary soldiers, Willie and Joe, slogging their way through European battlefields and, later, returning to postwar civilian life. Mauldin earned a Purple Heart* and the Legion of Merit* for his wartime service. After the war, the nation honored Mauldin with five honorary doctorates and a second Pulitzer, for a Cold War* editorial cartoon. Severe arthritis in both hands later limited his drawing ability but led to an interest in sculpting. He was featured in two notable films—*Up Front*, based on his best-selling book, and *The Red Badge of Courage*. Mauldin claims that he got his best ideas in the bathtub and that his cartoons required up to eight hours from initial concept to finished drawing. Born on 29 October 1921 in Mountain Park, New Mexico, he currently resides in Santa Fe, New Mexico.

References. Will Lang and Tom Durrance, "Mauldin," *Life*, 5 February 1945, 49–53. Bill Mauldin, *The Brass Ring*, 1971.

John R. Finch

MAXIM GUN

In 1884, Hiram Maxim, an American engineer, perfected the first fully automatic machine gun. Previous designs had relied on multiple barrels to increase rate of fire and had used hand-operated cranks or levers to work the gun. In contrast, the Maxim gun needed only a single barrel to deliver 600 rounds per minute, and it operated automatically once the trigger had been pressed. The Maxim gun employed the recoil caused by each exploding round to load, fire, and extract the next cartridge, and it used a water jacket to keep the barrel cool. When fired, the barrel slid back, allowing the spent cartridge to be ejected and a new one to be loaded. Maxim also devised a belt to feed cartridges into his gun. Nevertheless, each time the U.S. Army tested the Maxim gun, in 1888, 1890, and 1895, it found the gun too unreliable for field service. The Army subsequently adopted the .30 cal. Model 1904 Maxim gun.

References. David A. Armstrong, *Bullets and Bureaucrats*, 1982. Dolf L. Goldsmith, *The Devil's Paintbrush*, 1993.

Timothy C. Dunwoody

MEADE, GEORGE GORDON (1815–1872)

George Gordon Meade was born on 31 December 1815 at Cadiz, Spain, the son of an American merchant who had supported the Spanish cause during the Napoleonic Wars. He graduated nineteenth in a class of fifty-six from the U.S. Military Academy* in the class of 1835, but he did not pursue a military career and resigned from the Army in 1836 to become a civil engineer. In 1842, however, he changed of mind, reentered the Army, and served in the Mexican War.* He was promoted to brigadier general at the beginning of the Civil War*; the governor of Pennsylvania selected Meade to command one of the first brigades* raised in that state. He was severely wounded in the Peninsula Campaign* but later fought at Second Bull Run,* South Mountain, Antietam,* Fredericksburg,* and Chancellorsville,* where he commanded V Corps. In June 1863, Meade replaced Joseph Hooker* as commander of the Army of the Potomac,* just three days before the battle of Gettysburg.* Although the battle was a Union victory, Meade was criticized for failing to pursue and destroy Lee's army during its retreat. Meade offered to resign, but President Lincoln liked him and kept him in command of the Army of the Potomac, even after Ulysses S. Grant* was named general-in-chief. Meade worked well with Grant in the Overland and Petersburg* Campaigns.

After the war, Meade stayed in the Army and commanded the Military District of the Atlantic, with his headquarters at Philadelphia, where he died in 1872. George Meade was a leader of great character, a man who served honorably and bravely. He willingly subordinated himself when appropriate and accepted the responsibility of command when required.

References. Freeman Cleaves, *Meade of Gettysburg*, 1960. Theodore Lyman, *With Grant and Meade from the Wilderness to Appomattox*, 1994.

George Knapp

MEALS, READY TO EAT

Meals, Ready to Eat, or MREs, were adopted by the U.S. Army in the early 1980s to replace the C-ration* which had been in use since World War II.* The MRE consists of a meal entrée, dried fruit, a cracker pack, cheese, peanut butter or jelly spread, candy or a dessert cake, and a beverage powder pack. The ration also includes a sundry pack with coffee, toilet tissue, condiments, and a heater pack. Using a combination of foil-packaged, dehydrated, and ready-to-consume meals and components, the MRE eliminated the need for ration cans, reducing a single meal's weight to approximately one pound and prolonging the shelf life to ten years. Initially unpopular with soldiers due to limited menu choices and portion size, the MRE has undergone several modifications that have corrected deficiencies and added popular commercial components. MRE entree choices now include vegetarian meals for use in humanitarian operations.

References. Donna Miles, "MRE Feedback," *Soldiers*, November 1993, 48–49. Joseph A. Zanchi and Alan J. LaBrode, "Combat Ration Logistics" *Army Logistician*, January–February 1999, 144–149.

Robert J. Dalessandro

MECHANIZED INFANTRY

Mechanized infantry is the basic combat force that travels to battle and fights in tracked and wheeled vehicles. Troops conveyed to the battlefield in vehicles may dismount and fight alongside conventional infantry,* while the vehicles may remain in the battle area to provide fire support or to reembark the troops for movement elsewhere. Mechanized infantry provides speed, mobility, and maneuverability, and it adds protection to the combat force. Although various armies conducted some experimentation with mechanized infantry in World War I,* it did not appear as a significant force on the battlefield until World War II.*

References. John E. Foley, "Observations on Mechanized Infantry," *Infantry*, July–August 1986, 29–33. James M. Gibson, "A Case for Mechanized Infantry," *Military Review*, September 1970, 56–70. G. Harry Huppert, "Mechanized Infantry," *Armor*, July–August 1962, 43–45.

Krewasky A. Salter

MEDAL OF HONOR

The Medal of Honor is the highest decoration that can be awarded to a member of the U.S. armed forces. It originated during the Civil War,* with the Navy getting first approval on 21 December 1861. President Abraham Lincoln approved the Army medal on 12 July 1862, and Secretary of War* Edwin M. Stanton presented the first awards on 25 March 1863. When the U.S. Air Force became a separate service in 1947, an Air Force version was created. Until World War I,* the Medal of Honor was the only U.S. award for military heroism, which led to some abuses. In 1917, a board reviewed all citations and struck 911 names from the roll, their deeds having been of insufficient merit to have earned the medal. Two of those stricken were William F. Cody, known as "Buffalo Bill," who had received the award as a civilian scout for the Army, and Mary Walker, a Civil War contract surgeon and the only woman ever awarded the medal. Congress subsequently restored the medal to both Cody and Walker. As of May 1994, 3,420 Medals of Honor have been awarded to 3,401 recipients—200 of whom are still living. On 23 May 1994, the president presented posthumous Medals of Honor to widows of two Rangers* killed in Somalia during a firefight on 3 October 1993.

References. Hugh Kayser, *The Spirit of America*, 1982. *The Congressional Medal of Honor*, 1984. Joseph L. Schott, *Above and Beyond*, 1963.

John Reichley

MEDALS AND DECORATIONS

Medals and decorations are awarded in recognition of heroism, meritorious achievement, or meritorious service. Until 1918, the Medal of Honor* was the only decoration that the United States bestowed upon a soldier. The Distinguished Service Cross* (DSC) and Distinguished Service Medal (DSM), both established by President Woodrow Wilson in 1918, were joined by the Soldier's Medal* and the Distinguished Flying Cross in 1926. In 1932, the Silver Star* was established as a medal for battlefield heroism. The Air Medal, Bronze Star*medal; and Legion of Merit,* all established in World War II,* completed the wartime pyramid of honor. After World War II, the armed services established numerous medals and decorations for peacetime achievement and service. Soldiers may now receive awards for significant contributions to the effectiveness, morale, or readiness of their unit or organization and for personal achievement or service, including specific acts and sustained periods of exceptional leadership, command, or service.

The Army pyramid of honor (from highest to lowest) is: Medal of Honor, Distinguished Service Cross, Distinguished Service Medal, Silver Star, Legion of Merit, Distinguished Flying Cross, Soldier's Medal, Bronze Star, Purple Heart,* Meritorious Service Medal, Air Medal, Army Commendation Medal, and Army Achievement Medal. In addition to these medals, the Army awards a Good Conduct Medal to enlisted personnel, and campaign and expeditionary medals to all who meet established criteria—usually time and place related. A soldier may wear full-size medals or miniatures; most however, wear the corresponding ribbon.

References. Evans E. Kerrigan, *American War Medals and Decorations*, 1990. John E. Strandberg and Roger J. Bender, *The Call of Duty*, 1994.

Frederic L. Borch III

MEDIC

The term "medic," meaning physician or medical student, predates its military usage. In current Army parlance, it commonly refers to a medical specialist (MOS 91B), but it may also refer to any other direct medical care provider in an Army organization or hospital. In a broader context, the term may be used interchangably with medical personnel of other services, such as a U.S. Navy corpsman or a U.S. Air Force medical technician (MedTech), or with earlier U.S. Army designations, such as aidman. The origins of U.S. Army medics can be traced to the efforts of Brigadier General William Hammond, who organized a corps of enlisted hospital stewards in 1862. Until then, soldiers from nearby garrisons, without any knowledge, training, or understanding of medical requirements, were detailed to hospital work. With the establishment of the Medical

Department in 1887, the Army finally defined the role and began to recruit and train enlisted men as medical soldiers. Not until the 20th century, however, did the combat medic have a significant impact on the modern battlefield. First in World War I,* then increasingly in World War II,* Korea, and Vietnam, the highly trained, skilled, and dedicated medical specialist became an indispensable member of the combat team. His knowledge, the medical supplies he carried, and his willingness to risk his own life for the men with whom he served saved countless lives and bolstered the morale of all fighting soldiers.

References. Albert E. Cowdrey, *Fighting for Life*, 1994. Eloise Engle, *Medic*, 1967. Craig Roberts, *Combat Medic*, 1991. Terri Wiram, "Combat Medics," *Soldiers*, February 1983, 14–16.

MEDICAL BADGE. *See* Combat Medical Badge; Expert Field Medical Badge.

MEDICAL CORPS

Care of the Army's sick and wounded is the responsibility of the all-physician Medical Corps. The origins of the Medical Corps can be traced to the American Revolution,* when George Washington* requested medical support for the Continental Army.* Responding to Washington's request, on 25 July 1775 Congress created the Hospital Department, forerunner of today's Army Medical Department. In 1818, Congress established the position of Surgeon General* to centralize control of Army physicians, who did not hold military rank and were responsible directly to post commanders. Conditions for Army physicians on active duty changed in 1847, when they were given ranks and titles: surgeon, assistant surgeon, and medical inspector. Reserve doctors did not receive these honorifics until the creation of the Medical Reserve Corps in 1908. Today, the Chief, Medical Corps Affairs, is a brigadier general who also serves as special assistant to the Surgeon General for Medical Affairs. The corps sets and maintains physical standards for all uniformed personnel and provides clinical and preventive health care for active-duty, reserve, dependent, and retired military persons. In 1971, the Medical Corps launched a new program to train qualified enlisted men and women as physician's assistants (PAs). Upon completion of the program, graduates are appointed warrant officers* and provide medical care in combat units under the direct supervision of a Medical Corps officer.

References. Mary C. Gillett, *The Army Medical Department, 1865–1917*, 1995. Cole C. Kingseed, "The Battalion PA,"*Infantry*, November–December 1991, 6–8. Clarence McKittrick Smith, *The Medical Department*, 1956.

Trevor Brown

MEDICAL SERVICE CORPS

One of six corps of the Army Medical Department (AMED), the Medical Service Corps (MSC) is a diversified, multidisciplinary corps of officers whose purpose is to provide clinical, scientific, administrative, command, and support services to the AMED. Specialty areas include health services administration, tactical planning and operations, aeromedical evacuation, optometry, pharmacy, behavioral sciences, laboratory sciences, preventive medicine, audiology, and podiatry. Administrative support to the AMED dates to the apothecaries of the American Revolution.* Today's MSC, however, identifies its formal origin as the establishment on 30 June 1917 of a Sanitary Corps, consisting of officers with "special skill . . . in sanitary engineering . . . preventive medicine, or who possess other knowledge of special advantage to the Medical Department," including daily administration of hospital units. The Sanitary Corps went into reserve status after World War I* and was entirely replaced on 4 June 1920 by the Medical Administrative Corps (MAC). The MAC's focus was on the daily administration of hospital units. Its officers were required to have had five years enlisted service in the Medical Department, and they became hospital adjutants, registrars, and transportation officers. On 12 July 1943, Congress authorized a Pharmacy Corps. On 4 August 1947, the MSC replaced the Medical Administrative and Pharmacy Corps. Today, Medical Service Corps officers and warrant officers* operate one of the Army's most complex branches, with four mandated sections: Pharmacy, Supply, and Administration; Medical Allied Sciences; Sanitary Engineering; and Optometry.

References. Percy M. Ashburn, *A History of the Medical Department of the United States Army*, 1929. Richard V. N. Ginn, *The History of the U.S. Army Medical Service Corps*, 1997.

David A. Rubenstein

MEKONG DELTA

The Mekong Delta, a densely populated and fertile rice-producing area in the southernmost area of Vietnam, was an important Viet Minh breeding ground during the First Indochina War. President Ngo Dinh Diem of South Vietnam had divided the country into four tactical corps areas in 1956; he designated the sixteen provinces of the delta as IV Corps. Diem instituted a land reform movement, focused primarily on the delta, but it generally failed, and the government did not produce a more extensive reform until the passege of the Land-to-the-Tiller Law of 1970. The Viet Cong (VC) exploited the need for land reform in the delta, but they exacted heavy taxes and required mandatory military service.

In 1965 the U.S. Navy and Coast Guard began sea and inland-water interdiction of enemy shipments in the delta, Operations Market Time and Game Warden. The U.S. 9th Infantry Division moved into the delta in 1967 and worked closely with the Navy's Mobile Riverine Force in the interdiction campaign. Although set back by the Tet* offensive of 1968, General Creighton Abrams'* Accelerated Pacification Campaign of 1969 and the Cambodian incursion of 1970–1971 refocused attention on pacification of the delta. Following completion of Vietnamization and the Paris Peace accords, President Nguyen Van Thieu initiated a new pacification offensive in the delta in an effort to roll

back communist gains from the 1972 Eastertide offensive. After the abandonment of the northern provinces in 1975, Saigon and the delta briefly became the
last bastion of the Republic of Vietnam.

References. Victor J. Croizat, *The Brown Water Navy*, 1984. Thomas J. Cutler, *Brown
Water, Black Berets*, 1988. William J. Duiker, *The Communist Road to Power in Vietnam*, 1981.

Claude Sasso

MERRILL'S MARAUDERS

The 5307th Composite Unit (Provisional), better known as Merrill's Marauders, was activated on 3 October 1943 in the China-Burma-India Theater* (CBI)
to be the U.S. component of Major General Orde Wingate's long-range penetration operations behind Japanese lines. Code named "Galahad," the unit of
combat-experienced volunteers trained in India for operations in the rugged
jungles of northern Burma. In February 1944, the theater commander, Lieutenant
General Joseph W. Stilwell,* ordered the Marauders to conduct a series of end
runs around the Japanese positions in northern Burma, cut off those positions,
and establish a series of isolated roadblocks while Stilwell's Chinese divisions
crushed the Japanese. In a series of epic marches through dense jungles and up
and down steep mountains, the Marauders outflanked unit after unit of the Japanese army at Walawbum, Shaduzup, and Nhpum Ga, culminating in an attack
on Myitkyina. Assisted by Detachment 101 of the Office of Strategic Services*
(OSS), the force captured the strategic airfield at Myitkyina on 17 May, only to
face renewed Japanese attacks from the city. The resulting siege produced hundreds of casualties from combat and tropical diseases. Brigadier General Frank
Merrill, after whom the unit was named, had to be evacuated after his second
heart attack. On 10 August 1944, the Marauders were disbanded, and the survivors merged with the 475th Infantry and 124th Cavalry regiments to form the
Mars Task Force. Mars continued to advance to the south as far as Lashio. The
475th Infantry was inactivated in July 1945 in China. The Marauders campaign
credits include the India-Burma and Central Burma campaigns. The lineage of
Merrill's Marauders is maintained today by the 75th Ranger Regiment.

References. *Merrill's Marauders*, 1987. Charlton Ogburn, Jr., *The Marauders*, 1959.

Joseph R. Fischer

MERRITT, WESLEY (1836–1910)

Born in New York City on 16 June 1836, Wesley Merritt entered the U.S.
Army after graduation from the U.S. Military Academy* on the eve of the Civil
War.* In less than five years, he had been breveted a major general of volunteers
and commanded a cavalry* division* in action. After the war, Merritt reverted
to a Regular Army rank of lieutenant colonel and continued to serve in the
cavalry. In 1887, he completed a tour as superintendant of the Military Academy
and assumed command of the Department of the Missouri, as a brigader general.
In 1895, he assumed command of the Department of the East. When the United

States declared war on Spain in 1898, President William McKinley named Merritt to lead the U.S. Army's expeditionary force to the Philippines. Collaborating with U.S. naval forces and Filipino rebels, Merritt executed a successful attack against the Spanish garrison in Manila, forcing its surrender in August 1898. He resumed command of the Department of the East until his retirement in June 1900. He died in December 1910.

References. Don E. Alberts, *Brandy Station to Manila Bay*, 1981. Graham A. Cosmas, *An Army for Empire*, 1971.

Stephen D. Coats

MESS GEAR

During the Civil War,* soldiers were issued tin-plated iron cups and plates, but the U.S. Army did not have a standard pattern for such items. Standard-issue mess equipment, such as utensils and combination plate-pan, were developed in the decade following the Civil War. In the latter part of the 19th century, a pan with a folding handle and a tight-fitting cover that doubled as a plate, with standard utensils stored inside the pan, made up the Army mess gear. The more familiar oval-shaped mess kit first appeared with the Model 1910 Infantry Equipment. Officially named the Meat Can, the plate and pan were constructed for the first time of aluminum. An aluminum canteen and nesting cup with a folding handle replaced the tin cup. In 1918, the meat can was deepened. Early in World War II* an improved mess kit was issued. The plate was deepened again and compartmented, forming two smaller but more practical receptacles for food. The accompanying utensils—knife, fork, and spoon—were modified by adding an oval hole in their handles. This allowed temporary attachment to the mess-kit handle for dipping in wash water after use in the field. While aluminum shortages in 1942 caused some mess kits to made of steel, most wartime mess kits were still made of aluminum. Beginning in late 1944, the Army began to purchase stainless steel mess gear. Although the Army still issues mess gear to troops, today it frequently serves field meals on disposable paper plates with plastic flatware.

References. Stephen J. Allie, *All He Could Carry*, 1991. Robert W. Fisch, *Field Equipment of the Infantry 1914–1945*, 1989.

Stephen C. McGeorge

MESS HALL

Originally derived from Old French *mes*, meaning a portion of food or a prepared dish, in later usage a "mess" was a group of persons, usually a professional body, that took their meals together. Militarily the term applied first to dining arrangements aboard naval vessels, where seamen, petty officers, and officers ate in separate areas. Until the 1970s, "mess hall" was the proper term in the U.S. Army for the building or designated room where personnel took meals. Over the past half-century, however, the terms "mess" and "mess hall" have assumed pejorative connotations due to what has become a more common sense of the term "mess"—a disorderly clutter or chaos. In an attempt to correct the impression of eating in a disorderly or chaotic environment, the Army modernized its food service and determined that *dining facility* should replace *mess hall* in official terminology.

References. Aubrey S. Newman, *Follow Me*, 1990. Christopher Gebhardt Trump, "The Old Army Mess," *Infantry*, January 1960, 17–19. C. M. Virtue, *Company Administration*, 1953.

Lee Kruger

METT-T

METT-T is an acronym for the factors that must be considered during the planning and execution of tactical operations: Mission, Enemy, Terrain, Troops, and Time Available. *Mission* defines the who, when, where, why, and what of must be accomplished. *Enemy* concerns the estimates of the enemy's strength, location, equipment, capability, and most importantly, probable course of action. *Terrain* measures the effect of vegetation, soil type, climatic conditions, and physical environment on operations for both enemy and friendly forces. *Troops* analyzes the quality, level of training, morale, and the availability of weapons and critical equipment. Finally, *time available* measures the time required against what is available to plan, prepare, and execute operations for both friendly and enemy forces. U.S. Army planners and commanders employ this analytical framework as they plan and weigh possible courses of action and then conduct combat operations.

References. Thomas V. Morley and Anthony J. Tata, "The Mechanized Infantry Team in the Offense," *Infantry*, May–June 1990, 16–19. John R. Sutherland III, "The Platoon Team," *Infantry*, July–August 1994, 9–12.

Thomas Christianson

MEUSE-ARGONNE

From 26 September to 11 November 1918, the U.S. First Army,* commanded by General John J. Pershing,* conducted the most important U.S. campaign of World War I.* Conceived on 2 September amidst preparation for the St. Mihiel* attack, the Meuse-Argonne battle began just two weeks after St. Mihiel. The initial attack between the Meuse River and the Argonne Forest was delivered by three U.S. corps*—I, II, and V—composed of nine divisions.* After four days of intense battle, a halt was called to replace worn and disorganized units. From 4 to 11 October, a second attack, including the French XVI Corps' attack to clear the heights east of the Meuse. On 8 October, it pushed to the main enemy defenses, the Kriemhilde Stellung. After another short halt, fresh divisions penetrated this position by 16 October. By mid-October, both First Army and the enemy were exhausted. On 12 October, Pershing created the U.S. Second Army* and placed Major General Hunter Liggett* in command of First Army as of 16 October. For two weeks Liggett reorganized First Army in preparation for another attack. On 1 November he cracked through the German positions and began a pursuit of Germans withdrawing north of the Meuse near Sedan. On 4 November III Corps crossed the Meuse and attacked to the east, assisting the French XVII Corps clear the heights of the Meuse. First Army maintained constant pressure up to the hour of the armistice.

References. Paul F. Braim, *The Test of Battle*, 1987. Rexmond C. Cochrane, *The 1st Division in the Meuse-Argonne 1–12 October 1918*, 1957. Edward M. Coffman, *The War to End All Wars*, 1986.

Robert Ramsey

MEXICAN WAR

The war between the United States and the Republic of Mexico was the result of the continued westward expansion by American citizens pushing into the vast but sparsely settled territories of Mexico north of the Rio Grande–Gila River line (modern-day Texas, New Mexico, Arizona, and California). Pursuing an expansionist policy popularized by the phrase "Manifest Destiny," Washington politicians actively encouraged the growing westward movement of its citizens, hoping to follow the occupation with the incorporation of Mexican territory into the United States, either through negotiation or direct purchase from the Mexican government. Relations between the United States and Mexico deteriorated when Anglo-American settlers created an independent Republic of Texas in 1836— although the Mexicans refused to recognize Texas as anything other than a province of Mexico—and when the Americans elected the expansionist James K. Polk president in 1844. When the U.S. Congress voted to annex Texas in 1845, the two countries broke diplomatic relations, an action welcomed and approved by the government and people of Texas. By 13 May 1846, when President Polk signed the official declaration of war, U.S. and Mexican forces had already fought several battles along the Rio Grande.

Anticipating the imminent outbreak of hostilities, in the summer of 1845 Polk ordered brevet Brigadier General Zachary Taylor* and 1,500 soldiers to move to the Rio Grande. For several months, Taylor worked to build up his forces and establish a base of operations from which to support future action against the Mexican army. In April 1846, a Mexican force destroyed a small detachment of U.S. dragoons, prompting Taylor to strengthen his supply base and call for reinforcements. The first major engagement of the war occured on 8 May at Palo Alto. Although outnumbered two to one, Taylor used the devastating fire of his flying batteries* to defeat a force under General Mariano Arista. A few days later, at a dry riverbed called Resaca de la Palma, Taylor again defeated a Mexican force, this time by winning a series of sharp, confusing infantry actions in tangled underbrush and chaparral, where artillery could not effectively operate.

Subsequent to the declaration of war, President Polk and the general-in-chief, Winfield Scott,* devised a strategy employing three separate forces directed against the Mexican state. Breveted major general and given command of forces in Mexico, Taylor was to advance towards Monterrey* while a second column under Brigadier General John E. Wool, starting from the vicinity of San Antonio, would move to Chihuahua via Parras (later Wool diverted to join Taylor at Saltillo). The third force, under Colonel Stephen Watts Kearny, was to advance westward along the Santa Fe trail from Fort Leavenworth* to Spanish California. Part of Kearny's column, commanded by Colonel Alexander W. Doniphan,* was sent south to converge near Wood's and Taylor's forces via Chihauhau and Parras. Meanwhile, Scott gathered a force in the United States to conduct an amphibious landing at Vera Cruz,* from whence he planned to attack Mexico City.*

Despite supply difficulties and an acute shortage of wagon transport, Taylor's force established a base at Camargo in preparation for a movement on Monterrey. By the end of August 1846, Taylor had collected about 15,000 men, both Regulars and volunteers, from several states. The unhealthy Mexican climate, however, quickly produced sickness and disease that halved the number of men fit for field service. In mid-September less than 7,000 U.S. troops moved toward Monterrey, a principal Mexican garrison town of stone buildings and adobe huts protected by a citadel and several forts. The ensuing battle of Monterrey began on 19 September, when Taylor's troops arrived to confront a Mexican garrison of roughly the same size. Sending a strong detachment, led by a mounted unit of Texas Rangers, to seal off the enemy's main supply route* from Saltillo, Taylor attacked the city with infantry and artillery. The resulting house-to-house fighting ended on 24 September after U.S. artillery decimated a concentration of Mexican troops forming on the city's central plaza. Taylor accepted Monterrey's surrender but unwisely agreed to an eight-week armistice proposed by the retiring Mexican commander. When President Polk learned of the armistice he ordered Taylor to repudiate it, but by that time the damage had been done. The Mexicans had used the time to reconstitute their forces, gather reinforcements, and, under Antonio Lopez de Santa Anna, prepare to strike back.

After occupying the important road junction at the town of Saltillo, Taylor (now joined by Wool's column arriving from San Antonio) planned to establish a strong defensive line from Parras, through Saltillo and Monterrey, to Victoria. Polk, however, ordered Taylor to detach nearly half of his force to join in Scott's impending landings at Vera Cruz, evacuate Saltillo, and withdraw to Monterrey, where he was to conduct only defensive operations. Suspecting that these orders were merely a result of political maneuvering, Taylor refused to withdraw from his forward positions, even advancing farther in the direction of the approaching Mexican army. Santa Anna, at the head of 15,000 troops, moved toward Taylor's 4,000 men on 21 February 1847. The two armies clashed the next day about three miles south of Saltillo at the small hacienda of Buena Vista,* fighting the toughest action of the war. The terrain near the tiny ranch was characterized by steep gullies, deep ravines, and broken plateaus, it was covered with scrub and chaparral. Fingers of high ground led into the area from both flanks. Beginning with a Mexican artillery bombardment in the late afternoon of 22 February, the armies spent the remainder of the day parrying each other's maneuvers. The battle continued on the 23d, with each side gaining tactical advantages throughout the day. Several times the Mexicans broke the American positions but were thrown back by the timely arrival of fresh or repositioned troops and, especially, by devastating fire from one or more of the excellent U.S. field batteries. Major Braxton Bragg and his artillery battery, Colonel Jefferson Davis's* regiment* of Mississippi Rifles, and Taylor himself, a cool and fearless example under fire, helped maintain U.S. morale under the intense Mexican assaults. That evening, Santa Anna gave up the field and withdrew. Taylor had won the decisive battle in the north. The locus of action then shifted to Scott's campaign for Mexico City.

Scott's focus on the enemy's capital resembled numerous 18th-century European campaigns. His amphibious landing at Vera Cruz and subsequent capture of Mexico City not only was an outstanding example of tactical mobility and maneuver but ended the war. Scott's army of 13,000 Regulars and volunteers landed unopposed south of Vera Cruz on 9 March 1847, quickly investing the city with the help of a strong naval blockade. A heavy bombardment of Vera Cruz (aided significantly by naval guns borrowed from the fleet) forced the Mexican defenders to capitulate on 29 March. Scott moved inland on the nearly 300-mile journey to the enemy's capital on 8 April. Santa Anna, with 12,000 troops, prepared to oppose the U.S. advance at the rocky defile near Cerro Gordo along the national highway to Mexico City. Although Santa Anna's forces held a strong position, Scott discovered an alternate route around the Mexicans, thus avoiding battle. In this and other actions on the advance to Mexico City, Scott and his subordinate commanders consistently used their West Point–trained engineers (in this case, Captain Robert E. Lee*) to conduct reconnaissance of the unknown terrain and the Mexican positions. Scott moved the bulk of his forces to the flank and rear of Santa Anna's positions, and they were successful when they assaulted the next day, 18 April. Santa Anna withdrew after losing decisively.

Despite having his force reduced to less than 6,000 men by disease, sickness, and expiring enlistments of volunteers, Scott managed to continue to push inexorably toward Mexico City, occupying Puebla in May. Remaining there until reinforcements arrived from Vera Cruz, Scott moved out with 10,000 men on 7 August for the final push on the capital. Once again, excellent reconnaissance permitted Scott to take the Mexican positions at Contreras from the rear. On 20 August, he moved to assault the fortified bridges at Churubusco. The ensuing U.S. victory was costly (about 1,000 U.S. casualties), but Santa Anna lost a third of his remaining forces. On 7 September, after a two-week armistice cleverly arranged by the Mexican commander to rebuild his forces, Scott's final assault on Mexico City commenced. The U.S. forces defeated the Mexican defenders at Molino del Rey the following day, then stormed the castle of Chapultepec on 13 September. The next day the city surrendered. The Treaty of

Guadalupe Hidalgo, signed on 2 February 1848 and ratified by the U.S. Senate on 10 March, brought the Mexican War to an end, but the last U.S. troops did not march out of Mexico City until 12 June.

References. K. Jack Bauer, *The Mexican War, 1846–1848*, 1974. John S. D. Eisenhower, *So Far from God*, 1989.

Jerry D. Morelock

MEXICO CITY

The operational plan for the capture of Mexico City during the Mexican War* was the work of Winfield Scott,* commanding general of the U.S. Army and functioning as a one-man general staff. Despite the absence of maps, Scott landed south of the fortress city of Vera Cruz* on 9 March 1847. After a successful siege, he began a 260-mile westward advance, defeating General Santa Anna at Cerro Gordo, passing over the Sierra Madre mountains, and spending several months in the city of Pueblo awaiting reinforcements. Continuing his advance in August with only 10,738 troops, he approached the Mexican capital, defended by 30,000 soldiers. Scott bypassed a blocking position east of the city and swung south of Lake Chaico, where a staff engineer, Captain Robert E. Lee, found a path across the Pedregal, a fifteen-mile-wide lava bed. Crossing at night, Scott's troops seized the Mexican position at Contreras and fought their way across the Rio Churubusco despite determined resistance. Fearing he might create a spirit of national desperation, Scott agreed to an armistice. But after two weeks of negotiations, he resumed his offensive, winning a costly victory on the heights of the Molino del Rey. Scott subsequently deceived Santa Anna into expecting the final assault on the southern city gates but instead delivered his main blow from the west, storming Chapultepec as his columns entered the city via the San Cosme and Belden Gates. Santa Anna's army withdrew that night, and Scott, with 6,000 effectives, occupied Mexico City on 14 September 1847. The Duke of Wellington later called Scott "the greatest living soldier."

References. K. Jack Bauer, *The Mexican War, 1846–1848*, 1974. John S. D. Eisenhower, *So Far from God*, 1989.

Claude Sasso

MILES, NELSON APPLETON (1839–1925)

Beginning his military career as a captain of volunteers at the outbreak of the Civil War,* Nelson Appleton Miles participated in every major engagement of the Army of the Potomac* except Gettysburg.* He was cited for gallantry at Fair Oaks (Seven Pines*), Fredericsburg,* and Chancellorsville*; for his actions at Chancellorsville he was awarded the Medal of Honor* in 1892. Following the war he was commandant of Fort Monroe,* Virginia, where he had custody, and was criticized for his treatment, of former Confederate President Jefferson Davis.* In 1869 Miles became commander of the 5th U.S. Infantry. His subsequent service against the Indians on the western frontier was largely successful and added to his already popular (if self-promoted) reputation. Most notable were his successes during the Red River War of 1874–1875, forcing Sitting Bull into Canada and pacifying the Sioux under Crazy Horse; the defeat of the Nez Percé and capture of Chief Joseph in 1877; the pacification of the Bannocks in 1878; and the final surrender of Geronimo in 1886. Less favorably received, however, was his ungracious attitude toward Major General O. O. Howard* during the Nez Percé campaign, his actions during the Wounded Knee massacre of 1890, the suppression of the Pullman strike in Chicago in 1894, his quarrels with admirals and cabinet members, and his criticism of U.S. foreign policy. On the retirement of Lieutenant General John M. Schofield* in 1895, Miles became the last general-in-chief of the Army—the position was subsequently redesignated Chief of Staff.* Miles retired in August 1903. He published his autobiography in two volumes, in 1896 and 1911.

References. Arthur J. Amchan, *The Most Famous Soldier in America*, 1989. Virginia W. Johnson, *The Unregimented General*, 1962. Robert Wooster, *Nelson A. Miles and the Twilight of the Frontier Army*, 1993.

Jeffrey Prater

MILITARY ASSISTANCE AND ADVISORY GROUP

"Military assistance and advisory group" (MAAG) is one of the many names for defense organizations created to manage the transfer of military equipment, training, and developmental and economic assistance to friendly and allied nations under a variety of programs. Also called offices of defense cooperation (ODCs), military groups (MILGPS), and military liaison offices (MLOs), these security assistance organizations (SAOs), located throughout the world, are the primary points of contact for all security assistance–management functions. The basic legislation for security assistance is the Foreign Assistance Act of 1961, as amended, and the Arms Export Control Act, an update of the Foreign Military Sales Act of 1961. The SAO works for the ambassador or senior State Department representative in a country, the commander of the regional unified command, and the director of the Defense Security Assistance Agency, a Defense Department organization, more or less concurrently. These offices administer seven major programs, including foreign military sales and financing programs, direct commercial sales, and direct training (international military education and training).

References. Leonard D. Chafin, "Assignment MAAG," *Infantry*, January–February 1962, 52–53. Samuel T. Williams, "The Practical Demands of MAAG," *Military Review*, July 1961, 2–14.

J.G.D. Babb

MILITARY ASSISTANCE COMMAND, VIETNAM

In his State of the Union Message of 11 January 1962, President John F. Kennedy declared that the aggression bleeding South Vietnam was a "war of attempted subjugation." His determination to halt it was reflected in the upgrading of the Military Assistance and Advisory Group* (MAAG) in Saigon to a four-star joint command, the Military Assistance Command, Vietnam (MACV), in February 1962. As its first commander, General Paul D. Harkins had responsibility for equipping, training, and advising the South Vietnamese in an increased effort to defeat the Viet Cong. Harkins was recalled because of his firm opposition to the coup d'état against President Ngo Dinh Diem; he was replaced in June 1964 by General William C. Westmoreland.*

With Westmoreland's encouragement, the Johnson administration "Americanized" the war, deploying 540,000 troops to Vietnam. The Tet* offensive of 1968 produced a fundamental change in U.S. strategic direction; General Creighton W. Abrams* replaced Westmoreland and presided over MACV during the difficult period of Vietnamization and withdrawal. General Frederick C. Weyand succeeded Abrams in June 1972 and tried in vain to get supplemental aid from Congress for South Vietnam prior to its fall in 1975.

References. Jeffrey J. Clarke, *Advice and Support*, 1988. William C. Westmoreland, *A Soldier Reports*, 1976.

Claude Sasso

MILITARY ASSISTANCE COMMAND, VIETNAM-STUDIES AND OBSERVATIONS GROUP

Military Assistance Command, Vietnam-Studies and Observations Group (MACV-SOG) was a Joint Unconventional Warfare Task Force formed in January 1964 to conduct special operations throughout the entire Southeast Asia region. Using U.S. and South Vietnamese personnel, special operations teams conducted covert missions behind enemy lines. Missions included cross-border reconnaissance and interdiction; coastal raiding and infiltration; recovery of isolated, evading, or escaped U.S. personnel; support of guerrilla warfare; deception operations; and intelligence collection. Each special operations group (SOG) program was carefully compartmented from the other; personnel were assigned to cover units, such as the 5th Special Forces Group (Airborne) in South Vietnam or the 46th Special Forces Company (Airborne) in Thailand, while serving with SOG. Special Forces* personnel dominated the MACV-SOG structure, but personnel were also drawn from U.S. Navy Seal units, U.S. Air Force units, and indigenous forces. SOG conducted some of the most dangerous, and costly, deep-penetration missions of the Vietnam War.* Some units lost as much as 80 percent of their strength.

References. John L. Plaster, *SOG*, 1997. John K. Singlaub, *Hazardous Duty*, 1991. Shelby L. Stanton, *Green Berets at War*, 1985.

Richard Stewart

MILITARY COLLEGE OF SOUTH CAROLINA. *See* Citadel.

MILITARY HISTORY DETACHMENT

The Military History Detachment (MHD) is a self-contained, armed, fully mobile unit that collects, records, and documents military events for later historical analysis. MHD functions are carried out at any level from theater down to separate brigade.* The composition of the MHD is as follows:

Personnel	Equipment	Mission
Major—Military Historian	camera, tape recorder, M9 pistol	unit commander
Sergeant First Class—Photo Journalist	camera, video recorder, tape recorder, M-16 rifle*	NCOIC and photographic support
Sergeant—Executive Admin. Asst.	laptop computer, M-16 rifle and vehicle	admin. support, driver

The MHD is the only tactical military history unit designed to function in a combat environment.

References. James H. Ferguson, " 'Where the Action Is,' " *Army Digest*, August 1969, 56–58. John E. Jessup, Jr., and Robert W. Coakley, *A Guide to the Study and Use of Military History*, 1979, 1988.

Chris Clark

MILITARY HISTORY INSTITUTE

In 1967, the U.S. Army Military History Research Collection was established at the Army War College* to collect, preserve, and make available to military and civilian scholars documents, personal and official papers, and other sources, on the history of the U.S. Army. Redesignated the U.S. Army Military History Institute (MHI) in 1977, its scope has broadened to include sources relating to the U.S. Navy, the U.S. Air Force, the Army Reserve* and National Guard,* domestic and foreign conflicts, and the evolution of warfare and the military art. Located at Carlisle Barracks,* MHI is a complex of library and reference facilities, archives, and special collections, including 350,000 bound volumes. It is staffed by professional archivists, curators, and research specialists who maintain the collection; publish research aids, respond to public inquiries through interlibrary loan, copying services, and institute publications; and provide on-site research assistance to military and civilian scholars. MHI continues to acquire official sources, accept donations of private papers, diaries, and letters, and publish material of historical value to the U.S. Army.

References. Lawrence P. Crocker, *Army Officer's Guide*, 46th ed., 1993. John E. Jessup and Robert W. Coakley, *A Guide to the Study and Use of Military History*, 1979, 1988.

MILITARY INTELLIGENCE

Military Intelligence (MI) is the branch of the U.S. Army responsible for collecting, organizing, analyzing, and disseminating information about enemy forces. MI operations include human intelligence (HUMINT), signals intelligence (SIGINT), imagery intelligence (IMINT), counterintelligence (CI), and security of all types of sensitive information. MI traces its roots to the extended spy network and the Continental Light Dragoons who served as George Washington's* eyes and ears during the American Revolution.* Throughout most of the Army's early history, the cavalry* and topographic engineers carried out most intelligence functions. During the Civil War,* the Army hired civilian intelligence specialists, but technological developments forced both Union and Confederate armies to incorporate codes, ciphers, and countermeasures into their daily activities.

In 1885, after several decades without a permanent intelligence structure, the Army created a military information division under the Adjutant General* to keep track of world military developments. In 1889 the military attaché system was added to the division. Based on its success in the Spanish-American War,* military information became one of three permanent divisions of the new General Staff* in 1903. The division tested new technology, especially aerial photography and radio intercepts, that proved of considerable value during the Punitive Expedition* of 1916. In that year, however, the division merged with, and then was subordinated to, the U.S. Army war College,* virtually abolishing an organization that had rendered such notable service.

As U.S. entrance into World War I* approached, many Army leaders believed that the United States could get sufficient intelligence from the British and French. However, Colonel Ralph Van Dame (now known as the father of MI), disagreed and successfully pushed for a complete reorganization of the military intelligence structure. The revitalized Military Intelligence Division (MID) grew from two officers and two clerks in 1917 to 282 officers, 250 enlisted men, and over 1,100 civilians by November 1918. In addition to traditional intelligence, MID assumed a counterintelligence role as well.

In the interwar years, Army intelligence all but disappeared again. One of the few remnants, a code and ciphers section known as MI-8, existed until 1929, when the secretary of state disbanded it because "gentlemen do not read other gentlemen's mail." During World War II,* the Army created several agencies to carry out the critical intelligence missions, including the Military Intelligence Service, the Counter Intelligence Corps, and the Signal Intelligence Service. In World War II, the intelligence agencies broke the Japanese "Magic" code and the German command cipher Ultra, feats of inestimable value to the Allied victories. In 1962, the Army established the Intelligence and Security Branch, consolidating the increasing number of officers in intelligence fields. In July 1967, the Intelligence and Security Branch was formally redesignated the Military Intelligence Branch. Today, the U.S. Army Intelligence School and Training Center is located at Fort Hauchuca,* Arizona, the home of military intelligence.

References. Bruce W. Bidwell, *History of the Military Intelligence Division*, 1986. John Patrick Finnegan, *Military Intelligence*, 1998. Ralph H. Van Deman, *The Final Memoranda*, ed. Ralph E. Weber, 1988.

S. A. Underwood

MILITARY OCCUPATIONAL SPECIALTY

"Military occupational specialty" (MOS) designates a U.S. Army enlisted person's military occupation, including a job description at various skill levels, and establishes expectations of job performance. An MOS is an important tool for the initial selection and management of a soldier's training and career progression. MOS codes are five-digit number-letter sequences: the first two numbers indicate branch (11 for infantry,* 13 for artillery,* etc.); the third digit refers to specialty (for example, 13B is cannoneer, 13D is rocketeer, 13F is forward observer); and the final two numbers indicate skill level. Thus, a light-weapons infantry private is designated 11B10, while an infantry sergeant first class is an 11B40. Currently, the U.S. Army has approximately 317 MOSs in 33 career-management fields, of which 242 are considered entry-level MOSs.

References. Stephen J. Kirin and John D. Winkler, *The Army Military Occupational Specialty Database*, 1992. Donna Miles, "New Army, New MOSs," *Soldiers*, June 1993, 46–48. Harold Wool, *The Military Specialist*, 1968.

Jeffrey S. Shadburn

MILITARY OPERATIONS OTHER THAN WAR. *See* Operations Other Than War.

MILITARY POLICE CORPS

The Military Police (MP) heritage can be traced back to George Washington* and the Continental Army.* In 1776, a provost marshal* was appointed to deal with deserters, drunkards, and marauders who interfered with the army's mission, similar to the duties of the local sheriff during the time of William the Conqueror. Abolished at the end of the American Revolution,* the office was reestablished during the Civil War,* and the incumbent was given the title Provost Marshal General of the United States. In addition to the duties of his predecessor, the Provost Marshal was now charged with enforcing the draft laws, protecting railway depots, escorting POWs, and policing garrisons. The office was again abolished at the end of the Civil War. On 26 September 1941, the secretary of war* created the Military Police Corps, universally known as the MPs, with all of its previous missions plus several additional duties—for example, protecting supplies on the beaches and controlling traffic behind the lines. During the Korean War,* MPs assumed the responsibility for the refugee problem, and in Vietnam they provided security for the U.S. Embassy in Saigon.

Today's MP is a soldier and a lawman. He directs operations behind the lines, fights the deep battle when necessary, and works with civilian authorities during natural disasters and civil disturbances. The Military Police Corps Headquarters and School is located at Fort McClellan,* Alabama. The symbol of the Military Police Corps is two crossed Harpers Ferry pistols.

References. [Kathy Roe Coker], *The Military Police Corps at Fort Gordon, 1948–1975*, [1991]. Robert K. Wright, Jr., comp., *Military Police*, 1992.

Trevor Brown

MILITARY REVIEW

Military Review is a professional journal published by the U.S. Army Command and General Staff College* at Fort Leavenworth,* Kansas. Initially a small in-house publication, the *Instructors' Summary of Military Articles* appeared in 1922 to inform the faculty and students at the General Services School on the latest books and articles on military issues. The journal experienced several title changes, including *Review of Current Military Writings* in 1925, *Review of Current Military Literature* in 1931, *Quarterly Review of Military Literature* in 1932, and *Review of Military Literature* in 1933, before it became known as *Military Review* in September 1939. Published quarterly since September 1922, *Military Review* commenced monthly publication in April 1943. In 1945, at the request of a number of Latin American governments, *Military Review* began publishing simultaneous editions in Portugese and Spanish.

The first original article appeared in the *Review of Military Literature* in December 1933. Since then the journal has served as a forum for debate, discussion, and dissemination of ideas, theories, and proposals affecting the future of the U.S. Army, as well as reviews of articles and books of interest to the military professional. Budget constraints and downsizing in the U.S. Army forced *Military Review* to reduce publication first to bimonthly status, then to quarterly issues.

References. Jerold E. Brown, "Military Review," *Military Review*, November–December 1996, 59–66. Michael E. Unsworth, ed., *Military Periodicals*, 1990.

MILITIA ACT OF 1792

At the time of the American Revolution,* the thirteen English colonies in North America required all able-bodied white males to serve in the militia. Article I, section 8, of the new Constitution, ratified in 1789, established a new dual control between the federal and state governments over the militia. On 2 May 1792, Congress enacted legislation to enforce this constitutional requirement. "An Act to provide for calling forth the Militia to execute the laws of the Union, suppress insurrection and repel invasions," referred to as the Militia Act of 1792 (also called the Uniform Militia Act) provided that every free white male between the ages of eighteen and forty-five be enrolled in the state militia; it authorized the president to call forth the militia in specific circumstances. In the case of domestic unrest, the president would apply to the legislature of the state involved or, if the legislature was not in session, directly to the governor. The Act also permitted the president to call on militia from another state if forces within a state refused to suppress an insurrection. State militia were also permitted to serve alongside the Regular Army; the Act in that case subjected the militia to the same discipline under the Articles of War* and allotted it the same pay when serving with the Regular Army. Individuals who failed to obey orders to arms were subject to trial by court-martial and could suffer fines and imprisonment. Generally, the provisions of the Militia Act of 1792 went unimplemented throughout the 19th century. The Act did, however, remain in effect until passage of the Dick Act of 1903 created the modern National Guard.*

References. Richard H. Kohn, *Eagle and Sword*, 1975. John K. Mahon, *The American Militia*, 1960.

Michael G. Knapp

MINES

Mines are the weapons that wait—seemingly forever. During the Civil War,* buried mines were called "land torpedoes" and were normally fitted with sensitive percussion fuzes. Since the arrival of the tank in World War I,* the development of new and more powerful antitank and antipersonnel mines has been a top priority of all military forces. Today, there are an estimated eighty-five million land mines scattered around the world, and 150–200 people are killed or injured by old mines each week. Cambodia appears to be the most heavily mined, with 15–23 million mines; in the Mideast, 17–24 million mines are scattered in Iran, Iraq, and Kuwait. Recent public reports estimate worldwide mine production at ten million, or almost 30,000 per day. Advanced mines with self-destruct mechanisms may pose less of a hazard to civilians in future conflicts, but the race continues to make the next battlefield nearly impassable. Although a legitimate part of warfare when properly used, mines remain cheap, effective, and indiscriminate weapons.

References. Paul Davies, *War of the Mines*, 1994. K.J.W. Goad and D.H.J. Halsey, *Ammunition*, 1982. Stockholm International Peace Research Institute, *Anti-Personnel Weapons*, 1978.

John R. Finch

MINIÉ BALL

The Minié ball was developed by Claude-Etienne Minié, a French army officer, in 1849. It was adopted as the standard round in the U.S. Army in 1855. The Minié ball, as it is commonly called, is a cylindro-canodial lead round that made muzzle-loading rifles practical on the battlefield. Previous to its development, a rifleman had to load a patched-ball into his piece by pounding it in, to engage the grooves of the rifling. This process slowed the rate of fire to one round per minute, as compared to the three rounds per minute for the infantryman armed with a smooth-bore musket.* The Minié ball, which fits easily between the lands of the rifling, has a hollow base that expands into the grooves upon ignition. With this round, a soldier could fire three rounds per minute and increase his range to over 500 yards, in comparison with the 100-yard range of the smooth-bore musket. In response to the greater range capability of the infantry, William J. Hardee developed a new system of tactics.* He modified the earlier manual of arms, speeding up the soldier's movements, thus reducing the effect of range. However, the Civil War* soldier armed with the rifled musket firing the Minié ball was simply too effective to be neutralized by faster maneuver.

References. Jack Coggins, *Arms and Equipment of the Civil War*, 1962, 1990. William B. Edwards, *Civil War Guns*, 1962.

Steven J. Allie

MISSING IN ACTION

The term "missing in action" (MIA) is used in U.S. Army casualty reports to designate the status of soldiers whose whereabouts is unknown following contact or action with the enemy. "MIA" is intended to be a temporary status until an individual's actual status is determined. Most soldiers reported MIA will eventually be reclassified as killed in action (KIA), wounded in action (WIA), or prisoners of war* (POW); some will eventually return to duty; and a few may be reported as deserters. At the conclusion of every American war, a significant number of men were still listed as MIA. Typically, based on the presumption that all prisoners of war would be repatriated, the status of those not returned or accounted for, with few exceptions, has been changed to killed in action— no body recovered (KIA-NBR).

Following the end of the Vietnam War,* however, the fate of men initially reported as MIA and not subsequently returned in the exchange of prisoners following the Paris Peace Accord or whose remains have not been positively identified has become a national political issue. Amid rumors that some U.S. military personnel may have been detained in Southeast Asia after 1972 and suspicions that the U.S. government was not doing everything possible to account for these men, a small but highly vocal interest group, composed primarily of family members of a few men still listed as MIA, has kept the issue before the public. Today, missing in action is not only an official casualty reporting status but is closely identified with that current political cause; MIA has become synonymous with military personnel of the Vietnam War whose whereabouts and fates remain unknown.

References. Douglas L. Clarke, *The Missing Man*, 1979. Larry J. O'Daniel, *Missing in Action*, 1979.

MISSISSIPPI RIFLE

The U.S. Army adopted the Model 1841 rifle for use by flank or rifle companies attached to the line infantry.* It fired a .54-caliber round ball with an accurate range of over 300 yards. The rifle was popularized when it became the primary weapon of the First Mississippi regiment, commanded by Jefferson Davis,* during the Mexican War.* It was also the primary weapon of the mounted riflemen from 1846 through the late 1850s. In 1855 the weapon was rebored to accept the standard .58-caliber Minié ball,* and a lug was attached so that it could accept a bayonet.* The Mississippi rifle was used in this configuration throughout the Civil War.*

References. Arcadi Gluckman, *Identifying Old U.S. Muskets Rifles & Carbines*, 1959, 1965. James E. Hicks, *U.S. Military Firearms 1776–1956*, 1962.

Steven J. Allie

MITCHELL, WILLIAM "BILLY" (1879–1936)

William "Billy" Mitchell was the U.S. Army's first truly vocal supporter of airpower and its role on the modern battlefield. Entering the infantry* as a private in 1898, Mitchell served in both the Philippines and Cuba before being assigned to the aerial section of the Signal Corps* in 1915, as a captain. The following year, Mitchell learned to fly and was sent to France as an observer. When the United States entered World War I,* Mitchell was named air officer of the American Expeditionary Force* (AEF) and promoted to lieutenant colonel; in May 1918, Colonel Mitchell became I Corps air officer and was the first U.S. officer to fly over German lines. In September, he led a massed raid of 1,500 aircraft against the St. Mihiel* salient, and he led other raids against German rear areas during the Meuse-Argonne* offensive.

After the war, Mitchell aggressively called for the creation of a separate air arm and openly claimed that airplanes had made the battleship obsolete. Mitchell demonstrated the potential use of airplanes against battleships by sinking several captured German and old U.S. battleships in 1921 and 1923. Mitchell's subsequent charges of "criminal negligence" against the War Department* and the Navy following the crash of the dirigible *Shenandoah* in 1925 precipitated his court-martial and conviction for insubordination. He retired from service in 1926 but tirelessly continued to promote airpower until his death in 1936.

References. Burke Davis, *The Billy Mitchell Affair*, 1967. Alfred F. Hurley, *Billy Mitchell*, 1975.

Benjamin H. Kristy

MODIFIED TABLE OF ORGANIZATION AND EQUIPMENT. *See* Table of Organization and Equipment.

MONMOUTH

The 1778 alliance between France and the rebellious colonists prompted a British withdrawal from Philadelphia to New York. Evacuating Philadelphia in late June, Major General Henry Clinton marched his 8,000 British and Hessian troops and their baggage across central New Jersey. Although his officers expressed mixed opinions, George Washington,* seeking to strike Clinton's rear guard, sent about one third of his 12,000 men under Major General Charles Lee to intercept this force, while the main body closed. Initially opposing the plan, Lee vacillated before accepting command. On the morning of 28 June 1778, Lee's force engaged the British near Freehold, New Jersey, but Clinton had anticipated such an attack and wheeled his main force against Lee. In the developing confusion, Lee faltered and, when a few units fell back, ordered full retreat. Riding to the sound of the guns, Washington chastised Lee and deployed several regiments* to delay the enemy advance while he established a defensive line. Throughout the sultry afternoon, Baron Friedrich von Steuben's* drill and training at Valley Forge* paid off, for the Continentals* withstood artillery fire and repulsed several assaults. Washington attempted to outflank his opponent, but night fell before his forces were in position. Both sides declared a victory, each conservatively reporting some 350 casualties. Washington's army remained in control of the battlefield as the British withdrew that evening, but Clinton had stopped Washington's pursuit. This, the battle of Monmouth, was the last major battle in the northern theater; it demonstrated that the Continental line could meet the British on equal terms.

References. Michael D. Carter, "From Parade Ground to the Battlefield," *Field Artillery*, July–August 1998, 12–16. Samuel S. Smith, *The Battle of Monmouth*, 1964. William S. Stryker, *The Battle of Monmouth*, 1927.

Stanley Adamiak

MONTERREY

Late in August 1846, Major General Zachary Taylor* left his assembly area at Camargo on the Rio Grande with more than 6,000 troops for Saltillo, an important junction on the road south to Mexico City.* Monterrey (also Monterey), capital of Neuvo Leon and a principal garrison town of stone buildings and adobe huts protected by a citadel, known as the Black Fort, and several smaller forts, lay on Taylor's route of march. Before his force arrived at Monterrey, however, Mexican units occupied the town and began building additional fortifications. Not expecting a fight at Monterrey, Taylor had not brought siege guns, but he now faced a garrison roughly the same size as his own and he had to deal with it before proceeding.

The first contact between U.S. and Mexican troops came on 19 September, three miles north of Monterrey. The next day, Taylor sent a strong detachment of mounted Texas Rangers to seal off the main supply route from Saltillo and conducted a demonstration; he attacked the city with infantry and artillery on the 21st. A series of frontal assaults and maneuvers finally broke down the outer defenses, opening the way for Taylor's men to enter the town. U.S. artillery blasted the final concentration of Mexican troops, forming on the city's central plaza; house-to-house fighting ended on 24 September, when delegations from each side met to discuss terms of surrender. Taylor demanded the surrender of the garrison but accepted the evacuation of Monterrey and agreed to an eight-week armistice proposed by General Pedro de Ampudia, the Mexican commander. Many of Taylor's troops felt betrayed, and when President James Polk learned of the armistice he ordered Taylor to repudiate it, but by that time the damage had been done. The Mexican army, under Antonio Lopez de Santa Anna, had used the time to gather reinforcements and was prepared to strike back.

References. John S. D. Eisenhower, *So Far from God*, 1989. David Lavender, *Climax at Buena Vista*, 1966.

MONTGOMERY, RICHARD (1736–1775)

Richard Montgomery emerged as a talented leader in the American Revolution's* opening months. Born in Swoards, County Dublin, Ireland, the son of a member of Parliament, Montgomery attended St. Andrews and Trinity College, Dublin, before gaining a British army commission in 1756. A veteran of Louisbourg (1758), the Champlain Valley (1759), and the West Indies, Montgomery resigned as a captain in 1772 and moved to New York, where he married into the influential Livingston family and became a gentleman farmer. When the Revolution began, the politically active Montgomery reluctantly accepted a commission in the Continental Army,* serving as Major General Philip Schuyler's second in command for an invasion of Canada via Lake Champlain. When Schuyler fell ill, Montgomery pushed his ragged force through a string of victories over British posts, culminating with the capture of Montreal in November 1775. Montgomery and his 300 men then joined Colonel Benedict Arnold,* with 600 survivors of an overland trek through the Maine wilderness, in the siege of Quebec, the last British stronghold. Outnumbered, ill supplied, and facing expiring enlistments, the two commanders launched a two-pronged assault the night of 30 December, using a blizzard to achieve near-complete surprise. The attack failed when cannon fire killed Montgomery as he led a charge against a blockhouse and Arnold fell wounded. The British recovered and drove the Continentals from the city. British troops recognized Montgomery's body and buried it with full honors. At home, Montgomery became a hero and martyr.

References. Robert M. Hatch, *Thrust for Canada*, 1979. Hal T. Shelton, *General Richard Montgomery and the American Revolution*, 1994. A. L. Todd, *Richard Montgomery*, 1966.

Stanley Adamiak

MORNING REPORT

The term "morning report" can be traced to the 1890s, when Army Regulations provided that every company-sized unit maintain a "morning report book." The morning report became an official document regarding the status of every soldier assigned to the unit: arrivals, departures, promotions, detachments, leaves and other absences—both authorized and unauthorized—and casualties and losses. The company clerk's* first duty each morning was to publish the morning report and forward a copy to regiment* or battalion* headquarters. The information would then be compiled in a daily unit-strength report and passed to yet higher headquarters. DA Form 1, Morning Report, was one of the first standardized forms issued by the new Department of the Army,* and it became one of the most commonly used forms in U.S. Army history. DA Form 1 was declared obsolete in October 1978. Today, the information previously published in the morning report is electronically generated and maintained by the Standard Installation or Division Personnel System (SIDPERS).

References. Ches Schneider, *From Classrooms to Claymores*, 1999. C. M. Virtue, *Company Administration*, 1953.

MORRISON, JOHN F. (1857–1932)

Born in Charlottesville, New York, on 20 December 1857, John F. Morrison graduated from the U.S. Military Academy* in 1881. Commissioned in the infantry,* he served with the 20th Infantry and attended the Infantry and Cavalry School of Application* at Fort Leavenworth* before going to Kansas State Agricultural College as professor of military strategy and tactics in 1887. Returning to Fort Leavenworth, he served as an instructor until April 1898, when he was recalled to the 20th Infantry for the Spanish-American War.* Regarded as a "master of military tactics," Morrison returned to Leavenworth again in 1906, where he was instrumental in revamping the curriculum of the Staff College and the School of the Line. Graduates of these schools proudly labeled themselves "Morrison Men." Many of them, including George C. Marshall,* Hugh Drum, Stuart Heintzelmen, Harold B. Fiske, and James McAndrew, served in key positions in the American Expeditionary Force* (AEF) during World War I* and became leaders in the U.S. Army between the world wars. Morrison deployed to France in 1917 and assumed command of the 8th Division in March 1918. On 20 December 1921, John Morrison retired after forty years of service. His influence on the training of U.S. Army officers at Leavenworth had set the stage for victories long after he had passed from the scene.

References. Timothy K. Nenninger, *The Leavenworth Schools and the Old Army*, 1978. David Syrett, "The John F. Morrison Professor of Military History," *Military Review*, May 1983, 13–22.

Steven E. Clay

MORTAIN

After weeks of containment, the Allies erupted from the Normandy beachhead on 3 July 1944, turning a static military situation into a fluid war of maneuver. Needing time to plan and establish new defenses and to complete the production of new weapons systems, Hitler ordered Field Marshal Guenther von Kluge to prevent the Allies from quickly moving to the Seine, to hold firm along his front, and to prepare an offensive striking west to Avranches and reestablishing the German left flank on the Contentin coast. Kluge plundered the armor reserves along the entire Normandy front to assemble four panzer divisions, three to attack abreast through Mortain toward Avranches, and the fourth to pass though them and continue the attack to Avranches. Kluge scheduled the attack for the early morning of 7 August.

Mortain, a small French village of 1,600, is situated in wooded highlands of Manche Department. The U.S. 2d Battalion, 120th Infantry (2/120), 30th Infantry Division (ID), had moved onto the key terrain feature in the area, Hill 317, just east of Mortain, four hours before the German attack. Despite early confusion and repeated German assaults, the 2/120 employed supporting artillery fire and close air support* to hold Hill 317 throughout the day. Unable to sustain his attack, Kluge withdrew his now-exposed panzer division.

Some historians have claimed that Ultra decryption alerted the Allied command to the German offensive and that Lieutenant General Omar Bradley* laid a trap, but subsequent study has established that this information came too late to alert the 30th ID. The 2/120's successful defense was due rather to the American G.I.'s* outstanding skill, tenacity, and courage under fire.

References. Martin Blumenson, *Breakout and Pursuit*, 1961, 1984. Alwyn Featherson, *Saving the Breakout*, 1993.

John A. Hixson

MORTAR

During the siege of Constantinople in 1451, Mohammed II first employed mortars against enemy ships. Europeans adopted the mortar as a siege weapon early in the 16th century to supplement siege cannon. Originally the term referred to specialized howitzers, fired at angles greater than forty-five degrees, especially effective against targets with little overhead protection. By 1860, the U.S. Army had divided artillery into three basic types: guns, for low-trajectory firing; howitzers, for medium-trajectories, and mortars, for high-trajectory firing. By World War I,* with their relatively light weight, mechanical reliability, high trajectory, and effective penetration, mortars proved particularly useful when moving forward with the infantry assaulting enemy trenches. In the mid-1950s, as the Army developed the pentomic division,* the mortar's relatively limited range reduced its use in general support; nevertheless, by 1958 the Army had settled on the mortar's current role as a direct infantry-support weapon.

References. Peter Chamberlain and Terry Gander, *Mortars and Rockets*, 1975. J. W. Ryan, *Guns, Mortars & Rockets*, 1982.

Jeffrey S. Shadburn

MOTOR POOL

A motor pool is a collection of both wheeled and tracked motor vehicles, usually in one location, under the centralized control of a single organization, most frequently governmental or military units, it can also refer to the physical location where those vehicles are housed. The purpose of a motor pool is to make the most efficient use of available vehicles, provide security and accountability, and most effectively employ maintenance facilities and personnel. Support facilities for the vehicles, equipment, tools, washracks, fuel and oil distribution, hazardous waste collection, mechanical personnel and administrative offices are normally colocated with the motor pool.

References. Ronald M. Bufkin, "Identifying Quality Motor Sergeants," *Army Logistician*, March–April 1985, 34–35. Lana Ott, "Motor Pool," *Soldiers*, November 1979, 23–26.

Jeffrey S. Shadburn

MOUNTAIN HOWITZER

A mountain howitzer is a light artillery* piece capable of high-angle fire, specially designed to be easily broken down into component parts for transport by men or animals. It was first used by the French in the Peninsular Wars; other nations quickly adopted it to provide artillery support for units in rough terrain.

Adopted by the U.S. Army in 1841, the mountain howitzer first saw action in the Mexican War* and has been used in every American war since. Also known as pack howitzers (because of the packs used to secure the parts on mules), these reliable guns served the Army until the development of larger-caliber howitzers capable of movement by helicopter rendered them obsolete. Mountain howitzers are still in service with many underdeveloped nations, where units frequently operate in difficult or undeveloped terrain. Because of their small size and light weight, they are commonly seen on display in museums and military installations throughout the United States.

References. Boyd L. Dastrup, *King of Battle*, 1992. William A. Kupke, *The Indian and the Thunderwagon*, 1992.

Jeffrey S. Shadburn

MURPHY, AUDIE LEON (1924–1971)

Born in Hunt County, Texas, 28 May 1924, Audie Leon Murphy was awarded twenty-eight medals, including the Medal of Honor,* and is regarded as the most highly decorated U.S. soldier in World War II.* Murphy was a diminutive, underage enlistee who found himself in the infantry* after having been rejected for airborne training and by the U.S. Marines. After the usual training, Murphy joined the 3d Infantry Division's 15th Infantry Regiment in North Africa on the eve of the Allied invasion of Sicily. At first, Murphy's comrades called him "baby," because of his size and youth, and attempted to protect him from the ravages of combat, but Murphy proved to have what seemed to many a natural aptitude for infantry fighting. After Sicily, he fought with his regiment* through the Salerno landings in Italy, the Volturno River campaign, and later in the liberation of Rome after landing with his division* at Anzio.* During the Italian campaign, Murphy became widely known in his division for his expertise in combat. In the summer of 1944, Murphy participated in the Allied invasion of southern France. His chest already full of decorations for valor, he won the Distinguished Service Cross* (DSC) and the Medal of Honor during Seventh Army's* campaign across France. Promptly returned home and demobilized after the war, Murphy was lionized in the American press as the quintessential American military hero, an identity that he was never quite able to escape. His wartime exploits enabled him to embark upon a career in motion pictures, and at one time his was one of the more commercial names in Hollywood. During the 1960s his career and his personal life slowly eroded, but his wartime fame shone as brightly as ever. He died in a plane crash in 1971.

References. Don Graham, *No Name on the Bullet*, 1989. Harold B. Simpson, *Audie Murphy*, 1982. Charles Whiting, *Hero*, 1990.

Roger J. Spiller

MUSKET

In the middle of the 16th century, the Spaniards introduced a firearm heavier and longer than the previous standard arquebus. In the tradition of naming firearms after birds, this weapon was dubbed a mousequet, or sparrow hawk. By 1626, under the reign of the Swedish king, Gustavus Adolphus, the piece had been reduced in weight to about ten pounds, dispensing with the need for a portable rest or fork. The English referred to these refined, smooth-bore flintlock arms as "muskets." By the beginning of the 18th century, the musket, equipped with a plug bayonet* that fit into the end of the barrel, had made the pike totally obsolete. The bayonet was later fixed to a socket device, allowing the piece to be loaded and fired with the bayonet attached.

The standard musket round consisted of a one-ounce lead ball, .69 caliber, propelled by sixty grains of black powder. These weapons had a maximum effective range of a hundred yards, but they were not aimed. The soldiers would stand in massed formation, point their weapons downrange, and fire in volley. This would create the desired effect of concentrated firepower, presumably upon another massed formation. An assault with fixed bayonets followed the exchange of shot and sealed the victory.

The first U.S. musket was produced at the Springfield Arsenal* in 1795 and was a direct copy of the French pattern. In 1842 the percussion lock replaced the flintlock on the musket, making ignition more certain. Muskets with rifled barrels were called rifled muskets. However, breech-loading weapons with rifled barrels were called simply rifles.

References. Claud E. Fuller, *The Rifled Musket*, 1958. James E. Hicks, *U.S. Military Firearms, 1776–1956*, 1962.

Steven J. Allie

MY LAI

A number of hamlets in the Republic of Vietnam shared the name My Lai. My Lai 4 was one of a cluster of hamlets making up Son My village in the coastal lowlands of Quang Ngai Province, I Corps Tactical Zone. This hamlet became infamous as the site of the 16 March 1968 massacre of between 200 and 500 Vietnamese civilians by soldiers of Charlie Company, 1st Battalion, 20th Infantry, 11th Infantry Brigade (Light) of the 23rd (Americal) Division. Equally infamous was the coverup of the incident perpetrated by the brigade* and division* staffs. An investigation by the Army Criminal Investigation Division* and an Army board of inquiry, headed by Lieutenant General William Peers, brought the incident to light a year later. The Peers board produced a list of thirty persons, mostly officers (including the division commander), who knew of the atrocity; however, only fourteen individuals were charged with crimes. Charges against all of the accused were eventually dismissed or they were acquitted by courts-martial, except for the most junior officer, First Lieutenant William Calley, Jr. Calley, whose platoon allegedly killed some 200 women, children, and old men, was found guilty of murdering twenty-two civilians. Proclaimed by much of the public as a scapegoat, Calley was paroled in November 1974, after serving about a third of his ten-year sentence.

References. Jay W. Baird, ed., *From Nuremberg to My Lai*, 1972. Michael Bilton and Kevin Sim, *Four Hours in My Lai*, 1992. William R. Peers, *The My Lai Inquiry*, 1979. John Sack, *Lieutenant Calley*, 1971.

                                                                          Arthur T. Frame

N

NATIONAL DEFENSE ACT OF 1916

On 3 June, following a long and sometimes bitter debate and considerable disagreement between Congress and members of the Woodrow Wilson Administration, Congress passed the National Defense Act of 1916. While the act fell short of creating a great army equal to the European armies then at war, it established the foundations for national mobilization. It provided for a peacetime Regular Army of 175,000 men, to be implemented over a five-year period, and a 300,000-man wartime force. It increased the National Guard* to 400,000, required the Guard to comply with federal training and organizational standards, and made federal funds available to compliant Guard units. By requiring guardsmen to take a dual oath, the act permitted the president to call the Guard into federal service for duty abroad, without time limitation, during national emergencies. It implemented a then-popular idea with the creation of the Reserve Officer Training Corps* (ROTC) and the Officers' Reserve Corps. It further provided for an Enlisted Reserve Corps and a Volunteer Army to be raised in the event of war. Other provisions of the act dealt with mobilization and preparedness. Although the National Defense Act of 1916 was a compromise among contending interests, it was the most advanced and progressive defense measure Congress had passed to that time.

References. John Patrick Finnegan, *Against the Specter of a Dragon*, 1974. Allan R. Millett and Peter Maslowski, *For the Common Defense*, 1984.

Phil Bradley

NATIONAL DEFENSE ACT OF 1920

On 4 June 1920, Congress approved Public Law 242, an amendment to the National Defense Act of 1916.* Commonly referred to as the National Defense Act of 1920, the amendment created a template for the U.S. Army's contemporary structure. A reflection of wartime mobilization experiences, postwar budgetary pressures, and political wrangling, the legislation mandated an Army of the United States with a regular force of 280,000 men, with the National Guard* constituting the primary reserve force. A result of skillful lobbying by Guard proponents, this greatly expanded role for the Guard subsequently increased federal influence over Guard units. Greater federal supervision, improved and increased training, and uniform equipment requirements were the price of this elevated status.

The organized reserves, originally composed of World War I* veterans, constituted a second source of manpower for any future wartime expansion. During peacetime, these veterans would oversee skeleton divisions within nine designated corps areas. Each corps area consisted on one Regular Army division,* two National Guard divisions, and three Reserve divisions. This arrangement was consistent with the idea of an expansible Army, an Army that was by 1920 decidedly anti-Uptonian.

Finally, PL 242 accomplished two other notable feats. First, the extension of the Reserve Officer Training Corps* (ROTC) on college campuses provided a mechanism for a constant and fairly effective regeneration of the junior officer corps. Secondly, the Office of the Assistant Secretary of War became a nexus for military procurement planning. This arrangement reflected lessons learned during the last war and ultimately led to the creation of a planning staff charged with the assessment and coordination of industrial capacity with respect to projected wartime needs.

References. Jame E. Hewes, Jr., *From Root to McNamara*, 1975. John K. Mahon, *History of the Militia and the National Guard*, 1983. Alan R. Millett and Peter Maslowski, *For the Common Defense*, 1984.

Robert Rook

NATIONAL DEFENSE UNIVERSITY

On 16 January 1976, the Department of Defense* established the National Defense University (NDU) "to ensure excellence in professional military education and research in the essential element of national security." Located at Fort McNair, Washington, D.C., NDU initially consolidated two existing senior level schools, the National War College and the Industrial College of the Armed Forces.* The Armed Forces Staff College* became part of NDU in 1981, although its facilities remained in Norfolk, Virginia. Three academic centers have been subsequently established at NDU: the Institute for National Strategic Studies, coordinator of research activities; the Institute for Higher Defense Studies, a capstone course for general and flag officers and senior foreign service officers; and the International Fellows, a program for senior foreign officers. Responsible directly to the Joint Chiefs of Staff,* NDU is headed by a lieutenant general or vice admiral, while equivalent two-star officers serve as commandants of the three colleges. About 400 senior field-grade or equivalent officers, representing all of the armed services, other government executive agencies, and a number of allied armies, attend the annual ten-month course at the Fort McNair campus.

Half of these students have held battalion* or equivalent command, and most already hold graduate or professional degrees. Many of the graduates have served, or will serve, in joint assignments. The faculty is composed of both military and civilian academics and area experts. While attendance at NDU is not essential for further promotion in any of the armed services, most military officers consider a year at NDU a career-enhancing opportunity and a rewarding experience. The National Defense University is not accredited to grant degrees.

References. Stanley L. Falk, "The Little-Big School off Buzzard's Point," *Army*, April 1985, 46–50. Dennis Steele, "Higher Learning," *Soldiers*, March 1986, 21–24.

NATIONAL GUARD

The National Guard evolved in the decades after the Civil War* from the antebellum uniformed volunteer militia. The states employed the Guard to quell civil disorders, particularly labor conflicts, that periodically wracked late-19th-century America. Although support varied among the states, and financial support was rarely adequate, state funding assured the permanent existence of Guard units. While some Guard units perpetuated the antebellum social aspects of the militia, such as local fundraising for unit activities, some Guardsmen began to see themselves as a volunteer reserve to serve the nation in war. At first, they successfully lobbied Congress for funds to support their part-time training. Nevertheless, National Guard units, poorly equipped and inadequately trained as they were, provided the majority of volunteers that served in the Spanish-American War.* The military reforms that followed recognized the Guard as the nation's organized militia, and provided the state soldiers increasing federal dollars. The process began with the approval of the Militia Act of 1903, as amended in 1906 and 1908. Most Army officers, however, still rejected the National Guard's argument that it offered a reliable reserve. General Staff* studies and reports noted that the Guard's dual status as a state constabulary and federal reserve prevented the War Department* from training the Guard properly or using it overseas. From 1903 until passage of the National Defense Act of 1916,* the Guard and the War Department engaged in a sometimes bitter conflict over the Guard's place in national policy. The 1916 Act, as amended in 1920, ensured the Guard's role as a reserve component but greatly increased War Department control over its training, officer selection, and unit organization.

The test of the Guard's quality as a reserve came with mobilization. It failed that test in June 1916 when called to serve along the Mexican border, but it proved more valuable when mobilized a year later to provide the organizational structure and personnel (400,000 men) for seventeen divisions* of the American Expeditionary Force* (AEF). During the interwar years, the National Guard offered the only organized, partially trained reserve components that the General Staff could rely on for contingency planning purposes. These units formed the training organizations for draftees when mobilization began in 1940–1941.

In the post-1945 armed forces reorganizations, the National Guard successfully resisted attempts to eliminate it as a major reserve force and even expanded its presence, with the creation of the Air National Guard. While the Army Guard remained the chief ground-force reserve maintaining combat units, it nonetheless faced a rival in the reinvigorated Army Reserve.* During the Korean War* and the 1961 Berlin crisis mobilizations, for example, the Department of Defense* called up more Army reservists than Guardsmen. Reserve components were not used in the Vietnam War* until 1968, and even then only some 20,000 were mobilized. The refusal of President Lyndon Johnson's administration to call reservists unfortunately marked all reserve components as draft havens. Unprecedented civil disorder during the 1960s, notably urban civil rights upheavals and antiwar protests, placed a particular burden on the National Guard. While the Guard received over 90 percent of its funding from the federal government, it remained at home and served chiefly to quell civil disorder. Criticism fell on the state soldiers from all quarters.

In the reassessment of Army doctrine* and policy following the Vietnam War, the General Staff* developed the Total Force policy to ensure that in future conflicts the Army's reserve components would have to be mobilized. The staff organized the Army force structure so that it could not fight a war without calling up Guard and Reserve units, especially combat support and service support elements. By the late 1980s, Army plans even included National Guard roundout brigades assigned to active Army combat divisions. In 1991, Desert Storm* tested the Total Force and roundout concepts. Guard and Army Reserve combat and service support units met the demands of war; 33,000 Guardsmen deployed to the Gulf. Controversy exploded, however, when the General Staff deemed the mobilized Guard roundout brigades unfit for combat and refused to deploy them. Thus, the mutual suspicion and misunderstanding that soured relations between the National Guard and the Army in 1898 remains unresolved a century later.

References. Jerry Cooper, *The Rise of the National Guard*, 1997. Jim Dan Hill, *The Minute Man in Peace and War*, 1964. John K. Mahon, *History of the Militia and the National Guard*, 1983.

Jerry Cooper

NATIONAL GUARD ASSOCIATION OF THE UNITED STATES

In the fall of 1879, forty-three Civil War* veterans from fourteen former Union and Confederate states met at St. Louis to adopt a constitution for the National Guard Association of the United States (NGAUS), whose purpose was "to promote military efficiency throughout the active militia of the United States, and to secure united representation before Congress for such legislation as it may deem necessary for this purpose." The delegates elected George W. Wingate of New York president and Pierre G. T. Beauregard of Louisiana first vice president. For more than two decades, NGAUS struggled with financial hard times and inability to influence major legislation. The years of hard work and frustration, however, culminated with passage of the Dick Act* in 1903, which created the modern National Guard.* Throughout the 20th century, NGAUS has served as a major spokesman and an active congressional lobbyist for National Guard issues. NGAUS membership includes serving and retired National Guardsmen and many other Americans who believe in and support the concept of the citizen soldier in American life. The National Guard Association of the United States, headquartered in Washington, D.C., publishes a monthly magazine, *National Guard*, as a forum for ideas and issues of importance to the National Guard. Several thousand delegates and members attend the annual General Conference, held in a different city each year.

References. Allan C. Crist and W. D. McGlasson, "A Century of Service," *National Guard*, November 1978, 6–9. Les Pearson, "Muster in St. Louis . . . ," *National Guardsman*, May 1978, 18–19.

NATIONAL SECURITY ACT OF 1947

After four years of debate and compromise, on 26 July 1947 Congress passed the National Security Act of 1947, the most sweeping piece of defense legislation in more than a century and a half. It created the National Security Council (NSC), to advise the president on national security issues; the Central Intelligence Agency* (CIA), to collect intelligence and advise the NSC: and the National Security Resources Board, to advise the president concerning the coordination of military, industrial, and civilian mobilization in the event of war. It further created the National Military Establishment, to be headed by a secretary of defense,* a civilian appointee of the president. It established the U.S. Air Force, transferring to it the functions of the Air Corps* and the Army Air Forces,* and provided for chiefs of staff of the Air Force and Air National Guard. It reorganized the two older service departments, Army and Navy, and added a Department of the Air Force, each headed by separate secretaries. It formally created the Joint Chiefs of Staff* to act as primary military advisors to the president and secretary of defense. Finally, it established a Munitions Board and Research and Development Board to oversee national security issues in their respective fields. Almost immediately problems emerged with this new system, particularly the secretary of defense's ambiguous authority over the service chiefs and his lack of a staff and resources to accomplish the intent of Congress. Congress amended the act several times before the new structure became fully workable. Nevertheless, the National Security Act of 1947 remains one of the most sweeping reforms of national defense in American history.

References. Demetrios Caraley, *The Politics of Military Unification*, 1966. Paul Y. Hammond, *Organizing for Defense*, 1961.

Michael G. Knapp

NATIONAL SECURITY AGENCY

The National Security Agency (NSA) is responsible for intercepting and decoding foreign electronic transmissions and for developing methods to keep U.S. communications secure, including devising codes for classified material. It escaped publicity during the intelligence agency investigations of the mid-1970s in spite of a number of highly publicized incidents involving NSA missions, including the North Korean seizure of the USS *Pueblo*, an Israeli attack on an intelligence-gathering ship off the Palestine coast, and the North Vietnamese attack on two vessels in the Gulf of Tonkin. The National Security Agency is headquartered at Fort George G. Meade,* Maryland.

References. Henry M. Jackson, ed., *The National Security Council*, 1965. "National Security Agency," *Armed Forces Management*, November 1962, 103–105.

Jack Gifford

NATIONAL SIMULATION CENTER

The National Simulation Center (or NSC, also referred to as the Sim Center), located in the historic Beehive at Fort Leavenworth,* Kansas, provides simulation support to major military training exercises throughout the world. Through its numerous integration, research, and development functions, the Sim Center serves as the combat developer and integrator of live, virtual, and constructive requirements to ensure that soldiers are provided with state-of-the-art training and mission-rehearsal models, simulations, and simulators that inferface with operational battle command systems. As training costs increase and the availability of maneuver space is constrained, the U.S. Army looks more and more to realistic simulations to replicate combat scenarios. The current U.S. Army family of simulations is focused on varying levels of command and is constantly being upgraded for higher fidelity and functionality. They are also being integrated with simulations from the sister services to provide a joint and multinational environment. The National Simulation Center is the preeminent player in this U.S. Army initiative.

References. Keith E. Bonn, *Army Officer's Guide*, 48th ed., 1999. Colin L. McArthur, "Who's in Charge?" *Armed Forces Journal International*, December 1997, 34–35.

Lawyn C. Edwards

NATIONAL TRAINING CENTER

The National Training Center (NTC) was established in 1980 at Fort Irwin, California, as the U.S. Army's most advanced maneuver-exercise facility. Located on a thousand square miles of rugged Mojave Desert terrain, the NTC serves as the training ground for armor* and mechanized infantry* battalions* and their supporting combat support and service support elements. At the NTC, training units from posts around the United States fire their weapons in sophisticated live-fire exercises and fight mock battles with brigade-sized opposing force (OPFOR). Teams of observer-controllers use laser systems as well as video and position-location technology to control the exercise and provide feedback to training units. Despite early growing pains, the NTC became the Army's number-one success story of the 1980s and inspired the establishment of similar training centers at Hohenfels,* Germany, and Fort Chaffee,* Arkansas. The National Training Center is frequently cited as an important contributor to the U.S. Army's successful performance in Desert Storm.*

References. Anne W. Chapman, *The Origins and Development of the National Training Center 1976–1984*, 1992. James F. Dunnigan and Raymond M. Macedonia, *Getting It Right*, 1993. Hans Halberstadt, *NTC*, 1989.

Donald S. Stephenson

NEPTUNE

Operation Neptune was the code name for the naval component of Overlord.* Neptune included the movement to and the assault on the beaches of Normandy. A staff under Admiral Bertram Ramsey, the Allied Naval Commander in Chief, Expeditionary Force (ANCXF), developed the plans for the initial divison* landings on Utah, Omaha, Gold, Juno, and Sword Beaches—the first two U.S., the latter three British. The plan assigned two task forces to carry and escort the assault forces to their objectives. The Western Naval Task Force, under command of Rear Admiral Alan G. Kirk, USN, would support the U.S. forces, and the Eastern Naval Task Force, under Rear Admiral Sir Philip Vian, RN, would assist the British forces. A naval bombardment force was assigned to each of the five assault beaches. Operation Neptune employed 4,126 landing ships and craft and 1,213 warships.

References. Forrest C. Pogue, *The Supreme Command*, 1954. Max Schoenfeld, "The Navies and Neptune," in *D-Day 1944*, ed. Theodore A. Wilson, 1994.

James L. Isemann

NEW GUINEA

In 1942, New Guinea was strategically valuable as both a blocking position and a springboard between the Allies in Australia and the Japanese in the Philippines. Determined to retake the Philippines, General Douglas MacArthur,* Commander, Southwest Pacific Area* (SWPA), had to first wrest control of New Guinea from the Japanese. The Allied conquest of New Guinea can be divided into two separate but sequential campaigns. The offensive in eastern New Guinea from September 1942, when the first U.S. forces landed at Port Morseby, to mid-February 1944 entailed a 900 mile advance up the island's north coast. This part of the campaign included the bloody battles of Buna,* Gona, and Sanananda, and it concluded with the capture of Salamaua, Lae, and Finschafen. The campaign in Dutch New Guinea began in mid-April 1944 and ended the following August. In just over four months, the Allies advanced 1,200 miles from the Huon Peninsula to the western tip of Vogelkop Peninsula, fighting major battles at Hollandia and Biak Island. Some historians consider New Guinea the decisive campaign against the Japanese in World War II.* The fight for New Guinea cost the Allies 27,684 causalities, but the Japanese lost at least ten times that number. New Guinea became the springboard for MacArthur's promised invasion of the Philippines in October 1944.

References. Samuel Milner, *Victory in Papua*, 1957. Robert Ross Smith, *The Approach to the Philippines*, 1953, 1984.

John R. Kennedy

NEW MARKET

In the late spring of 1864, with the strength of the Union growing rapidly and the situation for the Confederacy becoming more desperate, the new general-in-chief of the Union Army, Ulysses S. Grant,* set his armies in motion. Grant intended to use his superior manpower and resources to overwhelm the South. One of the keys to his plan was the Shenandoah Valley; likewise, the Confederates had to hold the valley if they hoped to keep the North at bay. In March, during the same week, Major General John C. Breckenridge assumed command of the Confederate Department of West Virginia, and Major General Franz Sigel took command of the U.S. Department of West Virginia. Through April and early May, both sides sent additional forces into the valley and maneuvered for position. The maneuvering brought on numerous skirmishes and small engagements, but not until 15 May 1864 did the two armies meet.

The battle of New Market began with an artillery duel in the rain. Breckenridge's intention was to allow the Federals to attack him, but when the anticipated attack did not come, he ordered his troops, including the cadets of the Virginia Military Institute* (VMI), to move forward. Sigel's troops were still coming up and had not yet formed their defensive line when the Confederate assault drove them back. Sigel ordered a counterattack, but misconstrued orders, poor leadership, and piecemeal execution led to more confusion, and the Federals fell back. Sigel withdrew across the Shenandoah by early evening.

New Market has been called the "most important secondary battle" of the Civil War.* The Federal defeat left Robert E. Lee's* strategic flank secure and, according to some sources, prolonged the war.

References. William C. Davis, *The Battle of New Market*, 1975. Joseph W. A. Whitehorne, *The Battle of New Market*, 1988.

NEW ORLEANS

The War of 1812* was fought between the United States and Great Britain from June 1812 to the spring of 1815. The Treaty of Ghent ending the war, however, was signed in December 1814. In November 1814, Andrew Jackson* was sent to New Orleans to defend against a rumored British concentration in the Caribbean–Gulf of Mexico area. That same month, a force of 7,500 British soldiers under Major General Sir Edward Pakenham sailed from Jamaica to seize New Orleans and control the Mississippi River valley. Pakenham landed on 13 December and moved on New Orleans. Jackson's force of 5,100 ill-trained militia formed a defensive line of earth, timbers, and cotton bales along a canal south of the city. The British began bombarding the U.S. positions on 1 January and attacked on the 8th—unaware of the Treaty of Ghent. Jackson's militiamen poured a deadly fire from behind their entrenchments and repulsed the British attack. After sustaining 2,100 casualties, including Pakenham and his two senior surbordinates, and losing 500 prisoners of war,* the remaining British forces withdrew. Jackson lost seven killed and six wounded. This decisive victory, linked to the already completed peace treaty, convinced many Americans that the war had ended in triumph and contributed to the surge of nationalism in the postwar years.

References. Harry Albright, *New Orleans*, 1990. Frank L. Owsley, Jr., *Struggle for the Gulf Borderlands*, 1981. Robin Reilly, *The British at the Gates*, 1974.

James H. Willbanks

NEWBURGH CONSPIRACY

With the American Revolution* over, their pay months in arrears, their food and clothing accounts unsettled, and Congress having failed to make provisions for their pensions, a group of disgruntled Continental Army* officers planned a coup. Early in January 1783, a delegation of officers at Newburgh, New York, sent Congress a "memorial" regarding the aforementioned grievances. Major General Alexander McDougall headed the committee of senior officers that formulated this document, and it was he who took it to Congress. The organizer of the movement, however, was Colonel Walter Stewart, who informed the officers that Congress planned to dissolve the Army without settling their claims. He argued that the officers should band together and insist that Congress promptly pay all that had been promised them.

George Washington,* though aware that his officers were unhappy, suspected nothing ominous until 10 March, when he received a letter requesting his presence at a meeting of general and field officers. At this meeting he was given a copy of the fiery and rhetorical appeal known as the "First Newburgh Address." It suggested coercion of Congress. Washington in response called a meeting for 15 March. In the meantime, a second anonymous address appeared, less vehement in tone. On the 15th Washington met a delegation of officers and advised them to be patient and confident that Congress would honor their requests. His enormous influence calmed the hotheads; resolutions approving his counsel and deprecating the addresses were adopted. In 1823, Major John Armstrong, Jr., an officer on Major General Horatio Gate's staff, afterward a general, minister to France, and secretary of war,* admitted to writing the two addresses.

References. Douglas Southall Freeman, *George Washington*, vol. 5, 1952. Russell F. Weigley, *History of the U.S. Army*, 1967.

Michael Davis

NEZ PERCÉ WAR

The inital bloodshed in the Nez Percé War occurred between Nez Percé warriors and settlers on the Oregon, Washington, and Idaho borders in June 1877. The war became a series of running battles between the Nez Percé and the U.S. Army and its civilian volunteers. The Nez Percé withdrew 1,600 miles from the western area of Idaho, back and forth across the Montana boundary, into Yellowstone Park in Wyoming, and finally north through Montana to within forty miles of the Canadian border. U.S. troops, under Brigadier General Oliver O. Howard.* fought a number of engagements with the Nez Percé, but the Indians consistently managed to break contact and continue their flight. Howard was criticized because he could not catch the Nez Percé, but his troops had only one horse per man, while each Nez Percé had several ponies and could frequently change mounts. Howard was further hampered when the Nez Percé stole half of his pack train at Camas Meadows; he was forced to turn cavalry horses into pack animals.

Although Howard could not force a decisive engagement, he was able to use the telegraph to coordinate with other U.S. forces in the area to prevent their escape. A force under Colonel Nelson A. Miles* left Fort Keogh, Montana, at the convergence of the Tongue and Yellowstone Rivers, and intercepted the Nez Percé at the Bear Paw Mountain, just south of the Canadian border. Miles attacked, but the battle soon became a siege that lasted five days, allowing Howard time to arrive before Chief Joseph and 418 followers surrendered. Official casualty reports were 127 soldiers killed and 47 wounded, 151 Nez Percé killed and 88 wounded, and 50 civilian deaths.

References. Merrill D. Beal, *"I Will Fight No More Forever,"* 1963. Mark H. Brown, *The Flight of the Nez Perce*, 1967. Bruce Hampton, *Children of Grace*, 1994. David Lavender, *Let Me Be Free*, 1992.

L. Lynn Williams

NINETY-DAY WONDER

"Ninety-day wonder" refers to an officer who received a commission after a three-month course at an officer candidate school* (OCS). To meet the requirements of the 1941–1945 expansion, the Army commissioned thousands of qualified civilians and enlisted soldiers. First used derisively by graduates of the U.S. Military Academy,* who had spent four years earning their commissions, the term was revived during the Vietnam War,* when the Army once again substantially expanded its OCS programs.

References. Hanson W. Baldwin, "GI Gripes," *New York Times Magazine*, 31 March 1946, 12–13. Edward Gardner, Jr., "Ninety-Day Wonder," *Saturday Evening Post*, 14 November 1942, 14–15.

Randall N. Briggs

NINTH ARMY

Activated at Fort Sam Houston,* Texas, on 22 May 1944, Ninth Army participated in the major campaigns in the European Theater of Operations* (ETO) in 1944 and 1945. After serving as an expanded staff of the Fourth Army, a training command in the United States, for several months, the Ninth Army, including its commander, Lieutenant General William Hood Simpson, and his outstanding chief of staff, Major General James E. Moore, deployed to the United Kingdom in May 1944. Ninth Army entered combat in September, absorbing VIII Corps, then besieging the fortified city of Brest, France. Briefly taking command of units occupying the Ardennes region of Belgium and Luxembourg, situated between First and Third U.S. Armies, the Ninth soon relocated to the northernmost portion of the U.S. 12th Army Group sector. During the battle of the Ardennes* (December 1944–January 1945), Ninth Army dispatched seven divisions* and twenty-eight nondivisional combat units to the threatened area, including the 7th Armored Division, which conducted the critical defense of St. Vith. Ninth Army came under 21st Army Group (Field Marshal Barnard Law Montgomery) on 21 December 1944. Its finest exploits occurred after the battle of the Ardennes. Operation Grenade, the Roer River crossings, took place in February–March 1945; the Rhineland campaign followed close on its heels. Ninth Army participated in Montgomery's set-piece crossings of the northern Rhine near Wesel, once across the Rhine, it raced across Germany, becoming the first Allied unit to reach the Elbe River. As Ninth Army was preparing to attack Berlin, General of the Army Dwight D. Eisenhower* ordered Simpson to halt. The Ninth Army performed magnificently in Europe, earning praise from U.S. as well as British commanders. Plans to deploy Ninth Army to the Pacific to continue the war against Japan were cancelled when Japan surrendered. Ninth Army deactivated on 10 October 1945 at Fort Bragg,* North Carolina.

References. *Conquer*, 1947. Charles B. MacDonald, *The Siegfried Line Campaign*, 1963, 1984.

Jerry D. Morelock

NONAPPROPRIATED-FUND ACTIVITY

Nonappropriated-fund activity refers to any activity legally established to benefit military personnel and their dependents and Department of the Army* civilian employees located on military bases or reservations that are not incorporated in any state or the District of Columbia and do not operate with funds directly appropriated by Congress. Nonappropriated fund (NAF) activities (such as clubs, commissaries, post exchanges, theaters, and morale, welfare, and recreation (MWR) facilities) are subject to the authority of the secretary of the army* and *Army Regulations*, and they are instrumentalities of the United States.

References. Dan Daniel, "The Military Resale System," *Interservice*, Spring 1982, 12–19. J. M. Metzgar, "Nonappropriated Fund Activities Pay the Way," *Army Information Digest*, May 1961, 23–33.

NONCOMMISSIONED OFFICER

A noncommissioned officer (NCO) is an enlisted member of the armed forces appointed to a rank conferring leadership over other enlisted personnel. The NCO in the U.S. Army can be traced to the Continental Army* of 1775, as a unique blend of French, British, and Prussian traditions. The first document to standardize NCO duties was Inspector General* Friedrich von Steuben's* *Regulations for the Order and Discipline of the Troops of the United States*. It established duties for the NCO ranks of the period—corporal, sergeant, first sergeant, and quartermaster sergeant. In 1821, the War Department* directed that sergeants major and quartermaster sergeants wear a worsted chevron on each arm above the elbow, sergeants and senior musicians wear a chevron below the elbow on each arm, and corporals wear a chevron on the right arm only above the elbow. In 1832, Congress created the additional NCO rank of Ordnance Sergeant, and in 1902 the chevron was turned point up and reduced in size. In 1909, the War Department published the *Noncommissioned Officers Manual*, updating and defining NCO duties.

Prior to 1940, when many NCOs spent their entire careers within the same regiment,* regimental commanders were directly responsible for NCO promotions; the general-in-chief's permission was required for an NCO to transfer from one regiment to another without loss of stripes. New regulations in 1940 permitted NCOs to transfer from one unit to another while retaining their stripes. Professionalization of the NCO corps continued after World War II,* with increased emphasis on education and NCO training. In 1958, the Army added two additional NCO ranks with commensurate pay grades, E-8 and E-9, and by 1959 over 180,000 soldiers had attended NCO academies. The Army implemented the NCO Educational System during 1971 to prepare NCOs in subjects and skills necessary to enhance their performance in a modern force. These measures have resulted in the most professional and best educated NCO corps in history.

References. Arnold G. Fisch, Jr., and Robert K. Wright, Jr., eds., *The Story of the Noncommissioned Officer Corps*, 1989. Ernest F. Fisher, Jr., *Guardians of the Republic*, 1994. Frank J. Kaufman, "Roll Out the Leaders," *Army Digest*, March 1968, 17–19.

Andrew L. Giacomini, Jr.

NORTH ATLANTIC TREATY ORGANIZATION

The United States and the Soviet Union emerged as superpowers at the end of World War II.* Although allied during the war, relations had worsened and the two powers were at odds in the immediate postwar period. The result was the onset of the Cold War* and the uniting of Western Europe against a possible Soviet attack. On 4 April 1949, eight countries—Belgium, Canada, France, Great Britain, Luxembourg, the Netherlands, Norway, and the United States—signed a collective defense and security treaty creating the North Atlantic Treaty Organization (NATO). Later, other countries—Denmark, Greece, Iceland, Italy, Portugal, Spain, Turkey, and the Federal Republic of Germany (West Germany)—also signed the treaty. The inclusion of West Germany prompted the communist states of Europe to form the Warsaw Pact in 1955.

A major role for NATO was the declaration of a common defense for all members. An attack on one member would be considered an attack on all members. This pledge of unity was to be a deterrent against a future nuclear war, and the concept was incorporated into other treaties. Due to President Charles DeGaulle's desire to keep France independent of foreign control, on 29 March 1966 France gave notice of its intention to withdraw from the pact. France had earlier withdrawn its navy from NATO's integrated command structure. France's action, however, did not undermine the basic NATO mission. Following the collapse of communism in Eastern Europe and the dismantling of the Soviet Union, NATO has remained strong, and three former Warsaw Pact states have subsequently become members.

References. David Calleo, *The Atlantic Fantasy*, 1970. Don Cook, *Forging the Alliance*, 1989. Lawrence S. Kaplan, *NATO and the United States*, 1988. William Park, *Defending the West*, 1986.

Trevor Brown

NUCLEAR, BIOLOGICAL, AND CHEMICAL

The post–World War II* term "nuclear, biological, and chemical," or NBC, refers to the three weapons systems of mass destruction normally associated with the Cold War.* The roots of biological and chemical weapons, however, can be traced to earlier periods of warfare. Biological warfare is the employment of organisms, such as bacteria and viruses, to debilitate or destroy the human body by attacking its vital functions; biological weapons have been used in warfare since ancient times. Chemical warfare uses chemical agents to disable or kill humans; the origins of modern chemical weapons can be found in the rise of the chemical industry in the late 19th century. Nuclear weapons are of two types, fission and fusion. Based on theories proposed in the early 20th century by pure-research scientists, led by Albert Einstein, the United States produced the first fission weapons during World War II. In 1952 the United Stated detonated the first fusion device, many times more powerful than the fission bombs dropped on Hiroshima and Nagasaki. Today, the potential use of, and defense against NBC weapons are critical elements in national strategic planning, although the probability of their use seems to have eased somewhat since the end of the Cold War. Nuclear, Biological, and Chemical continues to be an integral part of the training, equipment, and deployment of U.S. Army forces around the world.

References. Randall Forsberg et al., *Nonproliferation Primer*, 1995. Terry J. Gander, *Nuclear, Biological & Chemical Warfare*, 1987. Robert G. Joseph and John F. Reichart, *Deterrence and Defense in a Nuclear, Biological, and Chemical Environment*, 1996.

O

O-1. *See* Bird Dog.

OFFICE OF STRATEGIC SERVICES

In July 1941, President Franklin Roosevelt authorized the establishment of the office of the Coordinator of Information (COI) and appointed Colonel (later Major General) William J. Donovan* to the post. The COI was to collect and process foreign intelligence; because there was no other office prepared to conduct special operations, it became involved in planning special operations, such as unconventional warfare, counterintelligence, psychological operations, propaganda, sabotage, subversion, and espionage. In July 1942, seven months after the U.S. entry into World War II,* the COI was reorganized as the Office of Strategic Services (OSS). In addition to intelligence and counterintelligence activities, the OSS created dozens of detachments, sections, operational groups, and teams to establish resistance movements, conduct sabotage and subversion operations, and spread propaganda. Jedburgh* teams of French (or Belgian), British, and U.S. agents parachuted into occupied France to contact and supply resistance elements. Second-generation Italians established contacts in Sicily and Italy to gather intelligence and sabotage German convoys and installations. Agents parachuted into Eastern Europe, especially Yugoslavia, to support partisans fighting the German army. Fifteen-man operational groups landed in southern France, Norway, Greece, and Italy to conduct hit-and-run attacks on the enemy in concert with the resistance. During the war, the OSS was a vital component of the Allied strategy of dissipating enemy resources, keeping liberation hopes alive in Europe and Asia, and inflicting material damage to selected targets. In October 1945, the OSS was abolished, only to be revived in another form as the Central Intelligence Agency* (CIA) in 1947. The OSS built the foundation for special operations in the U.S. Army.

References. David W. Hogan, Jr., *U.S. Army Special Operations in World War II*, 1992. R. Harris Smith, *OSS*, 1972

Richard Stewart

OFFICE OF STRATEGIC SERVICES OPERATIONAL GROUPS

On 23 December 1942, the Joint Chiefs of Staff* authorized the creation of operational groups (OGs) under the Office of Strategic Services* (OSS), consisting of specially selected and trained U.S. Army soldiers capable of waging war behind enemy lines. Each OG consisted of thirty enlisted and four officer volunteers, fluent in the language used where they would operate, whenever possible. Most OGs deployed as fifteen-man teams. OGs saw action in Italy, Yugoslavia, Greece, France, and Norway, where they operated against the Germans, and in the China-Burma-India* (CBI) theater against the Japanese. The OGs' performance was disproportionate to their numbers and resources. They could train guerrillas and coordinate guerrilla operations, conduct acts of direct sabotage, rescue downed airmen, and collect intelligence. The operational groups—also referred to as operations groups—officially ceased to exist when President Harry Truman issued an executive order on 20 September 1945 deactivating the OSS. However, much of the OG team structure, as well as its mission capabilities, reappeared in the U.S. Army Special Forces Operations Detachments with the activation of the Tenth Special Forces Group in 1952.

References. Bradley F. Smith, *Other OSS Teams*, 1989. R. Harris Smith, *OSS*, 1972.

Joseph R. Fischer

OFFICE OF THE CHIEF OF MILITARY HISTORY

In 1942, a number of government and military leaders, including President Franklin Roosevelt, began to voice an interest in preserving and recording an accurate and objective history of the the war, then in its third year. Responding to this growing concern, in the spring of 1943 Assistant Secretary of War John J. McCloy established an Historical Advisory Committee, including respected professional historians, to direct and coordinate the U.S. Army's historical effort. The committee recommended establishment of a central historical office within the U.S. Army to conduct the Army's program. Acting on the committee's recommendation, in August 1943 the Army created the nucleus of the Office of the Chief of Military History (OCMH). With support from the highest echelons of the Army's leadership the group of civilian historians launched a number of projects, including the "American Forces in Action" series. In late 1945, the office became a separate special-staff division, headed by a brigadier general. Assured of academic freedom and access to the widest possible range of documents and sources, the historians at OCMH commenced work on one of the most ambitious historical projects in history, *The United States Army in World War II* (the Green Books*)—a series that would take fifty years to complete. Over the next twenty-five years, OCMH assumed responsibility for numerous aspects of Army history, including archival holdings and unit lineages. In 1973, the Office of the Chief of Military History became the Center of Military History* (CMH).

References. Stetson Conn, "The Army's Historical Program," *Military Review*, May 1966, 40–47. John E. Jessup, Jr., and Robert W. Coakley, *A Guide to the Study and Use of Military History*, 1979, 1988. Mary Tanham, "The Gold Mine at OCMH," *Army*, January 1959, 38–41.

OFFICER CANDIDATE SCHOOL

The U.S. Army instituted officer training camps just prior to the U.S. entry into World War I* to meet the urgent need for commissioned officers. Descended from the earlier Plattsburg Movement,* initially the Officer Training Camps operated within divisional cantonments. However, the Army soon consolidated these camps in eight Officer Training Schools to improve the quality of officer candidates and newly commissioned lieutenants. The Officer Training Schools, later renamed Officer Candidate Schools (OCS), provided the bulk of commissioned officer during the war, but the War Department* suspended the program after the armistice. When the United States once again mobilized for war in July 1941, the Army reestablished OCS. During World War II,* OCS produced over 250,000 officers—the Army Air Forces* produced about the same number—many of whom maintained their commissions after the war. Each of the Army's branches operated schools, with the graduates normally assigned to that branch. During the Vietnam War,* OCS was a primary source of commissioned officers, especially for the combat arms. The number of Officer Candidate Schools has varied—to as high as twenty-five—with the Army's need; currently the Army operates only one, at Fort Benning,* Georgia.

References. Roger A. Beaumont and William P. Snyder, "A Fusion Strategy for Pre-Commissioning Training," *Journal of Political and Military Sociology*, Fall 1977, 259–277. Larry Lane, "Going for Gold Bars," *Soldiers*, February 1993, 37–41. Tom Williams, "A Gold Standard," *Soldiers*, July 1985, 46–50.

Lawyn C. Edwards

OFFICER EVALUATION REPORT

The officer evaluation report (OER) is the primary personnel management tool used to evaluate officer professionalism, performance, potential for promotion, selection for advanced schools, and future assignments in the U.S. Army. Generally, an officer receives one OER per year, covering his or her performance of duty during the previous year. The current OER form (DA Form 67–8) had its genesis in the early years of the 20th century. Before the Department of the Army* adopted the current system, evaluation reports consisted of informal letters from subordinate commanders to their respective army,* division,* brigade,* and regimental commanders. This rating system was judged ineffective, as it often led to generalities rather than specifics. For example, an 1813 performance letter characterized one officer as "the very dregs of the earth.

Unfit for anything under heaven. God only knows how the poor thing got an appointment."

References. William M. Causey, Jr., "Using the OER Support Form as a Management Tool," *Army Logistician*, March–April 1990, 30–34. Lawrence P. Crocker, *Army Officer's Guide*, 46th ed., 1993. Thomas A. Kolditz, "Inside the Professional Development System," *Field Artillery*, September–October 1997, 10–12.

Robert J. Dalessandro

OFFICIAL ARMY AND AIR FORCE REGISTER. *See Army Register.*

OFFICIAL ARMY REGISTER. *See Army Register.*

OH-6. *See* Cayuse.

OKINAWA

The Battle of Okinawa, one of the largest amphibious operations of World War II,* took place from 1 April to 22 June 1945. It proved to be the last major island battle between U.S. and Imperial Japanese forces in the Pacific war. The hilly and uneven terrain of Okinawa, sixty miles long and from two to eighteen miles wide, is a highly concentrated and compartmented combat environment. The U.S. Tenth Army, consisting of three Army infantry* divisions* and one Marine Corps division, organized into the XXIV Corps and III Amphibious Corps, landed on the Hagushi beaches on 1 April. The Imperial Japanese 32d Army, with two divisions, an independent mixed brigade, and a naval base force, defended the island. U.S. forces landed unopposed, met little resistance directly inland and to the north, and secured the northern two-thirds of the island by 18 April. Most of the Japanese force, however, was disposed in caves and bunkers in the southern third of Okinawa, where U.S. troops engaged them in a pitched battle lasting until 22 June, by which time the Japanese 32d Army had been more or less destroyed as an effective fighting force. Tenth Army losses mounted to more than 7,000 killed in action or died of wounds by the time fighting ended. Total Japanese losses were believed to be in the range of 110,000 soldiers killed in action, and an undetermined number of civilian residents of Okinawa.

References. Gerald Astor, *Operation Iceberg*, 1995. Robert Leckie, *Okinawa*, 1995. Hiromichi Yahara, *The Battle for Okinawa*, 1995.

Thomas M. Huber

OLD ARMY

"Old Army" refers to an army of an earlier period, usually the army before the last war. Veterans and old soldiers frequently speak of the Old Army in nostalgic terms, implying a distinct set of experiences, values, rigor, discipline, and comaraderie denied soldiers of the present generation. For historians of the U.S. Army, the phrase is generally associated with the peacetime Army of the

19th century. Some sources, however, occasionally use it when referring to the Army in the early 20th century or pre–World War II* period.

References. Patrick E. Andrews, "The Old Army," *Infantry*, September–October 1979, 31–34. Edward M. Coffman, *The Old Army*, 1986. Stanley L. Falk, "Feudin' and Fussin' in the Old Army," *Army*, November 1984, 57–61. *See also* Brown–Shoe Army.

OLD GUARD

The 3d United States Infantry is the oldest active infantry* unit in the Army. The unit traces its lineage to 3 June 1784, when the Continental Congress created one regiment* of 700 soldiers. In 1848, during the siege of Mexico City,* Major General Winfield Scott* gave the regiment its nickname when he said to members of his staff, "Gentlemen, take off your hats to The Old Guard of the Army."

In 1948, The Old Guard became the official ceremonial unit of the U.S. Army, responsible for ceremonies at the White House, the Pentagon,* and throughout the capital area. The regiment also maintains a twenty-four-hour vigil at the Tomb of the Unknown Soldier,* performs military funerals at Arlington National Cemetery,* provides the caisson and caparisoned horse for state funerals, and is the parent organization of the U.S. Army Drill Team and the Fife and Drum Corps.

The Old Guard has earned forty-two battle streamers in wars from 1794 through Vietnam.

References. Fielder P. Greer, "The Army's 'Old Guard,' " *Army Information Digest*, May 1956, 24–29. James A. Sawicki, *Infantry Regiments of the U.S. Army*, 1981.

Richard L. Kiper

101ST AIRBORNE DIVISION (AIR ASSAULT)

The 101st Airborne Division was activated on 15 August 1942 at Camp Clairborn, Louisiana. Reassigned to Fort Bragg,* North Carolina, the division* underwent many months of strenuous training before demonstrating its capabilities in a series of maneuvers in the summer of 1943. Upon completion of the exercises, the "Screaming Eagles" deployed to England and, on D-day, jumped into France and spent the next thirty-three days in combat. Following the Normandy campaign, the division returned to England to prepare for further operations. On 17 September, the 101st participated in Market-Garden, where its mission was to secure and hold the southern portion of the corridor from Eindhoven to Arnhem, Holland. Early in December, the division was sent to defend the town of Bastongne and halt the German drive through the Ardennes.*

After World War II,* the 101st was deactivated, reactivated as a training unit twice, and finally posted to Fort Campbell,* Kentucky, in September 1956. The 101st participated in numerous training exercises, both in the United States and abroad, over the next nine years. Between July 1965 and December 1967, all three brigades* of the 101st deployed to Vietnam. In addition to winning many

honors in Vietnam, the division moved toward an airmobile status, with helicopters replacing parachutes. When the 101st returned to Fort Campbell, its
evolution continued, as the air assault* concept replaced airmobility. In the fall
of 1990, the 101st responded once again to a national emergency and deployed
to the Persian Gulf for Desert Shield/Desert Storm.* Today, the 101st Airborne
Division (Air Assault) remains prepared to fight anywhere in the world.

References. Leonard Rapport and Arthur Northwood, Jr., *Rendezvous with Destiny*,
1948. Barry D. Smith, *101st Airborne Division in Colour Photographs*, 1993.

John Edgecomb

OPERATIONAL ART

Operational art is the military activity intermediate between tactics* (the art
of winning battles) and strategy* (the broad conduct of war). It comprehends
the range of activities involved in the design and conduct of campaigns and
major operations—selecting, sequencing, and coordinating practical actions so
that they contribute effectively to the overall purpose.

In the 19th century, the term "strategy" was employ to describe the sequencing of battles and engagements to achieve strategic purposes. Looked at from
another point of view, strategy involved the maneuvers prior to battle, designed
to ensure advantage on the battlefield, and those actions after the battle intended
to exploit the success won or mitigate the effects of loss. So long as the campaign was thought of as a series of battles and maneuvers arranged to lead to a
final, climactic engagement, all within a single season, this division of warfare
into matters of tactics and strategy appeared to be adequate. However, as the
scale of warfare grew with the effects of the democratic and industrial revolutions, single-season campaigns became a thing of the past. "Strategy" was used
increasingly to address the linkages between the battlefield and state, mobilization of manpower and industrial resources, and the guidance of the entire
national edifice. A new term was required to describe the principles of campaign
design and conduct. To this end, Soviet military theorists coined the phrase
"operational art." The other major continental power, Germany, tended to speak
of operations as a category of activity intermediate between strategy and tactics,
but without building a body of literature comparable to the Soviet Army's.

In the U.S. Army, operational art gained currency after the Vietnam War.*
This is easily explained as a response to the Army's belief that it had won all
of its battles in Vietnam but had still lost the war, a view first offered by Colonel
Harry Summers in his book *On Strategy*. While the view was comforting, it was
always dubious. Nonetheless, if the problem was that successful tactical engagements had not been properly brought to bear on the overall objective of the
war, it was clear that what was needed was a theory of how to do better. This
led to the search for a science of the use of battles for strategic purposes, and
then to the adoption of the Soviet concept—though most often using German
examples.

References. David M. Glantz, "Operation Art and Tactics," *Military Review*, December 1988, 32–40. Michael Howard, *The Causes of War and other Essays*, 2d ed., 1983. Clayton R. Newell and Michael D. Krause, eds., *On Operational Art*, 1994.

Richard Swain

OPERATIONS OTHER THAN WAR

With the end of the Cold War,* it quickly became apparent that many armed-force missions would soon fall into the ill-defined category that had been termed "low-intensity conflict"* (LIC). These missions would prevent or moderate conflicts rather than prosecute them. Thus, the Department of Defense* replaced the term LIC with a more appropriate (and less limiting) definition that encompasses a broader spectrum of future operations. Included under the umbrella of "operations other than war" (OOTW) are such actions as peacekeeping, peace enforcement, humanitarian assistance and disaster relief, stability operations, noncombatant evacuation operations, nation assistance, support to domestic civil authorities, arms control, security assistance, support to counterdrug operations, combatting terrorism, shows of force, support for insurgencies and counterinsurgencies, and attacks and raids.

According to the U.S. Army's Field Manual* (FM) 100–5, *Operations* (14 June 1993), OOTW "may precede and/or follow war or occur simultaneously with war in the same theater." FM 100–5 goes on to note that OOTW "may be conducted in conjunction with wartime operations to complement the achievement of strategic objectives" and that they are "designed to promote regional stability, maintain or achieve democratic end states, retain U.S. influence and access abroad, provide humane assistance to distressed areas, protect U.S. interests, and assist U.S. civil authorities." While the concept of OOTW was primarily an Army initiative, it elicited some interest in the other services, and the concept and its associated terminology continue to evolve. The Army has already modified the term by prefacing it with "Military."

References. George A. Joulwan, "Operations Other than War," *Military Review*, February 1994, 5–10. Dane L. Rota, "Combat Decision Making in 'Operations Other than War,'" *Military Review*, March–April 1996, 24–28.

Fred J. Chiaventone

ORDNANCE CORPS

The Ordnance Corps traces its lineage to the Ordnance Department, created by an act of Congress on 14 May 1812. This department replaced the Board of War and Ordnance, which had supervised material during the American Revolution.* The Corps has undergone many changes since 1812, joining the Artillery Corps at one time, then separating again. Its roles and missions have also changed repeatedly, with missions such as vehicle production and procurement moving back and forth between the Ordnance and Quartermaster Corps.* During World War I* and World War II,* the Ordnance Department maintained and operated arsenals throughout the United States, developing and producing equipment for the Army. Most of these facilities are now closed or in private hands. Currently, the Ordnance Corps provides maintenance, missile oversight, and ammunition expertise, including explosive ordnance disposal, for the Army. Headquartered at Aberdeen Proving Ground,* Maryland, the Corps maintains Rock Island Arsenal,* Illinois, and the Missile and Munitions Center at Redstone Arsenal, Alabama. These facilities train officers, NCOs, and enlisted personnel in all ordnance skills needed for assignments throughout the Army.

References. Constance McLaughlin Green, Harry C. Thompson, and Peter C. Roots, *The Ordnance Department*, 1955. James A. Huston, *The Sinews of War*, 1966.

Jim Martin

ORDNANCE RESEARCH AND DEVELOPMENT CENTER. *See* Aberdeen Proving Ground.

ORDNANCE RIFLE

Developed in 1861, the number of three-inch ordnance rifles in service in 1865 was exceeded only by that of the Napoleon 12-pounder. Like other rifled artillery of the period, the ordnance rifle was produced by cutting seven spiral grooves into the drilled-out solid core of a tube. A series of wrought-iron strips welded around the core, however, made the ordnance rifle stronger than most other rifled artillery pieces. More accurate than the smoothbore guns, the ordnance rifle was particularly effective for counterbattery fire.* It was also known as the Rodman rifle and the Griffen rifle. The ordnance rifle's major weakness was its inability to fire canister, due to scoring of the grooves. When the Army returned to the frontier after the Civil War.* the ordnance rifle proved too heavy for mobile warfare. The Army eventually replaced it with a much lighter 1.65-inch, breech-loading rifled gun.

References. James C. Hazlett, Edwin Olmstead, and M. Hume Parks, *Field Artillery Weapons of the Civil War*, 1983. Warren Ripley, *Artillery and Ammunition of the Civil War*, 1970.

Jeffrey S. Shadburn

OTIS, ELWELL STEPHEN (1838–1909)

A career soldier who rose to command U.S. Army forces in the Philippines at the turn of the century, Elwell Stephen Otis was born 25 March 1838 at Frederick City, Maryland. He graduated from Harvard Law School, joined the U.S. Army during the Civil War,* and distinguished himself as a brigade* commander in combat. After the war, Otis served on the frontier for nearly two decades. He helped organize the School for the Application of Infantry and Cavalry* at Fort Leavenworth,* commanded the Department of the Columbia, and rose to the rank of brigadier general. When the United States declared war against Spain in April 1898, the War Department* appointed Otis a major general of volunteers and dispatched him to San Francisco, where he managed the deployment of U.S. forces to the Philippines. He subsequently sailed for Manila and replaced Major General Wesley Merritt* as commander of the Department of the Pacific and military governor of the Philippine archipelago in August 1898. Otis directed U.S. Army operations against Filipino insurgents from February 1899 until May 1900, when he returned to the United States. Promoted to major general in the Regular Army in June 1900, Otis commanded the Department of the Lakes until his retirement in 1902. Elwell Otis died in 1909.

References. Thomas F. Burdett, "A New Evaluation of General Otis' Leadership in the Philippines," *Military Review*, January 1975, 79–87. John M. Gates, *Schoolbooks and Krags*, 1973.

Stephen D. Coats

OVERLORD

"Overlord" was the Allied codename for the invasion of Europe in World War II.* The Allies had amassed an army of forty-five divisions,* 6,000 aircraft, and 5,300 ships under the command of General Dwight D. Eisenhower.* Opposing the invasion were over fifty German divisions, ten of them armored, stretched along the Atlantic coast. Field Marshal Erwin Rommel, commanding forty of these divisions stationed along the Channel, spent the time before the impending invasion strengthening his position on the Atlantic Wall. For the Germans, who laid over four million mines,* the question was not if the invasion was coming but when and where. The Allies asked the same questions. Because of the limited range of the Allied fighter aircraft, the invasion had to take place between the Pas de Calais and Normandy. The Allies chose Normandy because of its relatively weaker defenses.

The invasion force sailed on the night of 5 June as 24,000 airborne troops took off for France to secure areas behind the landing beaches. The U.S. 82d and 101st Airborne Divisions landed around and to the south of Ste. Merè-Église, and the British 6th Airborne Division landed between Cabourg and the Orne River on the left in the predawn hours of 6 June. At dawn, the amphibious forces landed on five beaches, the Americans on Utah and Omaha on the right and the British and Canadians on Gold, Juno, and Sword on the left. By nightfall, all beachheads were secure and the troops had made contact with the airheads.

During the next five days, fighting intensified at Caen, where the British faced the Twelfth SS Division, and around Carentan, in the U.S. sector. By then, however, the Allies had linked all five beachheads and held a front sixty miles long and fifteen miles inland at its deepest point. The Allies had accomplished Overlord's initial objective.

References. Max Hastings, *Overlord*, 1984. John Keegan, *Six Armies in Normandy*, 1982.

Edward L. Maier III

P

P-38

"P-38" is a term commonly used by U.S. Army soldiers for a small, folding can-opener first issued in 1943 as part of the Hospital Five-in-One ration. Complaints against the the key opening system used on the World War II* K-ration* resulted in the P-38 becoming a standard item in the G-ration* in June 1944. The P-38 was issued with field rations until the Army adopted the Meals Ready to Eat* (MRE) in the mid-1980s. The origin of the term remains a mystery; however, one version states that soldiers boasted that it could open a can faster than the P-38 aircraft could fly.

References. Harold G. Moore and Joseph L. Galloway, *We Were Soldiers Once . . . and Young*, 1992. Erna Risch, *The Quartermaster Corps*, vol. 1, 1953.

Robert J. Dalessandro

PACIFIC OCEAN AREAS

Pacific Ocean Areas, also Pacific Ocean Area (POA), was one of three major Allied theaters of operations into which the Pacific was divided in April 1942. The other two were the Southwest Pacific Area* (SWPA), under the command of General Douglas MacArthur,* and the Southeast Pacific Area, commanded by Admiral John F. Shafroth. Established in 1941 as a defensive zone, the Southeast Pacific Area, encompassing the waters off the west coast of Central and South America, experienced little combat activity and has received minimal attention from historians. Under the command of Admiral Chester Nimitz, who was also Commander in Chief, U.S. Pacific Fleet (CINCPAC), POA included three subareas: North Pacific Area, Central Pacific Area, and South Pacific Area. The commanders of these areas operated directly under Nimitz. Just before the August 1942 landing on Guadalcanal,* the SWPA's boundary was moved slightly to the west, placing the southern Solomons inside the South Pacific

Area. Thus, POA occupied the area between SWPA and Southeast Pacific Area, north to the Aleutians.

References. Samuel Eliot Morison, *History of United States Naval Operations in World War II*, vols. 3 and 4, 1948–1949. Louis Morton, "Command in the Pacific," *Military Review*, December 1961, 76–88.

John A. Hixson

PACK HOWITZER. *See* Mountain Howitzer.

PALADIN

In the mid-1980s, the U.S. Army launched the howitzer improvement program (HIP) to upgrade the M109A2 and A3 howitzers, self-propelled, 155 mm,* stalwarts of the Army's heavy maneuver brigades* since the 1960s. In February 1980, the secretary of the Army* approved the new design, designated M109A6, for production. Named Paladin after the legendary knights of Charlemagne's court, the A6 was designed for responsiveness and survivability on the modern battlefield. It included the most advanced armament and cannon systems, the latest on-board navigation, fire control, and communications systems, improved suspension and hydraulics, a redesigned interior for efficiency and safety, and a kevlar liner for the turret. In July 1993, the 2d Battalion, 17th Field Artillery, became the first Army unit equipped with the new Paladins.

References. Kevin McAndrews, "Paladin Arrives on the Great Plains," *National Guard*, December 1996, 16–17. Ralph G. Reece and Todd J. Travas, "Paladin," *Field Artillery*, October 1990, 44–47.

PALMER, JOHN McAULEY (1870–1955)

John McAuley Palmer graduated from the U.S. Military Academy* in 1892 and was commissioned into the infantry* just as the Old Army* was seeing the last of frontier garrison life. Appointed the first professor of military science* (PMS) and tactics at the University of Chicago, Palmer rejoined his regiment* in time to see service in China during the Boxer Rebellion.* He later served in the Philippines after a tour on the faculty of the Military Academy. Palmer attended the school at Fort Leavenworth,* served on the General Staff,* and went to China and the Philippines once more before returning to Washington and the General Staff.

More than any other officer of his generation, Palmer believed in and advocated the idea of a citizen army. After returning to the General Staff, Palmer assisted in writing the Selective Service Act of 1917 and publicly supported the Plattsburgh movement.* His command of the 58th Infantry Brigade during a successful attack on the Hindenburg line in 1918 reinforced his conviction that America could rely on its citizen soldiers. Upon returning to the United States, Palmer advocated universal military training as well as an Army in which a citizen-based reserve and National Guard* units were integral to the defense of the United States. Congress incorporated many of his ideas into the National

Defense Act of 1920.* Palmer retired as a brigadier general in 1926 but returned to active duty in 1941. Once again, he advocated a citizen army rather than a Regular Army filled out with draftees. His belief that an army in a democracy must reflect its people remained unshakable until his death in 1955.

References. I. B. Holley, Jr., *General John M. Palmer, Citizen Soldiers, and the Army of a Democracy*, 1982. Jonathan House, "John McAuley Palmer and the Reserve Components," *Parameters*, September 1982, 11–18.

PANMUNJOM

The negotiations leading to an end of the fighting in the Korean War* were lengthy and bitter. The first talks began at the border town of Kaesong on 19 July 1951; they continued, with many interruptions, until the signing of the armistice two years later—a record for modern peace negotiations. From the beginning, the North Korean and Chinese delegates held higher political rank than their U.S. and Republic of Korea (ROK) counterparts. Unable to persuade the UN negotiators to accept the 38th parallel as the demarcation line, the Communists suspended the talks on 23 August, but when the Communist forces were badly battered on the battlefield they returned to the negotiations at the village of Panmunjom. Both sides came to realize that any attempt to seek victory in Korea would entail unacceptable costs. All major issues were agreed upon, but the talks stalled on the question of voluntary repatriation of prisoners of war.* This was an issue imcomprehensible to the Communists, who pointed out that the Geneva Convention provided for the speedy repatriation of all POWs. Realizing that they were suffering a propaganda defeat, the Communists finally dropped their opposition. However, ROK President Syngman Rhee, who bitterly opposed any armistice without reunification on his terms, released all Communist POWs in ROK camps in an attempt to sabotage any armistice. After the promise of substantial U.S. aid, Rhee dropped his opposition, and the armistice was signed on 27 July 1953. It remains in effect, unchanged, to this day.

References. Walter G. Hermes, *Truce Tent and Fighting Front*, 1966. William H. Vatcher, Jr., *Panmunjom*, 1958.

Stanley Sandler

PARACHUTE

The first military use of parachutes by the U.S. Army occurred in World War I* by members of American Expeditionary Force* (AEF) Balloon Corps* units. Parachutes allowed balloon observers to exit their baskets rapidly in case of aerial attack, which was important because the balloons were filled with highly flammable hydrogen gas. Air Service* pilots, however, were not issued parachutes, apparently based in the belief that they would bail out of their expensive and difficult-to-replace machines at the first sign of trouble. Although parachutes were in limited use at the time, Brigadier General William "Billy" Mitchell* proposed parachuting infantry* soldiers behind enemy lines in the anticipated 1919 offensive. The war ended, however, before such an operations could be conducted. Except for an Air Corps* parachute demonstration, where a machine gun and crew were dropped at Kelly Field in 1929, no further test of the paratroop concept occurred until 1940. Based on German army successes in Europe, the Army formed the Parachute Test Platoon at Fort Benning,* Georgia, in 1940. The next summer the Army organized three battalions* of parachute infantry as a Provisional Parachute Group, followed by the formation of an airborne division.* The utility of airborne and other special purpose units, however, continued to generate controversy throughout World War II.*

Army parachutes fall into three main categories: emergency escape parachutes for pilots and aircrew (ripcord activated); personnel parachutes for paratroops (static-line deployed); and cargo parachutes for aerial resupply. The two most common parachutes used by paratroops in World War II were the flat, circular-shaped T-5 and T-7 types. In the deployment sequence, the canopy deployed before the suspension lines, causing severe opening shock, sometimes sufficient to render the trooper unconscious. The addition of a deployment bag to the new T-10 type parachute in the early 1950s decreased opening shock by extending the suspension lines to their full length before deployment.

Until the introduction of the MC-1 series parachute in the 1970s, Army parachutes were virtually nonmaneuverable. The MC-1 allowed the trained jumper to avoid ground obstacles and negate the lateral drift caused by surface winds. Today, a substantial number of officers and enlisted men are jump qualified, and although many of them will never serve in airborne units, their familiarity and knowledge of parachuting is essential to U.S. Army readiness for any conflict in the future.

References. Gerard M. Devlin, *Paratrooper!* 1979. Edwin P. Hoyt, *Airborne*, 1979.

Stephen C. McGeorge

PARADE REST

At the position of parade rest a soldier remains silent and motionless, with his left foot twelve inches to the left of his right foot, legs straight, and hands clasped behind his back. If the soldier is armed with a rifle or musket,* the butt of the weapon rests on the ground by the right foot with the trigger facing to the front, while the muzzle, held in the right hand, is extended forward. The left hand is behind the back. The command "Parade Rest" can be given only while the soldier is at the position of attention.

Reference. P. S. Bond, *Essentials of Infantry Training*, 1934.

PARROTT GUN

In 1837, Captain Robert Parker Parrott resigned from the U.S. Army to become superintendant of the West Point Foundry. Over the next twenty-five years, the foundry became a principal supplier of ordnance for both the Army and Navy. By 1860, Parrott had developed a rifled cannon and soon put a ten-pounder into full production. The rifled cannon offered several advantages over the smooth-bore guns of the time: longer range, greater accuracy, and a more

effective impact. Numerous states, including Virginia, purchased Parrott guns—
or Parrott rifles, as they were also known—for their militias, and the Army
began to place orders for Parrotts after the Civil War* began. The wrought-iron
reinforcing band around the breech of the cast-iron tube distinguished the Parrott
from most other artillery pieces of the period. The Parrott was inexpensive to
manufacture, relatively simple to operate, stood up to rigorous campaigning and
could be produced in large numbers. Models appeared in a variety of calibers
from 2.9 to 8 inches for 10, 12, 20, 30, 60, 100, 200, 250, and 300 pound shells
(Parrotts are frequently referred to by the weight of the shell rather than the
bore diameter). Although the Parrott was not the best rifled cannon available
during the Civil War—the larger guns occasionally burst, killing their crews—it
was the most common, and it saw service in nearly every theater.

References. James C. Hazlett, Edwin Olmstead, and M. Hume Parks, *Field Artillery Weapons of the Civil War*, 1983. Warren Ripley, *Artillery and Ammunition of the Civil War*, 1970. Dean S. Thomas, *Cannons*, 1985.

PARTRIDGE, ALDEN (1785–1854)

The son of Samuel Partridge, a soldier in the American Revolution,* Alden
Partridge received an appointment to the U.S. Military Academy* by President
Thomas Jefferson in 1805 after attending Dartmouth College for several years.
Having completed all requirements, he graduated in October 1806 and was com-
missioned in the Corps of Engineers.* Assigned to the faculty at West Point,
Partridge taught mathematics and engineering for the entire eleven years of his
military career. Resigning from the Army as a captain. Partridge worked as a
surveyor before returning home to Norwich, Vermont, where he founded the
American Literary, Scientific and Military Academy, later chartered as Norwich
University. Partridge's association with Norwich was episodic, but his interest
in national defense persisted, and he worked for the establishment of numerous
other military academies in the northeast. Based on his observations during the
War of 1812,* he believed that the nation would have to rely on citizen soldiers
and that West Point could not provide sufficient trained officers in times of
crisis. In this respect, Partridge's ideas were far ahead of his time, but his concept of schools and academies, in which military training was a substantial
component, forshadowed a later period when the Reserve Officers' Training
Corps* (ROTC) would become part of the American higher education system.

References. William Arba Ellis, ed. and comp., *Norwich University*, vol. 1, *General History*, 1819–1911, 1911. Lester A. Webb, *Captain Alden Patridge and the United States Military Academy*, 1965.

PATCH, ALEXANDER M. (1889–1945)

The son of an Army officer, Alexander "Sandy" Patch entered the U.S. Military Academy* in 1909. Commissioned in the infantry* in 1913, Patch served
on the Mexican border during the Punitive Expedition* and in France with the
1st Division* in World War I.* Upon returning from Europe, Patch spent much

of his time in training and school assignments, where he developed a reputation as an outstanding trainer and leader. As a member of the Infantry Board in 1936, he participated in the development of the triangular division* concept. While commanding the Infantry Replacement Training Center at Camp Croft, South Carolina, in January 1942, Patch was named commander of Task Force 6814, the U.S. force then deploying to New Caledonia. Following a bout of pneumonia, Patch joined the task force and welded it into the new Americal Division.* On 9 December 1942, the Americal relieved the 1st Marine Division on Guadalcanal,* and the next month Patch was named commanding general of XIV Corps.

Patch returned to the United States in the spring of 1943 and once again turned to his specialty, training soldiers for war. In March 1944, Patch was designated to command the U.S. Seventh Army. He joined Seventh Army in Italy and led it in operation Dragoon,* the invasion of southern France. He was promoted to lieutenant general in August 1944. Under Patch, Seventh Army fought north, then east, linking up with Third Army* north of Dijon in September and Fifth Army* at the Brenner Pass the following May. Following Germany's surrender, the War Department* recalled Patch to the United States to train yet another army, Fourth Army, for the final assault of the war. However, Japan surrendered before Fourth Army could deploy to the Pacific. Patch, known as a soldier's general, a man of fierce integrity, and a strong disciplinarian, died suddenly of pneumonia on 21 November 1945 and is buried at West Point.

References. Truman R. Strobridge and Bernard C. Nalty, "From the South Pacific to the Brenner Pass," *Military Review*, June 1981, 41–48. William K. Wyant, *Sandy Patch*, 1991.

PATHFINDER

A pathfinder is a specially selected and trained, airborne qualified soldier, typically a private first class (PFC), whose primary mission is control of Army aircraft, both fixed and rotary-wing, in areas designated by support unit commanders. The need for pathfinders first became apparent when the 82d Airborne Division* drop over Sicily in 1943 scattered paratroopers over a fifty-mile radius. Early in 1944, the Army opened the first Pathfinder school at North Witham, England, to train pathfinders for Overlord.* After World War II,* the school moved to Fort Benning,* Georgia. In 1951, the U.S. Air Force assumed navigational drop-zone* responsibility, and the Army closed the Pathfinder School. The development of the air-mobile concept in the early 1960s, however, regenerated the need for Army pathfinders. Pathfinder units grew from two in 1963 to thirty in 1965. Pathfinders, whose motto is "Semper Primus" (always first), deploy as individuals or in small teams; they reconnoiter, select, and help prepared landing zones* (LZs); they provide voice, visual, and electronic assistance to landing aircraft; they provide weather and ground condition information; they control air traffic into and out of the LZ; and they assist in the assembly and direction of troops on the LZ until a senior officer assumes command. The Pathfinders School at Fort Benning offers a rigorous three-week course that qualifies graduates to serve in pathfinder units and wear the coveted pathfinder badge, the Winged Torch.

References. Edward M. Chamberlain, "Pathfinders," *Infantry*, January–February 1972, 32–35. Michael Honeycutt, "Pathfinders," *U.S. Army Aviation Digest*, August 1983, 26–28.

PATRIOT AIR DEFENSE SYSTEM

The Patriot air defense system's success in Desert Storm* quickly made it a household name. The Patriot program began in 1965, and the first missile was launched in 1970. The Army signed the contract to complete development of the Patriot in 1976, and testing concluded in 1981. After a follow-up evaluation, the Army deployed the Patriot in 1984. Manufactured by Raytheon Company, this surface-to-air missile (SAM) system replaced two outdated systems, the Nike Hercules and Hawk. It has been continually upgraded to counter new threats, such as stealth aircraft. A Patriot battery* consists of a radar* set, an antenna-mast-group vehicle, a AN/MQ-24 power plant, a control station, and eight remote launching stations. The rockets are 5.31 meters in length and rely on a single-stage solid-propellant (TX-486) motor for propulsion. The missile attains a speed in excess of Mach 3 and is armed with a high-explosive warhead. Although the Patriot performed admirably in Desert Storm, new evidence is emerging that problems exist with the system. Nevertheless, the United States and several other countries continue to use the Patriot.

References. Daniel O. Graham, "Patriot Missile Success over Scuds Has Application for SDI Program," *Officer.* May 1991, 36–38. Rudi Meller, "Patriot," *International Defense Review*, 1980, 495–499.

Trevor Brown

PATTON, GEORGE SMITH, JR. (1885–1945)

George Smith Patton, Jr., was born on 11 November 1885 into a family with a strong military heritage. He attended Viginia Military Institute* for one year before going to the U.S. Military Academy,* where he graduated with the class of 1909. Commissioned in the cavalry,* he was a superb horseman and competed in the modern pentathlon at the 1912 Olympics. Patton served as Major General John J. Pershing's* aide during the Punitive Expedition* in 1916; there his exploits included a gunfight in which he killed General Julio Cardenas and his orderly. Promoted to captain, Patton joined the American Expeditionary Force* (AEF), where he became the first member of the Tank Corps and organized a training center for tanks in France. After seeing action in the Meuse-Argonne,* Patton returned from Europe in 1919 as a colonel, with a Purple Heart* and Distinguished Service Cross.*

Reverting to his permanent rank of captain, Patton would not regain his wartime rank of colonel until 1938. As the United States began to rearm from 1940 to 1942, Patton commanded a brigade* 2d Armor Division, I Armored Corps, and helped organize a desert training center in California. Patton successfully commanded the western task force for Operation Torch,* landing in Morocco in November 1942. Following the disaster at Kasserine Pass,* General Dwight D. Eisenhower* selected Patton to command and rejuvenate II Corps in March 1943. Promoted to lieutenant general in April, Patton commanded Seventh Army* during the invasion of Sicily. Although Eisenhower reprimanded Patton for two incidents in which he slapped soldiers hospitalized for cambat fatigue, he summoned him to England in January 1944 to set up and command the dummy army in the deception plan for Overlord.* Patton landed in France in July and assumed command of Third Army* on 1 August. Under Patton, Third Army exploited the Allied breakout at Avranches, reduced German defenses in Britanny in a week, drove east into Lorraine and the Saar, and shifted north toward the Ardennes* to relieve Bastogne in December 1944.

In late January 1945, the Allies resumed the offensive. Patton conducted an active defense at the Siegfried Line,* captured Trier on 1 March, and drove toward Koblenz and Mannheim. Third Army crossed the Rhine on 22 March and continued a rapid movement toward Kassel. Prepared to take Prague, Patton was disappointed when a political agreement placed Prague in the Soviet sector of occupation. When he publicly refused to ban former Nazis from holding local administrative offices after the war, he was removed from command of Third Army. George Patton died in Heidelberg, Germany, on 21 December 1945 from injuries suffered in an automobile accident twelve days earlier. His name has become synonymous with relentless, aggressive tactics and pursuit.

References. Martin Blumenson. *Patton*, 1985. George Forty, *The Armies of George S. Patton*, 1996. Roger H. Nye, *The Patton Mind*, 1993. Charles M. Province, *The Unknown Patton*, 1983.

George Mordica II

PATTON TANK. *See* M48 Patton Tank.

PAY DEPARTMENT
Congress created the Pay Department on 16 June 1775, with the Paymaster General as its senior officer. James Warren was the first Paymaster General. In 1821, Colonel Nathan Townson became Paymaster General, a position he held for thirty-four years. The regulations and procedures that he instituted remained in force for nearly a century and reduced the cost of paying the troops to 1.3 percent of the amount paid. Ironically, the efficiency of his department ensured that it remained one of the smallest in the Army. Townson also forsaw the time when the Pay Department would be responsible for financial management as well as pay, a vision that became practical with the advent of computers. During the Civil War,* the Pay Department expanded to 447 paymasters, yet it maintained the highest standards under Paymaster Generals Andrews and Brice. Less than one half of 1 percent of all moneys dispatched failed to reach their intended

recipients. The Pay Department, with its Paymaster General, lost its identity when it was absorbed by the Quartermaster Corps* in 1912.

References. Maurice Matloff, ed., *American Military History*, 1969. Russell F. Weigley, *History of the United States Army*, 1967.

William H. Carnes

PEA RIDGE

After their victory at Wilson's Creek* in August 1861, Confederate forces remained in the Springfield, Missouri, area. On 10 February 1862, 11,000 Federal troops under Brigadier General Samuel Curtis moved toward Springfield, forcing the Confederates to fall back into Arkansas, where they were reinforced, and Major General Earl Van Dorn assumed command. Van Dorn then moved north with 17,000 men and on 6 March encountered Curtis's force occupying defensive positions about fifteen miles south of the Missouri border in the vicinity of Pea Ridge. Van Dorn decided against a frontal assault but instead, in a gruelling night march, moved his army onto the Federal eastern and western flanks. An eight-mile interval between elements, however, left Van Dorn with a precarious comand-and-control arrangement. The Confederate attack developed slowly on 7 March, and Curtis skillfully redeployed his units to counter the threat. On the Federal left, two Confederate generals were killed in quick succession, and their forces retired in disorder. Curtis's right flank was driven back almost a mile before reinforcements stabilized the situation and nightfall ended the fighting. An inadequate logistical system failed to resupply the exhausted Confederates, and with virtually no artillery ammunition, they withdrew the next morning in the face of renewed Federal attacks. The Federals did not pursue. Curtis lost approximately 1,400 men; Van Dorn lost 1,300, including 300 prisoners. The battle of Pea Ridge determined that the Union would retain control of Missouri.

References. William S. Bland and William M. Raymond, Jr., "Thunder in the Ozarks," *Field Artillery*, July–August 1998, 38–43. William L. Shea and Earl J. Hess, *Pea Ridge*, 1992.

Brian D. Moore

PEACEMAKER. *See* Colt Single-Action Army.

PENICILLIN

Although discovered in 1928, by the early 1940s penicillin was still being developed for mass production. Truly a revolutionary drug, it was the most effective antibiotic agent in the pharmacopeia of World War II.* Because of its recent emergence on the medical scene, penicillin dosage and therapy were poorly understood. This led to the idea that "more is better," and despite massive U.S. production, shortages persisted throughout the war. Most of the penicillin produced was reserved for military use. Penicillin was routinely administered to wounded soldiers early in the evacuation process. Hundreds of thousands of soldiers who in other wars would have died from wounds, postoperative infections, or bacterial disease owed their lives to penicillin. By contrast, German medical practitioners were only dimly aware of the benefits of penicillin and never developed mass production facilities. The result was a far higher rate of wound mortality among German soldiers.

References. Albert E. Cowdrey, *Fighting for Life*, 1994. J. D. Ratcliff, *Yellow Magic*, 1945.

Stephen C. McGeorge

PENINSULA CAMPAIGN

In early 1862, the Federal strategy for victory revolved around the capture of Richmond. President Abraham Lincoln continued to urge his new general in chief, Major General George B. McClellan,* to move against Confederate forces along the Rappahannock. McClellan feared that the overland approach would be highly fortified and too costly to carry by direct assault. He proposed a plan to bypass the bulk of Confederate forces by conducting an amphibious landing on the peninsula between the James and York Rivers, move up the peninsula, and achieve a junction with Major General Irvin McDowell's army, thus encircling the Confederate forces near Richmond. Lincoln favored the conventional approach but finally agreed. In mid-March, McClellan moved about 120,000 men to Fort Monroe* and on 3 April began his march toward Richmond.

At the Warwick River, Major General John B. Magruder and 15,000 Confederates waited. Although Magruder was vastly outnumbered, McClellan opted to lay siege to his line rather than risk assault. McClellan's failure to attack gave Joseph E. Johnston* the opportunity to reinforce Magruder. While McClellan laid siege, Johnston's force grew to 60,000 and two days prior to McClellan's opening bombardment, Johnston moved to better defensive positions around Richmond. On 5 May McClellan clashed with Johnston's rear guard; by 25 May McClellan was within sight of Richmond. He deployed three corps* south of the Chickahominy and three corps north to effect the junction with McDowell.

With McClellan astride the rain-swollen Chickahominy, Johnston saw an opportunity and struck McClellan's southern flank on 31 May. In the two-day battle of Seven Pines,* Johnston nearly enveloped McClellan's left. Although the Federals repulsed the Confederate attacks on both days and Johnston was seriously wounded, McClellan suffered heavy casualties and failed to capture Richmond. Johnston's replacement, Robert E. Lee,* went on the offensive and, in the Seven Days* battles, pushed the Federal forces back with heavy losses. McClellan's failure in the Peninsula campaign ultimately led to his relief by the frustrated Lincoln.

References. Joseph P. Cullen, *The Peninsula Campaign, 1862*, 1973. William J. Miller, ed., *The Peninsula Campaign*, 1997. Stephen W. Sears, *To the Gates of Richmond*, 1992.

Rebecca S. Witte

PENNSYLVANIA RIFLE

With its roots in the craftsmanship of German gunsmiths, the Pennsylvania rifle first appeared in colonial America in the 1740s. Most of the early production centered around Lancaster, Pennsylvania, although gunsmiths in Virginia and North Carolina also crafted the weapon for frontier hunters. The typical Pennsylvania rifle possessed an octagonal barrel at least forty inches long, in various calibers ranging from .52 to .65 inches. The Pennsylvania was unsuitable for close combat (it was not fitted for a bayonet,)* required a higher grade of powder than smoothbore muskets,* and took three times longer to load than smoothbore muskets. Nonetheless, a skilled Pennsylvania marksman could hit his mark at 200 yards, compared to eighty yards with a smoothbore.

While several European nations had experimented with rifles in warfare, the American colonists were the first to employ them extensively in combat. The colonists introduced the rifle early to the American Revolution,* although not without some consideration for the implications involved. One military writer, Lewis Nicola, wrote: "Using rifles in war is certainly savage and cruel, but the Americans may allege in their defense that law of absolute necessity, which supersedes all other obligations." The most famous U.S. unit to make use of the Pennsylvania rifle was Morgan's Rifles. Elements of Morgan's Rifles turned in remarkable feats of marksmanship at Saratoga* and during the Sullivan Expedition in 1779.

References. J. George Frederick, "The Kentucky Rifle Myth," *National Guardsman*, August 1951, 8–10. Henry J. Kauffman, *The Pennsylvania-Kentucky Rifle*, 1960.

Joseph R. Fischer

PENTAGON

By late 1941, Europe had been embroiled in war for almost two years, and it was becoming increasingly evident that the United States would not be able to stay out of the conflict indefinitely. Expansion of War Department* facilities was already under way. Most War Department offices were scattered about Washington, D.C., and the surrounding area in creaking, dilapidated, temporary buildings first occupied during World War I.* To manage the expansion effectively, planning began for a building that would house the defense community headquarters in a single location.

The site chosen was in Virginia near Arlington Cemetery. Planners felt this location was ideal for such a massive, temporary construction, as it would not disrupt the master plan for Washington's future development. The original site, nothing more than a wasteland of swamps and dumps, required over five million cubic yards of earthen fill. The first contract was awarded in August 1941, and construction began immediately. By May 1942, 500,000 square feet of offices were ready for occupancy, and by January 1943 construction was complete, at a cost of $83 million. The project consolidated War Department activities and returned the original investment within seven years. Because of its distinctive five-sided shape, the building became known as the Pentagon.

The Pentagon currently houses the Department of Defense,* the chairman of the Joint Chiefs of Staff,* the service chiefs, and approximately 23,000 personnel, about half civilians and half uniformed members of the armed forces. In 1993, the temporary facility celebrated its fiftieth anniversary. The term "Pentagon" is often used synonymously with the U.S. defense establishment.

References. Alfred Goldberg, *The Pentagon*, 1992. Perry M. Smith, *Assignment: Pentagon*, 1989.

Gary Bounds

PENTOMIC DIVISION

The 1950s pentomic division evolved from U.S. Army Chief of Staff* Matthew Ridgway's* belief that the nation's nuclear deterrence–massive retaliation strategy would fail. Ridgway and his successor, Maxwell D. Taylor,* explored ways to organize Army divisions* for both nuclear and nonnuclear battlefields, including the use of tactical nuclear weapons, to neutralize U.S. numerical inferiority compared to the Soviets. The new division was designed to provide maximum flexibility and survivability in the event of nuclear attack. Each division, airborne,* infantry,* and armor,* consisted of five battle groups; each battle group consisted of five companies,* and each company had five platoons.* (The recurring number five throughout the internal division structure suggested the term "pentomic division.") Each battle group included a headquarters and service company, to provide reconnaissance, maintenance, medical, and signal support, and a heavy mortar* battery.* The division included an Honest John rocket battery and five artillery batteries, to be attached to each battle group as required. In 1956, the 101st Airborne Division* became the first Army unit to adopt the pentomic concept.

The pentomic division concept ultimately failed tactically, because the span of control taxed even the best commanders; it was organized primarily for nuclear rather than conventional war; the support structure proved too weak to sustain the force; and it had no reserve. Moreover, when the Soviets fielded their own tactical nuclear weapons, Army thinkers realized that the pentomic division's tactical nuclear arsenal offered little advantage and could only result in a senseless stalemate. After January 1961, the Kennedy administration implemented a strategy* of flexible response* and the Army quickly shed the pentomic concept.

References. A. J. Bacevich, *The Pentomic Era*, 1986. James M. Gavin, *War and Peace in the Space Age*, 1958.

Walter E. Kretchik

PERRYVILLE

Following a summer of relative inactivity in Tennessee and northern Alabama, Confederate General Braxton Bragg, in coordination with a force under Major General Edmund Kirby Smith, invaded Kentucky in the fall of 1862. The Confederate advance prompted Major General Don Carlos Buell to give up his lethargic advance in western Tennessee and move back into Kentucky to defend his base at Louisville. Buell's slow-moving forces finally threatened Bragg, trying to install a pro-Confederate state government in Frankfort. Neither commander completely understood the dimensions of the pending battle along Doctor's Fork of the Chaplin River, near the small town of Perryville. The two armies, searching for water in the drought-parched landscape, met on 8 October 1962. A Federal division* commanded by Brigadier General Philip H. Sheridan* clashed with a Confederate corps under Major General Leonidas Polk. Polk's corps,* reinforced by Major General William J. Hardee's corps, pushed Major General Alexander McCook's Federal force back more than a mile but had less success with the other Federal forces nearby. As Buell prepared to continue combat on the 9th, Bragg led his forces away to Herrodsville and into Tennessee. One outcome of the campaign was the relief of the ultra-cautious Buell from his command. Polk, Hardee, and many of Bragg's officers became openly hostile to their commander. This dissension would do much to cripple Confederate efforts in the west for the remainder of the war.

References. Kenneth A. Hafendorfer, *Perryville*, 1981. James Lee McDonough, *War in Kentucky*, 1994.

Andrew N. Morris

PERSHING, JOHN JOSEPH (1860–1948)

John Joseph Pershing was born on 3 September 1860 in Linn County, Missouri, and graduated from the U.S. Military Academy* in 1886. He first served with the 6th Cavalry and later with the 10th Cavalry (Buffalo Soldiers*), where he received the nickname "Black Jack." He served in campaigns in New Mexico and Arizona against the Apache and in the Dakotas against the Sioux. From 1897 to 1898, he taught tactics* at the Academy. When the Spanish-American War* began, Pershing again served with the 10th Cavalry in Santiago,* Cuba. From 1899 to 1903, he filled various positions in the Philippines, where his actions against the Moros won him the admiration of President Theodore Roosevelt. Upon returning to the United States, Roosevelt promoted Pershing from captain to brigadier general, passing over 862 more senior officers. He commanded the Punitive Expedition* against Pancho Villa in 1916, a campaign that brought him national recognition. With the U.S. entry into World War I,* Pershing was named commander of the American Expeditionary Forces* (AEF), the first U.S. military force ever sent to fight in Europe. As AEF commander, Pershing was promoted to General of the Armies. From 1921 to 1924, Pershing served as the Army's Chief of Staff* and, after his retirement in 1924, as the chairman of the American Battle Monuments Commission. He was an early advocate of U.S. involvement in World War II,* although he took no active part in that war. Pershing died in 1948 and is buried in Arlington National Cemetery.*

References. Frederick Palmer, *John J. Pershing*, 1948. Donald Smythe, *Guerrilla Warrior*, 1973; and *Pershing*, 1986. Frank E. Vandiver, *Black Jack*, 2 vols., 1977.

John Edgecomb

PETERSBURG

On the morning of 4 May 1864, the new general in chief of the Union Army, Ulysses S. Grant,* put his great army into motion with the objective of finally bringing Robert E. Lee's* Army of Northern Virginia to battle and destroying it. Over the next six weeks, Grant and Lee dueled from the Rapidan to the James Rivers, Grant trying to force Lee into the open by moving around his right flank, Lee racing ahead of Grant to prepare and fight a series of brilliant defensive battles—Wilderness,* Spotsylvania,* North Anna, and Cold Harbor.* In spite of Lee's tactical successes, by the middle of June Grant had succeeded in moving around Richmond and began crossing the James. Grant now threatened the city of Petersburg, a vital communications center, twenty-three miles south of Richmond.

The siege of Petersburg began on 18 June 1864 and lasted until the end of March 1865. The two armies fought numerous engagements around the siege-works, as Grant sought a flank and Lee adroitly shored up his defenses wherever they were most threatened. Lee, the great master of maneuver, now proved that he was also "king of spades." Historians have observed that the siege of Petersburg forshadowed the future: in the siege lines around Petersburg one can see the specter of the trenches on the Western Front in 1915. On 29 March 1864, Grant once again set his armies in motion, and within a week Lee abandoned his defenses and Petersburg fell to the Union Army.

References. John Horn, *The Petersburg Campaign, June 1864–April 1965*, 1993. Henry Pleasants, Jr., and George H. Straley, *Inferno at Petersburg*, 1961.

Edward Shanahan

PETROLEUM, OILS, AND LUBRICANTS

Petroleum, oils, and lubricants, commonly referred to as POL, constitute Class III of the military classes of supply. The U.S. Army consumes large quantities of petroleum products, both in bulk and packaged forms. During peacetime, each service is responsible for planning and preparing for bulk-petroleum support to its own forces, including managing peacetime operating stocks and war reserves, and operating bulk storage, handling, and distribution facilities. During wartime (or in specific operations other than war* [OOTW]), the Army is responsible for the inland distribution of bulk fuels, including distribution to the Air Force and Marines. Inland distribution requires an Army organization structure capable of constructing, operating, and maintaining overland pipelines and facilities for bulk, nonpipeline fuels. Packaged POL products include lubricants, greases, hydraulic fluids, compressed gasses, and specialty items that are stored, transported, and issued in containers with capacites of fifty-five gallons or less.

References. John W. Ellis, "Welcome to the Petroleum Supply Battalion!" *Army Logistician*, January–February 1991, 34–36. Robert W. Metz, "Military Pipeline Operations," *Engineer*, no. 2, 1987, 16–18.

Lawyn C. Edwards

THE PHIL SILVERS SHOW. See Sergeant Bilko.

PHILIPPINE INSURRECTION

A couple of months after the December 1899 Treaty of Paris, which officially ended the Spanish-American War,* the United States became embroiled in another conflict in the Philippines. The seeds of this conflict had been sown a few years earlier when a secret society called the Katipunan rebelled against Spanish rule in the Philippines. In 1896, the Spanish granted the Filipinos certain freedoms, such as freedom of the press, in return for an armistice and the self-imposed exile of Emilio Aguinaldo, the Katipunan leader, who left for Hong Kong with forty of his most trusted lieutenants. In April 1898, a few days before the United States declared war against Spain, E. Spencer Pratt, the U.S. Consul General at Singapore, told Aguinaldo that if he returned to the islands and stirred up another revolt against the Spanish, the United States would grant his people independence. Spencer's offer did not have State Department authority.

Pratt notified Admiral George Dewey of the plan, and two weeks after the U.S. victory at Manila Bay, Aguinaldo arrived back in the Philippines and began assembling an insurgent army. The Filipinos quickly attacked and overthrew Spanish garrisons throughout the islands. The insurgents' continued success, and the distinct possibility that they might capture Manila, caused great concern in Washignton. When transports carrying Brigadier General Thomas Anderson and the vanguard of VIII Corps* steamed into Manila Bay and disembarked at the Cavite Navy Yard on 1 July 1898, insurgents had already surrounded the Philippine capital. To avoid future problems with the rebels, Anderson notified Aguinaldo that the United States recognized his military leadership but not his civil authority. Aguinaldo considered Anderson's remarks a violation of Pratt's and Dewey's promises.

On 15 July 1898, Major General Francis Greene's troop convoy reached Manila, and ten days later Major General Wesley Merritt* arrived at Cavite and assumed command of all U.S. expeditionary forces in the Philippines. Major General Arthur MacArthur's* regiment followed within a few days. Plans were quickly formulated for capturing the city, but Aguinaldo was not notified of the arrangements. Realizing that his troops could not advance on Manila without running into insurgent entrenchments, Merritt asked the rebel leader to order the insurgents to vacate the trenches to the south so that U.S. artillery* could be brought up and trained on the city. The night before the scheduled land and sea attack against Manila, Merritt notified Aguinaldo that the rebels must not enter the capital if U.S. forces captured the city, denying the rebels the honor due them as liberators of their own country. Early on 13 August the rebels began their attack on the Spanish defenses, then followed Anderson's advancing brigades* to occupy part of the Manila suburbs.

Believing now that the U.S. government never intended to give the Philippine Islands their independence, Aguinaldo determined to throw off U.S. rule before it became firmly established. Throughout January 1899, U.S. and insurgent forces faced each other; minor incidents were reported, but disputes were quickly settled. However, on 4 February an insurgent patrol was noticed crossing U.S. lines. When the Filipinos continued to advance despite several challenges, gunfire erupted all along the line. On hearing that his men were under attack, Aguinaldo immediately issued a declaration of war against the United States. U.S. forces soon defeated the untrained and poorly armed rebel soldiers and pushed them back into the mountains and thick jungles of central Luzon. With climate and terrain in their favor, however, the insurgents began to conduct a vicious guerrilla war. The mountain Igorot tribesmen, without guns, used their spears and long knives to ambush U.S. patrols.

Two years later, on 23 March 1901, a detachment of Army volunteers and native scouts under the command of Brigadier General Frederick Funston,* dressed in insurgent uniforms, enter Aguinaldo's camp at Palanan and captured the rebel leader. Although resistance to U.S. authority appeared to end, many Filipinos vowed to continue the fight for independence, and guerrilla activity persisted. Not until 4 July 1902 could President Theodore Roosevelt declare that the Philippine Insurrection had been crushed. The four years of war involved 100,000 U.S. troops, entailed 2,811 separate engagements, and cost 4,243 killed and 2,818 wounded. More than 16,000 insurgents died in the conflict.

When the southern islands broke out into open revolt, U.S. soldiers, who assumed that they were going home, were instead sent to remote outposts on Samar, Cebu, Mindanao, and Jolo. The fight to subdue the bolo-swinging Moro tribesmen on these malaria and cholera-infested islands dragged on for years. Troops of the 8th Infantry, commanded by Captain John J. Pershing,* finally ended the struggle when they defeated the Moros in the battle of Bagsak Mountain on Jolo Island on 15 June 1913. Casualties for this eleven-year period have never been adequately determined.

References. John M. Gates, *Schoolbooks and Krags*, 1973. Brian M. Linn, *The U.S. Army and Counterinsurgency in the Philippine War, 1899–1902*, 1989. Stuart C. Miller, *"Benevolent Assimilation,"* 1982.

A. B. Feuer

PHILIPPINE SCOUTS

Major General Elwell S. Otis* directed the formation of the first company* of Philippine Scouts (PS) in 1899. Challenged during the Philippine Insurrection* not only by a skillful adversary but by climate, terrain, and linguistic diversity, the U.S. Army quickly incorporated native collaborators into its fighting force, first as contract employees of the Quartermaster Department (U.S. Army Volunteers, paid from civilian funds), then as the Scouts. Macabebe natives, descended from Mexican troops brought to the Philippines by the Spanish in the 17th century, were initially recruited as Scouts, because they had assisted in the capture of the insurgent leader Emilio Aquinaldo. In 1901, Congress recognized the Scouts and made them part of the Regular Army, assumed responsibility for their pay and entitlements, and provided for three-year enlistments. Thereafter, all native tribes could contribute troops to the Scouts.

Originally formed in separate companies under the command of officers seconded from the U.S. Army, the Scouts were organized into battalions* in 1905. Native Scouts first received commissions as lieutenants in 1902, and in 1908 Filipinos were authorized admission to the U.S. Military Academy.* By 1941, sixteen of thirty-eight native Scout officers were Academy graduates. The National Defense Act of 1920* recognized the Scouts as a "permanent part of the military forces of the United States." In December 1920, the 45th and 57th Infantry Regiments (PS) were formed from the provisional 1st and 2d Philippine Infantry Regiments. In 1922, the so-called Philippine Division was formed, composed primarily of the Philippine Scouts, to provide a mobile defense force for the islands.

As the Philippine Commonwealth prepared for independence, the Scouts provided leaders and trainers for new Philippine army. When General Douglas MacArthur* assumed command of U.S. Army forces in the Far East on 26 July 1941, the Philippine Department included 22,532 men, of whom 11,972 were Philippine Scouts. More than 8,000 Scouts fell defending the Philippines in World War II,* some waging an effective guerrilla war against the Japanese occupation force; thousands of others became prisoners of war.* The Scouts were disbanded following Philippine independence in July 1946. In recognition of their service to the United States, the four Philippine Scout regiments—the 26th, 43d, 45th, and 57th—received Presidential Unit Citations.

References. John E. Olson and Frank O. Anders, *Anywhere-Anytime*, 1991. Russell Roth, *Muddy Glory*, 1981.

John A. Hixson

PHILIPPINES, FALL OF

The loss of the Philippines in 1942 was almost inevitable once Japan decided on war. The islands were close enough to provoke Japan but too far from the United States for any substantial reinforcement. The first Japanese landings in the Philippines took place on 8 December 1941, a few hours after an air strike on Clark Field reduced U.S. airpower in the western Pacific by half, an inexplicable "second Pearl Harbor." The Commander of U.S. Forces, Far East, Douglas MacArthur,* led a poorly trained, lightly armed Philippine army of 75,000 men—actually little more than a constabulary—plus the far more professional Philippine Scouts,* three U.S. Army regiments,* and smaller units, totalling 22,500 men. The debacle at Clark Field deprived MacArthur's forces of air cover and gave the Japanese their greatest single advantage.

After the initial landings at Lingayen Gulf, the Japanese moved east and south against the U.S. and Filipino forces. The Japanese, who had been fighting in China since 1937, held an advantage over the raw Filipinos and Americans, many of whom had difficulty adjusting to wartime challenges after decades of peace. The Filipinos regularly retreated under Japanese pressure, but they were rarely routed. Their battle performance compared more than favorably with British and Dutch retreats in Malaya and the East Indies. Filipino resistance at Bataan* and Corregidor* delayed the Japanese timetable of conquest by several months. The Japanese succeeded in pushing the Filipino-American force south into the Bataan Peninsula, and they occupied Manila before food and other supplies could be evacuated to Bataan. Cut off and unable to run the Japanese blockade, the army on Bataan suffered from a lack of transport, communications, medicine, food, ammunition, and reinforcements. The Japanese were also suffering from exhaustion and supply difficulties, and they were outnumbered by allied forces. They renewed their strength in March, however, with control of the air, they forced the Bataan garrison to surrender on 9 April. The fate of Americans on Bataan, many sick and starving already, was the infamous Bataan Death March,* the product of Japanese gross underestimation of number of prisoners of war* and their mindless contempt for troops so "dishonorable" as to surrender. Less than a month later, on 6 May 1942, the 14,000 man garrison on Corregidor, a World War I*–vintage fortress guarding Manila Bay, surrendered, ending the American military presence in the Philippines. Some of the outer islands did not capitulate until 9 June.

The fall of the Philippines was the greatest military disaster in U.S. history.

References. Louis Morton, *The Fall of the Philippines*, 1953. John Toland, *But Not in Shame*, 1961.

Stanley Sandler

PICKET'S MILL

After the battle of New Hope Church, Georgia, on 25 May 1864, Major General William T. Sherman* and General Joseph E. Johnston* probed each other's positions looking for weak spots to exploit. On the 27th, Major General O. O. Howard's* IV Corps, Army of the Cumberland,* searching for Johnston's right flank in the rugged terrain north of New Hope Church, encountered Major General Patrick R. Cleburne's Confederate infantry division* in dense woods near the small settlement of Pickett's Mill. By midafternoon, Howard, not knowing that Sherman had cancelled an order to attack, reported that he thought he had reached the enemy's flank and ordered an attack. William Hazen's 2d Brigade of Thomas Wood's 3d Division stepped off about 1630 and advanced through dense undergrowth until it made contact with Confederate cavalry skirmishers. Hazen's men pushed the Confederates back to a deep ravine dominated by a ridge about a hundred yards distant. Confederate infantry arriving on the ridge swept the low ground with a hail of lead, killing and wounding many of Hazen's surprised soldiers. The fighting went on for several hours. Wood sent another brigade, under Colonel William Gibson, forward to carry on the attack, but it too took severe losses. Yet a third brigade, under Colonel Frederick Knefler, was sent forward about 1830 to hold the Confederates until a defensive line could be established; it too took heavy casualties. Nightfall finally ended the day's action. Howard's corps lost approximately 1,600 men at Pickett's Mill and failed to turn the Confederate right flank.

References. Albert Castel, *Decision in the West*, 1992. Howell and Elizabeth Purdue, *Pat Cleburne, Confederate General*, 1973.

Edward Shanahan

PINEAPPLE GRENADE

Commonly called the "pineapple grenade" because of its cylindrical, serrated body, the defensive hand grenade Mark II was patterned after the French LeBlanc and British Mills hand grenades.* First introduced in World War I,* the Mark II had a cast-iron body, TNT filler, and a die-cast metal fuse assembly; it weighed twenty-two ounces. The fuse—a primer and striker held cocked by a sheet-metal level on top of a detonator charge of fulminate of mercury— screwed into the top of the pineapple. Release of the lever, held in place by a safety-pin ring, activated the spring-loaded striker, which struck the primer. Five seconds after the primer ignited, the detonator exploded, erupting the charge in the grenade. The pineapple body produced about a thousand lethal fragments over a radius of a hundred feet. An improved fuse, the M204, became available in 1944 and made the Mark II one of the most reliable grenades of World War II.* The Mark IIA1 pineapple grenade remained in U.S. Army service until the early 1960s.

Reference. Bruce N. Canfield, *U.S. Infantry Weapons of World War II*, 1994.

Michael G. Knapp

PISTOL, COLT .38

Introduced in 1900, the Browning-designed Colt .38 automatic pistol was the first of its type to be produced on a commercial scale in the United States. The .38-caliber round achieved an official velocity of 1,260 feet per second. The U.S. Army adopted the Model L .38 in 1902. The military model had an in-creased magazine capacity (eight rounds); a squarer, hard rubber butt handle; a slide stop to keep the action open after the last round was fired; a lanyard loop; and a "flying" pin—a pin shorter than the distance from hammer to primer. This recoil-operated semiautomatic had a locked breech that ejected the spent car-tridge and loaded a new round for the next shot. Manufactured from 1902 to 1928, the Model L .38 proved to be one of Colt's most reliable pistol designs.

References. Arcadi Gluckman, *United States Martial Pistols and Revolvers*, 1960. Ian V. Hogg, *Military Pistols & Revolvers*, 1987.

Robert S. Goings

PISTOL, COLT NAVY

The 1851 Colt Navy revolver was a hybrid of two previous Colt designs, the Colt .31 pistol and the .44 Dragoon.* Available in both .36 and .44 calibers, the Colt Navy quickly gained popularity, although Colt did not receive large government orders for it until 1854. The Navy was single action, with a round, six-shot, interchangable cylinder and a 7.5-inch-long octagonal barrel. In 1860, Colt created a new .44-caliber weapon, known as the Colt 1860 or the New Army Model, a redesign of the .44 Dragoon. The New Army Model was the most important handgun of the Civil War*; Colt manufactured over 200,000 of them. In 1861, Colt introduced the .36-caliber Navy Belt Pistol, by changing the 1851 Navy to a round barrel with a rachet-type loading lever.

References. Arcadi Gluckman, *United States Martial Pistols and Revolvers*, 1960. Nathan L. Swayze, *'51 Colt Navies*, 1967. R. L. Wilson, *Colt*, 1985.

Robert S. Goings

PISTOL, M1911A1, .45

Prior to the Spanish-American War* the U.S. Army replaced its .45-caliber single-action revolver with a newer .38-caliber revolver that had the advantage of being double action—that is, capable of being cocked and fired with a single squeeze of the trigger. The new revolver's reduced caliber and muzzle velocity, however, quickly proved to be a disadvantage in fierce fighting against Moro tribesmen and Filipino insurgents. The Moros, especially, their bodies tightly wrapped with vines serving as primitive body armor, were able to sustain numerous wounds and continue to fight.

An Army Ordnance board study released in 1904 recommended that a replacement sidearm be of a caliber not less than .45. Colt soon produced a modified version of John Browning's self-loading pistol in caliber .45—the ACP (Automatic Colt Pistol), designated the Model 1905. Following impressive field tests in 1906 and 1907, the Army tentatively accepted the design in 1908, and selected units received modified versions of the pistol, designated Model 1908, for further field tests. In 1911, the Army finally accepted the Model 1908 (redesignated Colt Model 1911) as its standard sidearm. Following service in World War I,* further modifications were effected, and the Colt Model 1911A1 became the personal sidearm that U.S. troops would carry into action until just prior to the Gulf War of 1990–1991. The Colt M1911A1 is a box-loading, magazine-fed, short-recoil-operated, semi-automatic pistol with an eight-round capacity. With a barrel length of five inches, an overall length of 8.62 inches, and a weight of 2.43 pounds, the 1911A1 fires a 230-grain bullet at a muzzle velocity of 860 feet per second. The 9 mm Beretta has replaced the Colt Model 1911A1 as the Army's standard sidearm.

References. Donald B. Bady, *Colt Automatic Pistols*, 1963. Ian V. Hogg, *Military Pistols & Revolvers*, 1987. R. L. Wilson, *Colt*, 1985.

Fred J. Chiaventone

PLATOON

The platoon is the smallest organizational element led by an officer, normally a second lieutenant. The platoon leader is assisted by a senior noncommissioned officer *(NCO), usually a sergeant first class, although sometimes a staff ser-

geant. A platoon usually consists of three or more squads.* A mechanized infantry* platoon currently includes four Bradley infantry fighting vehicles,* and
an armor platoon includes four M-1 Abrams* tanks. In nonmechanized infantry
units, a platoon typically consists of three rifle squads and a weapons squad.*
Three or more platoons, with a headquarters element, form a company* or
troop.*

References. Kenneth J. Ayers, "Structuring a Combat Maneuver Battalion," *Armor*,
May–June 1976, 50–51. James R. McDonough, *Platoon Leader*, 1985.

Andrew N. Morris

PLATTSBURG MOVEMENT

The Plattsburg movement resulted from the efforts of the U.S. Army General
Staff* and the Chief of Staff, Major General Leonard Wood,* to develop a
citizen-soldier training program between 1912 and 1916. Initially, two trial Student Military Instruction Camps, using 159 students primarily from local high
schools and colleges, were established during 1913 in Pacific Grove, California.
This was a low-cost program, with students paying for their own uniforms,
board, and travel. The Army provided all instruction and equipment during the
five-week encampment, and it offered training in basic marksmanship, patrolling, drilling, and combat survival skills. In 1915, Wood opened an additional
camp at Plattsburg, New York. Twelve hundred college students, businessmen,
and professionals between the ages of twenty and forty attended the Plattsburg
camp; thus the highly successful program became known as the "Plattsburg
movement." Two more camps were held that summer, with an additional 3,000
attendees. Using the Plattsburg model, 16,000 participants attended in 1916.
Eventually, the Plattsburg Movement trained over 90,000 officers. They became
the backbone of the rapid expansion of the Regular Army in World War I.*
The popular acceptance of the Plattsburg Movement directly influenced the establishment of the Reserve Officers' Training Corps* (ROTC) by the National
Defense Act of 1916.*

References. John G. Clifford, *The Citizen Soldiers*, 1972. Ralph B. Perry, *The Plattsburg Movement*, 1921.

Dwain Crowson

PLEIKU. *See* Ia Drang.

POLICE CALL

The term "police call" refers to the cleaning of an area, typically in and around
barracks, housing, and work stations. A police call is an informal formation,
normally under the supervision of a noncommissioned officer* (NCO), in which
soldiers are placed on line and move through the area picking up trash and
debris. On most Army posts, police calls are held daily, in the mornings.

Krewasky A. Salter

POMCUS

The concept of prepositioning necessary combat equipment at storage sites in likely theaters prior to the outbreak of war was embedded in U.S. Cold War* plans for a major war in Europe. Department of Defense* planners projected the need for ten additional divisions* in Europe within ten days of the outbreak of war; the political climate prevented the permanent stationing of such numbers of troops in Europe. The United States lacked the strategic lift to transport so quickly the necessary equipment for such a force; Prepositioning of Materiel Configured in Unit Sets, or POMCUS, allowed troops to be deployed without heavy equipment and be issued it upon arrival in Europe. Thus, the units would be made combat ready in the shortest possible time. Today, prepositioning of equipment has been extended to countries outside of Europe and ships that remain at sea near potential trouble spots. A more generic term, Army War Reserve (AWR), has replaced the term POMCUS. However, the concept and legacy of the original POMCUS organization is still a major part of U.S. military strategy.*

References. Larry L. Harless, "A POMCUS Primer," *Army Logistician*, March–April 1983, 6–9. Heike Hasenauer, "Europe's Metal Mountain," *Soldiers*, February 1994, 22–24.

Jim Martin

PORT GIBSON

After landing about 17,000 troops at Bruinsburg, Mississippi, on 30 April 1863, Major General Ulysses S. Grant* pushed inland toward Port Gibson, while William T. Sherman* marched south to join him. Around midnight Grant's advance guard made contact with Confederate forces as they approached the Shaifer House. This skirmishing halted the Federal advance and forced the units to deploy. On the morning of 1 May, fighting began anew as Federal columns attacked along two roads toward Magnolia Church. Throughout the morning, the intensity of fighting increased around the Shaifer House, and the battlelines expanded as both sides received reinforcements. Despite reinforcements, the Confederates had to concede the ridge line to the larger Federal force.

A mile and a half to the rear, two Confederate brigades established a blocking position between the White and Irwin branches of Willow Creek. The advancing Federals now concentrated twenty-one regiments* for a frontal assault on the Confederate position, slowly pushing it back and fending off a counterattack by the Confederate left. At the same time, the Confederate right had its hands full stopping another Federal division.* Once again, both sides were reinforced. Although the Federal attack unravelled in the maze of ravines and dense underbrush, its superior weight forced the Confederates to give way. By early evening, the Confederates retired from the field, and Grant reached Port Gibson. Losses for the battle were 787 Confederates and 875 Federals.

References. Jack D. Coombe, *Thunder along the Mississippi*, 1996. Terrence Winschel, "Grant's Beachhead for the Vicksburg Campaign," *Blue & Gray Magazine*, February 1994, 9–22.

Edward Shanahan

PORT HUDSON

Port Hudson, Louisiana, located between Baton Rouge and the mouth of the Red River, was a key strategic point in the defense of the Mississippi River and the site of the longest siege of the Civil War.* As early as April 1862, the Confederates began developing the defensive works around Port Hudson; they occupied it in force in August. When Ulysses S. Grant* launched his campaign to gain control of the Mississippi in the spring of 1863, 15,000 troops under Major General Nathaniel Banks ascended on Port Hudson, besieging a Confederate garrison of nearly 5,000 men on 23 May. Determined to take Port Hudson so that he could move north to meet Grant, Banks ordered his troops to assault the defenses on the morning of 27 May. In spite of the determined efforts by the Federals to break into the defenses, the Confederate lines held throughout the day, inflicting heavy losses on the attackers. Banks was unable to mount another assault on Port Hudson; the Confederates, however, were unable either to break out or lift the siege. Port Hudson surrender on 9 July, forty-eight days after the siege began and five days after Grant accepted the surrender of Vicksburg.* The entire length of the Mississippi was finally in Union hands.

References. Jack D. Coombe, *Thunder along the Mississippi*, 1996. Edward Cunningham, *The Port Hudson Campaign, 1862–1863*, 1963. Lawrence Lee Hewitt, *Port Hudson, Confederate Bastion on the Mississippi*, 1987.

POST-TRAUMATIC STRESS DISORDER. *See* Post-Traumatic Stress Syndrome.

POST-TRAUMATIC STRESS SYNDROME

Post-traumatic stress syndrome (PTSS) is a medical term dating from the Vietnam War.* It describes a collection of psychological symptoms arising from a delayed mental state marked by behavioral disorders originating in exposure to extreme stress. The term first appeared in the early 1970s, but the concept of adverse reactions to stress continuing long after the event has been a staple of medical theory for more than a century. As defined in medical literature, any stressful event, including combat, can cause PTSS. Post-traumatic stress syndrome is not to be confused with post-traumatic stress disorder (PTSD), which tends to be a product of more seriously dysfunctional behavior, is chronic, and resists treatments. Previous terminology for PTSS includes neurosis or traumatic neurosis, shell shock,* battle fatigue,* combat fatigue, old sergeant's syndrome, or, more generically, neuropsychiatric disorders. However, PTSS is distinguished somewhat from these earlier terms by virtue of the interval between the stress-inducing event and the onset of symptoms; thus in the years immediately following the Vietnam War, patients were more often said to have suffered from delayed stress syndrome. The medical community ultimately discarded this term in favor of post-traumatic stress syndrome or post-traumatic stress disorder, depending on the severity of the condition.

References. Charles R. Figley, ed., *Trauma and Its Wake*, 1985. William E. Kelly, ed., *Post-Traumatic Stress Disorder and the War Veteran Patient*, 1985.

Roger J. Spiller

POSTS ANDS FORTS

Historically, the U.S. Army has used a number of terms to define its installations, including camp, cantonment, barracks, fort, and post. "Post" and "fort" are the most common terms used today. A post is a military installation that permanently houses troops and is equipped with barracks, dining facilities, commissaries, hospitals, and all other facilities necessary to support troops for extended periods of time, and that is not within direct range of enemy forces. Posts are generally bounded by a fence or other demarcation and adhere to limited design requirements. A post may be the site of administrative as well as a military functions, and the military atmosphere may be somewhat relaxed.

In its historical context, a fort is a temporary structure designed to provide defense against an enemy attack. Forts generally conform to structural specifications, although the specifications vary with the fort's size, location, and mission. A fort may be as small as the a hilltop overlooking a strategic bypass, or as large as a small city. Larger and longer-established forts have earth, masonry, or palisade walls, watchtowers, obstacles on approaches, and developed infrastructures to support troops. Forts frequently serve as barriers to protect posts from enemy encroachment or to maintain lines of communications between posts.

In current U.S. Army usage, however, the terms post and fort have become synonymous. Fort Bragg,* Fort Polk,* and Fort Campbell,* for example, are not forts at all; in the traditional sense of the term, they are posts.

References. Dan Cragg, *Guide to Military Installations*, 4th ed., 1994. Francis Paul Prucha, *A Guide to the Military Posts of the United State, 1789–1895*, 1964.

Krewasky A. Salter

POWDER RIVER

The Powder River Battle was one of several fought during the Sioux Campaign of 1876, the most famous of them the Battle of the Little Bighorn* on 25–27 June. The Powder River Battle was a result of Brigadier General George Crook's* expedition north from Fort Fetterman, Wyoming, in February 1876. Colonel Joseph Reynolds's 3d Cavalry made contact with an Indian scouting element on 16 March near the Powder River in southeastern Montana, close to the Wyoming border. Reynolds followed the Indians and found their village that night. Reynolds planned to strike the village the next morning, with simultaneous attacks from two directions. Although coordinated assaults proved impossible, one force did manage to push the Indians out of their village, while the other force captured a herd of about 800 ponies. An Indian counterattack proved too much for the poorly led troops, and the Indians recaptured many of their ponies; Reynolds withdrew from the destroyed village and shot the ponies still in his possession. With four killed and six wounded, Crook and Reynolds returned to Fort Fetterman. Crook subsequently brought charges against Reynolds for mismanaging the battle. A court-martial found Reynolds guilty, thus ending his long military career.

References. Cyrus Townsend Brady, *Indian Fights and Fighters*, 1971. John S. Gray, *Centennial Campaign*, 1988. Fred H. Werner, *"The Soldiers Are Coming!"* 1982.

Chris Clark

POWER PACK

Power Pack was the code name for the U.S. military intervention in the Dominican Republic in 1965. In late April of that year, an attempted coup d'état, led by disgruntled Dominican military officers, triggered a civil conflict, the full fury of which was unleashed primarily in the capital, Santo Domingo. President Lyndon B. Johnson was determined to prevent a "second Cuba" in the Western Hemisphere, an allusion to the Marxist-Leninist regime Fidel Castro had imposed in Cuba since 1959. Informed by the U.S. Embassy in Santo Domingo that rebel forces in the Republic were falling increasingly under communist influence, Johnson ordered 2,000 U.S. Marines ashore to protect U.S. and foreign lives and property and, as Johnson later told the American people, to prevent a communist takeover of the country. Three brigades* from the 82d Airborne Division* followed within days. At its peak, the U.S. military presence in the Dominican Republic came to almost 24,000 troops, including airborne units, military police,* civil affairs* and psychological warfare experts, Green Berets,* and logistical personnel. After isolating the bulk of the rebel force in southeastern Santo Domingo, the U.S. ambassador, W. Tapley Bennett, and the military commander, Lieutenant General Bruce Palmer, received word that the White House desired a political settlement. In the ensuing days and weeks, U.S. troops, while the target of intermittent sniper fire, participated in humanitarian, civil affairs, and other stability operations. In late May, Palmer's forces were placed under an Inter-American Peace Force (IAPF), commanded by a Brazilian general. The IAPF enforced a ceasefire, created an environment for negotiations, lent military support to a provisional government created in September, and oversaw elections in June 1966. A new government was sworn in a month later, and the last intervention forces left the country in September.

References. Bruce Palmer, Jr., *Intervention in the Caribbean*, 1989. Lawrence A. Yates, *Power Pack*, 1988.

Lawrence A. Yates

PRESIDIO

The presidio, a "garrison or military fortification," was a central factor of Spanish colonialization in North America. As the Spanish sought to expand their territorial holdings, their expeditions in newly established provinces almost invariably began with the establishment of a governmental center. The fortified military post, or presidio, combined political, military, ecclesiastical, and economic functions providing for the concentration of troops, administrative officials, a Catholic mission, and a base for expanded mercantile enterprises. In addition to its mission of holding hostile native populations in check, the presidio served as a symbol of national power and deterred foreign incursions. The presidio had the added benefit of being the only type of settlement designed to accommodate families—a fact that quickly established presidios as the centers of Spanish life in its colonial holdings. In the United States, the most famous presidios were in California, at Santa Barbara, San Diego, Monterey, and San Francisco. The U.S. Army occupied some of these presidios after the Mexican War.* The latter two served as major Army posts until recently, when they were closed.

References. Janet R. Fireman, *The Spanish Royal Corps of Engineers in the Western Borderlands*, 1977. Neal Harlow, *California Conquered*, 1982.

Fred J. Chiaventone

PRIEST. *See* Howitzer, Self-Propelled, 105 mm M7.

PRINCIPLES OF WAR

Principles of war are commonly or doctrinally accepted general truths, or rules of thumb, about the conduct of war that, if respected *in their ensemble*, will tend to lead to success, and if ignored, to failure. Military thinkers generally agree that in any specific circumstances the individual principles take on different relative importance; indeed, some may have to be ignored entirely, while others are heavily determinate. Such guides were advocated most notably by the eighteenth-century theorist the Marshal de Saxe, in the preface to his *Reveries on the Art of War*. The late American strategic theorist, Bernard Brodie, in *Strategy in the Missile Age*, was highly critical of the entire idea of fixed principles of war. Brodie argued that such "hallowed 'principles' are essentially common sense propositions which are generally but by no means exclusively pertinent to the waging of war." The current list of pithy aphorisms common to most Western armies' official doctrines* are derived, more or less, from a list drawn up during World War I* and thereafter modified by Major General J.F.C. Fuller. The U.S. Army adopted Fuller's principles in the brief Training Regulation 10–5, *Doctrine, Principles, and Methods*, dated 23 December 1921. The entire topic of the "immutable principles" occupied less than a small page—the discussion, a single paragraph.

In contemporary U.S. military doctrine, principles are observed by brief but obligatory, ritual bows, often followed by quick relegation to the appendices of basic doctrinal manuals. The current principles of war in U.S. Army doctrine, taken from U.S. Army, FM 100-5, *Operations*, June 1993, are:

Objective	Unity of Command	Offensive
Security	Mass	Surprise
Economy of Force	Simplicity	Maneuver

There is little evidence of any organic connection between the vestigial remnants of Fuller's principles and their analogical descendants that address less traditional forms of political employment of military forces, principles of operations other than war* (OOTW). But military men are conservative and generally positivist thinkers, so public reverence to the "immutable principles" persists in military literature even into the 21st century. The principles of war remain useful as an easily mastered aid-memoire—one among many.

References. John I. Alger, *The Quest for Victory*, 1982. Donn A. Starry, "The Principles of War," *Military Review*, September 1981, 2–12.

Richard Swain

PRISONERS OF WAR

Generally, an enemy population is divided into two categories: civilians and those who are entitled to treatment as prisoners of war. Under the Geneva Conventions, prisoners of war are individuals who have fallen into the power of the enemy and are: members of the armed forces or militia of a party to the conflict; members of volunteer corps commanded by a person responsible for the actions of his subordinates, who wear a distinctive sign, carry arms openly, and conduct their operations in accordance with the law of war; persons who accompany the armed forces, who are not actually members but are authorized by the force they accompany, examples being war correspondents, civilian members of aircraft crews, and civilian contractors; and members of a *levee en masse*. A *levee en masse* results from a popular uprising in which inhabitants of a nonoccupied territory, upon approach of the enemy, take up arms to resist the invading force without having had time to organize themselves into regular units—provided that they carry arms openly and respect the law of war. Prisoners of war may not be killed for military convenience; they must be treated humanely; their persons and some personal effects must be respected; and they must be afforded medical treatment. Also, all prisoners of war must receive equal treatment regardless of their race, nationality, religious beliefs, or political opinions.

References. Tom Bird, *American POWs of World War II*, 1992. William E. S. Flory, *Prisoners of War*, 1942. Richard Garrett, *P.O.W.*, 1981.

PROFESSOR OF MILITARY SCIENCE

Congress authorized military training in colleges in 1870, although commissions were not authorized until the National Defense Act of 1916* established the Reserve Officers Training Corps* (ROTC). In order to provide professional leadership and instruction in the new ROTC programs, universities created the position of professor of military science (PMS), or professor of military science and tactics (PMST). Today, the PMS is appointed by the Army, with the university's concurrence, and serves as the chairman of the Military Science Department. The PMS, typically a lieutenant colonel, answers to the ROTC region commander, as well as to the dean of the college, and directs all aspects of the ROTC program, from curriculum development to military professional programs. His or her staff normally consists of Army and civilian personnel, involved in the recruiting, administration, budgeting, and supply areas of the program. The PMS's ultimate goal is to produce quality officers for the U.S. Army Reserve,* though exceptional students may be commissioned in the Regular Army.

References. Dean M. Benson, "The Army's Representative on Campus," *Army Information Digest*, March 1958, 18–23. Charles A. Goldman et al., *Staffing Army ROTC at Colleges and Universities*, 1999.

Claude Sasso

PROTECTIVE MOBILIZATION PLAN

In 1936, the Chief of Staff* of the Army initiated the Protective Mobilization Plan (PMP) to provide logistical and time-line guides to ensure a smoother mobilization than had occurred in previous periods of American history. The PMP was based on a three possible contingencies: first, to mobilize a protective force from the 118,000 enlisted strength as of 1933; second, to mobilize after reaching a strength of 165,000; and third, to mobilize based on the legislatively authorized but unfunded level of 280,000 men. Mobilization at the first level would require at least four months, probably six, and would provide no immediately available combat forces. The Army was too small to support both mobilization training and a combat force. Mobilization at the second level would take approximately the same period of time as the first and would also yield no combat-ready force. Only with the 280,000 men authorized by the National Defense Act of 1920* could the Army carry out both mobilization training and field at least one corps* for combat. The plans included provisions for calling up the National Guard* and Army reserves. Chief of Staff Douglas MacArthur* and his successor Malin Craig* accepted the second level as optimal, given the political and economic circumstances of the period. The Protective Mobilization Plan, although somewhat outdated by 1940, did provide an excellent body of detailed planning from which to mobilize for World War II.*

References. Richard M. Leighton and Robert W. Coakley, *Global Logistics and Strategy, 1940–1943*, 1955. R. Elberton Smith, *The Army and Economic Mobilization*, 1959.

John Broom

PROVIDE COMFORT

After the completion of Desert Storm,* U.S. Army Special Forces,* civil affairs,* and psychological operations* (PSYOPs) soldiers, and U.S. Marines were deployed to Turkey and northern Iraq on 7 April 1991 for Operation Provide Comfort. Their mission was to prevent the death, by starvation and exposure, of over 450,000 Iraqi Kurds who had rebelled against the regime of Saddam Hussein during the Gulf War. Over 1,700 Special Operations Forces* (SOF) personnel were instrumental in establishing refugee camps, rudimentary sanitary and hospital facilities, and distributing food. Operating out of remote and primitive facilities, U.S. Special Operations personnel worked with the local leadership to establish a sense of rapport and trust, and to facilitate basic camp organization. The SOF teams saved many lives, especially among the thousands of infants. After the situation stabilized, SOF teams established way-stations with food, medical care, and sanitary facilities, along the route back into Iraq. The refugees were persuaded to return home along safe routes mapped out by Special Operations Forces teams and publicized by PSYOP leaflets. By the end of July 1991, most Kurds had safely returned to their homes in northern Iraq.

References. John P. Abizaid, "Lessons for Peacekeepers," *Military Review*, March 1993, 11–19. Gordon W. Rudd, "Operation Provide Comfort," 1993.

Richard Stewart

PROVOST MARSHAL

The provost marshal is a staff officer who supervises the military police. In January 1776, George Washington* appointed Bartholomew Von Heer as Provost Martial (Marshal). His assignment was to patrol and maintain order in the rear area of the camp. In 1779, another provost force was organized to guard prisoners of war. Both forces were disbanded at the end of the American Revolution.* The next formal organization of the military police occurred during the Civil War.* On 3 March 1863, James B. Fry was appointed Provost Marshal General of the Army with responsibility for enforcing the new conscription laws. This office was discontinued in 1866. When the United States entered World War I,* Major Enoch H. Crowder was appointed Provost Marshal General to enforce the Selective Service Act, and a separate Provost Marshal General was appointed to enforce rules, protect rear areas, and care for prisoners of war for the American Expeditionary Force* in Europe. Congress refused to make the Provost Marshal a permanent branch of the Army, but it did authorize a military police branch from the Officers' Reserve Corps. On 31 July 1941, after the outbreak of World War II,* Major General Allen Guillon was appointed acting Provost Marshal. On 26 September 1941, the Military Police Corps* became a permanent branch of the Army. On 20 May 1974, the office of the Provost Marshal General was discontinued, and its duties were transferred to the office of the Deputy Chief of Staff for Personnel.

References. Thomas M. Moncure, Jr., "Marsena R. Patrick, Provost Marshal General of the Army," *Military Police*, December 1990, 23–25. Robert K. Wright, Jr., *Military Police*, 1992.

L. Lynn Williams

PSYCHOLOGICAL OPERATIONS

U.S. Army psychological operations (PSYOPS) began during the American Revolution,* when militiamen tossed leaflets to British troops on Breed's and

Bunker Hills,* promising the good life to those who would defect. But large-scale propaganda came with the advent of high-capacity printing presses and mass literacy at the beginning of the 20th century. The propaganda section of the American Expeditionary Force* (AEF) in France produced several million copies of leaflets that promised good treatment for defectors, warned of growing allied might, and called for political changes in Germany. German Field Marshal Paul von Hindenburg later admitted that allied leaflets had "poisoned" his troops.

Psychological warfare (as it came to be known) accelerated rapidly during World War II* and was waged by the U.S. Army in all theaters. The civilian Office of War Information also provided many strategic psychological warfare products, while the Office of Strategic Services* (OSS) carried out clandestine PSYOPS. All PSYOPS concentrated on the themes of good treatment, the miserable condition of the enemy in the field, the surrender pass, and, the most popular, the more-or-less truthful newsletter. For the first time, electronic loudspeakers and recordings were employed.

Although the Korean and Vietnam Wars were ideological conflicts, the Army continued to emphasize the more practical themes that had served well in past conflicts. By the time of the Vietnam War, newer technologies had made it possible to copy enemy diaries and photos in the field and drop choice excerpts over enemy lines in a matter of hours, and to use television to win over civilians. These familiar themes and methods were never put to better use than during Desert Shield/Desert Storm.* Iraqi commanders were deceived as to the true strategy of the coalition forces, and enemy troops, already demoralized, were talked out of their bunkers by PSYOPS teams; millions of leaflets assured of good treatment of prisoners.

The U.S. Army has identified several basic PSYOP principles. These include not denigrating or caricaturing the "brave," "decent" enemy soldier but instead drawing a distinction between him and his "bad" leaders; rarely making political demands; emphasizing the futility of continued resistance; and offering a pragmatic way out. Army PSYOPS has rarely sought to generate large numbers of prisoners of war* but rather to undermine enemy morale and fighting effectiveness.

References. Frank R. Barnett and Carnes Lord, eds., *Political Warfare and Psychological Operations*, 1989. Robert T. Holt and Robert W. van de Velde, *Strategic Psychological Operations and American Foreign Policy*, 1960. Ron D. McLaurin, ed., *Military Propaganda*, 1982.

Stanley Sandler

PUBLIC AFFAIRS OFFICER

The public affairs officer (PAO) is the staff officer responsible for managing the information needs of the unit, the military community, the soldier, and the public. PAO is an official position at U.S. Army posts and at division* and higher units. Commanders below division level frequently consider the PAO function sufficiently important to warrant appointment of an additional-duty officer. The PAO supervises the organization's public relations plan and ensures that the commander is kept informed of the possible impact of unit actions on those relations. He serves as the commander's official spokesman and is responsible for scheduling and routing media personnel within organization boundaries. He keeps soldiers and family members informed through newsletters and printed and broadcast media. He coordinates with the G-3 operations and G-5 civil affairs officers to ensure dissemination of truthful, yet security-conscious, information. He is also the organization's proponent for compliance with the Privacy Act of 1973 and the Freedom of Information Act. In the downsizing of the U.S. Army during the 1990s, civilians have replaced uniformed public affairs officers on many installations, still the Army has maintained the highest standards of public-affairs performance and integrity.

References. Michael S. Galloucis, "The Military and the Media," *Army*, August 1996, 14–18. William M. Hammond, "The Army and Public Affairs," *Parameters*, June 1989, 57–74. Charles W. McClain, Jr., and Garry D. Levin, "Public Affairs in America's 21st Century Army," *Military Review*, November 1994, 6–15.

Lawyn C. Edwards

PUNITIVE EXPEDITION

Between 1910 and 1920, the violence of the revolution in Mexico often spilled over the border into the United States. The worst case occurred on 9 March 1916, when Francisco "Pancho" Villa, a Mexican warlord chafing over U.S. recognition of his principal rival, launched a raid on Columbus, New Mexico,* with several hundred men. Elements of the U.S. 13th Cavalry, headquartered at Columbus, inflicted high casualties on the raiders and drove them off, but not before American lives and property had been lost. The next day, President Woodrow Wilson ordered the U.S. Army into Mexico to capture Villa and disperse his band. A force under Brigadier General John J. Pershing,* known as the Punitive Expedition, entered Mexico on 15 March. Pershing commanded 5,000 officers and men, a skeletonized division* that included four regiments* of cavalry, two infatntry* regiments, two field artillery* batteries,* support units, and—a sign of changing technology—eight biplanes and several trucks. Pershing dispatched flying cavalry columns after his quarry, but Villa, operating in familiar territory, proved elusive. The most serious engagement—and the last U.S. cavalry charge—took place at Carrizal, where Pershing's troops clashed with Mexican government troops also pursuing Villa. The ensuing bloodshed and threat of war with Mexico prompted President Wilson to call most of the National Guard* into federal service and to reinforce the border. Mindful that the United States could ill afford to become embroiled in hostilities with Mexico while Europe was in flames, Wilson also pursued a diplomatic course, urging his Mexican counterpart, Venustiano Carranza, to enter negotiations for the withdrawal of U.S. forces. Despite some areas of agreement, diplomacy failed to find a solution acceptable to both sides. By then, however, U.S. relations with

Germany had deteriorated to the point where Wilson had no recourse but to pull the troops out of Mexico in anticipation of the nation's becoming involved in the war in Europe.

By 5 February 1917, Pershing's troops were out of Mexico. The Punitive Expedition had failed to capture Villa, but it had applied enough pressure to disperse much of his force. From the outset, the expedition had been plagued by unhealthy climate, difficult terrain, inadequate communications, an extemporized logistical train, and restrictive political directives. In a more positive light, the whole episode allowed Army Regulars and National Guardsmen to receive training and experience that would serve them well on the European battlefield.

References. Clarence C. Clendenen, *The United States and Pancho Villa*, 1961. John S. D. Eisenhower, *Intervention!* 1993.

Lawrence A. Yates

PURPLE HEART

The Purple Heart is the oldest U.S. military decoration. It is awarded to members of the armed forces of the United States who are wounded in combat during operations against an enemy. It is also awarded posthumously to the next of kin of personnel killed or dead of wounds received in action. George Washington* created the award, originally called the Badge of Military Merit, in 1782; Congress reinstituted it as the Purple Heart in 1932, the two-hundredth anniversary of Washington's birth.

Elizabeth Will designed the Purple Heart medal. It consists of a gold-rimmed purple heart on which is affixed a gold-colored bust of George Washington, shown in profile. Above the heart is Washington's coat of arms, with two sprays of green leaves on either side of an enamel shield. The reverse of the medal is entirely of gold-colored metal, including the shield and leaves. Within the sculptured outer heart and below the shield is the inscription, set in three lines, "For Military Merit," with a space below for the recipient's name. The ribbon is deep purple with narrow white edges. Second and subsequent awards of the Purple Heart are denoted by gold star for Navy and Marine Corps personnel and by an oakleaf cluster for Army and Air Force personnel.

References. Frederic L. Borch III and F. C. Brown, *The Purple Heart*, 1996. Evans E. Kerrigan, *American War Medals and Decorations*, 1964.

James H. Willbanks

PUSAN PERIMETER

The defense of the Pusan perimeter marks one of the most dramatic moments in U.S. military history. Following the rapid collapse and retreat of the Republic of Korea Army (ROKA) before the assault of the much larger and better-equipped North Korean People's Army (NKPA), Lieutenant General Walton H. Walker, commanding the U.S. Eighth Army,* stabilized the situation by forming a thinly held line that ran ninety miles north from the Tsushima Strait and then sixty miles east to the Sea of Japan. The area encompassed by this line included the port of Pusan, which was the last available port for United Nations (UN) forces. The Pusan perimeter offered Walker several advantages: strong interior lines, the ability to shift a mobile reserve quickly wherever needed, and the capacity for rapid introduction of reinforcements. From 5 August to 15 September 1950, the UN forces within the perimeter withstood several heavy, but uncoordinated, NKPA attacks. The Pusan perimeter allowed the UN forces to regroup and reform, while sapping the strength of the overextended NKPA divisions facing them. General of the Army Douglas MacArthur's* dramatic Inchon* landing on 15 September 1950 was successful in part because the majority of the NKPA had been deployed and was, in effect, trapped along the Pusan perimeter. Simultaneously with the Inchon landings, the U.S. Eighth Army, lead by the 1st Cavalry Division, broke out from the Pusan perimeter and drove north and west toward Seoul. Their supply and communication line cut, the spent NKPA forces dissolved before the advancing UN forces and fled into the rugged countryside.

References. Clay Blair, *The Forgotten War*, 1987. Edwin P. Hoyt, *The Pusan Perimeter*, 1984.

Benjamin H. Kristy

PYLE, ERNEST TAYLOR (1900–1945)

Ernest Taylor "Ernie" Pyle was already a nationally known newspaper columnist when he volunteered as a war correspondent in 1942. Born in 1900 in Dana, Indiana, and a graduate of Indiana University, Pyle covered U.S. forces in North Africa, Sicily, Italy, France, and the Pacific. On 18 April 1945, he was killed by a Japanese sniper while accompanying the 77th Infantry Division fighting on the small island of Ie Shima during the Okinawa* Campaign.

Many historians consider Pyle's war reports the best of World War II.* He always sought out the forward units, sharing the deprivations, dangers, and company of the common soldiers he found there. He wrote most of his columns on these ordinary soldiers—their hardships, sacrifices, fears, humor, and humanity. He became America's most famous and most beloved war correspondent. Before and after his death, many of his columns were compiled in several volumes, including *Here Is Your War* (1943), *Brave Men* (1944), and *Last Chapter* (1946).

References. Lee G. Miller, *The Story of Ernie Pyle*, 1950. David Nichols, ed., *Ernie's War*, 1986.

Q

QUARTERMASTER CORPS

The Second Continental Congress authorized the first Quartermaster General of the Continental Army* on 16 June 1775. Following the established system of the British army, Congress directed that clothing for the Army be provided at its own expense, charging each soldier $1.65 per month, and that transportation wagons and teams be contracted with private drivers. Nevertheless, quartermasters provided most supplies for their troops on an ad hoc basis, with local agents purchasing what they could, for a commission. Just prior to the War of 1812* the Army and the War Department* realized that the system of military agents was unsatisfactory. Reforms provided for the appointment of forage masters, and individual contractors continued to supply rations to the mostly militia force. Sutlers, however, supplemented the sometimes meager and inadequate army rations. In 1818, a Subsistence Department replaced the old provisioning system used since the American Revolution,* and in 1842 the Quartermaster's Department assumed responsibility for the procurement, distribution, and issue of clothing. Rations remained under the separate Subsistence Department.

The Mexican War* of 1846–1848 strained the Army's limited resources and transportation assets, but the Army overcame substantial difficulties and met its continually expanding logistical demands. The Civil War* presented further challenges for the Quartermaster Department. The size of the Army swelled from under 20,000 to over two million men. The Army used railroads, inland river routes, and ocean transportation to sustain and supply troops as they advanced into the Confederacy. The Quartermaster Department also assumed responsibility for the care of the dead and for maintenance of national cemeteries* during this period.

The Army Appropriation Act of August 1912 created the modern Quartermaster Corps; it combined the Quartermaster, Pay, and Subsistence Departments and authorized 6,000 men for the procurement and distribution of all common-use items throughout the Army. This reform proved invaluable when the United States entered World War I* just a few years later. Peacetime retrenchment, however, inevitably followed the wartime expansion. Demobilization meant reduced funding and reliance on wartime surplus stocks, often obsolete or obsolescent equipment with little value in a future conflict. After World War II,* however, the Quartermaster Corps continued to grow to meet the complex needs of the U.S. Army during the Cold War.* In both the Vietnam War* and Desert Storm* the Quartermaster Corps accomplished unprecedented logistical feats, supplying virtually everything U.S. Army forces required over great distances. Through hard work and innovative techniques, the Quartermaster Corps continues to overcome all obstacles and fulfill the logistical requirements of the Army.

References. James A. Huston, *The Sinews of War*, 1966. Erna Risch, *Quartermaster Support of the Army*, 1962.

Ralph Nichols

QUEBEC

In 1759, British forces commanded by James Wolfe defeated an army under the marquis de Montcalm on the Plains of Abraham at the gates of Quebec (modern Quebec City). With its fall, New France came under British control, it was organized in 1761 as the province of Lower Canada. Situated where the St. Lawrence River narrows, Quebec was a veritable fortress whose guns dominated an important water trafficway into the interior of North America. The power that held the city virtually controlled the major supply route into the Great Lakes region. Anxious to ensure the loyalty of the French Canadians in any future Anglo-French conflict, Parliament passed the Quebec Act in 1774, guaranteeing the traditional rights of the Roman Catholic Church and protecting the French language. That same year, however, the winds of rebellion blew from New England into Lower Canada; the Continental Congress invited the people of Canada to join in the struggle to compel Britain to respect colonial rights.

Following the capture of Fort Ticonderoga* in 1775, Congress decided to force the issue. Quebec became the objective of an American expedition in 1775–1776. The rebels conducted a two-pronged attack. Former British officer Richard Montgomery* attacked north from Ticonderoga, while Benedict Arnold* approached along a difficult overland route far to the east. The combined army numbered about 1,000 poorly clothed, underfed, and inadequately armed volunteers, including over two hundred Canadians. The army's greatest assets, however, were its commanders, their leadership and force of will almost added a fourteenth star to the new flag. On 13 November 1775, Montreal fell to Montgomery, and on 3 December the two forces linked up outside Quebec. Without heavy guns to batter down Quebec's solid walls, the colonial forces were compelled to conduct a frontal assault. Attacking in a blinding snowstorm, the colonials enjoyed initial success, but they could not penetrate into the inner city. The attack collapsed shortly after Montgomery was killed in action. Arnold remained outside the city until May 1776, when the first British resupply ships appeared. Arnold then withdrew to Montreal and later across the border into New York. The Americans would not make another attempt on Quebec until the War of 1812.*

References. Harrison Bird, *Attack on Quebec*, 1968. George F. G. Stanley, *Canada Invaded*, 1973.

Richard Barbuto

R

RADAR

Radio detecting and ranging, or radar, is used to detect distant objects using very-high-frequency radio waves. Through analysis of waves reflected off an object, radar can determine position, velocity, and target characteristics. Although radar was developed through the efforts of a large number of researchers, Sir Robert Watson-Watt is usually credited with its development. Watson-Watt demonstrated the first practical radar system in 1935. In World War II,* the armed services quickly integrated radar into air defense systems and aviation operations. Radar provided the theater air picture, depicting both friendly and enemy air movement, missile and artillery fires, and other key data, such as enemy ground air defense status.

Today, radar is routinely used for missile control and launch-site detection. During Desert Storm,* Patriot* missile systems linked to radar networks responded rapidly to Iraqi Scud missile attacks. In addition to these common uses, new technology allows radar systems to play more nontraditional roles on the battlefield. The aircraft-mounted joint surveillance and target-attack radar system (JSTARS) provides airborne fire-direction information to ground units. JSTARS can observe troops and vehicle movements and concentrations and report them directly to ground or air-based weapon systems. During the Gulf War, JSTARS detected ground movements of enemy tank columns and truck convoys at ranges up to several hundred kilometers.

Today, Firefinder radars, available at the division* level, detect the location of enemy artillery* batteries firing on friendly units. Within seconds of firing, Firefinder is able to plot their positions and direct counterbattery fire.* Radar also has ground-force applications. Ground surveillance radar (GSR) can watch likely areas of enemy approach. Available to brigade* commanders, GSR can detect movement of individual enemy soldiers or groups and alert distant locations via radio nets. Surface interface radar (SIR), a ground-penetrating system, assists explosive ordnance and demolition teams in the detection and clearing of mines* and booby traps. SIR can identify both metallic and non-metallic mines by their shapes and characteristics. Additionally, SIR is used to detect tunnels along fixed defensive positions. In Korea, SIR has detected North Korean tunnels along the demilitarized zone* (DMZ).

References. David Kite Allison, *New Eye for the Navy*, 1981. Tony Devereux, *Messenger Gods of Battle*, 1991. Alfred Price, *The History of US Electronic Warfare*, 2 vols., 1984–1989.

Robert J. Dalessandro

RAINBOW DIVISION

Following the declaration of war in April 1917, the U.S. Army found itself critically short of trained divisions* that could be mobilized quickly. Major Douglas MacArthur,* then working on the General Staff,* proposed raising a division by drawing on the best National Guard* units across the country. Many Regular officers opposed the plan, they were suspicious of the democratic tendencies of Guard units and argued that Regular divisions would have to be raised to fight the war. With the support of the president, the secretary of war, and the newly appointed commander of the American Expeditionary Force* (AEF), MacArthur's plan was adopted. The new division's commanders and staff would be Regulars, but the nearly 28,000 men who began reporting to Camp Alvord L. Mills in the late summer of 1917 represented National Guard units from twenty-six states and the District of Columbia. Speaking at a press conference, MacArthur likened the new division, designated the 42d, to the structure of a rainbow spanning the nation—prompting one of the reporters to dub it the "Rainbow Division."

In France, the 42d participated in nearly every campaign of 1918: Champagne-Marne, Aisne-Marne, St. Mihiel,* Meuse-Argonne,* Champagne, and Lorraine. The division returned to the United States and demobilized at Camp Dix, New Jersey, in May 1919. Reconstituted in February 1943 in the Army of the United States, the 42d was reactivated at Camp Gruber, Oklahoma, on 14 July. Elements of the 42d arrived in France in time to see action before the end of December 1944, but the entire division was not in combat until 14 February 1945. Nevertheless, the 42d participated in the Rhineland and Central Europe campaigns. Returned to the United States, the 42d was again deactivated in June 1946. In March 1947, the division was reorganized and recognized as the New York National Guard.

The insignia of the Rainbow Division is a three-color—red, yellow, and blue—quadrant of the rainbow on a field of green.

References. James J. Cooke, *The Rainbow Division in the Great War, 1917–1919*, 1994. *42nd "Rainbow" Infantry Division*, 1946. *42nd "Rainbow" Infantry Division*, 1987.

RAINBOW PLANS

From 1920 to 1937, U.S. strategic contingency planning was based on a series of color-coded plans for war with various countries: orange for war against

Japan, red for war against Great Britain, green for war against Mexico, black for war against Germany, and so on. The color plans were essentially notional and did not necessarily reflect the evolution of events or the changing relations between the major world powers. As a new global conflict became increasingly apparent, the Joint Army-Navy Board* directed the respective staffs of the War Department* and Navy Department to develop a new generation of strategic plans that would more nearly meet U.S. defense requirements in a threatening world. Beginning in late 1938, members of the two staffs, along with representatives of the State Department, began work on Rainbow One, primarily concerned with defense of the Western Hemisphere. Over the next several years, planning evolved through Rainbows Two, Three, Four, and Five as the world situation changed and U.S. policy became clearer. Rainbow Five, the last of the Rainbow plans, identified the defense of the Western Hemisphere as the first priority, Great Britain and France as principal U.S. allies, and Europe as the primary theater in a future war. Rainbow Five became the basis for the U.S. position at the ABC-1 Conference between the U.S. and British staffs at the end of 1940 and thus the cornerstone for Allied strategic planning for World War II.* Although the plans were continually modified until the onset of war in December 1941, at which time the course of events dictated many operational decisions, the fundamentals of Rainbow Five remained intact throughout World War II.

References. Maurice Matloff and Edwin M. Snell, *Strategic Planning for Coalition Warfare, 1941–1942*, 1953. Steven T. Ross, *American War Plans, 1919–1941*, vols. 3 and 4, 1992.

John Broom

RANGERS

The earliest units in North America that called themselves Rangers were lightly armed raiding parties of colonial troops fighting against the Indians. British Major Robert Rogers formed and led the most famous of these units during the French and Indian War (1755–1763). Rogers's Rangers employed Indian tactics and fieldcraft to conduct long-range raids and reconnaissance missions against the Indians of New England. During World War II,* the U.S. Army created modern ranger battalions* to conduct raids and other high-risk missions. The 1st Ranger Battalion, commanded by Colonel William O. Darby, was formed on 19 June 1942 in Northern Ireland from volunteers. British commandos trained Darby's Rangers in hand-to-hand combat, patrolling, night operations, and small-boat operations. The 5307th Composite Unit (Provisional), popularly known as Merrill's Marauders,* formed in Burma and fought intense battles in the mud and rain of the Burmese jungles. Inactivated in 1944, the 5307th's remnants merged with the 475th Infantry Regiment, it was later activated as the 75th Ranger Regiment, thus maintaining the lineage of the original Marauders. The World War II Rangers fought in North Africa, Italy, France, Germany, and the Pacific. Because of their high casualty rates, the War Department* deactivated the Ranger battalions* at the end of the war.

The U.S. Army reactivated separate Ranger companies during the Korean and Vietnam Wars. Finally, in 1974 and 1984, the Army activated three new Ranger battalions and the 75th Ranger Regiment. The modern Rangers have seen action in Grenada, Panama, the Persian Gulf, Somalia, and Haiti. They remain the U.S. Army's premier light-infantry raiding force for airborne assaults, long-range raids, and deep penetrations.

References. David W. Hogan, Jr., *Raiders or Elite Infantry?* 1992. Michael J. King, *Rangers*, 1985.

Joseph R. Fischer

RAPIDO RIVER

The Rapido River, just north of Naples, Italy, was the site of an attempt by the 36th Infantry Division (Texas National Guard) to break through the formidable Gustav Line* in January 1944. The Fifth Army* commander, Lieutenant General Mark Clark,* scheduled the Rapido operation to coincide with the 22 January landing at Anzio.* Clark later stated that the real objective was not so much to break through the German line as it was to draw defenders away from the Anzio area. The U.S. chain of command questioned Clark's judgment on the possibility of assaulting the swiftly flowing Rapido River, with its steep banks and extensive minefields. Both the commander of the 36th Division, Major General Fred Walker, and his corps commander. Major General Geoffrey Keyes, offered alternative plans. Clark, however, insisted that the attack begin as scheduled, on the evening of 20 January.

The results of the two and a half days' attack were predictably disastrous. In spite of fierce German resistance, several hundred G.I.s* reached the opposite bank, only to be cut off and captured. Most soldiers in the tiny rubber and wooden assault boats were killed or wounded before crossing the river. The 36th Division lost an appalling 1,681 casualties, against insignificant German losses. Following the war, a congressional inquiry cleared Clark of incompetence at the Rapidio, noting that two German divisions did move from Rome to the Liri Valley, despite Walker's testimony critical of Clark's tactical judgment.

References. Martin Blumenson, *Bloody River*, 1970. Jeffrey Gaul, *Fighting 36th Infantry Division*, 1988.

Thomas Christianson

RAVEN OH-23

One of the U.S. Army's earliest helicopters, the OH-23/UH-12 Raven, manufactured by Hiller, was first flown in November 1947. Initially used as an observation helicopter, the Raven had a crew of one and could carry two passengers. The Raven's Lycoming VO-540 piston engine produced 340 horsepower to the two-bladed main rotor, for a maximum speed of eighty-three knots and a range of 676 kilometers. The bubble-shaped fusilage was 8.69 meters long, while the aircraft's overall length, including a twin-skid landing gear and tail boom, was 12.4 meters. The Raven was fairly light, with an empty weight of 798 kilograms and a gross weight of 1,270 kilograms. Hiller produced several variants of the Raven, for a variety of missions. The Raven is no longer in service with the U.S. Army.

References. *Army Aviation*, 1992. Stephen Harding, *U.S. Army Aircraft since 1947*, 1997.

Trevor Brown

RECOILLESS RIFLE

In the long history of artillery,* the recoilless rifle (RCR), also known as the recoilless gun, holds a special place on the battlefield, with a design and function unique to the 20th century. The RCR is unique not so much for its portability but its construction as a recoilless weapon. The RCR consists of a gun tube of varying lengths and calibers, the latter ranging from 75 to 106 mm; a venturi at the breech; and a number of mounting systems, including wheels, tripods, and vehicle mounts. Some RCRs are light enough to be man portable and shoulder fired. The gun is recoilless because about 80 percent of the propellant gases are expelled or bled off though the venturi at the breech, thus neutralizing backward movement or recoil. The remaining one-fifth of the propellant gas accelerates the small, lightweight projectile from the venturi down the tube, where it gains stability for its flat-trajectory flight. Making its first appearance in the opening days of World War II,* RCRs, have seen service in the Korean War,* the Vietnam War,* and Desert Storm.* The recoilless rifle continues to serve in the U.S. Army as a readily available source of firepower for both the infantryman and airborne troops against armored vehicles and fortifications.

References. L. B. Hedge, "More Punch for the Infantry," *Army Information Digest*, October 1955, 18–23. Richard M. Ogorkiewicz, "Recoilless Guns and Tanks," *Armor*, September–October 1953, 26–31.

Peter A. Kaiser

RECRUITING COMMAND

The origins of the U.S. Army Recruiting Command (USAREC) can be found in the U.S. Army Recruiting Service (USARS) established at the end of World War II.* For the first time following a major war, the U.S. Army prepared to meet its recruiting needs with a timely, focused program to keep its ranks filled. With the creation of the U.S. Air Force in 1947, USARS became the U.S. Army and Air Force Recruiting Service, a system that served the two services until 1954, when separate recruiting stations were established. In 1964, to streamline and improve recruiting operations, the Army implemented USAREC. Headquartered first at Hampton, Virginia, and later at Fort Sheridan, Illinois, USAREC is currently located at Fort Knox,* Kentucky. USAREC's primary mission is to recruit "high quality men and women to meet accession and special skill requirements" of the U.S. Army. A major general commands USAREC's 4,600

Regular Army and 1,300 Army Reserve* recruiters stationed around the world. Today, recruiting is a highly skilled, resource-intensive activity. U.S. Army Recruiting Command recruiters enlist approximately 70,000 men and women each year.

References. Peggy Flanigan, "No More Drummers and Fifers," *Soldiers*, February 1985, 6–8. Kenneth W. Simpson, "Recruiting Quality Soldiers for America's Army," *Army*, October 1994, 159–160.

RED BALL EXPRESS

The "Red Ball Express," a term borrowed from railway parlance, was a truck transport system employed by the U.S. Army during World War II* in Europe. It began operating on 25 August 1944, when the U.S. First and Third Armies rapid advance toward the Siegfried Line* overextended their logistical support. Since the French railway system had been damaged beyond immediate repair, the burden of supplying the armies was relegated to trucks. Two U.S. Army officers, Lieutenant Colonel Loren A. Ayers and Major Gordon K. Gravelle, were responsible for the implementation of the Red Ball Express. Its western terminus was at St. Lô, although the trucks often loaded supplies at the depots in Cherbourg. The eastern terminus was originally Chartres but was extended to Hirson and Sommesous at the beginning of September. Although the Red Ball Express consumed large quantities of fuel, vehicles, and spare parts, it supplied the armies with over 400,000 tons of supplies before it ceased operations on 16 November 1944.

References. Tory Billard, "The Red Ball Express," *Translog*, October 1976, 14–15. Steve R. Waddell, *United States Army Logistics, 1944*, 1994.

James L. Isemann

RED RIVER CAMPAIGN

In 1864, Major General Nathaniel Banks undertook a campaign to move up the Red River, capture Shreveport, and invade pro-Confederate Texas, in order to deter perceived French ambitions there. Although President Abraham Lincoln and Major General Henry W. Halleck* approved Banks's plan, Ulysses S. Grant,* newly promoted lieutenant general and general-in-chief of the Union Army, did not share their views on its importance, he set about limiting the time and troops allotted to conduct operations. Nevertheless, in concert with Rear Admiral David Dixon Porter's riverine navy, Banks set off up the Red River. The capture of Fort Derussy, an important Confederate stronghold, and several other successful engagements gave promise of a successful campaign. But the promise was short-lived. Traveling along the Red, and then striking out overland toward Shreveport with 30,000 men, Richard Taylor and Edmund Kirby Smith defeated Banks at Sabine Crossroads on 8 April. Retreating with his army back to Alexandria, Louisiana, Banks fought a series of engagements. Unable to get his gunboats back over the falls of the Red because of low water, Porter had to wait until Bank's troops could build a dam to raise the water level. Although

Union forces were victorious in most of the battles and engagements of the Red River Campaign, Banks had failed at Shreveport, and Texas remained under Confederate control.

References. Curt Anders, *Disaster in Deep Sand*, 1997. Ludwell H. Johnson, *Red River Campaign*, 1958.

Layton H. M. Pennington

REDEYE

Redeye is a heat-seeking, short-range, man-portable, surface-to-air missile defense system developed in the late 1950s and fielded by the U.S. Army in the mid-1960s. Developed and manufactured for the Army and Marine Corps by Convair-Pomona, ARGNA, and Philco, the system gave frontline units an organic air defense capability. Each combat-arms battalion* had four to six two-man Redeye teams. Redeye was derided by some critics as a "revenge weapon," because its short range (3.3 kilometers), slow speed (Mach 2.5), and limited ability to pick up the thermal signature of an incoming aircraft meant that it usually engaged after the enemy had made his attack. The lack of IFF (identification friend or foe) capability and the limits of the system placed great demands on the training of the teams. The Stinger,* which offered greater range, sensitivity, and an IFF capability, replaced Redeye in the 1980s.

References. James H. Brill, "Infantry Rocket Weapons," *Ordnance*, May–June 1966, 628–630. George J. Geiger, "Air Defense Missiles for the Army," *Military Review*, December 1969, 39–49. Carl Martin, "Redeye," *Army Digest*, June 1967, 48–51.

Kelvin Crow

REDOUBT NUMBER 10

Redoubts Numbers 9 and 10 were key defensive positions protecting the besieged British army at Yorktown,* under General Lord Cornwallis, from 28 September to 19 October 1781. After an intense artillery barrage, 400 light infantry troops under the command of Lieutenant Colonel Alexander Hamilton assailed Redoubt Number 10 at eight o'clock on the evening of 14 October 1781, taking the position after intense fighting that concluded with a bayonet* assault. French forces under the Comte de Rochambeau simultaneously attacked Redoubt Number 9. The success cost the Continentals nine killed and thirty-one wounded. When a British counterattack the next night failed to recapture Redoubt Number 10, Cornwallis opened negotiations that led to his surrender on 19 October, thus ending the siege of Yorktown. Redoubt Number 10 was the last major battle of the American Revolution.*

References. Howard H. Peckham, *The War for Independence*, 1958. Robert K. Wright, Jr., *The Continental Army*, 1983.

Chris Clark

REFORGER

An annual training and deployment exercise, REFORGER was an acronym for Return of Forces to Germany. Scheduled each autumn, REFORGER was designed to test the ability of the United States to deploy large air and ground forces from the continental U.S. (CONUS) to West Germany. Invariably, a series of tactical war games followed the deployment exercises, including both field training (FTX) and command-post exercises (CPX), designed to test and refine NATO tactical doctrine* and force interoperability. During the Cold War,* such exercises were conducted primarily for their political value, insofar as they were seen to demonstrate the U.S. resolve and ability to reinforce Western European countries to defeat any Warsaw Pact aggression.

References. Frank Cox, "REFORGER," *Soldiers*, April 1990, 21–26. Jack D. Jory, "Reforger I," *U.S. Army Aviation Digest*, May 1969, 32–35.

Fred J. Chiaventone

REGIMENT

One of the oldest combat unit designations, the regiment is an organization larger than a battalion* but smaller than a brigade.* The regiment essentially disappeared from the U.S. Army in the ROAD reorganization of the 1960s. Until that time, all combat units of the Army were tactically and administratively organic parts of regiments, whose lineages, and traditions could be traced to the earliest days of the republic. Since then, regimental designations have been preserved for tradition and sentimental reasons, but battalions are affiliated with brigades rather than regiments. Ostensibly, this is to allow easier cross-attachment within the division,* although there were numerous instances of battalions fighting detached from their parent regiments in World War II.*

Until the beginning of the 20th century, a regiment typically consisted of ten companies. During the reorganization for World War I,* battalions were created within the regiments. In World War II, when the brigade organization was dropped, the regiment was divided into three battalions and was directly subordinate to the division. The companies, however, were still consecutively lettered. The only remaining regiments in the U.S. Army are armored cavalry regiments (ACRs), one per heavy corps.* The Army attempted to establish a regimental system during the COHORT experiment of the early 1980s, but the final results were disappointing.

References. James A. Sawicki, *Infantry Regiments of the U.S. Army*, 1981. Elmer Schmierer, "Long Live the Regiment," *Army*, April 1957, 25–28. John W. Wike, "Our Regimental Heritage," *Army Information Digest*, February 1964, 50–56.

Andrew N. Morris

REGIMENTAL COMBAT TEAM

Until the Korean War,* the primary combat formation in the U.S. Army infantry* division* was the regiment.* During World War II,* the division's internal organization and equipment, and frequently its combat task organization, was modified to provide a more balanced combined-arms organization. This new grouping of units was called the regimental combat team (RCT). The basic building block of the RCT was still the regiment, consisting of a regimental headquarters and headquarters company,* a service company, antitank company, cannon company, and three infantry battalions,* with a total strength of 3,100 officers and men. RCTs were normally employed for missions in which there was a need to expand the combat potential of a single regiment. In such an event, a regiment was reinforced with a field artillery* battalion, a company of combat engineers,* an automatic-weapons antiaircraft battery, a medical company, a signal detachment, and frequently company-sized armor and cavalry formations. The result was a capable, flexible, and powerful combined-arms team. The predecessors of the regimental combat teams of World War II can be found in the subregions of the U.S. Army of 1792–1796.

References. Lewis I. Jeffries, "A Blueprint for Force Design," *Military Review*, August 1991, 20–31. Orville C. Shirey, *Americans*, 1946.

John A. Hixson

REGULAR ARMY. *See* United States Army.

REMAGEN BRIDGE

Named for General Erich Ludendorff and completed in 1916, the railroad bridge at Remagen, Germany, was the site of the first Allied crossing of the Rhine River in World Wat II.* On 7 March 1945 an element of the 9th Armored Division, attached to III Corps, First Army,* discovered that the Germans had not yet destroyed the bridge. Division* orders were to capture the bridge intact. As infantrymen of Combat Command B rushed toward the bridge, German engineers detonated explosive charges, but the bridge survived the explosion, and troops and equipment pushed across the damaged span. U.S. forces used the bridge until it collapsed on 17 March. By that time, however, the engineers had constructed a number of pontoon bridges to support the bridgehead on the east bank of the Rhine.

References. Ken Hechler, *The Bridge at Remagen*, 1957. David E. Pergrin and Eric Hammel, *First across the Rhine*, 1989.

James L. Isemann

REMOUNT SERVICE

Until the beginning of the 20th century, the U.S. Army purchased horses and mules for military service on an as-needed basis, usually by the post quartermasters at the various military installations. On 11 May 1908, Congress approved an act establishing the U.S. Army's Remount Service. The Remount Service became responsible for purchasing, training, and distributing healthy horses and mules to troops in the field, ending the practice of purchasing from local sources. The Remount Service operated three remount depots—Fort Reno, Oklahoma; Fort Royal, Virginia; and Fort Robinson, Nebraska—where the Quartermaster Corps* selected and purchased the required animals. Despite the Army's mechanization in the 1930s, the Remount Service continued to exist and expanded during World War II.* The Army Horse Breeding Program, supervised by the Remount Service, provided the Army with more than 230,000 foals before it was transferred to the U.S. Agricultural Service in 1948. The decline and ultimate dissolution of the horse cavalry* led to the disbandment of the Remount Service in 1949.

References. Maurice F. De Barneville, "The Remount Service in the A.E.F.," *Cavalry Journal*, April 1921, 130–144. Charles L. Scott, "The Remount Service," *Quartermaster Review*, September–October 1930, 13–16.

Layton H. M. Pennington

REORGANIZED OBJECTIVE ARMY DIVISION

In the early 1960s, the U.S. Army reformed its basic combat unit structure from the pentomic division* to the Reorganized Objective Army Division, or ROAD. In place of the pentomic battle group, the key to the ROAD organization was the maneuver battalion.* To its existing infantry,* armor,* and airborne* divisions, the Army added the mechanized division. All of these divisions had a common base: a cadre complete with command and staff and combat tactical, and logistical support elements. Each division had three brigade* headquarters and was assigned varying numbers and types of battalions, depending on its geographical location and missions it might be required to undertake. ROAD divisions were tailored to accomplish a variety of missions, and their mobility reflected the environments in which they operated. The reorganization improved the division's balance between nuclear and nonnuclear capabilities. An increase in conventional firepower—a 45 percent increase in 105 mm howitzers, a 17 percent increase in other artillery elements, a 100 percent increase in aircraft, and a 400 percent increase in recoilless rifles*—enhanced internal flexibility. The division's improved command and control structure allowed more effective use of resources, as well as expansion with the assignment of additional battalions.

The target date to reorganize all active Army divisions under ROAD tables of organizations was the end of fiscal year 1964. The Army expected substantial benefits from the reorganization, including: greater flexibility, through forces tailored to their environment: improved limited-war capability; increased nonnuclear firepower; enhanced tactical mobility; more mechanized forces for Europe; establishment of separate airborne brigades; improved command, control, and training of subordinate leaders; and more effective use of available resources.

References. Ralph E. Haines, Jr., "Division in a Hurry," *Army Information Digest*, August 1962, 43–49. Carl P. Keiser, "The ROAD Ahead," *Military Review*, January 1962, 2–6. Frank F. Rathbun, "On the Road to ROAD," *Infantry*, May–June 1963, 4–7.

Andrew L. Giacomini, Jr.

RESACA, GEORGIA

In May 1864, William T. Sherman's* invasion force of three armies was on the march in north Georgia, moving inexorably toward Atlanta. Avoiding the enemy's strong defenses north and west of Dalton, Sherman sent the Army of the Tennessee,* under Major General James B. McPherson,* to the right through Snake Creek Gap to flank the Confederate line. Meeting heavier resistance than expected and failing to take advantage of his numerical superiority, McPherson was repulsed at Resaca, Georgia, and withdrew to Snake Creek Gap. Both sides then rushed reinforcements into the area until almost the entire strengths of the two armies were facing each other near Resaca. The two armies sparred for three days, both sides making critical mistakes that added to the heavy casualties. When some of McPherson's troops finally succeeded in moving around the Confederate flank on the afternoon of 15 May, Joseph E. Johnston,* commanding the Confederate Army of Tennessee and Army of Mississippi, ordered a withdrawal late that evening and slipped away from Sherman's armies undetected.

References. George William Koon, ed., *Old Glory and the Stars and Bars*, 1995. Philip L. Secrist, *The Battle of Resaca*, 1998.

Edward Shanahan

RESERVE OFFICER TRAINING CORPS

The establishment of the Reserve Officer Training Corps (ROTC) came from a provision in the National Defense Act of 1916* that granted the federal government authority to manage reserve officer training at civilian colleges and to pool ROTC graduates into the Officers' Reserve Corps (ORC) for call-up in emergencies. During its first fifty years, decentralized administration and a lack of standardization, problems the framers of the 1916 act did not envision, plagued the ROTC program. Nevertheless, the reserve officer served as the backbone of Army combat leadership in World War II* and the Korean War.* When inefficient administration led to ROTC's failure to meet the demands of the Army during the Cold War* buildup, the Army gradually centralized control over, and standardized instruction for, ROTC.

In 1967, ROTC became a directorate, with increased emphasis and support from the Army Staff. In 1973, the Office of Deputy Chief of Staff for ROTC, U.S. Army (DSC-ROTC) and Training and Doctrine Command (TRADOC) assumed responsibility for ROTC and supervised the program through four regional headquarters. With changing public attitudes, elimination of the draft, and the end of the compulsory two-year military requirement for male students at land-grant colleges, ROTC again faced problems in quantity and quality. In 1986, the ROTC program came under the new Cadet Command.* Its mission was to "commission the future officer leadership of the United States Army." Cadet Command implemented major initiatives to standardize on-campus and camp training, tighten commissioning standards, and develop effective recruiting programs. Cadet Command's reforms resulted in over 32,000 commissions in the Army, National Guard,* and Army Reserve* between 1986 and 1990. The reduced requirement for officers in the Army, however, finally reached ROTC in 1993, with the elimination of ROTC at 120 schools and the 3d ROTC Region—2d and 4th Regions absorbed its functions. Currently, plans are under way to eliminate 2d ROTC Region and create ROTC Regions West and East. While ROTC will still be the largest peacetime officer-producing system, further reductions in the Army's end-strength may lead to further cuts in ROTC programs.

References. Wilbur M. Brucker, "Quality Is the Answer," *Army Information Digest*, February 1961, 2–15. Robert F. Collins, *Reserve Officers Training Corps*, 1986. Gene M. Lyons and John W. Masland, *Education and Military Leadership*, 1959.

Dwain Crowson

RESERVE OFFICERS ASSOCIATION

Following World War I* several members of the Officers' Reserve Corps (ORC) appeared before a congressional committee to support pending legislation. The chairman thanked them but said that since they did not represent an organization, their testimony carried little weight. As a consequence, an informal group of reserve officers, with the encouragement of General of the Armies John J. Pershing,* formed the Reserve Officers Association (ROA). The Association's stated purpose was to further national defense and promote the Officers' Reserve Corps as an important segment of that defense. At its first convention on 2 October 1922, Brigadier General Henry J. Reilly was elected president. By 1930, membership had grown to 18,178, 20 percent of the Officers' Reserve Corps's active members, and included members of the National Guard. In 1932, female officers were admitted. In the interwar years, the association lobbied for strong national defense and support for the Organized Reserve Corps. In 1949, the ROA opened its membership to reserve officers of all services, including the U.S. Coast Guard, and on 30 June 1950 Congress approved Public Law 595, the ROA charter. The Reserve Officers Association's recognized purpose is to support a military policy for the nation that provides "adequate security" and promotes "the development and execution" of that policy.

References. John T. Carlton and John F. Slinkman, *The ROA Story*, 1982. Richard Crossland and James T. Currie, *Twice the Citizen*, 1984.

Charles Heller

REST AND RECUPERATION

Although the practice of removing soldiers from the front lines to the relative peace and safety of rear areas for periods of rest is as old as warfare, the need became more compelling in the 19th and 20th centuries, when industrializing nations fielded armies that remained in the field or campaigned indefinitely. The modern practice of "rest and recuperation"—R&R—began in World War I,* when all armies periodically withdrew troops from the front for rest. The breaks not only rested soldiers but afforded logisticians opportunities to refit or upgrade unit arms, stores, and equipment. The practice continued in World War II,* when units from battalion* to division* rotated to the rear for periods of rest. During the Vietnam War,* the U.S. Army officially sanctioned a program, administered by U.S. Military Assistance Command, Vietnam* (MACV), to relieve every service member for seven days of R&R after 180 days of in-country service. Troops were offered transportation and accommodations at one of five official R&R sites: Honolulu; Hong Kong; Sydney, Australia; Bangkok, Thailand; and Kuala Lumpur, Malaysia. Hawaii was the most popular R&R location for married men, because commercial airlines offered military spouses special discount fares to that destination.

References. Carl Martin, "Where the Waiting Ends," *Soldiers*, January 1972, 29–31. Ches Schneider, *From Classrooms to Claymores*, 1999.

Keith B. Bartsch

RESTORE HOPE

U.S. and coalition forces conducted Operation Restore Hope in Somalia from 9 December 1992 to 4 May 1993. Pursuant to United Nations Security Council Resolution (UNSCR) 794, the force's mandate was to provide security for the delivery of humanitarian relief supplies. Initially a U.S. Joint Task Force (JTF) under the U.S. Central Command, built around I Marine Expeditionary Force and augmented by Army, Navy, Air Force, and special operations forces,* executed Restore Hope. The 10th Mountain Division was the Army component of the JTF. At the peak of the operation, U.S. forces consisted of 24,165 personnel, of which 6,728 were Army troops. As the operation took on a multinational character, an additional 13,770 troops from twenty-one nations joined U.S. forces in Somalia. The coalition force, known as UNITAF, brought Operation Restore Hope to a successful end on 4 May 1993, with the handover of the mission (now with an expanded mandate pursuant to UNSCR 814) to a UN force called UNOSOM II; UNOSOM II was smaller than UNITAF, with only a 1,200-man U.S. quick-reaction force and 17,200 total personnel.

References. Kenneth Allard, *Somalia Operations*, 1995. Walter S. Clarke, *Somalia*, 1992.

John T. Fishel

RETREAT

"Retreat" is a ceremony, rendered in the form of a bugle call,* firing of a cannon, and hand salute, honoring the U.S. flag when it is lowered in the evening. Retreat normally marks the end of the working day. The installation commander determines that exact time for retreat. The term originated from the French *retraite*. The bugle call is also of French origin and dates from the Crusades. In early American military tradition, retreat was sounded to remind sentries to begin challenging anyone approaching their posts throughout the night. For soldiers not on duty, the sounding of retreat signaled the time to return to quarters.

References. Lawrence P. Crocker, *Army Officer's Guide*, 46th ed., 1993. Aubrey S. Newman, *Follow Me*, 1990.

Kenneth Turner

RE-UP

Reenlistment is the most important and cost-effective method of maintaining a trained and experienced military force. Since soldiers in the U.S. Army have historically referred to enlisting as "signing up," the act of reenlisting is euphemistically referred to as "re-upping." In common soldier conversation, the term is sometimes accompanied by an obscene gesture. In spite of its original pejorative connotations, however, the Army has adopted "re-up" in its reenlistment programs. "Re-up pay" and "re-up bonus" are familiar terms to soldiers, and the officer or noncommissioned officer* (NCO) responsible for reenlistment counseling is frequently known as the Re-up Officer or Re-up NCO.

References. Alan Levy, Bernard Krisher, and James Cox, *Draftee's Confidential Guide*, 1957. "Re-up Law Headed for New Look," *Army-Navy-Air Force Journal*, 19 May 1956, 3.

Lawyn C. Edwards

REVEILLE

Reveille is a camp duty performed by musicians dating back to the 1600s. Reveille had two purposes in the American Revolution*: it was a signal to arise and prepare for the day, and it marked the cessation of challenging by the guards. Historically, reveille was not a single call but a series of six or more pieces strung together by a long drum roll. It began with "Three Camps," followed by "Slow Scotch," "The Austrian," "The Hessian," "The Dutch," and "Quick Scotch." "The Prussian" was sometimes used in place of "The Dutch," and "Finale" was sometimes added at the end. Various lyrics were sung to reveille including the following:

> I can't wake 'em up, I can't wake 'em up, I can't wake 'em up in the morning.
> I can't wake 'em up, I can't wake 'em up, I can't wake 'em at all.
> The corporal's worse than the private, the sergeant's worse than the corporal.
> The lieutenant's worse than the sergeant. And the captain's the worst of all.

References. Fairfax Downey, *Fife, Drum & Bugle*, 1971. Kenneth E. Olson, *Music and Musket*, 1981. William Carter White, *A History of Military Music in America*, 1944.

L. Lynn Williams

REVOLUTIONARY WAR. *See* American Revolution.

RIDGWAY, MATTHEW BUNKER (1895–1993)

Born on 3 March 1895 at Fort Monroe, Virginia, Matthew Bunker Ridgway graduated from the U.S. Military Academy* in 1917 and was commissioned in the infantry.* The son of a Regular Army colonel, Ridgway pursued a career during the interwar years marked by various assignments and slow but steady promotions. Like many officers of his generation, Ridgway rose to prominence in World War II.* He commanded the 82nd Airborne Division* in Italy in 1943 and during the Normandy landings in June 1944, where he jumped into the airhead at Ste. Mère Église with his paratroopers. He assumed command of XVIII Airborne Corps for the Allied breakout from Normandy.

After World War II, Ridgway served in various positions, including Deputy Chief of Staff, Headquarters, Department of the Army. The Korean War* once again provided Ridgway an opportunity to serve his country in a significant role. When Lieutenant General Walton Walker was killed in action, Ridgway assumed command of the badly demoralized Eighth Army.* Both contemporaries and historians have credited Ridgway's leadership with Eighth Army's eventual success in 1951. When President Harry Truman relieved General of the Army Douglas MacArthur* in April 1951, Ridgway was named Far East Commander and Commander in Chief of United Nations Command. Ridgway later became Supreme Allied Commander.

After returning to the United States, Ridgway rose to Chief of Staff* of the Army. Ridgway fought for funding for conventional forces, when the trend was to spend more heavily on nuclear forces. He opposed the "New Look" national strategic direction that the military pursued after the Korean War. Matthew Ridgway retired from the U.S. Army in 1955 after thirty-eight years of service. He passed away in 1993 at age ninety-eight.

References. Robert C. Alberts, "Profile of a Soldier," *American Heritage*, February 1976, 4–7. Jonathan M. Soffer, *General Matthew B. Ridgway*, 1998.

Krewasky A. Salter

RIFLED MUSKET, SPRINGFIELD, MODEL 1861

The model 1861 Springfield rifle musket and its slightly improved successor, model 1863, were the standard shoulder weapons of the Civil War.* First manufactured by the U.S. government armory in Springfield, Massachusetts—hence the name—the muzzle-loaded Springfield was fifty-six inches long, weighed about nine pounds, and fired a .58-caliber Minié ball.* Although Civil War combat ranges tended to be under 200 yards, well-drilled troops armed with Springfields could fire three rounds per minute accurately up to 500 yards, and the weapon was lethal beyond that range. The Springfield Arsenal and some twenty northern contractors produced more than 700,000 model 1861s and more than 500,000 model 1863s during the war.

References. Joseph G. Bilby, *Civil War Firearms*, 1996. Earl J. Coates and Dean S. Thomas, *An Introduction to Civil War Small Arms*, 1990. Claude E. Fuller, *The Rifled Musket*, 1958.

George Knapp

RINGGOLD SADDLE

Major Samuel Ringgold, an artillery* officer in the Regular Army, developed a saddle suitable for both dragoons and artillerymen. Although there were field tests in 1841, the Army did not adopt the Ringgold saddle until 1844. Only after the Army adopted the saddle did Ringgold apply for a patent (Number 3779, granted on 7 October 1844). The Army purchased a total of 1,147 Ringgold saddles between 1841 and 1845. The saddle was unpopular with both dragoons and artillerymen. Many officers privately purchased other saddles, because the Ringgold's sidebars gave their mounts sore backs. The Grimsley saddle* officially replaced the Ringgold in 1847. Samuel Ringgold died in the Mexican War.*

References. R. Stephen Dorsey and Kenneth L. McPheeters, *The American Military Saddle, 1776–1945*, 1999. Randy Steffen, *United States Military Saddles 1812–1943*, 1973.

L. Lynn Williams

RIVERINE OPERATIONS

The term "riverine operations" refers to operations conducted by specially organized, equipped, and trained forces along inland waterways and coastal areas comprising both extensive land and water surfaces. The purpose of riverine operations is to locate and destroy enemy forces in those areas, deny the enemy the use of those areas as transportation and communications routes, and secure and control them for friendly use. Riverine operations are frequently conducted jointly with U.S. Navy and Air Force units. The U.S. Army has conducted riverine operations throughout its history, most notably during the Civil War* along the Mississippi River, and during the Vietnam War;* when Army forces fought in the Mekong Delta and along South Vietnam's extensive coastline.

References. Thomas J. Cutler, *Brown Water, Black Berets*, 1988. Charles Dana Gibson and E. Kay Gibson, *Assault and Logistics*, vol. 2, 1995. Don Sheppard, *Riverine*, 1992.

ROCK ISLAND ARSENAL

Rock Island is located in the Mississippi River between the towns of Davenport, Iowa, and Rock Island, Illinois. The first construction on the island was Fort Montgomery, built in May 1816. In July 1862, Congress appropriated funds to build an arsenal on Rock Island. The first permanent building, the Clock Tower, was begun in 1863. Thomas J. Rodman, responsible for most of the design and construction, commanded the arsenal from 1865 until 1871. The arsenal's mission has been the production of items ranging from small articles of equipment for the infantry* and cavalry,* to recoil mechanisms for cannons and mounts for airplane guns. It was used as a prisoner of war* camp during the Civil War.* Rock Island Arsenal is presently the home of the U.S. Army Munitions and Chemical Command, and it continues to produce artillery components and weapons subsystems.

References. Thomas J. Slattery, *An Illustrated History of Rock Island Arsenal and Arsenal Island*, 1990. Martin S. Werngren, "Skills Spell Strength," *Army Digest*, September 1962, 60–62.

Jim Martin

ROCKET-PROPELLED GRENADE

The term "rocket-propelled grenade," or RPG, is derived from the Soviet *reaktivniy protivotankoviy granatomet*, an antitank rocket grenade launcher initially introduced in World War II.* First fielded by the Germans in World War II as the *panzerfaust*, the RPG provided infantry*units as low as the squad* an antitank weapon. RPGs have also been developed for use as small-unit antiaircraft defense and as a source of flat-trajectory firepower against fortifications. The RPG is basically a small, man-portable version of the often much larger recoilless rifle.* Both the recoilless rifle and RPG make use of the venturi effect, the expulsion of propellant gases from the rear of the gun-tube; the rocket grenade is loaded through the muzzle rather than the breech. More recent versions of the RPG, however, consist of a rocket enclosed in a sealed, disposable guntube that can be discarded after the rocket is fired. The U.S. Army's light antiarmor weapon, LAAW or LAW, used extensively during the Vietnam War,* and the more recent Soviet RPG-18 and 22, introduced in the Afghan War, are examples of this type of weapon. Typically, the rocket-propelled grenade has a caliber of 44 mm to 74 mm, is equipped with open sights and a pistol grip for ease of handling, is fired from the shoulder, and is served by a crew of two, a gunner and a loader.

References. Michael R. Harris, "Tactical Employment of the Shoulder-Fired Rocket," *Infantry*, November–December 1996, 29–32. Harold G. Moore and Joseph L. Galloway, *We Were Soldiers Once . . . and Young*, 1992.

Peter A. Kaiser

ROCKET LAUNCHER, 2.36-INCH, M1. *See* Bazooka.

RODMAN RIFLE. *See* Ordnance Rifle.

ROGERS' RANGERS. *See* Rangers.

ROME PLOW

"Rome Plow" refers to two innovative devices used by the U.S. Army at different periods of history. The first use of the term dates to the Civil War*: an enterprising inventor patented a plow that incorporated a small cannon above the plowshare. In theory, the farmer could ward off enemy attacks while continuing to work his fields near disputed areas. Unfortunately, the idea never caught on, and few if any Rome plows saw production.

The term was revived during the Vietnam War,* where it was popularly given to the D7E tractor, equipped with a protective cab and a special scrapper treecutting blade manufactured by the Rome Company of Rome, Georgia. Designed to clear undergrowth and trees, units used the Rome plow to clear lanes through minefields, remove vegetation to improve fields of fire, and enhance local roads and trails. The Rome plow became the backbone of unit engineer support and was one of the most effective weapons in the Vietnam War.

References. Rodney R. Gettig and James W. Dunn. "Land Clearing in Vietnam," *Engineer*, [1987], 45. Robert R. Ploger, *U.S. Army Engineers 1965–1970*, 1974.

                                                                                        Robert J. Dalessandro

ROOT, ELIHU (1845–1937)

Although never a soldier, Elihu Root deserves special recognition for his influence on the U.S. Army. A corporate lawyer by training, Root spent much of his life in public service as a senator and diplomat, and as secretary of war.* He was a close friend and advisor of Theodore Roosevelt during his years in New York politics. President William McKinley persuaded Root to serve as secretary of war, a position he held from 1899 through 1904. During his tenure Root was responsible for the administration of territories acquired by the United States during the Spanish-American War,* a task for which he was admirably suited. Under his direction, the Army provided efficient and enlightened governance for Puerto Rico, Cuba, and the Philippines—a feat for which Root received the Nobel Peace Prize in 1912. Root initiated and presided over a major reorganization of the U.S. Army, with the intent to redress gross inefficiencies revealed during the Spanish-American War. In addition to introducing the concept of the rotation of staff and line assignments, a practice that continues today, Root was instrumental in establishing the Army War College* (1900), the Command and General Staff School (1903), and the Army General Staff* (1903). After leaving the War Department,* Root served as secretary of state under President Roosevelt (1905), acted as a special emissary to the Kerensky government during the Russian Revolution (1917), helped frame the statutes establishing the World Court (1920), and was appointed by President Warren G. Harding to represent the United States at the Washington Arms Limitation Conference (1927).

References. James E. Hewes, Jr., *From Root to McNamara*, 1975. Philip C. Jessup, *Elihu Root*, 1938. Richard W. Leopold, *Elihu Root and the Conservative Tradition*, 1954.

                                                                                        Fred J. Chiaventone

ROSEBUD

On the morning of 17 June 1876, a large force of Sioux and Cheyenne warriors surprised more than 1,000 troops under the command of Brigadier General George Crook as they rested along Rosebud Creek near present-day Big Bend, Montana. Warned by his Crow and Shoshoni scouts in time to divert disaster, Crook took the offensive after repelling the initial Indian attack. Convinced that the Indians were acting to protect their nearby village, Crook split his force into three battalions* and established a command post* on a piece of high ground now known as Crook's Ridge. He sent Lieutenant Colonel William B. Royall, his second in command, northwest along Kollmar Creek to pursue a group of retreating warriors, and he sent Captain Anson Mills with six cavalry* companies* east along Rosebut Creek to locate and destroy the suspected village.

The battle, however, became desperate when the Sioux Royall had been pursuing turned and attacked his forward company at what is today known as Andrew's Point, more than a mile from Crook and the main body of the command. Surrounded on three sides, Royall's battalion was saved from destruction by friendly Crow and Shoshoni, who struck the Sioux from the east. Realizing the difficult situation Royall was in, Crook ordered Mills to return to the command while the infantry* provided covering fire under which Royall withdrew to a safer position. Mills's reappearance northwest of Crook's Ridge, near the Indian stronghold on Conical Hill, convinced the enemy to break off the action and leave the battlefield. Crook attempted to pursue the departing enemy, but Crow and Shoshoni scouts convinced him that the Sioux were preparing an ambush. Crook called off the pursuit and returned with his wounded to Goose Creek, where he stayed for the next six weeks awaiting reinforcement and re-supply.

The Battle of the Rosebud demonstrated a much higher degree of aggressiveness, coordination, and cooperation by the Indians—who had typically fought as individuals for status and honor—than had previously been seen in the Indian Wars.* Emboldened and stirred by their success at the Rosebud, the Sioux and Cheyenne achieved their greatest victory eight days later, at the Little Bighorn.*

References. Neil C. Mangum, *Battle of the Rosebud*, 1991. J. W. Vaughn, *With Crook at the Rosebud*, 1956.

Tamas Dreilinger

ROUGH RIDERS

On 22 April 1898, Congress approved an act authorizing the secretary of war* to raise three regiments* of volunteers to be commanded by Regular Army officers. The 1st U.S. Volunteer Cavalry was to become the most famous of these regiments. Theodore Roosevelt was first offered command of the new regiment, but he deferred to his more experienced friend and Regular officer Leonard Wood.* Roosevelt chose instead a lieutenant colonelcy and became second in command. Roosevelt subsequently resigned his position as assistant secretary of the Navy so he could devote himself fully to his new task. Newsmen quickly attached the alliterative nickname "Roosevelt's Rough Riders" to the assemblage of "young, good shots and good riders" enlisted by Wood and Roosevelt, then being organized and trained at San Antonio, Texas. At first, Roosevelt disapproved of the sobriquet, but eventually he took great pride in it.

The Rough Riders sailed from Tampa, Florida, on 13 June and disembarked nine days later at Daiquri, Cuba. Following their baptism of fire at Las Guasimas on 24 June, the Rough Riders continued with the general advance toward Santiago. When Brigadier General S.B.M. Young, 2d Brigade commander, fell seriously ill, Wood replaced him, and Roosevelt assumed command of the Rough Riders. On 1 July, during the assault on San Juan Heights, the Rough Riders earned undying fame for their charge up Kettle Hill, one of the two hills that flanked the main road to El Caney. Through myth and legend—in the making of which the future president of the United States had no small part—as well as heroism on the battlefield, the Rough Riders' charge has become one of the great epics of American history.

References. Virgil Carrington Jones, *Roosevelt's Rough Riders*, 1971. Theodore Roosevelt, *Theodore Roosevelt*, ed. Mario R. DiNunzio, 1994.

ROUNDUP

"Roundup" was the code name for a cross-Channel assault by Allied forces in World War II.* Related operations included the buildup of troops and resources in Great Britain prior to the invasion (Bolero*) and a contingency plan for a 1942 attack against Axis forces in France should Germany collapse precipitously or conditions on the Eastern Front become so critical that immediate pressure in the West became essential to keep the Soviet Union in the war (Sledgehammer*). Roundup involved forty-eight divisions* (thirty U.S. and eighteen British) and over 2,500 aircraft in an assault on the French coast northeast of the Seine, between Le Harve and Boulogne. The target date for Roundup was 1 April 1943.

Roundup became a source of continuing disagreement between U.S. and British military leaders. The U.S. Joint Chiefs of Staff* favored a 1943 assault on northwestern Europe, while their British counterparts, supported by Prime Minister Winston Churchill, advocated actions to defeat Axis forces in North Africa, followed by further operations in the Mediterranean. U.S. efforts to win approval for the American proposal—efforts that included an attempt to bluff the British by openly declaring that the United States ought to reconsider its "Europe First" strategy, failed in part due to President Franklin Roosevelt's desire to commit U.S. ground forces in combat in late 1942—too early to mount a major effort in northwest Europe with the limited Allied manpower and landing craft. At the January 1943 Casablanca Conference, the British gained the Joint Chiefs' support for a landing in Sicily. Provisions were also made during the conference to establish a command and planning organization (COSSAC) to plan 1943 operations against the northern coast of France in preparation for a major cross-Channel assault in 1944. By late spring 1943, plans to conduct Roundup were dropped in favor of a full-scale assault in 1944.

References. Kent Roberts Greenfield, ed., *Command Decisions*, 1959. Gordon A. Harrison, *Cross-Channel Attack*, 1951. Maurice Matloff, *Strategic Planning for Coalition Warfare, 1943–1944*, 1959.

Russell W. Glenn

RUCKSACK

Rucksack is an anglicized German military word (*ruck* = back, *sacke* = pack) for backpack. Made of material able to conform to the shape of the load, normally closed at the top with a drawstring and flap and equipped with a number of straps and external pockets, the rucksack is a popular piece of military and commercial outdoor equipment. The rucksack gained popularity over the standard packs, since it is generally flexible enough to assume the shape of the objects it carries. The U.S. Army has used rucksacks since World War II.* It replaced the field pack as a standard issue item in the 1970s.

References. David G. Faughan, "Lincloe System," *Infantry*, May–June 1973, 54–55. Robert W. Fisch, *Field Equipment of the Infantry, 1914–1945*, 1989.

Edwin Kennedy, Jr.

RULES OF ENGAGEMENT

Rules of engagement (ROEs) are directives derived from written policy to governing the circumstances in which combat is to be conducted and when force or combat actions should be employed. The Geneva Convention established the general rules of engagement—commonly referred to as the Laws of War. Its prohibitions include, but are not limited to, firing upon a descending paratrooper, damage and destruction to historical and religious establishments, and hostile acts against medical or Red Cross facilities. Rules of engagement, however, are normally written for specific military actions. For example, combat operations in Haiti may take on a different demeanor than those in Iraq, thus requiring different rules of engagement. In modern military operations, rules of engagement are often very complex and may change frequently. The U.S. Army commander on the scene is always responsible to see that his soldiers carefully observe the rules of engagement.

References. Lee E. DeRemer, "Leadership between a Rock and a Hard Place," *Airpower Journal*, Fall 1996, 87–94. Richard J. Grunawalt, "The JCS Standing Rules of Engagement," *Air Force Law Review*, 1997, 245–258.

Krewasky A. Salter

RUSSIAN INTERVENTION

U.S. participation in the allied intervention in the Russian civil war from 1918 to 1920 constitutes one of the least-known episodes in U.S. military history. Following the Bolshevik Revolution of 1917, at the allies' request President Woodrow Wilson reluctantly agreed to contribute forces to a combined intervention in Russia. Although Wilson's motives and goals are subjects of dispute, the nature and consequences of American participation are reasonably clear. The small U.S. forces deployed to Russia became embroiled, if only on the periphery, in the vast and bloody struggle between Reds and Whites. U.S. troops operated in two areas: in the Arctic, at and around Archangel, and in the general vicinity of Vladivostok, in the Far East. In the former instance, U.S. forces acted under British direction alongside British, French, and White Russian troops. In the Far East, the principal U.S. partners were the Japanese, with whom the U.S. had a distant and uneasy relationship. Overall, the intervention epitomized the difficulties that can beset coalition partners who are working at cross-purposes and without reliable intelligence, coordinated planning, or a clear chain of command. Allied troops began withdrawing from the Arctic in late 1919 and from the Far East in early 1920 (Japanese troops would be the last to leave), without having achieved any noteworthy military or political aims. Although it did not significantly affect the course of World War I* or the Russian Civil War, the intervention reinforced Bolshevik belief in the natural hostility of the capitalist powers and helped foster a siege mentality among the new rulers in the Kremlin. It later served Cold War* propaganda of the Soviet Union as apparent proof that the belligerence of the Western powers was to blame for the prevailing mistrust and animosity between East and West.

References. John Bradley, *Allied Intervention in Russia*, 1968. Richard Goldhurst, *The Midnight War*, 1978. Betty Miller Unterberger, ed., *American Intervention in the Russian Civil War*, 1969.

Robert F. Baumann

S

SAD SACK

"Sad Sack" is a character immortalized by *Yank** cartoonist Sergeant George Baker, a draftee and former Walt Disney artist, who first drew the pathetic private in 1942. The character symbolizes all the bewildered ex-civilians who blunder their ways through the mazes of army life. He is a G.I.* who means well but never does anything right. The epithet originated in common army usage of the time in which a sergeant would refer to the most worthless member of his unit as a "sad sack of shit." Sad Sack has come to mean any inept, bewildered person.

References. George Baker, "The Real Sad Sack," *New York Times Magazine*, 9 July 1944, 16–17. "Speaking of Pictures," *Life*, 31 December 1945, 8–10.

Randall N. Briggs

ST. MIHIEL

The St. Mihiel offensive marked the first time in World War I* that the U.S. Army fought as a unified force. The U.S. First Army* attacked on the morning of 12 September 1918 into the flanks of a sixteen-mile bulge in the French lines that ran from the heights of the Woervre to the Meuse River at St. Mihiel. Major General Hunter Liggett's* I Corps, on the extreme right of the U.S. line, and Major General Joseph T. Dickman's IV Corps attacked the eastern face of the bulge, while Major George H. Cameron's V Corps advanced into the western salient. The two prongs joined up at Vigneulles after a rapid advance on the morning of 13 September. When the pincers closed off the salient, the Americans captured 15,000 Germans and 443 guns at a cost of less than 8,000 U.S. casualties.

For the remainder of 13 and 14 September, the three U.S. corps* and the French 2nd Colonial Corps, which had applied pressure to the nose of the salient during the attack, advanced to face the Michel Line. The battle was then suspended to finalize preparations for the Meuse-Argonne* offensive.

References. Rexmond C. Cochrane, *The Use of Gas at St. Mihiel*, 1957. James H. Hallas, *Squandered Victory*, 1995.

Edward L. Maier III

SAM BROWNE BELT

Named after its designer, General Sam Browne of the British army, the Sam Browne belt is a leather military belt made to carry a number of accoutrements without falling or sagging. Its hallmark is the cross strap(s) designed by the one-armed general to hold pistol holster and sword. The belt proved so popular that it was adopted by the British and many other armies. The U.S. Army and Marines unofficially adopted the Sam Browne belt during World War I* as officer uniform* apparel. The belt gained great popularity with the officers serving in Europe, who called them "liberty belts." Military police promptly confiscated the belts upon debarkation, because General Payton March,* Chief of Staff* of the Army, did not like them. In 1921, however, General of the Armies John J. Pershing* had the belt made part of the official Army uniform. It remained a standard uniform item until 1941. Although no longer an official part of the U.S. Army uniform, the Marine Corps has retained it for use with its dress blue uniform.

References. Lawrence Stallings, *The Doughboys*, 1963. Randy Steffen, *The Horse Soldier 1776–1943*, vol. 4, 1979.

Edwin Kennedy, Jr.

SAN PIETRO

The small Italian village of San Pietro Infine, located at the foot of Monte Sammucro—which overlooks Highway 6 just south of the entrance to the Liri Valley, the primary axis of the Allied advance on Rome—was the scene of a bitter and costly battle in the late fall of 1943 between troops of Major General Fred Walker's 36th Infantry Division (ID) and German units fighting a holding action. When an attached ranger unit failed to take San Pietro at the end of November, Walker ordered an assault on the village. Battalions* from two infantry* regiments,* the 1st Italian Motorized Group, and attached rangers attacked San Pietro on 7 December but failed to take their objective after two days of heavy fighting. Walker ordered a second attack on San Pietro, this time utilizing an attached tank battalion and the 504th Parachute Infantry. Following preparations made by the combat engineers, the tanks and infantry attacked again on 14 December, finally succeeding in clearing the last German defenders by late evening of the 16th. The cost of taking San Pietro was high: the 36th ID suffered 1,200 casualties, plus several hundred casualties among the attached engineers, rangers, tankers, and paratroopers. The capture of San Pietro, however, did not immediately open the road to Rome. Progress up the Italian Peninsula continued to be at a very slow and costly pace.

References. Martin Blumenson, *Salerno to Cassino*, 1969. Chester G. Starr, *From Salerno to the Alps*, 1948.

SAND CREEK

Also known as the Sand Creek Massacre, the battle of Sand Creek occurred on 29 November 1864, when the 3d Colorado Cavalry and elements of the 1st Colorado Cavalry under Colonel John M. Chivington attacked a peaceful village of Cheyenne and Arapaho under chief Black Kettle. Chivington's surprise assault went forward despite the village, composed mostly of women and children, flying the Stars and Stripes and a white flag. The Village initially offered no resistance; only after the soldiers opened fire did the Indians put up a defense. The Colorado artillery cut the Cheyenne to pieces, and the cavalry hunted down the survivors. Chivington's order to take no prisoners resulted in the death of about 200 men, women, and children. The action was the object of one military and two congressional investigations during 1865. A Joint congressional committee condemned Chivington for his actions at Sand Creek, but he was never court-martialed. The consequence of the massacre was increased hostility between white settlers and enraged Cheyenne, Arapaho, and Sioux throughout the Plains region.

References. Bruce Cutler, *The Massacre at Sand Creek*, 1995. Stan Hoig, *The Sand Creek Massacre*, 1961.

Chris Clark

SANDCRAB. *See* Attu.

SANTA ROSA ISLAND. *See* Fort Pickens.

SANTEE SIOUX UPRISING

At the great council of Traverse des Sioux of 1851, the Santee Sioux relinquished possession of their lands, with the exception of a strip ten miles wide by 150 miles long. This reservation, or agency, lay adjacent to the Minnesota River in southwestern Minnesota. During the summer of 1862, having grown partially dependent upon government subsidies, the Sioux delayed the start of their annual buffalo hunt while awaiting the distribution of annuities. Bureaucratic red tape and inflexible government agents delayed issuing rations and goods, as the prime hunting season passed, the Santee grew ever more apprehensive and resentful. When hunting parties belatedly attempted to supplement stores for the winter, game proved exceedingly scarce. White and Santee relations, which had been remarkably good, began to sour. A chance encounter between a frustrated Santee hunting party and local settlers on 17 August 1862 ended in bloodshed, with several whites slain. The Sioux, fearing an indiscriminate response from the white communities, decided to strike first. The next day they moved against the whites.

Little Crow, a respected Sioux warrior who had initially counseled against violence, took charge and led a force of several hundred warriors against the garrison at Fort Ridgely and the town of New Ulm. Finding New Ulm heavily defended by settlers who had fled there for safety, the Sioux turned their attention to the 150-man garrison at nearby Fort Ridgely. Their attack on 20 August failed; the Sioux regrouped and launched a second assault two days later. This attack met with unexpectedly strong resistance from the 5th Minnesota Infantry, who used artillery to inflict heavy losses on the attacking warriors.

When Little Crow received word that Colonel H. H. Sibley and a detachment of the 6th Minnesota Infantry was moving to relieve the garrison, he broke off the attack and moved again toward New Ulm, hoping to destroy the town before Sibley's arrival, but this attack was also repulsed. The Sioux then began to withdraw toward the agencies. When the Indians bungled an ambush of the pursuing 6th Minnesota near Wood Lake, Little Crow sued for peace on 27 September. Warriors who had participated in the uprising were placed on trial, with 303 sentenced to death and sixteen given long prison terms. President Abraham Lincoln later commuted the death sentences of all but thirty-eight of the warriors, who were hanged at Fort Snelling* on 26 December 1862.

References. Ralph K. Andrist, *The Long Death*, 1964. Dee Brown, *Bury My Heart at Wounded Knee*, 1970.

Fred J. Chiaventone

SANTIAGO CAMPAIGN

Soon after the United States declared war against Spain on 25 April 1898, President William McKinley planned to send an expeditionary force to Havana, Cuba, but his strategy quickly changed on 28 May, when a small Spanish flotilla arrived off the east coast of Cuba and anchored in Santiago Harbor. The U.S. Navy immediately blockaded the entrance of Santiago Bay, and the newly formed V Corps, under Major General William Shafter, assembled at Tampa, Florida, and prepared to sail for Cuba. V Corps arrived off Santiago Bay on 22 June and began landing, without opposition, twenty miles east of the city.

Theodore Roosevelt's dismounted Rough Riders,* moving inland the following day, ran into a large Spanish force at Las Guasimas. After a fierce skirmish, the Spaniards abandoned their position and retreated toward Santiago. The U.S. troops continued to advance, on 24 June, they were about five miles from Santiago. Directly ahead lay fortified San Juan Hill and smaller Kettle Hill. On 30 June, after a short reconnaissance of enemy positions, Shafter divided his army, and at dawn the next day Brigadier General Henry Lawton's division* attacked the village of El Caney—a few miles north of Santiago—while Joseph Wheeler's and Jacob Kent's divisions assaulted San Juan Hill. Strategically, the attack on El Caney was a mistake; if the troops engaged at El Caney had been held in reserve, the heights and Santiago might have been captured the same day.

The Santiago campaign lasted less than a month, from 22 June to 17 July, yet it brought land warfare into the twentieth century. For the first time, machine guns supported an infantry* advance. The assault on San Juan Heights, backed by Lieutenant John Parker's Gatling gun* detachment, was the main factor in V Corps's victory. Although U.S. casualties were relatively light (290 killed and

1,600 wounded), more than 2,500 died from yellow fever, malaria, and other tropical diseases. Thus, the Army suffered total losses of 25 percent.

References. Jack Cameron Dierks, *A Leap to Arms*, 1970. A. B. Feuer, *The Santiago Campaign of 1898*, 1993.

A. B. Feuer

SARATOGA

In June 1777 Major General John Burgoyne's 8,000 British troops, Hessians, Loyalists, and Indians advanced southward across Champlain Valley toward the Hudson River and Albany, New York. After taking Fort Ticonderoga* in early July, the British advance slowed to a crawl as Colonial troops destroyed bridges, blocked roads, and defeated a foraging expedition near Bennington, Vermont. Along the Hudson, Major General Horatio Gates fortified Bemis Heights, blocking Burgoyne's advance. On 19 September Burgoyne tried to flank Gates's position, but forces led by Danial Morgan and Benedict Arnold* struck first in the Battle of Freeman's Farm. Although the field changed hands repeatedly, by nightfall the British controlled it—at a cost of some 600 casualties, twice the casualties of the Colonials. Burgoyne entrenched his forces to await relief he mistakenly believed to be en route from New York.

As Gates's forces swelled to more than 11,000, Burgoyne's Loyalists and Indians deserted. On 7 October the British probed the Colonial defenses, but Arnold rallied his forces and seized the redoubt, securing the British left. In the Battle of Bemis Heights, the Colonials inflicted a further 600 casualties, at a cost of 200 men. Burgoyne retreated northward to Saratoga (near Schuylerville, New York). Cut off and outnumbered, he surrendered his army on 17 October. The Colonial victory led to an alliance with France in February 1778, converting the revolution into a world war.

References. John R. Elting, *The Battles of Saratoga*, 1977. Rupert Furneaux, *The Battle of Saratoga*, 1971. Richard M. Ketchum, *Saratoga*, 1997.

Stanley Adamiak

SCHOFIELD, JOHN McALLISTER (1831–1906)

Born in New York on 28 September 1831, John McAllister Schofield received an appointment to the U.S. Military Academy* in 1849 from Illinois and graduated seventh of fifty-two cadets in his class. Commissioned in the artillery,* Schofield served in Florida before returning to West Point as an instructor. On duty in Missouri at the beginning of the Civil War,* he served as Brigadier General Nathaniel Lyon's chief of staff and saw action at Wilson's Creek,* where he won the Medal of Honor* (awarded in 1892). Appointed a brigadier general in November 1861, Schofield commanded the Federal militia in Missouri until April 1862, when he assumed command of the Army of the Frontier, Department of Missouri. Promoted to major general on 12 May 1863 (with an effective date of November 1862), Schofield commanded a division* of the Army of the Cumberland,* Department of Missouri, and XXIII Corps, Army of the Ohio,* during the Atlanta,* Franklin,* and Nashville* campaigns. Appointed a brigadier general in the Regular Army, he was serving under William T. Sherman* in North Carolina when the Civil War* ended. After the war, he served as Andrew Johnson's secretary of war* and superintendent of the Military Academy; he succeeded Philip H. Sheridan* as Commanding General* of the Army in 1888. Schofield retired from the Army in 1895 and published his memoirs, *Forty-Six Years in the Army*, two years later. He died at St. Augustine, Florida, on 4 March 1906.

References. James McDonough, *Schofield*, 1972. Russell F. Weigley, "The Military Thought of John M. Schofield," *Military Affairs*, Summer 1959, 77–84.

Edward Shanahan

SCHOFIELD BARRACKS

Schofield Barracks, located twenty-five miles north of Honolulu on the Leilahua Plain in central Oahu, the most populous island in the Hawaiian chain, was built in 1909 as a companion base to Fort Shafter, also on Oahu. Named for General John McAllister Schofield,* a highly respected corps* commander under William T. Sherman* in the Civil War* and secretary of war* under Andrew Johnson, Schofield Barracks has been the permanent home of the 25th Infantry Division (ID) since October 1941. Today, the 25th ID and the 45th Support Group, with approximately 15,000 military personnel, are the major tenants at this installation.

References. Dan Cragg, *Guide to Military Installations*, 4th ed., 1994. J. E. Theimer, "The U.S. Army in Hawaii," *Army Information Digest*, July 1960, 2–13.

J.G.D. Babb

SCHOOL FOR THE APPLICATION OF INFANTRY AND CAVALRY

Forerunner of the U.S. Army Command and General Staff College,* the School for the Application of Infantry and Cavalry was founded by Commanding General William T. Sherman* in 1881 to provide fundamental professional training for infantry* and cavalry* officers. (A school for artillery officers operated at Fort Monroe* as early as 1827.) One should not overestimate the importance of this early attempt at professional education on the basis of the success of its 20th-century successor schools. In fact, though Sherman's goal had been to offer a broad military education, the School of Application was little more than a company* officers' school, offering remedial work for officers whose precommissioning education had been limited or nonexistent, and basic instruction for subaltern officers preparing to become long-service officers in an army dispersed in company and troop posts on the frontier. Student selection was haphazard. Sherman personally traveled to Fort Leavenworth* to warn the students that poor performance could be rewarded by dismissal. Remedial academic instruction was eliminated in 1888, and the quality, if not the breadth, of the instruction appears to have improved steadily until the U.S. Infantry and

Cavalry School, as the School of Application was renamed in 1886, closed for the Spanish-American War.* The principal influence in these years was provided by Captains Arthur L. Wagner* and Eban Swift,* both of whom attempted to introduce European models and experience into the instruction. Swift developed the five-paragraph field order still used in the U.S. Army and introduced the applicatory method into Leavenworth instruction. Both Wagner and Swift played decisive roles in the development of Army education and the role of Leavenworth in that experience.

References. Elvid Hunt and Walter E. Lorence, *History of Fort Leavenworth*, 2d ed., 1937, 1981. Timothy K. Nenninger, *The Leavenworth Schools and the Old Army*, 1978.

Richard Swain

SCOTT, WINFIELD (1786–1866)

Winfield Scott was one of America's first internationally known military heroes. Dubbed "Old Fuss and Feathers" by his men for his stern and disciplined manner, he nevertheless became one of the most beloved commanders in U.S. history. Scott was born on 13 June 1786 on his father's farm near present-day Petersburg, Virginia. He attended the College of William and Mary and practiced law in Petersburg until 1808, when he accepted a commission as a captain in the U.S. Army.

Scott became a national hero during the War of 1812,* distinguishing himself during the battles of Chippawa* and Lundy's Lane.* He was wounded twice at Lundy's Lane, where his bravery earned him a medal from Congress and promotion to major general. Between the War of 1812 and the Mexican War,* Scott delved into politics, but there he enjoyed less success than on the battlefield. On the eve of the Mexican War, Scott was appointed general in chief of the Army. When hostilities commenced, however, President James K. Polk selected Zachary Taylor to lead the expedition to Mexico. Polk's reluctance to select Scott was fueled by his personal dislike of Scott, but eventually he ordered Scott to take command in the field. Scott planned and executed a daring amphibious landing at Veracruz* and then marched through the mountains to seize Mexico City.* This brilliant strategic action earned Scott another decoration from Congress and renewal of national praise.

Following the war, Scott made two unsuccessful bids for the presidency. In 1848, he lost the Whig nomination to his subordinate, Zachary Taylor, and in 1852 he was soundly defeated by Franklin Pierce. At the outbreak of the Civil War,* Scott was still commanding general* of the Army. Lincoln asked Scott to lead the Army in the field, but Scott declined due to failing health. He remained in Washington, supervising activities at the War Department* and developing a strategy to defeat the Confederacy. He alone foresaw the likelihood of a four-year war. He developed the Anaconda Plan,* which became the Federal strategy in 1864–1865. Upon the appointment of George B. McClellan* as commander of the Army of the Potomac,* Scott requested, and was granted, retirement on 31 October 1861. He had served his country for more than fifty years. Scott lived to see the end of the Civil War* and died at West Point on 29 May 1866. He is buried in the post cemetery.

References. John S. D. Eisenhower, *Agent of Destiny*, 1997. Charles Winslow Elliott, *Winfield Scott*, 1937. Timothy D. Johnson, *Winfield Scott*, 1998.

Robert J. Dalessandro

SEARCH AND DESTROY

In June 1964, Military Assistance Command, Vietnam* (MACV) adopted a new operational terminology that included "search and destroy," clearing, and securing operations. These operations were designed to find, fix in place, and destroy enemy forces, their base areas, and supply caches; they were originally intended to delineate the basic combat mission to be performed by South Vietnamese military forces. When U.S. forces arrived later in the Vietnam War,* search and destroy became the accepted mode of operation. The tactic was very simple in theory but very difficult in practice, as U.S. troops tried to find the enemy and bring him to battle. Search-and-destroy operations were a manifestation of the U.S. attrition strategy. Public repugnance toward the brutality implied by the term, in addition to vivid media accounts of destruction of Vietnamese villages, helped undermine support for the war.

References. John H. Hay, Jr., *Tactical and Materiel Innovations*, 1974. Dave Richard Palmer, *Summons of the Trumpet*, 1978. John Pimlott, ed., *Vietnam*, 1982.

James H. Willbanks

SECOND ARMY

General John J. Pershing* created the U.S. Second Army on 20 September 1918 at Toul, France. Under the command of Major General Robert L. Bullard,* Second Army was to prevent the Germans from flanking First Army* during the Lorraine campaign. Second Army remained in Europe on occupation duty until it was demobilized on 15 April 1919. Reactivated on 1 October 1933, Second Army assumed responsibility for the strategic area of the Great Lakes and the central northern frontier. During World War II,* Second Army did not deploy overseas but trained hundreds of thousands of troops, the equivalent of fifty divisions,* for America's war effort. In the postwar reorganization, Second Army became one of six armies in the continental U.S. Although its responsibilities continued to expand in the late 1950s and early 1960s, Second Army was deactivated on 1 January 1966, and its functions were consolidated in First Army. On 1 October 1983, Second Army was once again activated and was assigned to Forces Command.* With its headquarters at Fort Gillem, Georgia, Second Army oversees all Army Reserve* forces and training in eight southeastern states, Puerto Rico, and the Virgin Islands. Second Army's shoulder insignia is a numeral 2, upper half red and lower half white, on a green background. Its motto is *"Tout préparé."*

References. "A Salute to the Numbered U.S. Armies," *Army Information Digest*, October 1962, 32–39. Paula Anthony et al., "Armies and Corps," *Army*, October 1986, 330–343.

Trevor Brown

SECOND BULL RUN

In July 1862, Confederate General Robert E. Lee's* 80,000-man Army of Northern Virginia faced 90,000 Union soldiers under Major General George B. McClellan* moving toward Richmond along the peninsula from the southeast. The Army of Virginia, 50,000 men under Major General John Pope, was moving against the Confederate rear from the north. On 9 August, Major General Thomas J. "Stonewall" Jackson* slowed Pope, fighting him to a draw at Cedar Mountain. Learning that McClellan was withdrawing from the peninsula, Lee left only two brigades to face McClellan's overwhelming Union force and marched with the remainder of his army to join Jackson. Lee, seeking to defeat Pope before McClellan could join him, faced Pope across the Rappahannock River by 24 August.

Lee realized that if he remained on the defensive the combined Union armies would overwhelm him. Therefore, he sent Jackson on a wide move around the Union right to get behind Pope. Lieutenant General James Longstreet's* corps was to demonstrate against Pope and then follow Jackson. Jackson reached his objective, the Union supply depot at Manassas Junction, on 26 August with 24,000 men. Pope began concentrating his 75,000 men west of Manassas, effectively separating the two Confederate corps. Unfortunately, Pope largely ignored Longstreet and allowed Jackson to occupy a strong defensive position near the site of First Bull Run.* On 29 and 30 August Pope launched several attacks against Jackson, inflicting heavy casualties, but he could not force the Confederates from their defenses. As the attacks continued, Lee directed Longstreet to strike the left flank of the Union army. Jackson counterattacked and forced Pope's army to withdraw to Centerville. Lee then began planning the invasion of the north that would end at Antietam.*

References. Dennis Kelly, *Second Manassas*, 1983, 1987. Edward J. Stackpole, *From Cedar Mountain to Antietam*, 1959.

Richard L. Kiper

2D DIVISION

Organized at Bourmont, Haute-Marne, France on 26 October 1917, with one Army and one Marine brigade,* the 2d Division participated in six major World War I* campaigns, including Aisne-Marne, St. Mihiel,* and Meuse-Argonne.* After completing occupation duties near Coblenz, Germany, the division* moved to Fort Sam Houston,* Texas, where it participated in annual maneuvers at Camp Bullis each May from 1920 to 1939. In September 1937, the 2d Division was temporarily reorganized to test the Proposed Infantry Division (triangular division*) concept. It was further reorganized in January 1939 as the Provisional 2d Division to continue the tests. The Army adopted the triangular division as its basic infantry* organization in October 1939. Known as the "Indianhead Division," after the Indian's head with war bonnet displayed on its shoulder patch, the 2d Division participated in the 1940 and 1941 Louisiana Maneuvers* before deploying to Europe in World War II.* From 1944 to 1945, the 2d Division fought in five campaigns from Normandy to Central Europe After the war, the 2d was stationed at Forts Benning and Lewis before deploying to Korea, where its units fought in ten separate campaigns. Reorganized in South Korea from elements of the 1st Cavalry Division in 1965, the 2d Infantry Division is today the main U.S. combat force under the United Nations Command in Korea.

References. William J. Diehl, Jr., "2nd Infantry Division," *Infantry*, November–December 1978, 14–18. Rolfe L. Hillman, "Second to None," U.S. Naval Institute *Proceedings*, November 1987, 56–62. Oliver L. Spaulding and John W. Wright, *The Second Division American Expeditionary Force in France, 1917–1919*, 1937, 1989.

Steven E. Clay

SECOND DRAGOONS

The Second Regiment of Dragoons was activated in May 1836 by order of President Andrew Jackson. Beginning with service in the Seminole Wars,* the regiment* would amass fifty-six battle streamers from campaigns in the Mexican War,* Civil War,* Indian Wars,* Spanish-American War,* World War I,* World War II,* and Desert Storm.* Today, the descendant of the Second Dragoons, the Second Armored Cavalry Regiment, stationed at Fort Polk,* Louisiana, has the distinction of being the longest continually serving cavalry* regiment in the U.S. Army.

Fighting as part of the First Cavalry Division of the Army of the Potomac,* the Second U.S. Cavalry Regiment, as it was then known, fought at Gettysburg,* Chancellorsville,* and Antietam.* Elements of the regiment accompanied Major General Nelson A. Miles* in the Nez Percé War and the capture of Chief Joseph. During World War I, the regiment had the distinction of being the last U.S. cavalry unit to fight on horseback. Leaving the era of horse cavalry, the Second Cavalry Regiment fought as the tip of the spear in Lieutenant General George Patton's Third Army* during the drive across Europe, earning the nickname "the ghost of Patton's Army." During the Cold War,* the Second Armored Cavalry Regiment guarded 651 kilometers along the inter-German border. Deploying from Europe during Desert Shield, the regiment again found itself out in front, as the lead element of VII Corps's offensive push against the Iraqi army; it earned a Presidential Unit Citation.

References. David L. Fleming, *From Everglade to Cañon with the Second Dragoons*, 1911. James Hildreth, *Dragoon Campaigns to the Rocky Mountains*, 1836.

Jim Martin

SECOND INDOCHINA WAR. *See* Vietnam War.

SECOND SEMINOLE WAR. *See* Seminole Wars.

SECOND WAR OF INDEPENDENCE. *See* War of 1812.

SECRETARY OF DEFENSE

World War II* provided the major impetus for change in the command structure of U.S. forces. Bickering between the two services over strategy and the acquisition of military equipment led the president and Congress, along with key military leaders, to call for a greater unity in the command and management of the nation's armed forces. The secretary of defense was established by the National Security Act of 1947* as a cabinet level position; the role and power of the office have grown significantly over the years. In the original legislation, the secretary of defense was more or less coequal with the secretaries of Army, Navy, and Air Force. However, in the Defense Reorganization Act of 1958, the operational chain of command—president, secretary of defense, combatant commands—and the authority of the secretary over the Department of Defense* and the service secretaries were clarified. The Goldwater-Nichols Act* (Defense Reorganization Act) of 1986 further clarified and strengthened the role of the secretary of defense.

References. Alfred Goldberg, ed., *History of the Office of the Secretary of Defense*, 1984–1988. Douglas Kinnard, *The Secretary of Defense*, 1980. Carroll F. Miles, *The Office of the Secretary of Defense, 1947–1953*, 1988.

J.G.D. Babb

SECRETARY OF THE ARMY

A civilian appointee of the president, the secretary of the Army is chief of the Army establishment provided for under the Constitution. The president's nominee is confirmed by the Senate and serves at the pleasure of the president. The National Security Act of 1947* established the position of secretary of the Army, subsequent amendments and acts have defined the secretary's role within the constitutional concept of civilian control of the military. The secretary has primary responsibility for all Army affairs and reports directly to the secretary of defense.* With offices in the Pentagon,* the secretary of the Army is assisted by his principal deputy, the undersecretary, who acts as the acquisition executive, and five assistant secretaries and numerous administrative, fiscal, and bureau chiefs.

References. William Gardner Bell, *Secretaries of War and Secretaries of the Army*, 1982. Paul Y. Hammond, *Organizing for Defense*, 1961.

Lawyn C. Edwards

SECRETARY OF WAR

One of the original cabinet members, the secretary of war, along with the secretary of the Navy, served as a principal civilian advisor to the president until the National Security Act of 1947* reorganized the military and established the secretary of defense.* When the Army was created in June 1775, several boards and oversight organizations already existed. Congress established a War Office in 1781 and appointed Benjamin Lincoln* as the first "secretary at war," a term borrowed from the British. In August 1789, under the newly ratified Constitution, Congress established the War Department, changed the title of its head to "secretary of war," and made the position responsible to the president. Henry Knox, who had been serving as the secretary at war, stayed in the position. From 1789 until 1947, both military officers and civilians served in the office. In 1947, Kenneth C. Royall, the last secretary of war, became the first secretary of the Army.*

References. William Gardner Bell, *Secretaries of War and Secretaries of the Army*, 1982. Russell F. Weigley, *History of the United States Army*, 1967.

J.G.D. Babb

SECTION

The section is an organizational level between the squad* and platoon.* Before World War II,* platoons in the "square" division* typically organized into two sections of two squads each. Prior to the appearance of the M1 Abrams tank,* a platoon with five tanks consisted of two sections, heavy and light, with three and two tanks respectively. The current M1 platoon has two sections of two tanks. Mortar* and antitank sections are also found in the infantry* weapons platoon, where there is a mix of heavy weapons. A staff sergeant normally leads an infantry section, while the armor* platoon leader and platoon sergeant frequently double as section leaders in the tank platoon.

References. Anthony Cucolo and Dale S. Ringler, "Heavy Infantry," *Infantry*, September–December 1998, 7–10. Henry G. Morgan, Jr., "Stronger Fighting Teams in the Rifle Platoon," *Combat Forces Journal*, April 1952, 26–28.

Andrew N. Morris

SEEP

In 1941, the U.S. Army expressed interest in an amphibious version of the quarter-ton 4×4 truck, or Jeep,* then entering readiness for full-scale production. Mormon-Herrington, the Amphibious Car Company, and Ford Motor Company produced various prototype light amphibian vehicles throughout 1941. In September 1942, the Ford Model GPA, nicknamed the Seep, entered series production. The basic design was that of the Ford GPW (standard Jeep) enclosed in a reinforced sheet-metal hull—thus the epithet "Jeep in a bathtub." More than 12,500 GPAs came off the production line in 1942–1943 and saw service in both Europe and the Pacific theaters. The Seep could achieve a maximum speed of five mph in water and fifty mph on land. The enclosed-hull design made routine maintenance a major headache, and the Seep could swim in only the calmest waters without floundering.

References. Thomas Berndt, *Standard Catalog of Military Vehicles, 1940–1965*, 1993. Fred W. Crismon, *U.S. Military Wheeled Vehicles*, 1983.

Stephen C. McGeorge

SELECTIVE SERVICE SYSTEM

Compulsory military service has never been popular with the American people. The attempt to conscript men in the Civil War* was inefficient, led to draft riots in several cities, and was largely a failure. Nonetheless, when the United States entered World War I,* Congress accepted the War Department's* recommendation for mobilization through conscription, and in May it passed the Selective Service Act of 1917. To avoid the mistakes and inequities of the Civil War draft—purchased exemptions, substitutes, bounties, and War Department administration, for example—the act created the Selective Service System to implement the new conscription law. A system of local civilian boards, operating under general guidelines and with authority to grant selective exemptions, including exemptions for conscientious objection, relieved the War Department of direct responsibility for the draft and ensured that the program would remain generally corruption free. The nation raised nearly four million men for military service between May 1917 and November 1918.

The Selective Service System of World War I proved to be an effective and efficient method of mass mobilization. So successful was it that Congress re-created it with only minor changes when it passed the Selective Training and Service Act of 1940, more than a year before the United States entered World War II.* Except for a brief period in 1947, when Congress allowed the law to lapse, the System Service System established in 1940 provided the vast bulk of manpower for World War II, the Cold War,* and the Vietnam War.* Registering with the local Selective Service Board in the month of one's eighteenth birthday became an accepted obligation for an entire generation of Americans. Increasing opposition to conscription, fueled by the antiwar and civil rights movements in the late 1960s, and a growing sense that the draft was unfair—university students, married men, and sons of middle and upper–middle class families qualified for an array of exemptions that had not existed earlier—generated a national debate on the draft. Amid this turmoil, and after making several attempts at reform, including a lottery system, Congress allowed the Selective Service Act to expire in 1972. Although Congress did pass legislation requiring all eighteen year old males to register with the Selective Service System, the infrastructure that had made the system work so efficiently, including the local boards, had generally disappeared by 1974.

References. Martin Anderson, ed., *The Military Draft*, 1982. James W. Geary, *We Need Men*, 1991. Curtis W. Tarr, *By the Numbers*, 1981.

SELF-PROPELLED GUN

Many observers mistake self-propelled (SP) guns for tanks. A self-propelled gun is not a tank but an artillery gun carried on a motor carriage or, more commonly today, a main battle tank (MTB) chassis. As early as the 1920s, several armies experimented with mounting guns on motor carriages to give supporting artillery mobility and speed. The Germans were first to introduce a successful SP gun in combat, in World War II.* In 1941, the U.S. Army commenced development of the M7 Priest, a 105 mm gun mounted on an M4 Sherman tank chassis. After World War II, every major army developed and fielded SP guns. The new SP guns carried more armor for crew protection and mounted the guns in turrets for 360-degree fields of fire. In 1952, the U.S. Army began development of a more advanced generation of SP guns and took delivery of the first production models of the M109 (howitzer medium, self-propelled) with a 155 mm gun—perhaps the most successful SP gun in history—a decade later. After more than thirty years and several major upgrades, the M109 is still in service with the U.S. Army's field artillery.*

References. Christopher F. Foss, *Jane's World Armoured Fighting Vehicles*, 1977. Peter Williams, "The Future of the SP Gun," *NATO's Sixteen Nations*, April–May 1988, 65–66.

SEMINARY RIDGE

Located about three-quarters of a mile west of the small Pennsylvania town of Gettysburg,* a Lutheran seminary sits atop a gently rising slope known as Seminary Ridge. This ridge became the focal point in one of the great battles of American history. Union cavalry under Brigadier General John Buford occupied the heights overlooking Gettysburg on 30 June 1863. The next day, Confederate forces under Robert E. Lee* pushed the Federal troops off the ridge, through the streets of Gettysburg, and onto the high ground to the east. Arriving on the scene, Lee established his headquarters on the ridge and from there over the next two days directed the Confederate assaults against Union forces arrayed along Cemetery Ridge—parallel to Seminary Ridge—half a mile to a mile to the east. On the third day of the battle, Confederate infantry under George Pickett mounted a gallant but tragic attack across the open ground below Seminary Ridge. On 4 July, the Confederate infantry waited behind the breastworks on Seminary Ridge fòr an expected Federal attack, but it never came, and the remnants of Lee's army followed their supply and ambulance trains back across the Potomac into Virginia.

Today, Seminary Ridge is part of the Gettysburg National Military Park. Confederate Avenue runs for three miles along the ridgeline. Lutheran Theological Seminary still sits atop the ridge, along with Gettysburg College and seemingly countless markers to the soldiers who fought there.

References. Edwin B. Coddington, *The Gettysburg Campaign*, 1968. Warren W. Hassler, Jr., *Crisis at the Crossroads*, 1991. David G. Martin, *Gettysburg,* July 1, 1995.

Lawyn C. Edwards

SEMINOLE WARS

During the first half of the 19th century, the U.S. Army engaged in two wars with the loose-knit clans of the Seminole Indians of Florida. The first encounter came in 1817–1818, the consequence of the invasion of Spanish Florida by Andrew Jackson* and Edmund Gaines in an attempt to stop bloody Seminole raids across the border into Georgia. The First Seminole War is noted less for the combat between the Seminoles and the United States and its Creek allies than for the diplomatic furor created when Jackson executed two British citizens and captured several Spanish-held posts.

The Second Seminole War began when Jackson, now president, ordered ten companies into Florida to help federal and local agents evict about 5,000 Seminoles. This was part of the overall U.S. policy of relocating southern Indian tribes living east of the Mississippi River to western territories. The ambush and massacre of an Army column by a Seminole war party in December 1835 set off the war. Lasting until 1842, the hostilities marked the longest (and costliest) experience of the United States with unconventional warfare to that time.

At first the Army tried to subdue the Seminoles through conventional tactics,* employing large, heavily armed converging columns. These maneuvers, however, proved ineffective in the hot, swamplands inhabited by the small, elusive Seminole bands. Even when the Army could force its quarry to stand and fight, at the Battle of Okeechobee for example, the results proved inconclusive. Seven commanders tried without success to defeat the Seminoles. The eighth, Colonel William Worth, took charge in April 1841. Commanding 5,000 Regulars, he adopted small-unit, all-season search-and-destroy tactics aimed at Seminole villages and crops. By August 1842, over 4,000 Seminoles had been evicted from Florida. With fewer than 200 Seminoles remaining in the swamplands, the U.S. government called an end to the politically contentious war. The Seminoles have never signed a peace treaty formally ending the conflict.

References. Fairfax Downey, *Indian Wars of the U.S. Army, 1776–1865*, 1963. John K. Mahon, *History of the Second Seminole War 1835–1842*, 1967. Virginia Bergman Peters, *The Florida Wars*, 1979.

Lawrence A. Yates

SERGEANT BILKO

In 1955, CBS contracted with Broadway funnyman Phil Silvers and veteran television writer Nat Hiken to develop a new prime-time comedy series. The Silvers-Hiken collaboration produced Master Sergeant Ernie Bilko, a character who for many Americans became the stereotype of the unprincipled noncommissioned officer* (NCO) of the postwar Army. The classic barracks con man, Sergeant Bilko, whose "middle name is larceny," promoted innumerable schemes to separate unsuspecting soldiers from their hard-earned pay: bedmaking competitions with an entry fee, the Chester A. Arthur birthday benefit, a weekly contest to guess the number of AWOLs, and so forth. First titled *You'll Never Get Rich* then *The Phil Silvers Show* (also known as *The Sgt. Bilko Show*), the series was originally filmed at the old Du Mont Network studio in New York City. It aired on CBS opposite Milton Berle and was the first show to best Berle in the Trendex ratings. Sergeant Bilko remains an enduring caricature of the Army NCO.

References. Irving Settel, *A Pictorial History of Television*, 2d ed., 1983. Michael Winship, *Television*, 1988.

SERGEANT MAJOR

First established in the Continental Army* by Baron Friedrich von Steuben* on the Prussian model as the senior noncommissioned officer* (NCO) in the regiment,* the sergeant major (SGM) served as the primary assistant to the regimental adjutant. The SGM was closely conversant with the regiment's organization, administration, discipline, and drill, and he paid strict attention to the conduct and behavior of the soldiers. Today, the sergeants major of the U.S. Army have two primary functions. The sergeant major fills the senior NCO position from squadron* through army* level for each primary staff officer. The Command Sergeant Major, assigned to every commander from battalion* through major subordinate commands, serves as the commander's primary advisor for all matters relating to the unit's enlisted soldiers and command-group decisions. This position of responsibility provides the incumbant the visibility necessary to serve as role model for his subordinate NCOs and enlisted soldiers as well as mentor for officers of the command.

References. Robert B. Begg, "Sergeant Major," *Army*, January 1966, 37–39. Arnold G. Fisch, Jr., and Robert K. Wright, Jr., eds., *The Story of the Noncommissioned Officer Corps*, 1989.

Lawyn C. Edwards

SERGEANT MAJOR OF THE ARMY

Following the recommendation of the Sergeants Major Personnel Conference, Chief of Staff* Harold K. Johnson* issued General Order No. 29 on 4 July 1966, creating the position of Sergeant Major of the Army. A result of a desire of the Army's senior noncommissioned officers* to open a direct channel of communication between enlisted soldiers of all grades and the Chief of Staff,* the position was, in Johnson's words, "an ombudsman . . . a spokesman at the highest echelons . . . of the Army . . . to provide a recognition for the enlisted ranks." Not in the formal chain of command, the Sergeant Major of the Army serves as advisor to the Chief of Staff on issues, problems, and solutions affecting enlisted soldiers. He is selected and appointed by the Chief of Staff and serves at his pleasure. His office is in the Pentagon* in the Chief of Staff's suite.

References. William G. Bainbridge, *Top Sergeant*, 1995. Mark F. Gillespie et al., *The Sergeants Major of the Army*, 1995.

Lawyn C. Edwards

SERGEANT YORK

The M247 Sergeant York (also SGT York) was a twin 40 mm division air defense gun (DIVAD) designed in the late 1970s to replace the obsolescent 20 mm Vulcan air defense system. The team of Ford Aerospace and General Dynamics won the contract over several competing designs in 1978. The Sergeant York, named after the World War I* hero Alvin York, incorporated a main armament of two 40 mm guns in a two-man turret mounted on an M-48A5 tank chassis.

With a combat weight of 54,431 kg and a fuel capacity of 1,457 liters, Sergeant York had a maximum speed of 48 km/hr. It carried a three-man crew and included Doppler l-band search and tracking radar* to seek targets. However, the Sergeant York had serious technical limitations and production problems that led to cancelation of the project in the mid-1980s.

References. Blair Case, "Sergeant York Back on Track," *Air Defense Artillery*, Winter 1985, 9–13. J. Philip Geddes, "The US Army's Division Air Defense System," *International Defense Review*, 1981, 879–887. "SGT York," *Air Defense Artillery*, Winter 1984, 18–32.

Trevor Brown

SERVICEMEN'S READJUSTMENT ACT OF 1944. *See* G. I. Bill.

SERVICES OF SUPPLY

During the 18th century, this term was used to describe a wide range of logistical functions. Services of supply encompassed the duties normally associated with the Quartermaster General, including distribution, storage, and procurement of arms, ammunition, clothing, equipment, rations, and forage. Additionally, engineering functions, including construction of fortifications, fieldwork, and roads, as well as supply and repair of ordnance, medical services, and hospitalization, were included under the Quartermaster General's* purview. By the beginning of World War I,* specialization in the technical staff had resulted in a reduction. When General of the Armies John J. Pershing* reorganized the American Expeditionary Force* (AEF) staff in 1918, he designated a Commanding General, Services of Supply, with responsibility for procurement, transportation, supply, construction, and forestry. Construction responsibilities included only fixed facilities, such as depots and post facilities. Engineering missions in support of combat troops were performed solely by combat engineer units. Hospitalization and medical support fell under the Medical Department.*

World War II* saw a final change in the services of supply. In March 1942, Services of Supply became one of three independent agencies, under War Department* control, responsible for depots, oversight of procurement, production, distribution, storage of supplies, ports of embarkation, and quartermaster training schools. During the course of the war, changes in organization gradually diminished the responsibilities of the Services of Supply to operating forward and rear depots and ports of embarkation. Following World War II, the Quartermaster Corps* absorbed the Services of Supply. It eventually becoming part of the Army Material Command.

References. Johnson Hagood, *The Services of Supply*, 1927. James A. Huston, *The Sinews of War*, 1966. Erna Risch and Chester L. Kieffer, *The Quartermaster Corps*, vol. 2, 1955.

Robert J. Dalessandro

SEVEN DAYS

The series of battles in the Civil War* fought near Richmond between 25 June and 1 July 1862 are generally known as the Seven Days. As a result of General Joseph E. Johnston's* serious wounds at the battle of Fair Oaks, Jefferson Davis* appointed General Robert E. Lee* to command. On 25 June, three-fourths of Lee's forces gathered outside Mechanicsville. The next day, the first major battle of the Seven Days took place when Lee attacked Federal forces under Major General Fitz-John Porter. Lee had ordered Thomas J. "Stonewall" Jackson* to join him in the attack, but Jackson never arrived. When Porter learned of Jackson's approach, however, he fell back to Gaines' Mill. On 27 June, when Lee attacked Porter's troops, Jackson had still not arrived. The Battle of Gaines' Mill ended when the Confederates broke Porter's left flank and Jackson finally arrived to challenge the Federal right. Major General George B. McClellan* ordered Porter to fall back to the south bank of the Chickahominy. He subsequently directed a general withdrawal of troops to the James River.

Throughout 29 and 30 June, Lee continued to pursue and attack Federal troops, at the battles of Peach Orchard, Savage Station, White Oak Swamp, and Glendale–Frayser's Farm. Union counterattacks delayed Lee while Federal trains crossed White Oak Swamp. On 1 July, in the Battle of Malvern Hill, Lee once again attacked Porter's troops. Within two hours, the Confederates were halted with heavy losses. Nevertheless, in the series of brilliant maneuvers, Lee had managed to force McClellan to abandon his goal of taking Richmond by way of the Virginia Peninsula.

References. Clifford Dowdey, *The Seven Days*, 1964. William J. Miller, ed., *The Peninsula Campaign*, vol. 3, 1997.

Rebecca S. Witte

SEVEN PINES

The Battle of Seven Pines, also known as Fair Oaks, occurred on 31 May–1 June 1862, during the Peninsula Campaign.* Joseph E. Johnston,* commander of the Confederate army defending Richmond, planned to strike Major General George B. McClellan's* left wing, isolated south of the swollen Chickahominy River, six miles east of Richmond in the vicinity of Seven Pines. Johnston's plan called for James Longstreet's* division, reinforced by W.H.C. Whiting's division, to conduct the main attack along Nine Mile Road, while D. H. Hill's and Benjamin Huger's divisions conducted a secondary attack along the Williamsburg Road. Hill's and John B. Magruder's divisions would protect the army's left flank. Longstreet, however, misunderstood Johnston's oral orders, and the attack misfired from the start; the Confederate attack was executed piecemeal. Nevertheless, the Confederates pushed the Federals back through the village of Seven Pines until the arrival of Federal reinforcements brought the attack to a standstill. In the course of the first evening's fighting, Union musket fire struck and seriously wounded Johnston. Command passed temporarily to Gustavus W. Smith, who ordered a second attack for the next day. The attack the next morning, however, lacked determination, and the fighting ended by midday. Robert E. Lee, the new field commander, ordered a withdrawal that evening back toward Richmond. Confederate casualties were reported as 6,134, while Union losses were 5,031.

References. William J. Miller, *The Peninsula Campaign*, vol. 3, 1997. Stephen W. Sears, *To the Gates of Richmond*, 1992.

Edward Shanahan

SEVENTH ARMY

On 10 July 1943, while en route to the invasion of Sicily, I Armored Corps was redesignated the U.S. Seventh Army under the command of Lieutenant General George S. Patton, Jr.* It was the first U.S. field army* to see action in World War II.* In the Sicilian operations, Seventh Army units captured Palermo on 22 July, then raced the British Eighth Army for Messina, entering that city on the morning of 17 August. Seventh Army's next mission was the invasion of southern France, code named Anvil* (Dragoon*). Lieutenant General Mark Clark* briefly replaced Patton, who went to England to prepare for the coming cross-Channel attack, but Clark's duties as commander of U.S. Fifth Army* required his full-time attention in Italy: Lieutenant General Alexander Patch, a veteran of the fighting on Guadalcanal,* assumed command of Seventh Army on 2 March 1944.

On 15 August 1944, Seventh Army, composed of U.S. VI Corps, the 1st Allied Airborne Task Force, and a French armored force, landed on the French Riviera. Within a month, this combined force had liberated all of southern France and advanced to the Vosges Mountains. On 15 September, Seventh Army and the French First Army became the U.S. Sixth Army Group. In December 1944, Seventh Army extended its frontage in order to release a major portion of Patton's Third Army* for a counterattack against the German penetration in the Ardennes.* With the defeat of the Germans in the Ardennes, Seventh Army then resumed offensive operations—reducing the Colmar pocket in February, crossing the Rhine River on 26 March 1945, capturing Nuremberg on 20 April, and occupying Munich on 30 April. On 4 May, elements of Seventh Army crossed the Brenner Pass and linked up with Fifth Army troops.

Seventh Army performed occupation duty in Germany until 31 March 1946, when it was inactivated in Europe. Reactivated in November 1950, Seventh Army has since that time served as the principal U.S. ground force in Allied Command Europe.

References. Paula Anthony et al., "Armies and Corps," *Army*, October 1986, 330–343. Robert W. Komer, "The Rejuvenation of Seventh Army," *Armed Forces Journal International*, May 1983, 54–59. John Frayn Turner and Robert Jackson, *Destination Berchtesgaden*, 1975.

John A. Hixson

SHAKE 'N' BAKE

"Shake 'n' bake" was a pejorative term referring to hastily trained or newly assigned or promoted noncommissioned officers* (NCO) in combat units during the Vietnam War.* As the war expanded in 1967 and '68, increased ground combat and the commensurate increase in casualties required junior NCOs to fill leadership positions at the squad* and platoon* levels. The shortfall of NCOs was so great that specialist 4s (equivalent of corporal), who frequently lacked the seasoning and combat experience necessary to provide effective leadership, filled some squad-level positions. Poor leadership led to poor troop performance and a general decline in morale and discipline. In an attempt to confront the situation, the Army sent potential or newly promoted NCOs to a twenty-one–week leadership and advanced infantry* course at Fort Benning,* Georgia, prior to assignment to Vietnam. To improve the caliber of junior leaders already in the field in Vietnam, some units developed NCO-type schools to provide further leadership and combat-related training. Graduates of these schools were called "instant sergeants" or "shake 'n' bake" NCOs, after a popular packaged food product designed to reduce meal preparation time.

References. Jerome S. Berger, "Training Ground for Leadership," *Army Digest*, November 1967, 11–12. Frank J. Kaufman, "Roll Out the Leaders," *Army Digest*, March 1968, 17–19. Melvin Zais, "The New NCO," *Army*, May 1968, 72–76.

Chan Floyd

SHARPS CARBINE

The Sharps carbine was a breech-loading (loaded from the back of the bore), single-shot, .52-caliber weapon designed and manufactured by Christian Sharp. The first Sharps appeared in 1851; they were followed by a number of improved models over the next decade. The factory continued making the early models even after it had introduced newer versions, because the early model remained popular. For example, the 1853 Sharps were produced until late 1858 or early 1859, several years after the 1855 model had been introduced. These early Sharps models had on angled breech-loading mechanism. The most famous models of the carbine were the 1859 and the 1863. The 1859 model altered the breechblock position from a slant to a vertical position, at a right angle to the bore axis. The only alteration of the 1863 model, one required by the Ordnance Department,* was the removal of the patchbox from the carbine. During the Civil War,* the Sharps was a favorite among the U.S. Army's mounted units. The War Department* purchased more than 80,000 Sharps carbines during the war, but it chose not to arm the majority of its units with these modern weapons.

References. Earl J. Coates and John D. McAulay, *Civil War Sharps Carbines & Rifles*, 1996. Frank M. Sellers, *Sharps Firearms*, 1978. Winston O. Smith, *The Sharps Rifle*, 1943.

L. Lynn Williams

SHARPSBURG. *See* Antietam.

SHAWNEE H-21

The H-21 was a large, tandem-rotor, general-purpose helicopter powered by the Wright R-1820 radial engine. Officially named the Shawnee, most soldiers knew the H-21 as the "Flying Banana." It first flew in 1952, and in 1957 it set a closed-course distance record for helicopters, flying from San Diego to Washington, D.C., becoming in the process the first helicopter to refuel in flight. By 1959, the Army had received 334 Shawnees. Used extensively in the early years of the Vietnam War,* the Shawnee's limited lifting ability in the hot, humid environment eventually led the Army to replace it with newer, turbo-engine helicopters.

References. *Army Aviation*, 1992. Stephen Harding, *U.S. Army Aircraft since 1947*, 1997.

Randall N. Briggs

SHAYS' REBELLION

In 1786, a group of Massachusetts farmers, incensed by high taxes, high interest rates, and what they viewed as totally insensitive state government, marched on a county courthouse and closed it down. The leader of this minor act of violence was an American Revolution* veteran named Daniel Shays. Eventually he led his band to the Springfield Arsenal,* an act that prompted Congress to dispatch over 1,300 troops to put it down. This proved unnecessary, as the state militia was able to establish order well before the U.S. troops arrived. Shays' Rebellion is important in regard to the debate at the time on the Articles of Confederation and the movement to reform the government; the uprising occurred as states were deciding whether or not to send delegates to a meeting in Philadelphia to discuss modifications to the Articles. The subsequent meeting in Philadelphia, now known as the Constitutional Convention, proceeded not only to modify the Articles but to write the Constitution that all U.S. service members have sworn to protect and defend since its ratification in 1789.

References. Richard H. Kohn, *Eagle and Sword*, 1975. Lamar Middleton, *Revolt U.S.A.*, 1938, 1968.

Jim Martin

SHELL SHOCK

In 1914, only a few specialists had studied the medical aspects of psychology or psychiatry. These were new sciences, and even the leaders in the field, like Sigmund Freud, were just beginning to understand the dimensions of the human mind. One of the consequences of the horrendous battles at the outset of World War I* was the debilitation or incapacitation of large numbers of men with no apparent physical wounds. Believing that these men had been concussed by long periods of shelling, the medical community used the term "shell shock" to describe their condition. Most of them, in fact, suffered from psychoneuroses and psychosomatic disorders resulting from the extreme stress of combat in the trenches. Shell-shock symptoms included combinations of extreme nervousness, insomnia, tics, nightmares, depression, exhaustion, headaches, deafness, blindness, and paralysis of various limbs. Some shell-shock victims recovered fairly quickly and returned to duty after rest and hot meals;

others required long periods of hospitalization. When the American Expeditionary Force* (AEF) arrived in France in 1917, it borrowed much of its battlefield medical knowledge from the allies, including the diagnosis and treatment of shell shock.

Shell shock assumed negative connotations. Officers frequently suspected that malingerers feigned shell shock to avoid duty, and stronger, hardier soldiers looked down on men who "couldn't take it." Although the term was still in use in the early years of World War II,* both the desire to find a less pejorative term and a more sophisticated understanding of neuropsychiatry led to the introduction of other more accurate and acceptable terms, including battle fatigue* and post-traumatic stress disorder.

References. Hans Binneveld, *From Shell Shock to Combat Stress*, trans. John O'Kane, 1997. Arthur Hurst, "Mental Havoc in Wartime," *Science Digest*, February 1941, 1–9.

SHENANDOAH VALLEY

Confederate forces under the command of General Thomas "Stonewall" Jackson* maneuvered and fought a series of Union commands in the Shenandoah Valley from May to June 1862. The South took heart at Jackson's success, while the North took heed of its fears for Washington at a time when its main army, under Major General George B. McClellan,* was threatening the Confederate capitol at Richmond. The Valley was a granary for Southern troops in Virginia and an avenue by which those troops could threaten Washington. In the spring of 1862, McClellan's army moved by water to Fort Monroe* and then, very slowly, toward Richmond. The Confederates concentrated most of their troops against McClellan but left a small force under Jackson in the Valley to tie up as many Federals as possible. Jackson did this with great success. His command seldom numbered more than 10,000 men, yet he kept at least 40,000 Federals chasing him and guarding Washington.

After nearly sixty days of marching and countermarching, and several battles, Jackson left the Valley with his command and joined the main Confederate army near Richmond in time for a series of battles that forced McClellan away from the Confederate capitol. In the Shenandoah Valley Campaign, Jackson established himself as a major commander in the eastern theater. The campaign demonstrated what a relatively small force under the command of a bold leader can accomplish against long odds.

References. David G. Martin, *Jackson's Valley Campaign*, 1994. Robert G. Tanner, *Stonewall in the Valley*, 1976.

George Knapp

SHERIDAN, PHILIP HENRY (1831–1888)

After a one-year suspension for fighting, Philip Henry Sheridan graduated from the U.S. Military Academy* in 1853 and was commissioned in the infantry.* Sheridan served on the Rio Grande and in the Oregon Territory. In March 1861 he was promoted to first lieutenant. Serving as a staff officer in Missouri and later during the Corinth Campaign, he received a line assignment as colonel of the 2d Michigan Cavalry. He performed with distinction at Booneville, Perryville* Murfreesboro, the Tullahoma campaign,* Chickamauga,* Chattanooga,* Todd's Tavern, Winchester (Opequon), Fisher's Hill, Cedar Creek, Five Forks, Sayler's Creek, and Appomattox Court House. Following the Civil War,* Major General Sheridan was given command of the Military Division (later Department) of the Gulf until March 1867, when he assumed command of the Fifth Military District.

His harsh enforcement of Reconstruction measures in Texas and Louisiana led to his transfer the following September to the Department of the Missouri. In this capacity, Sheridan prosecuted campaigns against Cheyenne, Comanche, and Kiowa Indians. In 1869, a new position as commander of the Division of the Missouri brought a third star. From 1870 to 1871 Sheridan served as an observer with the Prussian army during the Franco-Prussian War. Upon his return, he directed campaigns against Indians on the southern plains under Nelson A. Miles* and Ranald S. McKinzie, and on the northern plains under Alfred H. Terry and Ceorge Crook.* After commanding the Military Division of the West and Southwest from 1878 to 1883, Sheridan succeeded Lieutenant General William T. Sherman as Commanding General* of the Army. Sheridan died in 1888, shortly after his promotion to the rank of general of the army and completion of his *Personal Memoirs of P. H. Sheridan.*

References. Paul A. Hutton, *Phil Sheridan and His Army*, 1985. Roy Morris, Jr., *Sheridan*, 1992.

Jeffrey Prater

SHERMAN, WILLIAM TECUMSEH (1820–1891)

William Tecumseh Sherman began his distinguished military career at the U.S. Military Academy,* graduating sixth in his class. A combat veteran of the Mexican War,* Sherman commanded a division* at First Bull Run,* where he sent in his battalions* piecemeal, a method that proved tactically ineffective. Later, realizing that emerging firepower had rendered the experience of the Mexican War obsolete, Sherman matured into one of the most innovative strategic thinkers and effective fighters of the Civil War.* Massed frontal assaults against often fortified positions gave way to an indirect approach, an attempt to return maneuver to the battlefield by attacking lines of communications and resources, and by applying overwhelming combat power at decisive points via strategic envelopment. Sherman proved to be master of this indirect approach in the Atlanta* and Carolina campaigns.

When Lieutenant General Ulysses S. Grant* became commanding general in 1864, he turned to Sherman to command the Military Division of the Mississippi (the western command), thus allowing Grant to focus on the East. President Abraham Lincoln finally had two capable theater commanders who would simultaneously apply unrelenting pressure against the Confederate armies. Sherman proved to be highly effective in executing this war of attrition. He defeated the armies of Generals Albert Sidney Johnston and Joseph E. Johnston* in the West, and he destroyed many of the remaining war resources of the Confederacy during his march through Georgia and South Carolina. Sherman's campaign of attrition struck at the Confederacy's capacity to wage war effectively against the Union and contributed to pinning the Confederate army under Lee around Petersburg, cut off from its lines of communication.

Sherman's acumen for waging war of attrition carried over into the next conflict in which he fought. In the campaign against the Sioux, Sherman continued to attack the enemy's capacity to wage war by destroying his logistical base. The 20th century historian and theorist Sir Basil H. Liddell Hart contended that Sherman's tactics displayed genius—the indirect approach in conjunction with war of attrition. Viewed in this light, perhaps Sherman anticipated the concept later known as *blitzkrieg*—the return of maneuver once again to the modern battlefield, featuring shock offensive action in a deep, strategic envelopment of enemy forces.

References. Mark Coburn, *Terrible Innocence*, 1993. John F. Marszalek, *Sherman*, 1993. James M. Merrill, *William Tecumseh Sherman*, 1971.

Ralph Nichols

SHERMAN M4 MEDIUM TANK

The Sherman M4 medium tank was a critical component of the Allied victory in World War II.* Built in greater numbers than any other U.S. tank in history, the M4 was simple, relatively rugged, and, most important, easy to mass produce. The M4A3, the most common variant (over 11,000 M4A3s were built), had a cast hull and turret, and either a low-velocity 75 mm or higher-powered 76 mm main gun. The M4 saw action in every major theater of the war and equipped not only the U.S. Army but the Free French, British, and Canadian armies. Because of its high profile, thin armor, and insufficient main gun, however, the Sherman had limited success against its German counterparts. However, the Allies had the luxury of being able to wage a war of attrition against the Axis tank forces, because the M4 could be produced in huge numbers. The basic M4 chassis was adapted for a variety of special uses, including self-propelled artillery, armored recovery vehicles,* flamethrowers, and amphibious assault tanks. Later models of the Sherman even saw action in the Arab-Israeli wars of 1967 and 1973.

References. Peter Chamberlain and Chris Ellis, *The Sherman*, 1969. R. P. Hunnicutt, *Sherman*, 1978.

Benjamin H. Kristy

SHERMAN'S MARCH

After the fall of Atlanta, Georgia, in September 1864, Major General William T. Sherman* rested his army for ten weeks; he then launched his march to the sea. Sending Major General George H. Thomas* back to defend Tennessee, Sherman took 62,000 soldiers and headed for Savannah, on the Atlantic coast.

Moving on several axes simultaneously, his army arrived at and wrecked Mil-ledgville on 22 to 24 November. The army continued its march essentially un-opposed, arriving at Savannah on 10 December. Sherman adopted a deliberate policy of devastating communications and transportation facilities; he also ap-propriated large quantities of food. His announced policy was to "make Georgia howl."

From Savannah, Sherman turned north into South Carolina and ultimately into North Carolina. These moves were also practically unopposed. The destruc-tion in South Carolina far surpassed that wrought on either Georgia or North Carolina, as it was regarded as the instigator of the war. One of the last major battles of the Civil War* was fought at Bentonville, North Carolina, between Sherman's army and 21,000 Confederate troops under General Joseph E. John-ston,* on 19 March 1865. When Sherman fended off Johnston's attack, oppo-sition to his march ended. Johnston surrendered to Sherman 26 April 1865 at Durham Station.

In six months of nearly continuous movement, Sherman's army had displayed a degree of operational sophistication and tactical ability that has rarely been equalled. His operations played a major role in ending the war through their impact on Southern logistics and morale.

References. John G. Barrett, *Sherman's March through the Carolinas*, 1956. Burke Davis, *Sherman's March*, 1980. Joseph T. Glatthaar, *The March to the Sea and Beyond*, 1985. Richard Wheeler, *Sherman's March*, 1978, 1991.

Andrew N. Morris

SHILOH

During the winter of 1861–1862, Federal forces under the direction of Major General Henry W. Halleck* began a series of maneuvers designed to capture western Tennessee and penetrate Confederate territory using the Tennessee and Cumberland River systems. The Confederates, under the overall command of General Albert Sidney Johnston, tried to hold their territorial boundaries, in accordance with their strategy of defense. After capturing Forts Henry and Don-elson* and the Tennessee state capitol at Nashville,* Halleck moved the Army of the Tennessee* by river to Pittsburg Landing. The army, about 43,000 strong and commanded by Ulysses S. Grant,* encamped and prepared for further op-erations against rail lines near Corinth, Mississippi, about twenty-five miles away. Johnston realized the danger and began concentrating all available forces at Corinth, assembling about 40,000 men. His plan was to strike Grant's en-campment before an additional Federal force under Major General Don Carlos Buell could arrive.

Johnston's hastily assembled and untried army attacked the Federal camps early on 6 April. It had good success, initially. Many Federal units, surprised and not entrenched, disintegrated, and the area around Pittsburg Landing became choked with soldiers who had fled the battlefield. Several factors, however, slowed the Confederate advance. Early in the battle the Confederate corps attacked one behind another and passed through each other to keep up the momentum. However, this created great confusion among the relatively inexperienced Confederate commanders. In the wooded terrain, broken by small fields and deep watercourses, formations became hopelessly disoriented and entangled. Some Federal units stood their ground and fought bravely, delaying the Confederate advance and giving Grant time to put together a last line of defense on dominating ground near Pittsburg Landing. About 2:30 in the afternoon, Johnston was killed while directing the action. General P.G.T. Beauregard assumed command and continued the advance, which finally halted about 6:00 P.M.

Beauregard expected to resume the offensive early on the 7th, but Buell, with 20,000 men, reinforced Grant during the night; Grant began his own attack at 7:30 A.M. The battle continued through the day, and the Federals regained much of the ground lost on the 6th. Beauregard hoped for reinforcements, but none came. He successfully disengaged and began withdrawing toward Corinth. Grant pursued but was checked by Confederate cavalry. Federal losses totaled 13,000 of 62,700 engaged, while the Confederates lost 10,700 of 40,300. After the battle, Halleck took personal command of the army in the field and began a series of slow advances resulting in the capture of Corinth at the end of May.

References. Larry J. Daniel, *Shiloh*, 1997. James Lee McDonough, *Shiloh*, 1977. Wiley Sword, *Shiloh*, 1974.

George Knapp

SHINGLE. *See* Anzio.

SHOOT AND SCOOT

"Shoot and scoot" refers to a fire-support survivability technique in which an artillery* or rocket unit moves immediately after firing before it receives counterbattery fire.* The technique originated with Soviet Katyusha rocket units during World War II.* The distinct signature of a Katyusha volley made detection fairly simple. Rather than relying on protection or deception against counterbattery fire, the Soviets developed a technique of moving to new firing locations within enlarged positions. NATO armies adopted "shoot and scoot" in the 1960s and '70s to protect nuclear-capable artillery. In U.S. Army tactical doctrine,* multiple-launch rocket systems (MLRS) and Paladin* (M109A6 howitzer) platoons* make similar survivability moves within larger areas immediately after firing. The ability to emplace quickly in new positions is critical to the unit's ability to prevent overall degradation in fire support.

References. J.B.A. Bailey, *Field Artillery and Firepower*, 1989. Barney Oldfield, "The Lance," *NATO's Fifteen Nations*, April–May 1975, 78–81.

Jeffrey S. Shadburn

SHORT-TIMER

As the term suggests, a short-timer is a soldier who has little time remaining in a tour of duty or an enlistment period. During World War II,* when all servicemen were under military control until the end of hostilities plus six months or until they became casualties, the term was rarely heard. During the Vietnam War,* however, when each soldier served a tour of one year in Southeast Asia, anyone with less than a particular number of days remaining, usually a hundred, considered himself to be "short." Short-timers were often admired by their buddies with longer periods yet to serve in country. The term short-timer is still used affectionately by soldiers approaching the end of their service obligations or current duty assignments.

References. Alan Levy, Bernard Krisher, and James Cox, *Draftee's Confidential Guide*, 1957. Ches Schneider, *From Classrooms to Claymores*, 1999.

Krewasky A. Salter

SIBLEY TENT

The Sibley tent, patterned after the plains Indian tipi, was submitted to the Quartermaster Department by Major Henry Hopkins Sibley, 2d U.S. Dragoons, in 1855. After successful field testing by the dragoons in 1856–1857, the War Department* officially adopted it in February 1858. A center pole attached at the base to an iron tripod supported the cone-shaped tent. The single smoke flap at the top allowed smoke and stale air to escape. Later, the conical sheet-iron Sibley stove was designed to fit beneath the tripod, replacing open fires for cooking and heating. The tent accommodated twelve men comfortably but could sleep up to twenty if necessary. The arrangement considered most healthful placed men like spokes of a wagon wheel, with their feet nearest the stove. Sibley received a royalty of five dollars per tent, until he joined the Confederate Army. The Army issued modified Sibley tents and stoves through World War II.*

References. Jack Coggins, *Arms and Equipment of the Civil War*, 1962, 1990. Randy Steffen, *The Horse Soldiers*, vol. 2, 1978.

Dana Prater

SIDEWINDER

The Aerial Intercept Missile Nine (AIM-9), commonly known as the Sidewinder, is a short-range infrared-guided weapon designed to detect and home on heat emissions generated by aircraft engines or exhausts. First tested in 1953 at the U.S. Naval Weapons Center at China Lake, California, the Sidewinder derived its name from the snakelike flight path it takes to its target. The self-guided AIM-9 permits the pilot or gunner freedom to maneuver after acquiring the target and firing the missile. It is carried on most U.S.-built fighter and attack aircraft, including some U.S. Army helicopter. The Army's Chaparral* air defense system is a ground-launched version of the Sidewinder. The AIM-9 is five inches in diameter and 113 inches long, has a wing span of fifteen inches, weighs 194 pounds, and has a range of eleven nautical miles. The Sidewinder has been adopted or copied by nations around the globe.

References. Tom Clancy, *Fighter Wing*, 1995. Bill Gunston, *An Illustrated Guide to Modern Airborne Missiles*, 1983.

                                                                            Chan Floyd

SIEGFRIED LINE

Der Westwall, as the Germans called it, was a line of defensive fortifications guarding the German frontier from the Swiss border in the south to the Dutch border in the north. Constructed at substantial cost in 1938 and 1939, the West Wall was a system of bunkers, pillboxes, antitank obstacles, dragons' teeth, minefields, magazines, and storehouses, three to four kilometers in depth, linked together by command centers and communication lines. It was intended to be an impregnable barrier against invasion from the west. British soldiers dubbed it the Siegfried Line, boasting in a 1939 ditty that they would hang their "dirty washing" on the Siegfried Line.

Although the Germans removed many of the guns originally emplaced in the West Wall to bolster other sites after the victories of 1940, and the units manning the fortifications were second and third-rate troops, the U.S. Army found the Siegfried Line quite formidable when it began advancing into its defenses in September 1944. The campaign to break through the Siegfried Line took more than seven months, entailed numerous battles—Aachen, Schmidt, the Huertgen Forest, and the Roer Plain, to name a few of the more costly battles—and concluded only when the defenders abandoned their final positions late in March 1945. U.S. Army casualties in the Siegfried Line campaign were more than 140,000, including more than 70,000 nonbattle losses from weather, disease, and exhaustion.

References. Charles B. MacDonald, *The Siegfried Line Campaign*, 1963, 1984. Charles Whiting, *Siegfried*, 1982.

SIGNAL CORPS

The U.S. Army was the first modern army to establish a separate branch specifically for signals and communications. In the Army appropriations bill for 1861, approved on 21 June 1860, Congress authorized one signal officer and two thousand dollars for equipment. Major (later Brigadier General) Albert J. Myer, a medical officer whose interest in sign language for the deaf had led him to devise a simple "wigwag" system using a flag or a torch to represent letters of the alphabet, was appointed the Army's first signal officer. The need for a better and more efficient signal system quickly became apparent in the Civil War.* To fill this need, Myer lobbied for a separate signal corps, and on 3 March 1863 Congress authorized a Signal Corps during the "present rebellion." During the conflict, the Signal Corps expanded the use of the electric telegraph, powered by wet-cell batteries and hand-cranked generators, and the use of balloons for both observation and delivery of messages.

Following the Civil War, however, the Signal Corps faced an uncertain future, although Congress did continue to authorize a chief signal officer. From 1870 to 1890, the Signal Corps organized and administered the Meteorological Service, which maintained hundreds of reporting stations across the United States. In 1881, First Lieutenant (later Major General and Chief Signal Officer) Adolphus Greeley led a scientific mission to the "farthest North" outpost at Lady Franklin Bay, north of the Arctic Circle. During the Spanish-American War,* the Signal Corps established the first telephone link between the president in Washington, D.C., and the Army commander at Santiago, Cuba. In 1908, the Army's new aviation section became part of the Signal Corps and, from 1914 to 1916, served on the Mexican border. During World War I,* the Signal Corp's role expanded to include radio transmissions, a pigeon service, and ground and aerial photography. Between the world wars, the Signal Corps conducted experiments in radar* and FM radio.

The Signal Corps played a major role in World War II.* It developed a worldwide system of radio communications as well as tactical radios small enough for one man to carry, yet powerful enough to transmit up to a mile. During the Cold War,* the Signal Corps continued to improve radio sets for use by tactical units and experimented with satellites for radio relay. Today, the Signal Corps has successfully linked ground and space systems to provide the U.S. Army the best communications of any army in the world.

References. Rebecca Robbins Raines, *Getting the Message Through*, 1996. Dulany Terrett, *The Signal Corps*, 1956.

Michael G. Knapp

SILVER STAR

The Silver Star is awarded to any person who, while serving in any capacity with the armed services, is cited for gallantry in action against an enemy of the United States. The required gallantry, while less than that required for the Medal of Honor* or Distinguished Service Cross,* "must nevertheless have been performed with marked distinction." The Silver Star was created in 1918 as a small silver "citation star," three-sixteenths of an inch in size. Soldiers who were cited for gallantry in action in "published orders from headquarters of a general officer" were permitted to wear the small star on the appropriate campaign medal. For example, soldiers cited for gallantry in World War I* wore the "citation star" on the ribbon of the World War I Victory Medal. The small size of the "citation star," however, made it very unpopular with soldiers, who wanted a separate, full-size medal for gallantry. As a result, Congress authorized the Silver Star medal in 1932. The obverse of the new award placed the existing silver "citation star" in the middle of a five-pointed gilt star; the reverse of the medal has the words "For Gallantry in Action." The Silver Star is the Army's third-ranking decoration for gallantry.

References. Evans E. Kerrigan, *American War Medals and Decorations*, 1964. John E. Strandberg and Roger J. Bender, *The Call of Duty*, 1994.

Frederic L. Borch III

SIOUX WAR (1866–1868)

In March 1866, representatives of the Brulé and Oglala Sioux arrived at Fort Laramie* to meet with agents of the U.S. government to discuss the future of their relations in the Powder River country. The government agents intended to negotiate a right of way for the newly opened Bozeman Trail,* which passed through Sioux hunting grounds on its way to the Montana gold fields. Under the influence of Spotted Tail, a Brulé chief, the Sioux had been inclined to cooperate, overriding the objections of Man-Afraid-of-His-Horse and his Oglalla faction.

However, the arrival of Colonel Henry B. Carrington and the 18th Infantry on 18 June 1866 shattered any hope for a peaceful resolution. Carrington was under orders to proceed into the Powder River country to construct a series of forts to secure passage along the Bozeman Trail, apparently unaware of the critical nature of the negotiations. Learning of Carrington's mission, the Oglalla chief Red Cloud joined Man-Afraid in accusing the government of negotiating in bad faith; he stormed out of the conference with a large number of warriors. Carrington proceeded to build Forts Phil Kearny, Reno, and C. F. Smith along the Bozeman Train and to assist emigrant trains. Almost immediately the Sioux embarked on a fierce campaign of raids and ambuscades that soon made the trail one of the most dangerous stretches on the frontier. The remote forts were dependent on small, escorted work details to gather provisions from the surrounding region; these work details, as well as cattle and horse herds, became prime targets for Sioux raiding parties. One such raid on a wood-cutting party on 21 December 1866 prompted a rescue foray by eighty soldiers and civilians under the command of Captain William J. Fetterman. The Sioux drew the unit into a devastating ambush from which not a man escaped.

Although the Army enjoyed subsequent successes at the Wagon Box* and Hayfield* fights the next year, the Sioux continued to harrass the beleaguered garrisons. The government finally accepted the futility of maintaining the Bozeman Trail and sent a Peace Commission to Fort Laramie in April 1868. In May of that year, Forts Phil Kearny, Reno, and C. F. Smith were ordered abandoned, and the last troops were withdrawn by the end of August. On 6 November 1868, Red Cloud arrived at Fort Laramie to sign a peace treaty. This was the only war in which the Sioux prevailed against the U.S. government.

References. Dorothy M. Johnson, *The Bloody Bozeman*, 1971. Remi Nadeau, *Fort Laramie and the Sioux Indians*, 1967. James C. Olson, *Red Cloud and the Sioux Problem*, 1965.

Fred J. Chiaventone

SIXTH ARMY

Constituted as Headquarters, Sixth Army, on 22 January 1943, this organization was activated three days later at Fort Sam Houston,* Texas. After moving into the Southwest Pacific Area* (SWPA), Sixth Army Headquarters was based in Brisbane, Australia. Sixth Army units were in almost constant combat from their first contact with the enemy at Milne Bay, New Guinea, from early 1943 until July 1945, when they finally cleared the Japanese from the northern Philippines. Sixth Army participated in fifteen amphibious operations, including twenty-two major assault landings. At the time Japan surrendered, Sixth Army was preparing for the invasion of Kyushu, Japan's southernmost island (Operation Olympic). For a brief time, Sixth Army participated in the occupation of Japan.

Deactivated on 28 January 1946, Sixth Army was reactivated at the Presidio* of San Francisco on 1 March 1946 as one of six Continental Armies of the Zone of the Interior.* Sixth Army's area of responsibility included eight western states. Over the next fifty years, the headquarters was responsible for active Army, Army Reserve,* and National Guard* unit training, support, and for oversight of mobilization and supply operations during the Korean War,* Vietnam War,* and numerous domestic relief operations. Headquarters, Sixth Army, was redesignated Sixth United States Army on 1 January 1957 and, on 29 September 1970, assumed responsibility for four additional western states. Sixth Army was inactivated on 23 June 1995.

References. Paula Anthony et al., "Armies and Corps," *Army*, October 1986, 330–343. Robert O. Bryan, "Guardian of the Golden West," *Army Digest*, June 1970, 4–9.

Russell W. Glenn

SKY TROOPER. *See* C-47.

SKYTRAIN. *See* C-47.

SLEDGEHAMMER

An unexecuted plan for a landing on the European continent in 1942, Sledgehammer would have placed eight to ten divisions* in France to relieve pressure on the Soviets during the summer of that year. U.S. participation would have been limited to two and a half divisions; Britain would have provided most of the forces. The shortage of landing craft* to supply the invasion force over the beaches was a problem, since there were no major ports in the area selected for the landings. Planners believed that it would take at least eight weeks to open a port for shipping, requiring an extended period of ship-to-shore support.

The plan was presented in England at a Defense Committee meeting in early 1942. The British government believed that an invasion force would face thirty to forty German divisions and that the enemy would be able to bring fresh divisions at double the rate that the Allies could land them. Thus, nothing could be done in Europe; the British preferred to look for a victory elsewhere. The United States, however, fearing the collapse of the Soviet Union during the coming summer campaign, had stabilized the situation in the Pacific by March 1942 and wanted action in Europe. President Franklin Roosevelt and his military advisors pressed the point and managed to get the British on 14 April 1942 to agree technically to accept large shipments of U.S. troops and to start preparing joints plans for an invasion when it became practical.

References. Walter Scott Dunn, Jr., *Second Front Now, 1943*, 1980. Maurice Matloff and Edwin M. Snell, *Strategic Planning for Coalition Warfare, 1941–1942*, 1953.

Luke Knowley

SLICK

"Slick" was a slang term commonly used during the Vietnam War* for (1) a helicopter without rockets or other external armament, used to carry troops and cargo; (2) a helicopter that landed on runners rather than wheels; and (3) a helicopter of any kind. In Vietnam, troop-carrying UH-1 Huey* slicks were frequently escorted by armed UH-1 "Hogs," which would lay down suppressive fire around the landing zone* to discourage opposition. The development of specially designed attack helicopters has since largely removed the armed utility helicopter from conventional forces, so the "slick" distinction is now less relevant.

References. Larry R. Lubenow, "Do You Read Me?" *Army*, May 1968, 51–53. Harold G. Moore and Joseph L. Galloway, *We Were Soldiers Once . . . and Young*, 1992.

Randall N. Briggs

SLIM BUTTES

Following the setbacks at the Rosebud* and the Little Bighorn* in June 1876, the punitive campaign against the Sioux, Cheyenne, and Arrapahoe stalled as the forces under Major General Alfred Terry and Brigadier General George Crook* reorganized and waited for reinforcements. Not until 5 August was a serious effort made to pursue the scattered tribes, and the pursuit was plagued by exhausted troops and dwindling supplies. As summer came to a close, torrential downpours and rapidly dropping temperatures replaced burning heat, straining the troops' endurance. Soldiers were reduced to eating their own horses and mules, on what veterans would later refer to as the "horsemeat march."

On 7 September, Crook ordered Captain Anson Mills to push south to Deadwood City with 150 of the fittest men of the 3rd Cavalry to obtain what supplies he could. En route, Mills stumbled onto American Horse's village of Sioux near Slim Buttes (near present-day Belle Fourche, South Dakota). Mills launched a dawn attack on 8 September, scattering the Sioux and capturing the village and a large store of provisions, but a prolonged fight ensued as the Sioux fired down on the troopers from the surrounding cliffs. Mills sent for reinforcements. A fierce firefight followed Crook's arrival, as the cavalrymen tried to force American Horse to surrender. After refusing three offers to negotiate, American Horse was mortally wounded and surrendered to Crook. Shortly thereafter Crazy Horse arrived with about 600 warriors and attempted to launch a counterattack, but heavy fire forced him to retreat up the nearby bluffs. The troops pursued the retreating braves, forcing them to break off the fight and retire from the field.

References. Jerome A. Greene, *Slim Buttes 1876*, 1982. Fred H. Werner, *The Slim Buttes Battle, September 9 and 10, 1876*, 2nd ed., 1981.

Fred J. Chiaventone

SNAFU

Originally an acronym for "situation normal, all fouled up," SNAFU is a World War II* soldier's expression used to describe sardonically the effects of fog and friction in war. First recorded in 1941, the term was brought into general usage by the returning troops upon demobilization in 1946. Today the term applies broadly to chaotic or confused situations where outcomes are drastically different from what is predicted or desired.

References. Paul Dickson, *War Slang*, 1994. Geoffrey Regan, *SNAFU*, 1993.

Kelvin Crow

SOLDIERS' AND SAILORS' CIVIL RELIEF ACT

In May 1918, Congress passed the first Soldiers' and Sailors' Civil Relief Act of 1918 (20 *Stat.* 440) to protect uniformed members of the armed forces and their families by postponing civil suits, judgments, attachments, garnishments, evictions, mortgages, foreclosures, installment payments, and prior tax obligations during terms of military service. It also provided protection against lapses or cancelation of life insurance and made the federal government responsible for any resulting losses to insurance companies. It safeguarded claims, leases, and land rights, mandated reemployment following honorable discharge, extended both local and federal statutes of limitation, and required court-appointed attorneys for military personnel who could not appear in person.

During the mobilization of 1940, Congress included some provisions of the Relief Act in its Joint Resolution calling up the National Guard* and Army Reserve* and, later, in the Selective Training and Service Act of 1940, which established the draft. On 17 October 1940, Congress approved the Soldiers' and Sailors' Civil Relief Act of 1940 (54 *Stat.* 1178), with only a few minor changes from the 1918 act. Congress has amended the Relief Act of 1940 numerous times since its passage, most recently in March 1991 (105 *Stat.* 34), broadening and expanding protection for serving members of the armed services. It remains in effect today.

References. Ganson J. Baldwin and John Kirkland Clark, Jr., *Legal Effects of Military Service under the Soldiers' and Sailors' Civil Relief Act of 1940*, 1940. James P. Pottorff, "Contemporary Applications of the Soldiers' and Sailors' Civil Relief Act," *Military Law Review*, Spring 1991, 115–140.

SOLDIER'S MEDAL

The Soldier's Medal is awarded to any soldier, sailor, airman, Marine, or allied military personnel who, while serving in any capacity with the U.S. Army, distinguishes himself by heroism not involving actual conflict with an enemy. This means that the Soldier's Medal is the Army's highest award for noncombat valor. The Soldier's Medal is not a lifesaving award, and it is not awarded solely on the basis of having saved a life; rather, the focus is on risk of life. Numerous awards of this decoration have been made to men and women who saved valuable government property or equipment from destruction or who risked their lives in an unsuccessful attempt to save another. One of the army's oldest awards, the Soldier's Medal was created by Act of Congress in 1926. Congress intended it to be the ground counterpart to the Distinguished Flying Cross.

References. Frederic L. Borch III and William R. Westlake, *The Soldier's Medal*, 1994. Evans E. Kerrigan, *American War Medals and Decorations*, 1964.

Frederic L. Borch III

SOUTHEAST ASIA TREATY ORGANIZATION

Created on 8 September 1954 with the signing of the Southeast Asia Collective Defense Treaty (also known as the Manila Pact), the Southeast Asia Treaty Organization, commonly referred to as SEATO, was a response to communist expansion in the region. Like members of the North Atlantic Treaty Organization,* SEATO members pledged to defend each other in the event one member came under attack by an outside force. SEATO headquarters was located in Bangkok, Thailand; members included Australia, France, Great Britain, New Zealand, Pakistan, the Philippines, and the United States. Although Cambodia, Laos, and South Vietnam were not members, they cooperated with SEATO. The organization, however, was hampered by a lack of effectiveness. When fighting broke out in Vietnam, in which the United States was increasingly involved, some members left the alliance. In 1972 Pakistan withdrew, and in 1975 France refused to continue its financial support. At the same time, Great Britain began to withdraw its forces from the region. On 30 June 1977, SEATO was formally dissolved.

References. Monro MacCloskey, *Pacts for Peace*, 1967. George Modelski, ed., *SEATO*, 1962.

Trevor Brown

SOUTHERN PLAINS WAR, 1868–1869

Precipitated by a series of Cheyenne raids on white settlements in western Kansas in the summer of 1868, the Southern Plains War eventually spread across western Kansas and Oklahoma, the panhandle of Texas, eastern Colorado, and southwestern Nebraska. Although both whites and Indians harbored legitimate grievances, the primary cause was the expansion of white culture and the attempt to restrict Indians to reservations. The war eventually involved bands of Cheyenne, Sioux, Arapahoe, Kiowa, and Comanche. In what became known as the "Winter Campaign," cavalry* and infantry* forces of Major General Philip H. Sheridan's* Division of the Missouri moved into the area, attacking the Indians in their villages at a time when they were vulnerable to the harsh weather conditions and their ponies lacked grass. Actions during the Southern Plains War included Beecher Island,* the Washita,* Soldiers Spring, Summit Springs, and numerous lesser skirmishes and engagements. The Army finally succeeded in convincing most of the bands to return to their reservations.

References. Richard H. Dillon, *North American Indian Wars*, 1983. William H. Leckie, *The Military Conquest of the Southern Plains*, 1963.

SOUTHWEST PACIFIC AREA

The rapid advance of Japanese forces southward into Malaya, Burma, the Netherlands Indies, and the Philippines in the first two months of 1942 effectively wrecked the American, British, Dutch, Australian Command (ABDA-COM), the Allied arrangement for defense of the Malay Barrier. In March 1942, the United States and Great Britain agreed to a new strategic arrangement in which the British assumed responsibility for the Middle East–Indian Ocean region and the U.S. assumed primary responsibility for the war in the Pacific. The U.S. Joint Chiefs of Staff* subsequently divided the Pacific into two main theaters: the Pacific Ocean Area (POA), with three subareas, North, Central, and South, under the the command of Admiral Chester Nimitz; and Southwest Pacific Area (SWPA), under the command of General Douglas MacArthur.* SWPA included Australia, the Philippines, New Guinea,* the Bismarck Archipelago, the western Solomons, and the Netherlands Indies (except Sumatra). MacArthur controlled all land, sea, and air forces within this theater; he formally announced his new command structure on 18 April 1942. Under MacArthur's leadership and with growing materiel and manpower resources from the United States, SWPA forces struck back at the Japanese in New Guinea in the waning months of 1942. Following success in New Guinea, Southwest Pacific Area forces met and defeated one Japanese force after another, recapturing much of what had been lost in the opening months of the war and leaving numerous isolated Japanese garrisons to wither behind the advancing American lines.

References. Richard M. Leighton and Robert W. Coakley, *Global Logistics and Strategy, 1940–1943*, 1955. Samuel Milner, *Victory in Papua*, 1957, 1989.

SPANISH-AMERICAN WAR

The Spanish-American War marked the emergence of the United States as a world power. Although fought mainly over the issue of Cuba, financial and political causes were also important. The rapid advance of U.S. productivity in the late 19th century had saturated home markets, and manufacturers and politicians quickly realized that America's future growth depended upon overseas trade. High import tariffs divided the American public into two camps—imperialists and anti-imperialists. The imperialists favored U.S. appropriation of overseas territories and coaling stations, naval bases, and a military presence abroad to protect U.S. investments and markets. Convinced that trade could best expand by peaceful means, the anti-imperialists opposed acquiring foreign territories. They believed that America should not imitate Europe's colonial greed. However, both sides realized that the opening of overseas markets was a way to avoid social and political problems at home; the 1893 depression and the end of western expansion caused many to think that the United States had reached its last frontier.

A rising tide of jingoism, led by Captain Alfred Thayer Mahan and Theodore Roosevelt, swept from coast to coast. "Yellow journalism," directed by William Randolph Hearst's *New York Journal* and Joseph Pulitzer's *New York World*, led to daily stories of Spanish brutality in Cuba. Editorial cartoonists portrayed Spain as a vicious beast. Hearst's famous remark to Frederic Remington upon sending the artist to Cuba, "You furnish the pictures, I'll furnish the war!" clearly revealed the arrogance of this new breed of newspaper publisher. Responsible officials in the William McKinley administration urged a peaceful solution to the Cuban problem, but the press hammered home the viewpoint that Spain was cowardly and weak—and would prove no match for the armed might of the United States.

The explosion of the USS *Maine* in Havana Harbor on 15 February 1898 was the catalyst that threw the United States into its most popular, and often most misunderstood, war. On 22 April, after a naval court of inquiry concluded that a submerged mine had destroyed the *Maine*, a naval blockade of Cuba was authorized. The U.S. Army was completely unprepared when President William McKinley officially declared war against Spain three days later. Over several years, the Army's strength had been steadily cut to about 28,000 Regulars, most of its forces were spread dangerously thin along the western frontier. McKinley issued a call for 200,000 volunteers and raised the authorized strength of the Regular Army to 65,000 men. But the archaic and dangerous policy of patronage commissions prevalent during the Civil War* continued. Regular Army junior officers often found themselves under the command of politically appointed colonels, whose only previous claim to fame was having been selected grand marshal of a Grand Army of the Republic parade.

"Remember the *Maine*," quickly became a national battle cry, and the public demanded immediate revenge. The War Department,* also caught up in the hysteria of the moment, decided to send an expeditionary force to Cuba as soon as possible, with little thought to the hazards of beginning a tropical campaign at the peak of the malaria and yellow fever season. The task of supplying a large force on such short notice completely overwhelmed the Quartermaster Corps.* Ordered in from the frontier, Regular Army regiments* were still wearing their winter uniforms; summer clothing never showed up. Thousands of cans of putrid beef, rotting in government warehouses since the Civil War and slapped with red paint to indicate that the contents were not for human consumption, were nevertheless issued to the troops. Freight trains, packed with supplies and provisions, lined up for miles along the single track leading to the port of Tampa; many carried no bill of lading, and their cars had to be opened and inventoried. The dock was a jumbled mass of confusion as cartons piled up on the pier; medical supplies, tents, arms, and ammunition were loaded on board any transport at hand. In most cases, no inventory was made of the cargo. As soon as one ship was loaded, another vessel moved into its vacated spot at the dock.

Suddenly, on 29 April a flotilla of Spanish warships under the command of Admiral Pascual Cevera y Topete was reported to have sailed from the Cape Verde Islands. Newspaper headlines screamed that the Spanish vessels had been ordered to bombard Boston Harbor and panic gripped the eastern United States. Under public pressure, Secretary of the Navy John D. Long divided Admiral William T. Sampson's blockade fleet. Commodore Winfield Scott Schley and three new battleships were sent to Hampton Roads, Virginia, to await the arrival of the latest "Spanish Armada."

On 1 May, Commodore George Dewey's Asiatic Squadron of six ships steamed into Manila Bay and destroyed ten Spanish men-of-war anchored there. Dewey blockaded Manila and waited over a month for U.S. Army troops to arrive. Not until 25 May did the first troops leave San Francisco for the Philippines. Meanwhile, Sampson carried on a loose blockade of Cuban waters, while Schley's formidable force of fighting ships waited for word of the arrival of Cervera's squadron off the east coast of the United States. On 28 May, despite Sampson's blockade, Cervera's flotilla managed to sneak into Santiago Harbor. Schley and his battleships immediately sailed from Hampton Roads to join Sampson's vessels covering the entrance to Santiago Bay.

A few days later, Major General William Shafter received orders to begin a military operation against the city of Santiago.* Shafter ordered V Corps, comprising eighteen regular and two volunteer infantry* regiments,* five regular cavalry* regiments (plus Theodore Roosevelt's Rough Riders)* six artillery* batteries,* and a Gatling gun* detachment—a total of 16,888 officers and men— to Cuba. On the night of 2 June, Navy Lieutenant Richmond Hobson and seven men made an unsuccessful attempt to sink the collier *Merrimac* across the entrance to Santiago Bay to trap the Spanish flotilla inside the harbor. On 10 June, 650 U.S. Marines landed at Guantanamo Bay to establish a coaling station for the blockade fleet; twelve days later, V Corps reached Cuba. Troops began landing at Daiquiri and Siboney, about twenty miles east of Santiago.

The first land skirmish of the war took place the following day, at Las Guasimas. The Spaniards withdrew toward Santiago before U.S. reinforcements could arrive. On 30 June, after a short reconnaissance of enemy positions, Shafter split his forces, sending Brigadier General Henry Lawton's division to attack El Caney, about forty miles from Santiago, while Brigadier General Joseph Wheeler's and Brigadier General Jacob Kent's divisions made a frontal assault on the main Santiago defenses at Kettle and San Juan Hills. By nightfall, the Americans were precariously entrenched on the ridges commanding the city; they had suffered 1,600 casualties.

With Santiago surrounded by U.S. land and sea forces, Admiral Cervera was ordered to try to save his ships by running the naval blockade. On 3 July, the Spanish vessels steamed out from the bay and headed east along the Cuban coast. Schley pursued and, in a running gun battle, destroyed Cervera's flotilla.

During the following two weeks, the two governments conducted peace negotiations. But while the talking went on, daily rains, yellow fever, malaria, and other tropical diseases began to take their toll on V Corps. By the time Santiago surrendered on 17 July, a quarter of Shafter's army had been killed or wounded, and practically every man in the water-filled trenches was too sick to fight. Fortunately, the Spaniards were unaware of the desperate situation facing the U.S. troops. On 12 August, Spain and the United States signed a peace protocol to end the fighting.

The Treaty of Paris, signed on 10 December 1898, officially ended the war. Spain granted Cuba its independence, ceded Guam and Puerto Rico, and sold the Philippine Islands to the United States for twenty million dollars.

References. James C. Bradford, ed., *Crucible of Empire*, 1993. Charles H. Brown, *The Correspondent's War*, 1967. Graham A. Cosmas, *An Army for Empire*, 1971. David F. Trask, *The War with Spain in 1898*, 1981.

A. B. Feuer

SPECIAL FORCES

Congressional interest in Special Operations Forces* (SOF) in the mid-1980s caused the Army to study the feasibility of creating a Special Forces (SF) branch. The desire to integrate SF into AirLand Battle* doctrine,* and increased emphasis on foreign internal defense (an SF mission), demanded a systematic approach to providing the best-trained soldiers possible. Such an approach would produce soldiers who were technically and tactically proficient, expert at SF missions, and aware of the capabilities and limitations of SF units at the tactical, operational, and strategic levels. On 9 April 1987, Secretary of the Army* John O. Marsh approved establishment of the Special Forces branch. Department of the Army* General Order Number 35, dated 19 June 1987, created the new branch.

Until the designation of Special Forces as a separate branch, officers and enlisted men assigned to special forces units were still required to maintain proficiency in their basic branches in order to be promoted. Earlier creation of Functional Area 18 (SF) had eliminated another difficulty for these soldiers, as prior to that time they had also to maintain proficiency in a functional area other than the branch. In effect, to be promoted SF soldiers had to be proficient in three areas rather than the two required of others in the Army. Special Forces is the Army's only nonaccession branch. Male officer volunteers must first complete a branch advanced course, the Special Forces Qualification Course. Upon graduation, the officers transfer from their basic branch to Special Forces branch.

References. Aaron Bank, *From OSS to Green Berets*, 1986. David Eshel, *Daring to Win*, 1992. Ian D. W. Sutherland, *Special Forces of the United States Army, 1952–1982*, 1990.

Richard L. Kiper

SPECIAL OPERATIONS FORCES

Special Operations Forces (SOF) cover the mission areas of counterterrorism, special reconnaissance, unconventional warfare, foreign internal defense, direct action, assistance to combat search and rescue, civil affairs, special operations aviation, and psychological operations.* U.S. Army Special Operations Forces are the units that perform these missions. SOF units include U.S. Army Rangers,* U.S. Army Special Forces,* Civil Affairs, Psychological Operations Groups, Special Operations Support, and Special Operations Aviation. Special Operations Forces are mission-tailored to conduct sensitive and low-key missions in peace and war, in any climate or condition, in support of national interests.

References. Geoffrey T. Barker, *A Concise History of U.S. Army Special Operations Forces with Lineage and Insignia*, 2d ed., 1993. John M. Collins, *Special Operations Forces*, 1994. Stanley Sandler, *To Free from Oppression*, 1994.

Richard Stewart

SPENCER RIFLE

The Spencer rifle was a seven-shot repeating arm that fired rim-fire .56-caliber rounds loaded in a tube magazine in the stock. Developed in 1861, the Spencer was not the first repeating weapon used by the U.S. Army, but, in both its rifle and carbine versions, was the most extensively used repeating arm during the Civil War.* The U.S. Ordnance Department purchased over 42,000 Spencers, both rifles and carbines, and thirty million cartridges manufactured by the Spencer Rifle Company and the Burnside Rifle Company. A later .50-caliber Spencer was issued by the U.S. Army as late as 1874.

References. Joseph G. Bilby, *Civil War Firearms*, 1996. William B. Edwards, *Civil War Guns*, 1962. Glenn W. Sunderland, *Wilder's Lightning Brigade . . . and Its Spencer Repeaters*, 1984.

Steven J. Allie

SPOTSYLVANIA

Following the indecisive Battle of the Wilderness* on 5–6 May 1864, Ulysses S. Grant,* instead of pulling the Army of the Potomac* back to recover and refit, turned southward toward Richmond. His immediate goal was to reach the crossroads at Spotsylvania Court House, putting his army on Robert E. Lee's* right flank, between the Army of Northern Virginia and Richmond. After dark on the 7th, Grant and Major General George G. Meade* pulled the Army of the Potomac, three corps with a fourth corps covering the force, out of line and began a general movement southward. After several skirmishes en route, Federal infantry arrived near Alsop, just northwest of Spotsylvania Court House, on the morning of the 8th. They found Confederate infantry hastily entrenched across their route of advance: Lee had won the race to the key crossroads. Over the next ten days, the armies maneuvered and countermaneuvered as they attempted to find the respective opposing flanks and attacked and counterattacked in numerous bitter engagements. Finally, exhausted, they dug in to face each other. Two days later both armies left the field around Spotsylvania, without a clear victory or defeat. Federal losses were more than 17,500, while the Confederates lost between 9,000 and 10,000 men. The message, however, was clear to Lee:

Grant, unlike the previous commanders of the Army of the Potomac, would not fall back but would continue to fight, whatever his losses.

References. Joseph P. Cullen, *Where a Hundred Thousand Fell*, 1966. Gary W. Gallagher, ed., *The Spotsylvania Campaign*, 1998. William D. Matter, *If It Takes All Summer*, 1988.

Edward Shanahan

SPRINGFIELD ARSENAL

The Springfield Arsenal was one of the original depositories for weapons in the United States. It was located in Springfield, Massachusetts, a geographical position well suited for weapons storage and manufacture. During Shays' Rebellion* in 1786, the Arsenal became a focal point of discontent. Angry mobs, led by Daniel Shays and motivated by severe economic depression, directly threatened the Arsenal; in January 1787, a force of local militia repulsed them. Several days later reinforcements arrived to end the disturbance. Although the numerous militia units were quickly disbanded, two federally supported artillery* companies* remained, and one of the companies was permanently quartered at the Arsenal. The two units represented the first augmentation of the Regular Army.

Originally proposed by Alexander Hamilton and Henry Knox to provide for the "public manufacture of arms and powder," Springfield became the first officially established national armory in 1794. Production at the Springfield Arsenal, however, remained relatively low, with foreign sources supplying substantial proportions of U.S. munitions needs. The Arsenal later became known for the creation and production of a series of weapons that bore the name Springfield.

References. Chris L. Dvarecka, "Springfield Armory," *Army Information Digest*, July 1954, 41–48, and "Weapons on Parade," *Army Information Digest*, September 1955, 39–43.

Lee W. Eysturlid

SPRINGFIELD RIFLE

In 1901 the U.S. Army bgan a series of studies to find a replacement for the Krag-Jorgenson.* A design based on the Manlicher two-lug design was employed to strengthen the receiver assembly, and a five-round magazine, with a stripper clip, directly below the receiver facilitated quick loading. The .30-caliber center-fire case, with head or rim ammunition, made removal of jammed cases easier. The improved rifle went into production in 1903. So that it could be used for all branches, the Springfield's barrel was shortened to twenty-four inches for the production version. The original bayonet* was in fact the cleaning rod beneath the barrel; it could be pulled out and secured with a latch. In 1905 an eighteen-inch knife bayonet replaced the rod bayonet. In 1906, the rifle was rechambered to accept the new .30-caliber model 1906 ammunition. The 1903 Springfield was the standard U.S. Army weapon until the M1 Garand* replaced it in 1936, but the U.S. Army continued to issue 1903s throughout World War II* as a grenade launcher and sniper rifle. Many contractors manufactured the 1903 Springfield in different variations, and it is still heralded as one of the most accurate rifles ever produced.

References. William S. Brophy, *The Springfield 1903 Rifles*, 1985. Arcadi Gluckman, *Identifying Old U.S. Muskets Rifles and Carbines*, 1959, 1965. James E. Hicks, *U.S. Military Firearms, 1776–1956*, 1962.

Steven J. Allie

SQUAD

The squad is the basic maneuver element in the infantry.* The term also describes small organizational elements in other branches. Typically a squad consists of ten or eleven soldiers broken into two fire teams; it is led by a squad leader, usually a staff sergeant or sergeant. Squad weapons typically include two grenade launchers (M203), one or two squad automatic weapons (M240), and M-16 rifles.* For special missions, the squad can be equipped with many types of specialized weapons, from heavy machine guns to antitank missiles. In some cases, two or more squads are organized into a section.* More often, three or more squads make up a platoon.*

References. Douglas K. Lehmann and Robert J. O'Neil, "Two Views on the Rifle Squad," *Infantry*, May–June 1980, 18–21. Dandridge M. Malone, "The Squad," *Army*, February 1976, 12–16.

Andrew N. Morris

SQUARE DIVISION

The War Department* officially adopted the "square division" as its basic infantry* division* on 8 August 1917, shortly after the United States entered World War I.* The War Department combined the recommendations of a board headed by Colonel Chauncey B. Baker, input from the American Expeditionary Force* (AEF) staff, and the results of its own research to produce the square-division table of organization. The square division consisted of two infantry brigades,* each comprising two infantry regiments* of three battalions* each— thus two brigades, four regiments, and twelve battalions. The division included an artillery* brigade, a cavalry* squadron,* two machine-gun battalions, an engineer regiment, a signal battalion, a medical department, and a brigade-sized logistical support element (the division trains). With a personnel strength of 27,123 officers and men, the division was twice as large as most French, British, and German divisions of the day. Designed for trench warfare, its great size enabled the square division to stay in contact with enemy forces for extended periods.

The origins of the term "square division" are more difficult to uncover. The term was not used to describe the table of organization of 8 August 1917, and it does not appear to have been used during World War I. The term came into general use during the 1930s, when the Army contemplated changing its divisional organization from the four-regiment square division to the three-regiment "triangular" division.* The 1941 edition of *Field Manual 100–5: Operations* used the terms square and triangular to distinguish between these two tables of organization, which were both used in 1941.

References. John C. Binkley, "A History of US Army Force Structuring," *Military Review*, February 1977, 67–82. James G. Harboard, *The American Army in France, 1917–1919*, 1936.

Scott McMeen

STAFF DUTY OFFICER

The staff duty officer (SDO) serves as the unit command and control monitor during off-duty hours, including weekends and holidays. He is the direct representative of the unit's commander and is charged with personally handling matters requiring continuous attention, both of a normal and emergency nature. The staff duty officer is usually assigned by roster to this official duty and is detailed to be constantly available during a specified period of time.

Bill Knight

STAFF RIDE

The staff ride program is designed to prepare military leaders for modern war through the in-depth study of historical battles and campaigns. The study of past examples of warfare allows leaders to hone combat skills during periods of peace. Comprehensive study of key leaders and role playing on the battlefield drive home the unchanging dynamics of warfare. Originally developed by Captain Arthur L. Wagner* at the School for the Application of Infantry and Cavalry* at Fort Leavenworth,* Kansas, in the 1890s, the staff ride is employed today at a wide range of Army schools, beginning with cadet programs and continuing through the Army War College.* Staff rides are conducted in three phases: preliminary study—comprehensive classroom study of the battle; field study—a visit to the actual battlefield; and integration—discussion of lessons gleaned from both classroom and the field study and their application to modern warfare.

Reference. William G. Robertson, *The Staff Ride*, 1987.

Robert J. Dalessandro

STANDING OPERATING PROCEDURES

Standing operating procedures (SOPs) are sets of instructions that dictate the procedures to be used for actions that can be executed in a set manner without loss of effectiveness. Examples of activities frequently governed by SOPs are tactical drills and frequently repeated actions (e.g., submission of award requests, setup of command posts). Examples of SOPs are Rules of engagement* and report formats. This standardization reduces the necessity of repeating such information in plans and orders. Procedures stated in SOPs are applicable unless ordered otherwise. Organizations often have a field SOP (FSOP) for use during operations or training away from garrison, and an administrative SOP covering routine administrative matters.

References. Randall A. Soboul, "A Framework for SOPs," *Infantry*, July–August 1992, 12–13. Peter G. Williams, "SOPs That Work," *Infantry*, November–December 1984, 37–38.

Russell W. Glenn

STANTON, EDWIN McMASTERS (1814–1869)

A lawyer by profession and an abolitionist by upbringing, Edwin McMasters Stanton (1814–1869) was a "War Democrat" when President Abraham Lincoln appointed him secretary of war* in January 1862. Although Republicans in the administration questioned his politics at first, Stanton became one of the most ardent workers for the Union cause. Perhaps the most competent secretary of war since John C. Calhoun,* he reformed and reorganized the War Department,* ridding the department of corruption, incompetence, and inefficiency. He worked closely with the Joint Committee on the Conduct of the War, increased internal security, and strengthened the War Department's control over the armies in the field.

Stanton was a demanding and sometimes difficult man to work with. He was not always well liked and had frequent clashes with colleagues and subordinates. He continued in the cabinet after Lincoln's death but disagreed with Andrew Johnson over Reconstruction policies. When Johnson attempted to fire him in February 1868, Stanton refused to leave office. The crisis led to Johnson's impeachment by the House, but the Senate failed to convict. Stanton then resigned and resumed his private law practice. President Ulysses S. Grant* later nominated, and the Senate confirmed, Stanton to the Supreme Court, but he died before he could take his seat.

References. Fletcher Pratt, *Stanton*, 1953. Benjamin P. Thomas and Harold M. Hyman, *Stanton*, 1962.

STARLIGHT SCOPE

Developed at several U.S. Army research and development laboratories from the mid-1950s to the mid-1960s, the Army began fielding starlight scopes in Vietnam in late 1967 and early 1968. The starlight scope was the first-generation passive night-vision device, which does not rely on the emission of light sources, such as flares, searchlights, or infrared equipment, but gathers and intensifies natural light sources (starshine, moonlight, and skyglow), thus rendering it undetectable to the enemy. The starlight scope is actually an image-intensifyer tube using energized electrons to enhance and project the gathered light onto a screen so that it can be seen by the viewer. The image the viewer sees is 40,000 times brighter than the light entering the tube. Three models were available by 1968: the AN/PVS-2, a small scope for individual use or attachment to a shoulder weapon; the AN/TVS-2, for use with a crew-served weapon; and the AN/TVS-4, a medium-range observation scope. The starlight scope did not com-

pletely solve the U.S. Army's problems in night operations in the Vietnam War,*
but it offered the soldier a valuable tool in taking back the initiative the enemy
had enjoyed after dark.

    References. Robert G. McClintic, "Rolling Back the Night," *Army,* August 1969, 28–
35. "Night Vision Equipment," *Field Artilleryman,* March 1971, 32–36.

STARS AND STRIPES

Stars and Stripes was established as the official service newspaper of the
American Expeditionary Force* (AEF) in World War I.* The first number was
printed in Paris on 8 February 1918, and the paper appeared weekly thereafter
until 13 June 1919. At its height, circulation reached 522,000. Captain Guy T.
Viskinski was the managing editor throughout most of the paper's early run; a
large number of the staff, including Alexander Woolcott and Harold Ross, went
on to notable postwar careers in journalism. In World War II,* *Stars and Stripes*
resumed publication, but due to the truly global nature of the conflict, it was
published in multiple editions worldwide. Perhaps the most famous World War
II staff member was Bill Mauldin,* creator of Willie and Joe.* Mauldin's cartoons were among the most popular features of the paper, while the "B-Bag"
(bitch bag) column raised the ire of some senior officers. The vast majority of
the *Stars and Stripes* staff were enlisted men, who tended to champion the
enlisted view of Army life in general. Chief editors of the various editions
retained a high degree of editorial freedom.

    Today, *Stars and Stripes* continues publication in both Pacific and European
editions and serve as "America's Hometown Paper for those Serving Overseas."
Unlike its wartime predecessor, the current staff is primarily civilian. The paper
has lost much of its military flavor.

    References. Alfred Emile Cornebise, *Ranks and Columns,* 1993, and *The Stars and
Stripes,* 1984. Steve Harding, "Changes Ahead for the *Stars and Stripes,*" *Soldiers,* September 1997, 2–3.

                                                            Stephen C. McGeorge

STEEL POT

"Steel pot" is the common term for the M-1 helmet. In June 1941, the M-1
replaced the World War I* Model 1917, and the 1930 Model 1917A1 (which
added an improved lining and chin strap). The steel pot is among the most
distinctive helmets of all time, and it remained in service in the U.S. Army from
1941 through the early 1980s, when the PASGT (Personnel Armor System
Ground Troops), or the Kevlar helmet, replaced it.

    As early as 1917–1918, the Army undertook research to design a more pro-
tective and comfortable helmet than the British-inspired Model 1917. It tested
a variety of prototypes. By 1940, with war looming on the horizon, the Infantry
Board endorsed the need for a new helmet. The steel helmet-shell was designed
first, with a specific requirement that it provide greater protection particularly
to the sides and back of the head. The liner/suspension system remained a problem until a meeting between the Riddell Company (designer of sports equipment

and patent holder on a new plastic football helmet) and a member of the Infantry Board resulted in the novel idea of resting a separate plastic liner unside the steel shell. The liners themselves went through a number of manufacturing variations between late 1941 and early 1942. These included cloth and fiber liners (which were fragile and tended to turn mushy in jungle climates), low-pressure cloth and resin liners, and finally a high-pressure cloth and phenolic liner, using a process developed by the Westinghouse Company.

The steel pot with its separate liner offered several advantages over the earlier designs with fixed liners. The liner could be worn alone as a lightweight and military-appearing headgear when not in combat. The steel pot itself could serve a variety of useful functions: washbasin, entrenching tool, field stool, and cooking pot (although this use was frowned upon, as it destroyed the temper of the steel and burned off the dull-painted finish).

References. Chris Arnold, *Steel Pots*, 1997. Mark A. Reynosa, *The M-1 Helmet*, 1996.

Stephen C. McGeorge

STEUBEN, FRIEDRICH WILHELM LUDORF GERHARD AUGUSTIN, BARON VON (1730–1794)

Friedrich von Steuben, born on 17 September 1730 in Magdeburg, served in the Prussian army as a staff officer under Frederick the Great during the Seven Years' War. He was forced to retire as a captain in 1764 in the demobilization following the Treaty of Paris. He then spent a number of years as a chamberlain to a minor German prince. In 1777, Steuben offered his services to the Continental Congress, through Benjamin Franklin and Silas Deane. In their letter to Congress they inflated Steuben's rank to lieutenant general to improve his apparent value to the colonial cause.

In February 1778, Steuben arrived at Valley Forge* to take charge of drilling the Continental Army.* As acting inspector general,* he standardized and greatly simplified training and tactics,* thus improving efficiency and morale among the Continentals. In May, Congress confirmed his appointment as inspector general* and promoted him to major general. He quickly became the Army's supreme administrator and virtual chief of staff to George Washington.* In March 1779 Congress approved publication of Steuben's *Regulations for the Order and Discipline of the Troops of the United States*, which became the standard drill manual for the Continental Army and early U.S. Army.

In 1783, von Steuben, one of the organizers of the Society of Cincinnati, became a citizen of the United States. He died on 28 November 1794 and is buried in Steuben County, New York.

References. Joseph R. Riling, *Baron von Steuben and His Regulations*, 1966. Horst Ueberhorst, *Friedrich Wilhelm von Steuben 1730–1794*, 1981.

Timothy C. Dunwoody

STILWELL, JOSEPH WARREN (1883–1946)

Known for his fighting skills and direct manner that earned him the nickname "Vinegar Joe," Joseph Warren Stilwell was born in Palatka, Florida, on 19

March 1883 and graduated from the U.S. Military Academy* in 1904, thirty-second in a class of 124. For his first assignment, Stilwell chose the Philippines, where he saw action in the continuing U.S. effort to pacify the country. During World War I,* he served as a corps* intelligence officer with the American Expeditionary Force* (AEF). After the war, Stilwell was the first officer sent by the Military Intelligence Division to China for language training. He spent several tours of duty in China: as an assistant to the military attaché (1919–1923), as a battalion* commander in the 15th Infantry Regiment in Tianjin (1926–1929), and as military attaché (1935–1939). In January 1942, General George C. Marshall turned to Stilwell, at the time a corps commander, to head the U.S. effort to strengthen China and keep it in the war against Japan.

Stilwell went to China with orders to serve as chief of staff* to Chiang Kai-shek, the president of China and commander of the Chinese army. Soon he also became commander of U.S. Army forces in the China-Burma-India theater.* Directed to increase the effectiveness of U.S. aid to China and improve the efficiency of the Chinese army, Stilwell struggled to reform the Chinese army and have it engage the Japanese. However, Chiang wanted to preserve his forces for use against the Communists in the war he knew would follow Japan's defeat, and he therefore resisted reforms that would undermine his personal control over the army. Tension between the two grew until October 1944, when Chiang sent a request to Roosevelt asking that Stilwell be replaced.

Stilwell left China a deeply frustrated man. But his actions in the CBI had captured the imagination of the American public, and in their minds he was a hero. In January 1945 he was appointed commander of Army Ground Forces* in the United States, and in June, when Lieutenant General Simon Buckner, Jr., was killed on Okinawa, he assumed command of Tenth Army. Stilwell accepted the surrender of Japanese forces on the island and when the war ended was preparing to lead the Tenth Army in the invasion of Japan. He died in 1946.

References. Charles F. Romanus and Riley Sunderland, *Stilwell's Mission to China*, 1953. Barbara W. Tuchman, *Stilwell and the American Experience in China, 1911–45*, 1971.

Gary Bjorge

STIMSON, HENRY LEWIS (1867–1950)

Henry Lewis Stimson was brought into President Franklin Roosevelt's cabinet as secretary of war* in July 1940, despite his advanced age and his Republican politics. Stimson had held this post previously under President William Howard Taft (1911–1913) and had served as President Herbert Hoover's secretary of state (1929–1933). A strong preparedness advocate, Stimson had served as a colonel of artillery with the American Expeditionary Force* (AEF) in World War I.*

Known for his moral intensity, Stimson worked closely with General George C. Marshall* on the challenges of mobilization and organization as the United States prepared to enter World War II.* He supported Lend-Lease, especially for Great Britain, urged Marshall to speed the development of radar,* and encouraged Admiral Ernest J. King to employ Army aircraft in antisubmarine warfare. He opposed Treasury Secretary Henry Morganthau's plan to remove German industry after the war and pursuaded Roosevelt to moderate it.

Stimson's supervision of the Manhattan project, particularly his recommendations to President Harry Truman, were important. He had the old and culturally important Japanese city of Kyoto deleted from the list of atomic-bomb targets and was among a few key advisors who recommended retaining Japan's emperor in order to preclude a series of more costly battles like Iwo Jima and Okinawa.* He understood that the emperor's influence was needed to end the war and that the longer the war lasted in the Far East, the more influence the Soviets would demand at the peace table. His sage advice made him the only man to serve in four presidents' cabinets.

References. Richard N. Current, *Secretary Stimson*, 1954. Godfrey Hodgson, *The Colonel*, 1990. Elting E. Morison, *Turmoil and Tradition*, 1960.

Claude Sasso

STINGER

The stinger is a man portable, shoulder-fired, infrared-homing, short-range air defense missile system. Developed in the 1970s and fielded in the early 1980s, Stinger replaced the Redeye* missile system. With a head-on capability Redeye lacked, Stinger can defend against both fixed-wing aircraft and helicopters attacking at all angles and is generally deployed as a divisional forward-area weapon in all types of terrain. Its two-man crew visually acquires the target and electronically determines if it is friend or foe. The system notifies the gunner when it locks on the target, by emitting a distinctive sound. The gunner discards the launch tube after firing. Currently the Avenger system, which mounts four Stinger missiles on a pod attached to the HMMWV,* is replacing the older Stinger.

References. Wilburn D. Essary, "Stinger! for Potent Air Defense," *Marine Corps Gazette*, May 1984, 69–74. Oliver D. Street III and Kenneth N. Brown, "Army Air Defense," *Army*, May 1980, 24–29.

Thomas Christianson

STONES RIVER

After Christmas 1862, Major General William S. Rosecrans's Army of the Cumberland* moved out of Nashville to attack Braxton Bragg's Confederate Army of Tennessee at nearby Murfreesboro. Though delayed by a cavalry force under Brigadier General Joseph Wheeler, Rosecrans had closed with his opponent and was preparing to attack, on New Year's Eve, when Bragg struck first at Stones River. Bragg swept the Federal's right flank under Major General Alexander McCook and drove it back upon Rosecrans's headquarters, behind Major General George H. Thomas's* corps.* Thomas held, but the day was a success for the Confederates.

The next day, 1 January 1863, both sides waited for the other to move, but neither was willing to initiate action. On 2 January, Bragg tried to sweep around the Federals' left flank, but his assault quickly failed when Rosecrans refused to retreat and appeared to have been reinforced. After receiving a letter urging him to pull back, Bragg met with his senior officers and decided to retire to new positions to the south. Rosecrans was allowed to claim victory by his possession of the battlefield. His success revived Union morale at a critical time. For the Confederacy, the batte exacerbated tensions among the senior officers of the Army of Tennessee, a factor that would cost them dearly during the coming summer.

References. Peter Cozzens, *No Better Place to Die*, 1990. David R. Logsdon, comp. and ed., *Eyewitnesses at the Battle of Stones River*, 1989. Grady McWhiney, *Braxton Bragg and Confederate Defeat*, vol. 1, *Field Command*, 1969.

Andrew N. Morris

STONY POINT

Nicknamed "Little Gibraltar" by its British occupiers, Stony Point was a well fortified outpost situated at the southern terminus of the Hudson Highlands, a scant twelve miles from the key fortress at West Point. Its continued occupation by the British was a cause of concern for George Washington.* A spy penetrated the fort and noted that the defenses were incomplete and vulnerable in several areas. Rather than permit the British to finish preparing the position, Washington set Major General Anthony Wayne to plan a way to storm it. Relying on the newly created light infantry corps, consisting largely of troops from Pennsylvania, Virginia, and Connecticut, Wayne assaulted Stony Point on the night of 16 July 1779. Wayne's Continentals attacked in two columns, the left column asttacking from the north while the right column penetrated the fortifications from the west, taking the British sentries by surprise. Although the fort's defenders made a determined effort to hold their positions, the Continentals had penetrated too far through the outer string of abattis to be stopped.

References. Henry B. Dawson, *The Assault on Stony Point by General Anthony Wayne, July 16, 1779*, 1863. Henry P. Johnston, *The Storming of Stony Point on the Hudson*, 1971.

Joseph R. Fischer

STRATEGY

Strategy is the art of employing one's resources to gain one's ends. In the later 20th-century military lexicon, strategy involves direction at the highest levels. It encompasses selecting objectives likely in their accomplishment to achieve the goals of policy; the distribution of resources among the tasks; and the establishment of the political environment that will permit the most efficient utilization of available means. Operational art* and tactics* are lesser included activities within the concept of strategy, with operational art serving to link the lowest concept with the highest, the part with the whole. In his book *Soldiers* *and Soldiering*, Field Marshal Sir Archibald Wavell compared strategy to bidding in bridge, and tactics to playing the hand. Wavell's metaphor has the virtue of illustrating the instrumental relationship in the hierarchy of actions and purposes.

The age of total wars, with the total involvement of civil society, first served to expand the term, drawn from the Greek word for general, *strategos*. The development of weapons capable of striking and instantly destroying the heart of the enemy state turned the idea of strategy on it head. The purpose of strategy became *not* fighting, rather than fighting with skill. During the 1950s and early 1960s, strategy and deterrence became almost synonymous. The realization that nuclear weapons had not ended war as we knew it, brought about by the U.S. failure in Vietnam and the Israeli success in the Middle East, revived in conventional military strategy, but by then the old term had been stretched beyond recall. Hence the development of the operational art.

References. Michael Howard, *The Causes of War and Other Essays*, 1983. Edward N. Luttwak, *Strategy*, 1987. Peter Paret, ed., *Markers of Modern Strategy*, 1986.

Richard Swain

STRIKER. *See* Dogrobber.

STUART, JAMES EWELL BROWN (1833–1964)
Born in Patrick County, Virginia, on 6 February 1833, James Ewell Brown "Jeb" Stuart graduated from the U.S. Military Academy* thirteenth of forty-six in the class of 1854. He served in the 1st Cavalry on the frontier in the Indian Wars* and in the Kansas border conflicts; he was Robert E. Lee's* aide during John Brown's raid at Harpers Ferry.* He resigned his commission in May 1861 to join his home-state troops. Stuart commanded the Confederate cavalry in Virginia and devoted much of his time making that force tactically and operationally superior to its Federal counterpart. Along the way he became the epitome of the Southern cavalier. He conducted a raid that took him completely around the Federal army in the Peninsula Campaign* of 1862. His command was the "eyes and ears" of Lee's army and did excellent work in reconnaissance and intelligence gathering. After Chancellorsville,* the Federal cavalry surprised and attacked Stuart's unit in the Battle of Brandy Station. Later, Stuart led a portion of his corps on a ride around the Union army at Gettysburg.* but his action drew considerable criticism, as it resulted in Lee's loss of operational intelligence about the location and movements of the Federal army. Stuart's cavalry fought in the Wilderness* and at Spotsylvania.* On 11 May 1864, Stuart was mortally wounded leading his cavalry against a large Federal force at Yellow Tavern, not far from Richmond. He died the next day. An outstanding leader, personally brave, and a man of great endurance, Stuart was deeply religious and somewhat vain. His death was a great loss to the Confederacy.

References. Emory M. Thomas, *Bold Dragoon*, 1986. Robert J. Trout, *They Followed the Plume*, 1993.

George Knapp

STUART TANK. *See* M5 Stuart Tank.

SULFA DRUGS

Antibacterial sulfa drugs were first included in the individual first aid kits issued to U.S. soldiers in World War II.* The first aid kit consisted of a Carlisle compress wound dressing in a hermetically sealed metal container with sulfanilimide powder to be applied topically to the wound before dressing, and sulfadiazine tablets to be administered orally, provided the wounded soldier was conscious. Clinical experience during the war raised doubts as to whether the sulfa regimen should be continued in the first aid treatment. Sulfa powder tended to make the wound "dirtier," obscuring the extent of tissue damage and in some cases delaying natural wound closure. Oral sulfa drugs caused negative reactions in a percentage of individuals. Also, sulfa drugs were not as effective as the newly discovered miracle drug penicillin.* Still, they were administered to casualties proceeding through medical evacuation channels and saved innumerable lives through the prevention of wound infection.

References. E. C. Andrus et al., eds., *Advances in Military Medicine*, vol. 2, 1948. Graham A. Cosmas and Albert E. Cowdry, *The Medical Department*, 1992.

Stephen C. McGeorge

SULLIVAN EXPEDTION

In the latter months of 1778, Iroquois and Tory raids devastated a number of Pennsylvania and New York frontier settlements. In the spring of 1779, George Washington* sent Major General John Sullivan to punish the Indians and take hostages against further raids. After several months of preparation, Sullivan and a force of nearly 4,000 Continentals invaded the homelands of the Six Nations. Implementing a well prepared deception plan, Sullivan led four brigades* along two axes. One brigade under Brigadier General James Clinton moved down the Susquehanna River from Lake Otsego, while Sullivan and the remaining three brigades proceeded up the Susquehanna from the Wyoming Valley (present-day Wilkes-Barre, Pennsylvania). After meeting at the Indian village of Tioga (present-day Athens, Pennsylvania), the combined force proceeded into Iroquois territory, torching forty villages and destroying approximately 160,000 acres of corn. On 29 August, the Iroquois, along with John Butler's Tory rangers, attempted to stop Sullivan near Newtown (present-day Elmira, New York) but failed. However devastating the campaign, the expedition failed to knock the Iroquois out of the war, because the extensive devastation bound the Iroquois even more closely to the British in order to survive the impending winter. With the coming of spring, Iroquois raiding parties resumed their assaults on frontier settlements.

References. Joseph R. Fischer, *A Well-Executed Failure*, 1997. Barbara Graymont, *The Iroquois in the American Revolution*, 1972. Charles P. Whittemore, *A General of the Revolution*, 1961.

Joseph R. Fischer

SUMTER, THOMAS (1734–1832)

Known as the "Carolina gamecock" for his feisty and combative manner, Thomas Sumter was one of three partisan leaders who came to prominence following the defeat of Continental Army* units under Major General Horatio Gates at Camden, South Carolina, in August 1780. Sumter and his men waged a concerted war against British posts, striking Fort Grandby, Bellville, Fort Watson, Fort Motte, and Orangeburg in succession. Sumter, however, demonstrated a most inadequate understanding of how partisan warfare could contribute to the operations of conventional military forces. He showed no interest in co-ordinating his operations with Major General Nathanael Greene* following the return of the Continental Army to the Carolinas. Thus, Sumter's efforts fell short of providing the best return for the effort expended. After the American Revolution,* Sumter served in both the U.S. House of Representatives and Senate. Fort Sumter in Charleston Harbor was named for Thomas Sumter.

References. Robert D. Bass, *Gamecock*, 1961. Anne King Gregorie, *Thomas Sumter*, 1931.

Joseph R. Fischer

SUPREME HEADQUARTERS ALLIED EXPEDITIONARY FORCE

Under the direction of the Supreme Allied Commander in the European Theater of Operations* (ETO) in World War II, General of the Army Dwight D. Eisenhower, *SHAEF—the combined U.S.-British and Allied headquarters for the conduct of operations in northwest Europe from 1944 to 1945—became the most successful coalition headquarters in history. The nucleus of the SHAEF staff was formed in early 1943 under Lieutenant General Sir Frederick E. Morgan, designated chief of staff* to the Supreme Allied Commander (COSSAC), after the Casablanca Conference agreed that Overlord* (the invasion of Nazi-occupied Europe) would take place in 1944. This planning cell eventually evolved into the full staffed SHAEF headquarters after the announcement of Eisenhower's appointment as supreme commander in December 1943.

Formed by the U.S.-British Combined Chiefs of Staff under the guiding principle of unity of command in each theater of war, Eisenhower's new headquarters in the ETO was organized along standard staff-section lines, with each section having either a U.S. or British head and a deputy head from the other nation. Under Ike's hand, SHAEF became the model of an integrated coalition headquarters.

In February 1944, the Combined Chiefs of Staff issued a directive to SHAEF that gave the organization the mission to "enter the continent of Europe, and, in conjunction with the other United Nations, undertake operations aimed at the heart of Germany and the destruction of her armed forces." On 6 June 1944, forces under SHAEF command began the invasion of France and set about accomplishing that mission. In less than a year, SHAEF had succeeded in destroying German resistance in the West, occupying that country west of the Elbe River and accepting the unconditional surrender of all remaining German forces in the zone of operations. On 7 May, Eisenhower cabled the Combined Chiefs of Staff on behalf of SHAEF that "the mission of this Allied Force was fulfilled at 0241, local time, May 7th 1945." Ike formally dissolved SHAEF at 0001 hours, 14 July 1945, in Frankfurt, Germany.

References. Stephen E. Ambrose, *The Supreme Commander*, 1970. Forrest C. Pogue, *The Supreme Command*, 1954. Russell F. Weigley, *Eisenhower's Lieutenants*, 1981.

Jerry D. Morelock

SUPREME WAR COUNCIL

In October 1917, two disasters struck the allies, then locked in a death struggle with the Central Powers: the near collapse of the Italian army at Caporetto and the Bolshevik seizure of power in Russia. Early in November, the British, French, and Italian heads of state, meeting at Rapollo, decided to establish a Supreme War Council (Conseil Supérieur de Guerre) to adopt and maintain "policy for the Allies in the prosecution of the war." The council consisted of the heads and one other member of the governments then at war with Germany. Although created out of a military crisis, the Supreme War Council proved not to be the unified command many thought essential to a successful continuation of the war. While President Woodrow Wilson strongly supported unity of military control, neither France nor Great Britain was prepared to hand over power to a military command that might act contrary to its national interest. A proposal to replace the prime ministers with the allied commanders in chief and chiefs of staff only generated additional controversy. At various times, Major General Tasker Bliss and Colonel Edward M. House represented the Wilson administration at council meetings, while Wilson turned his attention to other issues. After the armistice in November 1918, the Supreme War Council merged into the Supreme Council of the Peace Conference.

References. Edward M. Coffman, *The War to End All Wars*, 1986. Charles Seymour, *American Diplomacy during the World War*, 1964.

SURGEON GENERAL

As early as July 1775, the Continental Congress had appointed a director general and chief physician of the Continental Army,* who was responsible for the health care of the Army and reported directly to the Continental Congress. Over the next forty years, medical care for the Army was steeped in politics and controversy. Finally, in 1818 Congress authorized the position of Surgeon General, placing U.S. Army medical officers under the control of a medical professional to ensure standardization of skills and reporting. The new position also provided medical officers a venue outside of their normal chain of command to bring health issues to the attention of senior Army leaders. Today, the Surgeon General presides over the Medical Department and serves as advisor to the Chief of Staff* of the Army on all matters affecting the Army's health. He is responsible for setting standards for individuals enlisting, reenlisting, or separating from service and for overseeing the health needs of Army families, including preventive medical care. The chiefs of the Dental Corps,* Veterinary Corps,* Medical Service Corps,* Medical Specialist Corps, and a special assistant for Medical Corps Affairs assist the Surgeon General in his duties. The Surgeon General is a lieutenant general in the Medical Corps nominated by the president and confirmed by Congress. The Surgeon General of the Army is not to be confused with the Surgeon General of the United States, which is a civilian position.

References. Mary Gillett, *The Army Medical Department 1865–1917*, 1995. James A. Huston, *The Sinews of War*, 1966.

Lawyn C. Edwards

SWIFT, EBAN, JR. (1854–1938)

After graduating from the U.S. Military Academy* in 1876, Eban Swift, Jr. joined his regiment for service in the West and participated in several major campaigns. Unlike his contemporary, Arthur L. Wagner,* Swift spent his first seventeen years serving with his regiment, with only a short tour as an aide to Major General Wesley Merritt.* He arrived at Fort Leavenworth* in 1893 to serve as an assistant instructor. Although he would return to Leavenworth twice more as a senior instructor and commandant, this initial tour was his most significant. Swift developed a standard system of tactical procedures based on German models for both tactical problem solving and orders preparation. The system not only facilitated instruction at Fort Leavenworth itself but also provided a useful tool for the field army* in the conduct of operations. The basic elements of his system are still in use today by the U.S. Army, especially the five-paragraph field order. Swift also pioneered the use of the war game in the U.S. Army, following a lead from the German army *Kriegspiel*. Using a looser system of rules than was typical of most German versions, Swift used the war game to teach students how to apply tactical decision making under simulated conditions that approximated reality. Swift went on to serve in numerous positions, including service on the Mexican border during the 1916 Punitive Expedition* and in staff positions during World War I.* Eban Swift retired in 1918 after more than forty years of service and died in Washington, D.C., in 1938.

References. Timothy Nenninger, *The Fort Leavenworth Schools and the Old Army*, 1978. Carol Reardon, *Soldiers and Scholars*, 1990.

John Broom

T

TABLE OF ORGANIZATION AND EQUIPMENT

The table of organization and equipment (TOE) sets the authorized number of soldiers, including their military occupational specialties* (MOS), and major durable, nonconsumable equipment items for each unit performing a function or mission in the U.S. Army. Normally, however, units operate under a modified table of organization and equipment (MTOE). The term "table of organization and equipment" may be used synonymously with the term "establishment," and it is frequently shortened to "table of organization."

References. Lewis I. Jeffries, "A Blueprint for Force Design," *Military Review*, August 1991, 20–31. Bolko G. Zimmer, "TOE, MTOE, and TDA," *Army Logistician*, May–June 1988, 13–15.

TACTICAL OPERATIONS CENTER

The tactical operations center, or TOC, is the main command post* for U.S. Army units from battalion* to the corps.* It is the nerve center of the unit and directs the unit's action. The TOC's primary purpose is to assist the unit commander in his command and control functions. The members of the commander's staff within the TOC, responsible for their assigned areas of expertise, receive, analyze, coordinate, and disseminate information necessary for mission accomplishment. Typical areas within the TOC include operations, intelligence, personnel, logistics, communications, and a planning cell for future activities. There is no rigid organization or specified physical configuration for a TOC; but each commander organizes his TOC to meet requirements for specific missions.

References. Douglas R. Boulter, "Defending the TOC," *Armor*, March–April 1983, 37–39. Malcolm M. Jameson, "Tactical Operations Center," *Military Review*, November 1956, 52–59.

Kenneth Turner

TACTICS

Tactics is the art of winning battles or engagements (small battles with only cumulative effects). In a broader sense, tactics comprehend actions taken to solve problems that require the creative employment of tools of some sort to achieve an immediate end. Historically, the term has been applied to two sorts of activity found in war. *Minor tactics* has involved the employment of units of a single arm on the battlefield. The methods of minor tactics have been most affected by the evolution of the means of war, the nature of the weapons with which soldiers have been armed, though most often the modification of minor tactics has followed the evolution of technology by some distance. Military men have been almost criminally slow to change their behavior in response to major developments in conditions of the battlefield. The slow adaptation to the effects of rifled musketry is only one of the most prominent examples.

Grand tactics has involved the employment of large units and combined arms on the battlefield by senior commanders. Although grand tactics too has been influenced by technology, prior to the 20th century the effects of changes in weapon capabilities have been indirect. That is, they have been derivative, arising from the limitations or possibilities existing at the level of minor tactics. It is the successes, or at least the effects of the actions of small units, that are the means of the grand tactician.

Minor tactics truly fight. Grand tactics employs combat, seeking to set the conditions of engagements in terms of time, place, relative strength, and duration, to achieve success in battle. Battles, historically, were conceived to be combats isolated in time and space. As industrialization and other social and political developments changed the nature of combat in the 19th century, battles tended to be prolonged and less identifiable in strict terms of time and space. Minor tactics tended to become the province of smaller and smaller elements, as formations became articulated in response to the effects of firepower. Today, squad* and team leaders (leaders of five to ten men) practice minor tactics. They employ fire effects directly against the enemy. Company* commanders (leaders of 100 men) employ units and effects of all arms. The concepts of grand tactics and minor tactics have become merged into the single term "tactics," used to describe the methods of direct combat with an enemy.

References. J.F.C. Fuller, *The Conduct of War, 1789–1961*, 1961. Archer Jones, *The Art of War in the Western World*, 1987. Tom Wintringham, *The Story of Weapons and Tactics from Troy to Stalingrad*, 1943.

Richard Swain

TA-50

TA-50 is a soldier term for field equipment—rucksack,* equipment belt, ammunition pouches, suspenders, and so on—in use since the 1960s. The term is derived from the Common Table of Allowances* (CTA) 50–900, the quartermaster* supply document listing of all common individual equipment items.

TA-50 is commonly used to refer to web gear,* LCE (load-carrying equipment), and LBE (load-bearing equipment).

Stephen C. McGeorge

TANK DESTROYER, M10

The tank destroyer, M10, was one in a series of early World War II* expedients designed to counter the German panzer threat. Standardized in May 1942 and originally designated the three-inch gun motor carriage, the M10 was a versatile and reliable modification to the standard M4A2 Sherman medium tank chassis. It mounted the high velocity three-inch M7 gun in an open-top, hand-operated, 360-degree traversable turret. The M10 had an operational weight of thirty-two tons, including a crew of five and fifty-four rounds of three-inch ammunition. Its principal disadvantages were its weight and lack of power traverse for the turret. Built in two versions, the M10 was produced by both General Motors and Ford Motor Company. A 375-horsepower, twin-six diesel engine powered the General Motors version, giving it a top speed of thirty miles per hour, with a maximum 50 percent grade-climbing ability. The M10's fording depth was thirty-six inches. The M10A1 variant produced by Ford Motor Company was powered by a five-hundred-horsepower Ford V-8 tank engine, providing approximately the same performance as the GM engine.

References. Charles M. Baily, *Faint Praise*, 1983. Emory A. Dunham, *Tank Destroyer History*, 1946. Christopher R. Gabel, *Seek, Strike, and Destroy*, 1985.

David Zoellers

TANK DESTROYER, M18

In early 1942, the Tank Destroyer Board began the search for the "ideal tank destroyer" to replace the M10. The Ordnance Department looked at some 200 proposed designs before selecting the T49 for further development. The T49 met the basic mobility specifications using a Christie-type suspension, two Buick engines, and a 57 mm gun. When Brigadier General Andrew Bruce, commander of the Tank Destroyer Center, insisted on a 75 mm gun, the carriage was redesigned and designated the T67. By January 1943, when the War Department* ordered the first 1,000 T70s, the new 76 mm gun had been adopted, along with numerous modifications to the chassis, including a Wright radial engine that replaced the two Buicks. Even after the new M18—the official designation—went into production, modifications continued, 157 in all. The M18 was the first armored fighting vehicle designed as a tank destroyer. It had a power-traverse turret, was lighter and more maneuverable than its predecessor, and, with a top speed of over forty-five mph, was the fastest tracked vehicle in World War II.* The M18 received its baptism of fire in Italy, where it proved superior in every way to the tank destroyer, M10,* then in general service. The M18 earned the nickname "Hellcat" for its aggressive performance. More than 2,500 Hellcats were built before the War Department canceled production in October 1944.

References. Christopher R. Gabel, *Seek, Strike, and Destroy*, 1985. Lonnie Gill, *Tank Destroyer Forces, World War II*, 1992.

TANK DESTROYER, M36

The M36 tank destroyer was the most heavily gunned of the World War II* antitank vehicles designed to implement the tank destroyer doctrine* of massed, aggressive defense from ambush. As the tank destroyer, M-18,* was being developed, a dispute arose over the arming of the tank destroyer with a 90 mm gun. The Ordnance Department decided to proceed with another variant of the Sherman M4 medium tank,* with a shielded 90 mm antiaircraft gun mounted in place of the turret. This version was cumbersome and ineffective. However, Ordnance Department experiments proved that the 90 mm gun could be adapted to the three-inch gun mount in the turret of a tank destroyer, M10.* Additional modifications resulted in a vehicle that was actually lighter than the M10 and slightly more mobile. The tank destroyer force still objected to the vehicle but had little choice but to accept it.

The M36 was standardized in April 1944 and entered production in June. It shared many components with the M10 tank destroyer and the M4 Sherman tank. It proved itself a valuable addition to the armored vehicle fleet in the Ardennes* the following December. The M36's 90 mm gun was the only mobile gun in the U.S. Army that proved capable of dealing on nearly even terms with the German Panther and Tiger tanks.

References. Charles M. Baily, *Faint Praise*, 1983. Emory A. Dunham, *Tank Destroyer History*, 1946. Christopher R. Gabel, *Seek, Strike, and Destroy*, 1985.

John Broom

TARHE. *See* Flying Crane.

TASK FORCE SMITH

Task Force Smith was the first U.S. Army element to make contact with the North Korean People's Army (NKPA) during the Korean War.* Named after Lieutenant Colonel Charles B. "Brad" Smith, Task Force Smith consisted of 440 officers and men of Smith's 1st Battalion, 21st Infantry, Battery A, 52d Field Artillery Battalion, and other units from the 24th Infantry Division. Smith's battalion was alerted at 2245 hours, 30 June 1950, at Camp Wood, Japan, for deployment to Korea. After moving to Korea by air and sea, Task Force Smith boarded trains and headed north to Taejon. Meeting with Brigadier General John Church, commander of General of the Army Douglas MacArthur's* Advance Command and Liaison Group in Korea (ADCOM), Smith received the following orders: "We have a little action up here (Osan). All we need is some men up here who won't run when they see tanks. We're going to move you up to support the Republic of Korea (ROK) soldiers and give them moral support."

Along with several of his subordinate commanders, Smith conducted a forward reconnaissance and selected an initial blocking position three miles north of Osan. Smith moved his task force forward and by the early hours of 5 July was in position. At 0700 Smith's artillery engaged the lead elements of the NKPA's Fourth Division. The U.S. artillery did not faze the enemy's T-34 (Soviet) tanks, but it did cause the accompanying infantry to dismount and deploy into battle formation. As the T-34s continued south, Task Force Smith engaged them with 2.36-inch rocket launchers (bazookas)* and 75 mm recoilless rifles.* Both were ineffective; many bazooka rockets either failed to detonate because of age or simply bounced off the T-34s' armor plating. One of the 105 mm howitzers of A Battery, 52nd Field Artillery Battery, deployed forward in an antitank ambush role with six high-explosive antitank (HEAT) rounds, succeeded in disabling three T-34s before it was knocked out by enemy fire. Once this gun was eliminated, the T-34s continued southward umimpeded.

By 1000 hours, Task Force Smith was under intense enemy fire, with the enemy infantry attempting to conduct an envelopment. As his position became untenable, Smith withdrew in some disarray, with his troops attempting to withdraw individually or in small groups. By the time Task Force Smith regrouped two days later, it had lost five officers and 148 men killed or missing in action* (MIA). But Task Force Smith had delayed the North Korean advance for several days, buying critical time for the United States to deploy additional forces to Korea.

References. Roy E. Appleman, *South to the Naktong, North to the Yalu*, 1961. Roy K. Flint, "Task Force Smith and the 24th Division," in *America's First Battles, 1776–1965*, ed. Charles E. Heller and William A. Stofft, 1986.

John Edgecomb

TAYLOR, MAXWELL D. (1901–1987)

Maxwell D. Taylor was a daring pioneer of airborne troops in World War II* and later a chief U.S. strategist during the Vietnam War.* Born in Keytesville, Missouri, in 1901, he attended the U.S. Military Academy* and graduated fourth in the class of 1922. Early in World War II Taylor assisted in organizing the 82d Airborne Division* and was its artillery commander in the battle for Sicily. In the fall of 1943, he volunteered for one of the most dangerous missions of the war, when General Dwight D. Eisenhower* needed a highly placed emissary to meet with agents of the Italian premier, Marshal Pietro Badoglio, in German-occupied Rome to determine if that city was vulnerable to a U.S. airborne assault. Taylor infiltrated through the German lines and discovered that an attack would be too risky. His mission gained him much notice and earned him a Silver Star,* command of the 101st Airborne Division,* and promotion to major general.

On D-day, Taylor parachuted with his division into Normandy and later jumped with the 101st into Holland in Operation Market-Garden.* During the Ardennes* campaign in December 1944, Taylor's surrounded unit valiantly held out against the Germans at Bastogne.

From 1955 to 1959, Taylor served as Chief of Staff* of the Army. An ardent but unsuccessful proponent of flexible response,* Taylor emphasised the use of balanced conventional forces in lieu of massive nuclear deterrence. During the Kennedy and Johnson administrations, Taylor assumed a number of important positions, including chairman of the Joint Chiefs of Staff* (1962) and ambassador to the Republic of Vietnam (1964). As advisor to President Lyndon Johnson, Taylor participated in decisions both accelerating the Vietnam War* and, later, in initiating U.S. disengagement. He died in 1987.

References. Douglas Kinnard, *The Certain Trumpet*, 1991. John M. Taylor, *General Maxwell Taylor*, 1989. Maxwell D. Taylor, *Swords and Plowshares*, 1972.

Donald L. Gilmore

TAYLOR, ZACHARY (1784–1850)

Born 1784 in Monticello, Virginia, Zachary Taylor spent his boyhood in Kentucky before enlisting in the Army in 1806. He was commissioned a first lieutenant in the infantry* in 1808 and served almost continuously thereafter, advancing to the rank of major general. Known as "Old Rough and Ready," Taylor commanded troops in the field in the War of 1812,* the Black Hawk War,* and the Second Seminole War,* in which he won promotion to brigadier general. In June 1845, President James Polk ordered Taylor to occupy land on the Mexican border near the Rio Grande. When the Mexican War* began, he captured Matamoros and defeated the Mexicans at Monterrey* on 23 September 1846. As commander of the Army of the Rio Grande, he disobeyed Polk's orders to remain on the defensive, overcoming the army of Antonio Lopez de Santa Anna at Buena Vista.*

Taylor emerged as a hero from the Mexican War and in 1848 won the Whig nomination for the presidency on the fourth ballot. He defeated the Democratic candidate, Lewis Cass, in the general election. Taylor's administration was marked by the signing of the Clayton-Bulwer Treaty, in which the U.S. and England agreed never to obtain exclusive control over the isthmian canal or exercise dominion over any part of Central America. In the developing controversy over slavery, Taylor argued that the territories acquired in the Mexican War should seek statehood without regard to the slavery issue. His attitude, however, was opposed by the southern Whigs. In 1850, while the issue was under debate, Taylor became ill and died.

References. K. Jack Bauer, *Zachary Taylor*, 1985. Brainerd Dyer, *Zachary Taylor*, 1946, 1967. Holman Hamilton, *Zachary Taylor*, 2 vols., 1941–1951.

Michael Davis

TEMPORARY DUTY

The term "temporary duty" (TDY) refers to duty at a location other than a soldier's permanent duty station. Members of the armed forces are detailed by official orders that direct them, after the TDY period, either to return to their permanent duty station or report to a new duty station. TDY is usually associated with duty performed for periods up to 180 days. TDY frequently sends personnel to short-term schools, official meetings and seminars, and temporary assignments with another unit or installation. Normally a service member is provided a travel allowance and reimbursement of extraordinary expenses while on temporary duty.

Reference. Danny M. Branch, "Watch Those TDY Orders!" *TIG Brief*, January–February 1995, 6–7. Lawrence P. Crocker, *Army Officer's Guide*, 46th ed., 1993.

Bill Knight

TEN-IN-ONE RATION

The ten-in-one ration derived its name from the number of soldiers it could feed: it consisted of ten meals in one package, thus it could provide one meal for ten men, two meals for five men, and so forth. While considered a combat ration, the ten-in-one was designated for small-group feeding, such as gun crews and tank crews. Weighing approximately forty-five pounds and requiring a small stove and basic mess gear to prepare, the ten-in-one was generally impractical for frontline units except in static situations. The ten-in-one ration consisted primarily of commercially packaged, brand-name canned goods and accessories, including cigarettes, matches, bulk sugar, and condensed milk. The lunch components were standard K-rations,* but the breakfast and supper menus were group-prepared items, including whole wheat cereal, canned bacon, ham, pork tenderloin, hamburgers, stew, hash, and assorted vegetables. The ten-in-one was probably the most popular of all World War II* field rations.

References. Erna Risch, *The Quartermaster Corps*, vol. 1, 1953. Harold W. Thatcher, *The Development of Special Rations for the Army*, 1944.

Stephen C. McGeorge

TET

On 30 January 1968, the North Vietnamese and Viet Cong (VC) launched a general offensive throughout South Vietnam designed to destroy the Army of the Republic of Vietnam (ARVN) and rally the civilian population for a general uprising against the South Vietnamese government. The communist forces struck five major cities, thirty-six provincial capitals, sixty-four district capitals, and fifty hamlets. In addition, they attacked Ton Son Nhut Air Base and penetrated the U.S. Embassy compound in Saigon.

Both communist and South Vietnamese leaders had agreed to a cease-fire to celebrate Tet, the beginning of the lunar new year and an important holiday for Vietnamese as a period of ancestor worship. Despite the cease-fire, however, military intelligence had received indications of an impending attack. This intelligence was disregarded, as U.S. commanders did not believe the enemy capable of launching a major attack. Furthermore, the commanders were focused on the siege of the U.S. Marines at Khe Sanh. U.S. and ARVN troops quickly drove the communist forces from the cities, except for Hue, which was occupied until 25 February. Hue's liberation came too late for some 5,800 civilians, many of whom had been executed by the North Vietnamese and Viet Cong. Losses in the offensive were approximately 52,000 Communists, 11,600 ARVN soldiers, and 9,300 U.S. and other free-world forces.

Although a decisive military defeat for the North, the results of Tet were far reaching. After Tet, U.S. public opinion turned further against the war; President Lyndon Johnson refused to authorize the increased level of troop commitments sought by the Military Assistance Command, Vietnam* (MACV). On 31 March, on national television, Johnson announced a partial bombing halt and stated that he would not seek reelection to the presidency.

References. Eric M. Hammel, *Fire in the Streets*, 1991. Don Oberdorfer, *Tet!* 1971. James J. Wirtz, *The Tet Offensive*, 1991.

Richard L. Kiper

THIRD ARMY

The U.S. Third Army was organized in November 1918 at Ligny-en-Barrois, France. It served as the principal army of occupation in Europe following World War I* until it was deactivated on 2 July 1919. Prior to World War II,* Third Army was reactivated at Fort Sam Houston,* Texas. It saw service during World War II in the Normandy, northern France, Rhineland, Ardennes-Alsace, and Central Europe campaigns. Third Army is remembered during this period for Patton's initiative during the Ardennes* and the subsequent crossing of the Rhine River. Following World War II, Third Army remained on occupation duty in France until 1947.

Returning to the United States, Third Army was redesignated as Headquarters and Headquarters Company, Third U.S. Army in 1957 and ultimately inactivated in October 1973. Reactivated at Fort McPherson,* Georgia, on 1 December 1982, Third Army serves as headquarters of the Army component of U.S. Central Command (CENTCOM), a joint service command having responsibility for the Middle East. During Desert Shield and Desert Storm,* Third Army, under the command of Lieutenant General John J. Yeosock, controlled all U.S. ground forces. Today, Third Army is stationed at Fort McPherson, with elements forward in Kuwait serving as the Army's component command for CENTCOM.

References. Robert S. Allen, *Lucky Forward*, 1947. George Forty, *Patton's Third Army at War*, 1978, 1990. Richard Swain, *"Lucky War,"* 1994.

Robert J. Dalessandro

38TH PARALLEL

On 15 August 1945, the 38th degree of north latitude, known as the 38th parallel, became the boundary between North and South Korea. This division reflected the joint decision of the United States and the Soviet Union to divide temporarily the Korean Peninsula, part of the Japanese empire since 1905, into zones of occupation following Japan's surrender at the end of World War II.* Two U.S. Army colonels, Robert T. Stevens and Dean Rusk, serving in the Army General Staffs* Policy Section, Strategy and Planning Group, Operations

Division, and both future cabinet secretaries, determined the 38th parallel as a dividing line. Soviets troops had entered Korea almost a month before the first U.S. units arrived. Thus Steven and Rusk moved deliberately to prevent the Red Army from occupying the entire peninsula. The 38th parallel divided Korea roughly in half and was acceptable to both sides. Although the 38th parallel was militarily indefensible, by October 1945 the Soviets had fortified the border and stopped travel between the two zones. The division remained an international border until the outbreak of the Korean War* in June 1950.

Reference. Roy E. Appleman, *South to the Naktong, North to the Yalu*, 1961.

J. Tom Ashworth

THOMAS, GEORGE H. (1816–1870)

Born in Southhampton County, Virginia, on 31 July 1816, George H. Thomas won an appointment to the U.S. Military Academy* in 1836 and graduated twelfth of forty-two cadets in 1840. Commissioned in the artillery,* he served in the Second Seminole War* and the Mexican War,* where he was twice breveted for gallantry. He returned to West Point as an instructor and later served in the 2d Cavalry. Promoted to lieutenant colonel in April 1861, colonel a week later, and brigadier general of volunteers in August, Thomas commanded a brigade* in the Shenandoah Valley during First Bull Run* and the 1st Division, Army of the Ohio,* from December 1861 to September 1862. Promoted to major general of volunteers in April 1862, he commanded XIV Corps, Army of the Cumberland,* during the Stones River,* Tullahoma,* and Chickamauga* campaigns. At Chickamauga, Thomas earned the sobriquet "the Rock of Chickamauga" for his stand on Snodgrass Hill, where he was credited with saving the Army of the Cumberland* from destruction. Promoted to brigadier general in the Regular Army in October 1863, Thomas commanded the Army of the Cumberland when it drove Braxton Bragg's forces off Missionary Ridge* during the Chattanooga campaign, then led William T. Sherman's* center during the Atlanta campaign.* Subsequently promoted to major general, Thomas commanded the Department of Tennessee until 1867. He died on 28 March 1870 in San Francisco.

References. Freeman Cleaves, *Rock of Chickamauga*, 1949. Francis F. McKinney, *Education in Violence*, 1961, 1991.

Edward Shanahan

TIPPECANOE

The Battle of Tippecanoe on 7 November 1811 marked the beginning of open warfare between Tecumseh's Indian Confederation and the United States, nearly eight months before the declaration of war against Great Britain in the War of 1812.* In 1809, William Henry Harrison,* then governor of the Indian Territory, negotiated with a group of chiefs for the cession of three million acres of Indian lands. Tecumseh, a leader with far-ranging vision, refused to recognize the treaty, claiming that these chiefs could not cede land that all Indians held in common. While Tecumseh was away persuading other tribes to join forces to limit white expansion and preserve the Indian way of life, Harrison decided to act against his territorial seat of power, Prophetstown, at the confluence of the Wabash and Tippecanoe Rivers.

In his absence, Tecumseh's brother Tenskwatawa (the Prophet) led Tecumseh's warrior followers who lived at Prophetstown. With 350 Regulars and 550 Indiana and Kentucky militia volunteers, Harrison approached Prophetstown to assert U.S. sovereignty over the disputed land through a show of force. On 6 November Tenskwatawa sent a delegation proposing a conference the following day. Harrison agreed and encamped his force in a hollow quadrilateral, his men sleeping in battle formation with their weapons at their sides. At 0400, Tecumseh's warriors surrounded Harrison's camp and opened fire. Tenskwatawa had convinced them that the soldiers' bullets were harmless. The troops returned fire and the battle continued into the daylight, when Harrison ordered a mounted attack that broke up the Indian force. Having suffered over 30 percent casualties, Harrison withdrew back to Vincennes, his territorial capital. After this engagement many western Indians joined Tecumseh, who moved toward open alliance with the British. The battle of Tippecanoe convinced many Americans on the western frontier, already suspicious of British involvement with the Indians, that British influence among the Indians must be removed, by force if necessary.

References. Harrison Bird, *War for the West, 1790–1813*, 1971. Fairfax Downey, *Indian Wars of the U.S. Army 1776–1865*, 1963. John K. Mahon, *The War of 1812*, 1972.

Richard Barbuto

TOMB OF THE UNKNOWN SOLDIER

Lying at rest on the grounds of Arlington National Cemetery are the remains of three unknown U.S. soldiers under the inscription, "HERE RESTS IN HONORED GLORY AN AMERICAN SOLDIER KNOWN BUT TO GOD." After World War I,* a grateful nation, seeking a way to remember those who had lost their lives in the nation's wars, established the tomb as a permanent memorial. A World War I serviceman chose the first unknown from the American cemeteries of France, the remains were brought back to the United States and laid to rest on Armistice Day 1921. The tomb was completed ten years later. After the Korean War,* Congress decided to honor the unknowns from that war and World War II.* Again, two veterans chose the unknown soldiers that were to represent their respective wars. In 1958, these remains were laid to rest in Arlington. In 1984, remains representing soldiers lost in Vietnam were laid to rest next to comrades-in-arms, but this body was subsequently removed when evidence of its identity came to light. An honor guard keeps watch over the tomb twenty-four hours a day. Between October and March, sentries change every hour; from April to September, they change every half hour. The tomb, made of polished Colorado marble, is also known as the Tomb of the Unknowns.

References. Philip Bigler, *In Honored Glory*, 1987. John Vincent Hinkel, *Arlington*, 1965. James Edward Peters, *Arlington National Cemetery*, 1986.

Trevor Brown

TORCH

Operation Torch, the November 1942 Allied invasion of North Africa, was the largest amphibious operation attempted to that date in World War II.* Torch was based on several rationale: Soviet insistance on a second front to relieve pressure on them; to bring French colonial possessions into the war against the Axis and prevent their being controlled by the Axis; to open the Mediterranean almost completely to Allied shipping and provide a jump-off point for operations into southern Europe; to relieve pressure on the British Eighth Army in Egypt; and to fulfill President Franklin Roosevelt's political desire to have U.S. troops engaged against Germany by the end of 1942. The U.S. Chiefs of Staff favored a direct cross-Channel attack in early 1943, but the British preferred a peripheral strategy. The final impetus for Operation Torch was the defeat of the British Eighth Army in a spectacular tank battle with German forces at Knightsbridge in Libya on 13 June 1942 and the subsequent fall of Tobruk on 21 June, followed by the rapid advance of Field Marshal Erwin Rommel's army toward Alexandria and the Suez Canal. British intransigence and the lack of Allied resources for a cross-Channel attack convinced the United States to support Operation Torch in 1942.

Torch's objectives were the occupation of Tunisia to prevent reinforcement and resupply of German forces operating in Libya, and the building of a force in French Morocco to strike into Spanish Morocco and protect the Straits of Gibraltar should Spanish or Axis forces threaten there through the Iberian Peninsula. To achieve these goals, U.S. and British assault forces conducted near-simultaneous amphibious landings to seize the ports and airfields at Casablanca, Oran, and Algiers. After buildup and consolidation, forces from Algiers drove east to occupy Tunisia and cut German lines of communications, while forces from Oran and Casablanca joined to establish the striking force in French Morocco to protect Gibraltar. While the landings and buildup were essentially successful, a rapid German response prevented a quick advance by the Allies and caused the U.S. debacle at Kasserine Pass.*

References. William B. Breuer, *Operation Torch*, 1985. Arthur Layton Funk, *The Politics of Torch*, 1974. Norman Gelb, *Desperate Venture*, 1992.

Arthur T. Frame

TOTAL ARMY

The term "Total Army" was coined by General Creighton Abrams* to describe the close integration of the Active Army, Army Reserve* and the National Guard* during his tenure as Chief of Staff.* Abrams's intent was to delegate sufficient support assets to the reserve components to ensure that in any future large military endeavor, the reserve components would have to be called to active duty very quickly after the commitment of the active forces. Abrams's purpose was to preclude the Vietnam-type situation of very limited call-ups of reserve components, in order to ensure that the nation as a whole would be committed to any future conflict. This was accomplished by transferring certain combat-critical functions, especially those of a logistical nature, to the reserve components. Examples of such units are postal companies and detachments, civil affairs* units, psychological operations* units, port management units, and water purification units. The concept was broadened under subsequent Chiefs of Staff to include round-out or round-up reserve component combat brigades for active divisions,* as well as increasing the readiness of reserve component units by speeding the fielding of modern equipment to Reserve and Guard units.

References. Philip A. Brehm, *Restructuring the Army*, 1992. Robert L. Petruschell, James H. Bigelow, and Joseph G. Bolten, *Overview of the Total Army Design and Cost System*, 1993.

John Broom

TOTAL QUALITY MANAGEMENT

In 1988, Secretary of Defense* Frank Carlucci mandated Total Quality Management (TQM) for all military services. TQM grew out of a number of systemic problems and failures confronting American business during the increasingly competitive late 1970s and early 1980s. TQM is directed toward the delivery of continuously improved products and services to the final consumer. It employs both new and proven management techniques, including decentralization of decision making, efficiency and elimination of waste, and the philosophy that quality must be built into a product or service from its inception. To achieve TQM, all assets from workers to management must be dedicated to this goal. TQM was not just another "buzzword" or a fad program. While Carlucci's mandate most immediately affected Department of Defense* (DOD) agencies that dealt or interfaced with outside industry and contractors on a regular basis, such as the U.S. Army's Acquisition Corps,* the essential principles of Total Quality Management would influence Army leaders as they built the Army of the next century.

References. Frank L. Lewis, *Introduction to Total Quality Management in the Federal Government*, 1991. John Rhea, "Total Quality Management," *National Defense*, January 1990, 25–27. James H. Saylor, *TQM Field Manual*, 1992.

TRAINING AND DOCTRINE COMMAND

To increase efficiency and deal with a number of pressing issues, in 1973 the U.S. Army reorganized the U.S. Continental Army Command* (CONARC), which supervised all Army activities ranging from recalling units from Vietnam to overseeing the Reserve Officer Training Corps* (ROTC) program. CONARC was divided into two organizations: U.S. Army Forces Command* (FORSCOM), which would oversee the operation of units assigned to the United States; and the U.S. Army Training and Doctrine Command (TRADOC), which assumed responsibility for military training and policy. All but two Army training centers and schools, the U.S. Military Academy* and the U.S. Army War College,* came under TRADOC authority. In 1976, TRADOC published FM 100–5, *Operations*, providing a uniform policy for field operations. Subsequent iterations of FM 100–5 continue to define the way the U.S. Army will fight in the event of war. TRADOC headquarters is currently located at Fort Monroe,* Virginia.

References. William E. DePuy, "TRADOC," *Army*, October 1973, 31–34. Frederick M. Franks, Jr., "TRADOC at 20," *Army*, October 1993, 46–55. Paul H. Herbert, *Deciding What Has to Be Done*, 1988.

Rebecca S. Witte

TRANSPORT AIRCRAFT

At the beginning of World War II,* the U.S. Army adapted existing civil air transport aircraft for military use. Notable examples of transport aircraft utilized prior to the establishment of the U.S. Air Force in 1947 were the Curtiss Commando (C-46), Douglas Skytrain (C-47),* and the relatively large four-engine Douglas Skymaster (C-54). These rugged aircraft were used in all theaters by both the U.S. Army Air Forces* and the U.S. Navy, as well as several U.S. allies. In fact, some of these aircraft are still flying today, soldiering on in their original roles. Cargo areas of these types could be configured in many different ways. Seats and litters could be hung from the interior walls for transporting troops and casualties. Boxes, barrels, and crates were secured to the cargo bay deck with straps. Bulk deliveries of bagged items and commissary stores— potatoes, fresh vegetables, or flour, for example—could simply be stacked in the cargo bay until full, thus minimizing the danger of inflight slippage and obviating any requirement to tie down the cargo. If items such as trucks or storage tanks proved too large for the aircraft's doors, these items were cut apart or disassembled and rewelded upon arrival at their destination. In addition to aircraft built expressly as transports, military necessity also prompted the conversion of bombers to the transport role. Notable examples here include the Boeing B-17, the North American B-25, and the Consolidated B-24, all of which did transport service during World War II. With the establishment of the U.S. Air Force as a separate service in 1947, military airlift and all fixed-wing transport aircraft became the Air Force's responsibility.

References. John D. Carter, "The Air Transport Command," in *The Army Air Corps in World War II*, vol. 7, ed. Wesley Frank Craven and James Lea Cate, 1958. Clayton Knight, *Lifeline in the Sky*, 1957. Charles E. Miller, *Airlift Doctrine*, 1988.

Keith B. Bartsch

TRANSPORTATION CORPS

Before World War II,* several branches shared responsibility for transportation assets in the U.S. Army. The unprecedented nature of the mobilization in 1941 and early 1942, however, quickly demonstrated the inadequacy of this system. In March, 1942, the Army established the Transportation Service to deal with its growing transportation needs and the requirement to work even more closely with the U.S. Navy, whose ships would carry the materiel and men to the battlefields of the world. The need for even more centralization and control of transportation assets and the rapid expansion of the transportation service itself led to the establishment of the Transportation Corps on 31 July 1942. The Transportation Corps has become one of the key combat service support branches in the U.S. Army. Transportation officers have been involved in the planning and implementation of every operation and deployment, whether overseas or in the continental United States, since 1942. The branch insignia*—a ship's wheel encircling a flanged wheel on a rail, a wing, and a U.S. highway marker shield—is indicative of the varied missions the Transportation Corps is called on to undertake. The U.S. Army Transportation School and headquarters of the Transportation Corps are located at Fort Eustis, Virginia.

References. Benjamin King, Richard C. Briggs, and Eric R. Criner, *Spearhead of Logistics*, 1994. Howard F. Schlitz, "Army Transportation Corps," *Defense Transportation*, September–October 1970, 30–34.

Trevor Brown

TRAPDOOR SPRINGFIELD

The Trapdoor Springfield was the standard long arm of the U.S. Army from the early 1870s until replaced by the Krag-Jorgenson* in the 1890s. Based on modification of the 1861 and 1863 model .58-caliber rifled muskets,* the First Allin Alteration (Allin Conversion*) allowed for the breech-loading of a metallic cartridge by means of a forward-hinged "trapdoor" just in front of a hammer mechanism (the release catch replaced the muzzle-loader's percussion nipple). In 1866 the older musket was rechambered for caliber .50–70 ammunition and issued to infantry units. The first effective use of this weapon was at the Hayfield* and Wagon Box* fights (1–2 August 1867) along the Bozeman Trail,* where their rapid-fire devastated attacking Sioux and Arapaho warriors, who expected to face the slower-firing muzzle-loading muskets.* In 1873, the Springfield Armory began producing a long rifle chambered for a .45–70 cartridge and a carbine firing a .45–55 cartridge for cavalry use. Early models used copper-cased, Benet cup, inside-primed cartridges, which were found to be irregular in manufacture—the thin-walled copper was prone to heat expansion and rupture in rapid-fire situations. The use of leather-loop cartridge belts, which promoted the formation of verdigris on the rounds, compounded this problem and contributed to the incidence of fouled and jammed weapons. Effective range was claimed to be 1,100 yards, but accuracy was doubtful beyond 300 yards. The 1873 Trapdoor Springfield remained in service until the end of the century.

References. Kenneth M. Hammer, *The Springfield Carbine on the Western Frontier*, 1970. James E. Hicks, *U.S. Military Firearms, 1776–1956*, 1962.

Fred J. Chiaventone

TRENCH FOOT

Trench foot, or immersion foot, is a condition similar to frostbite caused by enforced immobility of the extremities in cold and wet conditions for prolonged periods. The first symptom is a burning sensation; if untreated, the feet become numb, blacken, and rot. Although the malady had been noted during Napoleon's Moscow campaign and among British soldiers before Sevastopol, it became known as trench foot during World War I,* when conditions in the trenches caused thousands of cases and decimated many units. Armies tried to combat trench foot by prescribing changes of socks and footwear, duckboards to keep soldiers out of the water, and rotation of units to rest camps in the rear. Trench foot continued to be a serious medical problem in World War II*; it accounted for more than 4 percent of all nonbattle injuries. In Italy and Europe, trenchfoot threatened to overwhelm the medical support system. Similar conditions were known as jungle rot in the Pacific during World War II and "paddy foot" during the Vietnam War.*

References. Graham A. Cosmas and Albert E. Cowdrey, *The Medical Department*, 1992. Albert E. Cowdrey, *Fighting for Life*, 1994.

Kelvin Crow

TRENTON

George Washington* displayed his military genius by mounting an assault on Hessian-occupied Trenton, New Jersey, on Christmas Day, 1776. He chose a time when his army's fortunes were at a low ebb—it had been routed from New York, and his troops were leaving as their enlistments expired—and a season in which 18th-century armies considered it bad form to campaign. Surprise was essential to Washington's plans. Under cover of darkness, his men crossed the ice-choked, flooded Delaware River. The freezing men then faced a nine-mile march to Trenton. After raking the town's street with artillery, the Continentals went in with bayonets* among the confused Hessians, recovering from a traditional German all-day Christmas Eve celebration. After about three-quarters of an hour, the mortally wounded Hessian commander, Colonel Johann (or Johannes) Rall, ended the fighting with the surrender of his sword. The Continentals counted thirty officers, 861 troopers, and "a band of musicians" as prisoners. Trenton not only retrieved rebel military fortunes in the Pennsylvania–New Jersey area of operations but gave new heart to the patriots when they needed it most.

References. William Dwyer, *The Day Is Ours!* 1983. Samuel S. Smith, *The Battle of Trenton*, 1965. Kemble Widmer, *The Christmas Campaign*, 1975.

Stanley Sandler

TRIANGULAR DIVISION

"Triangular division" was an informal designation given to the infantry* division* organization employed by the U.S. Army during World War II.* The term was derived from the division structure: three infantry regiments,* or regimental combat teams,* constituted the division's major maneuver combat elements. With about 14,000 men, this triangular structure proved less cumbersome and more flexible than the four-regiment, 28,000-man square division* of World War I.* It also allowed commanders to engage the enemy with most of their combat strength (two regiments) and still maintain a substantial reserve of one regiment—the classic two up, one back* tactical deployment still widely used by the Army today.

Lieutenant General Lesley J. McNair,* chief of Army Ground Forces* during World War II, is recognized as the chief architect of the triangular division. His experience during World War I and during a series of War Department* reorganization studies in the 1930s convinced him that the infantry division must be lean and offensively oriented, unencumbered by anything not essential. Although modified somewhat in practice, McNair's ideas proved generally sound. The triangular division proved sufficiently flexible and effective to achieve victory in all combat theaters.

References. John C. Binkley, "A History of US Army Force Structuring," *Military Review*, February 1977, 67–82. Kent Roberts Greenfield, Robert R. Palmer, and Bell I. Wiley, *The Organization of Ground Combat Troops*, 1947. Jonathan M. House, *Toward Combined Arms Warfare*, 1984.

Scott McMeen

TROOP

Throughout its early history, the U.S. Army officially designated the subordinate units of infantry* and cavalry* regiments* as companies. In 1883, the Army officially adopted "troop" to replace company as the subordinate unit of the cavalry regiment. Many historians and writers, however, use the term when referring to cavalry units before 1883. The Army has retained the term "troop" for company-sized units in armored cavalry squadrons* and armored cavalry regiments.*

References. James A. Sawicki, *Cavalry Regiments of the US Army*, 1985. Randy Steffen, *The Horse Soldiers*, vol. 3, 1978.

Andrew N. Morris

TROPIC LIGHTNING

The 25th Infantry Division (ID), "Tropic Lightning," was constituted in August 1941 at Schofield Barracks,* Hawaii. Throughout its history the 25th ID has been associated with Hawaii and the Pacific theater, and it is still stationed at Schofield Barracks. The 25th ID fought on Guadalcanal,* the Northern Solomons, and Luzon in World War II,* in the Korean War* from 1950 to 1953, and in the Vietnam War* from 1966 to 1971. The division* derives its nickname from its distinctive insignia, a yellow lightning flash on a red taro leaf for the shoulder patch. The division crest* displays a red and gold lightning bolt in front of an erupting volcano surrounded by two palm leaves. The lightning bolt is symbolic of the manner in which the division carries out its missions. In Vietnam, U.S. troops dubbed the Tropic Lightning Division the "Electric Strawberry" (the shape of a taro leaf resembles the outline of a strawberry), a term that could be used both pejoratively and respectfully.

References. Eric M. Bergerud, *Red Thunder, Tropic Lightning*, 1993. Richard Fitzpatrick, Bill Baumann, and Duquesne Wolf, *Twenty-fifth Infantry Division*, 1988.

TRUCKS

U.S. Army efforts to take advantage of motor trucks as a means of military transport date back as far as 1900, with the most energetic proponents of mechanization being the technical service branches, such as the Signal Corps.* The first operational test of motor trucks took place in 1916–1917 during the Punitive Expedition,* when Brigadier General John J. Pershing's* forces utilized a bewildering variety of motor vehicles in the pursuit of Pancho Villa. Early machines proved unreliable, a situation compounded by the lack of standardization, resulting in extreme difficulty in managing spare parts and repair facilities. Nonetheless, Ford, Dodge, White, and FWD (Four Wheel Drive Company) machines seemed the most promising makes based on experience in Mexico.

In World War I,* mechanization became a necessity. The Army again used an amazing array of vehicles, both stateside and overseas with the American Expeditionary Force* (AEF). Again spare parts problems were predictable. Each branch of the Army procured more or less whatever was available in the way of commercial motor trucks. For example, the Medical Department* was responsible for motor ambulance procurement and settled on GMC to produce a standard heavy ambulance, while the Ford Model T was the basis of the light ambulance. The Ordnance Department* procured vehicles relating specifically to ordnance material, such as Holt tractors for heavy artillery prime-movers and Dodge and White trucks for use as mobile repair shop vehicles. General transport vehicles were the responsibility of the Quartermaster Corps,* and they initially included virtually every make then in production. In all, the Army was using roughly 300 makes and models of trucks in 1917–1918.

The need for a standard, general-purpose cargo truck was clearly evident. The solution came when U.S. truck manufacturers cooperated in the development of the Standard B, or Liberty, Truck in 1917. Some fifteen truck manufacturers, working from one basic design provided by the Quartermaster Corps, built approximately 9,450 trucks, 7,600 of which were delivered overseas. The first series' rated capacity was three tons; later series were rated at five tons. The Standard B holds the best claim to be the Army's first standardized cargo truck; with minor improvements, it continued to serve the Army into the early 1930s.

Although the industrial capacity of the U.S. auto industry was expanding for war prior to the attack on Pearl Harbor, little progress was made in developing a newer standard-model Army truck before 1941. By 1941, however, the Army had settled on a design for its most famous transport vehicle, the 2½-ton 6×6 truck, the "deuce and a half,"* known as the "workhorse of the Army." Over 800,000 deuce and a halfs were built, the majority by GMC (Models GMC-CCKW 352 and 353). Nevertheless, requirements always exceeded production capabilities. The deuce and a half remained the primary tactical truck for decades, and many of the trucks produced during World War II* remained in service in allied armies as late as the 1980s. Except for the newer models with diesel engines, the deuce and a halfs of the 1960s and 1970s looked remarkably like their predecessors. The general trend in military trucks has been toward larger cargo capacities (five tons and greater) and improved off-road mobility. In addition, many larger-capacity cargo trucks now include some type of built-in material handling equipment, such as hoists, lifts, and telescoping cranes.

References. Marc K. Blackburn, "A New Form of Transportation," 1992. Fred Crismon, *U.S. Military Wheeled Vehicles*, 1983. Erna Risch, *The Quartermaster Corps*, vol. 1, 1953.

Stephen C. McGeorge

TULLAHOMA CAMPAIGN

After numerous exhortations from the president, secretary of war,* and general in chief,* Major General William S. Rosecrans's Army of the Cumberland* finally advanced from its position in and around Murfreesboro, Tennessee, on 25 June 1863. In a campaign of maneuver that lasted until the Fourth of July, in some of the worst rains that middle Tennessee had ever experienced, the Federals forced General Braxton Bragg's Confederate Army of Tennessee out of its prepared positions around Shelbyville and Tullahoma, Tennessee, across the Cumberland Plateau, and into Chattanooga. The total cost to Rosecran's army was 560 men. Bragg lost over 1,634 prisoners, but his corps* actually finished the campaign stronger than it started, thanks to the soldiers who returned to the colors when they heard that their army was under attack. As a partial response to this catastrophe, the Confederate government ultimately reinforced Bragg's army with units from both Virginia and Mississippi. On the other hand, Rosecrans made enemies in Lincoln's administration by his prickliness. They would wait for a stumble to seek their revenge.

References. Benjamin Franklin Cooling, *Fort Donelson's Legacy*, 1997. William B. Feis, "The Deception of Braxton Bragg," *Blue & Gray*, October 1992, 10–21.

Andrew N. Morris

TUNNEL RAT

The term "tunnel rat" was first used in Vietnam in the early 1960s to describe a soldier who searched enemy tunnels. Extensive tunnel systems, often dating back to the 1940s, were used throughout Vietnam from Khe Sahn to Cu Chi, where the soil and the water table allowed; they were major obstacles to finding and engaging Viet Cong forces. Tunnels were dug in as many as four layers, with many chambers, sometimes running for miles. Booby traps, dead ends, and concealed passageways hampered penetration of these systems. The tunnel rats' effectiveness later led to the establishment of units within divisions* to carry out the mission systematically. Combat in the tunnels was personal and deadly. Tunnel rats explored with only a flashlight, a knife or a bayonet,* and a pistol.

References. Tom Mangold and John Penycate, *Tunnel Warfare*, 1987, and *The Tunnels of Cu Chi*, 1985.

William H. Carnes

25TH INFANTRY DIVISION. *See* Tropic Lightning.

201 FILE

Officially called a DA Form 201, Field Personnel File, this "hard copy" folder has defined a soldier's legal military status since the late 1940s. It includes a record of the soldier's enlistment date(s), security clearance, promotions, awards, orders, military occupation specialty* (MOS) awards and orders, and Servicemen's Group Life Insurance. Information is divided into three broad areas: a permanent section, which contains promotions and orders; an action-pending section, which includes requests for overseas assignments; and a temporary section, containing all material pertaining to a soldier's current assignment. Material in the temporary section is transferred to other parts of the 201 file as given to the soldier, as appropriate, or at the end of an assignment. The current 201 file is under review and is expected to be replaced shortly with electronic storage devices, either CD-ROM or credit-card style.

Reference. Bill G. Evans, "Personnel Paperwork," *Army*, May 1967, 52, 58–60, 64.

William H. Carnes

TWO UP—ONE BACK

"Two up—one back" describes a widely employed tactical formation, well suited to the triangular division* and used by nearly every command echelon from platoon* through corps.* In both offensive and defensive operations, commanders typically place two of their major subordinate units forward, in contact with the enemy, and keep the third one in reserve. In the offense, one of the forward units is designated for the main attack and receives the bulk of the command's resources to assist it. The other unit stands ready to be committed when and where the commander directs. The reserve may also be used to deal with unforseen emergencies. In the defense, the commander typically divides his assigned sector between two of his subordinate units, keeping his third unit in reserve, to be committed as he directs.

The term sometimes includes the words "scouts out." This implies the deployment of a reconnaissance/security force forward of the main body, with the mission of providing information on the enemy defenses or early warning of the enemy's approach. The two up—one back formation is so commonly used that it has become a cliché, but its inherent simplicity and flexibility continue to make it popular and effective.

Reference. William E. DePuy, " 'One-Up and Two-Back'?" *Army*, January 1980, 20–25. Harold G. Moore and Joseph L. Galloway, *We Were Soldiers Once . . . and Young*, 1992.

Scott McMeen

U

UH-60. *See* Black Hawk.

UNIFIED COMMANDS

Unified commands, first described and authorized in the National Security Act of 1947,* provide for operational control of the nation's combat forces. A unified command, headed by a commander in chief (CINC), is composed of forces from two or more services. These commands are normally organized to conduct operations either within a specific geographical area or with a strategic capability, and they have broad continuing missions. The number and type of unified commands are not set by law or regulation. The president and the Joint Chiefs of Staff* share the responsibility to establish unified commands. The Unified Command Plan (UCP), approved by the president, establishes the commands, outlines the missions and specific tasks, and designates the geographic area of responsibility, if appropriate. The UCP also outlines the common responsibilities of the CINCs.

Currently, there are nine unified commands. Five are geographical: U.S. Joint Forces Command (previously Atlantic Command ACOM), Central Command (CENTCOM), European Command (EUCOM), Pacific Command (PACOM), and Southern Command (SOUTHCOM). Four have worldwide responsibilities: Space Command (SPACECOM), Special Operations Command (SOCOM), Strategic Command (STRATCOM), and Transportation Command (TRANSCOM). In addition, unified commands have subunified commands: U.S. Forces, Korea (USFK) and Special Operations Command, Pacific (SOCPAC) are two examples.

References. Joseph W. Prueher, "Warfighting CINCS in a New Era," *Joint Force Quarterly*, Autumn 1996, 48–52. Charles S. Robb, "Examining Alternative UCP Structures," *Joint Force Quarterly*, Winter 1996–1997, 85–93.

J.G.D. Babb

UNIFORM

A uniform is a distinctive garb or dress of the same material, cut, style, and color worn by all members of military or naval force. Since ancient times, commanders have dressed their armies in like clothing and accoutrements to foster discipline, pride, and esprit de corps, differentiate friend from foe, and present an imposing facade to the enemy. Beginning with the uniform George Washington* designed for his troops in the Continental Army,* the evolution of U.S. Army uniforms has reflected the external influences during each period of time, the practical requirements of the diverse environments in which the Army has operated, and progress in textiles and military technology. *AR 670-1, Wear and Appearance of Army Uniforms and Insignia* currently prescribes the authorized uniform for officers and enlisted personnel in the U.S. Army. There are three basic types of uniforms: dress, service, and utility. Service uniforms are further defined as Class A, B, and C. Each uniform has a specific purpose and function. Some uniforms, such as the Army blues, reflects the heritage of Army uniforms, while others (the Class B uniform, for example) have been designed for the modern workplace. Today, proposed uniform changes initiated throughout the chain of command are reviewed and approved by the Army uniform board.

References. John R. Elting and Michael McAlee, eds., *Military Uniforms in America*, 1974–1978. Martin Windrow and Gerry Embleton, *Military Dress of North America, 1665–1970*, 1973.

UNIFORM CODE OF MILITARY JUSTICE

Enacted by Congress in May 1950, the Uniform Code of Military Justice (UCMJ) is that portion of Title 10, S801 *et seq. United States Code*, that concerns the administration of the military justice system. Specific provisions address apprehension and restraint, nonjudicial punishment, court-martial jurisdiction, composition of courts-martial, pretrial procedure, trial procedure, sentences, post-trial procedure and review of courts-martial, punitive articles, miscellaneous provisions, and the Court of Military Appeals.*

References. William T. Generous, Jr., *Swords and Scales*, 1973. Frederick Barnays Wiener, *The Uniform Code of Military Justice*, 1950.

UNIFORM MILITIA ACT. *See* Militia Act of 1792.

UNIT FUND

Every U.S. Army unit from company* to major command is authorized a unit fund to purchase supplies, services, and equipment items not available through government sources but that contribute to the entertainment, recreation, comfort, and education of unit members. Profits from post nonappropriated fund (NAF) activities,* such as post exchanges and theaters, support unit funds, which are typically used to purchase sports equipment, day-room furnishings, awards and prizes, and distinctive unit insignia* for the good of the entire organization. The unit commander has sole responsibility for operation and maintenance of the unit fund, although he may appoint a custodian. A unit fund council, composed of at least one officer or warrant officer* and two enlisted person appointed by the commander, meet quarterly to advise the commander and oversee the fund. *AR 215-1, The Administration of Morale, Welfare and Recreation Activities and Nonappropriated Fund Intrumentalities* and *AR 215-2, The Management ond Operation of Army Morale, Welfare and Recreation Activities and Nonappropriated Fund Intrumentalities* govern the maintenance and accountability of unit funds.

References. Lawrence P. Crocker, *Army Officer's Guide*, 46th ed., 1993. C. M. Virtue, *Company Administration*, 22d ed., 1953.

UNITED SERVICE ORGANIZATIONS

In World War I,* a number of volunteer organizations provided social and recreational support services for American troops in the United States and Europe. When the nation began mobilizing for World War II,* some of these organizations stepped forward again to serve America's servicemen, but the unprecedented magnitude of the mobilization meant that no single agency could provide the needed services. When President Franklin Roosevelt determined that welfare and recreational services should be provided by civilian rather than government agencies, six organizations formed the United Service Organizations—universally known as the USO. Since 1941, in both war and peace, the USO has served men and women of the U.S. armed forces around the world. While the government occasionally makes facilities available on military bases, the USO is supported solely by voluntary contributions from the American people. The USO is best known for sponsoring celebrity road shows; Bob Hope, Marilyn Monroe, Martha Raye, and scores of other big-name stars have reached out to American service people from Korea to Desert Storm.* The six organizations that make up the United Service Organizations are the Young Men's Christian Association (YMCA), National Catholic Community Service, National Jewish Welfare Board, Young Women's Christian Association (YWCA), the Salvation Army, and the Travelers Aid Association.

References. Frank Cox, "USO: Serving Those Who Serve," *Soldiers*, February 1990, 50–52. David Millman, "Everyone's USO," U.S. Naval Institute *Proceedings*, December 1997, 74–76.

UNITED STATES ARMY

The United States Army, or U.S. Army, is the army or armies referred to in Article I, Section 8 of the Constitution of the United States. The term "Army of the United States" is frequently encountered in the historical literature and may be used synonymously with United States Army, but there are also instances in which the former refers to a component of the United States Army. In August 1789, Congress maintained continuity with the past by creating a War Department* similar to that which had existed under the Articles of Confederation and confirming Henry Knox, secretary of the previous department, as secretary of war.* In September 1789, Congress adopted the First American Regiment and several artillery* battalions,* the first units to serve under the banner of the United States of America. Today the United States Army includes the Regular Army, the National Guard,* and the Army Reserve,* all persons appointed, enlisted, or inducted in the Army without specification of component; and all persons serving in the Army under call or conscription under any provision of law, including members of the National Guard of the states, territories, and the District of Columbia, when in the service of the United State pursuant to call as provided by law.

References. Maurice Matloff, ed., *American Military History*, rev. ed., 1989. Allan R. Millett and Peter Maslowski, *For the Common Defense*, 1984. Russell F. Weigley, *History of the United States Army*, 1967.

UNITED STATES ARMY, EUROPE

United States Army, Europe (USAREUR), is the major command responsible for logistical and administrative support of U.S. Army units operating in Europe, Africa, and portions of the Middle East. It is a component of European Command (EUCOM) and is combined with Headquarters, Seventh Army.* USAREUR's origins can be found in European Theater of Operations,* U.S. Army (ETOUSA), created in 1942 to control forces assigned to the forthcoming invasion of Europe and placed under the command of General Dwight D. Eisenhower.* Currently, USAREUR is headquartered in Heidelberg, Germany.

References. Robert D. Howe and William D. O'Malley, *USAREUR Force Structure*, 1993. Michael Skinner, *USAREUR*, 1989.

Kelvin Crow

U.S. ARMY PARACHUTE TEAM. *See* Golden Knights.

UNITED STATES ARMY RESERVE COMMAND

The U.S. Army Reserve Command (USARC) was established in 1991 to command, control, and support all U.S. Army Reserve* (USAR) troops in the continental United States, except psychological operations,* civil affairs,* and special forces* units. In 1995, USARC reorganized its command and control by replacing twenty Army Reserve Commands (ARCOMs) with ten Regional Support Commands (RSCs), three Regional Support Groups (RSGs), and thirty-seven specialized commands/units (institutional training divisions, exercise divisions, general officer commands, garrison support units, etc.). Three ARCOMs were still located outside of the continental United States: Hawaii, Puerto Rico, and Germany. The RSCs command, control, and support units in given geographical areas. The others command, control, and support units in specific functions, such as medical, logistical, engineer, training, and installation or base operations, to name a few. This recent reorganization brings USARC in line with the new end-strength, enhances its ability to train and mobilize Army Reserve units, and reflects its expertise in combat support and combat service support functions.

References. Frank A. Edens, "Major Command or Major Subordinate Command Is Question for Army Reserve," *Officer*, December 1992, 35–41, and "Strong and Ready," *Officer*, January 1994, 13–15.

Bill Knight

U.S. ARMY SERGEANTS MAJOR ACADEMY

The Vietnam War* exposed a number of weaknesses in noncommissioned officer* (NCO) preparation in the U.S. Army, especially the "Shake 'n' Bake"* system, which turned out enlisted leaders without sufficient seasoning in the military. After reexamining its needs, the Army created the NCO education system, a progressive system of schools to prepare NCOs from corporal (E-4) to command sergeant major (E-9) for their increasing leadership roles. In 1972, the U.S. Army established the U.S. Army Sergeants Major Academy (USASMA) at Fort Bliss,* Texas, the highest level in the NCO education system. USASMA's mission is to prepare NCOs selected for sergeant major for positions of greater responsibility throughout the defense establishment. The student body includes U.S. Army, Marine, Navy, Air Force, and Coast Guard NCOs and qualified international NCOs. The curriculum focuses on leadership, resource management, training, and military operations. The academy also offers a command sergeant major's course, a first sergeant's* course, a staff battle NCO course, and a command sergeants major spouses' course. In 1987, the Sergeants Major Academy moved from temporary quarters to a permanent, modern facility with two academic wings, a headquarters and administrative wing, a lecture center, and a learning resource center and library.

References. L. James Binder, "Conscience, Voice of a Corps," *Army*, July 1992, 29–30. Jamie Cavazos and Floyd Harrington, "Ultimate for NCOs," *Soldiers*, August 1976, 22–25.

U.S. ARMY TECHNICAL MOBILITY REQUIREMENTS BOARD. *See* Howze Board.

U.S. DISCIPLINARY BARRACKS

Established at Fort Leavenworth,* Kansas, in buildings originally used as a quartermaster depot, the United States Military Prison began operation on 15 May 1875. Prior to this time, military prisoners were incarcerated in various regional prisons and lock-ups, often under deplorable and inhumane conditions. Twice in its history the institution came under control of the U.S. Department of Justice: from 1895 until 1906 it was used for civilian prisoners, and in 1929 it again passed to civilian control as the Leavenworth Penitentiary Branch. The facility reverted to U.S. Army control in November 1940 and was reestablished as the U.S. Disciplinary Barracks (USDB, or DB).

The DB is today the only maximum security confinement facility in the Department of Defense,* and it is the oldest penal institution in the federal system. Its maximum capacity is 1,503 inmates, although the average population is only 1,360. The majority of inmates are incarcerated for their first offense; the average sentence length is just over twelve years. Prisoners represent all branches of the armed services and all ranks and grades from private (E-1) to colonel (0-6). The most prominent prior rank of offenders is sergeant (E-5), with an average of seventy-seven months of service prior to commission of offense. Upon arrival, most new inmates are placed in what the DB calls medium custody. With good behavior and willingness to work in one of the DB's industries or services, inmates may be elevated to minimum custody, still within the prison walled area but able to enjoy increased privileges. The DB provides a range of academic and vocational training, available to inmates on a voluntary basis. The highest-custody grade, called trustee custody, is dependent on progress during confinement and the nature of the offense. Trustees are housed outside the walled area of the prison. Due to the age and condition of the existing facility, a new DB is currently being constructed adjacent to the original prison.

References. Charles G. Cavanaugh, Jr., "Behind the Walls," *Soldiers*, June 1983, 48–52. Lisa DeCicco, "Disciplinary Duty," *Soldiers*, August 1992, 6–8. Alan Moore, "Life inside Leavenworth," *Soldiers*, September 1997, 23–25.

Keith B. Bartsch

U.S. ENGINEER SCHOOL. *See* Engineer School of Application.

U.S. INFANTRY AND CAVALRY SCHOOL. *See* School for the Application of Infantry and Cavalry.

U.S. MILITARY ACADEMY

Established on 16 March 1802, at West Point, New York, the U.S. Military Academy (USMA) sprang from the vision of the nation's founding fathers. It had two imperatives: to produce professional officers and to ensure that they were unshakably loyal to the Constitution. George Washington* thought the former reason paramount, while Thomas Jefferson had the latter concept foremost in mind.

At first the Academy barely survived, but it flourished after the abysmal performance of U.S. arms in the War of 1812* demonstrated the abiding need for ready leaders. Although never without critics, the Academy has had an enormous effect on the Army, and even on the country. Its small size quite belies its importance. The impact—in peace and war—rests in large measure on West Point's adaptation to changing national needs. Historians credit it with the professionalization of the Army in the 19th century. Also, for many years it was America's only engineering school, and its graduates were instrumental in exploring, mapping, and building the country. In the 20th century, graduates led the way in flight, including the exploration of space. West Point's motto—Duty, Honor, Country—has become the ethos of the Army itself.

The school's martial reputation got its first major boost when graduates were credited with providing the crucial junior leadership that made possible the brilliant U.S. victory in the Mexican War.* In the Civil War,* West Pointers dominated the top positions on both sides, and in all subsequent wars graduates have filled a large percentage of the higher echelons of military leadership. Nevertheless, their numbers represent only a small proportion of all officers. In the Cold War,* for example, the large standing force required far more officers than West Point could turn out, even after the size of the Corps of Cadets doubled to some 4,400 students in the early 1970s.

After the Cold War, the student body was cut to 4,000. Although few minorities attended until after World War II,* today's cadets come from every corner of the United States, and they mirror American society. Women entered in 1976. The 1,000th black and the 1,000th woman both graduated in the class of 1991. Graduates go directly to active duty and serve a minimum of six years. The Academy's purpose is "to provide the nation with leaders of character who serve the common defense." The degree to which it has met that expectation is reflected in its reputation. It is acclaimed and imitated worldwide.

References. Stephen E. Ambrose, *Duty, Honor, Country*, 1966. James R. Endler, *Other Leaders, Other Heroes*, 1998. George S. Pappas, *To the Point*, 1993.

Dave R. Palmer

U.S. SANITARY COMMISSION

At the beginning of the Civil War* the federal government was unable to cope with the suffering of soldiers from sickness and wounds. In response, numerous civilian organizations, generally dominated by women, came into existence to offer both preventative care and treatment. In April 1861 a former Army surgeon, using the British Army Sanitary Commission model from the Crimean War, sought to consolidate the efforts of the various groups. In June 1861, the Surgeon General* accepted the Sanitary Commission's assistance. Its services were extended not only to the sick and wounded but to prisoners of war.* The commission's activities were varied and included such things as supplying writing and reading materials, bed clothes, spirits, mosquito netting, and even ice; its volunteer doctors accompanied the field armies with medical supplies, including anesthetics and surgical instruments. The commission established a hospital directory for relatives seeking information on wounded soldiers. Its inspectors monitored sanitary conditions in camps and reported on hospital conditions and prisoner of war camps. The War Department,* however, saw the commission as a challenge to its authority and frequently interfered in its activities. The U.S. Sanitary Commission was a forerunner of the American Red Cross.

References. Mary Gillett, *The Army Medical Department 1818–1865*, 1987. William Quentin Maxwell, *Lincoln's Fifth Wheel*, 1956.

Charles Heller

UPTON, EMORY (1839–1881)

Emory Upton was born 27 August 1839 near Batavia, New York, and graduated from the U.S. Military Academy* in 1861, eighth in his class. He served in all three branches of the Army during the Civil War* and had been breveted major general of volunteers by war's end. His most notable moment came on 10 May 1864 at Spotsylvania Court House, Virginia, where he led a surprise attack with twelve regiments* against a sector of breastworks known as the "Bloody Angle." His command enjoyed initial success, but it was not properly supported and withdrew. The army copied Upton's technique two days later with an assault that enjoyed early success, though it eventually stalled after suffering nearly 7,000 casualties.

Upton was wounded at the Battle of Winchester while commanding a division.* He recovered and finished the war commanding a cavalry* division during Wilson's raid into Alabama and Georgia. After the war, he reverted to the rank of captain but was soon promoted to lieutenant colonel, second in command of the newly raised 25th Infantry Regiment (Colored). He served as commandant of cadets at the U.S. Military Academy* from 1870 until 1875 and was commanding officer of the Presidio* in San Francisco from 1875 until his death by his own hand on 15 March 1881.

Upton wrote several important works, including *The Armies of Asia and Europe, Infantry Tactics*, and *The Military Policy of the United States*. The last work remained unpublished until 1904.

References. Stephen E. Ambrose, *Upton and the Army*, 1964. Wallace E. Walker, "Emory Upton and the Army Officer's Creed," *Military Review*, April 1981, 65–68.

George Knapp

URGENT FURY

Urgent Fury was the code name for the U.S. invasion of Grenada in October 1983. Since 1979, the New Jewel Movement (a Marxist-Leninist organization strongly supported by Cuba, the Soviet Union, and various radical governments and groups) ruled that island. President Ronald Reagan, alarmed by the shipment of large quantities of Eastern bloc weapons to the island and by a number of construction projects with military overtones (in particular, the building of a large aircraft runway at Port Salines, in the southwestern corner of the island), declared Grenada "a Soviet-Cuban colony being readied as a major military bastion" for the export of revolution. In mid-October 1983, when Grenada's prime minister and his followers were executed by an even more radical faction within the New Jewel Movement, Reagan responded to an appeal from several eastern Caribbean countries to restore order and authorized U.S. military action.

Plans for military operations initially focused on the evacuation of several hundred U.S. citizens on the island. Quickly, however, the mission expanded to include the overthrow of the New Jewel regime and its replacement with a democratic government. As the mission grew, so did the force involved. U.S. Marines, paratroopers, rangers,* elite special operations forces,* and air and naval units participated in the invasion. A joint task force, commanded by Vice Admiral Joseph Metcalf, directed the action. To ensure that Metcalf had expert advice on the conduct of the land operations, the Army offered the services of

Major General H. Norman Schwarzkopf, commander of the 24th Infantry Division (Mechanized).

After a delay, the invasion began shortly after dawn on 25 October. Elements from Battalion Landing Team 2/8 Marines (2d Battalion, 8th Marine Regiment) quickly seized an airfield on the eastern coast and began to secure the northern half of the small (131-square-mile) island. Elsewhere, Operation Urgent Fury proceeded less smoothly. Certain special operations at St. Georges, the capital city, on the west coast, ran into trouble and required assistance from the Marines and other forces. At Port Salines, the rangers dropped onto the still uncompleted runway and ran into stiff resistance from Grenada'a People's Revolutionary Army and, more menacingly, from a well-armed group of several hundred Cuban "construction workers." Under fire, the rangers cleared the airstrip and moved out toward an enclave of American students. That afternoon, the first elements of what would grow into a two-brigade force from the U.S. Army's 82d Airborne Division* began landing at Salines. Despite the fighting that ensued over the next several days, neither side suffered excessive casualties. Of the nearly 20,000 U.S. service personnel who participated in the operation, eighteen lost their lives. Cuban and Grenadian deaths numbered forty-five. By 2 November, the fighting was over, the U.S. citizens had been evacuated, the New Jewel Movement toppled; most of the invasion force was redeployed. Problems in the area of joint, or multiservice, operations overshadowed the success of Operation Urgent Fury and helped fuel U.S. military reforms in the mid-1980s.

References. Mark Adkin, *Urgent Fury*, 1989. Daniel P. Bolger, *Americans at War, 1975–1986*, 1988. Peter M. Dunn and Bruce W. Watson, eds., *American Intervention in Grenada*, 1985.

Lawrence A. Yates

USO. *See* United Service Organizations.

UTE WAR

The Ute War was the result of efforts of Nathan Meeker, Indian agent to the White River Utes, to assimilate the Utes into white society, and of the Colorado legislature's attempts to have the Utes removed to the Indian Territories. By 1879 the situation was quite explosive. The spark that set off the war was the murder of Meeker and seven other men at the White Water Agency. Although the Utes had never fought against the United States—they considered themselves allies, having fought with the Army against the Navajo and Cheyenne—they prepared to meet the soldiers whom, they knew, the U.S. Army would send against them. In response to an earlier request by Meeker for assistance, Major Thomas Thornburgh and one company* of the 3d Cavalry, two companies of the 5th Cavalry, and one company of the 4th Infantry (153 soldiers and 25 civilians) left Fort Steele, Wyoming, on 21 September 1879. Knowing the strength of the white soldiers; the Utes struck first, attacking Thornburgh's column at Milk River on 29 September, killing twelve and wounding forty-three soldiers, and killing all of the horses and mules. Without any means of escape, the besieged troops, including a company from the 9th Cavalry, suffered more casualties. When the remainder of the 5th Cavalry arrived on 5 October, the Utes retreated into the nearby mountains and awaited reprisals. Negotiations precluded additional loss of life, however, and the issues were resolved on 10 November. The Utes ultimately agreed to resettlement and were removed to Utah by 1881.

References. Marshall Sprague, *Massacre*, 1957. Fred H. Werner, *Meeker*, 1985.

Layton H. M. Pennington

V

VALCOUR ISLAND

Early in the American Revolution* the British saw the Hudson River valley as the geographical key to success. In 1776, believing that control of the Hudson would split the colonies and lead to their piecemeal defeat, one army under William Howe prepared to attack up the Hudson River from New York while another under Guy Carlton attacked south toward Lake Champlain. Meanwhile, Benedict Arnold* hastily gathered local militia, sailors, and craftsmen and in three months launched a flotilla of fifteen vessels armed with a total of eighty-four guns on Lake Champlain. Aware of Arnold's growing strength, Carlton wrestled with the problems of preparing his force, which included the man-of-war *Inflexible*. On 11 October, Carlton's fleet of twenty-five vessels slammed into Arnold's smaller flotilla. Arnold anchored his vessels in a concave formation in the channel east of Valcour Island to concentrate his fire on the British. Although Arnold's men fought bravely, by dark superior British firepower had taken a heavy toll on the Colonials, and Indians allied with the British controlled the land flanks, preventing escape to the rear. Arnold held a council of war and decided to fight through the British fleet. Thanks to the darkness, fog, and fatigue of the enemy, Arnold's force escaped in the night. Two days later the British caught up with the remnants of Arnold's flotilla and destroyed it. Although Carlton thus succeeded in eliminating colonial naval power from Lake Champlain, the battle of Valcour Island put British plans far behind schedule. With winter approaching and Howe still in New York City, Carlton gave up his campaign and returned to Canada.

References. Harrison Bird, *Navies in the Mountains*, 1962. Ralph Nading Hill, *Lake Champlain*, 20th ann. ed., 1995.

S. A. Underwood

VALLEY FORGE

Valley Forge was the winter camp of George Washington's* Continental Army* between 19 December 1777 and 19 June 1778. Washington chose this location on the west bank of the Schuykill River twenty-two miles northwest of Philadelphia for his 11,000 man army as a compromise between conducting a winter campaign against the British who occupied Philadelphia and retiring to a place better suited for winter quarters. By placing his encampment in the vicinity of Philadelphia, Washington threatened General William Howe's army. Washington's decision, however, brought a heavy price. The troops that endured the cold winter at Valley Forge lacked many basic necessities, including food and clothing. The conditions at Valley Forge can be attributed to the breakdown of logistics, the inflated Continental currency, and the farmers who sold their crops to the British or to civilians. During the winter months, eight to ten soldiers deserted each day. On 23 February 1778, Baron Friedrich von Steuben* arrived at Valley Forge and succeeded in instilling discipline and military order. Von Steuben instructed the Continentals in the use of the bayonet* and introduced other tactical improvements. By the summer of 1778, Washington's army was prepared to meet the British army on a more equal footing.

References. Alfred Hoyt Bill, *Valley Forge*, 1952. Noel F. Busch, *Winter Quarters*, 1974. John F. Reed, *Valley Forge*, 1969.

James L. Isemann

VALVERDE

Early in 1862, Confederate President Jefferson Davis* saw an opportunity to sever the lines of communications between Washington and the western states and territories and open up the West to the Confederacy. He ordered Henry H. Sibley to lead a Confederate force into New Mexico, take Forts Filmore, Craig, and Union, and drive the Federals from the territory. After the Federal garrison abandoned Fort Filmore, Sibley's troops made contact with Colonel Edward Canby's force at Fort Craig. Sibley knew that Fort Craig was too strong for a frontal assault and therefore ordered his troops to flank the fort and move northward to the ford at Valverde. Sibley's movement threatened Canby's supply route and drew the Federals out of the fort to protect it. This led to the most notable action of the campaign. Fought on 21 February 1862, the battle at Valverde began at the ford as Canby's troops challenged the Confederate position. Although Union troops failed to rout the Confederates, they drove back a counterattack by the Mounted Texans. After several hours, Thomas Green led the Confederates in a frontal assault, which failed. Colonel Kit Carson and Major Thomas Duncan staged a massive counterattack, unintentionally opening an unprotected area in the Union line; Confederate troops captured a Union battery.* Canby then retreated to Fort Craig, and Sibley claimed victory. The Confederates lost thirty-six killed and 160 wounded from their force of 2,600 men; Federal losses were sixty-nine killed and 160 wounded of 3,810 men engaged. The Confederates, however, failed to drive the Federal forces from the territory.

References. Paul I, Kliger, "The Confederate Invasion of New Mexico," *Blue & Gray*, June 1994, 8–20. John Taylor, *Bloody Valverde*, 1995.

Rebecca S. Witte

VAN FLEET, JAMES ALWARD (1892–1994)

James Alward Van Fleet was born in Coytesville, New Jersey, and graduated from the U.S. Military Academy* in 1915—the "class the stars fell on." He served in the Punitive Expedition* in 1916 but missed action in World War I.* In World War II,* he held division* and corps* commands in the European Theater of Operations* (ETO). As head of the U.S. Army mission to Greece, he was instrumental in reinvigorating the Greek army in its victorious 1947–1949 campaign against communist guerillas.

In April 1951, Van Fleet succeeded Lieutenant General Matthew B. Ridgway* as Eighth Army* commander in Korea, following President Harry Truman's recall of General of the Army Douglas MacArthur.* Van Fleet inherited a stable battle line, reflecting a political and military situation in which neither side was willing to provoke a wider war or face the heavy casualties that would result from any further attempt to win the conflict. The sides conducted on-off armistice negotiations while fighting.

Van Fleet was ordered to maintain the military status quo and to sustain the Republic of Korea Army (ROKA), still recovering from its heavy defeat in 1950–1951. By the end of 1952, ROKA troops comprised almost three-fourths of his army, but they remained shaky to the end of the war. Van Fleet, increasingly frustrated with this "fighting while negotiating" posture, complained that it affected the morale of his troops and was no way to fight communist aggression. Nevertheless, Washington vetoed his offensive moves. Somewhat embittered, Van Fleet left Korea and the U.S. Army in 1953, maintaining that the United States could have won the Korean War* relatively easily if it had had the will.

References. Clay Blair, *The Forgotten War*, 1987. Walter G. Hermes, *Truce Tent and Fighting Front*, 1966. Callum A. MacDonald, *Korea*, 1987.

Stanley Sandler

VERACRUZ

When Woodrow Wilson became president of the United States in March 1913, the three-year-old revolution in Mexico had just entered a more violent phase with the assassination of the liberal president, Francisco Indalécio Madero by General Victoriano Huerta. Wilson refused to recognize Huerta's increasingly dictatorial regime and, as civil strife in Mexico intensified, tried to engineer the strongman's removal from power. On 9 April 1914, Mexican soldiers in Tampico arrested several U.S. sailors, including two who they took at gunpoint off a Navy whaleboat flying the U.S. flag. The sailors were soon released, and the episode would have been closed, except that the U.S. admiral off shore demanded reparations and that Wilson elected to use the incident (together with the approach of a German ship carrying arms for Huerta) as a pretext to intervene militarily in the revolution. On 21 April, U.S. bluejackets landed at Veracruz. Their mission was to seize the customs house and prevent the shipment of supplies to Huerta.

Wilson expected U.S. forces to be welcomed by those fighting Huerta. Instead, the bluejackets and marines had to take Veracruz by force, while Huerta's opponents denounced U.S. interference. Shocked by the bloodshed, Wilson ordered an Army brigade* under Major General Frederick Funston* to Veracruz, and the Navy turned over to the Army responsibility for the city's occupation. Shunning pressures for a full-scale intervention and a march on Mexico City, Wilson refused to commit an Army division* but sought rather to negotiate the removal of U.S. forces. As diplomats wrangled to this end, U.S. Marines in Veracruz provided security to Army troops engaged in overhauling the city's administrative, judicial, sanitation, and penal systems. U.S. troops evacuated Veracruz in November 1914.

References. John S. D. Eisenhower, *Intervention!* 1993. Robert E. Quirk, *An Affair of Honor*, 1962. Jack Sweetman, *The Landing at Veracruz*, 1968.

Lawrence A. Yates

VETERAN RESERVE CORPS

Confronted with a critical manpower shortage in the spring of 1863, the War Department* established the Invalid Corps for officers and enlisted men who were no longer fit for frontline duty but volunteered for further service. Organized in separate companies,* battalions,* and regiments* of men available for any duty except combat, and men suited only for very light work, the corps performed services as prison and building guards, hospital orderlies, clerks, and administrators. In response to objections to the term "Invalid," the War Department redesignated the Invalid Corps the Veteran Reserve Corps in 1864. More than 60,000 men served in the corps during the Civil War,* with a peak strength of more than 30,000 in April 1865, releasing a substantial number of physically fit men to combat units.

References. Marvin A. Kriedberg and Merton G. Henry, *History of Military Mobilization in the United States Army, 1775–1945*, 1955. Maurice Matloff, ed., *American Military History*, 1969.

VETERANS ADMINISTRATION

On 21 July 1930, President Herbert Hoover issued Executive Order No. 5398 establishing the Veterans Administration (VA) as the agency of the U.S. government that would administer benefits prescribed by Congress for veterans and their families. The new agency consolidated the responsibilities of several existing agencies, including the United States Veterans' Bureau, the National Home for Disabled Volunteer Soldiers, and the Bureau of Pensions. Initially, the VA administered pensions, insurance, and medical care for veterans and their widows. In World War II,* however, Congress greatly expanded veteran benefits, including the Vocational Rehabilitation Act (1943) and the G.I. Bill* of Rights (1944), which provided readjustment, educational, and guaranteed loans to veterans during their transition back into civilian life. Headquartered in Washington, D.C., the VA maintained regional and district offices throughout the United States to serve its constituents. To most Americans, the many veterans hospitals and medical centers represented the daily presence of the VA.

Following the Vietnam War,* scandals, questions about its operations, and numerous veterans' complaints regarding treatment and quality of services dogged the Veterans Administration. Reforms in the late 1970s and early 1980s remedied some of these problems, but others persisted. Responding to the demands of veterans organizations, Congress passed legislation in 1987 creating the cabinet-level Department of Veteran Affairs, headed by a Secretary of Veteran Affairs, at last giving veterans' issues representation at the highest level of the government. The new department came into existence on 25 October 1988.

References. Robert Klein, *Wounded Men, Broken Promises*, 1981. James A. McDonnell, Jr., "The Veterans Administration," *Air Force Magazine*, August 1980, 99.

Trevor Brown

VETERANS DAY

The observation of Veterans Day traces its origin to the conclusion of World War I.* At 1100 hours, 11 November 1918, the allies and Germany signed an armistice effectively ending the war. Great Britain, Canada, France, and the United States set aside 11 November as Armistice Day, to be celebrated as a day of rememberance for fallen soldiers of the Great War. This tradition continued after World War II.* U.S. and Canadian citizens observe a moment of silence at 1100 on the eleventh day of the eleventh month, Armistice Day (referred to as Remembrance Day in Canada). Great Britain observes Armistice Day on the Sunday nearest 11 November and calls it Remembrance Sunday.

In 1954, President of the United States and former Allied commander in Europe Dwight D. Eisenhower* signed legislation officially designating 11 November as Veterans Day, honoring all veterans. Special ceremonies to the fallen are held at Arlington National Cemetery and military shrines throughout the country. Veterans organizations, like the American Legion* and Veterans of Foreign Wars, sponsor parades and tributes to veterans. Veterans Day is also a traditional day for naturalization ceremonies.

References. Adrian Gregory, *The Silence of Memory*, 1994. A. P. Sanford and Robert H. Schauffler, *Armistice Day*, 1928.

Thomas Christianson

VETERINARY CORPS

The Army Veterinary Corps is a component of the Army Medical Service Corps* and is responsible for safeguarding the health of humans as well as animals. The birthplace of U.S. military veterinary medicine can be traced to the early U.S. cavalry.* The heritage of Veterinary Corps officers is specifically traced to horseshoers and farriers who acted as animal nurses in the Old Army.* Congressional legislation of 1792 provided that each of the four troops of light dragoons would have one farrier to care for the ailments of horses. The Army Veterinary Corps today has three major tasks: to inspect the foods used by the military, including its processing and the establishments producing them; to provide a comprehensive animal service; and to ensure that the various veterinary laboratory functions concerned with food and research are conducted properly.

References. William Henry Harrison Clark, *The History of the United States Army Veterinary Corps in Vietnam, 1962–1973* [1991]. Louis A. Merillat and Delwin M. Campbell, *Veterinary Military History of the United States*, 1935. Everett B. Miller, *United States Army Veterinary Service in World War II*, 1961.

Michael Davis

VICKSBURG

The Vicksburg Campaign was a crucial event in the Civil War.* Preliminary land operations began in November 1862, when forces under Major General Ulysses S. Grant,* concentrated at Grand Junction, Tennessee, pushed General John C. Pemberton's Confederate army south toward Vicksburg. In a poorly coordinated effort, Admiral David G. Farragut and Major General Nathaniel P. Banks moved up the Mississippi to threaten Baton Rouge from the south. In December, Grant sent an expedition under Brigadier General William T. Sherman* to attack the Chickasaw Bluffs, north of Vicksburg. Heavy losses to Sherman's forces, continual harrassment of Federal lines of communications by Nathan Bedford Forrest's* Confederate cavalry, and the capture of his major supply base at Holly Springs, Mississippi, dealt Grant severe blows and resulted in Confederate control of the Mississippi River from Vicksburg to Baton Rouge at year's end.

Throughout the winter and early spring of 1863, Grant continued to probe around Vicksburg in an effort to outflank the city's defenses. Initially Grant accomplished little in the rain-flooded and swampy region. Gunboats under Admiral David D. Porter operating from north of Vicksburg and under Farragut from south of Baton Rouge, however, succeeded in clearing Confederate river traffic from the previously protected part of the Mississippi and thus isolated the Confederate garrison at Port Hudson* from Pemberton and the defenders of Vicksburg.

By April, Pemberton had about 50,000 men scattered about on the east bank of the river, while Grant had roughly the same number on the west bank. Leaving Sherman's force above Vicksburg, Grant moved his army to Hard Times below Vicksburg. Sending Colonel Benjamin H. Grierson on his famous raid through Mississippi to further confuse and disrupt Confederate communications, on 30 April Grant crossed the river below Grand Gulf* on Porter's boats. Recalling Sherman and consolidating his forces, Grant cut his lines of communications and fought a series of battles beginning at Port Gibson* against the Grand Gulf garrison on 1 May; captured Jackson, Mississippi, and prevented a linkup between Pemberton and General Joseph E. Johnston* in the Black River Campaign, from 7 to 19 May; and forced Pemberton back into the Vicksburg defenses at the Battle of Champion Hill* on 16 May. Grant finally settled in for a seige of Vicksburg on 19 May.

The Vicksburg defenders and civilians, trapped and near starvation, were under continuous bombardment and in a hopeless situation. General Pemberton, believing Grant's forces were preparing for a general assault, surrendered on 4 July 1863. On hearing of Vicksburg's fate, Port Hudson surrendered on the 9th. As President Abraham Lincoln remarked, the Mississippi River now "flowed unvexed" to the sea. Grant had split the Confederacy in half.

References. James R. Arnold, *Grant Wins the War*, 1997. Edwin C. Bearss, *The Campaign for Vicksburg*, 1985–1986. Shelby Foote, *The Beleaguered City*, 1963, 1995.

George Mordica II

VICTORY PROGRAM

The Victory Program was the manpower and industrial mobilization plan that guided the growth of the U.S. Army in World War II.* Changing mobilization requirements and the Lend-Lease program rapidly upset plans developed during the 1930s. Based on a series of requests for planning data, Chief of Staff* George C. Marshall* directed the War Plans Division* to prepare a manpower mobilization and industrial-utilization plan to be used as guidance for contracts and planning. The plan, prepared in ninety days by Lieutenant Colonel Albert C. Wedemeyer,* was both a mobilization plan and a strategic concept.

Wedemeyer's primary obstacle was the difficulty of determining strategic requirements, as no clear strategy* had been articulated at the time. Strong isolationist sentiment prevented a public statement of strategic intentions in the event of war, as that would appear to be actual preparation for war. Therefore, Wedemeyer had to be circumspect in researching probable U.S. strategic goals and objectives in the event of hostilities. He began by applying concepts he had learned or developed over years of professional education. He identified four questions that demanded answers for his estimate of required material and manpower: (1) What was the national strategic objective in the event of war with Germany? (2) What military strategy would be devised to accomplish that objective? (3) What naval, air, and land forces would be required to accomplish that military strategy? and (4) How would the land forces be raised, equipped, and trained to support the military strategy?

Wedemeyer's analysis led to an estimate for 8.7 million men in the Army and Army Air Forces,* organized into 215 maneuvers divisions.* The plan hypothesized a large number of divisions organized into task forces to accomplish the strategic objective of entering the European continent and to provide a strategic reserve for contingencies, especially the Pacific theater. Since the projected number of U.S. divisions was lower than the anticipated number available to Germany, particularly if the Soviet Union collapsed (as seemed likely in the summer of 1941), Wedemeyer proposed using airpower and armored formations to counterbalance the larger number of German divisions. In fact, the United

States raised only ninety divisions by 1945. While Wedemeyer's estimate of the total number of divisions required was significantly high, the manpower totals were incredibly accurate. The difference was to some extent made up by the continued resistance of the Soviets and by the decision to rely on individual replacements rather than a rotation of units in and out of combat. The war became much more logistically intensive than Wedemeyer had imagined, yet his plan was quite flexible and allowed for this change, while still bringing order and system to an otherwise chaotic and ever-changing mobilization process. By balancing U.S. industrial needs with the needs of all the services, as well as Lend-Lease needs of the Allies, Wedemeyer was able to prepare a blueprint for victory that continues to provide a model of strategic and mobilization planning fifty years later.

References. Keith E. Eiler, ed., *Wedemeyer on War and Peace*, 1987. Charles E. Kirkpatrick, *An Unknown Future and a Doubtful Present*, 1990. Steven T. Ross, ed., *American War Plans*, vol. 5, 1992.

John Broom

VIETNAM WAR

U.S. Army involvement in the Vietnam War, sometimes called the Second Indochina War, can be traced through five distinct phases: the combined French-U.S. advisory phase (1950–1955); the U.S. advisory phase (1955–1964); force buildup and combat phase (1965–1967); large-unit offensive combat operations (1967–1969); and Vietnamization (1969–1973). The first phase began with the arrival of the U.S. Military Assistance and Advisory Group* (MAAG) Indochina to oversee distribution of U.S. aid to the French, fighting the communist Viet Minh. From the beginning, U.S. policy supported the development of an independent, indigenous Vietnamese army and a U.S. role in its organization and training. The French raised indigenous Vietnamese units commanded and led by French officers and NCOs but refused any U.S. role in their training and accepted only minimal American advice on the conduct of operations. When in May 1954 the fall of Dien Bien Phu appeared imminent, the French agreed to place U.S. advisors with Vietnamese units, and in early June the French formally asked the United States to join them in organizing and training the Vietnamese army.

The situation in South Vietnam was anything but stable after the Geneva Accords of 1954. The state of Vietnam had gained independence, but the French remained without a timetable for withdrawal. French and U.S. objectives did not coincide, but despite mutual distrust the two powers agreed on a binational training organization under the overall authority of the French Commander in Chief, Indochina, and the direct command of the chief of the U.S. MAAG. Established on 12 February 1955, this integrated command lasted less than six months. By June 1955 the French were gone, and creating and training a South Vietnamese army became entirely a U.S. Army task.

While the South Vietnamese government sought stability, communists in the South began to rebuild and consolidate their political and military apparatus. Beginning in 1956, the Viet Cong (VC) initiated a program of political agitation and subversion. Through 1957 and into 1958, insurgent incidents increased. U.S. officials misread the insurgency, believing it a diversion for a conventional attack across the demilitarized zone separating North and South Vietnam. In 1959, scattered and sporadic acts of terror evolved into a sustained campaign. By 1960, the Vietnamese and the U.S. Army advisors found themselves embroiled in an insurgency assisted by the communists in the North.

Prior to 1960, U.S. Army advisors were involved primarily in training and high-level staff work. In 1960 they began advising ground combat units in the field, at the regimental level. In 1961 Army advisors were assigned to battalion* level, and by 1964 they were working with paramilitary forces. To coordinate all U.S. military support activities in South Vietnam, the U.S. government established the Military Assistance Command, Vietnam* (MACV) in 1962. MACV would eventually consolidate all support and advisory activities and swallow up the MAAG. Gradually, U.S. advisors became directly involved in combat. After the fall of President Ngo Dinh Diem in November 1963 and the tumultuous coup-riddled year that followed, the U.S. Army introduced combat units into South Vietnam. By 1964 the Army of the Republic of Vietnam (ARVN) had grown to 250,000, and U.S. support had grown apace to 23,000 advisors.

Between the arrival of the first Army combat units in 1965 and their withdrawal in 1973, seven U.S. Army divisions* (1st Cavalry,* 1st Infantry,* 4th Infantry,* 9th Infantry,* 35th Infantry, 101st Airborne,* and 23d Infantry [Americal] in order of deployment); four separate brigade-sized units (173d Airborne, 199th Light Infantry, 11th Armored Cavalry, and 1st Brigade, 5th Infantry Division), a 24,000-man aviation brigade, and the 5th Special Forces Group served in Vietnam. At the height of U.S. involvement in 1968–1969, nearly 360,000 U.S. Army troops were in South Vietnam conducting large-scale search-and-destroy* operations, while ARVN forces were relegated to counterinsurgency.

In late 1969, after sustaining casualty ratios equal to those suffered in other major U.S. conflicts, the Nixon administration announced the gradual withdrawal of U.S. forces from Vietnam and the assumption of responsibility for the war by the South Vietnamese—Vietnamization, as it became known. The gradual withdrawal, accompanied by continued battle casualties, lasted until January 1973, when both sides signed the Paris Peace Accords. The last U.S. soldier was killed in action in Vietnam on 27 January 1973. Sixty days after the peace accords were signed, North Vietnam released the American prisoners of war* held in its jails. Over 58,000 Americans were killed in Vietnam and nearly 2,500 servicemen were listed as missing in action; many of these are still unaccounted for.

References. Jeffrey J. Clarke, *Advice and Support*, 1988. George C. Herring, ed., *America's Longest War*, 2d ed., 1986. Bruce Palmer, Jr., *The 25-Year War*, 1984. Dave Richard Palmer, *Summons of the Trumpet*, 1978. Ronald H. Spector, *Advice and Support*, 1983. Shelby L. Stanton, *The Rise and Fall of an American Army*, 1985.

Arthur T. Frame

VINCENNES

Located on the Wabash River in present-day southern Indiana, Vincennes was the site of a French, and later British, outpost known as Fort Sackville. During his campaign to end the Indian menace in the Ohio valley during the American Revolution,* George Rogers Clark* twice captured Fort Sackville. In the summer of 1778, a small contingent of Clark's men marched 240 miles across Illinois to occupy Fort Sackville. When Henry Hamilton (known as "the hair buyer"), the British commander in the region, learned of Clark's success, he moved a force of 400 Regulars, volunteers, and Indians to retake the fort. Receiving the news of Vincennes's loss in January 1779, Clark determined immediately to recapture the outpost. He built a boat to carry his artillery and provisions up the Ohio and raised two companies of local French volunteers to supplement his small force. Clark's force departed Kaskaskia in the dead of winter and, despite widespread flooding, marched 240 miles through rain, snow, and chest-deep, frozen swamps in seventeen days—the last seven without food—to reach Vincennes. Arriving without meeting his supply boat, Clark prepared to attack. He detailed his best riflemen to shoot the British pickets and approached the fort in darkness. With most of his Regulars wounded or killed, Hamilton surrendered.

Although on the periphery of the war, the capture of Vincennes and Clark's actions contributed to the loss of British control in the Ohio valley. More importantly, control of the Ohio valley led to the addition of vast tracts of land, larger than the original thirteen colonies, to the new nation. Neither Clark nor his men received any compensation for their epic campaign until after Clark's impoverished death in 1818.

References. August Derleth, *Vincennes*, 1968. Joseph Henry Vandenburgh Somes, *Old Vincennes*, 1962.

S. A. Underwood

VIRGINIA MILITARY INSTITUTE

Founded in 1839, the Virginia Military Institute (VMI) is a four-year, state-supported military college, often called the "West Point of the South." VMI alumni have played a major role in all of the nation's conflicts since its founding. General of the Army George C. Marshall* is perhaps VMI's most distinguished graduate, rising to Chief of Staff* of the Army during World War II* and holding subsequent positions as secretary of state and secretary of defense.* VMI's famous professors include Lieutenant Colonel Thomas J. "Stonewall" Jackson* and the oceanographer Matthew Fontaine Maury. During the Civil

War,* VMI became an important source for both drill cadets and officers in the Confederacy. In May 1864, the VMI Corps of Cadets fought in the battle of New Market,* contributing to the Confederate victory and capturing a Federal gun; cadet casualties numbered ten dead and forty-seven wounded. The victory only temporarily held Federal forces in check, however; by June Major General David Hunter's force operating in the Shenandoah Valley burned and severely damaged VMI.

Today, VMI continues to provide leaders to all of the armed services. In 1990, the Department of Justice ordered VMI to admit women, and after a bitter fight in the courts, VMI complied. In 1998 the first female cadet graduated from VMI.

References. Henry A. Wise, *Drawing Out the Man*, 1978. Jennings C. Wise, *Sunrise of the Virginia Military Institute as a School of Arms*, 1958.

Robert J. Dalessandro

VOLCKMANN, RUSSELL (1911–1982)

Russell Volckmann was born in Iowa in 1911 and graduated from the U.S. Military Academy* in 1934. He is considered by some to be the true father of special operations. Serving in the Philippines at the beginning of World War II,* he refused to surrender. Leaving his unit on Bataan,* Volckmann made his way through Japanese lines, avoiding enemy positions and movements. Reaching northern Luzon, he set out to reorganize the nascent Philippine resistance into seven geographical districts. He organized five regiments* of guerrillas, totalling some 20,000 Filipinos and Americans. This force tied down several Japanese divisions and provided vital intelligence to Allied headquarters in Australia.

After the Leyte landing on 20 October 1944, Volckmann prepared his units to close with the enemy forces, about 50,000 troops. He emphasized ambush, night operations, sabotage, demolitions, and small-unit training. Due to the courage of Volckmann's guerrillas, General Douglas MacArthur* found little resistance to his landing at Lingayen Gulf. For his bravery and leadership in the Philippines, Volckmann received the Bronze Star,* the Silver Star,* and the Distinguished Service Cross.*

After World War II, Volckmann developed the U.S. doctrine and policies of unconventional warfare forces, worked to establish a special warfare directorate within the Army General Staff,* and helped activate the first Special Forces* unit at Fort Bragg.* He drafted the documents that would become FM 31–20, *Combatting Guerilla Forces* (February 1951), and FM 31–21, *Organization and Conduct of Guerilla Warfare* (October 1951). In late 1951, Major General Robert A. McClure recruited Volckmann to work in the Special Operations Division of McClure's newly created Office of the Chief of Psychological Warfare. The period he spent as a staff officer there was critical in the development of U.S. doctrine* and policy relating to unconventional warfare. His work, along with that of others, led to the relocation of the Psychological Warfare Center to Fort

Bragg and the establishment of the nineteenth Special Forces Group (Airborne), the U.S. Army's first regular unconventional-warfare fighting unit. He died in 1982.

References. Alfred Paddock, Jr., *U.S. Army Special Warfare*, 1982. R. W. Volckmann, *We Remained*, 1954.

Richard Stewart

VULCAN

Development of the Vulcan air defense system began in 1964. The United States eventually developed two versions of the systems: the M163, a self-propelled model, and the M167, a towed model. The M163 is an M113 armored personnel carrier* fitted with a one-man, electrically driven turret mounting the Vulcan gun and its fire control system. The Vulcan gun is a 20 mm, six-barrel derivative of a cannon originally designed for the Lockheed F-104 Starfighter. It has two rates of fire, 1,000 and 3,000 rounds per minute, and it is capable of firing in preset bursts of either 10, 30, 60 or 100 rounds. Maximum effective range against aircraft is 1,200 meters and against ground targets is 2,200 meters. The Vulcan system can traverse a complete 360 degrees, depress five degrees below horizontal, and elevate to eighty degrees.

References. Joseph Berk, *The Gatling Gun*, 1991. E.W.D. Bunke, "The Vulcan for Air Defense," *National Defense*, November–December 1973, 244–246. William D. Kilgore, "Air Defense Protection for the Division," *Military Review*, February 1975, 37–50.

David Zoellers

W

WAGNER, ARTHUR LOCKWOOD (1853–1905)

Arthur Lockwood Wagner graduated from the U.S. Military Academy* in 1875 and served for the next six years with the 6th Infantry on the frontier. Between 1881 and 1885 he served as professor of military science* at Louisiana State University and East Florida Seminary. A prolific and effective writer, he was already known as one of the intellectual officers in the Army. In 1886, following another year with his regiment,* he arrived at Fort Leavenworth,* Kansas, where he served as assistant instructor in the School for the Application of Infantry and Cavalry.* From this time Wagner's career centered around Leavenworth and the Army's educational system. He served successively as instructor, department head, assistant commandant, and finally as the president of the newly formed Army War College* in Washington, D.C. Wagner was not only an outstanding instructor he was also an effective writer, preparing several historical studies and tactical manuals. Starting from European works on the military art, Wagner pioneered a genre of American military literature that went far beyond the earlier writers, who merely translated European works or, in some cases, plagiarized European sources. His literary contributions alone would have made him an important figure in the evolution of U.S. Army professionalization.

Wagner went far beyond that, however, to become one of the principal designers of what has come to be known as the applicatory method, a combination of study followed by practical exercises in the classroom and the field. He took this model of instruction from the German army, adapting it to U.S. Army needs and conditions. Wagner, a firm believer in the use of history to illustrate principles, pioneered the use of the staff ride,* visiting battlefields to study strategic and tactical decision making on the actual terrain. After leaving Leavenworth, Wagner went to the Adjutant General's Office in the War Department,* then served on Major General William R. Shafter's staff in Cuba during the Spanish-

American War.* Wagner assisted Elihu Root* in formulating plans for a General Staff* and a modern Army education system. After another brief tour at Leavenworth, Wagner returned to Washington as senior director at the newly established Army War College. The next year, however, still at the War College, Wagner died from tuberculosis in his fifty-third year.

References. Timothy K. Nenninger, *The Fort Leavenworth Schools and the Old Army*, 1977. Carol Reardon, *Soldiers and Scholars*, 1990.

John Broom

WAGON BOX FIGHT

On 2 August 1867, a force of 800–1,200 Indians led by the great Oglala chief Red Cloud attacked woodcutting parties working six miles northwest of Fort Phil Kearny.* The woodcutters and their military escort defended a corral made by placing fourteen wagon boxes that had been removed from their running apparatus in an oval sixty to seventy feet long and twenty-five to thirty feet wide. Some woodcutters were forced to fight their way to the corral from the pinery, suffering several casualties in the process. The Indians made at least one mounted attack and probably two attacks on foot from a coulee, or dry streambed, that gave them cover to within a short distance of the corral. The defenders, armed with the new Springfield Allin Conversion* breech-loading rifles and a substantial stock of ammunition, suffered seven killed and two wounded. The attackers' losses were estimated at sixty killed and an unknown number wounded. The Indians withdrew when a relief party from Fort Phil Kearny appeared with a cannon.

References. Cyrus Townsend Brady, *Indian Fights and Fighters*, 1971. Jerry Keenan, *The Wagon Box Fight*, 3d ed., 1992.

Jack Gifford

WAINWRIGHT, JONATHAN MAYHEW (1883–1953)

Jonathan Mayhew Wainwright was born in Walla Walla, Washington, in 1883 and graduated from the U.S. Military Academy* in 1906. He was assigned to the cavalry* and served in the Philippines from 1909 to 1910. During World War I,* he served on the staff of the 82d Division in France. In 1940 he returned to the Philippines, with the mission of defending northern Luzon. After the Japanese landed in December 1941, Wainwright's troops retreated into prepared positions on Bataan, in accordance with the prewar plans. When General Douglas MacArthur* left the Philippines in March 1942, Wainwright assumed command of all U.S. forces in the islands. With no hope of relief, on 6 May Wainwright surrendered his remaining forces and became a prisoner of war.* He was held in Manchuria until the end of the war. In a moment of personal triumph, however, on 2 September 1945, Wainwright stood next to MacArthur on board the USS *Missouri* as the emperor's delegate signed the official surrender of the Japanese Empire to the Allied powers. For his service, Wainwright was awarded the Medal of Honor.* After World War II,* he commanded Fourth

Army. Retiring in 1947, Wainwright settled in San Antonio, Texas, where he died on 2 September 1953.

References. John Jacob Beck, *MacArthur and Wainwright*, 1947. Duane Schultz, *Hero of Bataan*, 1981.

John Edgecomb

WALKER DRAGOON .44. *See* Colt "Walker" Dragoon Pistol.

WALTER REED ARMY MEDICAL CENTER

Located between Rock Creek Park and Georgia Avenue in the District of Columbia, on the site of an Army general hospital first opened to patients on 1 May 1909, Walter Reed Army Medical Center (WRAMC) is one of the most modern medical facilities of its kind in the world. In 1923, Chief of Staff* John J. Pershing* designated the hospital the Army Medical Center. In 1951, it was renamed in honor of Major Walter Reed, the Army physician who had helped conquer typhoid and yellow fever (and had died prematurely at age fifty-one in 1902). WRAMC has three primary missions: patient care, education, and medical research. It treats more than 1,000 outpatients each day and admits more than 22,000 patients each year. A number of institutes and other subordinate units, including the Walter Reed Army Institute of Research, the Armed Forces Institute of Pathology, and the Army Office for Defense Medical Information, accomplish WRAMC's other missions. In 1977, the Medical Center moved into a new 1,280-bed, 1,120,000-square-foot, seven-story complex. Today, Walter Reed Army Medical Center is staffed by nearly 5,000 active-duty and 4,000 civilian personnel.

References. John H. Kenworthy, "A New Walter Reed Army Medical Center," *Military Engineer*, January–February 1975, 29–31. Brian Sullivan, "WRAMC," *Soldiers*, July 1979, 6–10.

WAR DEPARTMENT

Congress established a War Department in February 1781 under the Articles of Confederation. The agency did not assume a major role until the Constitution took effect in August 1789. Theoretically, the War Department, through the secretary of war,* administered and directed the land forces in the name of the president as commander in chief.* However, the department failed to develop any administrative effectiveness until 1815. Disagreements over military policy, inadequate financing, varying strengths of the Army, and the absence of dynamic leadership retarded institutional development. The woeful performance of the land forces during the War of 1812* demonstrated that the War Department, and in consequence the Army as well, remained ineffective.

Dramatic change came when John C. Calhoun* became secretary of war (1817–1825). Calhoun initiated reforms that endured into the 20th century. Drawing on legislation approved during the War of 1812, the South Carolinian organized the uniformed chiefs of the Army's administrative and logistical bureaus into a staff. This provided a unified management system that also gave the secretary of war access to military men to advise him on the technical and fiscal needs of the Army. Calhoun also created the position of Commanding General* to set the professional tone of the Army and, in theory, direct combat operations. While Congress rejected his expansible army plan, Calhoun had demonstrated that an active secretary of war could shape military policy.

Calhoun's reorganization served the Army well, giving it institutional stability and fostering a new sense of professionalism. In other respects, however, his legacy plagued the Army for the rest of the century. The bureau chiefs became powerful figures, overshadowing secretaries of war, who came and went frequently—thirty men between 1825 and 1899, few of whom matched Calhoun in intellect or political stature. The bureau chiefs, conversely, remained in office for many years. The position of the Commanding General compounded the problem, as most secretaries of war rarely conferred with the Commanding General, leaving him largely irrelevant to the peacetime operations of the Army, and sometimes even in war. War Department organization also made it difficult to merge management and combat functions. None of the staff elements prepared war plans. When conflict came, the peacetime routine failed initially to cope with manpower mobilization, supply, and strategic deployment. The disruptions of war in 1846, 1861, and 1898 illustrated graphically the great management vacuum in the War Department.

The leadership of Secretary of War Edwin M. Stanton eventually overcame the pressing demands of the Civil War,* but the failures during the Spanish-American War* led to the most significant military reforms since the early 1820s. Secretary of War Elihu Root* won congressional approval for a general staff* system and replacement of the Commanding General with a Chief of Staff* in 1903. While it took a decade for Root's reforms to mature, the General Staff/Chief of Staff system allowed the War Department to begin contingency war planning. It led as well to close collaboration between secretaries of war and Chiefs of Staff, who publicly lobbied for the adoption of a permanent military policy. While not entirely satisfactory to the War Department, congressional approval of the National Defense Act of 1916,* as amended in 1920, gave the nation a military policy that in its broader provisions prevailed into the 1940s.

Despite its imperfections, the new, centralized War Department management system proved flexible enough to administer selective service, organize a mass army, and send an expeditionary force to France in World War I.* Insufficient funding, the need to plan for industrial mobilization, and the advent of military aviation compounded War Department planning and management difficulties when the United States entered World War II.* Fighting a two-front, global war requiring combined air, sea, and land operations necessitated drastic War Department reorganization and expansion and led to the creation of a Joint Chiefs of Staff* system to coordinate interservice efforts. The nation's new position as a world leader in the late 1940s brought major reorganization to the management of the armed services. When Congress approved the National Security Act of 1947,* it abolished the War Department and replaced it with the Department of the Army,* a component of the new Department of Defense.*

References. James E. Hewes, Jr., *From Root to McNamara*, 1975. Allan R. Millett and Peter Maslowski, *For the Common Defense*, 1984. Russell F. Weigley, *History of the United States Army*, enlarged ed., 1984.

Jerry Cooper

WAR OF 1812

The War of 1812, sometimes referred to as the Second War of Independence, was the first attempt by the new national government to wage war against a major power. The causes of this conflict were many, but they were generally rooted in the economic struggle between Britain and Napoleonic France. The Royal Navy seized American ships and cargoes on the seas, while French customs agents did the same in European ports under French control. Adding insult to injury, the British seized crewmen from American ships stopped on the high seas, claiming that they were subjects of the Crown. These flagrant violations of U.S. sovereignty roused national passions. American determination to expand westward also brought conflict with Native Americans. British authorities understood the value of Indian warriors, and British agents sought alliances with Indians living within U.S. borders in the event of war. American frontiersmen saw the British machinations as a diabolical plot to incite war with the Indians, and they concluded the best remedy was to add Canada to the Union. Meanwhile, the charismatic Tecumseh sought to unite the Indians in an effort to halt further white settlement. In November 1811, William Henry Harrison,* governor of the Indiana Territory, burned Tecumseh's capital city on the Tippecanoe River, driving Tecumseh and his followers into open alliance with the British.

The leaders of the Democratic Republican prowar faction—the "War Hawks," as they were known—persuaded a majority of their fellow congressmen to declare war against Great Britain in June 1812. At war with France since 1793, Britain had a powerful war machine, with more than 350,000 Britons in uniform—the U.S. Army had fewer than 7,000 men. The Royal Navy, with nearly 600 vessels, enjoyed an unsurmountable advantage over the U.S. Navy. The young republic had only seven frigates, ten sloops of war, and sixty-two gunboats for coastal defense. However, the U.S. had the advantage of waging war while Britain was already fully occupied with Napoleon. Thus, U.S. strategy* was to seize Canada quickly. The four provinces that then made up Canada had a population one-twelfth that of the United States, and the British army had only 10,000 regulars in North America, most of them defending the port of Halifax in Nova Scotia and the fortress of Quebec in Lower Canada. To the War Hawks, Canada appeared an easy target. Once captured, President James Madison could trade it back to Britain in exchange for a recognition of neutral rights; failing that, he could ask Congress to annex Canada outright.

Congress authorized an expansion of the Army to 35,000 men. However, recruiting proceeded slowly; suitable recruits were more inclined to join a volunteer unit for six months than to enlist as a Regular for five years. The Regular Army was scattered at posts on the frontier and the seacoast. The senior officers were largely American Revolution* veterans, including the ranking major general, Henry Dearborn. Dearborn devised a plan, a three-pronged attack to seize Canada before the winter snows, and commanded the main force gathering in northern New York. Militia Major General Stephen van Rennselaer commanded on the Niagara River, while Brigadier General William Hull commanded the Army of the Northwest. All three forces were to invade simultaneously, thus dividing the British defensive effort, but the plan, workable in theory, collapsed as each commander followed his own timetable.

Hull's poorly supplied army crossed into Canada from Detroit on 12 July. Major General Isaac Brock, the British commander in the province of Upper Canada, joined forces with Tecumseh and, although outnumbered, maneuvered Hull out of Canada and forced him to surrender his army at Detroit. Van Rennselaer ordered his army across the Niagara River and into the village of Queenstown on 13 October. Brigadier General Alexander Smyth, a Regular, refused to support his militia superior and withheld his brigade.* Other militiamen invoked their constitutional right not to be ordered outside the national boundaries. Although Brock was killed while leading a counterattack, the British captured nearly all Americans brave enough to cross the river. In November, Dearborn crossed the border north of Plattsburgh with thousands of raw recruits, but after an indecisive skirmish decided to withdraw from Canada. Smyth, who had taken command from the failed Rennselaer, made the final attempt to invade Canada in 1812. On two occasions, he ordered troops embarked; both times he declined to give the order to cross. The following year Smyth's name disappeared from the Army's rolls. The invasion of Canada failed for a variety of reasons. Senior leaders were incompetent and insufficiently aggressive; Secretary of War* William Eustis was incapable of directing the war effort on land; the supply system was in a shambles; the Army was untrained; and the militia was ill disciplined.

What little success the United States enjoyed in 1812 occurred on the high seas. The Navy and privateers captured hundreds of merchantmen. More surprising, however, was a string of U.S. victories in ship-to-ship actions. These triumphs brought undeniable glory, yet they hardly mattered, as the Royal Navy inexorably tightened its blockade of the Atlantic coast, sealing much of the Navy and merchant fleet in port.

The year 1813 opened with yet another disaster, when the British and their Indian allies defeated a force of Kentuckians on the River Raisin. They then twice laid siege to Fort Meigs, on the Maumee River, but failed to take it. Meanwhile, Commodore Oliver Hazard Perry managed to build a fleet on Lake Erie and, on 10 September 1813, won a decisive victory over a British flotilla. William Henry Harrison, who had taken command from the hapless Hull, followed Perry's achievement with a powerful invasion into western Upper Canada.

Near Moraviantown, on the River Thames, Harrison destroyed a combined British-Indian force and killed Tecumseh, whose dream of an Indian Confederation died with him.

Also in 1813, Madison replaced Eustis with John Armstrong, who understood the importance of the fact that the British were supplied along the St. Lawrence River and the Great Lakes. Severing this supply line meant the eventual defeat of forces to the west; the farther east the cut, the more decisive the effect. Important results would follow the capture of Montreal, and the war would be won when Quebec fell. Unfortunately, Dearborn's main force was too small and too poorly trained to seize either of these cities. Therefore, Armstrong reluctantly allowed Dearborn to conduct operations along Lake Ontario. Assisted by the U.S. Navy, Dearborn raided York and went on to take Fort George, at the western end of the lake. Recovering from this setback, the British defeated U.S. forces at Stoney Creek and Beaver Dams in June. Madison finally relieved Dearborn, while Armstrong planned a two-pronged attack against Montreal. Major General James Wilkinson led 8,000 men down the St. Lawrence, while Major General Wade Hampton, starting on Lake Champlain, moved 4,000 men along the Chateaugay River toward the St. Lawrence. The British, again with inferior numbers, turned back both forces, stopping Hampton only fifteen miles from the St. Lawrence and Wilkinson at Crysler's Farm.

In 1813 the war exploded in an unforseen arena. The Creek Indians, settled largely in Alabama, had a string of grievances against the white authorities. When a few thousand Creeks, known as Red Sticks, decided to strike the governor of Tennessee directed Andrew Jackson,* a militia commander, to punish them. The Creek uprising ended in March 1814 at Horseshoe Bend, when Jackson devasted the Creek Nation.

Napoleon's defeat at Leipzig in 1813 meant the release of large numbers of experienced British soldiers for operations in North America. In London, the mood was for punishing the upstart Americans, and British strategy envisioned widely dispersed offensives. At sea, the fleet would support major raids on the U.S. coast; in the North, an army would move from Montreal toward Albany; and in the South, another large force would seize Mobile or New Orleans. The war was Britain's to win.

U.S. prospects were not entirely bleak, however, for two years of war had witnessed many improvements in the Army, most significantly in generalship as younger men who had proven themselves on campaign replaced Revolution-era veterans. Armstrong persuaded Madison to make one more attempt to seize Canada before British power appeared in force in North America. On 3 July, Major General Jacob Brown's division* crossed the Niagara River and captured Fort Erie. Two days later, a U.S. force defeated an equal number of British regulars and Canadian militia at Chippawa.* Brigadier General Winfield Scott's* superbly trained brigade carried the bulk of the fight. When Major General Gordon Drummond confronted Brown on 25 July at Lundy's Lane,* adjacent to Niagara Falls, the bloodiest battle of the war yet occurred. When decisive victory eluded the Americans, they returned to Fort Erie, where they withstood a seven-week siege before forcing Drummond to withdraw. There the New York militia proved their bravery and redeemed their earlier disgrace at Queenstown. George Izard, another new brigadier, crossed the Niagara in October but was also unable to win a decisive battle. Although improved generalship and fighting skill failed to drive the British out of Canada, it did prevent disaster in the face of powerful British counterattacks.

In August, 4,500 British troops landed at Benedict, Maryland, drove off a hastily assembled body of defenders at Bladensburg, and burned the public buildings of Washington. The British reembarked and in September attempted to capture Baltimore; they were thwarted by Fort McHenry,* guarding Baltimore Harbor. Sir George Prevost, Governor General of British North America, personally led 11,000 combat-hardened British regulars and a small naval flotilla south toward Plattsburgh. In Plattsburgh Bay, a squadron under Captain Thomas McDonough defeated the British flotilla. With the loss of his navy, Prevost could not supply his invasion force, and he retreated northward.

New Orleans was the target of the final British attempt to punish the United States. In December 1814, Admiral Sir Alexander Cochrane sailed sixty vessels and 14,000 troops into Lake Borgne. Major General Sir Edward Pakenham, an experienced and trusted subordinate of the Duke of Wellington, brought his army through the bayous and onto a plain only nine miles from New Orleans. On 8 January 1815, Pakenham ordered a frontal assault against Andrew Jackson's lines of Regulars, volunteers, militia, Indians, and pirates. The result was a disaster for British arms: 2,500 casualties out of 6,000 men engaged. To the misfortune of many—including Pakenham, killed at the head of his men—word of the peace treaty signed at Ghent on Christmas Eve had not yet reached the opposing forces.

The Treaty of Ghent did not speak to the causes of the war, which disappeared with the end of war in Europe. More importantly, the United States never again invaded Canada, nor did British naval officers impress American sailors. With newfound confidence gained at Chippawa and New Orleans, the Army looked forward to the nation's march westward. For astute observers of national policy, however, the cost of military unpreparedness was obvious—needless loss of life and treasure.

References. John R. Elting, *Amateurs, To Arms!* 1991. Donald R. Hickey, *The War of 1812*, 1989. John K. Mahon, *The War of 1812*, 1972. J.C.A. Stagg, *Mr. Madison's War*, 1983.

Richard Barbuto

WAR PLAN ORANGE

War Plan Orange, primarily written by the U.S. Navy for a war with Japan, was part of the series of hypothetical war plans begun by the United States in the early 1900s. Among other plans in the series were Plan Red (war with Britain), Plan Green (war with Mexico), and Plan Black (war with Germany).

Orange planning began in 1906 with the rise of tensions over immigration policies between the U.S. and Japan, it continued until 1939, when it was superceded by the more comprehensive Rainbow Plans,* set against a variety of enemies, including coalitions involving the United States. The Rainbow series, as it applied to the Pacific theater, was heavily influenced by Plan Orange.

Although variously cautious and bold, Plan Orange was remarkably consistent in that it projected an initial defense against Japanese expansion followed by a midocean counteroffensive from one island group to the next. The war would culminate with the dictation of terms to a blockaded and bombarded Japan. The projected timeline for this entire process was two to three years, given a war with Japan alone.

The Army's portion of War Plan Orange was necessarily limited, as it was admitted early on that the Navy could not transport and protect reinforcements for the Philippines. The garrison there was to hold out as long as possible without relief. Army counteroffensives were to be limited to the seizure of island bases for naval use and the accumulation of reserves for the reconquest of the Philippines and for a possible, though unlikely, invasion of the Japanese home islands. Plan Orange was remarkably prophetic in its broad context, although the two-ocean war slowed it down, and the initial Japanese offensives were more wide-ranging and successful than projected. The basic outlines of the Allied counteroffensives followed the outlines of War Plan Orange, and the plan's concentration on isolating Japan, followed by an intensive bombardment, prefigured the actual second and third phases of the war.

References. Edward S. Miller, *War Plan Orange*, 1991. Mark S. Watson, *Chief of Staff*, 1950; 1985.

John Broom

WAR PLANS DIVISION

The Army General Staff,* established during the Elihu Root* reforms of 1903, emerged from World War I* with a greatly enhanced reputation for effectiveness. When General of the Armies John J. Pershing* became Chief of Staff* in 1921, he further strengthened the structure, with a new War Plans Division (WPD). The role of the WPD was to address strategic planning issues and related preparations in case of war. Prior to World War II,* the WPD drafted a number of contingency plans in the event of war with individual countries. The most notable of these color plans was War Plan Orange* for war with Japan. The War Plans Division was also to provide the nucleus of any wartime general headquarters that would direct military operations during a future conflict. During World War II, the expanded War Plans Division, renamed the Operations Division (OPD), became General George C. Marshall's* command post a de facto superior general staff for the direction of overseas operations. In 1946, internal changes within the Army restored the General Staff to its prewar position, eliminated the OPD, and reestablished the prewar structure of five coequal divisions.

References. Maurice Matloff, ed., *American Military History*, rev. ed, 1989. Maurice Matloff and Edwin M. Snell, *Strategic Planning for Coalition Warfare, 1941–1942*, 1953.

Gary Bounds

WARRANT OFFICER

Congress created the Warrant Officer Corps on 7 July 1896. Traditionally, the rank had served as a culmination of a lifetime of enlisted service in a technical field. A warrant officer was recognized as the senior specialist in a military occupational specialty* (MOS). Initially composed of engineering specialists, the Warrant Officer Corps expanded to include band leaders, clerical, administrative, maintenance, and aviation specialists. Today's definition of a warrant officer is best expressed by the Warrant Officer Study Group, convened by the Chief of Staff* on 24 June 1985. It stated that a warrant officer is "an officer appointed by warrant by the Secretary of the Army* based on a sound level of technical and tactical competence. The warrant officer is a highly specialized expert and trainer who, by gaining progressive levels of expertise and leadership, operates, maintains, administers, and manages the Army's equipment, support activities, or technical services."

Reference. Lawrence P. Crocker, *Army Officer's Guide*, 46th ed., 1993.

Robert J. Dalessandro

WASHINGTON, GEORGE (1732–1799)

Raised from the age of eleven by a verbally abusive single parent, George Washington left home at an early age. Failing in his attempt to join the Royal Navy at fourteen, he became a surveyor at seventeen and entered military service, with an appointment as a major of Virginia militia, before his twenty-first birthday. Campaigns against French and Indian forces in the western wilderness provided his military schooling. In far-ranging independent operations, he became known internationally—and suffered his first defeats. Combined operations with British regulars saw him play key roles in Major General Edward Braddock's disaster in 1755 and in General John Forbes's victory in 1758. Although a colonel commanding Virginia's colonial regiment, he failed to gain integration into the regular army and resigned.

When the American Revolution* broke out, the Continental Congress appointed Washington commander in chief* of the Continental Army.* He faced the daunting task of raising an army even as he had to employ it. The army had to be recruited, equipped, trained, sustained, and led into battle—with neither a body of experience nor a corps of professional leaders to build on. By indomitable will and matchless force of character, he succeeded against all odds. More than anyone before or since, he *was* the army.

Personally courageous and charismatic, able under the full weight of adversity to keep his eye unwaveringly on the objective, at once flexible in planning and forceful in execution, capable of learning from setbacks, and having a rare balance between prudence and aggressiveness, he was a complete general. At the tactical level, he was competent; operationally, he was sound and sometimes superb; strategically, he was brilliant. He was one of the few to see that a revolution has two parts: winning the war and shaping the peace. He blocked a scheme that might have turned the army against the government; he defined what the peacetime military establishment ought to be; and he played a central role in creating in the Constitution a powerful chief executive who would be commander in chief of the nation's armed forces. As president, he worked constantly to bolster the country's military strength, molding the core elements of the defense establishment—which remains in being after two centuries.

He never stopped working for a strong military. "To be prepared for war is one of the most effectual means of preserving the peace," he warned. The last letter he wrote was in support of establishing a military academy.

References. John R. Alden, *George Washington*, 1984. Trevor N. Deputy. *The Military Life of George Washington*, 1969. James T. Flexner, *George Washington*, 1965–1972.

Dave R. Palmer

WASHITA

Washita was one of several battles fought during the Southern Plains War* of 1868–1869; it typified the Army's concept of total war and winter campaigning against the Indians following the Civil War.* Under orders from Major General Philip H. Sheridan,* Lieutenant Colonel (Brevet Major General) George A. Custer* and 800 men of the 7th Cavalry attacked fifty-one lodges of Black Kettle's Cheyenne on the Washita River (in present-day Oklahoma); it was the same band that Colonel John Chivington and his Colorado cavalry had savaged at Sand Creek* in 1864. After trailing a large war party, Custer and his men found Black Kettle's village and attacked at dawn on the morning of 27 November 1868. The village was quickly siezed, although skirmishing continued throughout the morning. One group of fifteen cavalrymen under Major Joel H. Elliott, pursuing a group of Cheyennes, was cut off and annihilated by a larger force of Indians from Cheyenne, Arapaho, Kiowa, and Comanche villages downstream. Custer destroyed Black Kettle's tipis, food, robes, weapons, and other winter necessities, including over 800 ponies. By the end of the day, however, Custer's supply train had become vulnerable, his men were without overcoats, and he had wounded and captive women and children to care for. As a result, he chose not to search for Elliott's group, for which he would later be severely criticized. Custer mounted his men and turned toward the remaining Indian villages, forcing the warriors to return to defend their camps. As night fell, Custer turned from the Washita Valley, arriving at Camp Supply on 2 December 1868.

References. Cyrus Townsend Brady, *Indian Fights and Fighters*, 1971. Stan Hoig, *The Battle of the Washita*, 1976.

Jeffrey Prater

WEAPONS SQUAD

The weapons squad is a combat element of the infantry,* airborne, or air assault rifle platoon* designed to provide intensive suppressive or supporting fires for the maneuver rifle squads.* It consists of a squad leader, two machine gunners equipped with M60s or other light machine guns, two assistant machine gunners, two antitank gunners equipped with antitank weapons, and two assistant antitank gunners.

References. Anthony A. Cucolo and Dale S. Ringler. "Heavy Infantry." *Infantry.* September–December 1998, 7–10. Harold G. Moore and Joseph L. Galloway, *We Were Soldiers Once . . . and Young,* 1992.

Andrew N. Morris

WEB GEAR

Experimentation with woven cotton webbing as a material for cartridge belts, slings, suspenders, pouches, and other military accoutrements began in the late 1870s. Cotton webbing offered advantages over leather belts and equipment, including lighter weight, greater durability, and elimination of verdigris on brass cartridges. The name most commonly associated with cotton webbing is Anson Mills, a Civil War* and Indian Wars* officer who developed and sold to the U.S. Army a number of designs for woven belts. By 1912, cotton web gear had become standard issue for most individual equipment items, except holsters, which continued to be leather. In the mid-1960s, nylon began to replace cotton in the production of web gear.

References. R. Stephen Dorsey, *American Military Belts and Related Equipments,* 1984. Harold G. Moore and Joseph L. Galloway, *We Were Soldiers Once . . . and Young,* 1992.

Stephen C. McGeorge

WEDEMEYER, ALBERT COADY (1897–1989)

Albert Coady Wedemeyer succeeded General Joseph Stilwell* as commander of U.S. troops in the China-Burma-India theater* in World War II.* During his career he served mainly in staff posts; his prewar experience included service in China, the Philippines, and Europe, where he spent two years at the German Kriegsakademie (staff college). He was involved in organizing the expansion of the U.S. Army in 1940 and in 1941 was appointed to the war plans branch of the General Staff,* where he was involved in planning strategy and policy. In 1943, Wedemeyer went to the Southeast Asia Command as deputy chief of staff to British Admiral Lord Mountbatten. Wedemeyer represented the supreme commander during several decision-making conferences that changed the strategy for the invasion of Japan from a seaborne to a land and air campaign. In 1944 he replaced Stilwell in China and served as chief of staff to Chiang Kai-shek, with whom he got along better than Stilwell had. He remained in this post until 1946, when he retired.

References. Keith E. Eiler, ed., *Wedemeyer on War and Peace*, 1987. Jonathan Spence, *To Change China*, 1969. William Stueck, *The Wedemeyer Mission*, 1984.

Luke Knowley

WEST POINT. *See* U.S. Military Academy.

WESTMORELAND, WILLIAM CHILDS (1914–)

William Childs Westmoreland's career spanned three wars and much of a fourth: World War II,* the Korean War,* the Vietnam War,* and the Cold War.* His career started in the days of horse-drawn artillery and ended in the era of air mobility. Born in Spartanburg, South Carolina, in 1914, the only child of a local businessman, he went to the Citadel* for a year, then to the U.S. Military Academy.* He graduated in 1936 into the field artillery* and saw action as a field-grade officer in North Africa and Sicily and from Normandy to Germany. Switching to airborne infantry* after World War II, he led the 187th Airborne Regimental Combat Team in Korea and was promoted to brigadier general in 1952. Peacetime posts included command of the 101st Airborne Division,* high-level duties in the Pentagon,* superintendant of the U.S. Military Academy, and command of XVIIIth Airborne Corps. He went to Vietnam in January 1964 as the deputy commander and became commander in June. He oversaw the buildup of U.S. forces and led the overall effort for the next four years. He was initially very successful, but his star waned as the war dragged on inconclusively. He remained loyally supportive of civilian leaders despite their misgivings about the war, and his reputation remains linked to the lost cause. He served four years as Chief of Staff* of the Army, retiring in 1972. He ran unsuccessfully for governor of South Carolina. Thereafter he devoted himself to explaining the Vietnam War and to aiding Vietnam veteran organizations across the country.

References. Ernest B. Furgurson, *Westmoreland*, 1968. Samuel Zaffiri, *Westmoreland*, 1994.

Dave R. Palmer

WESTPORT

On 19 September 1864, Confederate Major General Sterling Price, commander of the Army of Missouri, began a campaign toward St. Louis to rally men to the Confederate cause and obtain needed supplies. Hastily gathered Union reinforcements forced Price to turn west toward Kansas City, but his mission could still succeed if he captured the Union military stores at Fort Leavenworth,* Kansas. Two Union columns of about 20,000 men each, commanded by Major General Samuel Curtis, converged on Price's force of about 10,000. Initial contact east of Kansas City along the Little Blue River and at Byram's Ford across the Big Blue River on 21 and 22 October forced Price to occupy a defensive line along Brush Creek near Westport, Missouri, facing north toward the city. Price left a cavalry force under Major General John Marmaduke facing east to contest Major General Alfred S. Pleasonton's crossing of the Big Blue.

Early on 23 October Price attacked Curtis, while Pleasonton attempted a crossing at Byram's Ford against Marmaduke. Fighting along Brush Creek was indecisive until a farmer showed Curtis a hidden ravine by which Union forces could envelop Price's left. The Confederate line held until about 1300, when simultaneous attacks all along the front and pressure from Pleasonton, who had succeeded in driving Marmaduke away from Byram's Ford, left Price no choice except to withdraw. Incomplete casualty reports indicate about 492 Confederate dead, wounded, and captured during the three-day fight, and Union losses of about 200. Price began a retreat but was confronted and badly mauled two days later at Mine Creek, Kansas. Curtis called off the pursuit in early November, when the remnants of Price's army reached the Arkansas River in eastern Oklahoma.

References. Fred L. Lee, ed., *The Battle of Westport*, 1982. Howard N. Monnett, *Action before Westport, 1864*, 1964.

Richard L. Kiper

WHITE PLAINS

After General William Howe's British and Hessian forces drove the Colonials from New York City in September 1776, and after a skirmish at Harlem Heights, George Washington* retreated northward and entrenched his 14,000 men on hills overlooking White Plains. With his right flank anchored on the Bronx River and his left on Mill Pond, Washington awaited Howe's 16,000 strong pursuit force, hoping his foe would launch a costly frontal assault. On 28 October, skirmishes occurred before the Colonial positions, but the awaited frontal attack never came. Instead, Howe focused on Chatterton Hill, across the Bronx River, which dominated Washington's position. Almost too late, Washington realized the high ground's significance and rushed reinforcements to aid two militia regiments* guarding it. Though the Continentals repulsed repeated British attacks, a force of Hessian and British dragoons routed the militia holding Washington's right, forcing the defenders to withdraw. Fortunately, the British did not emplace artillery on the heights or challenge their main position, as the Continentals feared. Under cover of a rainstorm, Washington withdrew farther northward. The British had taken a hill at a cost of some 200 casualties, while inflicting at least 150 on their foes. Though defeated, Washington felt that the battle had improved morale, for his forces had not fled but stood firm until ordered to retire.

References. Israel Mauduit, *Conduct of Sir William Howe*, 1927, 1971. Richard F. Snow, "Standoff at White Plains," *American Heritage*, 1973, 41–44.

Stanley Adamiak

WILDERNESS

The Battle of the Wilderness was the first in a series of battles during the Overland campaign fought between the Union Army of the Potomac* and the Confederate Army of Northern Virginia. Lieutenant General Ulysses S. Grant's* plan was to maneuver toward the Confederate capital at Richmond. He knew that Robert E. Lee* would move to protect the city. Grant crossed the Rapidan River west of Fredericksburg, Virginia, on 4 May 1864 and moved south into the area known as the Wilderness. Lee's Army of Northern Virginia lay in wait farther to the west. Lee discovered Grant's move and ordered attacks on his line of march, but neither side knew exactly where the other was. Consequently, the battle developed piecemeal as Federal and Confederate commands arrived on the field and deployed for battle.

The Wilderness was a poorly developed area with few settlements and fewer roads and trails. Thick scrub and second-growth forest dominated the terrain. Few places existed where artillery could be effective, so engagement ranges were the closest of the Civil War.* Lee's initial attacks caused the Federals to stop moving south and reorient to the west from their line of march. The battle developed slowly, as units groped their way forward into contact with the enemy. Meanwhile, units became disoriented, and organizations lost cohesion. Command and control was difficult. By the evening of 5 May, the opposing battle lines lay just west of the clearing at Wilderness Tavern and stretched four miles from north of the Orange Court House Turnpike southeastward to an unfinished railroad line south of the Orange Plank Road. Grant prepared to attack on the morning of 6 May. Lee brought up reinforcements but neglected to make adequate preparations in the southern part of his line along the Orange Plank Road. Federal attacks early on the 6th made good headway until Lee's reserves arrived and counterattacked, restoring the situation by about noon. After that, neither side gained an advantage.

Casualties were high, the Federals losing 17,700 men killed, wounded, and missing. The Confederates lost 7,500. Many expected the Federals to withdraw north of the Rapidan and develop a new campaign. Grant, however, began a series of skillful maneuvers toward Richmond that kept the armies generally in contact with each other for the next two months, during which nearly 100,000 more soldiers on both sides became casualties.

References. Gary W. Gallagher, ed., *The Wilderness Campaign*, 1997. Gordon C. Rhea, *The Battle of the Wilderness*, 1994. Noah Andre Trudeau, *Bloody Roads South*, 1989.

George Knapp

WILLIE AND JOE

Willie and Joe were the beloved World War II* characters created *by Stars and Stripes* cartoonist Bill Mauldin.* Willie and Joe first appeared in the 45th Infantry Division's newspaper, where Mauldin originally served as a soldier-journalist. Willie and Joe were archetypical infantry* grunts who experienced all of the pain, suffering, frustration, cynicism, comradeship, and satisfaction of a job well done that every G.I.* experienced. Through Willie and Joe, Mauldin brought an understanding of war to the level of the common soldier and raised morale by allowing soldiers to laugh at themselves.

References. Bill Mauldin, *Up Front*, 1945, and *The Brass Ring*, 1971.

Steven J. Allie

WILSON'S CREEK

In the summer of 1861, Brigadier General Nathaniel Lyon aggressively pursued pro-Southern state forces under Governor Claiborne Jackson and General Sterling Price, who withdrew across Missouri and kept their command intact. After skirmishes at Booneville, Carthage, and Crane Creek, Lyon held Springfield, while Price and Jackson camped nearby waiting for reinforcements. Brigadier General Ben McCullough arrived in early August with reinforcements from Arkansas, Louisiana, and Texas, bringing the Confederate force to twice Lyon's strength. Price and McCullough argued over leadership but finally agreed to move on Springfield. Lyon, dispairing at lack of reinforcements and supplies, determined to withdraw to his base at Rolla. His subordinates, however, convinced him to attack the Confederates, now camped just ten miles southwest along Wilson's Creek. Lyon divided his outnumbered command and attacked early on 10 August. The Confederates were initially surprised but slowly recovered. After six hours of seesaw fighting, including the rout of a Union flanking column under Colonel Franz Sigel, Lyon was killed leading a charge. Shortly afterward the Federals withdrew to Springfield and then to Rolla. The Confederates occupied Springfield on the 11th, then procrastinated. McCullough decided to return to Arkansas with his command; Price continued north to capture Lexington but could manage no more before winter set in.

Wilson's Creek was a Confederate tactical victory, and it had the same practical effect as First Bull Run,* fought just nineteen days earlier. It forced the Union leadership to recognize the potential danger of losing Missouri and eliminated any Northern notions of a quick and easy victory over secession.

References. Edwin C. Bearss, *The Battle of Wilson's Creek*, 1988. William R. Brooksher, *Bloody Hill*, 1995.

George Knapp

WINTER CAMPAIGN 1868–1869. *See* Southern Plains War.

WOMEN'S ARMY AUXILIARY CORPS. *See* Women's Army Corps.

WOMEN'S ARMY CORPS

On 14 May 1942, after the Japanese attack on Pearl Harbor on 7 December 1941 and the U.S. declaration of war, Congress established the Women's Army Auxiliary Corps. Its mission was to obtain and train women for administrative positions to release men for duty in combat divisions.* The corps operated so successfully that on 1 September 1943 Congress gave it military status as part of the Army of the United States and renamed it the Women's Army Corps (WAC). By the end of World War II,* the Army had assigned women to duties in administration, communications, medical care, maintenance, air operations, supply, and intelligence both in the United States and overseas. Over 140,000 women served in the WAC during the war. Senior Army generals like Dwight D. Eisenhower* praised their service and asked Congress in 1946 to include the WAC in the Regular Army, thus making it a permanent career field for women. Although the idea was opposed by some legislators, in June 1948 Congress authorized women to serve in the Regular Army and the Organized Reserve Corps. To satisfy opponents of the new law, Congress precluded women from serving in combat units, from commanding men, and from being promoted to general.

Despite the restrictions, however, thousands of patriotic women made the Army their careers during the next three decades. WAC strength reached 9,000 by 1960 and 12,500 by 1970. The end of selective service in 1972 created a serious challenge for recruiters to meet the Army's manpower needs. American women were more than ready to help fill this need. To enhance their career opportunities, Congress and the Army eliminated many of the restrictions concerning their service (commanding men, promotion to general, etc.). By October 1978, WAC strength had increased to 52,000. In that month, Congress responded to pressure from the women's liberation movement, which considered placing women in a separate corps discriminatory, to eliminate the Women's Army Corps as a separate part of the Army. Thereafter, women's training, assignments, and promotions were assimiliated into programs with those of men. They were no longer known as WACs but merely as women in the Army. Their history and traditions as a proud corps of the Army live on in the hearts of former members and at the Women's Army Corps Museum at Fort McClellan,* Alabama.

References. Bettie J. Morden, *The Women's Army Corps, 1945–1978*, 1990. Mattie E. Treadwell, *The Women's Army Corps*, 1954.

Bettie J. Morden

WOOD, LEONARD (1860–1927)

Born in New Hampshire in 1860 and trained as a doctor at Harvard, Leonard Wood entered military service in 1885. Winning notice for his courage during the successful 1886 expedition to capture Geronimo, his career nevertheless remained unspectacular until the Spanish-American War.* Thanks to his friendship with Theodore Roosevelt, Wood was given command of the 1st Volunteer Cavalry, the Rough Riders.* Promoted to brigade* command and appointed governor of Cuba in 1900, he earned his first star by reforming Cuban education, law, medicine, and government. Sent to the Philippines in 1904 as governor of Moro Province to pacify the Moros, Wood assumed command of the Philippine Division in 1908.

Appointed Chief of Staff* of the Army in 1910, Wood won a critical struggle with Adjutant General* Fred Ainsworth that permitted him to reorganize the General Staff.* With the aid of Secretary of War* Henry Stimson, Wood won congressional approval to organize the first four peacetime divisions.* He was, however, frustrated that he could not do more to create a true mobilization capability. During World War I,* Wood commanded the Department of the East and skillfully employed the New York media in promoting a citizen army. His outspoken criticism of the nation's lack of preparedness for large-scale war, and of General John J. Pershing* in particular, forestalled any wartime command.

In 1920, Leonard Wood narrowly lost the Republican nomination for president to Warren G. Harding, who appointed him governor of the Philippines. He died in that office in 1927, leaving a legacy of effective Army reform and government service.

References. Hermann Hagedorn, *Leonard Wood*, 1931. Jack C. Lane, *Armed Progressive*, 1978.

Claude Sasso

WORLD WAR I

World War I began in August 1914 for most European countries. From the beginning, President Woodrow Wilson's neutrality policy sought to avoid U.S. involvement. This was made impossible when in 1917 Germany declared an unrestricted submarine campaign threatening U.S. shipping. On 2 April Wilson, reelected the previous fall on the slogan "He Kept Us Out of War," asked for a declaration of war. Congress voted for war on 6 April. At that time, the U.S. Army consisted of 128,000 Regulars and 67,000 National Guardsmen demobilizing along the Mexican border. Regiments* were the basis of the Army; divisions* and larger units, such as corps* and armies,* existed only on paper. No plans existed for military operations overseas or for mobilization of a larger force in the United States. By European standards of size, equipment, and experience, the U.S. Army was insignificant. It was, however, backed by a tremendous industrial and manpower potential. By the 11 November 1918 armistice nineteen months later, the U.S. Army was 3.7 million strong, with two million men serving in the American Expeditionary Force* (AEF) in France.

Secretary of War* Newton D. Baker oversaw the massive efforts to raise, house, clothe, equip, train, and ship U.S. forces for service in France, with the assistance of Army Chief of Staff Hugh L. Scott and Assistant Chief of Staff Tasker Bliss.* In response to British and French requests for an immediate military response, Baker designated Major General John J. Pershing* as the AEF commander in chief and sent him with a small staff to France in late May 1918. Arriving in June, they were immediately followed by four regular infantry* regiments,* which were organized into the 1st Division* in France. The 2d Division,* consisting of a Marine and an Army brigade,* was formed in France in the spring of 1918. All other divisions were raised in the United States and shipped to France. In France, the AEF staff quickly developed three documents that provided the War Department* an AEF master plan—a general organization calling for a million-man, separate American army by July 1918; a logistical system to support the AEF; and a shipping priority schedule to maintain a balance between combat and support organizations.

Efforts to organize and manage a rapid expansion of the U.S. Army were fraught with misconceptions as to what was needed and what was possible; with misunderstandings about what was said and what was meant; and with mistakes in judgment, both in France and in the United States. The War Department, reorganized in 1903 by the Root reforms, split responsibilities between bureau chiefs and the General Staff. This organization proved inadequate to meet the diverse, complex, and massive demands of mobilization. Several reorganizations, along with personnel changes, were necessary to create a War Department capable of meeting the demands of the war. At the armistice, General Payton C. March,* named Army Chief of Staff* in February 1918, oversaw a War Department that subordinated bureau chiefs to four general staff sections—Operations; Military Intelligence; Purchase, Storage, and Traffic; and War Plans. These agencies worked closely with the AEF, with units in the United States, and with civilian industrial and transportation agencies.

On 19 May 1917, Congress passed the Selective Service Act. All male citizens and resident aliens between twenty-one and thirty years of age were to register with local draft boards. Unlike conscription during the Civil War,* there were no bounties, substitutes, or purchased exemptions. Local draft boards, administered by civilians, decided who would fill their quotas for the military and who would work in industry. Almost three million men were conscripted into military service, with millions of others working in war industries. During the war, 67 percent of all soldiers were drafted, compared to only 6 percent in the Civil War.* The composition of the Army changed dramatically. In April 1917, the Army was two-thirds Regular and one-third federalized National Guardsmen. At the armistice, it was 77 percent National Army (draftees), 10 percent National Guard,* and 13 percent Regular.

Even with the draft, finding officers in adequate numbers and quality remained a major problem. The initial 5,800 Regular and 3,200 National Guard officers were insufficient to meet the requirement for almost 200,000 officers. "Inexperienced but enthusiastic" described most officers. Only one of every six officers had prior military experience, three attended the ninety-day Officer Training Couse, and two had little or no training, having received a commission based upon their civilian technical skills.

Volunteers and draftees were organized into fifty-four divisions* of 28,000 men each. Forty-two of these divisions deployed to France. Twenty-nine divisions—seven Regular Army, eleven National Guard, and eleven National Army—saw combat. To overcome tensions and eliminate confusions created by the three types of units, in August 1918 the War Department declared that henceforth only the United States Army existed; references to Regular Army, National Guard, National Army, and Reserve Corps were to be discontinued. In France, however, it proved easier to declare the existence of the U.S. Army than to eliminate the pride, prejudice, and distinctiveness of Regulars, National Guardsmen, and National Army draftees.

Establishing facilities for mobilization and training divisions was one of the first challenges the War Department faced. Using cost-plus contracts, thirty-two posts were established by the winter of 1917. Sixteen National Guard camps were established in the South, where the soldiers generally lived under canvas. In addition, sixteen National Army cantonments were established with semipermanent wooden buildings. Clothing, feeding, equipping, and transporting these units placed tremendous strain upon the War Department bureaus. Each struggled, with notable failures as well as successes, particularly during the first nine months of the war.

Divisions were shipped to France based on training status and availability of shipping. Just as the AEF depended upon the allies for equipping the AEF, the Shipping Control Committee depended on them for transporting the AEF to France. Despite the efforts of the Emergency Fleet Corporation to beg, borrow, and steal shipping, inadequate tonnage slowed the AEF buildup. During the first thirteen months of the war, only 500,000 Americans arrived in France. After May 1918, the last six months of the war, when the British provided more ships, 1.5 million Americans arrived, nearly 50 percent in British vessels. This massive influx disrupted AEF plans for a balanced force yet provided the manpower for a separate U.S. sector and a major contribution to ending the war in 1918.

Unlike in World War II,* the United States was not an arsenal for the allies during World War I. Economic mobilization suffered the same difficulties as military mobilization. Uncertain, constantly changing requirements from both the allies and the AEF complicated effective management. Lack of bureaucratic machinery to interconnect civilian industry, government agencies, and the War Department further complicated the process. The General Munitions Board, formed in April 1917, was ineffective. The War Industries Board (WIB), established in July, floundered until Bernard Baruch became its chairman in May 1918. Within the War Department, Major General George W. Goethals, first as Quartermaster General* and then as Director of Purchase, Storage, and Traffic, greatly improved War Department effectiveness. Yet when Baker offered Pershing the services of Goethals to command the AEF Services of Supply* (SOS), Pershing refused, placing Major General James G. Harbord in command of the SOS instead. This highlights Pershing's concern for his own authority and his strong belief that he, as the AEF commander, was senior to the Chief of Staff* in Washington. March, on the other hand, provided the AEF tremendous support; he saw the Chief of Staff as senior to any field commander. Baker worked to prevent this conflict from interfering with the war effort.

After the armistice, the War Department faced the same problem as at the beginning of the war, only in reverse. Demobilization required many of the skills and systems developed to support the war effort. Fortunately, demobilization went more smoothly than mobilization. By the end of June 1919, 2.7 million soldiers had returned to civilian life.

References. Kathleen Burk, *Britain, America and the Sinews of War; 1914–1918*, 1985. Edward M. Coffman, *The War to End All Wars*, 1986. David M. Kennedy. *Over Here*. 1980. James L. Stokesbury, *A Short History of World War I*, 1981.

Robert Ramsey

WORLD WAR II

World War II brought the U.S. Army to levels of size and power unsurpassed in its history. When Germany invaded Poland in September 1939, the Army numbered only 190,000 officers and men, equipped largely with World War I* weapons and gear. Although some modest expansion and modernization followed the outbreak of war in Europe, the Army's first real step toward rearmament was in response to Germany's lightning conquest of France in May and June 1940. An alarmed Congress authorized the induction of reservists in August 1940 and in September passed the nation's first peacetime conscription act. By 7 December 1941, when the United States entered the war, the Army numbered 1.6 million men, organized into thirty-five divisions;* not until 1943 did the Army approach its full wartime strength of roughly eight million men— about two million in the Army Air Forces,* two million in ground combat units, and four million in training, logistics, and administration. At full strength, the Army fielded ninety combat divisions; sixty-six of these were infantry* divisions, eighteen from the National Guard.* There were also sixteen armored, five airborne, and two cavalry* divisions, and one mountain division. In addition, the Army had a multitude of smaller artillery, engineer, tank, tank destroyer, and antiaircraft units that reinforced specific divisions as needed.

In terms of doctrine,* the U.S. Army in World War II developed the infantry-artillery team—small, light, and mobile infantry units amply supported by heavier weapons at the company,* battalion,* and regimental levels. Emphasis was on maneuver and the envelopment of enemy positions. U.S. artillery,* arguably the finest in the world, possessed transportation and communication assets that allowed it to accompany the infantry without losing its ability to quickly mass fires on critical targets. The tank occupied an ambiguous position in U.S. doctrine, being viewed as both a support to the infantry and as an independent weapon. The spirit of Army doctrine was to attack and destroy the enemy's forces.

The chain of command for the World War II Army extended from President Franklin D. Roosevelt to Secretary of War* Henry L. Stimson, then to Army Chief of Staff* George C. Marshall.* General Marshall exercised command over Army troops in the combat theaters through the Operations Division of the General Staff.* Two other headquarters under his authority were responsible for troops within the United States: Army Ground Forces,* under LTG Lesley J. McNair,* organized troops into units and supervised their training; Army Service Forces, under Lieutenant General Brehon B. Sommervell, directed the logistical support for a war effort that literally circled the globe. In addition, the Army Air Forces, under Lieutenant General Henry H. Arnold,* served in both operational and administrative capacities as the Army's quasi-independent air arm.

When the Japanese attack on Pearl Harbor catapulted the United States into war, the Army had completed only the initial stages of its mobilization. However, Army garrisons were already in danger spots from Iceland to the Philippines. The Philippines garrison, including the Philippine Division and some 160,000 Filipinos, was the first to make contact with enemy ground troops, when the Japanese invaded Luzon in December 1941. Americans and Filipinos fought tenaciously in a hopeless cause for five months, capitulating in May 1942 in the worst defeat in U.S. Army history.

Within four months, however, the Army, along with the Navy, Marines, and other Allied forces, began limited counteroffensives against the overextended Japanese. Under General Douglas MacArthur,* U.S. and Australian forces opened in September 1942 an offensive in New Guinea* that lasted until July 1944 and eventually involved eleven Army divisions. Lieutenant General Walter Krueger's* Sixth Army* became MacArthur's principal ground force head-quarters in New Guinea. A Navy and Marine counteroffensive in the Solomon Islands involved four other Army divisions. Far to the north, a single Army division evicted the Japanese from the Aleutians during the summer of 1943.

Meanwhile, the Army began its war against Germany on 8 November 1942, with the Anglo-U.S. invasion of North Africa, Operation Torch,* under Lieu-tenant General Dwight D. Eisenhower.* Inexperienced U.S. troops suffered a sharp defeat at Kasserine Pass* in February 1943 but recovered to play a major role in the final offensive that led to the capture of 250,000 Axis troops in May. Five U.S. divisions fought in North Africa.

The Allies quickly followed up their victory in Tunisia with an invasion of Sicily on 10 July 1943. With troops of the British Eighth Army, Lieutenant General George S. Patton, Jr.'s* Seventh Army* landed five divisions on the beaches of southern Sicily, while an airborne division parachuted behind the coastal defenses. Sicily was secured on 17 August, and the Allies turned their attention to the Italian mainland. Following British landings at the toe of Italy, Lieutenant General Mark Clark's* Fifth Army* landed at Salerno on 9 September 1943, inaugurating a protracted and bitterly fought campaign in which weather and terrain were as formidable as the enemy. At year's end, Fifth Army, with the British Eighth Army on its right, was stalemated in the vicinity of Cassino. An Allied amphibious assault at Anzio,* intended to turn the German defensive position, only created another deadly stalemate. Rome finally fell to Fifth Army on 4 June 1943, but the Allied pursuit toward the Po River valley ran up against yet another German defensive line in the Appenine Mountains. By this time, both the Allies and the Germans had drawn down their forces in Italy in favor of the campaign in France. Not until April 1945, with the arrival of new divisions, did the Allies break through to the Po and close out the costly and controversial Italian campaign. This forgotten war involved a total of eleven U.S. divisions and lasted an agonizing twenty months.

To General Marshall and the Army high command, the campaigns in North Africa, Sicily, and Italy were costly distractions from the main business at hand, a cross-Channel invasion of France, followed by a decisive campaign to destroy Germany's military might. Fundamentally, this was the mission for which the Army had been raised, organized, and trained; it called for the largest assemblage of U.S. Army forces in history. The buildup of these forces in England began in 1942, but many of the early-arriving units were drawn off for the North African campaign, while the demands of the Pacific theater diverted others. But in Autumn 1943 the buildup began in earnest, with U.S. divisions arriving at a rate of two per month. In January 1944, when Eisenhower assumed the duties of supreme commander for the invasion of Europe, eleven U.S. divisions were in England; by D day, 6 June, there were twenty, with even more to follow.

Nine Allied divisions, including five U.S. divisions (three infantry and two airborne) in Lieutenant General Omar N. Bradley's* First Army,* performed the D day assault. Thirteen more infantry and five armored divisions joined Bradley's command during the bitter beachhead fighting. On 1 August, Bradley assumed command of the newly activated 12th Army Group, composed of the First Army under Lieutenant General Courtney H. Hodges* and the Third Army* under George Patton. Lieutenant General William Simpson's Ninth Army,* activated on 5 September, saw service under both the 12th and British 21st Army Groups in the course of the campaign. No fewer than fifty-four divisions served under the 12th Army Group at various times.

On 15 August 1944 U.S. and French forces under Lieutenant General Alexander Patch's Seventh Army* landed on France's Mediterranean coast. By 15 September, Lieutenant General Jacob L. Devers' 6th Army Group commanded the U.S. Seventh and French First Armies, with three U.S. and seven French divisions. At the war's end, Devers counted sixteen U.S. and ten French divisions in his order of battle.

Autumn 1944 found three Allied army groups poised on the western frontiers of Germany: the British 21st in the north, the 12th in the center, and the 6th on the Allied right. In December, when the German Ardennes* offensive ruptured the 12th Army Group's line, Eisenhower committed twenty-six U.S. divisions (600,000 troops) to restore the front, in the largest battle in U.S. Army history. U.S. forces first crossed the Rhine on 7 March 1945, encircled the Ruhr industrial region on 1 April, and met the Soviets near the Elbe River on 25 April. In the closing days of the war, Bradley's 12th Army Group amassed forty-eight divisions and 1.3 million men, the largest exclusively U.S. field command in history.

Ultimately, the U.S. Army's war against Germany involved a total of sixty-nine divisions—forty-seven infantry, sixteen armored, four airborne, and one cavalry. By comparison, the Pacific war required the services of twenty-two Army divisions—twenty infantry, one airborne, and one cavalry. The greater part of the Army's ground forces in the Pacific served in MacArthur's Southwest Pacific Area* (SWPA), which, after securing New Guinea, commenced the liberation of the Philippines on 20 October 1944. Eighteen divisions under Walter Krueger's Sixth Army and Lieutenant General Robert L. Eichelberger's* Eighth Army* waged this second Philippine campaign. Three other divisions fought under Navy and Marine Corps leadership in the western Pacific, most notably in the Marianas. Finally, the campaign for Okinawa,* which began on 1 April

1945, involved four Army and two Marine divisions under the command of Lieutenant General Simon B. Buckner's Tenth Army.

The greatest land campaign of the Pacific war never took place. Three field armies* made up of divisions drawn from both European and Pacific theaters were in the process of assembling for an invasion of the Japanese home islands when the atomic bombing of Hiroshima and Nagasaki ended the war. The Manhattan Project,* which had produced the atomic bombs at a cost of two billion dollars and had employed a work force of 120,000 people, was an Army responsibility.

The U.S. Army in World War II was one of the most powerful military forces ever to wage war. It was perhaps the most lavishly equipped and supplied army in history, with 88,000 tanks, 89,000 artillery pieces, 2,383,000 trucks, 2,680,000 machine guns, 6,552,000 rifles, and consuming no fewer than forty billion rounds of small-arms amunition. Financially, World War II cost the War Department $167 billion. In human terms, the Army (exclusive of the Army Air Forces) suffered 832,000 casualties, of which 143,000 were killed in action.

References. A. Russell Buchanan, *The United States and World War II*, 1964. Robert Leckie, *Delivered from Evil*, 1987. Charles B. MacDonald. *The Mighty Endeavor*, 1969. Gerhard L. Weinberg, *A World at Arms*, 1994.

Christopher R. Gabel

Y

YANK

Founded in April 1942 by Col. Hyman Munson of the U.S. Army's Special Service Division, *Yank* was a U.S. Army publication for enlisted personnel. Its specialty was documentary photography. Printed in plants throughout the world, its reporters and photographers were enlisted men who wrote and photographed from the point of view of the common soldier. *Yank* ceased publication at the end of World War II,* by which time it (like its better known counterpart *Stars and Stripes**) had a circulation in the millions and was distributed in all major theaters of operation.

References. Alfred Emile Cornebise, *Ranks and Columns*, 1993. Steve Kluger, *Yank*, 1991.

Luke Knowley

YARDBIRD

Yardbird was a term applied to any hapless or unfortunate soldier, but usually a new private, who habitually committed minor misdeeds in formations, failed inspections for trivial errors, or ran afoul of the first sergeant* and frequently found himself on extra duty or menial labor details when his buddies were off duty or on pass. The yardbird was commonly the object of jokes and butt of unit humor. In World War II,* the term Sad Sack* generally replaced yardbird to denote the most pathetic soldier in a camp or unit, although the term yardbird was still heard in the 1960s.

References. George Bristol, "Shavetail Tells All," *New York Times Magazine*, 14 February 1943, 10. Marion Hargrove, *See Here, Private Hargrove*, 1942.

YELLOWSTONE EXPEDITION. *See* Centennial Campaign.

YORK, ALVIN (1887–1964)

One remarkable feat of heroism in France's Argonne Forest during World War I* made Alvin York a household name in postwar America. The son of

the rural backwaters of Tennessee's Cumberland Mountains, York's hard upbringing and simple creed were complicated on the eve of the war by his conversion to a small Christian sect opposed to violence. When the United States
entered the war, York at first asked for deferment as a conscientious objector*
but later accepted the draft. He was sent overseas with the 82d Division* in
May 1918. He fought in the St. Mihiel* offensive that summer and in early
October was with his unit when it was pinned down by fire from a German
machine gun battalion. Leading a small party to envelop the enemy's position,
York and his men were themselves taken under fire by another group of enemy
soldiers. As his men took cover, York coolly shot one enemy soldier after another until their commander attempted to rush York's position. York killed
another six enemy soldiers, after which their battalion commander offered surrender. Using the battalion commander to order his other machine-gunners to
surrender as they returned to friendly U.S. lines, York was credited with capturing 132 enemy troops in all. In the process, he had killed twenty-five enemy
and silenced thirty-five enemy machine guns. For this feat, York was awarded
the Medal of Honor.*

York's rustic modesty won the affection of his countrymen after the war. He
refused to capitalize upon his fame, retiring instead to his mountain home. Only
the prospect of earning enough money to support local church and educational
projects convinced him finally to permit the making of a film of his life on the
eve of World War II.* York's final years were plagued by ill health and financial
difficulties, none of which seemed to tarnish the image that had been given birth
that day in the Argonne Forest.

References. David D. Lee, *Sergeant York*, 1985. Amy Lynch, "A Gift for Sergeant
York," *American History*, December 1998, 18–24.

Roger J. Spiller

YORKTOWN

The siege of Yorktown was the decisive battle of the American Revolution,*
George Washington's* overall grasp of the strategic situation, his use of com-
bined French and Continental forces, and French sea power led to this unpar-
alleled victory. The siege began 28 September 1781 with the investment of the
British force in Yorktown by an allied force of 9,500 Continentals and 7,800
French troops under Washington's command. The French commander, Comte
de Rochambeau, had placed himself at Washington's disposal for the campaign.
The British forces, numbering about 8,000 men, were under the command of
Lord Charles Cornwallis.

On 21 May 1781, Washington and Rochambeau held a meeting and concluded
that the British strength lay in New York and Chesapeake Bay. They decided
that if Admiral Francois de Grasse's fleet could cut the sea lines between the
two, they would then conduct a land and sea campaign against one or the other.
When Cornwallis occupied Yorktown and the French fleet headed north, Washington recognized an opportunity to destroy Cornwallis and began a series of

forced marches to get into position. On 30 August, de Grasse arrived off York-town and disembarked 3,000 French reinforcements under the command of General Marquis de Lafayette. The subsequent French naval victory at the Battle of the Virginia Capes sealed the fate of the British forces at Yorktown. The British Admiral Thomas Graves retired to New York, leaving command of the sea to the French.

In the face of superior numbers and hoping that reinforcements would soon arrive, on 30 September Cornwallis withdrew to his inner fortifications. On 9 October the allied bombardment began, and five days later two key British redoubts were stormed and taken, one by the Continentals, the other by the French, in rare night attacks. A British counterattack launched on the 16th failed. Cornwallis now realized that the end was near and a storm prevented a planned evacuation of some of his forces across the York River. As the British band played "The World Turned Upside Down," the British garrison marched out and laid down their arms. With the British surrender, military action in the Revolution ended. Admiral Graves arrived on 24 October with 7,000 British reinforcements, but he was too late.

References. Burke Davis, *The Campaign That Won America*, 1970. Thomas J. Fleming, *Beat the Last Drum*, 1963. Henry Lumpkin, *From Savannah to Yorktown*, 1981. John Selby, *The Road to Yorktown*, 1976

George Mordica II

YUMA PROVING GROUND

Located on more than one million acres twenty-six miles northeast of Yuma, Arizona, Yuma Proving Ground is one of the largest facilities operated by the U.S. Army. Established in 1943 as the Yuma Test Branch under the Corps of Engineers* for testing vehicles, bridges, boats, and other equipment, the facility was deactivated in 1950, but reactivated the next year as the Yuma Test Station. Redesignated the Yuma Proving Ground in 1963, today the facility is a Class II installation with a permanent party of 375 officers and enlisted men and over 1,000 civilian personnel. Among other activities, the U.S. Army Parachute Team, the Golden Knights,* conduct their annual winter training at Yuma Proving Ground.

References. Dan Cragg, *Guide to Military Installations*, 4th ed., 1994. John Valceanu, "YPG," *Soldiers*, August 1999, 4–8.

Z

ZONE OF THE INTERIOR

The Zone of the Interior (ZI) in World War I* comprised that area of U.S. territory not included in the theater of operations. Its mission was to exploit and develop the national resources in men and material required for military purposes to supply the means required by the field commanders to achieve victory. The concept of a ZI was reestablished in World War II* with three separate commands to provide trained forces, equipment and supplies, and the means to transport them overseas.

References. R. Elberton Smith, *The Army and Economic Mobilization*, 1959. United States Army, Army War College, Historical Section, *Order of Battle of the Land Forces in the World War*, vol. 3, *Zone of the Interior*, 1931–1949, 1988.

ZOUAVE

In the United States during the 1850s it was popular to form militia companies for patriotic and social functions. It was then in vogue to copy the new light rifle drill and the uniforms* used by the French Algerians in North Africa known as Zouaves. In the U.S., militia Zouave units sported colorful uniforms complete with baggy trousers, open-front coats, gaiters, and tasseled caps. When the Civil War* began, some of these units formed into U.S. volunteer regiments,* while others, like Wheat's Louisiana Tiger Zouaves who fought at First Bull Run,* joined the Confederate cause. Because of the expense of maintaining the elaborate uniforms in the field, most of these units eventually adopted the regular issue uniforms provided by their respective governments.

References. Jack Coggins, *Arms and Equipment of the Civil War*, 1962, 1990. Frederick P. Todd, *American Military Equipage 1851–1872*, 1980.

Steven J. Allie

APPENDIX A:
ABBREVIATIONS AND
ACRONYMS

AAA	antiaircraft artillery
AAF	Army Air Forces
AAFES	Army and Air Force Exchange System
ACAV	armored cavalry assault vehicle
ACOM	Atlantic Command
ACR	armored cavalry regiment
ADA	air defense artillery
AEF	American Expeditionary Force
AFF	Army Field Forces
AFSC	Armed Forces Staff College
AG	Adjutant General
AGF	Army Ground Forces
AIM-9	Aerial Intercept Missile Nine (Sidewinder)
AIT	advanced individual training
AMED	Army Medical Department
AMMISCA	American Military Mission to China
ANC	Army Nurse Corps
ANCXF	Allied Naval Commander in Chief, Expeditionary Force
APC	armored personnel carrier
APTF	army physical fitness test
ARCOM	Army Commendation Medal; Army Reserve Command
ARTEP	Army Training and Evaluation Program
ARV	armored recovery vehicle
ARVN	Army of the Republic of Vietnam

ASF	Army Service Forces
AUSA	Association of the United States Army
AVG	American Volunteer Group
AWOL	absent without leave
AWR	Army War Reserve
BCD	Bad Conduct Discharge
BCT	Basic Combat Training
BCTP	Battle Command Training Program
BN	battalion
BNOC	Basic Noncommissioned Officer Course
CAC	Coast Artillery Corps
CAD	Civil Affairs Division
CAR	Chief, Army Reserve
CAS	close air support
CAS^3	Combined Arms Services and Staff School
CATF	China Air Task Force
CAV	cavalry
CBI	China, Burma, India (theater)
CCC	Civilian Conservation Corps
CCS	Combined Chiefs of Staff
CCT	combat control team
CENTCOM	U.S. Central Command
CG	commanding general
CGSC	Command and General Staff College
CGSOC	Command and General Staff Officers Course
CGSS	Command and General Staff School
CI	counterintelligence
CIA	Central Intelligence Agency
CIB	Combat Infantryman's Badge
CID	Criminal Investigation Division
CIDG	Civilian Irregular Defense Group
CINC	commander in chief
CINCPAC	Commander in Chief, Pacific
CJCS	Chairman, Joint Chiefs of Staff
CMC	Commandant of the Marine Corps
CMH	Center of Military History
CNO	Chief of Naval Operations

CO	commanding officer; conscientious objector
CofS	chief of staff
COI	coordination of information
COLT	combat observation laser team
CONARC	Continental Army Command
CONUS	continental United States
COSCOM	Corps Support Command
COSSAC	Chief of Staff to the Supreme Allied Commander
CP	command post
CPX	command post exercise
CSAF	Chief of Staff of the Air Force
CSI	Combat Studies Institute
CTA	common tables of allowances
CWS	Chemical Warfare Service
DA	Department of the Army
DB	Disciplinary Barracks
DIA	Defense Intelligence Agency
DISCOM	Division Support Command
DIVARTY	division artillery
DMZ	demilitarized zone
DOD	Department of Defense
DSC	deputy chief of staff; Distinguished Service Cross
DSCOPS	Deputy Chief of Staff Operations
DVA	Department of Veterans Affairs
DZ	drop zone
EIB	Expert Infantryman's Badge
ETO	European Theater of Operations
ETOUSA	European Theater of Operations for the U.S. Army
EUCOM	European Command
FA	Field Artillery
FAC	forward air controller
FADAC	Field Artillery Digital Automatic Computer
FCE	fire control element
FDC	fire direction center
FEBA	forward edge of the battle area
FFAR	folding-fin aerial rocket
FLIR	forward-looking infrared

FM	field manual
FO	forward observer
FOD	field officer of the day
FORSCOM	U.S. Army Forces Command
FSCL	fire support coordination line
FSOP	field standing operating procedure
FTX	field training exercise
GHQ	General Headquarters
GHQAF	General Headquarters Air Force
GS	General Staff
GSR	ground surveillance radar
HE	high-explosive
HEAT	high-explosive, antitank
HEDP	high-explosive, dual-purpose
HET	heavy equipment transporter
HMMWV	high-mobility multipurpose wheeled vehicle
HUMINT	human intelligence
IAPF	Inter-American Peace Force
ICAF	Industrial College of the Armed Forces
ID	infantry division
IET	initial entry training
IFF	identification friend and foe
IFV	infantry fighting vehicle
IG	Inspector General
IMINT	imagery intelligence
IPB	intelligence preparation of the battlefield
JAG	Judge Advocate General
JCEWS	Joint Command, Control, and Electronics Warfare School
JCS	Joint Chiefs of Staff
JCSOC	Joint and Combined Staff Officers School
JPC	Joint Planning Committee
JROTC	Junior Reserve Officer Training Corps
JRTC	Joint Readiness Training Center
JSTARS	Joint Surveillance Target Attack Radar System
JTF	joint task force
KATUSA	Korean Augmentation of the United States Army
KIA	killed in action

KIA-NBR	killed in action, no body recovered
KP	kitchen police
LAAW	light antiarmor weapon
LAW	light antitank weapon
LBE	load-bearing equipment
LCE	load-carrying equipment
LCF	landing craft, flak
LCG	landing craft, gun
LCI	landing craft, infantry
LCM	landing craft, mechanized
LCR	landing craft, rocket
LCT	landing craft, tank
LCVP	landing craft, vehicle, personnel
LIC	low-intensity conflict
LRRP	long-range reconnaissance patrol
LSD	landing ship, dock
LSF	landing ship, fighter direction
LSH	landing ship, headquarters
LSI	landing ship, infantry
LSR	landing ship, rocket
LST	landing ship, tank
LZ	landing zone
M	mechanized
MAAG	Military Assistance and Advisory Group
MAC	Medical Administrative Corps
MACV	Military Assistance Command, Vietnam
MACV-SOG	Military Assistance Command, Vietnam–Special Operations Group
MBT	main battle tank
METT-T	mission, enemy, terrain, troops, and time
MHD	Military History Detachment
MHI	Military History Institute
MI	military intelligence
MIA	missing in action
MID	Military Intelligence Division
MILGP	military group
MLO	military liaison officer
MOS	military occupational specialty

MP	military police
MPH	miles per hour
MPRS	Military Pay Records System
MRE	Meals Ready to Eat
MSC	Medical Service Corps
MSR	main supply route
MTOE	modified table of organization and equipment
MWR	Morale, Welfare, and Recreation
NAF	nonappropriated fund
NATO	North Atlantic Treaty Organization
NBC	nuclear, biological, and chemical
NCA	National Command Authorities
NCO	noncommissioned officer
NDA	National Defense Act
NDU	National Defense University
NG	National Guard
NGAUS	National Guard Association of the United States
NKPA	North Korean People's Army
NP	neuropsychiatric
NSA	National Security Agency
NSC	National Simulation Center; National Security Council
NTC	National Training Center
NVA	North Vietnamese Army
OCAC	Office of the Chief of the Air Corps
OCAR	Office of the Chief, Army Reserve
OCMH	Office, Chief of Military History
OCS	Officer Candidate School
ODC	Office of Defense Cooperation
OER	Officer Efficiency Report
OG	operations group
OOTW	operations other than war
OPFOR	opposing force
ORC	Officers' Reserve Corps
ORDC	Ordnance Research and Development Center
OSS	Office of Strategic Services
OSUT	one-station unit training
PA	physician's assistant

PAC	Personnel Administration Center
PACOM	Pacific Command
PAO	Public Affairs Officer
PJME	Professional Joint Military Education
PMP	Preventive Mobilization Plan
PMST	professor of military science and tactics
POA	Pacific Ocean Area
POC	platoon operations center; point of contact
POL	petroleum, oils, and lubricants
POMCUS	Prepositioning of Material Configured in Unit Sets
POW	prisoner of war
PS	Philippine Scouts
PSYOPS	psychological operations
PTSD	post-traumatic stress disorder
PTSS	post-traumatic stress syndrome
PX	post exchange
PZ	pick-up zone
QM	quartermaster
QMC	Quartermaster Corps
RADAR	radio detecting and ranging
R&R	rest and recuperation
RCR	recoilless rifle
RCT	regimental combat team
REFORGER	Return of Forces to Germany
RGT	regiment
ROA	Reserve Officers Association
ROAD	Reorganized Objective Army Division
ROE	rules of engagement
ROK	Republic of Korea
ROKA	Republic of Korea Army
ROTC	Reserve Officer Training Corps
RPG	rocket-propelled grenade
RSC	regional support command
RSG	regional support group
SAM	surface-to-air missile
SAO	Security Assistance Organization
SCP	School of Command Preparation

SDO	staff duty officer
SEATO	Southeast Asia Treaty Organization
SF	Special Forces
SIGINT	signals intelligence
SIR	surface interface radar
SNAFU	situation normal, all fouled up
SOCOM	Special Operations Command
SOCPAC	Special Operations Command, Pacific
SOF	Special Operations Forces
SOP	standard operating procedure
SOUTHCOM	Southern Command
SPG	self-propelled gun
SSS	Selective Service System
STRATCOM	Strategic Command
SWPA	Southwest Pacific Area
TDA	table of distribution and allowances
TDY	temporary duty
TOC	tactical operations center
TOE	table of organization and equipment
TOW	tube-launched, optically tracked, wire-guided missile
TQM	total quality management
TRADOC	Training and Doctrine Command
TRANSCOM	Transportation Command
UCMJ	Uniform Code of Military Justice
UN	United Nations
UNSCR	United Nations Security Council Resolution
USACIDC	U.S. Army Criminal Investigation Command
USAPAC	United States Army, Pacific
USAR	United States Army Reserve
USARC	United States Army Reserve Command
USAREC	United States Army Recruiting Command
USAREUR	United States Army, Europe
USARS	United States Army Recruiting Service
USDB	U.S. Disciplinary Barracks
USFK	United States Forces, Korea
USMA	United States Military Academy
USN	United States Navy

USO	United Service Organizations
USSOCOM	U.S. Special Operations Command
VA	Veterans Administration
VC	Viet Cong
VMI	Virginia Military Institute
WAC	Women's Army Corps
WD	War Department
WIA	wounded in action
WPD	War Plans Division
WRAMC	Walter Reed Army Medical Center
XO	executive officer
YMAC	Young Men's Christian Assocation
YWCA	Young Women's Christian Association
ZI	Zone of the Interior

APPENDIX B:
RANKS AND GRADES IN THE U.S. ARMY

The Congress of the United States establishes the grade and rank structure for the armed forces of the United States. Officers and warrant officers* are appointed to grades, and enlisted personnel and noncommissioned officers* (NCO) are assigned ranks. Ranks and grades in each of the services correspond to pay grades, which are uniform throughout the five military services: Army, Navy, Air Force, Marine Corps, and Coast Guard. Each service determines the terminology and insignia or designation for the ranks and grades of its members. The chart below shows the current grades and ranks recognized by the U.S. Army, the official abbreviation for each, and the corresponding pay grade.

Pay Grade	Rank or Grade	Official Abbreviation
	General of the Army[1]	GENA
O–10	General	GEN
O–9	Lieutenant General	LTG
O–8	Major General	MG
O–7	Brigadier General	BG
O–6	Colonel	COL
O–5	Lieutenant Colonel	LTC
O–4	Major	MAJ
O–3	Captain	CPT
O–2	First Lieutenant	1LT
O–1	Second Lieutenant	2LT
W-5	Chief Warrant Officer	CW5
W-4	Chief Warrant Officer	CW4
W-3	Chief Warrant Officer	CW3
W-2	Chief Warrant Officer	CW2

[1]There are no current living service members at this grade.

W-1	Warrant Officer	WO1
E-9	Sergeant Major of the Army	SMA
	Command Sergeant Major	CSM
	Sergeant Major	SGM
E-8	First Sergeant	1SG
	Master Sergeant	MSG
E-7	Sergeant First Class	SFC
E-6	Staff Sergeant	SSG
E-5	Sergeant	SGT
E-4	Corporal	CPL
	Specialist	SPC
E-3	Private First Class	PFC
E-2	Private	PV2
E-1	Private	PVT

SOURCES

Abbott, Henry L. *Early Days of the Engineer School of Application*. Washington, D.C.: Engineer School of Application, 1904.

Abbott, Steve. "High in the Rockies." *Soldiers* 7 (July 1978): 34–38.

Abizaid, John P. "Lessons for Peacekeepers." *Military Review* 73 (March 1993): 11–19.

"Acquisition Corps Established." *Army Logistician* (May–June 1990): 2–3.

Adams, Daniel B. "The New M48 Tank." *Infantry School Quarterly* 44 (October 1954): 98–112.

Adams, James. *Secret Armies: Inside the American, Soviet and European Special Forces*. New York: Atlantic Press, 1987.

Adamson, Hans Christian. *Rebellion in Missouri, 1861: Nathaniel Lyon and His Army of the West*. Philadelphia and New York: Chilton, 1961.

Addington, Larry H. "The U.S. Coast Artillery and the Problem of Artillery Organization, 1907–1954." *Military Affairs* 30 (February 1976): 1–6.

Adkin, Mark. *Urgent Fury: The Battle for Grenada*. Lexington, MA., and Toronto: Lexington Books, 1989.

Adleman, Robert H., and George Walton. *The Devil's Brigade*. Philadelphia: Chilton, 1966.

Albertine, Connel. *The Yankee Doughboy*. Boston: Branden Press, 1968.

Alberts, Don E. *Brandy Station to Manila Bay: A Biography of General Wesley Merritt*. Austin, TX: Presidial Press, 1981.

Alberts, Robert C. "Profile of a Soldier: Matthew B. Ridgway." *American Heritage* 27 (February 1976): 4–7.

Albright, Harry. *New Orleans: Battle of the Bayous*. New York: Hippocrene Books, 1990.

Albright, John, John A. Cash, and Allan W. Sandstrum. *Seven Firefights in Vietnam*. Washington, D.C.: Office of the Chief of Military History, 1970.

Alden, John Richard. *George Washington: A Biography*. Baton Rouge: Louisiana State University Press, 1984.

———. *A History of the American Revolution*. New York: Alfred A. Knopf. 1972.

———. *The South in the Revolution, 1763–1789*. Vol. 3 of *A History of the South*.

Edited by Wendell Holmes Stephenson and E. Merton Coulter. Baton Rouge: Louisiana State University Press, 1957.

Alexander, Bevin. *Lost Victories: The Military Genius of Stonewall Jackson.* New York: Henry Holt, 1992.

Alger, John I. *The Quest for Victory: The History of the Principles of War.* Westport, CT: Greenwood Press, 1982.

Allard, C. Kenneth. *Command, Control, and the Common Defense.* New Haven, CT: Yale University Press, 1990.

———. *Somalia Operations: Lessons Learned.* Washington, D.C.: National Defense University Press, 1995.

Allen, Francis J. *The Concrete Battleship: Fort Drum, El Fraile Island, Manila Bay.* Missoula, MT: Pictorial Histories Publishing, 1988.

Allen, Robert S. *Lucky Forward: The History of Patton's Third U.S. Army.* New York: Vanguard Press, 1947.

Allie, Steven J. *All He Could Carry: US Army Infantry Equipment, 1839–1910.* [Fort Leavenworth, KS]: Frontier Army Museum, 1991.

Allison, David Kite. *New Eye for the Navy: The Origin of Radar at the Naval Research Laboratory.* Washington, D.C.: Naval Research Laboratory, 1981.

Amaral, Anthony A. *Comanche: The Horse That Survived the Custer Massacre.* Los Angeles: Westernlore Press, 1961.

Ambrose, Stephen E. *Duty, Honor, Country: A History of West Point.* Baltimore: Johns Hopkins Press, 1966.

———. *Eisenhower.* 2 vols. New York: Simon and Schuster, 1983–1984.

———. *Halleck: Lincoln's Chief of Staff.* Baton Rouge: Louisiana State University Press, 1962.

———. *The Supreme Commander: The War Years of General Dwight D. Eisenhower.* Garden City, NY: Doubleday, 1970.

———. *Undaunted Courage: Meriwether Lewis, Thomas Jefferson, and the Opening of the American West.* New York: Simon and Schuster, 1996.

———. *Upton and the Army.* Baton Rouge: Louisiana State University Press, 1964.

Amchan, Arthur J. *The Most Famous Soldier in America: A Biography of Lt. Gen. Nelson A. Miles. 1839–1925.* Alexandria, VA: Amchan Publications, 1989.

Ammer, Christine. *Fighting Words: From War, Rebellion, and Other Combative Capers.* New York: Dell Publishing, 1989.

Anders, Curt. *Disaster in Deep Sand: The Red River Expedition.* Indianapolis: Guild Press of Indiana, 1997.

Anderson, Martin, ed. *The Military Draft: Selected Readings on Conscription.* Stanford, CA: Hoover Institute Press, 1982.

Andress, Harry C. "The Bradley Challenge." *Infantry* 81 (January–February 1991): 18–21.

Andrews, Owen. *A Moment of Silence: Arlington National Cemetery.* Washington, D.C.: Elliott and Clark Publishing, 1994.

Andrews, Patrick E. "The Old Army." *Infantry* 69 (September–October 1979): 31–34.

Andrist. Ralph K. *The Long Death: The Last Days of the Plains Indian.* New York: Macmillan, 1964.

Andrus, E. C., C. S. Keefer, D. W. Bronk, J. S. Lockwood, G. A., Carden, Jr., J. T. Wearn, and M. C. Winternitz, eds. *Advances in Military Medicine Made by Amer-*

ican Investigators Working under the Sponsorship of the Committee on Medical Research. Vol. 1. Boston: Little, Brown, 1948.

Anthony, Paula, Romana Danysh, Wayne M. Dzwonchyk, Rebecca Robbins, and John B. Wilson. "Armies and Corps." *Army* 36 (October 1986): 330–343.

Appleman, Roy E. *East of Chosin: Entrapment and Breakout in Korea, 1950*. College Station: Texas A&M University Press, 1987.

———. *Escaping the Trap: The US Army X Corps in Northeast Korea, 1950*. College Station: Texas A&M University Press, 1990.

———. *South to the Naktong, North to the Yalu (June–November 1950)*. Washington, D.C.: Office of the Chief of Military History, 1961.

Arms, L. R. *A Short History of the NCO*. Fort Bliss, TX: U.S. Army Sergeants Major Academy, [1989].

Armstrong, David A. *Bullets and Bureaucrats: The Machine Gun and the United States Army, 1861–1916*. Westport, CT: Greenwood Press, 1982.

Army Aviation: Cub to Comanche. Westport, CT: Army Aviation Publications, 1992.

Arnold, Chris. *Steel Pots: The History of America's Steel Combat Helmets*. San Jose, CA: R. James Binder, 1997.

Arnold, H. H. *Global Mission*. New York: Harper and Brothers, 1949.

Arnold, James R. *Grant Wins the War: Decision at Vicksburg*. New York: John Wiley and Sons, 1997.

Ashburn, Percy M. *A History of the Medical Department of the United States Army*. Boston: Houghton Mifflin, 1929.

Astor, Gerald. *Operation Iceberg: The Invasion and Conquest of Okinawa in World War II*. New York: Donald I. Fine, 1995.

Atkeson, Edward B. "New Life for Duster." *Army* 14 (August 1963): 45–46.

Atkinson, Rick. *Crusade: The Untold Story of the Persian Gulf War*. Boston: Houghton Mifflin, 1993.

Avendano, Numa P. "Fort Sill Fifty Years Ago." *Field Artillery Journal* (March–April 1978): 44–47.

Avins, Alfred. *The Law of AWOL*. New York: Oceana Publications, 1957.

Axelrod, Alan. *Chronicle of the Indian Wars: From Colonial Times to Wounded Knee*. New York: Prentice Hall, 1993.

Ayers, Kenneth J. "Structuring a Combat Maneuver Battalion." *Armor* 85 (May–June 1976): 50–51.

Babits, Lawrence E. *A Devil of a Whipping: The Battle of Cowpens*. Chapel Hill: University of North Carolina Press, 1998.

Bacevich, A. J. *The Pentomic Era: The US Army between Korea and Vietnam*. Washington, D.C.: National Defense University Press, 1986.

Bachtel, Charles L. "The KATUSA Program."*Signal* 23 (December 1968): 42–44.

Bady, Donald B. *Colt Automatic Pistols, 1896–1955*. Los Angeles: Borden Publishing, 1963.

Bahnsen, John C. "The Shadow War in the Army's Orderly Rooms." *Army* 37 (January 1987): 14–17.

Bailey, J.B.A. *Field Artillery and Firepower*. Oxford: Military Press, 1989.

Baily, Charles M. *Faint Praise: American Tanks and Tank Destroyers during World War II*. Hamden, CT: Archon Books, 1983.

Bainbridge, William G. *Top Sergeant: The Life and Times of Sergeant Major of the Army William G. Bainbridge*. New York: Fawcett Columbine, 1995.

Baird, Jay W., ed. *From Nuremberg to My Lai*. Lexington, MA: D.C. Heath, 1972.

Bakeless, John. *Background to Glory: The Life of George Rogers Clark*. Philadelphia: J. B. Lippencott, 1957.

Baker, A. D., III. *Allied Landing Craft of World War Two*. Annapolis, MD: Naval Institute Press, 1944, 1985.

Baker, Charles R. "The Rifle Squad's Artillery." *Infantry* 59 (September–October 1969): 39–41.

Baker, George. "The Real Sad Sack." *New York Times Magazine* (9 July 1944): 16–17.

Baker, Harold D., Jr. "Hand-Receipt Procedures." *Infantry* 86 (November–December 1996): 41–44.

Baker, Richard W., ed. *The ANZUS States and Their Region: Regional Policies of Australia, New Zealand, and the United States*. Westport, CT: Praeger, 1994.

Baldwin, Ganson J., and John Kirkland Clark, Jr., *Legal Effects of Military Service under the Soldiers' and Sailors' Civil Relief Act of 1940 . . . and upon Procedure in All State and Federal Courts*. New York: n.p., 1940.

Baldwin, Hanson W. "GI Gripes—Causes and Cures." *New York Times Magazine*, 31 March 1946, 12–13.

Baldwin, Truxton R. "The Improved Chinook." *U.S. Army Aviation Digest* 13 (December 1967): 22–27.

Ball, Desmond. "Improving Communications Links between Moscow and Washington." *Journal of Peace Research* 28 (May 1991): 135–159.

Ball, Edmund F. *Staff Officer with the Fifth Army: Sicily, Salerno and Anzio*. New York: Exposition Press, 1958.

Ball, Harry P. *Of Responsible Command: A History of the U.S. Army War College*. Carlisle Barracks, PA: Alumni Association of the United States Army War College, 1984.

Bank, Aaron. *From OSS to Green Berets: The Birth of Special Forces*. Novato, CA: Presidio, 1986.

Bant, Bruce. "EIB: Only the Best." *Soldiers* 33 (July 1978): 28–31.

Barker, Geoffrey T. *A Concise History of US Army Special Operations Forces with Lineage and Insignia*. Vol. 1. 2d ed. Tampa, FL: Anglo-American Publishing, 1993.

Barnett, Frank R., and Carnes Lord, eds. *Political Warfare and Psychological Operations: Rethinking the US Approach*. Washington, D.C.: National Defense University Press, 1989.

Barnouw, Erik. *Tube of Plenty: The Evolution of American Television*. New York: Oxford University Press, 1975.

Barrett, John G. *Sherman's March through the Carolinas*. Chapel Hill: University of North Carolina Press, 1956.

Bartlett, Irving H. *John C. Calhoun: A Biography*. New York: W. W. Norton, 1993.

Bass, Robert D. *Game Cock: The Life and Campaigns of General Thomas Sumter*. New York: Holt. Rinehart and Winston, 1961.

———. *Swamp Fox: The Life and Campaigns of General Francis Marion*. Columbia, SC: Sandlapper Press, 1972.

Bauer, K. Jack. *The Mexican War, 1846–1848*. New York: Macmillan, 1974.

———. *Zachary Taylor: Soldier, Planter, Statesman of the Old Southwest*. Baton Rouge: Louisiana State University Press, 1985.

Baumgartner, Richard A. *Kennesaw Mountain, June 1864: Bitter Standoff at the Gibraltar of Georgia.* Huntington, WV: Blue Acorn Press, 1998.

Baya, G. Emery. "Army Organization Act of 1950." *Army Information Digest* 5 (August 1950): 28–37.

Beal, Merrill D. *"I Will Fight No More Forever": Chief Joseph and the Nez Perce War.* Seattle: University of Washington Press, 1963.

Bearss, Edwin. *The Battle of Wilson's Creek.* [Diamond, MO]: Wilson's Creek National Battlefield Foundation, 1988.

———. *The Campaign for Vicksburg.* 3 vols. Dayton, OH: Morningside, 1985–1986.

———. "Civil War Operations in and around Pensacola: Part II." *Florida Historical Quarterly* 39 (January 1961): 231–255.

Beaumont, Roger A., and William P. Snyder. "A Fusion Strategy for Pre-Commissioning Training." *Journal of Political and Military Sociology* 5 (Fall 1977): 259–277.

Beck, Alfred M., Abe Bortz, Charles W. Lynch, Lida Mayo, and Ralph F. Weld. *The Corps of Engineers: The War against Germany. United States Army in World War II.* Washington, D.C.: Center of Military History, 1985.

Beck, John Jacob. *MacArthur and Wainwright: Sacrifice of the Philippines.* Albuquerque: University of New Mexico Press, 1974.

Becker, Quinn S. "The 'We Care People' in Army Medicine." *Army* 36 (October 1986): 240–245.

Beer, Francis A., ed. *Alliances: Latent War Communities in the Contemporary World.* New York: Holt, Rinehart and Winston, 1970.

Begg, Robert B. "Sergeant Major." *Army* 16 (January 1966): 37–39.

Belenky, Gregory, ed. *Contemporary Studies in Combat Psychiatry.* Westport, CT: Greenwood Press. 1987.

Bell, James A. "Grizzly Flight—We Do It Right: 30 Years of Safety Excellence." *U.S. Army Aviation Digest* (July–August 1994): 18–20.

Bell, William Gardner. *Commanding Generals and Chiefs of Staff, 1775–1987: Portraits & Biographical Sketches of the United States Army's Senior Officers.* Washington, D.C.: Center of Military History, 1987.

———. *Quarters One: The United States Army Chief of Staff's Residence, Fort Myer, Virginia.* Washington, D.C.: Center of Military History, 1988.

———. *Secretaries of War and Secretaries of the Army: Portraits & Biographical Sketches.* Washington, D.C.: Center of Military History, 1982.

Belote, James H., and William M. Belote. *Corregidor: The Saga of a Fortress.* New York: Harper and Row, 1967.

Bendetsen, Karl R. "A Plan for Army Reorganization." *Military Review* 33 (January 1954): 39–60.

Benson, Dean M. "The Army's Representative on Campus." *Army Information Digest* 13 (March 1958): 18–23.

Bercovitch, Jacob, ed. *ANZUS in Crisis: Alliance Management in International Affairs.* New York: St. Martin's Press, 1988.

Berger, Jerome S. "Training Ground for Leadership." *Army Digest* 22 (November 1967): 11–12.

Bergerud, Eric M. *Red Thunder, Tropic Lightning: The World of a Combat Division in Vietnam.* Boulder, CO: Westview Press, 1993.

Berk, Joseph. *The Gatling Gun: 19th Century Machine Gun to 21st Century Vulcan.* Boulder, CO: Paladin Press, 1991.

Berndt, Thomas. *Standard Catalog of U.S. Military Vehicles, 1940–1965*. Iola, WI: Krause Publications, 1993.

Berry, William E. J. *U.S. Bases in the Philippines: The Evolution of the Special Relationship*. Boulder, CO: Westview Press, 1989.

Betz, John J., Jr. "Brown Shoe Army Payday." *Army* 39 (February 1989): 54–57.

Biddle, A. J. Drexel. "This Is AUSA." *Army Information Digest* 14 (October 1959): 32–36.

Bidwell, Bruce W. *History of the Military Intelligence Division, Department of the Army General Staff: 1775–1941*. Frederick, MD: University Publications of America, 1986.

Bigelow, Donald Nevius. *William Conant Church & the Army Navy Journal*. New York: Columbia University Press, 1952.

Bigler, Philip. *In Honored Glory: Arlington National Cemetery: The Final Post*. Arlington, VA: Vandamere Press, 1987.

Bilby, Joseph G. *Civil War Firearms: Their Historical Background, Tactical Use and Modern Collecting and Shooting*. [Conshohocken, PA]: Combined Books, 1996.

Bill, Alfred Hoyt. *Valley Forge: The Making of an Army*. New York: Harper and Brothers, 1952.

Billard, Tory. "The Red Ball Express: Stay on the Ball—Keep 'Em Rolling!" *Translog* 9 (October 1976): 14–15.

Billias, George Athan, ed. *George Washington's Generals*. New York: William Morrow, 1964.

Bilton, Michael, and Kevin Sim. *Four Hours in My Lai*. New York: Viking, 1992.

Binder, L. James. "Conscience, Voice of a Corps." *Army* 42 (July 1992): 29–30.

Binder, T. James. "Their Battlefield Is the Courtroom." *Army* 34 (November 1984): 48–52.

Binkin, Martin, and William W. Kaufmann. *U.S. Army Guard and Reserve: Rhetoric, Realities, Risks*. Washington, D.C.: Brookings Institution, 1989.

Binkley, John C. "A History of US Army Force Structuring." *Military Review* 57 (February 1977): 67–82.

Binneveld, Hans. *From Shell Shock to Combat Stress: A Comparative History of Military Psychiatry*. Translated by John O'Kane. Amsterdam: Amsterdam University Press, 1997.

Bird, Harrison. *Attack on Quebec: The American Invasion of Canada, 1775*. New York: Oxford University Press, 1968.

———. *Navies in the Mountains: The Battles on the Waters of Lake Champlain and Lake George, 1609–1814*. New York: Oxford University Press, 1962.

———. *War for the West, 1790–1813*. New York: Oxford University Press, 1971.

Bird, Tom. *American POWs of World War II: Forgotten Men Tell Their Stories*. Westport, CT: Praeger, 1992.

Blackbeard, Bill, and Martin Williams, eds. *The Smithsonian Collection of Newspaper Comics*. Washington, D.C.: Smithsonian Institution Press, 1977.

Blackburn, Marc K. "A New Form of Transportation: The Quartermaster Corps and Standardization of the United States Army's Motor Trucks, 1907–1939." Ph.D. diss., Temple University, 1992.

Blackmore, Howard L. *British Military Firearms, 1650–1850*. London: Herbert Jenkins, 1961.

Blair, Clay. *The Forgotten War: America in Korea 1950–1953*. New York: Times Books, 1987.

Blair, John G. "CONARC: Organization with a Mission." *Army Information Digest* 10 (October 1955): 14–17.

Blake, Geoffrey N., John Calahan, and Steven Young. "OPFOR Observations from the JRTC." *Infantry* 85 (January–February 1995): 30–35.

Bland, William S., and William M. Raymond, Jr. "Thunder in the Ozarks: The Battles of Wilson's Creek and Pea Ridge." *Field Artillery* (July–August 1998): 38–43.

Bliven, Bruce, Jr. *Battle for Manhattan*. New York: Henry Holt, 1956.

Bluhm, Raymond K., Jr., and James B. Motley. *The Soldier's Guidebook*. Washington, D.C.: Brassey's, 1995.

Blumenfeld, Aaron. "Airland Battle Doctrine: Evolution or Revolution?: A Look Inside the U.S. Army." B.A. Thesis, Princeton University, 1989.

Blumenson, Martin. *Anzio: The Gamble That Failed*. New York: Curtis Books, 1963.

———. *The Battle of the Generals: The Untold Story of the Falaise Pocket—The Campaign That Should Have Won World War II*. New York: William Morrow, 1993.

———. *Bloody River: The Real Tragedy of the Rapido*. Boston: Houghton Mifflin, 1970.

———. *Breakout and Pursuit. United States Army in World War II: The European Theater of Operations*. Washington, D.C.: Center of Military History, 1961, 1984.

———. *Kasserine Pass*. New York: Jove Publications, 1983.

———. *Mark Clark*. New York: Congdon and Weed, 1984.

———. " 'A Most Remarkable man.' " *Army* 18 (August 1968): 18–26.

———. *Patton: The Man behind the Legend, 1885–1945*. New York: William Morrow, 1985.

———. *Salerno to Cassino. United States Army in World War II: The Mediterranean Theater of Operations*. Washington, D.C.: Office of the Chief of Military History, 1969.

Bolger, Daniel P. *Americans at War, 1975–1986: An Era of Violent Peace*. Novato, CA: Presidio, 1988.

———. *Scenes from an Unfinished War: Low-Intensity Conflict in Korea, 1966–1969*. Leavenworth Paper Number 19. Fort Leavenworth, KS: Combat Studies Institute, 1991.

Bond, O. J. *The Story of the Citadel*. 1936. Reprint. Greenville, SC: Southern Historical Press, 1989.

Bond, P. S. *Essentials of Infantry Training*. Harrisburg, PA: Military Service Publishing, 1934.

Bonn, Keith E. *Army Officer's Guide*. 48th ed., Mechanicsburg, PA: Stackpole Books, 1999.

Borch, Frederic L., III, and F. C. Brown. *The Purple Heart: A History of America's Oldest Military Decoration*. Tempe. AZ: Borch and Westlake Publishing, 1996.

Borch, Frederic L., III, and William R. Westlake. *The Soldier's Medal: A History of the U.S. Army's Highest Award for Non-Combat Valor*. Tempe, AZ: Borch and Westlake Publishing, 1994.

Borklund, C. W. *The Department of Defense*. New York: Praeger, 1968.

Borthick, David, and Jack Britton. *Medals, Military and Civilian of the United States*. Tulsa, OK: M.C.N. Press, 1984.

Boulter, "Defending the TOC." *Armor* 92 (March–April 1983): 37–39.

Bourke, John G. *On the Border with Crook*. 1891. Reprint. Lincoln: University of Nebraska Press, 1971.

Bowers, John. *Chickamauga and Chattanooga: The Battles That Doomed the Confederacy*. New York: HarperCollins, 1994.

————. *Stonewall Jackson: Portrait of a Soldier*. New York: William Morrow, 1989.

Bowman, William, Roger Little, and G. Thomas Sicilia, eds. *The All-Volunteer Force after a Decade: Retrospect and Prospect*. Washington, D.C.: Pergamon-Brassey's 1986.

Boyce, Paul. "The Army's Investigators." *Soldiers* 51 (September 1996): 40–43.

Boyd, Thomas. *Light-Horse Harry Lee*. New York: Charles Scribner's Sons, 1931.

Braddy, Haldeen. *Pancho Villa at Columbus: The Raid of 1916*. El Paso: Texas Western Press, 1965.

Bradford, James C., ed. *Crucible of Empire: The Spanish-American War & Its Aftermath*. Annapolis, MD: Naval Institute Press, 1993.

Bradley, John, *Allied Intervention in Russia*. New York: Basic Books, 1968.

Bradley, John H., and Jack W. Dice. *The Second World War: Asia and the Pacific*. Wayne, NJ: Avery Publishing Group, 1984.

Bradley, Omar N., and Clay Blair. *A General's Life: An Autobiography by General of the Army Omar N. Bradley*. New York: Simon and Schuster, 1983.

Brady, Cyrus Townsend. *Indian Fights and Fighters*. Lincoln: University of Nebraska Press, 1971.

Braim, Paul F. *The Test of Battle: The American Expeditionary Forces in the Meuse-Argonne Campaign*. Newark: University of Deleware Press, 1987.

Bralley, Neal H. "Improving Battle Command Skills: The Brigade Command and Battle Staff Training Program." *Military Review* 75 (November–December 1995): 49–52.

Branch, Danny M. "Watch Those TDY Orders!" *TIG Brief* 47 (January–February 1995): 6–7.

Brandt, Clare. *The Man in the Mirror: A Life of Benedict Arnold*. New York: Random House, 1994.

Branley, Bill. "I'm Going Where?" *Soldiers* 36 (November 1981): 31–33.

Brehm, Philip A. *Restructuring the Army: The Road to a Total Force*. Carlisle, PA: Strategic Studies Institute, 1992.

Breuer, William B. *Death of a Nazi Army: The Falaise Pocket*. New York: Stein and Day, 1985.

————. *The Great Raid on Cabanatuan: Rescuing the Doomed Ghosts of Bataan and Corregidor*. New York: John Wiley and Sons, 1994.

————. *Operation Dragoon: The Allied Invasion of the South of France*. Novato, CA: Presidio, 1987.

————. *Operation Torch: The Allied Gamble to Invade North Africa*. New York: St. Martin's Press, 1985.

Brill, James H. "Infantry Rocket Weapons." *Ordnance* 50 (May–June 1966): 628–630.

Brinckerhoff, Sidney B. *Boots and Shoes of the Frontier Soldier, 1865–1893*. Tucson: Arizona Historical Society, 1976.

Bristol, George. "Shavetail Tells All." *New York Times Magazine*, 14 February 1943, 10.

Britton, Jack, ed. *Uniform Insignia of the United States Military Forces*. Tulsa, OK: M.C.N. Press, 1980.

Brooksher, William R. *Bloody Hill: The Civil War Battle of Wilson's Creek*. Washington, D.C.: Brassey's, 1995.

Brophy, Leo P., and George J. B. Fisher. *The Chemical Warfare Service: Organizing for War. United States Army in World War II: The Technical Services*. Washington, D.C.: Office of the Chief of Military History, 1959.

Brophy, Leo P., Wyndham D. Miles, and Rexmond C. Cochrane. *The Chemical Warfare Service: From Laboratory to Field. United States Army in World War II: The Technical Services*. Washington, D.C.: Office of the Chief of Military History, 1959.

Brophy, William S. *The Krag Rifle*. 2d ed. Highland Park, NJ: Gun Room Press, 1986.

———. *The Springfield 1903 Rifles: The Illustrated, Documented Story of the Design, Development, and Production of All the Models, Appendages, and Accessories*. Harrisburg, PA: Stackpole Books, 1985.

Brown, Charles H. *The Correspondents' War: Journalists in the Spanish-American War*. New York: Charles Scribner's Sons, 1967.

Brown, Dee. *Action at Beecher Island*. Garden City, NY: Doubleday, 1967.

———. *Bury My Heart at Wounded Knee: An Indian History of the American West*. New York: Holt, Rinehart and Winston, 1970.

———. *The Fetterman Massacre: Formerly Fort Phil Kearny: An American Saga*. Lincoln: University of Nebraska Press, 1971.

Brown, Frederic J. *Chemical Warfare: A Study in Restraints*. Princeton, NJ: Princeton University Press, 1968.

Brown, Jerold E. "Military Review: 75 Years of Service." *Military Review* 76 (November–December 1996): 59–66.

Brown, M. L. *Firearms in Colonial America: The Impact on History and Technology, 1492–1792*. Washington, D.C.: Smithsonian Institution Press, 1980.

Brown, Mark H. *The Flight of the Nez Perce*. New York: G. P. Putnam's Sons, 1967.

Brown, Michael. "All-Terrain Post." *Soldiers* 40 (March 1985): 13–17.

———. "Graf on Target." *Soldiers* 40 (January 1985): 23–25.

Brownlee, Romie L., and William J. Mullen III. *Changing an Army: An Oral History of General William E. DePuy, USA Retired*. Carlisle Barracks, PA: U.S. Military History Institute, [1986].

Brucker, Wilbur M. "Quality Is the Answer: The Role of ROTC in the Supreme Contest of Our Times." *Army Information Digest* 16 (February 1961): 2–15.

Bryan, Robert O. "Guardian of the Golden West." *Army Digest* 25 (June 1970): 4–9.

Buchanan, A. Russell. *The United States and World War II*. 2 vols. New York: Harper and Row, 1964.

Buchanan, John. *The Road to Guilford Courthouse: The American Revolution in the Carolinas*. New York: John Wiley and Sons, 1997.

Buffkin, Ronald M. "Identifying Quality Motor Sergeants." *Army Logistician* 17 (March–April 1985): 34–35.

Bunke, E.W.D. "The Vulcan for Air Defense." *National Defense* 58 (November–December 1973): 244–246.

Bunker, W. B. "Why the Army Needs Wings." *Army* 6 (March 1956): 19–23.

Burdett, Thomas F. "A New Evaluation of General Otis' Leadership in the Philippines." *Military Review* 55 (January 1975): 79–87.

Burhans, Robert D. *The First Special Service Force: A War History of the North Americans, 1942–1944*. 1947. Reprint. Nashville, TN: Battery Press, 1981.

Burk, Kathleen. *Britain, America and the Sinews of War, 1914–1918.* Boston: George Allen and Unwin, 1985.

Burk, Robert F. *Dwight D. Eisenhower: Hero and Politician.* Boston: Twayne Publishers, 1986.

Burton, E. Milby. *The Siege of Charleston, 1861–1865.* Columbia: University of South Carolina Press, 1970.

Busch, Noel F. *Winter Quarters: George Washington and the Continental Army at Valley Forge.* New York: Liveright, 1974.

Butler, David F. *United States Firearms: The First Century, 1776–1875.* New York: Winchester Press, 1971.

Bykofsky, Joseph, and Harold Larson. *The Transportation Corps: Operations Overseas. United States Army in World War II: The Technical Services.* Washington, D.C.: Office of the Chief of Military History, 1957.

Byrd, Martha. *Chennault: Giving Wings to the Tigers.* Tuscaloosa: University of Alabama Press, 1987.

Byrne, Edward M. *Military Law.* 3d ed. Annapolis, MD: Naval Institute Press, 1981.

Callahan, Raymond. *Burma, 1942–1945.* Newark: University of Delaware Press, 1979.

Calleo, David. *The Atlantic Fantasy: The U.S., NATO, and Europe.* Studies in International Affairs Number 13. Baltimore: Johns Hopkins Press, 1970.

Cameron, John R. "Turf Philosophy Hard on Doctrine Cohesion." *Army* 32 (August 1982): 20–23.

Camilleri, Joseph A. *The Australia New Zealand US Alliance: Regional Security in the Nuclear Age.* Boulder, CO: Westview Press, 1987.

Canfield, Bruce N. *U.S. Infantry Weapons of World War II.* Lincoln, RI: Andrew Mowbray Publishers, 1996.

Cannan, John. *The Antietam Campaign, August–September 1862.* Rev. ed. Conshohocken, PA: Combined Books, 1994.

Cannon, M. Hamlin. *Leyte: The Return to the Philippines. United States Army in World War II: The War in the Pacific.* Washington, D.C.: Office of the Chief of Military History, 1954.

Cantor, Louis. "The Creation of the Modern National Guard: The Dick Act of 1903." Ph.D diss., Duke University, 1963.

Caraley, Demetrios. *The Politics of Military Unification: A Study of Conflict and the Policy Process.* New York; Columbia University Press, 1966.

Carlton, John T., and John F. Slinkman. *The ROA Story: A Chronicle of the First 60 Years of the Reserve Officers Association of the United States.* Washington, D.C.: Reserve Officers Association of the United States, 1982.

Carpenter, John A. *Sword and Olive Branch: Oliver Otis Howard.* Pittsburgh: University of Pittsburgh Press, 1964.

Carter, Anthony, and John Walter. *The Bayonet: A History of Knife and Sword Bayonets, 1850–1970.* New York: Charles Scribner's Sons, 1974.

Carter, Michael D. "From Parade Ground to the Battlefield: Henry Knox and the Battle of Monmouth." *Field Artillery* (July–August 1998): 12–16.

Carter, Samuel, III. *The Siege of Atlanta, 1864.* New York: St. Martin's Press, 1973.

Carter, William H. *The Life of Lieutenant General Chaffee.* Chicago: University of Chicago Press, 1917.

Case, Blair. "Sergeant York Back on Track." *Air Defense Artillery* (Winter 1985): 9–13.

Castel, Albert. *Decision in the West: The Atlanta Campaign of 1864.* Lawrence; University Press of Kansas, 1992.

Catton, Bruce. *Grant Moves South.* Boston: Little, Brown, 1960.

Causey, William M., Jr. "Using the OER Support Form as a Management Tool." *Army Logistician* (March–April 1990): 30–34.

Cavanaugh, Charles G., Jr. "Behind the Walls." *Soldiers* 38 (June 1983): 48–52.

Cavazos, Jaime, and Floyd Harrington. "Ultimate For NCOs." *Soldiers* 31 (August 1976): 22–25.

Cavazos, Richard E. "FORSCOM Hones as It Modernizes." *Army* 32 (October 1982): 34–39.

Cave Brown, Anthony. *The Last Hero: Wild Bill Donovan.* New York: Times Books, 1982.

Chafin, Leonard D. "Assignment MAAG." *Infantry* 52 (January–February 1962): 52–53.

Challener, Richard D. *Admirals, Generals, and American Foreign Policy, 1898–1914.* Princeton, NJ: Princeton University Press, 1973.

Chamberlain, Edward M. "Pathfinders: First In—Last Out." *Infantry* 62 (January–February 1972): 32–35.

Chamberlain, Peter, and Chris Ellis. *British and American Tanks for World War II: The Complete Illustrated History of British, American and Commonwealth Tanks, Gun Motor Carriages and Special Purpose Vehicles, 1939–1945.* 2d U.S. ed. New York: Arco Publishing, 1981.

———. *Pictorial History of Tanks of the World, 1915–45.* Harrisburg, PA: Stackpole Books, 1972.

———. *The Sherman.* New York: Arco Publishing, 1969.

Chamberlain, Peter, and Terry Gander. *Machine Guns.* New York: Arco Publishing, 1974.

———. *Mortars and Rockets.* New York: Arco Publishing, 1975.

Chamberlain, Samuel E. *My Confession.* New York: Harper and Brothers, 1956.

Chapman, Anne W. *The Origins and Development of the National Training Center, 1976–1984.* Fort Monroe, VA: Office of the Command Historian, United States Army Training and Doctrine Command, 1992.

Chappell, Gordon. *The Search for the Well-Dressed Soldier, 1865–1890.* Museum Monograph No. 5. Tucson: Arizona Historical Society, 1972.

Chase, Joseph Cummins. *Soldiers All: Portraits and Sketches of the Men of the A.E.F.* New York: George H. Doran, 1920.

Chermol, Brian H. "Battle Fatigue." *Infantry* 74 (January–February 1984): 13–15.

Chinn, George M. *The Machine Gun: History, Evolution, and Development of Manual, Automatic, and Airborne Repeating Weapons.* Vol. 1. Washington, D.C.: Government Printing Office, 1951.

Christianson, Thomas E. "Triple A." *Air Defense Artillery* (May–June 1994): 8–16.

Chwialkowski, Paul. *In Caesar's Shadow: The Life of General Robert Eichelberger.* Westport, CT: Greenwood Press, 1993.

Clancy, Tom. *Armored Cav: A Guided Tour of an Armored Cavalry Regiment.* New York: Berkley Books, 1994.

———. *Fighter Wing: A Guided Tour of an Air Force Combat Wing.* New York: Berkley Books, 1995.

Clark, Gregory R. *Words of the Vietnam War: The Slang, Jargon, Abbreviations, Acronyms, Nomenclature, Nicknames, Pseudonyms, Slogans, Specs, Euphemisms,*

Double-talk, Chants, and Names and Places of the Era of United States Involvement in Vietnam. Jefferson, NC: McFarland, 1990.

Clark, Mark W. *Calculated Risk.* New York: Harper and Brothers, 1950.

Clark, William Henry Harrison. *The History of the United States Army Veterinary Corps in Vietnam, 1962–1973.* Roswell, GA: W. H. Wolfe Associates, [1991].

Clarke, Douglas L. *The Missing Man: Politics and the MIA.* Washington, D.C.: National Defense University Research Directorate, 1979.

Clarke, Jeffrey J. *Advice and Support: The Final Years, 1965–1973. United States Army in Vietnam.* Washington, D.C.: Center of Military History, 1988.

Clarke, Jeffrey J., and Robert Ross Smith. *Riviera to the Rhine. United States Army in World War II: The European Theater of Operations.* Washington, D.C.: Center of Military History, 1993.

Clarke, Walter S. *Somalia: Background Information for Operations Restore Hope, 1992–93.* Carlisle Barracks, PA: U.S. Army War College, 1992.

Clary, David A., and Joseph W. A. Whitehorne. *The Inspectors General of the United States Army, 1777–1903.* Washington, D.C.; Office of the Inspector General and Center for Military History, 1987.

Clayton, Michael. *Jeep.* North Pomfret, VT: David and Charles, 1982.

Cleaves, Freeman. *Meade of Gettysburg.* Norman: University of Oklahoma Press, 1960.

———. *Old Tippecanoe: William Henry Harrison and His Times.* New York: Charles Scribner's Sons, 1939.

———. *Rock of Chickamauga: The Life of General George H. Thomas.* Norman: University of Oklahoma Press, 1949.

Clendenen, Clarence C. *The United States and Pancho Villa: A Study in Unconventional Diplomacy.* Ithaca, NY: Cornell University Press, 1961.

Clifford, John G. *The Citizen Soldiers: The Plattsburg Training Camp Movement, 1913–1920.* Lexington: University Press of Kentucky, 1972.

Cline, Ray S. *Washington Command Post: The Operations Division. United States Army in World War II: The War Department.* Washington, D.C.: Office of the Chief of Military History, 1951.

Coakley, Robert W., and Richard M. Leighton. *Global Logistics and Strategy, 1943–1945. United States Army in World War II: The War Department.* Washington, D.C.: Office of the Chief of Military History, 1968.

Coates, Earl J., and John D. McAulay. *Civil War Sharps Carbines & Rifles.* Gettysburg, PA: Thomas Publications, 1996.

Coates, Earl J., and Dean S. Thomas. *An Introduction to Civil War Small Arms.* Gettysburg, PA: Thomas Publications, 1990.

Coates, K. S., and W. R. Morrison. *The Alaska Highway in World War II: The U.S. Army of Occupation in Canada's Northwest.* Norman: University of Oklahoma Press, 1992.

Coburn, Mark. *Terrible Innocence: General Sherman at War.* New York: Hippocrene Books, 1993.

Cochran. Thomas B., William M. Arkin, and Milton M. Hoenig. *Nuclear Weapons Databook.* Vol. 1, *U.S. Nuclear Forces and Capabilities.* Cambridge, MA: Ballinger Publishing, 1983.

Cochrane, Rexmond C. *The 1st Division in the Meuse-Argonne, 1–12 October 1918.* Gas Warfare in World War I, Study Number 3. U.S. Army Chemical Corps Historical

Studies. Army Chemical Center, MD: U.S. Army Chemical Corps Historical Office, 1957.

————. *The Use of Gas at St. Mihiel: The 90th Division, September 1918.* Gas Warfare in World War I, Study Number 5. U.S. Army Chemical Corps Historical Studies. Army Chemical Center, MD: U.S. Army Chemical Corps Historical Office, 1957.

Coddington, Edwin B. *The Gettysburg Campaign: A Study in Command.* New York: Charles Scribner's Sons, 1968.

Coffey, Thomas M. *HAP: The Story of the U.S. Air Force and the Man Who Built It, General Henry H. "HAP" Arnold.* New York: Viking Press, 1982.

Coffman, Edward M. *The Hilt of the Sword: The Career of Peyton C. March.* Madison: University of Wisconsin Press, 1966.

————. *The Old Army: A Portrait of the American Army in Peacetime, 1784–1898.* New York: Oxford University Press, 1986.

————. *The War to End All Wars: The American Military Experience in World War I.* Madison: University of Wisconsin Press. 1986.

Coggins, Jack. *Arms and Equipment of the Civil War.* 1962. Reprint. Wilmington, NC: Broadfoot Publishing, 1990.

Cohen, Stan. *The Trail of '42: A Pictorial History of the Alaskan Highway.* Missoula, MT: Pictorial Histories Publishing, 1979.

Coit, Margaret L. *John C. Calhoun: American Portrait.* Boston: Houghton Mifflin, 1950.

[Coker, Kathy Roe.] *The Military Police Corps at Fort Gordon, 1948–1975: A Commemorative History.* Fort Gordon, GA: Office of the Command Historian, U.S. Army Signal Center and Fort Gordon, [1991].

Cole, Alice C., Alfred Goldberg, Samuel A. Tucker, and Rudolph A. Winnacker, eds. *The Department of Defense: Documents on Establishment and Organization, 1944–1978.* Washington, D.C.: Office of the Secretary of Defense, 1978.

Cole, Donald. *The Presidency of Andrew Jackson.* Lawrence: University Press of Kansas, 1993.

Cole, Hugh M. *The Ardennes: Battle of the Bulge.* United States Army in World War II: The European Theater of Operations. Washington, D.C.: Office of the Chief of Military History, 1965.

Coleman, J. D. *Pleiku: The Dawn of Helicopter Warfare in Vietnam.* New York: St. Martin's Press, 1988.

Coles, Harry L. *The War of 1812.* Chicago: University of Chicago Press, 1965.

————, and Albert K. Weinberg. *Civil Affairs: Soldiers Become Governors. United States Army in World War II: Special Studies.* Washington D.C.: Office of the Chief of Military History, 1964.

Coll, Blanche D., Jean E. Keith, and Herbert H. Rosenthal. *The Corps of Engineers: Troops and Equipment. United States Army in World War II: The Technical Services.* Washington, D.C.: Center of Military History, 1988.

Collins, Arthur S., Jr. *Common Sense Training: A Working Philosophy for Leaders.* Novato, CA: Presidio, 1978.

————. "Take It—Don't Leave It." *Army* 12 (December 1974): 8–9.

————. "Walter Krueger: An Infantry Great." *Infantry* 73 (January–February 1983): 14–19.

Collins, Barry W. "Covering Force." *Soldiers* 42 (December 1987): 34–36.

Collins, J. Lawton. *Lightning Joe: An Autobiography.* Baton Rouge: Louisiana State University Press, 1979.

Collins, John M. *American and Soviet Military Trends since the Cuban Missile Crisis*. Washington, D.C.: Center for Strategic and International Studies, 1978.

————. *Special Operations Forces: An Assessment*. Washington, D.C.: National Defense University Press, 1994.

Collins, Robert F. *Reserve Officers Training Corps: Campus Pathways to Service Commissions*. New York: Rosen Publishing Group, 1986.

Conger, A. L. *The Rise of U.S. Grant*. New York: Da Capo Press. 1931, reprint 1996.

Conger, Roger N., James M. Day, Joe B. Frantz, Kenneth F. Neighbours, W. C. Nunn, Ben Procter, Harold B. Simpson, and Dorman H. Winfrey. *Frontier Forts of Texas*. Waco, TX: Texian Press, 1966.

The Congressional Medal of Honor: The Names, the Deeds. Forest Ranch, CA: Sharp and Dunnigan Publications, 1984.

Conn, Stetson. "The Army's Historical Program." *Military Review* 46 (May 1966): 40–47.

————. "Guardian of the Pacific: The Army in Hawaii, 1849–1945." *Army Information Digest* 7 (July 1960): 14–23.

————, Rose C. Engelman, and Byron Fairchild. *Guarding the United States and Its Outposts. United States Army in World War II: The Western Hemisphere*. Washington, D.C.: Office of the Chief of Military History, 1964.

Connelly, Thomas L. *Army of the Heartland: The Army of Tennessee*. Baton Rouge: Louisiana State University Press, 1967.

————. *The Marble Man: Robert E. Lee and His Image in American Society*. New York: Alfred A. Knopf, 1977.

Conquer: The Story of the Ninth Army, 1944–1945. Washington, D.C.: Infantry Journal Press, 1947.

Conrad, Thomas E. "Fort Benning, Home of the Infantry: A Bicentennial Review." *Infantry* 65 (May–June 1975): 24–30.

Cook, Blanche Wiesen. *The Declassified Eisenhower: A Divided Legacy*. Garden City, NY: Doubleday, 1981.

Cook, Don. *Forging the Alliance: NATO, 1945–1950*. New York: Arbor House/William Morrow, 1989.

Cooke, James J. *The Rainbow Division in the Great War, 1917–1919*. Westport, CT: Praeger, 1994.

Cooling, Benjamin Franklin, ed. *Case Studies in the Development of Close Air Support*. Washington, D.C.: Office of Air Force History, 1990.

————. *Fort Donelson's Legacy: War and Society in Kentucky and Tennessee, 1862–1863*. Knoxville: University of Tennessee Press, 1997.

————. *Forts Henry and Donelson: The Key to the Confederate Heartland*. Knoxville: University of Tennessee Press, 1987.

Coombe, Jack D. *Thunder along the Mississippi: The River Battles That Split the Confederacy*. New York: Sarpedon, 1996.

Cooper, Jerry. *The Rise of the National Guard: The Evolution of the American Militia, 1865–1920*. Lincoln: University of Nebraska, 1997.

Corn, Vollney B., Jr. "The Counterfire Battle: Shoot First to Win." *Army* 39 (July 1989): 39–41.

Cornebise, Alfred Emile. *Ranks and Columns: Armed Forces Newspapers in American Wars*. Westport, CT: Greenwood Press, 1993.

———. *The Stars and Stripes: Doughboy Journalism in World War I*. Westport, CT: Greenwood Press, 1984.

Corr, Edwin G., and Stephen Sloan, eds. *Low-Intensity Conflict: Old Threats in a New World*. Boulder, CO: Westview Press, 1992.

Corwin, Edward S. *The President: Office and Powers, 1787–1957: History and Analysis of Practice and Opinion*. New York: New York University Press, 1957.

———. *Presidential Power and the Constitution: Essays*. Edited by Richard Loss. Ithaca, NY: Cornell University Press, 1976.

———. *Total War and the Constitution: Five Lectures Delivered on the William W. Cook Foundation at the University of Michigan, March 1946*. 1947. Essay Index Reprint Series. Freeport, NY: Books for Libraries Press, 1970.

Cosmas, Graham A. *An Army for Empire: The United States Army in the Spanish-American War*. Columbia: University of Missouri Press, 1971.

——— and Albert E. Cowdrey. *The Medical Department: Medical Service in the European Theater of Operations. United States Army in World War II: The Technical Services*. Washington, D.C.: Center of Military History, 1992.

Costello, Gene. "Black Hawk." *United States Army Aviation Digest* 24 (February 1978): 34–39.

Coumbe, Arthur T., and Lee S. Harford. *U.S. Army Cadet Command: The 10 Year History*. Fort Monroe, VA: Office of the Command Historian, U.S. Army Cadet Command, 1996.

Cowdrey, Albert E. *Fighting for Life: American Military Medicine in World War II*. New York: Free Press, 1994.

Cox, Charles W., III. "CAS^3." *Military Police Journal* 13 (Spring 1986): 41–42.

Cox, Frank. *Enlisted Soldier's Guide*. 4th ed. Mechanicsburg, PA: Stackpole Books, 1996.

———. *NCO Guide*. 4th ed. Harrisburg, PA: Stackpole Books, 1992.

———. "REFORGER: Not 'Jess' Another Exercise." *Soldiers* 45 (April 1990): 21–26.

———. "USO: Serving Those Who Serve." *Soldiers* 45 (February 1990): 50–52.

Cox, Jacob D. *Sherman's March to the Sea: Hood's Tennessee Campaign & the Carolina Campaigns of 1865*. New York: Da Capo Press, 1994.

Cozzens, Peter. *No Better Place to Die: The Battle of Stones River*. Urbana: University of Illinois Press, 1990.

———. *The Shipwreck of Their Hopes: The Battles for Chattanooga*. Urbana: University of Illinois Press, 1994.

———. *This Terrible Sound: The Battle of Chickamauga*. Urbana: University of Illinois Press, 1992.

Cragg, Dan. *Guide to Military Installations*, 4th ed. Mechanicsburg, PA: Stackpole Books, 1994.

Craven, Wesley Frank, and James Lea Cate, eds. *The Army Air Forces in World War II*. 7 vols. Chicago: University of Chicago Press, 1948–1958.

Cray, Ed. *General of the Army: George C. Marshall, Soldier and Statesman*. New York: W. W. Norton, 1990.

Crego, Arthur Van Voorhis. *City on the Mesa: The New Fort Bliss, 1890–1895*. Fort Bliss, TX: n.p., 1969.

Crismon, Fred W. *U.S. Military Tracked Vehicles*. Osceola, WI: Motorbooks International Publishers, 1992.

———. *U.S. Military Wheeled Vehicles*. Sarasota, FL: Crestline Publishing, 1983.

Crist, Allan G, and W. D. McGlasson. "A Century of Service." *National Guard* 32 (November 1978): 6–9.

Crocker, Lawrence P. *Army Officer's Guide.* 46th ed. Mechanicsburg, PA: Stackpole Books, 1993.

Croizat, Victor. *The Brown Water Navy: The River and Coastal War in Indo-China and Vietnam, 1948–1972.* Poole, Dorset, U.K.: Blandford Press, 1984.

Cromartie, Eugene R. "Boosting Combat Readiness by Fighting Crime in the Army." *Army* 39 (October 1989): 152–155.

Crossland, Richard B., and James T. Currie. *Twice the Citizen: A History of the United States Army Reserve, 1908–1983.* Washington, D.C.: Office of the Chief, Army Reserve, 1984.

Crouch, Thomas W. *A Yankee Guerrillero: Frederick Funston and the Cuban Insurrection, 1896–1897.* [Memphis, TN]: Memphis State University Press, 1975.

Crow, Duncan, ed. *American AFVs of World War II.* Armored Fighting Vehicles in Profile (AFVs of the World Series), vol. 4. Garden City, NY: Doubleday, 1972.

Crowl, Philip A., and Edmund G. Love. *Seizure of the Gilberts and Marshalls.* United States Army in World War II: The War in the Pacific. Washington, D.C.: Office of the Chief of Military History, 1955.

Cucolo, Anthony A., and Dale S. Ringler. "Heavy Infantry: Let's Revive Its Lethality." *Infantry* 88 (September–December 1998): 7–10.

Culkin, Dennis. "David and Goliath." *Defense & Foreign Affairs* 12 (February 1984): 24–26.

Cullen, Joseph P. *The Peninsula Campaign, 1862: McClellan & Lee Struggle for Richmond.* Harrisburg, PA: Stackpole Books, 1973.

———. *Where a Hundred Thousand Fell: The Battles of Fredericksburg, Chancellorsville, the Wilderness, and Spotsylvania Court House.* National Park Service Historical Handbook Series No. 19. Washington, D.C.: Government Printing Office, 1966.

Cunningham, Edward. *The Port Hudson Campaign, 1862–1863.* [Baton Rouge]: Louisiana State University Press, 1963.

Current, Richard N. *Secretary Stimson: A Study in Statecraft.* New Brunswick, NJ: Rutgers University Press, 1954.

Cutler, Bruce. *The Massacre at Sand Creek: Narrative Voices.* Norman: University of Oklahoma Press, 1995.

Cutler, Thomas J. *Brown Water, Black Berets: Coastal and Riverine Warfare in Vietnam.* Annapolis, MD: Naval Institute Press, 1988.

Dalfiume, Richard M. *Desegregation of the U.S. Armed Forces: Fighting on Two Fronts, 1939–1953.* Columbia: University of Missouri Press, 1969.

Dallek, Robert. *The American Style of Foreign Policy: Cultural Politics and Foreign Affairs.* New York: Alfred A. Knopf, 1983.

Daniel, Dan. "The Military Resale System: Its Past . . . Its Present . . . Does It Have a Future?" *Interservice* 2 (Spring 1982): 12–19.

Daniel, Larry J. *Shiloh: The Battle That Changed the Civil War.* New York: Simon and Schuster, 1997.

Dary, David. *Comanche.* Public Education Series No. 5. Lawrence: University of Kansas Publications, 1976.

Dastrup, Boyd L. *The Field Artillery: History and Sourcebook.* Westport, CT: Greenwood Press, 1994.

————. *King of Battle: A Branch History of the U.S. Army's Field Artillery.* Fort Monroe, VA: Office of the Command Historian, U.S. Army Training and Doctrine Command, 1992.

————. *The U.S. Army Command and General Staff College: A Centennial History.* Leavenworth and Manhattan, KS: J. H. Johnston III and Sunflower University Press, 1982.

Davies, Paul. *War of the Mines: Cambodia, Landmines and the Impoverishment of a Nation.* Boulder, CO: Pluto Press, 1994.

Davis, Burke. *The Billy Mitchell Affair.* New York: Random House, 1967.

————. *The Campaign That Won America: The Story of Yorktown.* New York: Dial Press, 1970.

————. *The Cowpens–Guilford Courthouse Campaign.* Philadelphia: J. B. Lippencott, 1962.

————. *Sherman's March.* New York: Random House, 1980.

Davis, Franklin M., Jr. *Come as a Conqueror: The United States Army's Occupation of Germany, 1945–1949.* New York: Macmillan, 1967.

Davis, Richard G. *The 31 Initiatives: A Study in Air Force-Army Cooperation.* Air Staff Historical Study. Washington, D.C.: Office of Air Force History, 1987.

Davis, William C. *Battle at Bull Run: A History of the First Major Campaign of the Civil War.* Garden City, NY: Doubleday, 1977.

————. *The Battle of New Market.* Garden City, NY: Doubleday, 1975.

————. *Jefferson Davis: The Man and His Hour.* New York: HarperCollins, 1991.

Daws, Gavan. *Prisoners of the Japanese: POWS of World War II in the Pacific.* New York: William Morrow, 1994.

Dawson, Henry B. *The Assault on Stony Point by General Anthony Wayne, July 16, 1779.* Cambridge: H. O. Houghton, 1863.

Dawson, W. Forrest, comp. and ed. *Saga of the All Americans.* Atlanta, GA: Albert Love Enterprises, 1946.

De Barneville, Maurice F. "The Remount Service in the A.E.F." *Cavalry Journal* 30 (April 1921): 130–144.

DeCicco, Lisa. "Disciplinary Duty." *Soldiers* 47 (August 1992): 6–8.

Dellinger, George C. "1st Infantry Division." *Infantry* 68 (March–April 1978): 18–23.

DePuy, William E. " 'One-Up and Two-Back'?: Reexamining an Old Law." *Army* 30 (January 1980): 20–25.

————. "TRADOC: A New Command for An Old Mission." *Army* 23 (October 1973): 31–34.

DeRemer, Lee E. "Leadership between a Rock and a Hard Place: ROE." *Airpower Journal* 10 (Fall 1966): 87–94.

Derleth, August. *Vincennes: Portal to the West.* Englwood Cliffs, NJ: Prentice-Hall, 1968.

D'Este, Carlo. *Bitter Victory: The Battle for Sicily, 1943.* New York: E. P. Dutton, 1988.

————. *Fatal Decision: Anzio and the Battle for Rome.* New York: HarperCollins, 1991.

————. *World War II in the Mediterranean, 1942–1945.* Chapel Hill, NC: Algonquin Books, 1990.

Devereux, Tony. *Messenger Gods of Battle: Radio, Radar, Sonar: The Story of Electronics in War.* London: Brassey's, 1991.

Devlin, Gerard M. *Back to Corregidor: America Retakes the Rock*. New York: St. Martin's Press, 1992.

———. *Paratrooper! The Saga of U.S. Army and Marine Parachute and Glider Combat Troops during World War II*. New York: St. Martin's Press, 1979.

———. *Silent Wings: The Saga of U.S. Army and Marine Combat Glider Pilots during World War II*. New York: St. Martin's Press, 1985.

Dexter, Dennis D., and Russell B. Shor. "From Zama to Hokkaido." *Army Digest* 25 (August 1970): 14–19.

Dickson, Paul. *War Slang: Fighting Words and Phrases of Americans from the Civil War to the Gulf War*. New York: Pocket Books, 1994.

Diehl, William J. "2nd Infantry Division." *Infantry* 68 (November–December 1978): 14–18.

Dierks, Jack Cameron. *A Leap to Arms: The Cuban Campaign of 1898*. Philadelphia: J. B. Lippencott, 1970.

Dillon, Lester R., Jr. *American Artillery in the Mexican War, 1846–1847*. Austin, TX: Presidial Press, 1975.

Dillon, Richard H. *Meriwether Lewis: A Biography*. New York: Coward-McCann, 1965.

———. *North American Indian Wars*. New York: Facts on File, 1983.

DiNardo, R. L., and Albert A. Nofi, eds. *James Longstreet: The Man, the Soldier, the Controversy*. Conshohocken, PA: Combined Publishing, 1998.

DiNunzio, Mario R., ed. *Theodore Roosevelt: An American Mind: A Selection from His Writings*. New York: St. Martin's Press, 1994.

Dodge, Griffin N. "When New Fatigues Come In, Can #10 Cans Be Far Behind?" *Army* 33 (September 1983): 44–49.

Donnelly, Thomas, Margaret Roth, and Caleb Baker. *Operation Just Cause: The Storming of Panama*. New York: Lexington Books, 1991.

Donnini, Frank P. *ANZUS in Revision: Changing Defense Features of Australia and New Zealand in the Mid-1980s*. Maxwell Air Force Base, AL: Air University Press. 1991.

Doolittle, James H., with Carroll V. Glines. *I Could Never Be So Lucky Again: An Autobiography*. New York: Bantam Books, 1991.

Dorsey, R. Stephen. *American Military Belts and Related Equipment*. Union City, TN: Pioneer Press, 1984.

———, and Kenneth L. McPheeters. *The American Military Saddle, 1776–1945*. Eugene, OR: Collector's Library, 1999.

Dougan, Clark, and Stephen Weiss. *The American Experience in Vietnam*. New York: W. W. Norton, 1988.

Doughty, Robert A. *The Evolution of US Army Tactical Doctrine, 1946–76*. Leavenworth Paper No. 1. Fort Leavenworth, KS: Combat Studies Institute, 1979.

Dowdey, Clifford. *The Seven Days: The Emergence of Lee*. Boston: Little, Brown, 1964.

Downey, Fairfax. *Fife, Drum & Bugle*. Fort Collins, CO: Old Army Press, 1971.

———. *Indian Wars of the U.S. Army, 1776–1865*. Garden City, NY: Doubleday, 1963.

———. *Storming of the Gateway: Chattanooga, 1863*. New York: David McKay, 1960.

———, and Jacques N. Jacobsen, Jr. *The Red/Bluecoats: The Indian Scouts, U.S. Army*. Fort Collins, CO: Old Army Press, 1973.

Dreux, William B. *No Bridges Blown*. Notre Dame, IN: University of Notre Dame Press, 1971.

Driver, J. P. "Hand Grenade: 1775–1963," *Marine Corps Gazette* 47 (March 1963): 43–45.

Duiker, William J. *The Communist Road to Power in Vietnam*. Boulder, CO: Westview Press, 1981.

Dunham, Emory A. *Tank Destroyer History*. Studies in the History of Army Ground Forces, No. 29. [Washington, D.C.]: Historical Section, Army Ground Forces, 1946.

Dunlay, Thomas W. *Wolves for the Blue Soldiers: Indian Scouts and Auxiliaries with the United States Army, 1860–90*. Lincoln: University of Nebraska Press, 1982.

Dunlop, Richard. *Behind Japanese Lines: With the OSS in Burma*. Chicago: Rand McNally, 1979.

———. *Donovan: America's Master Spy*. Chicago: Rand McNally, 1982.

Dunn, Peter M., and Bruce W. Watson, eds. *American Intervention in Grenada: The Implications of Operation "Urgent Fury."* Boulder, CO: Westview Press, 1985.

Dunn, Walter Scott, Jr. *Second Front Now, 1943*. University, AL: University of Alabama Press, 1980.

Dunne, David M. "The Engineer School: Past and Present." *Military Engineer* 41 (November–December 1949): 411–416.

Dunnigan, Brian Leigh. *Forts within A Fort: Niagara's Redoubts*. Youngstown, NY: Old Fort Niagara Association, 1989.

———. *A History and Guide to Old Fort Niagara*. Youngstown, NY: Old Fort Niagara Association, 1985.

Dunnigan, James F., and Albert A. Nofi. *Shooting Blanks: War Making That Doesn't Work*. New York: William Morrow, 1991.

Dunnigan, James F., and Raymond M. Macedonia. *Getting It Right: American Military Reforms after Vietnam to the Persian Gulf and Beyond*. New York: William Morrow, 1993.

Dunstan, Simon. *Vietnam Choppers: Helicopters in Battle 1950–1975*. London: Osprey Publishing, 1988.

Dupre, Flint O. *Hap Arnold: Architect of American Air Power*. Air Force Academy Series. Carroll V. Glines, gen. ed. New York: Macmillan, 1972.

Dupuy, R. Ernest. "The Concrete Battleship." *Army* 23 (August 1973): 28–32.

———. *Men of West Point: The First 150 Years of the United States Military Academy*. New York: William Sloane Associates, 1951.

Dupuy, Trevor N. *The Military Life of George Washington: American Soldier*. New York: Franklin Watts, 1969.

Dvarecka, Chris L. "Springfield Armory: Pioneer in Small Arms." *Army Information Digest* 9 (July 1954): 41–48.

———. "Weapons on Parade." *Army Information Digest* 10 (September 1955): 39–43.

Dwyer, William M. *The Day Is Ours! November 1776–January 1777: An Inside View of the Battles of Trenton and Princeton*. New York: Viking Press, 1983.

Dyer, Brainerd. *Zachary Taylor*. 1946. Reprint. New York: Barnes and Noble, 1967.

Dykeman, Wilma. *With Fire and Sword: The Battle of Kings Mountain*. Washington, D.C.: National Park Service, 1991.

Eaton, Clement. *Jefferson Davis*. New York: Free Press, 1977.

Eby, Cecil. *"That Disgraceful Affair," or the Black Hawk War*. New York: W. W. Norton, 1973.

Edens, Frank A. "Major Command or Major Subordinate Command Is Question for Army Reserve." *Officer* 68 (December 1992): 35–41.

———. "Strong and Ready." *Officer* 70 (January 1994): 13–15.

Edward, John E. *Combat Service Support Guide.* 2d ed. Harrisburg, PA: Stackpole Books, 1993.

Edwards, William B. *Civil War Guns: The Complete Story of Federal and Confederate Small Arms: Design, Manufacture, Identification, Procurement, Issue, Employment, Effectiveness, and Postwat Disposal.* Harrisburg, PA: Stackpole, 1962.

Eiler, Keith E., ed. *Wedemeyer on War and Peace.* Stanford, CA: Hoover Institution Press, 1987.

Eisenhower, Dwight D. *At Ease: Stories I Tell to Friends.* Garden City, NY: Doubleday, 1967.

Eisenhower, John S. D. *Agent of Destiny: The Life and Times of General Winfield Scott.* New York: Free Press, 1997.

———. *Intervention! The United States and the Mexican Revolution, 1913–1917.* New York: W. W. Norton, 1993.

———. *So Far from God: The U.S. War with Mexico, 1846–1848.* New York: Random House, 1989.

Eisnitz, Sheldon R. "Challenge with Choice: Four Ways to an Army Commission." *Army Information Digest* 20 (August 1965): 38–47.

Eller, Cynthia. *Conscientious Objectors and the Second World War: Moral and Religious Arguments in Support of Pacifism.* Westport, CT: Praeger, 1991.

Elliott, Charles Winslow. *Winfield Scott: The Soldier and the Man.* New York: Macmillan, 1937.

Elliott, J. F. "The Great Western: Sarah Bowman, Mother and Mistress to the U.S. Army." *Journal of Arizona History* 30 (Spring 1987): 1–26.

Elliott, Robert F. "Commitment or Cop Out?" *Soldiers* 26 (November 1971): 4–6.

Ellis, John W. "Welcome to the Petroleum Supply Battalion!" *Army Logistician* (January–February 1991): 34–36.

Ellis, William Arba, ed. and comp. *Norwich University, 1819–1911: Her History, Her Graduates, Her Roll of Honor.* Vol. 1, *General History, 1819–1911.* Montpelier, VT: Capital City Press, 1911.

Elting, John R. *Amateurs to Arms! A Military History of the War of 1812.* Chapel Hill, NC: Algonquin Books, 1991.

———. *The Battle of Bunker's Hill.* Monmouth Beach, NJ: Philip Freneau Press, 1975.

———. *The Battles of Saratoga.* Monmouth Beach, NJ: Philip Freneau Press, 1977.

———, and Michael McAfee, eds. *Military Uniforms in America.* 4 vols. 1974–1988.

Emmett, Chris. *Fort Union and the Winning of the Southwest.* Norman: University of Oklahoma Press, 1965.

Endler, James R. *Other Leaders, Other Heroes: West Point's Legacy to America beyond the Field of Battle.* Westport, CT: Praeger, 1998.

Engle, Eloise. *Medic: America's Medical Soldiers, Sailors and Airmen in Peace and War.* New York: John Day, 1967.

Eppinga, Jane. *Henry Ossian Flipper: West Point's First Black Graduate.* Plano: Republic of Texas Press, 1996.

Epstein, Miles Z. "Seventy-Five Years for God and Country." *The American Legion* 137 (September 1994): 42–44.

Escott, Paul D. *After Secession: Jefferson Davis and the Failure of Confederate Nationalism*. Baton Rouge: Louisiana State University Press, 1978.

Eshel, David. *Daring to Win: Special Forces at War*. London: Arms and Armour, 1992.

Essary, Wilburn D. "Stinger! For Potent Air Defense." *Marine Corps Gazette* 68 (May 1984): 69–74.

Ethell, Jeffrey L., Robert Grinsell, Roger Freeman, David A. Anderton, Frederick A. Johnsen, Alex Vanagas-Baginski, and Robert C. Mikesh. *The Great Book of World War II Airplanes*. New York: Bonanza Books, 1984.

Evans, Bill G. "Personnel Paperwork: The Administration of Personnel Affairs in the Combat Division Is Both Centralized and Decentralized." *Army* 17 (May 1967): 52, 58–60, 64.

Evinger, William R., ed. *Directory of U.S. Military Bases Worldwide*. 3d ed. Phoenix, AZ: Oryx Press, 1998.

Ewald, William Bragg, Jr. *Who Killed Joe McCarthy?* New York: Simon and Schuster, 1984.

Ezell, Edward Clinton. *The Great Rifle Controversy: Search for the Ultimate Infantry Weapon from World War II through Vietnam and Beyond*. Harrisburg. PA: Stackpole Books, 1984.

———. *Small Arms of the World: A Basic Manual of Small Arms*. 11th rev. ed. Harrisburg, PA: Stackpole Books, 1977.

Falk, Stanley L. *Bataan: The March of Death*. New York: W. W. Norton, 1962.

———. *Decision at Leyte*. New York: W. W. Norton, 1966.

———. "Feudin' and Fussin' in the Old Army." *Army* 34 (November 1984): 57–61.

———. "The Little-Big School off Buzzard's Point." *Army* 35 (April 1985): 46–50.

Farley, James J. *Making Arms in the Machine Age: Philadelphia's Frankford Arsenal, 1816–1870*. University Park, PA: Pennsylvania State University Press, 1994.

Faughan, David G. "Lincloe System: A New Infantry Pack." *Infantry* 63 (May–June 1973): 54–55.

Faulk, Odie B., and Laura E. Faulk. *Fort Hood: The First Fifty Years*. Temple, TX: Frank W. Mayborn Foundation, 1990.

Fawcett, John M., Jr. "Which Way to the FEBA?" *Airpower Journal* 6 (Fall 1992): 14–24.

Featherson, Alwyn. *Saving the Breakout: The 30th Division's Heroic Stand at Mortain, August 7–12, 1944*. Novato, CA: Presidio, 1993.

Fehrenbach, T. R. *This Kind of War: A Study in Unpreparedness*. New York: Macmillan, 1963.

Feis, William B. "The Deception of Braxton Bragg: The Tullahoma Campaign, June 23–July 4, 1863." *Blue & Gray* 10 (October 1992): 10–21.

Fellowes-Gordon, Ian. *The Magic War: The Battle for North Burma*. New York: Charles Scribner's Sons, 1971.

Fenstemacher, Edgar R., and Eugene R. Webb. "From Musket to M1." *Infantry School Quarterly* 43 (July 1953): 22–31.

Ferguson, James H. "The Military Historian Goes 'Where the Action Is.' " *Army Digest* 24 (August 1969): 56–58.

Feuer, A. B. *The Santiago Campaign of 1898: A Soldier's View of the Spanish-American War*. Westport, CT: Praeger, 1993.

"Fifty-Year-Old Edgewood Arsenal Develops New Equipment." *Ordnance* 53 (July–August 1968): 30.

Figley, Charles R. *Trauma and Its Wake: The Study and Treatment of Post-traumatic Stress Disorder.* New York: Brunner/Mazel, 1985.

Finn, James, ed. *Conscience and Command: Justice and Discipline in the Military.* New York: Random House, 1971.

Finnegan, John Patrick. *Against the Specter of a Dragon: The Campaign for American Military Preparedness, 1914–1917.* Contributions in Military History Number 7. Westport, CT: Greenwood Press, 1974.

———. *Military Intelligence. Army Lineage Series.* Washington, D.C.: Center of Military History, 1998.

Fireman, Janet R. *The Spanish Royal Corps of Engineers in the Western Borderlands: Instrument of Bourbon Reform, 1764–1815.* Glendale, CA: Arthur H. Clark, 1977.

"The First Annual Meeting of the Association of the U.S. Army." *Armed Forces Chemical Journal* 9 (November–December 1955): 38–39.

Fisch, Arnold G., Jr., and Robert K. Wright, Jr., eds., *The Story of the Noncommissioned Officer Corps: The Backbone of the Army.* Washington, D.C.: Center of Military History, 1989.

Fisch, Robert W. *Field Equipment of the Infantry, 1914–1945.* Sykesville, MD: Greenberg Publishing, 1989.

Fischer, Edward. *The Chancy War: Winning in China, Burma, and India, in World War Two.* New York: Orion Books, 1991.

Fischer, Joseph R. *A Well-Executed Failure: The Sullivan Campaign against the Iroquois, July–September 1779.* Columbia: University of South Carolina Press, 1997.

Fishel, John T. *Civil Military Operations in the New World.* Westport, CT: Praeger, 1997.

Fisher, Ernest F., Jr. *Cassino to the Alps. United States Army in World War II: The Mediterranean Theater of Operations.* Washington, D.C.: Center of Military History, 1989.

———. *Guardians of the Republic: A History of the Noncommissioned Officer Corps of the U.S. Army.* New York: Ballantine Books, 1994.

Fisher, Vardis. *Suicide or Murder? The Strange Death of Governor Meriwether Lewis.* Denver: Alan Swallow, 1962.

Fitzpatrick, Jim. *The Bicycle in Wartime: An Illustrated History.* Washington, D.C.: Brassey's, 1998.

Fitzpatrick, Richard, Bill Baumann, and Duquesne Wolf. *Twenty-fifth Infantry Division: Tropic Lightning.* Paducah, KY: Turner Publishing, 1988.

Flanagan, Edward M., Jr. *Battle for Panama: Inside Operation Just Cause.* Washington, D.C.: Brassey's, 1993.

———. *Corregidor: The Rock Force Assault, 1945.* Novato, CA: Presidio, 1988.

Flanigan, Peggy. "No More Drummers and Fifers." *Soldiers* 40 (February 1985): 6–8.

Fleming, David L. *From Everglade to Cañon with the Second Dragoons: A Commemorative Address.* Governors Island, NY: Journal Military Service Institute, 1911.

Fleming, Peter. *The Siege at Peking.* New York: Harper and Brothers, 1959.

Fleming, Thomas J. *Beat the Last Drum: The Siege of Yorktown, 1781.* New York: St. Martin's Press, 1963.

———. *Now We Are Enemies: The Story of Bunker Hill.* New York: St. Martin's Press, 1960.

Fletcher, Marvin E. *America's First Black General: Benjamin O Davis, Sr, 1880–1970.* Lawrence: University Press of Kansas, 1989.

Flexner, James T. *George Washington*. 4 vols. Boston: Little, Brown, 1965–1972.
———. *The Traitor and the Spy: Benedict Arnold and John André*. 1953. Boston: Little, Brown, 1975.
Flipper, Henry Osian. *The Colored Cadet at West Point, Autobiography of Henry Osian Flipper, U.S.A.: First Graduate of Color from the U.S. Military Academy*. 1878. New York: Johnson Reprint, 1968.
Florentin, Eddy. *The Battle of the Falaise Gap*. Translated by Mervyn Savill. New York: Hawthorn Books, 1967.
Flory, William E. S. *Prisoners of War: A Study in the Development of International Law*. Washington, D.C.: American Council on Public Affairs, 1942.
Flynn, George Q. *Lewis B. Hershey: Mr. Selective Service*. Chapel Hill: University of North Carolina Press, 1985.
Foley, John E. "Observations on Mechanized Infantry." *Infantry* 76 (July–August 1986): 29–33.
Foner, Jack D. *Blacks and the Military in American History: A New Perspective*. New York: Praeger, 1974.
Foote, Shelby. *The Beleaguered City: The Vicksburg Campaign, December 1862–July 1863*. 1963. New York: Modern Library, 1995.
Ford, Daniel. *Flying Tigers: Claire Chennault and the American Volunteer Group*. Washington, D.C.: Smithsonian Institution Press, 1991.
Forsberg, Randall, William Driscoll, Gregory Webb, and Jonathan Dean. *Nonproliferation Primer: Preventing the Spread of Nuclear, Chemical, and Biological Weapons*. Cambridge, MA: MIT Press, 1995.
"Fort Devens: Defending the Cradle of Liberty." *Army Digest* 21 (June 1966): 51–52.
Fortner, Joe A., Jules T. Doux, and Mark A. Peterson. "Bring on the HETs! Operational and Tactical Relocation of Heavy Maneuver Forces." *Military Review* 72 (January 1992): 36–45.
Forty, George. *The Armies of George S. Patton*. London: Arms and Armour, 1966.
———. *Fifth Army at War*. New York: Charles Scribner's Sons, 1980.
———. *Patton's Third Army at War*. 1978. London: Arms and Armour, 1990.
"Forty-nine Years for Edgewood Arsenal." *Ordnance* 52 (July–August 1967): 90.
42nd Rainbow Infantry Division. Paducah, KY: Turner Publishing, 1987.
42nd "Rainbow" Infantry Division: A Combat History of World War II. Baton Rouge, LA: Army and Navy Publishing, 1946.
Foss, Christopher F. *Jane's World Armoured Fighting Vehicles*. New York: St. Martin's Press, 1977.
Foss, Christopher F., and T. J. Gander. *Infantry Weapons of the World*. New York: Charles Scribner's Sons, 1977.
Foster, Gregory D. "Educating for the 21st Century." *National Defense* 76 (March 1992): 14–17.
Fowle, Herb "Chick." *The Men of the Terrible Green Cross*. Hillsdale, MI: Herb Fowle, 1991.
Francillon, René J. *McDonnell Douglas Aircraft since 1920*. London: Putnam. 1979.
Frank, Richard B. *Guadalcanal*. New York: Randon House, 1990.
Franks, Frederick M., Jr. "TRADOC at 20: Where Tomorrow's Victories Begin." *Army* 43 (October 1993): 46–55.
Fraser, Walter J., Jr. *Patriots, Pistols, and Petticoats: "Poor Sinful Charles Town"* dur-

ing the American Revolution. 2d. ed. Columbia: University of South Carolina Press, 1993.

Frazer, Robert W. *Forts of the West: Military Forts and Presidios, and Posts Commonly Called Forts, West of the Mississippi River to 1898.* Norman: University of Oklahoma Press, 1965.

Frederick, J. George. "The Kentucky Rifle Myth." *National Guardsman* 5 (August 1951): 8–10.

Freeman, Douglas Southall. *George Washington: A Biography.* 7 vols. New York: Charles Scribner's Sons, 1948–1957.

French, William F. "Who Is Kilroy?" *Saturday Evening Post* 20 October 1945, 6.

"FT. McClellan: 46 Years of Service." *Armed Forces Chemical Journal* 17 (March 1963): 18–22.

Fuller, Claude E. *The Rifled Musket.* Harrisburg, PA: Stockpole, 1958.

Fuller, J.F.C. *The Conduct of War, 1789–1961: A Study of the Impact of the Franch, Industrial, and Russian Revolutions on War and Its Conduct.* New Brunswick, NJ: Rutgers University Press, 1961.

Funk, Arthur Layton. *The Politics of Torch: The Allied Landings and the Algiers Putsch, 1942.* Lawrence: University Press of Kansas, 1974.

Furgurson, Ernest B. *Chancellorsville, 1863.* New York: Alfred A. Knopf, 1992.

———. *Westmoreland: The Inevitable General.* Boston: Little, Brown, 1968.

Furneaux, Rupert. *The Battle of Saratoga.* New York: Stein and Day, 1971.

Futch, Ovid L. *History of Andersonville Prison.* [Gainesville]: University of Florida Press, 1968.

Futrell, Robert F. *Ideas, Concepts, Doctrine: Basic Thinking in the United States Air Force, 1907–1960.* Maxwell Air Force Base, AL: Air University Press, 1989.

Gabel, Christopher R. *Seek, Strike, and Destroy: U.S. Army Tank Destroyer Doctrine in World War II.* Leavenworth Paper No. 12. Fort Leavenworth, KS: Combat Studies Institute, 1985.

———. *The U.S. Army GHQ Maneuvers of 1941.* Washington, D.C.: Center of Military History, 1991.

Gallagher, Gary W., ed. *Lee: The Soldier.* Lincoln: University of Nebraska Press, 1996.

———, ed. *The Spotsylvania Campaign.* Military Campaigns of the Civil War. Chapel Hill: University of North Carolina Press, 1998,

———, ed. *The Wilderness Campaign.* Chapel Hill: University of North Carolina Press, 1997.

Gallagher, James J. *Low-Intensity Conflict: A Guide for Tactics, Techniques, and Procedures.* Harrisburg, PA: Stackpole Books, 1992.

Gallagher, Tag. *John Ford: The Man and His Films.* Berkeley: University of California Press, 1986.

Galloucis, Michael S. "The Military and the Media." *Army* 46 (August 1996): 14–18.

Gander, Terry J. *Bazooka: Hand-Held Hollow-Charge Anti-Tank Weapons.* Classic Weapons Series. New York: Military Book Club, 1998.

———. *Nuclear, Biological & Chemical Warfare.* London: Ian Allan, 1987.

Gardner, Edward, Jr. "Ninety-Day Wonder." *Saturday Evening Post,* 14 November 1942, 14–15.

Garfield, Brian. *The Thousand-Mile War: World War II in Alaska and the Aleutians.* Garden City, NY: Doubleday, 1969.

Garland, Albert N. "The Combat Infantryman Badge." *Infantry* 86 (July–August 1996): 17–21.

———. "Reflections of a Veteran Foot Soldier." *Army* 42 (June 1992): 39–41.

Garrett, Richard. *P.O.W.* London: David and Charles, 1981.

Garth, Timothy. "The Future Is Now: A Profile of the M1A2 Abrams." *Armor* 101 (March–April 1992): 26–28.

Gates, John M. *Schoolbooks and Krags: The United States Army in the Philippines, 1898–1902*. Contributions in Military History Number 2. Westport, CT: Greenwood Press, 1973.

Gaul, Jeffrey. *Fighting 36th Infantry Division*. Paducah, KY: Turner Publishing, 1988.

Gavin, James M. *War and Peace in the Space Age*. New York: Harper and Brothers, 1958.

Geary, James W. *We Need Men: The Union Draft in the Civil War*. Dekalb: Northern Illinois University Press, 1991.

Geddes, J. Philip. "High Mobility: An Urgent Requirement for the US Armed Forces." *International Defense Review* 15 (5/1982): 581–584.

———. "The US Army's Division Air Defense System." *International Defense Review* 14 (1981): 879–887.

Gehring, Stephen P. *From the Fulda Gap to Kuwait: U.S. Army, Europe and the Gulf War*. Washington, D.C.: Department of the Army, 1998.

Geiger, George J. "Air Defense Missiles for the Army." *Military Review* 49 (December 1969): 39–49.

Gelb, Norman. *Desperate Venture: The Story of Operation Torch, the Allied Invasion of North Africa*. New York: William Morrow, 1992.

Generous, William T., Jr. *Swords and Scales: The Development of the Uniform Code of Military Justice*. Port Washington, NY: Kennikat Press, 1973.

Germane, Gayton E., Joseph O. Carter, and William E. Rogers. *A New Concept of Transportation Movement: A System for Cargo Movement in the Communications Zone*. Fort Eustis, VA: U.S. Army Transportation Research and Engineering Command, 1959.

Gervasi, Tom. *America's War Machine: The Pursuit of Global Dominance*. New York: Grove Press, 1984.

Gettig, Rodney R., and James W. Dunn. "Land Clearing in Vietnam." *Engineer* 17 ([1987]): 45.

Gibson, Charles Dana, and E. Kay Gibson. *Assault and Logistics: Union Army Coastal and River Operations, 1861–1866*. Vol. 2, *The Army's Navy Services*. Camden, ME: Ensign Press, 1995.

Gibson, James M. "A Case for Mechanized Infantry." *Military Review* 50 (September 1970): 56–70.

Gildner, Gray M. "The Chickasaw Bayou Campaign." MMAS thesis, U.S. Army Command and General Staff College, 1991.

Gill, Lonnie. *Tank Destroyer Forces, World War II*. Paducah, KY: Turner Publishing, 1992.

Gillespie, Mark F., Glen R. Hawkins, Michael B. Kelly, and Preston E. Pierce. *The Sergeants Major of the Army*. Washington, D.C.: Center of Military History, 1995.

Gillett, Mary C. *The Army Medical Department, 1818–1865*. Army Historical Series. Washington, D.C.: Center of Military History, 1987.

————. *The Army Medical Department, 1865–1917*. Army Historical Series. Washington, D.C.: Center of Military History, 1995.

————. *The Army Medical Department, 1775–1818*. Army Historical Series. Washington, D.C.: Center of Military History, 1981.

Gillie, Mildred Hanson. *Forging the Thunderbolt: A History of the Development of the Armored Force*. Harrisburg, PA: Military Service Publishing, 1947.

Ginn, Richard V. N. *The History of the U.S. Army Medical Service Corps*. Washington, D.C.: Office of the Surgeon General and Center of Military History, 1997.

Gioglio, Gerald R. *Days of Decision: An Oral History of Conscientious Objectors in the Military during the Vietnam War*. Trenton, NJ: Broken Rifle Press, 1989.

Glantz, David M. "Operational Art and Tactics." *Military Review* 68 (December 1988): 32–40.

Glasgow, Matt. "Bullets, Beaches and Bayonets: A Look at Fort Ord." *Soldiers* 34 (June 1979): 45–48.

Glatthaar, Joseph T. *The March to the Sea and Beyond: Sherman's Troops in the Savannah and Carolinas Campaigns*. New York: New York University Press, 1985.

Glines, Carroll V., ed. *Lighter-than-Air Flight*. New York: Franklin Watts, 1965.

Gluckman, Arcadi. *Identifying Old U.S. Muskets, Rifles & Carbines*. Harrisburg, PA: Stackpole Books, 1959, 1965.

————. *United States Martial Pistols and Revolvers*. Harrisburg, PA: Stackpole Books, 1960.

Goad, K.J.W., and D.H.J. Halsey. *Ammunition (including Grenades and Mines)*. Oxford, U.K.: Brassey's Publishers, 1982.

Goebel, Dorothy Burne. *William Henry Harrison: A Political Biography*. Indianapolis: Historical Bureau of the Indiana Library and Historical Department, 1926.

Goldberg, Alfred, ed. *History of the Office of the Secretary of Defense*. 4 Vols. Washington, D.C.: Historical Office, Office of the Secretary of Defense, 1984–1997.

————, ed. *A History of the United States Air Force, 1907–1957*. Princeton, NJ: D. Van Nostrand, 1957.

————. *The Pentagon: The First Fifty Years*. Washington, D.C.: Historical Office, Office of the Secretary of Defense, 1992.

Goldhurst, Richard. *The Midnight War: The American Intervention in Russia, 1918–1920*. New York: McGraw-Hill, 1978.

Goldman, Charles A., Bruce R. Orvis, Michael G. Mattock, and Dorothy A. Smith. *Staffing Army ROTC at Colleges and Universities: Alternatives for Reducing the Use of Active-Duty Soldiers*. Santa Monica, CA: RAND, 1999.

Goldsmith, Dolf L. *The Devil's Paintbrush: Sir Hiram Maxim's Gun*. 2d ed. Toronto: Collector Grade Publications, 1993.

Goldstein, Julius. " 'Invincible' Lt. Gen. Lesley J. McNair." *Army* 49 (August 1999): 43–44.

Good, Karen E. " 'Ghostbusters' in the Saudi Desert: Operating Heavy Equipment Transporters." *Army Logistician* (May–June 1993): 14–17.

Gourley, Scott R. "US Army Transports in Transition: Expanding the Utility of the Wheeled Vehicle." *Armed Forces Journal International* 130 (May 1993): 38–40.

————. "M113A3: Catch Me . . . If You Can." *Armada International* 16 (August–September 1992): 22.

Govan, Gilbert E., and James W. Livingood. *A Different Valor: The Story of General Joseph E. Johnston, C.S.A.* Indianapolis: Bobbs-Merrill, 1956.

Gow, Ian. *Okinawa 1945: Gateway to Japan*. Garden City, NY: Doubleday, 1985.

Grady, John E. "No More Pickup Games." *Army* 44 (July 1994): 28–30.

Graham, Daniel O. "Patriot Missile Success over Scuds Has Applications for SDI Program." *Officer* 67(May 1991): 36–38.

Graham, Don. *No Name on the Bullet: A Biography of Audie Murphy*. New York: Viking Press, 1989.

Grant, Bruce. *American Forts, Yesterday and Today*. New York: E. P. Dutton, 1965.

Graves, Donald E. *The Battle of Lundy's Lane: On the Niagara in 1814*. Baltimore: Nautical and Aviation Publishing, 1993.

Gray, John S. *Centennial Campaign: The Sioux War of 1876*. Norman: University of Oklahoma Press, 1988.

———. *Custer's Last Campaign: Mitch Boyer and the Little Bighorn Reconstructed*. Lincoln: University of Nebraska Press, 1991.

Graymont, Barbara. *The Iroquois in the American Revolution*. Syracuse, NY: Syracuse University Press, 1972.

Green, Constance McLaughlin, Harry C. Thomson, and Peter C. Roots. *The Ordnance Department: Planning Munitions for War. United States Army in World War II: The Technical Services*. Washington, D.C.: Office of the Chief of Military History, 1955.

Greene, Jerome A. *Slim Buttes, 1876: An Episode of the Great Sioux War*. Norman: University of Oklahoma Press, 1982.

———. *Yellowstone Command: Colonel Nelson A. Miles and the Great Sioux War, 1876–1877*. Lincoln: University of Nebraska Press, 1991.

Greene, Joseph I. *What You Should Know about Army Ground Forces*. New York: W. W. Norton, 1943.

Greenfield, Kent Roberts, ed. *Command Decisions*. New York: Harcourt, Brace, 1959.

———, Robert R. Palmer, and Bell I. Wiley. *The Organization of Ground Combat Troops. United States Army in World War II: The Army Ground Forces*. Washington, D.C.: Historical Division, Department of the Army, 1947.

Greer, Fielder P. "The Army's 'Old Guard.' " *Army Information Digest* 11 (May 1956): 24–29.

Gregorie, Anne King. *Thomas Sumter*. Columbia, SC: R. L. Bryan, 1931.

Gregory, Adrian. *The Silence of Memory: Armistice Day 1919–1946*. Oxford, U.K.: Berg Publishers, 1994.

Griess, Thomas E. "Dennis Hart Mahan: West Point Professor and Advocate of Military Professionalism, 1830–1871." Ph.D. diss., Duke University, 1968.

Griffis, Fletcher H. "Revamping Fort Drum." *Military Engineer* 78 (September–October 1986): 502–505.

Griffith, Paddy. *Battle Tactics of the Civil War*. New Haven, CT: Yale University Press, 1989.

Griffith, Robert K., Jr. *The U.S. Army's Transition to the All-Volunteer Force, 1968–1974*, Army Historical Series. Washington, D.C.; Center of Military History, 1997.

Groom, Winston. *Shrouds of Glory: From Atlanta to Nashville: The Last Great Campaign of the Civil War*. New York: Atlantic Monthly Press, 1995.

Groueff, Stephane. *Manhattan Project: The Untold Story of the Making of the Atomic Bomb*. Boston: Little, Brown, 1967.

Grunawalt, Richard J. "The JCS Standing Rules of Engagement: A Judge Advocate's Primer." *Air Force Law Review* 42 (1997): 245–258.

Grupp, Larry. *Claymore Mines: Their History and Development.* Boulder, CO: Paladin Press, 1993.

Gudmens, Jeffrey J. "The M60 Machinegun: Training and Employment." *Infantry* 84 (March–April 1994): 39–41.

Gudmundsson, Bruce I. *On Artillery.* Westport, CT: Praeger, 1993.

"A Guide to Army Equipment in Field Use or Development." *Army* 18 (November 1968): 134–136.

Gunston, Bill. *An Illustrated Guide to Military Helicopters.* New York: Arco Publishing, 1981.

———. *An Illustrated Guide to Modern Airborne Missiles.* New York: Arco Publishing, 1983.

Haas, Irvin. *Citadels, Ramparts & Stockades: America's Historic Forts.* New York: Everest House, 1979.

Hafendorfer, Kenneth A. *Perryville: Battle for Kentucky.* Owensboro, KY: McDowell Publications, 1981.

Hagan, Barry L. *"Exactly in the Right Pace": A History of Fort C. F. Smith Montana Territory, 1866–1868.* El Segundo, CA: Upton and Sons, 1999.

Hagedorn, Hermann. *Leonard Wood: A Biography.* 2 vols. New York: 1931.

Hagerman, Edward. *The American Civil War and the Origins of Modern Warfare: Ideas, Organization, and Field Command.* Bloomington: Indiana University Press, 1988.

Hagood, Johnson. *The Services of Supply: A Memoir of the Great War.* Boston: Houghton Mifflin, 1927.

Haines, Ralph E., Jr. "Division in a Hurry." *Army Information Digest* 17 (August 1962): 43–49.

———. "Vast CONARC: Forger of Men and New Ideas." *Army* 22 (October 1972): 26–33.

Hake, Janet. "Fort Lewis and Other Sites of the Sound." *Soldiers* 34 (February 1979): 46–49.

Halberstadt, Hans. *Green Berets: Unconventional Warriors.* Novato, CA: Presidio Press, 1988.

———. *NTC: A Primer of Modern Land Combat.* Novato, CA: Presidio Press, 1989.

Halbert, H. S., and T. H. Ball. *The Creek War of 1813 and 1814.* Chicago: Donohue and Henneberry, 1895.

Hall, Steve. *Fort Snelling: Colossus of the West.* St. Paul: Minnesota Historical Society, 1987.

Hallas, James H. *Squandered Victory: The American First Army at St. Mihiel.* Westport, CT: Praeger, 1995.

Hallinan, Ulick. "From Operation Cobra to the Liberation of Paris: American Offensive Operations in Northern France, 25 July–25 August 1944." Ph.D. diss., Temple University, 1988.

Hamilton, Edward P. *Fort Ticonderoga: Key to a Continent.* Boston: Little, Brown, 1964.

Hamilton, Holman. *Zachary Taylor.* 2 Vols. Indianapolis: Bobbs-Merrill, 1941–1951.

Hammel, Eric M. *Chosin: Heroic Ordeal of the Korean War.* Novato, CA: Presidio Press, 1990.

———. *Fire in the Streets: The Battle for Hue, Tet 1968.* Chicago: Contemporary Books, 1991.

———. *Guadalcanal: Starvation Island.* New York: Crown Publishers, 1987.

Hammer, Kenneth M. *The Springfield Carbine on the Western Frontier.* Bellevue, NB: Old Army Press, 1970.

[Hammett, Dashiell, et al] *The Capture of Attu: Tales of World War II in Alaska as Told by the Men Who Fought There*. Anchorage: Alaska Northwest Publishing, 1944. 1984.

Hammond, Paul Y. *Organizing for Defense: The American Military Establishment in the Twentieth Century*. Princeton, NJ: Princeton University Press, 1961.

Hammond, William M. "The Army and Public Affairs: Enduring Principles." *Parameters* 19 (June 1989): 57–74.

Hampton, Bruce. *Children of Grace: The Nez Perce War of 1877*. New York: Henry Holt, 1994.

Handy, Mary Olivia. *History of Fort Sam Houston*. San Antonio, TX: Naylor, 1951.

Hankinson, Alan. *First Bull Run 1861: The South's First Victory*. Osprey Military Campaign Series 10. London: Osprey Publishing, 1991.

Hara, Steve. "Fort Rucker." *Soldiers* 43 (March 1988): 19–21.

———. "The Polkword: New." *Soldiers* 40 (December 1985): 13–16.

———. "Show Me Fort Wood." *Soldiers* 41 (August 1986): 6–8.

———. "Tomorrow's Battles Fought Today." *Soldiers* 40 (June 1985): 36–39.

Harboard, James G. *The American Army in France, 1917–1919*. Boston: Little, Brown, 1936.

Harclerode, Peter. *Arnhem: A Tragedy of Errors*. London: Arms and Armour Press, 1994.

Harding, Stephen. *U.S. Army Aircraft since 1947: An Illustrated Reference*. Atglen, PA: Schiffer Publishing, 1997.

Harding, Steve. "Changes Ahead for the *Stars and Stripes*." *Soldiers* 52 (September 1997): 2–3.

Hargrove, Marion. *See Here, Private Hargrove*. New York: Henry Holt, 1942.

Harless, Larry. "A POMCUS Primer." *Army Logistician* 15 (March–April 1983): 6–9.

Harlow, Neal. *California Conquered: War and Peace on the Pacific, 1846–1850*. Berkeley: University of California Press, 1982.

Harrell, Ben. "Toward a Total Land Combat System." *Army* 16 (October 1966): 57–61.

Harrington, Nancy, and Edward Doucette. "Army after Next and Precision Airdrop." *Army Logistician* 31 (January–February 1999): 46–49.

Harris, Michael R. "Tactical Employment of the Shoulder-Fired Rocket." *Infantry* 8 (November–December 1996): 29–32.

Harris, Sean E. "Company Fire Support Matrix—Getting It Right at the First Line of the Fight." *Field Artillery* (May–June 1997): 17–20.

Harrison, Gordon A. *Cross-Channel Attack. United States Army in World War II: The European Theater of Operations*. Washington, D.C.: Office of the Chief of Military History, 1951.

Harrison, Lowell H. *George Rogers Clark and the War in the West*. Lexington: University Press of Kentucky, 1976.

Hart, Herbert M. *Pioneer Forts of the West*. Seattle: Superior Publishing, 1967.

———. *Tour Guide to Old Western Forts*. Boulder, CO: Pruett Publishing, 1980.

Hasenauer, Heike. "Bragg 2000." *Soldiers* 49 (June 1994): 24–25.

———. "Building Up Bragg." *Soldiers* 52 (June 1997): 28–31.

———. "Europe's Metal Mountain." *Soldiers* 49 (February 1994): 22–24.

———. "Fort Riley History." *Soldiers* 46 (April 1991): 38–41.

Hassler, Warren W., Jr. *Commanders of the Army of the Potomac*. Baton Rouge: Louisiana State University, 1962.

————. *Crisis at the Crossroads: The First Day at Gettysburg.* 1970. Reprint. Gettysburg, PA: Stan Clark Military Books, 1991.

————. *General George B. McClellan: Shield of the Union.* Baton Rouge: Louisiana State University Press, 1957.

Hastings, Max. *Overlord: D-Day and the Battle for Normandy.* New York: Simon and Schuster, 1984.

Hatch, Gardner N., ed. *4th Infantry "Ivy" Division: Steadfast and Loyal.* Paducah, KY: Turner Publishing, 1987.

Hatch, Robert M. *Thrust for Canada: The American Attempt on Quebec in 1775–1776.* Boston: Houghton Mifflin, 1979.

Hattaway, Herman, and Archer Jones. *How the North Won: A Military History of the Civil War.* Urbana: University of Illinois Press, 1983.

Hauser, William L. "Fire and Maneuver in the Delta." *Infantry* 60 (September–October 1970): 12–15.

Hausrath, Alfred H. "Civil Affairs and Military Government." In *A Survey of Military Institutions*, ed. Roger W. Little. Vol. 2. Chicago: Inter-University on Armed Forces and Society, 1969.

Havinghurst, Walter. *George Rogers Clark: Soldier in the West.* New York: McGraw-Hill, 1952.

Hay, John H., Jr. *Tactical and Materiel Innovations.* Vietnam Studies. Washington, D.C.: Department of the Army, 1974.

Hazlett, James C., Edwin Olmstead, and M. Hume Parks. *Field Artillery Weapons of the Civil War.* Newark: University of Delaware Press, 1983.

Hearn, Chester G. *Six Years of Hell: Harpers Ferry during the Civil War.* Baton Rouge: Louisiana State University, 1996.

Hebert, Walter H. *Fighting Joe Hooker.* Indianapolis; Bobbs-Merrill, 1944.

Hechler, Ken. *The Bridge at Remagen.* New York: Ballantine Books, 1957.

Hedge, L. B. "More Punch for the Infantry." *Army Information Digest* 10 (October 1955): 18–23.

Hedren, Paul L. *Fort Laramie in 1876: Chronicle of a Frontier Post at War.* Lincoln: University of Nebraska Press, 1988.

Heiberg, H.H.D. "Organize a Mechanized Force." *Armor* 85 (September–October 1976): 8–11.

Heller, Charles E., and William A. Stofft, eds. *America's First Battles, 1776–1965.* Lawrence: University Press of Kansas, 1986.

Hendrickson, Robert. *Sumter: The First Day of the Civil War.* Chelsea. MI: Scarborough House, 1990.

Hennessy, Juliette A. *The United States Army Air Arm, April 1861 to April 1917.* Washington, D.C.: Office of Air Force History, 1985.

Henry, Charles R. "New Acquisition Corps Enhances DOD Procurement Functions." *Defense 92* (July–August 1992): 53–55.

Herbert, Paul H. *Deciding What Has to Be Done: General William E. DePuy and the 1976 Edition of FM 100–5.* Leavenworth Papers Number 16. Fort Leavenworth, KS: Combat Studies Institute, 1988.

Hermes, Walter G. *Truce Tent and Fighting Front.* Washington, D.C.: Office of the Chief of Military History, 1966.

Herr, John K., and Edward S. Wallace. *The Story of the U.S. Cavalry. 1775–1942.* Boston: Little, Brown, 1953.

Herring, George C., ed. *America's Longest War: The United States and Vietnam, 1950–1975.* 2d ed. New York: Alfred A. Knopf, 1986.

Hewes, James E., Jr. *From Root to McNamara: Army Organization and Administration. 1900–1963.* Special Studies. Washington, D.C.: Center of Military History, 1975.

Hewitt, Lawrence Lee. *Port Hudson, Confederate Bastion on the Mississippi.* Baton Rouge: Louisiana State University Press, 1987.

Hickey, Donald R. *The War of 1812: A Forgotten Conflict.* Urbana: University of Illinois Press, 1989.

Hicks, James E. *U.S. Military Firearms, 1776–1956.* La Canada, CA: James E. Hicks and Sons, 1962.

Higginbotham, Don. *The War of American Independence: Military Attitudes, Policies, and Practice, 1763–1789.* New York: Macmillan, 1971.

Higgins, Trumbull. *Soft Underbelly: The Anglo-American Controversy over the Italian Campaign, 1939–1945.* New York: Macmillan, 1968.

Hildreth, James. *Dragoon Campaigns to the Rocky Mountains: Being a History of the Enlistment, Organization, and First Campaigns of the Regiment of United States Dragoons; Together with Incidents of a Soldier's Life, and Sketches of Scenery and Indian Character. By a Dragoon.* New York: Wiley & Long, 1836.

Hill, Jim Dan. *The Minute Man in Peace and War: A History of the National Guard.* Harrisburg, PA: Stackpole, 1964.

Hill, Ralph Nading. *Lake Champlain: Key to Liberty.* 20th ann. ed. Woodstock, VT: Countryman Press, 1995.

Hillman, Rolfe L. "Second to None: The Indianheads." U.S. Naval Institute *Proceedings* 113 (November 1987): 56–62.

Hinkel, John Vincent. *Arlington: Momment to Heroes.* Englewood Cliffs, NJ: Prentice-Hall, 1965.

Hinshaw, Arned L. *Heartbreak Ridge: Korea, 1951.* Westport, CT: Praeger, 1989.

Hiro, Dilip. *Desert Shield to Desert Storm: The Second Gulf War.* New York: Routledge, 1992.

Hobart, F.W.A., ed. *Jane's Infantry Weapons.* London: Jane's Yearbooks, 1975.

Hodges, Warren D. "New Role for Aberdeen." *Ordnance* 56 (September–October 1971): 132–135.

Hodgson, Godfrey. *The Colonel: The Life and Wars of Henry Stimson, 1867–1950.* New York: Alfred A. Knopf, 1990.

Hofmann, George F., and Donn A. Starry, eds. *Camp Colt to Desert Storm: A History of U.S. Armored Forces.* Lexington: University Press of Kentucky, 1999.

Hogan, David W., Jr. *Raiders or Elite Infantry? The Changing Role of the U.S. Army Rangers from Dieppe to Grenada.* Westport, CT: Greenwood Press, 1992.

———. *U.S. Army Special Operations in World War II.* Washington, D.C.: Center of Military History, 1992.

Hogan, Michael J., ed. *The End of the Cold War: Its Meaning and Implications.* Cambridge, U.K.: Cambridge University Press, 1992.

Hogg, Ian V. *A History of Artillery.* London: Hamlyn, 1974.

———. *Military Pistols & Revolvers.* Dorset: Arms and Armour Press, 1987.

Hogg, Ian V., and John Weeks. *Military Small Arms of the 20th Century: A comprehensive Illustrated Encyclopedia of the World Small Calibre Firearms, 1900–1977.* London: Arms and Armor Press, 1977.

Hoig, Stan. *The Battle of the Washita: The Sheridan-Custer Indian Campaign of 1867–69.* Garden City, NY: Doubleday, 1976.

———. *The Sand Creek Massacre.* Norman: University of Oklahoma Press, 1961.

Holbrook, Stewart H. *Ethan Allen.* Portland, OR: Binfords and Mort, 1958.

Holley, I. B., Jr. *General John M. Palmer, Citizen Soldiers, and the Army of a Democracy.* Contributions in Military History, Number 28. Westport, CT: Greenwood Press, 1982.

Holt, Dean W. *American Military Cemeteries: A Comprehensive Illustrated Guide to the Hallowed Grounds of the United States, including Cemeteries Overseas.* Jefferson, NC: McFarland, 1992.

Holt, Robert T., and Robert W. van de Velde. *Strategic Psychological Operations and American Foreign Policy.* Chicago: University of Chicago Press, 1960.

Holtzoff, Alexander. "Administration of Justice in the United States Army." *New York University Law Quarterly Review* 22 (January 1947): 1–18.

Honeycutt, Michael. "Pathfinders: Then, Now, and Fututre." *U.S. Army Aviation Digest* 29 (August 1983): 26–28.

Honeywell, Roy J. *Chaplains of the United States Army.* Washington D.C.: Office of the Chief of Chaplains, 1958.

Horn, John. *The Petersburg Campaign, June 1864–April 1865.* Conshohocken, PA: Combined Books, 1993.

Horn, Stanley F. *The Decisive Battle of Nashville.* Baton Rouge: Louisiana State University Press, 1956.

Hough, Franklin B., ed. *The Siege of Charleston by the British Fleet and Army under the Command of Admiral Arbuthnot and Sir Henry Clinton which Terminated with the Surrender of That Place on the 12th of May, 1780.* 1867. Reprint. Spartanburg, SC: Reprint, 1975.

House, Jonathan M. "John McAuley Palmer and the Reserve Components." *Parameters* 12 September 1982): 11–18.

———. *Toward Combined Arms Warfare: A Survey of 20th Century Tactics, Doctrine, and Organization.* Research Survey No. 2. Fort Leavenworth, KS: U.S. Army Command and General Staff College, 1984.

Howard, Michael. *The Causes of Wars and Other Essays.* 2d ed. Cambridge, MA: Havard University Press, 1983.

Howe, Robert D., and William D. O'Malley. *USAREUR Force Structure: Adapting to a Changing World.* Santa Monica, CA: RAND, 1993.

Howze, Hamilton H. "The Mobile Branch." *Armor* 77 (January–February 1968): 4–9,

Hoyt, Edwin P. *Airborne: The History of American Parachute Forces.* New York: Stein and Day, 1979.

———. *Guadalcanal.* New York: Military Heritage Press, 1982.

———. *The Pusan Perimeter: Korea, 1950.* New York: Stein and Day, 1984.

———. *Storm over the Gilberts: War in the Central Pacific: 1943.* New York: Van Nostrand Reinhold, 1978.

Huddleston, Joe D. *Colonial Riflemen in the American Revolution.* York, PA: George Shumway Publishers, 1978.

Hughes, John T. *Doniphan's Expedition: An Account of the U.S. Army Operations in the Great American Southwest.* Chicago: Rio Grange Press, 1962.

Hugus, David K. "Counterbattery: The Decisive Mission." *Armed Forces Journal International* 127 (October 1989): 105–110.

Hunnicutt, R. P. *Abrams: A History of the American Main Battle Tank*. Vol. 1. Novato, CA: Presidio, 1990.

————. *Patton: A History of the American Main Battle Tank*. Vol. 1. Novato, CA: Presidio, 1984.

————. *Sherman: A History of the American Medium Tank*. Novato, CA: Presidio, 1978.

————. *Stuart: A History of the American Light Tank*. Vol. 1. Novato, CA: Presidio, 1992.

Hunt, Elvid, and Walter E. Lorence. *History of Fort Leavenworth, 1827–1937*. 2d ed. 1937. Reprint. Fort Leavenworth, KS: Fort Leavenworth Historical Society, 1981.

Huppert, G. Harry. "Mechanized Infantry." *Armor* 7 (July–August 1962): 43–45.

Hurley, Alfred F. *Billy Mitchell: Crusader for Air Power*. New ed. Bloomington Indiana University Press, 1975.

Hurst, Arthur. "Mental Havoc in Wartime." *Science Digest* 9 (February 1941): 1–9.

Hurst, Jack. *Nathan Bedford Forrest: A Biography*. New York: Alfred A. Knopf, 1993.

Huston, James A. *The Sinews of War: Army Logistics, 1775–1953*. Army Historical Series. Washington D.C.: Office of the Chief of Military History, 1966.

Hutton, Paul. *Phil Sheridan and His Army*. Lincoln: University of Nebraska Press, 1985.

————, ed. *Soldiers West: Biographies from the Military Frontier*. Lincoln: University of Nebraska press, 1987.

Hymoff, Edward. *Fourth Infantry Division, Vietnam*. New York: M. W. Lads Publishing, [1968].

Hyson, John M., Jr. *The United States Military Academy Dental Service: A History, 1825–1920*. West Point, NY: U.S. Military Academy, 1989.

Inker, Harry. "Improved EIB: The Standard of Excellence." *Infantry*. 75 (March–April 1985): 15–17.

Ivey, Robert A. "Tough Lessons Learned at the JRTC." *Military Intelligence* 16 (April–June 1990): 15–18.

Jackson, Henry M., ed. *The National Security Council: Jackson Subcommittee Papers on Policy-Making at the Presidential Level*. New York: Praeger; 1965.

Jackson, John W. *With the British Army in Philadelphia, 1777–1778*. San Rafael, CA: Presidio, 1979.

Jacobs, James B. *Socio-Legal Foundations of Civil-Military Relations*. New Brunswick: Transaction Books, 1986.

Jacobs, Jeffrey A. *The Future of the Citizen-Soldier Force: Issues and Answers*. Lexington: University Press of Kentucky, 1994.

Jacobs, William A. "Tactical Air Doctrine and AAF Close Air Support in the European Theater, 1944–1945." *Aerospace Historian* 27 (Spring–March 1980): 35–49.

James, D. Clayton. *The Years of MacArthur*. 3 vols. Boston: Houghton Mifflin, 1970–1985.

Jameson, Malcolm M. "Tactical Operations Center." *Military Review* 36 (November 1956): 52–58.

Jeffcott, George F. *United States Army Dental Service in World War II*. Washington D.C.: Office of the Surgeon General, 1955.

Jeffreys-Jones, Rhodri. *The CIA and American Democracy*. New Haven, CT: Yale University Press, 1989.

Jeffries, Lewis I. "A Blueprint for Force Design." *Military Review* 71 (August 1991): 20–31.

Jellison, Charles. *Ethan Allen: Frontier Rebel*. Syracuse, NY: Syracuse University Press, 1969.

Jenkins, D.H.C. "Operating the Bradley Infantry Fighting Vehicle." *International Defense Review* 15 (1982): 1203–1206.

Jerzykowski, Dale P. "A 'Lifer' Has His Say." *Soldiers* 26 (August 1971): 42–43.

Jessup, John E., Jr., and Robert W. Coakley. *A Guide to the Study and use of Military History*. Washington D.C.: Center of Military History, 1979, 1988.

Jessup, Philip C. *Elihu Root*. 2. vols. New York: Dodd, Mead, 1938.

Johnson, Dorothy M. *The Bloody Bozeman: The Perilous Trail to Montana's Gold*. New York: McGraw-Hill, 1971.

Johnson, Eric S. "RAH-66 Comanche—Eyes and Ears for the 21st Century." *Field Artillery* (May–June 1996): 22–25.

Johnson, Forrest Bryant. *Raid on Cabanatuan*. Las Vegas, NV: Thousand Autumns Press, 1988.

Johnson, Lawrence H., III. *Winged Sabers: The Air Cavalry in Vietnam, 1965–1973*. Harrisburg, PA: Stackpole Books, 1990.

Johnson, Ludwell H. *Red River Campaign: Politics and Cotton in the Civil War*. Baltimore: Johns Hopkins Press, 1958.

Johnson, Melvin M, Jr., and Charles T. Haven. *Automatic Arms: Their History, Development and Use*. New York: William Morrow, 1941.

Johnson, Sandee Shaffer, ed. *Cadences: The Jody Call Book*. 2 Vols. Canton, OH: Daring Press, 1983–1986.

Johnson, Thomas E. "Reconstitution: A Combat Force Multiplier." *Military Review* 69 (September 1989): 36–47.

Johnson, Timothy D. *Winfield Scott: The Quest for Military Glory*. Lawrence: University Press of Kansas, 1998.

Johnson, Virginia W. *The Unregimented General: A Biography of Nelson A. Miles*. Boston: Houghton Mifflin, 1962.

Johnston, Henry P. *The Battle of Harlem Heights, September 16, 1776, with a Review of the Events of the Campaign*. London: Macmillan, 1897.

———. *The Storming of Stony Point on the Hudson: Midnight, July 15, 1779*. 1900. Reprint. New York: Da Capo Press, 1971.

Johnston, J. H., III, ed. and comp. *Early Leavenworth and Fort Leavenworth: A Photographic History*. Leavenworth, KS: J. H. Johnston III, 1977.

———. *Leavenworth: Beginning to Bicentennial*. Leavenworth, KS: J. H. Johnston III, 1976.

Jones, Archer. *The Art of War in the Western World*. Urbana: University of Illinois Press, 1987.

Jones, Evan. *Citadel in the Wilderness: The Story of Fort Snelling and the Old Northwest Frontier*. New York: Coward-McCann, 1966.

Jones, Vincent C. *Manhattan: The Army and the Atomic Bomb*. United States Army in World War II: Special Studies. Washington, D.C.: Center of Military History, 1985.

Jones, Virgil Carrington. *Roosevelt's Rough Riders*. Garden City, NY: Doubleday, 1971.

Jory, Jack D. "Reforger 1." *U.S. Army Aviation Digest* 15 (May 1969): 32–35.

Joseph, Robert G., and John F. Reichart. *Deterrence and Defense in a Nuclear, Biological, and Chemical Environment*. Washington, D.C.: National Defense University, 1996.

Joulwan, George A. "Operations Other than War: A CINC's Perspective." *Military Review* 74 (February 1994): 5–10.

Kahn, E. J., Jr. *McNair: Educator of an Army*. Washington. D.C.: Infantry Journal, 1945.

Kaplan, Lawrence S. *NATO and the United States: The Enduring Alliance*. Boston: Twayne Publishers, 1988.

Karnow, Stanley. *In Our Image: America's Empire in the Philippines*. New York: Random House, 1989.

Kaser, Tom. "More than Gold: Fort Knox." *Travel*, September 1962, 49–52.

Kauffman, Henry J. *The Pennsylvania-Kentucky Rifle*. Harrisburg, PA: Stackpole, 1960.

Kaufman, Frank J. "Roll Out the Leaders: New Model NCOs Take to the Field." *Army Digest* 23 (March 1968): 17–19.

Kayser, Hugh. *The Spirit of America: The Biographies of Forty Living Congressional Medal of Honor Recipients*. Palm Springs, CA: ETC Publications, 1982.

Keating, Bern. *The Flamboyant Mr. Colt and His Deadly Six-Shooter*. Garden City, NY: Doubleday, 1978.

Keating, Gerald. "Buglers and Bugle Calls in the U.S. Army." *Army History* (Summer 1993): 16–17.

Keegan, John. *Six Armies in Normandy: From D-Day to the Liberation of Paris, June 6th–August 25th, 1944*. New York: Viking Press, 1982.

Keenan, George E., and Paul R. Reed. "Do We Need an Exec?" *Infantry* 52 (July–August 1962): 34–35.

Keenan, Jerry. *The Wagon Box Fight*. 3d ed. Boulder, CO: Lightning Tree Press, 1992.

Keiser, Carl P. "The ROAD Ahead: An Introduction to the Reorganization of the Army Division." *Military Review* 42 (January 1962): 2–6.

Kelly, Dennis. "Atlanta Campaign: Mountains to Pass, a River to Cross: The Battle of Kennesaw Mountain and Related Actions from June 10 to July 9, 1864." *Blue & Gray* 8 (June 1989): 8–12.

———. *Second Manassas: The Battle and Campaign*. 1983. Reprint. [Conshohocken, PA]: Eastern Acorn Press, 1987.

Kelly, Francis J. *U.S. Army Special Forces, 1961–1971*. Vietnam Studies. Washington, D.C.: Department of the Army, 1985.

Kelly, William E., ed. *Post–Traumatic Stress Disorder and the War Veteran Patient*. Brunner/Mazel Psychological Stress Series No. 5. New York: Brunner/Mazel, 1985.

Kennedy, David M. *Over Here: The First World War and American Society*. New York: Oxford University Press, 1980.

Kennett, Lee. *G.I.: The American Soldier in World War II*. New York: Charles Scribner's Sons, 1987.

Kenworthy, John H. "A New Walter Reed Army Medical Center." *Military Engineer* 67 (January–February 1975): 29–31.

Keon, Michael. *Korean Phoenix: A Nation from the Ashes*. Englewood Cliffs, NJ: Prentice/Hall International, 1977.

Kerrigan, Evans E. *American Badges and Insignia*. New York: Viking Press, 1967.

———. *American War Medals and Decorations*. New York: Viking Press, 1964.

Kerscher, Thomas E. "The Rebirth of Fort Polk." *Military Engineer* 67 (November–December 1975): 329–330.

Ketchum, Richard M. *Decisive Day: The Battle for Bunker Hill: An Expanded and Fully*

Illustrated Edition of the Battle for Bunker Hill. Garden City, NY: Doubleday, 1974.

———. *Saratoga: Turning Point of America's Revolutionary War.* New York: Henry Holt, 1997.

Killgore, William D. "Air Defense Protection for the Division." *Military Review* 55 (February 1975): 37–50.

Kimball, Jeffrey. "The Battle of Chippawa: Infantry Tactics in the War of 1812." *Military Affairs* 31 (Winter 1967–68): 169–186.

King, Benjamin, Richard C. Briggs, and Eric R. Criner. *Spearhead of Logistics: A History of the United States Army Transportation Corps.* Fort Eustis, VA: U.S. Army Transportation Center, 1994.

King, Charles. *Campaigning with Crook.* Norman: University of Oklahoma Press, 1964.

King, Michael J. *Rangers: Selected Combat Operations in World War II.* Leavenworth Papers No. 11. Fort Leavenworth, KS: Combat Studies Institute, 1985.

Kingseed, Cole C. "The Battalion PA." *Infantry* 81 (November–December 1991): 6–8.

———. "The Falaise-Argentan Encirclement: Operationally Brilliant, Tactically Flawed." *Military Review* 64 (December 1984): 2–11.

———. "A 'Formidable Array of Warriors,' " *Army* 46 (May 1996): 46–53.

Kinnard, Douglas. *The Certain Trumpet: Maxwell Taylor & The American Experience in Vietnam.* New York: Brassey's (US), 1991.

———. *The Secretary of Defense.* Lexington: University Press of Kentucky, 1980.

Kirin, Stephen J., and John D. Winkler. *The Army Military Occupational Specialty Database.* Santa Monica, CA: RAND, 1992.

Kirkpatrick, Charles E. *An Unknown Future and a Doubtful Present: Writing the Victory Plan of 1941.* Washington, D.C.: Center of Military History, 1990.

———. *Archie in the A.E.F.: The Creation of the Antiaircraft Service of the United States Army, 1917–1918.* [Fort Bliss, TX]: U.S. Army Air Defense Artillery School, 1984.

Kitchens, John. "Camp Rucker Selected as Home of Army Aviation." *U.S. Army Aviation Digest* (January/February 1994): 30–39.

Kleber, Brooks E. "The Educator of the Army." *Army* 30 (July 1980): 50–54.

———, and Dale Birdsell. *The Chemical Warfare Service: Chemicals in Combat, United States Army in World War II: The Technical Services.* Washington D.C.: Office of the Chief of Military History, 1966.

Klein, Robert. *Wounded Men, Broken Promises.* New York: Macmillan, 1981.

Kliger, Paul I. "The Confederate Invasion of New Mexico." *Blue & Gray* 11 (June 1994): 8–20.

Kluger, Steve. *Yank: World War II from the Guys Who Brought You Victory.* New York: St. Martin's Press, 1991.

Knickerbocker, H. R., Jack Thompson, Jack Belden, Don Whitehead, A. J. Liebling, Mark Watson, Cy Peterman, Iris Carpenter, R. E. Dupuy, and Drew Middleton. *Danger Forward: The Story of the First Division in World War II.* 1947. Reprint. Nashville, TN: Battery Press, 1980.

Knight, Clayton. *Lifeline in the Sky: The Story of the U.S. Military Air Transport Service.* New York: William Morrow, 1957.

Knight, Kenneth R. "DRS: A Battery Commander's Perspective." *Field Artillery Journal* 47 (January–February 1979): 44–47.

Knox, Donald. *Death March: The Survivors of Bataan*. New York: Harcourt Brace Jovanovich, 1981.

Koehler, Franz A. *Special Rations for the Armed Forces, 1946–53*. QMC Historical Studies Series II, No. 6. Washington, D.C.: Historical Branch. Office of the Quartermaster General, 1958.

Kohn, Richard H. *Eagle and Sword: The Federalists and the Creation of the Military Establishment in America, 1783–1802*. New York: Free Press, 1975.

Kolasheski, Richard F. "Division Restructuring: A Battalion Commander's View." *Armor* 87 (November–December 1978): 18–23.

Kolditz, Thomas A. "Inside the Professional Development System: The New OER." *Field Artillery* (September–October 1997): 10–12.

Komer, Robert W. "The Rejuvenation of Seventh Army." *Armed Forces Journal International* 120 (May 1983): 54–59.

Koon, George William, ed. *Old Glory and the Stars and Bars: Stories of the Civil War*. Columbia: University of South Carolina Press, 1995.

Korb, Lawrence J. *The Joint Chiefs of Staff: The First Twenty-five Years*. Bloomington: Indiana University Press, 1976.

Kreidberg, Marvin A., and Merton G. Henry. *History of Military Mobilization in the United States Army, 1775–1945*. Washington, D.C.: Department of the Army, 1955.

Krisman, Michael J. "Huey Is the Bird Known as the 'Can Do' Helicopter." *Army Digest* 21 (July 1966): 12–16.

Kroesen, Frederick J. "What Should a Command Post Do?" *Army* 43 (January 1993): 32–35.

Krueger, Walter. *From Down Under to Nippon: The Story of Sixth Army in World War II*. Washington, D.C.: Combat Forces Press, 1953.

Kupke, William A. *The Indian and the Thunderwagon*. Silver City, NM: William A. Kupke, 1992.

Lafeber, Walter. *America, Russia, and the Cold War, 1945–1980*. 4th ed. New York: John Wiley and Sons, 1980.

Lane, Jack C. *Armed Progressive: General Leonard Wood*. San Rafael, CA: Presidio Press, 1978.

Lane, Larry. "Going for Gold Bars." *Soldiers* 48 (February 1993): 37–41.

Lang, Will, and Tom Durrance. "Mauldin: His Tough, Realistic Drawings of GIs at Front Make Him Top Cartoonist of War." *Life*, 5 February 1945, 49–53.

Langley, Michael. *Inchon Landing: MacArthur's Last Triumph*. New York: Times Books, 1979.

Lanning, Michael Lee. *Inside the LRRPS: Rangers in Vietnam*. New York: Ivy Books, 1988.

Larson, Norman O. "Faster Landing Craft." U.S. Naval Institute *Proceedings* 92 (February 1966): 128–133.

Lash, Jeffrey N. *Destroyer of the Iron Horse: General Joseph E. Johnston and Confederate Rail Transport, 1861–1865*. Kent, OH: Kent State University Press, 1991.

Latour, Charles. "Small Arms." *NATO's Fifteen Nations* 19 (June–July 1974): 62–68.

Launius, Roger D. *Alexander William Doniphan: Portrait of a Missouri Moderate*. Columbia: University of Missouri Press, 1997.

Lavender, David. *Climax at Buena Vista: The American Campaign in Northeastern Mexico, 1846–47.* Philadelphia: J. B. Lippencott, 1966.

———. *Let Me Be Free: The Nez Perce Tragedy.* New York: HarperCollins, 1992.

Lawton, Manny. *Some Survived.* Chapel Hill, NC: Algonquin Books, 1984.

Leckie, Robert. *Delivered from Evil: The Saga of World War II.* New York: Harper and Row, 1987.

———. *None Died in Vain: The Saga of the American Civil War.* New York: HarperCollins, 1990.

———. *Okinawa: The Last Battle of World War II.* New York: Viking, 1995.

Leckie, William H. *The Buffalo Soldiers: A Narrative of the Negro Cavalry in the West.* Norman: University of Oklahoma Press, 1967.

———. *The Military Conquest of the Southern Plains.* Norman: University of Oklahoma Press, 1963.

Lee, David D. *Sergeant York: An American Hero.* Lexington: University Press of Kentucky, 1985.

Lee, Fred L., ed. *The Battle of Westport: October 21–23, 1864.* Kansas City, MO: Westport Historical Society, 1982.

Lee, Ulysses. *The Employment of Negro Troops. United States Army in World War II: Special Studies.* 1966. Washington, D.C.: Center of Military History, 1986.

Lehman, John. *Making War: The 200-Year-Old Battle between the President and Congress over How America Goes to War.* New York: Charles Scribner's Sons, 1992.

Lehmann, Douglas K., and Robert J. O'Neil. "Two Views on the Rifle Squad." *Infantry* 70 (May–June 1980): 18–21.

Leighton, Richard M., and Robert W. Coakley. *Global Logistics and Strategy, 1940–1943. United States Army in World War II: The War Department.* Washington D.C.: Office of the Chief of Military History, 1955.

Leinbaugh, Harold P., and John D. Campbell. *The Men of Company K: The Autobiography of a World War II Rifle Company.* New York: William Morrow, 1985.

Le Mon, Warren J. "Fort Benjamin Harrison: Home Base for Educational and Administrative Activities." *Army Information Digest* 20 (November 1965): 17–24.

Leonard, Steven M. "Steel Curtain: The Guns on the la Drang." *Field Artillery* (July–August 1998): 17–20.

Leopold, Richard W. *Elihu Root and the Conservative Tradition.* Edited by Oscar Hanlin. Boston: Little, Brown, 1954.

Lerwill, Leonard L. *The Personnel Replacement System in the United States Army.* Washington, D.C.: Department of the Army, 1954.

Levy, Alan, Bernard Krisher, and James Cox. *Draftee's Confidential Guide: How to Get Along in the Army.* Bloomington: Indiana University Press, 1957.

Lewis, Frank L. *Introduction to Total Quality Management in the Federal Government.* Washington, D.C.: Office of Personnel Management, Federal Total Quality Institute, 1991.

Lewis, Thomas A. *The Guns of Cedar Creek.* New York: Harper and Row, 1988.

Liddell Hart, Basil H. *Reputations: Ten Years After.* 1928. Reprint. Freeport, NY: Books for Libraries Press, 1968.

Linderman, Gerald F. *Embattled Courage: The Experience of Combat in the American Civil War.* New York: Free Press, 1987.

Linn, Brian M. "Guerrilla Fighter: Frederick Funston in the Philippines, 1900–1901." *Kansas History* 10 (Spring 1987): 2–16.

————. *The U.S. Army and Counterinsurgency in the Philippine War, 1899–1902*. Chapel Hill: University of North Carolina Press, 1989.

Livengood, Gale C. "The Story of the BAR." *Infantry School Quarterly* 42 (April 1953): 67–69.

Locher, James R., III. "Taking Stock of Goldwater-Nichols." *Joint Force Quarterly* (Autumn 1996): 10–16.

Lockhart, Christopher E. "Modern Dragoons: Bradley Mechanized Infantry." *Infantry* 82 (November–December 1992): 33–35.

Logsdon, David R., comp. and ed. *Eyewitnesses at the Battle of Stones River*. Nashville, TN: David R. Logsdon, 1989.

Longacre, Edward G. *Army of Amateurs: General Benjamin F. Butler and the Army of the James, 1863–1865*. Mechanicsburg, PA: Stackpole Books, 1997.

Lord, Walter. *The Dawn's Early Light*. New York: W. W. Norton, 1972.

Lowden, John L. *Silent Wings at War: Combat Gliders in World War II*: Washington, D.C.: Smithsonian Institution Press, 1992.

Lubenow, Larry R. "Do You Read Me?" *Army* 18 (May 1968): 51–53.

Luellig, Paul P., Jr. "Arsenals." *Field Artillery Journal* 42 (March–April 1974): 50–53.

Lumpkin, Henry. *From Savannah to Yorktown: The American Revolution in the South*. Columbia: University of South Carolina Press, 1981.

Lurie, Jonathan. *Arming Military Justice*. Vol. 1: *The Origins of the United States Court of Military Appeals, 1775–1950*. Princeton, NJ: Princeton University Press, 1992.

Lustyik, Andrew F. *Civil War Carbines: From Service to Sentiment*. Aledo, IL: World-Wide Gun Report, 1962.

Luttwak, Edward N. *Strategy: The Logic of War and Peace*. Cambridge, MA: Belknap Press of Harvard University Press, 1987.

Lutz, Catherine, and Lesley Bartlett. *Making Soldiers in the Public Schools*. Philadelphia: American Friends Service Committee, 1995.

Luvaas, Jay, and Harold W. Nelson, eds. *The U.S. Army War College Guide to the Battles of Chancellorsville and Fredericksburg*. Carlisle, PA: South Mountain Press, 1988.

Lyman, Theodore. *With Grant and Meade from the Wilderness to Appomattox*. Lincoln: University of Nebraska Press, 1994.

Lynch, Amy. "A Gift for Sergeant York." *American History* 33 (December 1998): 18–24.

Lynch, William R., III. "The Eight-Day ARTEP FTX." *Military Review* 64 (December 1984): 12–22.

Lynn, John A., ed. *Feeding Mars: Logistics in Western Warfare from the Middle Ages to the Present*. Boulder, CO: Westview Press, 1993.

Lyons, Gene M., and John W. Masland. *Education and Military Leadership: A Study of the R.O.T.C.* Princeton, NJ: Princeton University Press, 1959.

"M60-Series 7.62-mm Machine Gun." *Army* 42 (June 1992): 52–53.

"M109-Series 155-mm Self-Propelled Howitzers." *Army* 42 (May 1992): 53–54.

McAndrews, Kevin. "The Hohenfels Experience." *National Guard* 50 (February 1996): 20–24.

————. "Paladin Arrives on the Great Plains." *National Guard* 50 (December 1996): 16–17.

McArthur, Colin L. "Who's in Charge?" *Armed Forces International* 135 (December 1997): 34–35.

McCaffrey, George W. "Progress toward Decentralized Command." *Military Review* 31 (November 1951): 45–52.

McChristian, Douglas C. *The U.S. Army in the West, 1870–1880: Uniforms, Weapons, and Equipment*. Norman: University of Oklahoma Press, 1995.

McClain, Charles W., Jr., and Garry D. Levin. "Public Affairs in America's 21st Century Army." *Military Review* 74 (November 1994): 6–15.

McClintic, Robert G. "Army Artillery Slims Down." *Army Digest* 24 (May 1969): 28–29.

———. "Rolling Back the Night." *Army* 19 (August 1969): 28–35.

MacCloskey, Monro. *Hallowed Ground: Our National Cemeteries*. New York: Richards Rosen Press, 1968.

———. *Pacts for Peace: UN, NATO, SEATO, CENTO and OAS*. New York: Richards Rosen Press, 1967.

———. "Paths to a Commission." *Army* 15 (December 1964): 35–39.

McDevitt, Kenneth A. "Why Standardize Command Posts?" *Military Review* 70 (July 1990): 54–59.

MacDonald, Callum A. *Korea: The War before Vietnam*. New York: Free Press, 1987.

MacDonald, Charles B. *The Mighty Endeavor: American Armed Forces in the European Theater in World War II*. New York: Oxford University Press, 1969.

———. *The Siegfried Line Campaign. United States Army in World War II: The European Theater of Operations*. Washington D.C.: Center of Military History, 1963, 1984.

McDonnell, James A., Jr. "The Veterans Administration: Fifty Years of Caring." *Air Force Magazine* 63 (August 1980): 99.

McDonough, James Lee. *Chattanooga—A Death Grip on the Confederacy*. Knoxville: University of Tennessee Press, 1984.

———. *Schofield: Union General in the Civil War and Reconstruction*. Tallahassee: Florida State University Press, 1972.

———. *Shiloh: In Hell before Night*. Knoxville: University of Tennessee Press, 1977.

———. *War in Kentucky: From Shiloh to Perryville*. Knoxville: University of Tennessee Press, 1994.

———, and Thomas L. Connelly. *Five Tragic Hours: The Battle of Franklin*. Knoxville: University of Tennessee Press, 1983.

McDonough, James R. *Platoon Leader*. Novato, CA: Presidio Press, 1985.

McFeely, William S. *Grant: A Biography*. New York: W. W. Norton, 1981.

MacGregor, Morris J., Jr. *Integration of the Armed Forces, 1940–1965*. Defense Studies Series. Washington, D.C.: Center of Military History, 1981.

McKenzie, James B., Jr. "Challenges for the Aviation Branch." *U.S. Army Aviation Digest* 30 (December 1984): 10–13.

McKinney, Francis F. *Education in Violence: The Life of George H. Thomas and the History of the Army of the Cumberland*. Chicago: American House, 1961, 1991.

Macksey, Kenneth, and John H. Batchelor. *Tank: A History of the Armoured Fighting Vehicle*. New York: Ballantine Books, 1971.

McLaurin, Ron D., ed. *Military Propaganda: Pschological Warfare and Operations*. New York: Praeger, 1982.

McLeod, Mavis. "Best in the Business: Junior ROTC Program." *Corrections Today* 58 (April 1996): 16.

McMichael, William H. "The Best Kept Secret in the Army." *Soldiers* 46 (December 1991): 46–49.

McMurry, Richard M. *The Road past Kennesaw: The Atlanta Campaign of 1864*. Washington, D.C.: Office of Publications, National Park Service. 1972.

McNamara, Walter W. "You and Your Commissary: Facts and Answers on a Benefit That Is an Integral Part of Your Pay." *Airman* 6 (June 1962): 15–18.

McNeil, Alex. *Total Television: The Comprehensive Guide to Programming from 1948 to the Present*. 4th ed. New York: Penguin Books, 1996.

McPherson, James M. *Battle Cry of Freedom: The Civil War Era*. New York: Oxford University Press, 1988.

McWhiney, Grady. *Braxton Bragg and Confederate Defeat*. Vol. 1, *Field Command*. New York: Columbia University Press, 1969.

————, and Perry D. Jamieson. *Attack and Die: Civil War Military Tactics and the Southern Heritage*. Tuscaloosa: University of Alabama Press, 1982.

Maddox, Bobby J. "Army Aviation Branch Implementation." *U.S. Army Aviation Digest* 29 (August 1983): 2–9.

Madej, W. Victor, ed. *U.S. Army Order of Battle*. Vol. 1, *European Theater of Operations, 1943–1945*. Allentown, PA: Game Publishing, 1983.

Magyera, Stephen N., Jr. "Troubleshooting the New Division Organization." *Military Review* 57 (July 1977): 53–60.

Mahler, Michael D. *Ringed in Steel: Armored Cavalry, Vietnam 1967–68*. Novato, CA: Presidio, Press, 1986.

Mahon, John K. *The American Militia: Decade of Decision, 1789–1800*. University of Florida Monographs, Social Sciences No. 6. Gainesville: University of Florida Press, 1960.

————. *History of the Militia and the National Guard*. The Macmillan Wars of the United States. New York: Macmillan, 1983.

————. *History of the Second Seminole War, 1835–1842*. Gainesville; University of Florida Press, 1967.

————. *The War of 1812*. Gainesville; University of Florida Press, 1972.

————, and Romana Danysh. *Infantry, Part I, Regular Army*. Army Lineage Series. Washington D.C., Center of Military History, 1972.

Mallonée, Richard C., II, ed. *The Naked Flagpole: Battle of Bataan from the Diary of Richard C. Mallonée*. Novato, CA: Presidio, 1980.

Malone, Dandridge M. "The Squad." *Army* 26 (February 1976): 12–16.

Maney, R. Wayne. *Marching to Cold Harbor: Victory and Failure, 1864*. Shippensburg, PA: White Mane Publishing, 1995.

Mangold, Tom, and John Penycate. *Tunnel Warfare*. New York: Bantam Books, 1987.

————. *The Tunnels of Cu Chi*. New York: Random House, 1985.

Mangum, Neil C. *Battle of the Rosebud: Prelude to the Little Bighorn*. El Segundo, CA: Upton and Sons, 1991.

Mann, JoAnn. "On Leave and Pass." *Soldiers* 30 (May 1975): 16–17.

Manning, Don. "Getting to Know an Old Standby: The .50 Caliber." *Army* 42 (March 1992): 36–38.

Manwaring, Max G., ed. *Uncomfortable Wars: Toward a New Paradigm of Low Intensity Conflict*. Boulder, CO: Westview Press, 1991.

March, Peyton C. *The Nation at War*. 1932. Reprint. Westport, CT: Greenwood Press, 1970.

Marcy, Randolph B. *The Prairie Traveler*. Formerly *A Hand-Book for Overland Expeditions: With Maps, Illustrations, and Itineraries of the Principal Routes between the Mississippi and the Pacific*. 1859. Reprint. Williamstown, MA: Corner House Publishers, 1968.

Marlin, R. B. "The M-79." *Infantry* 53 (March-April 1963): 31–40.

Marmion, Harry A. *Selective Service: Conflict and Compromise*. New York: John Wiley and Sons, 1968.

Marshall, John Douglas. *Reconciliation Road: A Family Odyssey of War and Honor*. Syracuse, NY: Syracuse University Press, 1993.

Marshall, S.L.A. *Bringing Up the Rear: A Memoir*. Edited by Cate Marshall. San Rafael, CA: Presidio, 1979.

———. *Crimsoned Prairie: The War between the United States and the Plains Indians during the Winning of the West*. New York: Charles Scribner's Sons, 1972.

———. *The River and the Gauntlet: Defeat of the Eighth Army by the Chinese Communist Forces, November, 1950, in the Battle of the Chongchong River, Korea*. New York: William Morrow, 1953.

Marszalek, John F. *Sherman: A Soldier's Passion for Order*. New York: Free Press, 1993.

Martin, Carl. "Redeye: It Swats Five out of Five." *Army Digest* 22 (June 1967): 48–51.

———. "Where the Waiting Ends." *Soldiers* 27 (January 1972): 29–31.

Martin, David G. *Gettysburg, July 1*. Conshohocken, PA: Combined Books, 1995.

———. *Jackson's Valley Campaign: November 1861–June 1862*. Great Campaigns. Conshohocken, PA: Combined Books, 1994.

Martin, Joel W. *Sacred Revolt: The Muskogee's Struggle for a New World*. Boston: Beacon Press, 1991.

Martin, Ralph G. *The GI War, 1941–1945*. Boston: Little, Brown, 1967.

Marvel, William. *Andersonville: The Last Depot*. Chapel Hill: University of North Carolina Press, 1994.

———. *Burnside*. Chapel Hill: University of North Carolina Press, 1991.

Masland, John W., and Laurence I. Radway. *Soldiers and Scholars: Military Education and National Policy*. Princeton, NJ: Princeton University Press, 1957.

Massaquoi, Hans J. "Maj. Gen. Wallace C. Arnold: Gung-Ho on 'Building Better Young Americans.' " *Ebony* 47 (September 1992): 90.

Mathias, Frank F. *G.I. Jive: An Army Bandsman in World War II*. Lexington: University of Kentucky Press, 1982.

Matloff, Maurice, ed. *American Military History*. Army Historical Series. Washington, D.C.: Office of the Chief of Military History, rev. ed., 1989.

———. *Strategic Planning for Coalition Warfare, 1943–1944, United States Army in World War II: The War Department*. Washington, D.C.: Office of the Chief of Military History, 1959.

———. and Edwin M. Snell. *Strategic Planning for Coalition Warfare, 1941–1942. United States Army in World War II: The War Department*. Washington, D.C.: Office of the Chief of Military History, 1953.

Matter, William D. *If It Takes All Summer: The Battle of Spotsylvania*. Chapel Hill: University of North Carolina Press, 1988.

Mattern, David B. *Benjamin Lincoln and the American Revolution*. Columbia: University of South Carolina Press, 1995.

Mauduit, Israel. *Conduct of Sir William Howe*. 1927. Reprint. Eyewitness Accounts of the American Revolution. [New York]: New York Times, 1971.

Mauldin, Bill. *The Brass Ring*. New York: W. W. Norton, 1971.

———. *Up Front*. New York: Henry Holt, 1945.

Maurer, Maurer. *Aviation in the U.S. Army, 1919–1939*. Washington, D.C.: Office of Air Force History, 1987.

Maxwell, William Quentin. *Lincoln's Fifth Wheel: The Political History of the United States Sanitary Commission*. New York: Longmans, Green, 1956.

Mayo, Lida. *Bloody Buna*. Garden City, NY: Doubleday, 1974.

Medhurst, Martin J. *Dwight D. Eisenhower: Strategic Communicator*. Great American Orators, Number 19. Westport, CT: Greenwood Press, 1993.

Melia, Tamara Moser. "James B. McPherson and the Ideals of the Old Army." Ph.D. diss., Southern Illinois University, 1987.

Meller, Rudi. "Patriot: The US Army's Mobile Air-Defense Missile System Nears Production." *International Defense Review* 13 (1980): 495–499.

Meloy, G. S., Jr. "The Eighth Army Story." *Army Information Digest* 18 (June 1963): 3–13.

Merillat, Louis A., and Delwin M. Campbell. *Veterinary Military History of the United States: With A Brief Record of the Development of Veterinary Education, Practice, Organization and Legislation*. 2 vols. Chicago: Veterinary Magazine, 1935.

Merrill, James M. *William Tecumseh Sherman*. Chicago: Rand McNally, 1971.

Merrill, Perry H. *Roosevelt's Forest Army: A History of the Civilian Conservation Corps, 1933–1942*. Montpelier, VT: Perry H. Merrill, 1981.

Merrill's Marauders. Paducah, KY: Turner Publishing, 1987.

Messick, Hank. *King's Mountain: The Epic of the Blue Ridge 'Mountain Men' in the American Revolution*. Boston: Little, Brown, 1976.

Metz, Leon C. *Desert Army: Fort Bliss on the Texas Border*. Rev. ed. El Paso, TX: Mangan Books, 1988.

———. *Fort Bliss: An Illustrated History*. El Paso, TX: Mangan Books, 1981.

Metz, Robert W. "Military Pipeline Operations." *Engineer* 17 no. 2 (1987): 16–18.

Metzgar, J. M. "Nonappropriated Fund Activities Pay the Way." *Army Information Digest* 16 (May 1961): 23–33.

Middlebrook, Martin. *Arnhem 1944: The Airborne Battle, 17–26 September*. Boulder, CO: Westview Press, 1994.

Middleton, Lamar. *Revolt U.S.A.* 1938. Reprint. Freeport, NY: Books for Libraries Press, 1968.

Miers, Earl S. *The Web of Victory: Grant at Vicksburg*. New York: Alfred A. Knopf, 1955.

Miles, Carroll F. *The Office of the Secretary of Defense, 1947–1953: A Study in Administrative Theory*. New York: Garland Publishing, 1988.

Miles, Donna. "AAFES Turns 100." *Soldiers* 50 (July 1995): 50–52.

———. "Hail the New Hohenfels." *Soldiers* 45 (October 1990): 44–48.

———. "MRE Feedback." *Soldiers* 48 (November 1993): 48–49.

———. "New Army, New MOSs." *Soldiers* 48 (June 1993): 46–48.

Miller, Charles E. *Airlift Doctrine*. Maxwell Air Force Base, AL: Air University Press, 1988.

Miller, Don. "The Handlebar Infantry." *Army* 30 (September 1980): 38–40.

Miller, Edward S. *War Plan Orange: The U.S. Strategy to Defeat Japan, 1897–1945*. Annapolis, MD: Naval Institute Press, 1991.

Miller, Everett B. *United States Army Veterinary Service in World War II*. Washington, D.C.: Office of the Surgeon General, 1961.

Miller, John, Jr. *Cartwheel: The Reduction of Rabaul. United States Army in World War II: The War in the Pacific*. Washington, D.C.: Office of the Chief of Military History, 1959.

Miller, John E. "Training and Educating Leaders for the Future: The New CGSOC Curriculum." *Military Review* 71 (January 1991): 10–17.

———, and Daniel P. Bolger. "Going Deep: Division Air Assault Operations." *Military Review* 73 (April 1993): 2–12.

Miller, Lee G. *The Story of Ernie Pyle*. New York: Viking Press, 1950.

Miller, Stuart C. *"Benevolent Assimilation": The American Conquest of the Philippines, 1899–1903*. New Haven, CT: Yale University Press, 1982.

Miller, William J., ed. *The Peninsula Campaign*. 3 vols. Campbell, CA: Savas Publishing, 1997.

Millett, Allan R. *The General: Robert L. Bullard and Officership in the United States Army, 1881–1925*. Contributions in Military History, Number 10. Westport, CT: Greenwood Press, 1975.

———, and Peter Maslowski. *For the Common Defense: A Military History of the United States of America*. New York: Free Press, 1984.

Millet, Allan R., and Williamson Murray, eds. *Military Effectiveness*. 2 vols. Mershon Center Series on Defense and Foreign Policy. Boston: Unwin Hyman, 1988.

Millett, Allan R., Mackubin Thomas Owens, Bernard E. Trainor, Edward C. Meyer, and Robert Murray. *The Reorganization of the Joint Chiefs of Staff: A Critical Analysis*. Washington, D.C.: Pergamon-Brassey's International Defense Publishers, 1986.

Millman, David. "Everyone's USO." U.S. Naval Institute *Proceedings* 123 (December 1997): 74–76.

Milner, Samuel. *Victory in Papua. United States Army in World War II: The War in the Pacific*. Washington, D.C.: Office of the Chief of Military History, 1957, 1989.

Mitcham, Samuel W., Jr., and Friedrich von Stauffenberg. *The Battle of Sicily*. New York: Orion Books, 1991.

Mitchell, Joseph B. *Military Leaders in the American Revolution*. McLean, VA: EPM Publications, 1967.

Mitz, Rick. *The Great TV Sitcom Book*. New York: Richard Marek Publications, 1980.

Modelski, George, ed. *SEATO: Six Studies*. Vancouver, Canada: Publication Centre, University of British Columbia, 1962.

Moncure, Thomas M., Jr. "Marsena R. Patrick, Provost Marshal General of the Army." *Military Police* (December 1990): 23–25.

Monnett, Howard N. *Action before Westport, 1864*. Kansas City, MO: Westport Historical Society, 1964.

Moore, Alan. "Life inside Leavenworth." *Soldiers* 52 (September 1997): 23–25.

———. "Redeveloping Fort McClellan." *Soldiers* 51 (June 1996): 15–16.

Moore, Harold G., and Joseph L. Galloway. *We Were Soldiers Once . . . and Young: Ia Drang: The Battle That Changed the War in Vietnam*. New York: Random House, 1992.

Morden, Bettie J. *The Women's Army Corps, 1945–1978.* Washington, D.C.: Center of Military History, 1990.

Morelock, George L., Jr. "Army Aviation."*Military Review* 35 (January 1956): 53–64.

Morelock, Jerry D. *Generals of the Ardennes: American Leadership in the Battle of the Bulge.* Washington, D.C.: National Defense University Press, 1994.

Morgan, Henry G., Jr. "Stronger Fighting Teams in the Rifle Platoon." *Combat Forces Journal* 2 (April 1952): 26–28.

Morgan, J. McDowell. *Military Medals and Insignia of the United States.* Glendale, CA: Griffin-Patterson Publishing, 1941.

Morison, Elting E. *Turmoil and Tradition: A Study of the Life and Times of Henry L. Stimson.* Boston: Houghton Mifflin, 1960.

Morison, Samuel Eliot. *History of United States Naval Operations in World War II.* 15 vols. Boston: Little, Brown, 1947–1962.

Morley, Thomas V., and Anthony J. Tata. "The Mechanized Infantry Team in the Offense." *Infantry* 80 (May–June 1990): 16–19.

Morris, Eric. *Corregidor: The End of the Line.* New York: Stein and Day, 1981.

Morris, Roy, Jr. *Sheridan: The Life and Wars of General Phil Sheridan.* New York: Crown Publishers, 1992.

Morrow, R. C. "Does the Fire Team Need Reorganizing?" *Marine Corps Gazette* 53 (February 1969): 28–30.

Mortensen, Daniel R. *A Pattern for Joint Operations: World War II Close Air Support, North Africa.* Historical Analysis Series. Washington, D.C.: Office of Air Force History and Center for Military History, 1987.

Morton, Julie Jenkins. "Trusting to Luck: Ambrose E. Burnside and the American Civil War." Ph.D. diss., Kent State University, 1992.

Morton, Louis. "Command in the Pacific: 1941–45." *Military Review* 41 (December 1961): 76–88.

———. *The Fall of the Philippines. United States Army in World War II: The War in the Pacific.* Washington, D.C.: Office of the Chief of Military History, 1953.

Mosch, Theodore R. *The G.I. Bill: A Breakthrough in Educational and Social Policy in the United States.* Hicksville, NY: Exposition Press, 1975.

Moser, Don. *China-Burma-India.* Alexandria, VA: Time-Life Books, 1978.

Moskos, Charles C., and John Whiteclay Chambers II, eds. *The New Conscientious Objection: From Sacred to Secular Resistance.* New York: Oxford University Press, 1993.

Mosley, Leonard. *Marshall: Hero for Our Times.* New York: Hearst Books, 1982.

Murphy, James L. "More on Claymore." *Marine Corps Gazette* 50 (September 1966): 42–44.

Murray, G. Patrick. "Courtney Hodges: Modest Star of World War II." *American History Illustrated* 7 (January 1973): 12–25.

Murray, R. C. *Golden Knights: The History of the U.S. Army Parachute Team.* Canton, OH: Daring Books, 1990.

Murray, Robert A. *Fort Laramie: "Visions of a Grand Old Post."* Fort Collins, CO: Old Army Press, 1974.

Nadeau, Remi. *Fort Laramie and the Sioux Indians.* Englewood Cliffs, NJ: Prentice-Hall, 1967.

Nalty, Bernard C. *Strength for the Fight: A History of Black Americans in the Military.* New York: Free Press, 1986.

"National Security Agency." *Armed Forces Management* 9 (November 1962): 103–105.

Nauroth, Tony. "In the Shadow of Cheyenne Mountain." *Soldiers* 46 (August 1991): 48–51.

Nelms, Douglas W. "The Awesome Apache." *Army* 37 (January 1987):38–47.

Nelson, Harold W. "CMH: Keeper of the Flame, Teacher to Army of '90s." *Army* 40 (October 1990): 208–210.

Nelson, Otto L., Jr. *National Security and the General Staff.* Washington D.C.: Infantry Journal Press, 1946.

Nenninger, Timothy K. "The Experimental Mechanized Forces." *Armor* 78 (May–June 1969): 33–39.

———. *The Leavenworth Schools and the Old Army: Education, Professionalism, and the Officer Corps of the United States Army, 1881–1918.* Contributions in Military History, Number 15. Westport, CT: Greenwood Press, 1978.

Nevins, Allan. *Frémont: Pathmaker of the West.* New York: D. Appleton-Century, 1939.

Newell, Clayton R., and Michael D. Krause, eds. *On Operational Art.* Washington D.C.: Center for Military History, 1994.

Newman, Aubrey S. *Follow Me: The Human Element in Leadership.* Novato, CA: Presidio, Press, 1981, 1990.

Nichols, David, ed. *Ernie's War: The Best of Ernie Pyle's World War II Dispatches.* New York: Random House, 1986.

Nichols, Roger. *Black Hawk and the Warrior's Path*, Arlington, IL: Harlan Davidson, 1992.

"Night Vision Equipment." *Field Artilleryman* (March 1971): 32–36.

Nolan, Keith William. *Into Laos: The Story of Dewey Canyon Lamson 719; Vietnam 1971.* Novato, CA: Presidio Press, 1986.

Noland, Chuck. "What Money Can't Buy." *Soldiers* 26 (November 1971): 24–25.

Nolte, M. Chester, ed. *Civilian Conservation Corps: The Way We Remembered It, 1933–1942.* Paducah, KY: Turner Publishing, 1990.

Nosworthy, Brent. *The Anatomy of Victory: Battle Tactics 1689–1763.* New York: Hippocrene Books, 1990.

Nye, Roger H. *The Patton Mind: The Professional Development of an Extraordinary Leader.* Garden City, NY: Avery Publishing, 1993.

Nye, W. S. *Carbine and Lance: The Story of Old Fort Sill.* Norman: University of Oklahoma Press, 1937.

Oberdorfer, Don. *Tet!* Garden City, NY: Doubleday, 1971.

O'Daniel, Larry J. *Missing in Action: Trail of Deceit.* New Rochelle, NY: Arlington House Publishers, 1979.

Ogburn, Charlton, Jr. *The Marauders.* New York: Harper and Brothers, 1959.

Ogorkiewicz, Richard M. "Recoilless Guns and Tanks." *Armor* 62 (September–October 1953): 26–31.

Oldfield, Barney. "The Lance: 'Shoot and Scoot.' " *NATO's Fifteen Nations* 20 (April–May 1975): 78–81.

Oliver, Norman. "The Honorable Thing to Do." *Soldiers* 38 (September '1983): 34–36.

Olson, James C. *Red Cloud and the Sioux Problem.* Lincoln: University of Nebraska Press, 1965.

Olson, James S., and Randy Roberts. *Where the Domino Fell: America and Vietnam, 1945 to 1990.* New York: St. Martin's Press, 1991.

Olson, John E. *O'Donnell: Andersonville of the Pacific*. Lake Quivira, KS: J. E. Olson, 1985.

————, and Frank O. Anders. *Anywhere-Anytime: The History of the Fifty-seventh Infantry (PS)*. [San Antonio, TX]: J. E. Olson, 1991.

Olson, Keith W. *The G.I. Bill, the Veterans, and the Colleges*. Lexington: University Press of Kentucky, 1974.

Olson, Kenneth E. *Music and Musket: Bands and Bandsmen of the American Civil War*. Contributions to the Study of Music and Dance, Number 1. Westport, CT: Greenwood Press, 1981.

Orgill, Douglas. *The Gothic Line: The Autumn Campaign in Italy, 1944*. London: Heinemann, 1967.

Osterhoudt, Henry Jerry. "The Evolution of U.S. Army Assault Tactics, 1778–1919: The Search for Sound Doctrine." Ph.D. diss., Duke University, 1986.

Ott, Lana. "Motor Pool." *Soldiers* 34 (November 1979): 23–26.

————. "Secrets of Fort Huachucha." *Soldiers* 34 (May 1979): 17–20.

————. "Spit & Polish." *Soldiers* 35 (May 1980): 6–9.

Owen, John, ed. *Brassey's Infantry Weapons of the World 1979*. 2d ed. London: Brassey's Publishers, 1979.

Owens, Bobby. *The Diamond: "The Power behind the Throne."* N.p. 1993.

Owsley, Frank L., Jr. *Struggle for the Gulf Borderlands: The Creek War and the Battle of New Orleans, 1812–1815*. Gainesville: University of Florida Press, 1981.

Pack, S.W.C. *Operation "Husky": The Allied Invasion of Sicily*. New York: Hippocrene Books, 1977.

Paddock, Alfred H., Jr. *US Army Special Warfare: Its Origins: Psychological and Unconventional Warfare, 1941–1952*. Washington, D.C.: National Defense University Press, 1982.

Pagonis, William G., and Jeffrey L. Cruikshank. *Moving Mountains: Lessons in Leadership and Logistics from the Gulf War*. Boston: Harvard Business School Press, 1992.

Palmer, Bruce, Jr. *Intervention in the Caribbean: The Dominican Crisis of 1965*. Lexington: University Press of Kentucky, 1989.

————. *The 25-Year War: America's Military Role in Vietnam*. Lexington: University Press of Kentucky, 1984.

Palmer, Dave Richard. *Summons of the Trumpet: U.S.-Vietnam in Perspective*. San Rafael, CA: Presidio Press, 1978.

————. *The Way of the Fox: American Strategy in the War for America, 1775–1783*. Contributions in Military History Number 8. Westport, CT: Greenwood Press, 1975.

Palmer, Frederick. *Bliss, Peacemaker: The Life and Letters of General Tasker Howard Bliss*. New York: Dodd, Mead, 1934.

————. *John J. Pershing: General of the Armies*. Harrisburg, PA: Military Service Publishing, 1948.

Palmer, Robert R., Bell I. Wiley, and William R. Keast. *The Procurement and Training of Ground Combat Troops*. United States Army in World War II: The Army Ground Forces. Washington, D.C.: Office of the Chief of Military History, 1948.

Pancake, John S. *1777: The Year of the Hangman*. University, AL: University of Alabama Press, 1977.

Pappas, George S. *Prudens Futuri: The US Army War College, 1901–1967.* Carlisle Barracks, PA: Alumni Association of the US Army War College, [1967].

————. *To the Point: The United States Military Academy, 1802–1902.* Westport, CT: Praeger, 1993.

Paret, Peter, ed. *Makers of Modern Strategy from Machiavelli to Nuclear Age.* Princeton, NJ: Princeton University Press, 1986.

Park, William. *Defending the West: A History of NATO.* Boulder, CO: Westview Press, 1986.

Parker, Robert M., Jr. "M-60A1: Name Enough." *Armor* 74 (July–August 1965): 33–40.

Partin, John W., ed. *A Brief History of Fort Leavenworth, 1827–1983.* Fort Leavenworth, KS: Combat Studies Institute, 1983.

Patch, Joseph Dorst. *A Soldier's War: The First Infantry Division, A.E.F. (1917–1918).* Corpus Christi, TX: Mission Press, 1966.

Patterson, J. Steve. "CAS[3]: Investment in the Future." *Military Review* 74 (May 1994): 24–28.

Pearson, Les. "Muster in St. Louis . . ." *National Guardsman* 32 (May 1978): 18–19.

Peckham, Howard H. *The War for Independence: A Military History.* Chicago: University of Chicago Press, 1958.

Peers, W. R. *The My Lai Inquiry.* New York: W. W. Norton, 1979.

Pencak, William. *For God and Country: The American Legion, 1919–1941.* Boston: Northeastern University Press, 1989.

Pengelley, Rupert. "M109 Modernization Moves." *International Defense Review* 23 (1990): 193–195.

Pergrin, David P., and Eric Hammel. *First across the Rhine: The 291st Engineer Combat Battalion in France, Belgium, and Germany.* New York: Atheneum, 1989.

Perret, Geoffrey. *Old Soldiers Never Die: The Life of Douglas MacArthur.* Holbrook, MA: Adams Media, 1996.

————. *Ulysses S. Grant: Soldier & President.* New York: Random House, 1997.

Perry, Ralph B. *The Platsburgh Movement: A Chapter of America's Participation in the World War.* New York: E. P. Dutton, 1921.

Peters, James Edward. *Arlington National Cemetery: Shrine to America's Heroes.* Kensington, MD: Woodbine House, 1986.

Peters, Virginia Bergman. *The Florida Wars.* Hamden, CT: Archon Books, 1979.

Petruschell, Robert L., James H. Bigelow, and Joseph G. Bolten. *Overview of the Total Army Design and Cost System.* Santa Monica, CA: RAND, 1993.

Piemonte, Robert V., and Cindy Gurney, eds. *Highlights in the History of the Army Nurse Corps.* Washington, D.C.: Center of Military History, 1987.

Pimlott, John, ed. *Vietnam: The History and the Tactics.* New York: Crescent Books, 1982.

————. *Vietnam: The Decisive Battles.* New York: Macmillan Publishing Company, 1990.

Piston, William G. *Lee's Tarnished Lieutenant: James Longstreet and His Place in Southern History.* Athens: University of Georgia Press, 1987.

Place, J. A. *The Western Films of John Ford.* Secaucus, NJ: Citadel Press, 1974.

Plaster, John L. *SOG: The Secret Wars of America's Commandos in Vietnam.* New York: Simon and Schuster, 1997.

Pleasants, Henry, Jr., and George H. Straley. *Inferno at Petersburg.* Philadelphia: York: Chilton, 1961.

Ploger, Robert R. *U.S. Army Engineers, 1965–1970. Vietnam Studies.* Washington, D.C.: Department of the Army, 1974.

Poe, Perry. "How's Air Mobility?" *Army* 13 (June 1963): 25–28.

Pogue, Forrest C. *George C. Marshall.* 4 vols. New York: Viking Press, 1963–1987.

————. *The Supreme Command. United States Army in World War II: The European Theater of Operations.* Washington, D.C.: Office of the Chief of Military History, 1954.

Poling, Kevin D. "M1A2 Update: Training and Doctrine Observations from Saudi Arabian NET Training on the M1A2." *Armor* 105 (May–June 1996): 16–20.

Pottorff, James P. "Contemporary Applications of the Soldiers' and Sailors' Civil Relief Act." *Military Law Review* 132 (Spring 1991): 115–140.

Prater, Phil. "The Good Neighbor Post." *Soldiers* 47 (March 1992): 34–36.

Pratt, Fletcher. *Stanton: Lincoln's Secretary of War.* New York: W. W. Norton, 1953.

Price, Alfred. *The History of US Electronic Warfare.* 2 vols. [Arlington, VA]: Association of Old Crows, 1984–1989.

Prokopowicz, Gerald John. "All For the Regiment: Unit Cohesion and Tactical Stalemate in the Army of the Ohio, 1861–1862." Ph.D. diss., Harvard University: 1994.

Province, Charles M. *The Unknown Patton.* New York: Bonanza Books, 1983.

Prucha, Francis Paul. *A Guide to the Military Posts of the United States, 1789–1895.* Madison: State Historical Society of Wisconsin, 1964.

Prueher, Joseph W. "Warfighting CINCs in a New Era." *Joint Force Quarterly* (Autumn 1996): 48–52.

Purcell, Victor. *The Boxer Uprising: A Background Study.* Cambridge, U.K.: Cambridge University Press, 1963.

Purdue, Howell and Elizabeth. *Pat Cleburne, Confederate General: A Definitive Biography.* Hillsboro, TX: Hill Junior College Press, 1973.

Quinn, Mike. "K. P." *Soldiers* 38 (June 1983): 18–19.

Quirk, Robert E. *An Affair of Honor: Woodrow Wilson and the Occupation of Veracruz.* Lexington: University of Kentucky Press, 1962.

Raines, Edgar F., Jr. "Major General J. Franklin Bell, U.S.A.: The Education of a Soldier, 1856–1899." *Register of the Kentucky Historical Society* 83 (Autumn 1985): 315–346.

Raines, Rebecca Robbins. *Getting the Message Through: A Branch History of the U.S. Army Signal Corps.* Army Historical Series. Washington, D.C.: Center of Military History, 1996.

Randall, Willard Sterne. *Benedict Arnold: Patriot and Traitor.* New York: William Morrow, 1990.

Ranelagh, John. *The Agency: The Rise and Decline of the CIA.* New York: Simon and Schuster, 1986.

Rankin, Hugh F. *Francis Marion: The Swamp Fox.* New York: Thomas Y. Crowell, 1973.

Rapport, Leonard, and Arthur Northwood, Jr. *Rendezvous with Destiny: A History of the 101st Airborne Division.* Enl. ed. Sweetwater, TN: Headquarters, 101st Airborne Division Association, 1948.

Ratcliff, J. D. *Yellow Magic: The Story of Penicillin.* New York: Random House, 1945.

Rathbun, Frank F. "On the Road to ROAD." *Infantry* 53 (May–June 1963): 4–7.

————. "The Rifle in Transition." *Army* 14 (August 1963): 19–25.

Raymond, Richard, III. "St. Clair's Defeat: Rout on the Wabash." *Army* 33 (December 1983): 62–65.

Reardon, Carol. *Soldiers and Scholars: The U.S. Army and the Uses of Military History, 1865–1920*. Lawrence: University Press of Kansas, 1990.

Reece, Ralph G., and Todd J. Travas. "Paladin." *Field Artillery* (October 1990): 44–47.

Reed, John F. *Valley Forge: Crucible of Victory*. Monmouth Beach, NJ: Philip Freneau Press, 1969.

Regan, Geoffrey. *SNAFU: Great American Military Disasters*. New York: Avon Books, 1993.

Reilly, Robin. *The British at the Gates: The New Orleans Campaign in the War of 1812*. New York: G. P. Putnam's Sons, 1974.

Reinberg. Linda. *In the Field: The Language of the Vietnam War*. New York: Facts on File, 1991.

Remini, Robert V. *The Life of Andrew Jackson*. New York: Harper and Row, 1988.

"Re-Up Law Heads for New Look." *Army-Navy-Air Force Journal* 93 (19 May 1956): 3.

Reynolds, Quentin. *The Amazing Mr. Doolittle: A Biography of Lieutenant General James H. Doolittle*. New York: Appleton-Century-Crofts, 1953.

Reynosa, Mark A. *The M-1 Helmet: A History of the U.S. M-1 Helmet in World War II*. Arglen, PA: Schiffer Military History, 1996.

Rhea, Gordon C. *The Battle of the Wilderness, May 5–6, 1864*. Baton Rouge: Louisiana State University Press, 1994.

Rhea, John. "Total Quality Management: Myths and Realities." *National Defense* 74 (January 1990): 25–27.

Rhodes, Richard. *The Making of the Atomic Bomb*. New York: Simon and Schuster, 1986.

Richardson, Doug. *AH-1: Cobra*. Modern Fighting Aircraft, vol. 13. New York: Prentice Hall, 1987.

Richelson, Jeffrey. *The U.S. Intelligence Community*. Cambridge, MA: Ballinger Publishing, 1985.

Rickey, Don, Jr. *Forty Miles a Day on Beans and Hay: The Enlisted Soldier Fighting the Indian Wars*. Norman: University of Oklahoma Press, 1963.

Riley, Jacob L., Jr. " 'What Is a Corps?" *Military Review* 36 (October 1956): 12–19.

Riling, Joseph R. *Baron von Steuben and His Regulations, including a Complete Facsimile of the Original Regulations for the Order and Discipline of the Troops of the United States*. Philadelphia: Ray Riling Arms Books, 1966.

Ripley, Warren. *Artillery and Ammunition of the Civil War*. New York: Van Nostrand Reinhold, 1970.

RisCassi, Robert W. "Doctrine for Joint Operations in a Combined Environment: A Necessity." *Military Review* 77 (January–February 1997): 103–114.

Risch, Erna. *The Quartermaster Corps: Organization, Supply, and Services*. Vol. 1 *United States Army in World War II: The Technical Services*. Washington, D.C.: Office of the Chief of Military History, 1953.

———. *Quartermaster Support of the Army: A History of the Corps, 1775–1939*. Washington, D.C.: Quartermaster Historians' Office, 1962.

———, and Chester L. Kieffer. *The Quartermaster Corps: Organization, Supply, and Services*. Vol. 2, *United States Army in World War II: The Technical Services*. Washington, D.C.: Office of the Chief of Military History, 1955.

Robb, Charles S. "Examining Alternative UCP Structures." *Joint Force Quarterly* (Winter 1996–1997): 85–93.

Roberts, Craig. *Combat Medic: Vietnam*. New York: Pocket Books, 1991.

Roberts, Kenneth. *The Battle of Cowpens: The Great Morale-Builder*. Garden City, NY: Doubleday, 1958.

Roberts, Mary M. *The Army Nurse Corps, Yesterday and Today*. [Washington, D.C.]: United States Army Nurse Corps, [1957].

Roberts, Robert B. *New York's Forts in the Revolution*. Rutherford, NJ: Fairleigh Dickenson University Press, 1980.

Roberts, William R. "Loyalty and Expertise: The Transformation of the Nineteenth-Century American General Staff and the Creation of the Modern Military Establishment." Ph.D. diss., Johns Hopkins University, 1979.

Robertson, William G. *The Staff Ride*. Washington, D.C.: Center of Military History. 1987.

Robinson, Anthony Preston, and Ian V. Hogg. *Weapons of the Vietnam War*. New York: Gallery Books, 1983.

Robinson, Charles M., III. *A Good Year to Die: The Story of the Great Sioux War*. New York: Random House, 1995.

Robinson, Jerry. *The Comics: An Illustrated History of Comic Strip Art*. New York: G. P. Putnam's Sons, 1974.

Robles, Philip K. *United States Military Medals and Ribbons*. Rutland, VT: Charles E. Tuttle, 1971.

Robson, George L., Jr. "Claymore." *Infantry* 50 (January 1960): 14–16.

Roche, Bill. "The Real McCoy." *Soldiers* 45 (January 1990): 42–44.

Rodenbough, Theophilus F., comp. *From Everglade to Cañon with the Second Dragoons (Second United States Cavalry): An Authentic Account of Service in Florida, Mexico, Virginia, and the Indian Country, including the Personal Recollections of Prominent Officers. With an Appendix Containing Orders, Reports and Correspondence, Military Records, Etc.* New York: D. Van Nostrand, 1875.

Rogers, Bernard W. *Cedar Falls–Junction City: A Turning Point*. Vietnam Studies. Washington, D.C.: Department of the Army, 1974.

Roland, Charles P. *An American Iliad: The Story of the Civil War*. Lexington: University Press, of Kentucky, 1991.

Rolle, Andrew. *John Charles Frémont: Character as Destiny*. Norman: University of Oklahoma Press, 1991.

Romanus, Charles F., and Riley Sunderland. *Stilwell's Mission to China. United States Army in World War II: China-Burma-India Theater*. Washington; D.C.: Office of the Chief of Military History, 1953.

Romjue, John L. *From Active Defense to AirLand Battle: The Development of Army Doctrine, 1973–1982*. Fort Monroe, VA: Historical Office, United States Army Training and Doctrine Command, 1984.

Roosevelt, Theodore. *Theodore Roosevelt: An American Mind, a Selection from His Writings*. Edited by Mario R. DiNunzio. New York: St. Martin's Press, 1994.

Ropp, Ralph E. "Ft. Polk: Cinderella Story in Louisiana." *Army* 28 (April 1978): 46–50.

Rosen, Robert N. *Confederate Charleston: An Illustrated History of the City and the People during the Civil War*. Columbia: University of South Carolina Press, 1994.

Ross, Steven T., ed. *American War Plans, 1919–1941*. 5 vols. New York: Garland Publishing, 1992.

Rossie, Jonathan G. *The Politics of Command in the American Revolution*. Syracuse, NY: Syracuse University Press, 1975.

Rota, Dane L. "Combat Decision Making in 'Operations Other Than War.' " *Military Review* 76 (March–April 1996): 24–28.

Roth, Russell. *Muddy Glory: America's "Indian Wars" in the Philippines*. West Hanova, MA: Christopher Publishing House 1981.

Rovin, Jeff. *The Great Television Series*. South Brunswick: A. S. Barnes, 1977.

Rowe, Gregory P. "Integrating IPB into Paragraph Three (and Other OPORD Briefing Techniques)." *Armor* 101 (January–February 1992): 44–46.

Royster, Charles. *Light-Horse Harry Lee and the Legacy of the American Revolution*. New York: Alfred A. Knopf, 1981.

Rudd, Gordon William. "Operation Provide Comfort: Humanitarian Intervention in Northern Iraq, 1991." Ph.D. diss., Duke University, 1993.

Rundell, Walter, Jr. *Military Money: A Fiscal History of the U.S. Army Overseas in World War II*. College Station: Texas A&M University Press, 1980.

Ruppenthal, Roland G. *Logistical Support of the Armies*. 2 vols. *United States Army in World War II: The European Theater of Operations*. Washington, D.C.: Office of the Chief of Military History, 1953–1959.

Russell, W. H. "Before the Fire Team." *Marine Corps Gazette* 68 (November 1984): 71–78.

Ryan, Cornelius. *A Bridge Too Far*. New York: Simon and Schuster, 1974.

Ryan, J. W. *Guns, Mortars & Rockets*. Battlefield Weapons Systems and Technology Series, vol. 2. Oxford, U.K.: Brassey's Publishers, 1982.

Sack, John. *Lieutenant Calley: His Own Story*. New York: Viking Press, 1971.

Salmond, John A. *The Civilian Conservation Corps, 1933–1942: A New Deal Case Study*. Durham, NC: Duke University Press, 1967.

"A Salute to the Numbered U.S. Armies." *Army Information Digest* 17 (October 1962): 32–39.

Sandler, Stanley. *To Free from Oppression: A Concise History of U.S. Army Special Forces, Civil Affairs, Psychological Operations, and the John F. Kenedy Special Warfare Center and School*. [Fort Bragg, NC]: United States Army Special Operations Command, Directorate of History and Museums, 1994.

Sandwich, Brian. *The Great Western: Legendary Lady of the Southwest*. Southwestern Studies No. 94. El Paso: Texas Western Press, 1991.

Sanford, A. P., and Robert H. Schauffler, eds. and comps. *Armistice Day: An Anthology of the Best Prose and Verse on Patriotism, the Great War, the Armistice—Its History, Observance, Spirit and Significance: Victory, the Unknown Soldier and His Brothers, and Peace. With Fiction, Drama, Pageantry and Programs for Armistice Day Observance*. New York: Dodd, Mead, 1928.

Sarf, Wayne Michael. *The Little Bighorn Campaign: March–September 1876*. Great Campaigns. Conshohocken, PA: Combined Books, 1993.

Sarnecky, Mary T. "A History of Volunteerism and Patriotism in the Army Nurse Corps." *Military Medicine* 154 (July 1989): 358–384.

Sawicki, James A. *Cavalry Regiments of the US Army*. Dumfries, VA: Wayne Publications, 1985.

———. *Infantry Regiments of the U.S. Army*. Dumfries, VA: Wayne Publications, 1981.

Saylor, James H. *TQM Field Manual*. New York: McGraw-Hill, 1992.

Scales, Robert H., Jr. *Certain Victory: United States Army in the Gulf War.* Washington, D.C.: Office of the Chief of Staff, 1993.

Schaffel, Kenneth. *The Emerging Shield: The Air Force and the Evolution of Continental Air Defense, 1945–1960.* Washington, D.C.: Office of Air Force History, 1991.

Schaller, Michael. *Douglas MacArthur: The Far Eastern General.* New York: Oxford University Press, 1989.

Schildt, John W. *Drums along the Antietam.* Parsons, WV: McLain Printing, 1972.

Schiltz, Howard F. "Army Transportation Corps: Twenty-Eight Years of Translation." *Defense Transportation* 26 (September–October 1970): 30–34.

Schmidt, Blaise X., and Lawrence E. Broughton. " 'We Mean Business.' " *Field Artillery Journal* 53 (July–August 1985): 23–25.

Schmierer, Elmer. "Long Live the Regiment." *Army* 7 (April 1957): 25–28.

Schneider, Ches. *From Classrooms to Claymores: A Teacher at War in Vietnam.* New York: Ivy Books, 1999.

Schott, Joseph L. *Above and Beyond: The Story of the Congressional Medal of Honor.* New York: G. P. Putnam's Sons, 1963.

Schreier, Konrad F., Jr. *Standard Guide to US World War II Tanks & Artillery.* Iola, WI: Krause Publications, 1994.

———. "The 'Long Tom' Story." *Ordnance* 52 (November–December 1967): 281–283.

Schubert, Frank N. *Black Valor: Buffalo Soldiers and the Medal of Honor, 1870–1898.* Wilmington, DE: Scholarly Resources, 1997.

———. *Buffalo Soldiers, Braves and the Brass: The Story of Fort Robinson, Nebraska.* Shippensberg, PA: White Mane Publishing, 1993.

———, ed. *The Nation Builders: A Sesquicentennial History of the Corps of Topographical Engineers, 1838–1863.* Fort Belvoir, VA: Office of History, United States Army Corps of Engineers, 1988.

Schultz, Duane. *The Maverick War: Chennault and the Flying Tigers.* New York: St. Martin's Press, 1987.

———. *Hero of Bataan: The Story of General Jonathan M. Wainwright.* New York: St. Martin's Press, 1981.

Scott, Charles L. "The Remount Service: What It Has Done for the Cavalry, the Riding Horse, Industry and the Farmer." *Quartermaster Review* 10 (September–October 1930): 13–16.

Scott, Robert Garth. *Into the Wilderness with the Army of the Potomac.* Rev. and enl. ed. Bloomington: Indiana University Press, 1992.

Sears, Stephen W. *Chancellorsville.* Boston: Houghton Mifflin, 1996.

———. *George B. McClellan: The Young Napoleon.* New York: Ticknor and Fields, 1988.

———. *Landscape Turned Red: The Battle of Antietam.* New Haven, CT: Ticknor & Fields, 1983.

———. *To the Gates of Richmond: The Peninsula Campaign.* New York: Ticknor and Fields, 1992.

Secrist, Philip L. *The Battle of Resaca: Atlanta Campaign, 1864.* Macon, GA: Mercer University Press, 1998.

Sedar, Robert P. "Employing the IFV." *Infantry* 71 (September–October 1981): 33–37.

Selby, John. *The Road to Yorktown.* New York: St. Martin's Press, 1976.

———. *Stonewall Jackson as Military Commander.* London: B. T. Batsford, 1968.

Sellers, Frank. *Sharps Firearms.* North Hollywood, CA: Beinfeld Publishing, 1978.

Serven, James E. *Colt Firearms from 1836.* Harrisburg, PA: Stackpole Books, 1954, 1979.

Settel, Irving. *A Pictorial History of Television.* 2d ed. New York: Frederick Ungar Publishing, 1983.

Seymour, Charles. *American Diplomacy during the World War.* Hamden, CT: Archon Books, 1964.

Seymour, Digby Gordon. *Divided Loyalties: Fort Sanders and the Civil War in East Tennessee.* Knoxville: University of Tennessee Press, 1963.

"SGT York: Air Defense Gun." *Air Defense Artillery* (Winter 1984): 18–32.

Shea, William L., and Earl J. Hess. *Pea Ridge: Civil War Campaign in the West.* Chapel Hill: University of North Carolina Press, 1992.

Sheehan, Fred. *Anzio: Epic of Bravery.* Norman: University of Oklahoma Press, 1964.

Sheehan, Neil. *A Bright Shining Lie: John Paul Vann and America in Vietnam.* New York: Random House, 1988.

Sheldon, Walter J. *Hell or High Water: MacArthur's Landing at Inchon.* New York: Macmillan, 1968.

Shelton, Hal T. *General Richard Montgomery and the American Revolution: From Red-coat to Rebel.* New York: New York University Press, 1994.

Sheppard, Don. *Riverine: A Brown-Water Sailor in the Delta 1967.* Novato, CA: Presidio Press, 1992.

Sherry, Michael S. *The Rise of American Air Power: The Creation of Armageddon.* New Haven, CT: Yale University Press, 1987.

Shirey, Orville C. *Americans: The Story of the 442d Combat Team.* Washington D.C.: Infantry Journal Press, 1946.

Shoemaker, Robert M. "The Changeover to 'Go to War' Management." *Army* 30 (October 1980): 28–32.

Shortal, John F. *Forged by Fire: General Robert L. Eichelberger and the Pacific War.* Columbia: University of South Carolina Press, 1987.

Simpson, Charles M., III. *Inside the Green Berets: The First Thirty Years: A History of the U.S. Army Special Forces.* Novato, CA: Presidio Press, 1983.

Simpson, Harold B. *Audie Murphy: American Soldier.* Dallas, TX: Alcor Publishing, 1982.

Simpson, Kenneth W. "Recruiting Quality Soldiers for America's Army." *Army* 44 (October 1994): 159–160.

Sinclair, Andrew. *John Ford.* New York: Dial Press, 1979.

Singlaub, John K. *Hazardous Duty: An American Soldier in the Twentieth Century.* New York: Summit Books, 1991.

Siuru, Bill. *The Huey and Huey Cobra.* Blue Ridge Summit, PA: Tab Books, 1987.

Skaggs, David C. "The KATUSA Experiment: The Integration of Korean Nationals into the U.S. Army, 1950–1965." *Military Affairs* 38 (April 1974): 53–58.

———, and Robert S. Browning, III, eds. *In Defense of the Republic: Readings in American Military History.* Belmont, CA: Wadsworth Publishing, 1991.

Skelton, Ike. "JPME: Are We There Yet?" *Military Review* 72 (May 1992): 2–9.

Skelton, William B. "The Commanding General and the Problem of Command in the United States Army, 1821–1841." *Military Affairs* 34 (December 1970): 117–122.

Skinner, Michael. *USAREUR: The United States Army in Europe.* Novato, CA: Presidio Press, 1989.

Slattery, Thomas J. *An Illustrated History of the Rock Island Arsenal and Arsenal Island;
Parts One and Two.* Rock Island, IL: Historical Office, U.S. Army Armament,
Munitions and Chemical Command, 1990.

Smith, Barry D. *101st Airborne Division in Colour Photographs.* Europa Militaria No.
13. London: Windrow and Greene, 1993.

Smith, Bradley F. *Other OSS Teams.* Covert Warfare, No. 5. New York: Garland Publishing, 1989.

Smith, Clarence McKittrick. *The Medical Department: Hospitalization and Evacuation,
Zone of the Interior. United States Army in World War II: The Technical Services.*
Washington, D.C.: Office of the Chief of Military History, 1956.

Smith, Merritt Roe. *Harpers Ferry Armory and the New Technology: The Challenge of
Change.* Ithaca, NY: Cornell University Press. 1977.

Smith, Perry M. *Assignment Pentagon: The Insider's Guide to the Potomac Puzzle Pal-
ace.* McLean, VA: Pergamon-Brassey's International Defense Publishers, 1989.

Smith, R. Elberton. *The Army and Economic Mobilization. United States Army in World
War II: The War Department.* Washington, D.C.: Office of the Chief of Military
History, 1959.

Smith, Robert Ross. *The Approach to the Philippines. United States Army in World War
II: The War in the Pacific.* Washington, D.C.: Office of the Chief of Military
History, 1953, 1984.

———. *Triumph in the Philippines. United States Army in World War II: The War
Department.* Washington, D.C.: Office of the Chief of Military History, 1963.

Smith, Samuel S. *The Battle of Brandywine.* Monmouth Beach, NJ: Philip Freneau Press,
1976.

———. *The Battle of Monmouth.* Monmouth Beach, NJ: Philip Freneau Press, 1964.

———. *The Battle of Trenton.* Monmouth Beach, NJ: Philip Freneau Press, 1965.

Smith, Winston O. *The Sharps Rifle: Its History, Development and Operation.* New York:
William Morrow, 1943.

Smoke, Richard. *National Security and the Nuclear Dilemma: An Introduction to the
American Experience.* Reading, MA: Addison-Wesley Publishing, 1984.

Smythe, Donald. *Guerrilla Warrior: The Early Life of John J. Pershing.* New York:
Charles Scribner's Sons, 1973.

———. *Pershing: General of the Armies.* Bloomington: Indiana University Press, 1986.

Snow, Richard F. "Standoff at White Plains." *American Heritage* 24 (April 1973): 41–
44.

Soboul, Randall A. "A Framework for SOPs." *Infantry* 82 (July–August 1992): 12–13.

Soffer, Jonathan M. *General Matthew B. Ridgway: From Progressivism to Reaganism,
1895–1993.* Westport, CT: Praeger, 1998.

Somes, Joseph Henry Vanderburgh. *Old Vincennes: The History of a Famous Old Town
and Its Glorious Past.* New York: Graphic Books, 1962.

Sorley, Lewis. "Creighton Abrams and Active-Reserve Integration in Wartime." *Parameters* 21 (Summer 1991): 35–50.

———. *Honorable Warrior: General Harold K. Johnson and the Ethics of Command.*
Lawrence: University Press of Kansas, 1998.

———. *Thunderbolt: General Creighton Abrams and the Army of His Times.* New York:
Simon and Schuster, 1992.

Spaller, Ruth J. "Earning the Badge." *Soldiers* 49 (June 1994): 42–43.

Sparks, Mike. "M113s Maximize Mechanized Infantry Mobility and Firepower in Contingency Ops." *Armor* 104 (January–February 1995): 6–14.

Spaulding, Lyman, and John W. Wright. *The Second Division, American Expeditionary Force in France, 1917–1919.* 1937. Reprint. Nashville, TN: Battery Press, 1989.

"Speaking of Pictures . . . : Sad Sack Stumbles His Way to End of War." *Life*, 31 December 1945, 8–10.

Spector, Ronald. *Advice and Support: The Early Years, 1941–1960. United States Army in Vietman.* Washington, D.C.: Center of Military History, 1983.

———. *Eagle Against the Sun: The American War with Japan.* New York: Free Press, 1984.

Spence, Jonathan. *To Change China: Western Advisers in China 1620–1960.* Boston: Little, Brown, 1969.

Spiller, Roger J. "John C. Calhoun as Secretary of War, 1817–1825." Ph.D. diss., Louisiana State University, 1977.

———. "War History and the History Wars: Establishing the Combat Studies Institute." *Public Historian* 10 (Fall 1988): 65–81.

Sprague, Marshall. *Massacre: The Tragedy at White River.* Boston: Little, Brown, 1957.

Sprock, Phyllis. "Fredom's Fort." *Soldiers* 43 (January 1988): 20–23.

Stackpole, Edward J. *Chancellorsville: Lee's Greatest Battle.* Harrisburg, PA: Stackpole, 1958.

———. *The Fredericksburg Campaign: Drama on the Rappahannock.* 2d ed. Harrisburg, PA: Stackpole Books, 1991.

———. *From Cedar Mountain to Antietam: August–September, 1862: Cedar Mountain—Second Manassas—Chantilly—Harpers Ferry—South Mountain—Antietam.* Harrisburg, PA: Stackpole, 1959.

———. *They Met at Gettysburg.* Harrisburg, PA: Stackpole, 1956.

Stagg, J.C.A. *Mr. Madison's War: Politics, Diplomacy, and Warfare in the Early American Republic, 1783–1830.* Princeton, NJ: Princeton University Press, 1983.

Stallard, Patricia Y. *Glittering Misery: Dependents of the Indian Fighting Army.* Norman: University of Oklahoma Press, 1992.

Stallings, Laurence. *The Doughboys: The Story of The AEF, 1917–1918.* New York: Harper and Row, 1963.

Stanley, George F. G. *Canada Invaded, 1775–1776.* Toronto: Hakkert, 1973.

———. *The War of 1812: Land Operations.* Canadian War Museum Historical Publication No. 18. Ottawa: Macmillan of Canada, 1983.

Stanley, Gregory, and David Snodgrass. "BCTP: Warfighting Exercises Strengthen Battlefield Performance." *Engineer* 26 (August 1996): 32–35.

Stanton, Shelby L. *Anatomy of a Division: The 1st Cav in Vietnam.* Novato, CA: Presidio Press, 1987.

———. *Green Berets at War: U.S. Army Special Forces in Southeast Asia, 1956–1975.* Novato, CA: Presidio Press, 1985.

———. *Rangers at War: Combat Recon in Vietnam.* New York: Orion Books, 1992.

———. *The Rise and Fall of an American Army: U.S. Ground Forces in Vietnam, 1965–1973.* Novato, CA: Presidio Press, 1985.

———. *U.S. Army Uniforms of World War II.* Harrisburg, PA: Stackpole Books, 1991.

Starr, Chester G. *From Salerno to the Alps: A History of the Fifth Army, 1943–1945.* Washington, D.C.: Infantry Journal Press. 1948.

Starry, Donn A. *Mounted Combat in Vietnam*. Vietnam Studies. Washington, D.C.: Department of the Army, 1978.

―――. "The Principles of War." *Military Review* 61 (September 1981): 2–12.

Staudenmaier, William O. "Division Air Defense." *Infantry* 64 (September–October 1974): 10–12.

Steele, Dennis. "The Golden Knights: Army's 'Hands-On' Goodwill Emissaries." *Army* 39 (August 1989): 36–39.

―――. "Higher Learning." *Soldiers* 41 (March 1986): 21–24.

―――. "The 1994 Air Assault Challenge." *Army* 45 (January 1995): 14–20.

Steffen, Jerome O. *William Clarke: Jeffersonian Man on the Frontier*. Norman: University of Oklahoma Press, 1977.

Steffen, Randy. *The Horse Soldiers, 1776–1943*. 4 vols. Norman: University of Oklahoma Press, 1977–1979.

―――. *United States Military Saddles, 1812–1943*. Norman: University of Oklahoma Press, 1973.

Stein, Barry Jason. *U.S. Army Heraldric Crests: A Complete Illustrated History of Authorized Distinctive Unit Insignia*. Columbia: University of South Carolina Press, 1993.

Stephenson, Roy R. "Road to Downfall: Lam Son 719 and U.S. Airmobility Doctrine." Ph.D. diss., University of Kansas, 1991.

Stern, Gary M., and Morton H. Halperin, eds. *The U.S. Constitution and the Power to Go to War: Historical and Current Perspectives*. Contributions in Military Studies, No. 150. Westport, CT: Greenwood Press, 1994.

Stevens, R. Blake. *U.S. Rifle M14: From John Garand to the M21*. 2d rev. ed. Modern U.S. Military Small Arms Series, vol. 1. Cobourg, Ont.: Collector Grade Publications, 1995.

Stewart, Miller J. "Army Laundresses: Ladies of the 'Soap Suds Row.' " *Nebraska History* 51 (Winter 1980): 421–436.

Stockholm International Peace Research Institute. *Anti-Personnel Weapons*. London: Taylor and Francis, 1978.

Stohlman, Robert F., Jr. *The Powerless Position: The Commanding General of the Army of the United States, 1864–1903*. Manhattan. KS: Military Affairs/Aerospace Historian Publishing, 1975.

Stokesbury, James L. *A Short History of World War I*. New York: William Morrow, 1981.

Stoler, Mark A. *George C. Marshall: Soldier-Statesman of the American Century*. Boston: Twayne Publishers, 1989.

Stonesifer, Roy P., Jr. "The Forts Henry-Heiman and Fort Donelson Campaigns: A Study of Confederate Command." Ph.D. diss., Pennsylvania State University, 1965.

Strahan, Jerry E. *Andrew Jackson Higgins and the Boats That Won World War II*. Baton Rouge: Louisiana State University Press, 1994.

Straight, Michael. *Trial by Television and Other Encounters*. New York: Devon Press, 1979.

Strandberg, John E., and Roger J. Bender. *The Call of Duty: Military Awards and Decorations of the United States of America*. San Jose, CA: R. James Bender Publishing, 1994.

Street, Oliver D., III, and Kenneth N. Brown. "Army Air Defense: A New Role." *Army* 30 (May 1980): 24–29.

Strobridge, Truman R., and Bernard C. Nalty. "From the South Pacific to the Brenner Pass: General Alexander M. Patch." *Military Review* 61 (June 1981): 41–48.

Stryker, William S. *The Battle of Monmouth.* Edited by William Starr Myers. Princeton, NJ: Princeton University Press, 1927.

Stubbs, Mary Lee, and Stanley Russell Connor. *Armor-Cavalry. Part I: Regular Army and Army Reserve.* Army Lineage Series. 1969. Reprint. Washington, D.C.: Center of Military History, 1984.

Stuckey, John D. "Echelons above Corps." *Parameters* 13 (December 1983): 39–41.

Stueck, William. *The Wedemeyer Mission: American Politics and Foreign Policy during the Cold War.* Athens: University of Georgia Press, 1984.

Sullivan, Brian. "WRAMC: In Pusuit of Excellence." *Soldiers* 34 (July 1979): 6–10.

Sullivan, Charles J. *Army Posts & Towns: The Baedeker of the Army.* Burlington, VT: Free Press Interstate Printing, 1935.

Sullivan, George. *Modern Combat Helicopters.* New York: Facts on File, 1993.

Sunderland, Glenn W. *Wilder's Lighting Brigade . . . and its Spencer Repeaters.* (Previously published as *Lightning at Hoovers Gap.*) Washington, IL: Book Works: 1984.

Sunderland, Riley. *Evolution of Command and Control Doctrine for Close Air Support.* [Washington, D.C.]: Office of Air Force History, 1973.

Sutherland, Ian D. W. *Special Forces of the United States Army, 1952–1982.* San Jose, CA: R. James Bender Publishing, 1990.

Sutherland, John R., III. "The Platoon Team." *Infantry* 84 (July–August 1994): 9–12.

Swain, Richard M. *"Lucky War": Third Army in Desert Storm.* Fort Leavenworth, KS: U.S. Army Command and General Staff College Press, 1994.

Swanberg, W. A. *First Blood: The Story of Fort Sumter.* New York: Charles Scribner's Sons, 1957.

Swartz, Oretha D. *Service Etiquette.* 4th ed. Annapolis, MD: Naval Institute Press, 1988.

Swayze, Nathan L. *'51 Colt Navies.* Yazoo City, MS: Gun Hill Publishing, 1967.

Sweetman, Jack. *The Landing at Veracruz, 1914: The First Complete Chronicle of a Strange Encounter in April 1914, When the United States Navy Captured and Occupied the City of Veracruz, Mexico.* Annapolis, MD: United States Naval Institute, 1968.

Sword, Wiley. *Embrace an Angry Wind: The Confederate's Last Hurrah: Spring Hill, Franklin, and Nashville.* New York: HarperCollins, 1991.

———. *Mountains Touched with Fire: Chattanooga Besieged, 1863.* New York: St. Martin's Press, 1995.

———. *Shiloh: Bloody April.* New York: William Morrow, 1974.

Symonds, Craig L. *Joseph E. Johnston: A Civil War Biography.* New York: W. W. Norton, 1992.

Syrett, David. "The John F. Morrison Professor of Military History." *Military Review* 63 (May 1983): 13–22

Talbott, Orwin C. "The Home Where Nobody Ever Rests." *Army* 20 (March 1970): 34–41.

Tan, Chester C. *The Boxer Catastrophe.* New York: Columbia University Press, 1955.

Tan Pei-Ying. *The Building of the Burmaz Road.* New York: McGraw-Hill, 1945.

Tanham, Mary. "The Gold Mine at OCMH." *Army* 9 (January 1959): 38–41.

Tanner, Robert G. *Stonewall in the Valley: Thomas J. "Stonewall" Jackson's Shenandoah Valley Campaign, Spring 1862.* Garden City, NY: Doubleday, 1976.

Tararine, J.-G. Jeudy M. *The Jeep*. New York: Vilo, 1981.

Tarr, Curtis W. *By the Numbers: The Reform of the Selective Service System, 1970–1972*. Washington, D.C.: National Defense University Press, 1981.

Taylor, George. "Army Gets Improved Tank Recovery Vehicle." *Army Logistician* (January–February 1993): 34–35.

Taylor, Gerri. "Fort Crossroads." *Soldiers* 41 (May 1986): 34–36.

Taylor, John. *Bloody Valverde: A Civil War Battle on the Rio Grande, February 21, 1862*. Albuquerque: University of New Mexico Press, 1995.

Taylor, John M. *General Maxwell Taylor: The Sword and the Pen*. New York: Doubleday, 1989.

Taylor, Maxwell D. *Swords and Plowshares*. New York: W. W. Norton, 1972.

Teetor, Paul R. *A Matter of Hours: Treason at Harper's Ferry*. Rutherford, NJ: Fairleigh Dickenson University Press, 1982.

Tenney, Lester I. *My Hitch in Hell: The Bataan Death March*. Washington, D.C.: Brassey's, 1995.

Terrett, Dulany. *The Signal Corps: The Emergency (to December 1941)*. *United States Army in World War II: The Technical Services*. Washington, D.C.: Office of the Chief of Military History, 1956.

Thatcher, Harold W. *The Development of Special Rations for the Army*. [Washington D.C.]: Historical Section, General Administration Services Division, Office of the Quartermaster General, 1944.

Thayer, Theodore. *Nathanael Greene: Strategist of the American Revolution*. New York: Twayne Publishers, 1960.

Theimer, J. E. "The U.S. Army in Hawaii." *Army Information Digest* 15 (July 1960): 2–13.

Thomas, Ann Van Wynen, and A. J. Thomas, Jr. *The War-Making Powers of the President: Constitutional and International Law Aspects*. Dallas, TX: SMU Press, 1982.

Thomas, Benjamin P., and Harold M. Hyman. *Stanton: The Life and Times of Lincoln's Secretary of War*. New York: Alfred A. Knopf, 1962.

Thomas, Dean S. *Cannons: An Introduction to Civil War Artillery*. Gettysburg, PA: Thomas Publications, 1985.

Thomas, Emory M. *Bold Dragoon: The Life of J.E.B. Stuart*. New York: Harper and Row, 1986.

———. *Robert E. Lee: A Biography*. New York: W. W. Norton, 1995.

Thompson, Leroy. *The All Americans: The 82nd Airborne*. New Abbot, Devon, U.K.: David and Charles Publishers, 1988.

Thompson, Loren B., ed. *Low-Intensity Conflict: The Pattern of Warfare in the Modern World*. Lexington, MA: Lexington Books, 1989.

Thompson, Tommy. *The Citadel: Then and Now*. Louisville, KY: Harmony House, 1993.

Tierney, Richard K. "The Flying Crane." *U.S. Army Aviation Digest* 10 (November 1964): 12–15.

Tiffany, Allen L. "Proposed Rapidly Deployable, Tactically Mobile, Motorized Infantry Brigade." *Military Review* 74 (February 1994): 74–77.

Tillotson, Lee S. *The Articles of War Annotated*. Harrisburg, PA: Military Service Publishing, 1942.

———. *Index-Digest and Annotations to the Uniform Code of Military Justice*. 4th ed. Harrisburg, PA: Military Service Publishing, 1956.

Todd, A. L. *Richard Montgomery: Rebel of 1775*. New York: David McKay, 1966.

Todd, Frederick P. *American Military Equipage, 1851–1872: A Description by Word and Picture of What the American Soldier, Sailor and Marine of These Years Wore and Carried, with Emphasis on the American Civil War*. New York: Charles Scribner's Sons, 1980.

Toguchi, Robert M, and James Hogue. "The Battle of Convergence in Four Dimensions." *Military Review* 72 (October 1992): 11–20.

Toland, John. *But Not in Shame: The Six Months after Pearl Harbor*. New York: Random House, 1961.

———. *In Mortal Combat: Korea, 1950–1953*. New York: William Morrow, 1991.

Tolson, John J. *Airmobility, 1961–1971*. Washington D.C.: Department of the Army, 1973.

Tousey, Thomas G. *Military History of Carlisle and Carlisle Barracks*. Richmond, VA: Dietz Press, 1939.

Townsend, Joseph. *The Battle of Brandywine*. Eyewitness Accounts of the American Revolution. New York: The New York Times and Arno Press, 1969.

Traas, Adrian George. *From the Golden Gate to Mexico City: The U.S. Army Topographical Engineers in the Mexican War, 1846–1848*. Washington, D.C. Office of History, Corps of Engineers and Center of Military History, 1993.

Trask, David F. *The War with Spain in 1898*. New York: Macmillan, 1981.

Treadwell, Mattie E. *The Women's Army Corps. United States Army in World War II: Special Studies*. Washington D.C.: Office of the Chief of Military History, 1954.

Tretler, David A. "The Making of a Revolutionary General, Nathanael Greene: 1742–1779." Ph.D. diss., Rice University, 1986.

Trohoske, Keith. "The Beat of a Different Drum." *Soldiers* 42 (October 1987): 34–36.

Trout, Robert J. *They Followed the Plume: The Story of J.E.B. Stuart and His Staff*. Mechanicsburg, PA: Stackpole Books, 1993.

Troy, Thomas F. *Donovan and the CIA: A History of the Establishment of the Central Intelligence Agency*. Frederick, MD: University Publication of America, 1981.

Trudeau, Noah Andre. *Bloody Roads South: The Wilderness to Cold Harbor, May–June 1864*. Boston: Little, Brown, 1989.

Trulock, Alice Rains. *In the Hands of Providence: Joshua L. Chamberlain and the American Civil War*. Chapel Hill: University of North Carolina Press, 1992.

Trump, Christopher Gebhardt. "The Old Army Mess: A Whimsical Glance at the Old Army Institution 40 Years Ago." *Infantry* 50 (January 1960): 17–19.

Truong, Ngo Quang. *The Easter Offensive of 1972*. Indochina Monographs. Washington, D.C.: Center of Military History, 1980.

Tuchman, Barbara W. *Stilwell and the American Experience in China, 1911–45*. New York: Macmillan, 1971.

Tucker, Glenn. *Chickamaugu: Bloody Battle in the West*. Dayton, OH: Morningside Press, 1961.

Tucker, Phillip Thomas. *The Forgotten "Stonewall of the West": Major General John Stevens Bowen*, Macon, GA: Mercer University Press, 1997.

Turley, Gerald H. *The Easter Offensive: Vietnam, 1972*. Novato, CA: Presidio Press, 1985.

Turner, John Frayn, and Robert Jackson. *Destination Berchtesgaden: The Story of the United States Seventh Army in World War II*. New York: Charles Scribner's Sons, 1975.

Turner, Stansfield. *Secrecy and Democracy: The CIA in Transition.* Boston: Houghton Mifflin, 1985.

Ueberhorst, Horst. *Friedrich Wilhelm von Steuben, 1730–1794.* München, FRG: Heinz Moos, 1981.

Underwood, Jeffrey S. *The Wings of Democracy: The Influence of Air Power on the Roosevelt Administration, 1933–1941.* College Station: Texas A & M University Press, 1991.

United States Army. Field Manual 22–6. *Guard Duty.* Washington, D.C.: Headquarters, Department of the Army, 1971.

United States Army Chaplainey. 5 vols. Washington, D.C.: Office of the Chief of Chaplains, 1977–1997.

United States Army. Corps of Engineers. *The History of the US Army Corps of Engineers.* [Washington D.C.]: Corps of Engineers [1986].

United States Army. Finance School. *History and Organization of the Finance Corps.* Fort Benjamin Harrison, IN: United States Army Finance School, 1971.

United States Army. Office of the Judge Advocate General. *The Army Lawyer: A History of the Judge Advocate Generals' Corps, 1775–1975.* Washington, D.C.: Government Printing Office, [1975].

United States Army. 2d Infantry Division. *Combat History of the Second Infantry Division in World War II.* 1946. Reprint. Nashville, TN: Battery Press, 1979.

United States Army. War College, Historical Division. *Order of Battle of the United States Land Forces in the World War.* Vol. 3, *Zone of the Interior.* 3 parts. 1931–1949. Reprint. Washington, D.C.: Center of Military History, 1988.

United States. Department of Defense. Joint Publication 3–57. *Doctrine for Joint Civil Affairs.* Washington, D.C.: Joint Chiefs of Staff, 1995.

United States. War Department. Historical Division [John M Baker and George F. Howe]. *The Capture of Makin, 20 November–24 November 1943.* American Forces in Action Series. 1946. Reprint. Washington, D.C.: Center of Military History, 1990.

Unsworth, Michael E., ed. *Military Periodicals: United States and Selected International Journals and Newspapers.* Historical Guides to the World's Periodicals and Newspapers. Westport, CT: Greenwood Press, 1990.

Unterberger, Betty Miller, ed. *American Intervention in the Russian Civil War.* Problems in American Civilization. Lexington, MA: D.C. Health, 1969.

Urwin, Gregory J. W. *The United States Infantry: An Illustrated History, 1775–1918.* London: Blandford Press, 1988.

Utgoff, Victor. *The Challenge of Chemical Weapons: An American Perspective.* New York: St. Martin's Press, 1991.

Utley, Robert M. *Cavalier in Buckskin: George Armstrong Custer and the Western Military Frontier.* Norman: University of Oklahoma Press, 1988.

———. *Frontier Regulars: The United States Army and the Indian, 1866–1891.* New York: Macmillan, 1973.

———, and Wilcomb E. Washburn. *The American Heritage History of the Indian Wars.* New York: American Heritage Publishing, 1977.

Valceanu, John. "YPG: The Army's Desert Test Center." *Soldiers* 54 (August 1999): 4–8.

Van Deman, Ralph H. *The Final Memoranda: Major General Ralph H. Van Deman, USA Ret., 1865–1952: Father of U.S. Military Intelligence.* Edited by Ralph E. Weber. Wilmington, DE: Scholarly Resources, 1988.

Vandiver, Frank E. *Black Jack: The Life and Times of John J. Pershing.* 2 vols. College Station: Texas A & M University Press, 1977.

Van Horne, Thomas B. *History of the Army of the Cumberland: Its Organization, Campaigns, and Battles Written at the Request of Major-General George H. Thomas Chiefly from His Private Military Journal and Official and Other Documents Furnished by Him.* 1875. Reprint. Wilmington, NC: Broadfoot Publishing, 1988.

Vatcher, William H., Jr. *Panmunjom: The Story of the Korean Military Armistice Negotiations.* New York: Praeger, 1958.

Vaughn, J. W. *Indian Fights: New Facts on Seven Encounters.* Norman: University of Oklahoma Press, 1966.

————. *With Crook at the Rosebud.* Lincoln: University of Nebraska Press, 1956.

Virtue, C. M. *Company Administration: Including Personnel Management, Unit Records, Supply and Mess, and the Personnel Section, including Career Guidance and Personnel Management, Personnel Records and Pay.* 22d ed. Harrisburg, PA: Military Service Publishing, 1953.

Volckmann, R. W. *We Remained: Three Years behind the Enemy Lines in the Philippines.* New York: W. W. Norton, 1954.

Volkman, Ernest. *Warriors of the Night: Spies, Soldiers, and American Intelligence.* New York: William Morrow, 1985.

Waddell, Steve R. *United States Army Logistics: The Normandy Campaign, 1944.* Contributions in Military Studies, No. 155. Westport, CT: Greenwood Press, 1994.

Wagner, Robert E. "Active Defense and All That." *Military Review* 60 (August 1980): 4–13.

Wahl, Paul. *Carbine Handbook: The Complete Manual and Guide to U.S. Carbine, Cal. .30, M1.* New York: Arco Publishing, 1964.

————, and Donald R. Toppel. *The Gatling Gun.* New York: Arco Publishing, 1965.

Walker, Glenn D. "First U.S. Army: A New Challenge." *Army* 23 (October 1973): 72–76.

Walker, Richard R. "Fielding the Black Hawk: A Logistics Alternative." *Army Logistician* 9 (November–December 1977): 24–25.

Walker, Wallace E. "Emory Upton and the Army Officer's Creed." *Military Review* 61 (April 1981): 65–68.

Wallace, Anthony F. C. *The Long, Bitter Trail: Andrew Jackson and the Indians.* New York: Hill and Wang, 1993.

Wallace, Willard M. *Soul of the Lion: A Biography of General Joshua L. Chamberlain.* 1960. Reprint. Gettysburg, PA: Stan Clark Military Books, 1991.

————. *Traitorous Hero: The Life and Fortunes of Benedict Arnold.* 1954. Reprint. Freeport, NY: Books for Libraries Press, 1970.

Walton, George. *Sentinel of the Plains: Fort Leavenworth and the American West.* Englewood Cliffs, NJ: Prentice-Hall, 1973.

Watson, Bruce W., and Peter G. Tsouras, eds. *Operation Just Cause: The U.S. Intervention in Panama.* Boulder, CO: Westview Press, 1991.

Watson, Mark S. *Chief of Staff: Prewar Plans and Preparations. United States Army in World War II: The War Department.* Washington, D. C: Office of the Chief of Military History, 1950, 1985.

Webb, Henry W. "The Story of Jefferson Barracks." *New Mexico Historical Review* 21 (July 1946): 185–208.

Webb, Lester A. *Captain Alden Partridge and the United States Military Academy, 1806–1833*. Northport, AL: American Southern, 1965.

Webster, Donald B., Jr. *American Socket Bayonets, 1717–1873*. Ottawa: Museum Restoration Service, 1964.

Weigley, Russell F. *Eisenhower's Lieutenants: The Campaign of France and Germany, 1944–1945*. Bloomington: Indiana University Press, 1981.

———. *History of the United States Army*. Enlarged ed. Bloomington: Indiana University, 1984.

———. "The Military Thought of John M. Schofield." *Military Affairs* 23 (Summer 1959): 77–84.

———. *The Partisan War: The South Carolina Campaign of 1780–1782*. Tricentennial Booklet, No. 2. Columbia: University of South Carolina Press, 1970.

Weinberg, Gerhard L. *A World at Arms: A Global History of World War II*. Cambridge, U.K.: Cambridge University Press, 1994.

Weiner, Ed, and Editors of *TV Guide*. *The TV Guide TV Book: 40 Years of the All-time Greatest: Television Facts, Fads, Hits, and History*. New York: HarperCollins, 1992.

Weinert, Richard P., Jr. *A History of Army Aviation: 1950–1962*. Edited by Susan Canedy. Fort Monroe, VA: Office of the Command Historian, United States Army Training and Doctrine Command, 1991.

———, and Robert Arthur. *Defender of the Chesapeake: The Story of Fort Monroe*. 3d rev. ed. Shippensburg, PA: White Mane Publishing, 1989.

Weisberger, Bernard A. *Cold War, Cold Peace: The United States since 1945*. New York: American Heritage Publishing, 1984.

Weland, Gerald. *O. O. Howard, Union General*. Jefferson, NC: McFarland, 1995.

Welch, Richard E., Jr. *Response to Imperialism: The United States and the Philippine–American War, 1899–1902*. Chapel Hill: University of North Carolina Press, 1979.

Welcher, Frank J. *The Union Army, 1861–1865: Organization and Operations*. 2 vols. Bloomington: Indiana University Press, 1989–1993.

Werner, Fred H. *Meeker—The Story of the Meeker Massacre and the Thornburgh Battle, September 29, 1879*. Greeley, CO: Werner Publications. 1985.

———. *The Slim Buttes Battle, September 9 and 10, 1876*. 2d ed. [Greeley, CO]: Werner Publications, 1981.

———. "The Soldiers Are Coming!": The Reynolds Battle, March 17, 1876*. Greeley, CO: Werner Publications, 1982.

Werngren, Martin S. "Skills Spell Strength." *Army Digest* 17 (September 1962): 60–62.

Werrell, Kenneth P. *Archie, Flak, AAA, and Sam*. Maxwell Air Force Base, AL: Air University Press, 1988.

Wert, Jeffrey D. *Custer: The Controversial Life of George Armstrong Custer*. New York: Simon and Schuster, 1996.

———. *From Winchester to Cedar Creek: The Shenandoah Campaign of 1864*. Carlisle, PA: South Mountain Press, 1987.

———. *General James Longstreet: The Confederacy's Most Controversial Soldier—A Biography*. New York: Simon and Schuster, 1993.

West, Luther C. *They Call It Justice: Command Influence and the Court-Martial System*. New York: Viking Press, 1977.

Westmoreland, William C. *A Soldier Reports*. Garden City, NY: Doubleday, 1976.

Westwood, James T. "Maneuver: A Broad Concept." *Military Review* 63 (March 1983): 15–19.

Wheeler, Richard. *Sherman's March*. 1978. Reprint. New York: HarperPerennial, 1991.

Whelan, Richard. *Drawing the Line: The Korean War, 1950–1953*. Boston: Little, Brown, 1990.

White, B. T. *Tanks and Other Armored Fighting Vehicles of World War II*. New York: Exeter Books, 1983.

[White, Stephen H.] "Editor's Page." *Infantry* 47 (April 1957): 2.

White, William Carter. *A History of Military Music in America*. New York: Exposition Press, 1944.

Whitehorne, Joseph W. A. *The Battle of New Market*. Washington, D.C., Center in Military History, 1988.

———. *The Inspectors General of the United States Army, 1903–1939*. Washington D.C.: Office of the Inspector General and Center of Military History, 1998.

Whiting, Charles. *Hero: The Life and Death of Andre Murphy*. Chalsea, MI: Searborough House, 1990.

———. *Kasserine: First Blood*. New York: Stein and Day, 1984.

———. *Siegfried: The Nazis' Last Stand*. New York: Stein and Day, 1982.

Whitley, James R. "Unit Training Management: An Approach to a Dilemma." *Military Review* 60 (August 1980): 53–58.

Whitman, John W. *Bataan: Our Last Ditch: The Bataan Campaign, 1942*. New York: Hippocrene Books, 1990.

Whittemore, Charles P. *A General of the Revolution: John Sullivan of New Hampshire*. New York: Columbia University Press, 1961.

"Who Is 'Kilroy'?" *New York Times Magazine*, 12 January 1947, 30.

Widmer, Kemble. *The Christmas Campaign: The Ten Days of Trenton and Princeton*. New Jersey's Historical Experience 22. Trenton: New Jersey Historical Commission, 1975.

Wiener, Frederick Bernays. *The Uniform Code of Military Justice: Explanation, Comparative Text, and Commentary*. Washington D.C.: Combat Forces Press, 1950.

Wike. John W. "Our Regimental Heritage: A Soldier's Link with Tradition." *Army Information Digest* 19 (February 1964): 50–56.

Williams, F.D.G. *SLAM: The Influence of S.L.A. Marshall on the United States Army*. TRADOC Historical Monograph Series. Fort Monroe, VA: Office of the Command Historian, United States Army Training and Doctrine Command, 1990.

Williams, Peter. "The Future of the SP Gun." *NATO's Sixteen Nations* 33 (April–May 1988): 65–66.

Williams, Peter G. "SOPs That Work." *Infantry* 74 (November–December 1984): 37–38.

Williams, Samuel T. "The Practical Demands of MAAG." *Military Review* 41 (July 1961): 2–14.

Williams, T. Harry. *Lincoln and His Generals*. New York: Alfred A. Knopf, 1952.

———. *McClellan., Sherman and Grant*. 1962. Reprint. Westport. CT: Greenwood Press, 1976.

Williams, Tom. "A Gold Standard." *Soldiers* 40 (July 1985): 46–50.

———. "Mountains, Glaciers and Rivers." *Soldiers* 39 (August 1984): 42–45.

Willinger, Kurt, and Gene Gurney. *The American Jeep in War and Peace*. New York: Crown Publishers, 1983.

Willis, John T. "The United States Court of Military Appeals: Its Origins, Operation and Future." *Military Law Review* 55 (Winter 1972): 39–93.

Wills, Brain Steel. *A Battle from the Start: The Life of Nathan Bedford Forrest.* New York: HarperCollins, 1992.

Wilson, Arthur R. *Field Artillery Manual.* Vol. 2. Rev. ed. Menasha, WI: George Banta Publishing, 1928.

Wilson, George C. *Mud Soldiers: Life inside the New American Army.* New York: Charles Scribner's Sons, 1989.

Wilson, Gerald C. "Simple Little Things." *Soldiers* 45 (April 1990): 50–52.

Wilson, John B., comp. *Armies, Corps, Divisions and Separate Brigades.* Army Lineage Series. Washington, D.C: Center of Military History, 1987.

———. *Maneuver and Firepower: The Evolution of Divisions and Separate Brigades.* Washington, D.C.: Center of Military History, 1998.

———. "Influences on U.S. Army Divisional Organization in the Twentieth Century." *Army History* (Fall 1996): 1–7.

Wilson, Leonard R. "The Chinook: A Personal View." *U.S. Army Aviation Digest* 10 (April 1964): 18–20.

Wilson, R. L. *Colt: An American Legend: The Official History of Colt Firearms from 1836 to the Present.* New York: Artabras Publishers, 1990.

Wilson, Theodore A., ed. *D-Day 1944.* Lawrence: University Press of Kansas, 1994.

Windrow, Martin, and Gerry Embleton. *Military Dress of North America, 1665–1970.* New York: Charles Scribner's Sons, 1973.

Winschel, Terrence. "Grant's Beachhead for the Vicksburg Campaign: The Battle of Port Gibson, May 1, 1863." *Blue & Gray* 11 (February 1994): 9–22.

Winship, Michael. *Television.* New York: Random House, 1988.

Wintringham, Tom. *The Story of Weapons and Tactics from Troy to Stalingrad.* Boston: Houghton Mifflin, 1943.

Wiram, Terri. "Combat Medics: First Aid to the Rescue." *Soldiers* 38 (February 1983): 14–16.

———. "Fort Sam: Yesterday & Today." *Soldiers* 38 (March 1983): 46–48.

Wirtz, James J. *The Tet Offensive: Intelligence Failure in War.* Ithaca, NY: Cornell University Press, 1991.

Wise, Henry A. *Drawing Out the Man: The VMI Story.* Charlottesville: University Press of Virginia, 1978.

Wise, Jennings C. *Sunrise of the Virginia Military Institute as a School of Arms.* Lexington, VA: Jennings C. Wise, 1958.

Witt, Christopher, and David L. Priddy. "Target: Chaparral!!" *Air Defense Magazine* (January–March 1977): 6–11.

Witze, Claude. "The Howze Board Issue Is Joined." *Air Force and Space Digest* 46 (May 1963): 14–16.

Wood, Alan. *History of the World's Glider Forces.* Wellingborough, Northamptonshire, U.K.: Patrick Stephens, 1990.

Wool, Harold. *The Military Specialist: Skilled Manpower for the Armed Forces.* Baltimore: Johns Hopkins Press, 1968.

Wooley, Richard W. "A Short History of Identification Tags." *Quartermaster Professional Bulletin* (December 1988): 16–17.

Wooster, Robert. *Nelson A. Miles and the Twilight of the Frontier Army.* Lincoln: University of Nebraska Press, 1993.

————. *Soldiers, Sutlers, and Settlers: Garrison Life on the Texas Frontier*. College
 Station: Texas A&M University Press, 1987.
Wormser, Richard. *The Yellowlegs: The Story of the United States Cavalry*. Garden City,
 NY: Doubleday, 1966.
Wormuth, Francis D., and Edwin B. Firmage, with Francis P. Butler. *To Chain the Dog
 of War: The War Power of Congress in History and Law*. Dallas, TX: Southern
 Methodist University Press, 1986.
Wright, John M., Jr. "Fort Benning 1918–1968." *Infantry* 58 (September–October 1968):
 4–11.
Wright, Robert K., Jr. *The Continental Army*. Washington, D.C.: Center of Military
 History, 1983.
————, comp. *Military Police*. Army Lineage Series. Washington, D.C.: Center of Mil-
 itary History, 1992.
Wyant, William K. *Sandy Patch: A Biography of Lt. Gen. Alexander M. Patch*. Westport,
 CT: Praeger, 1991.
Wyman, Willard G. "New and Old Tasks of CONARC." *Army* 8 (December 1957): 40–
 44.
Yahara, Hiromichi. *The Battle for Okinawa*. Translated by Roger Pineau and Masatoshi
 Uehara. New York: John Wiley and Sons, 1995.
Yates, Lawrence A. *Power Pack: U.S. Intervention in the Dominican Republic, 1965–
 1966*. Leavenworth Papers No. 15. Fort Leavenworth, KS: Combat Studies Insti-
 tute, 1988.
Yenne, Bill. *McDonnell Douglas: A Tale of Two Giants*. New York: Crescent Books,
 1985.
Young, Donald J. *The Battle of Bataan: A History of the 90-Day Siege and Eventual
 Surrender of 75,000 Filipino and United States Troops to the Japanese in World
 War II*. Jefferson, NC: McFarland, 1992.
Young, Kenneth Ray. *The General's General: The Life and Times of Arthur MacArthur*.
 Boulder, CO: Westview Press, 1994.
Zaffiri, Samuel. *Hamburger Hill, May 11–20, 1969*. Novato, CA: Presidio Press, 1988.
————. *Westmoreland: A Biography of General William C. Westmoreland*. New York:
 William Morrow, 1994.
Zais, Melvin. "The New NCO." *Army* 18 (May 1968): 72–76.
Zanchi, Joseph A., and Alan J. LaBrode. "Combat Ration Logistics: From Here to Eter-
 nity." *Army Logistician* 31 (January–February 1999): 144–149.
Zedric, Lance Q. "Prelude to Victory—The Alamo Scouts." *Army* 44 (July 1994): 49–
 52.
————. *Silent Warriors of World War II: The Alamo Scouts Behind Japanese Lines*.
 Ventura, CA: Pathfinder Publishing of California, 1995.
Zierdt, John G. "Missiles vs. Armor." *Ordnance* 51 (November–December 1966): 268–
 271.
Zimmer, Bolko G. "TOE, MTOE, and TDA—What's the Difference?" *Army Logistician*
 [20] (May–June 1988): 13–15.

INDEX

Page numbers for main entries appear in boldface type.

624

INDEX

Surgeon General, 21, 148, **460–461**, 487; dental care by, 141
Surgeon General of Medical Affairs, 304
Surgeon General of the United States, 21, 148, 460–461
Susquehanna River, 458
Sutler, 29
"Swamp Fox," 296–297
Swift, Eban, 415, **461**
Sword Beach, 335, 350
Sykes, Major George, 174

T-34, 466
Table of basic allowances, 122
Table of distribution and allowances, 122
Table of equipment, 122
Table of organization, 122
Table of organization and equipment, 42, 122, 245, **462**
Tactical air controller party, 204. *See also* Close air support
Tactical exercise without troops, 210
Tactical Operations Center, **462**
"Tactical Problems," 245–246
Tactics, 456, **463**
TA-50, **463–464**
Taft, President William Howard, 454
Taku, 65, 87, 352
Talladega, 133
Tallahatchee, 133
Tampa, Florida, 405, 444
Tank Corps, 357. *See also* Armor
Tank Destroyer and Tactical Firing Center, 186, 206
Tank Destroyer Center, 464
Tank destroyer, M10, **464**
Tank destroyer, M18, **464–465**
Tank destroyer, M36, **465**
Tarhe, 178
Tarleton, Colonel Banastre, 131
Task Force Faith, 99
Task Force 160, 280
Task Force 6814, 356
Task Force Smith, 159, **465–466**
Tay Ninh Province, 258
Taylor, Lieutenant General Richard, 392
Taylor, Maxwell D., 159, 362, **466–467**

Taylor, Zachary, xv, 49, 70, 139, 181, 309–310, 322, 415, **467**
Tecumseh, 228, 470, 507, 509
Tecumseh's Indian Confederation, 470
Television series, 115,164, 300
Teller, Edward, 296
Temporary duty, **467–468**
Ten-in-one ration, **468**
Tennessee Valley Authority, 101
Tenskwatawa (the Prophet), 471
Tenth Air Force, 145
Tenth Army, 345, 454, 526
10th Special Forces Group, 183, 220, 343
Terry, Major General Alfred, 84, 136, 279, 431, 440
Tet, 305, 314, **468–469**
Texas Rangers, 310
Texas, Republic of, 309
Thames River (Canada), 509; Battle of the, 228
Thieu, President Nguyen Van, 305
Third Army, 2, 13, 144, 164, 193, 233, 270, 338, 358, 392, 427, **469**, 525
38th Parallel, 268–269, 353, **469–470**
Thomas, George H., 33, 93, 95, 206, 207, 262, 432, 455, **470**
Thornburgh, Major Thomas, 489
Thurman, General Maxwell R., 259
Tiger tank, 465
Tippecanoe, 228, **470–471**, 507
Tobruk, 472
Todd's Tavern, 431
Tomb of the Unknown Soldier, 23, 346, **471**
Ton Son Nhut Air Base, 468
Topographical Engineers, 116, 212. *See also* Corps of Engineers; U.S. Topographical Corps
Torch, 175, 358, **472**
Torrijos, General Omar, 259
Tory Rangers, 458
Total Army, **472–473**
Total Force, 41, 332. *See also* Total Army
Total Quality Management, **473**
Totopotomy Creek, 111
TOW, 110, 232
Townson, Colonel Nathan, 358

ABOUT THE EDITOR
AND CONTRIBUTORS

STANLEY ADAMIAK is Assistant Professor in the Department of History and Geography at Central Oklahoma University, Edmond, Oklahoma.

STEPHEN J. ALLIE is Director, Frontier Army Museum, Fort Leavenworth, Kansas.

J. TOM ASHWORTH is a law student at Drake University in Des Moines, Iowa.

J. G. D. BABB, Lieutenant Colonel, U.S. Army Retired, is Associate Professor, Department of Joint and Multinational Operations, U.S. Army Command and General Staff College, Fort Leavenworth, Kansas.

RICHARD BARBUTO, Lieutenant Colonel, U.S. Army Retired, is Department Manager, Northrop Grumman, Fort Leavenworth, Kansas.

KEITH B. BARTSCH, Lieutenant Colonel, USAF, is Commander, 19th Air Support Operations Squadron (ACC), Fort Campbell, Kentucky.

WILLIAM E. BASSETT, Lieutenant Colonel, U.S. Army Retired, was formerly Instructor, Combat Studies Institute, U.S. Army Command and General Staff College, Fort Leavenworth, Kansas.

ROBERT F. BAUMANN is Professor of History, Combat Studies Institute, U.S. Army Command and General Staff College, Fort Leavenworth, Kansas. He is the coauthor of *Invasion, Intervention, "Intervasion": A Concise History of the U.S. Army in Operation Uphold Democracy*.

GARY BJORGE is Professor of History, Combat Studies Institute, U.S. Army Command and General Staff College. Fort Leavenworth, Kansas. He is the author of *Merrill's Marauders: Combined Operations in Northern Burma in 1944*.

FREDERIC L. BORCH III, Lieutenant Colonel, U.S. Army, is coauthor of *The Soldier's Medal: A History of the Army's Highest Award for Non-Combat Valor* and *The Purple Heart: A History of America's Oldest Military Decoration*.

GARY BOUNDS, Lieutenant Colonel, U.S. Army Retired, is Deputy for Concepts, Doctrine, and Force Development, Office of the Deputy Chief of Staff for Operations and Plans for the Army Staff.

PHIL BRADLEY, Lieutenant Colonel, U.S. Air Force, is AC 130 Gunship Air Crew, Air Force Special Operations Command, Hurlburt Field, Florida.

RANDALL N. BRIGGS, Major, U.S. Army Retired, is Adjunct Professor, Tulsa Community College, Tulsa, Oklahoma.

JOHN BROOM is historical consultant and Adjunct Professor, Kansas City Kansas Community College, Kansas City, Kansas.

JEROLD E. BROWN is Professor of History, Combat Studies Institute, U.S. Army Command and General Staff College, Fort Leavenworth, Kansas. He is the author of *Where Eagles Land.*

TREVOR BROWN is Project Manager, Academic Resource Center, Fort Riley, Kansas.

WILLIAM H. CARNES is Historian and Curator, U.S. Army Finance Corps Museum, Fort Jackson, South Carolina.

FRED J. CHIAVENTONE, Major, U.S. Army Retired, was formerly Instructor of International Security Affairs, Department of Joint and Combined Operations, U.S. Army Command and General Staff College, Fort Leavenworth, Kansas. He is the author of *A Road We Do Not Know.*

THOMAS CHRISTIANSON, Lieutenant Colonel, U.S. Army Retired, was formerly Instructor, Combat Studies Institute, U.S. Army Command and General Staff College.

CHRIS CLARK, Major, U.S. Army Retired, is Manager, IMS Health Strategy Technologies, Atlanta, Georgia.

STEVEN E. CLAY, Lieutenant Colonel, U.S. Army, is Executive Officer, Combat Studies Institute, U.S. Army Command and General Staff College, Fort Leavenworth, Kansas.

STEPHEN D. COATS, Major, U.S. Army Retired, is Professor, Department of Joint and Multinational Operations, U.S. Army Command and General Staff College, Fort Leavenworth, Kansas.

ROBERT E. CONNOR, Major, U.S. Army Retired, was formerly Instructor, Combat Studies Institute, U.S. Army Command and General Staff College.

ROD COOLEY, Major, U.S. Army Retired, is a student of military history and a frequent speaker on military topics. He lives in Colorado Springs, Colorado.

JERRY COOPER is Professor of History, University of Missouri-St. Louis. He is the author of *The Army and Civil Disorder: Federal Military Intervention in Labor Disputes, 1877–1900* (1980); *Citizens as Soldiers: A History of the North Dakota National Guard* (1986); and *The Militia and National Guard in America Since Colonial Times: A Research Guide* (1993).

KELVIN CROW, Major, U.S. Army Retired, is a business consultant. He was formerly Instructor, Combat Studies Institute, U.S. Army Command and General Staff College, Fort Leavenworth, Kansas. He is the author of *The Concept of Common Training*.

DWAIN CROWSON, Lieutenant Colonel, ARNGUS Retired, was formerly Instructor, Combat Studies Institute, U.S. Army Command and General Staff College, Fort Leavenworth, Kansas.

ROBERT J. DALESSANDRO, Lieutenant Colonel, U.S. Army, is Chemical Officer, Combined Arms Doctrine Directorate, U.S. Army Command and General Staff College, Fort Leavenworth, Kansas.

MARK H. DANLEY served in the 101st Airborne Division (Air Assault).

MICHAEL DAVIS is a doctoral candidate in history at Kansas State University, Manhattan, Kansas.

DON DENMARK, Lieutenant Colonel, U.S. Army, Retired, was formerly PMS, Kansas University, Lawrence, Kansas.

TAMAS DREILINGER, Major, U.S. Army, Retired, is Instructor, Enterprise State Junior College, Enterprise, Alabama.

TIMOTHY C. DUNWOODY is a doctoral candidate at Purdue University, West Lafayette, Indiana.

JOHN EDGECOMB, Lieutenant Colonel, U.S. Army, Retired, is Instructor and Coach, Howe Military School, Howe, Indiana.

LAWYN C. EDWARDS, Colonel, U.S. Army, is Director, Combat Studies Institute, U.S. Army Command and General Staff College, Fort Leavenworth, Kansas.

LEE W. EYSTURLID is Instructor at the Indiana Academy, Ball State University, Muncie, Indiana.

A. B. FEUER is a freelance journalist and military writer. He is the author of *The Santiago Campaign of 1898: A Soldier's View of the Spanish-American War* (1993); *General Chennault's Secret Weapon: The B-24 in China* (1992); and numerous other books.

JOHN R. FINCH, Lieutenant Colonel, U.S. Army Retired, was formerly Instructor, Combat Studies Institute, U.S. Army Command and General Staff College.

JOSEPH R. FISCHER teaches school in Selinsgrove, Pennsylvania.

JOHN T. FISHEL is Professor, Center for Hemispheric Defense Studies, National Defense University. He is the author of *Civil Military Operations in the New World* (1997), and coauthor of *Invasion, Intervention, "Intervasion": A Concise History of the U.S. Army in Operation Uphold Democracy*.

CHAN FLOYD, Lieutenant Colonel USAF, is Chief of Staff, 23d Operations Support Squadron, Pope Air Force Base, North Carolina.

ARTHUR T. FRAME, Lieutenant Colonel, U.S. Army Retired, is Professor, Department of Joint and Multinational Operations, U.S. Army Command and General Staff College, Fort Leavenworth, Kansas.

JAMES E. FRANKLIN teaches history in Fort Atkinson, Wisconsin.

CHRISTOPHER R. GABEL is Professor of History, Combat Studies Institute, U.S. Army Command and General Staff College, Fort Leavenworth, Kansas. He is the author of *The U.S. Army GHQ Maneuvers of 1941* (1991); and *Seek, Strike, Destroy: U.S. Army Tank Destroyer Doctrine in World War II* (1985).

ANDREW L. GIACOMINI, JR., Lieutenant Colonel, USAF, is Deputy Director, Air Force Element, U.S. Army Command and General Staff College, Fort Leavenworth, Kansas.

JACK GIFFORD, retired, was a POW during the Korean War. He was formerly Professor of History, Combat Studies Institute, U.S. Army Command and General Staff College. Fort Leavenworth, Kansas.

DONALD L. GILMORE is Senior Editor, Combat Studies Institute, U.S. Army Command and General Staff College, Fort Leavenworth, Kansas.

RUSSELL W. GLENN, Lieutenant Colonel, U.S. Army Retired, is Senior Defense and Political Analyst, RAND.

ROBERT S. GOINGS manages a computer graphics company in Lafayette, Louisiana.

CHARLES HELLER, Colonel, U.S. Army Reserve Retired, is Professor, Military and Strategic Studies, Washburn University, Topeka, Kansas.

JOHN A. HIXSON, Lieutenant Colonel, U.S. Army Retired, is Training Analyst, Logicon-RDA, Battle Command Training Program, Fort Leavenworth, Kansas. He is the author of *Combined Operations in Peace and War* (1982).

THOMAS M. HUBER is Professor of History, Combat Studies Institute, U.S. Army Command and General Staff College, Fort Leavenworth, Kansas. He is the author of *Japan's Battle of Okinawa, April-June 1945; Strategic Economy in Japan.*

JAMES L. ISEMANN is a doctoral candidate at Kansas State University, Manhattan, Kansas, and Instructor of History, Southeast Community College, Lincoln, Nebraska.

PETER A. KAISER is a graduate student in Library Science at University of North Texas, Denton, Texas.

DANIEL G. KARIS, Lieutenant Colonel, U.S. Army Retired, is Operations Officer, OGA-LOGICON, BCTP, Fort Leavenworth, Kansas.

EDWIN KENNEDY, JR., Lieutenant Colonel, U.S. Army Retired, is Senior Army Instructor, Leavenworth (Kansas) High School JROTC.

JOHN R. KENNEDY, Lieutenant Colonel, U.S. Army Retired, is Assistant Director of Faculty, Baker University, Overland Park, Kansas.

JOHN KING, Colonel, U.S. Army, is Dental Corps Historian, Fort Sam Houston, Texas.

RICHARD L. KIPER, Lieutenant Colonel, U.S. Army Retired, was formerly Instructor, Combat Studies Institute, U.S. Army Command and General Staff College.

GEORGE KNAPP, Major, U.S. Army, Retired, was formerly Instructor, Combat Studies Institute, U.S. Army Command and General Staff College.

MICHAEL G. KNAPP is Associate Archivist, Middlebury College, Middlebury, Vermont.

BILL KNIGHT, Lieutenant Colonel, U.S. Army Retired, is Proposal, Program & International Sales Manager, COTS Marketing & Business Development, Government Program, Allied Signal, Inc., Olathe, Kansas.

LUKE KNOWLEY is a doctoral candidate at Purdue University, West Lafayette, Indiana.

WALTER KRETCHIK, Lieutenant Colonel, U.S. Army Retired, was formerly instructor, Combat Studies Institute, U.S. Army Command and General Staff College, Fort Leavenworth, Kansas.

BENJAMIN H. KRISTY is a graduate student at Kansas State University, Manhattan, Kansas, and a recipient of the Marine Corps Historical Foundation Master's Thesis Fellowship.

LEE KRUGER, Lieutenant Colonel, U.S. Army, is assigned to Headquarters, European Command.

STEPHEN C. McGEORGE, Major, U.S. Army Retired, is Director, Oregon Military Museum, Camp Withycombe, Clackamas, Oregon.

SCOTT McMEEN, Major, U.S. Army Retired, was formerly Instructor, Combat Studies Institute, U.S. Army Command and General Staff College.

EDWARD L. MAIER III is a doctoral candidate at Kansas State University, Manhattan, Kansas.

JIM MARTIN, Lieutenant Colonel, U.S. Army Retired, is Director of Instruction and Technology, School of Professional and Graduate Studies, Baker University, Overland Park, Kansas.

BRIAN D. MOORE, Colonel, U.S. Marine Corps Retired, is Director of Warfighting Studies, U.S. Army War College, Carlisle Barracks, Pennsylvania.

BETTIE J. MORDEN, Colonel, U.S. Army Retired, former Deputy Director of the Women's Army Corps and Women's Army Corps Historian, is President of the Women's Army Corps Foundation.

GEORGE MORDICA II, U.S. Army Retired, is Combat Operations Analyst, Center For Army Lessons Learned, Fort Leavenworth, Kansas.

JERRY D. MORELOCK, Colonel, U.S. Army Retired, is Director, Winston Churchill Memorial and Library, Westminster College, Fulton, Missouri.

ANDREW N. MORRIS, Lieutenant Colonel, U.S. Army Retired, was formerly Instructor, Combat Studies Institute, U.S. Army Command and General Staff College.

RALPH NICHOLS, Lieutenant Colonel, U.S. Army, is Instructor, Combined Arms Services and Staff School, U.S. Army Command and General Staff College, Fort Leavenworth, Kansas.

DAVE R. PALMER, Lieutenant General, U.S. Army Retired, is President, Walden University, Minneapolis, Minnesota. He is the author of *The River and the Rock* (1969); *The Way of the Fox* (1975); *Summons of the Trumpet* (1978); and *1794* (1994).

LAYTON H. M. PENNINGTON, Lieutenant Colonel, is U. S. Army, Plans Officer, V Corps, Heidelberg, Germany.

DANA PRATER is Curator, Trail End State Historic Site, Sheridan, Wyoming.

JEFFREY PRATER, Lieutenant Colonel, USAF Retired, is Vice President, Fort Phil Kearney/Bozeman Trail Association, Sheridan, Wyoming.

JOHN QUINLIVAN, Lieutenant Colonel, U.S. Army, is Deputy Commander for Admissions, Lawrence Joel Army Health Clinic, Fort McPherson, Georgia.

ROBERT RAMSEY, Lieutenant Colonel, U.S. Army Retired, was formerly Instructor, Combat Studies Institute, U.S. Army Command and General Staff College. Fort Leavenworth, Kansas.

JOHN REICHLEY, Major, U.S. Army Retired, is Visitor Coordination Officer, U.S. Army Command and General Staff College, Fort Leavenworth, Kansas.

DANNY E. RODEHAVER is a graduate student at Kansas State University, Manhattan, Kansas.

ROBERT ROOK is Assistant Professor of History, Fort Hays State University, Hays, Kansas.

DAVID A. RUBENSTEIN, Colonel, U.S. Army, is Commander, 21st Combat Support Hospital, Fort Hood, Texas.

KREWASKY A. SALTER, Major, U.S. Army, is Executive Officer, 1-3 ADA, 3d Infantry Division, Fort Stewart, Georgia.

STANLEY SANDLER is the author of *The Emergence of the Modern Capital Ship* (1979); and *Segregated Skies: The All-Black Squadrons of the USSAF in World War II* (1992).

MARY T. SARNECKY, Colonel, U.S. Army Retired, is writing volume two of *A History of the U.S. Army Nurse Corps.*

CLAUDE SASSO, Major, U.S. Army Retired, is Adjunct Professor, William Jewell College, Liberty, Missouri.

DOUGLAS P. SCALARD, Lieutenant Colonel, U.S. Army Retired, was formerly History Instructor, Combat Studies Institute, U.S. Army Command and General Staff College, Fort Leavenworth, Kansas.

JEFFREY S. SHADBURN, Lieutenant Colonel, U.S. Army, was formerly History Instructor, Combat Studies Institute, U.S. Army Command and General Staff College, Fort Leavenworth, Kansas.

EDWARD SHANAHAN, Lieutenant Colonel, U.S. Army, Retired, is Education Specialist, U.S. Army Reserve Command, Fort McPherson, Georgia.

ROGER J. SPILLER is George C. Marshall Professor of Military History, U.S. Army Command and General Staff College, Fort Leavenworth, Kansas.

DONALD S. STEPHENSON, Lieutenant Colonel, U.S. Army, is Instructor, Combat Studies Institute, U.S. Army Command and General Staff College, Fort Leavenworth, Kansas.

RICHARD STEWART is Chief, Histories Division, U.S. Army Center of Military History, Fort McNair, Washington, D.C.

RICHARD SWAIN, Colonel, U.S. Army Retired, is the former Director, Combat Studies Institute, U.S. Army Command and General Staff College, Fort Leavenworth, Kansas.

KENNETH TURNER, Lieutenant Colonel, U.S. Army, is Commander 3rd Psychological Operations Battalion (Airborne), Fort Bragg, North Carolina.

S. A. UNDERWOOD, Major, U.S. Army, is Commander, NATO Special Intelligence Force, Mons, Belgium.

JAMES H. WILLBANKS, Lieutenant Colonel, U.S. Army Retired, is Professor, Department of Joint and Multinational Operations, U.S. Army Command and General Staff College, Fort Leavenworth, Kansas.

L. LYNN WILLIAMS is a graduate student at the University of Nebraska-Lincoln and editorial assistant for Great Plains Research.

REBECCA S. WITTE is an archeologist and historical consultant at Fort Leavenworth, Kansas.

LAWRENCE A. YATES is Chief, Historical Services, Combat Studies Institute, U.S. Army Command and General Staff College, Fort Leavenworth, Kansas.

DAVID ZOELLERS, Lieutenant Colonel, U.S. Army, is Joint Staff Action Officer, AIR, Land, Sea Application Center, Langley Air Force Base, Virginia.